CLYMER®
MANUALS

HONDA
VT1100 SERIES • 1995-2007

WHAT'S IN YOUR TOOLBOX?

 You Tube™

Copyright ©2007 Penton Business Media, Inc.

FIRST EDITION
First Printing December, 2004

SECOND EDITION
First Printing July, 2007
Second Printing April, 2009
Third Printing March, 2013

Printed in U.S.A.

CLYMER and colophon are registered trademarks of Penton Business Media, Inc.

ISBN-10: 1-59969-141-8

ISBN-13: 978-1-59969-141-1

Library of Congress: 2007931297

AUTHOR: Ron Wright.

TECHNICAL PHOTOGRAPHY: Ron Wright.

TECHNICAL ILLUSTRATIONS: Steve Amos.

WIRING DIAGRAMS: Bob Meyer and Lee Buell.

EDITOR: Lee Buell.

PRODUCTION: Julie Jantzer-Ward.

TOOLS AND EQUIPMENT: K & L Supply Co. at www.klsupply.com.

COVER: Mark Clifford Photography at www.markclifford.com.

Associate Publisher James Grooms

EDITORIAL

Content Director
James Grooms

Editor
Steven Thomas

Associate Editor
Rick Arens

Authors
Ed Scott
Ron Wright
Michael Morlan
George Parise
Jay Bogart

Illustrators
Bob Meyer
Steve Amos
Errol McCarthy
Mitzi McCarthy

MARKETING

Marketing Manager
Steven Thomas

SALES

Sales Manager–Powersport/Marine/I&T
Matt Tusken

CUSTOMER SERVICE

Customer Service Manager
Terri Cannon

Customer Service Representatives
Becky Bigham
Dinah Bunnell
April LeBlond
Sherry Rudkin

PRODUCTION

Director of Production
Dylan Goodwin

Group Production Manager
Greg Araujo

Project Managers
Darin Watson
Adriane Wineinger

Production Editor
Ashley Bally

Associate Production Editor
Samantha Collins

P.O. Box 12901, Overland Park, KS 66282-2901 • 800-262-1954 • 913-967-1719

More information available at *clymer.com*

CONTENTS

QUICK REFERENCE DATA

MOTORCYCLE INFORMATION

MODEL:_____YEAR:_____

VIN NUMBER:_____

ENGINE SERIAL NUMBER:_____

CARBURETOR SERIAL NUMBER OR I.D. MARK:_____

TIRE INFLATION PRESSURE[1]

	Front psi (kPa)	Rear psi (kPa)
Up to 90 kg (200 lb.) load		
VT1100C	33 (225)	33 (225)
VT1100C2		
ACE		
1995-1996	33 (225)	33 (225)
1997-on	29 (200)	33 (225)
Shadow Sabre	29 (200)	33 (225)
VT1100C3	29 (200)	29 (200)
VT1100T	33 (225)	33 (225)
From 90 kg (200 lb.) load to the maximum weight limit[2]		
VT1100C	33 (225)	41 (280)
VT1100C2		
ACE	33 (225)	41 (280)
Shadow Sabre	29 (200)	41 (280)
VT1100C3	29 (200)	41 (280)
VT1100T	33 (225)	36 (250)

1. Tire inflation pressure for original equipment tires. Refer to Table 1 in Chapter Eleven for OEM tire brands and tire sizes. Aftermarket tires may require different inflation pressures. Refer to tire manufacturer's specifications.
2. Refer to Table 3 (Vehicle Weight Specifications) in Chapter One for the maximum weight limit for each model.

RECOMMENDED LUBRICANTS AND FUEL

Brake fluid	DOT 4 brake fluid
Control cables	Cable lubricant
Cooling system	Honda HP Coolant or equivalent[1]
Engine oil[2]	
Classification	
JASO T 903 standard rating	MA
API classification	SG or higher[3]
Viscosity rating	
1995-2006	SAE 10W-40
2007-on	SAE 10W-30

(continued)

RECOMMENDED LUBRICANTS AND FUEL (continued)

Final drive unit	Hypoid gear oil, SAE No. 80
Fork oil	Pro Honda Suspension Fluid SS-8 or equivalent 10 wt fork oil
Fuel	Unleaded gasoline with a pump octane number of 86 or higher

1. Coolant must not contain silicate inhibitors as they can cause premature wear to the water pump seals. Refer to text for further information.
2. Do not use oil with molybdenum additives.
3. API SG or higher classified oils not specified as ENERGY CONSERVING can be used. Refer to text for additional information.

ENGINE OIL CAPACITY

	Liters	U.S. qt.
Engine oil change only		
VT1100C2 ACE and	3.3	3.5
VT1100C3		
1998-2000	3.3	3.5
2001-2002	2.9	3.1
All other models	2.9	3.1
Engine oil and filter change		
VT1100C2 ACE	3.5	3.7
VT1100C3		
1998-2000	3.5	3.7
2001-2002	3.1	3.3
All other models	3.1	3.3
After engine disassembly		
VT1100C2	4.2	4.4
VT1100C3		
1998-2000	4.2	4.4
2001-2002	3.8	4.0
All other models	3.8	4.0

COOLANT CAPACITY

	Liters	U.S. qt.
Radiator and engine	2.0	2.1
Reserve tank	0.39	0.41

FINAL DRIVE UNIT OIL CAPACITY

	MI	U.S. oz.
Oil change	130	4.4
After drive unit disassembly	150	5.1

FRONT FORK OIL SPECIFICATIONS

Fork oil capacity	
VT1100C	449 ml (15.2 U.S. oz.)
VT1100C2	
ACE	
1995-1998	482 ml (16.3 U.S. oz.)
1999	495 ml (16.7 U.S. oz.)
Sabre	538 ml (18.2 U.S. oz.)
VT1100C3	488 ml (16.5 U.S. oz.)
VT1100T	497 ml (16.8 U.S. oz.)
Fork oil level	
VT1100C	173 mm (6.8 in.)
VT1100C2	
ACE	
1995-1998	151 mm (5.9 in.)
1999	139 mm (5.5 in.)
Sabre	108 mm (4.3 in.)
VT1100C3	151 mm (5.9 in.)
VT1100T	140 mm (5.5 in.)
Fork oil type	Pro-Honda Suspension Fluid SS-8 or 10 wt. fork oil

TUNE-UP SPECIFICATIONS

Carburetor synchronization	
Base carburetor	No. 1 (rear carburetor)
Maximum vacuum difference	40 mm Hg (1.6 in. Hg)
Choke valve adjustment distance	10-11 mm (0.39-0.43 in.)
Clutch lever free play	10-20 mm (3/8-3/4 in.)
Cylinder number	No. 1 (rear)
	No. 2 (front)
Engine compression	1275 ± 196 kPa (185 ± 28 psi) @ 300 rpm
Engine firing order	
VT1100C2 ACE	
Front	315°
Rear	405°
VT1100C3	
1998-2000	
Front	315°
Rear	405°
2001-2002	
Front	225°
Rear	495°
All other models	
Front	495°
Rear	225°
Engine idle speed	1000 ± 100 rpm
Ignition timing	
F mark	
VT1100C and VT1100T	12° BTDC @ 1000 rpm
VT1100C2	
ACE	6.5° BTDC @ 1000 rpm
Shadow Sabre	11.5° BTDC @ 1000 rpm
VT1100C3	6.5° BTDC @ 1000 rpm
Spark plug gap	0.8-0.9 mm (0.031-0.035 in.)

(continued)

Spark plug type	
NGK	
Standard	DPR7EA-9
Cold climate*	DPR6EA-9
Extended high speed riding	DPR8EA-9
Denso	
Standard	X22EPR-U9
Cold climate*	X20EPR-U9
Extended high speed riding	X24EPR-U9
Throttle grip free play	2-6 mm (5/64-1/4 in.)

*Ambient temperature below 5° C (41° F).

MAINTENANCE TORQUE SPECIFICATIONS

	N•m	in.-lb.	ft.-lb.
Clutch cable locknut	10	88	–
Coolant drain bolt	13	115	–
Engine oil drain bolt	29	–	22
Final drive oil drain bolt	12	106	–
Final drive oil filler cap	12	106	–
Fork drain bolt	8	71	–
Oil filter cartridge[1]	10	88	–
Oil pressure switch[2]	12	106	–
Spark plug	14	124	–
Timing hole cap[3]	18	159	–

1. Lubricate threads and O-ring with engine oil.
2. Apply silicone sealant to switch threads as described in text. Do not tighten further if leakage occurs.
3. Lubricate threads with grease.

CHAPTER ONE

GENERAL INFORMATION

This detailed and comprehensive manual covers the Honda VT1100 models from 1995-2007. Refer to **Table 1** for specific models. The text provides complete information on maintenance, tune-up, repair and overhaul. Hundreds of original photographs and illustrations created during the complete disassembly of the motorcycle guide the reader through every job. All procedures are in step-by-step form and designed for the reader who may be working on the motorcycle for the first time.

MANUAL ORGANIZATION

A shop manual is a tool and as in all Clymer manuals, the chapters are thumb tabbed for easy reference. Main headings are listed in the table of contents and the index. Frequently used specifications and capacities from the tables at the end of each individual chapter are listed in the *Quick Reference Data* section at the front of the manual. Specifications and capacities are provided in U.S. standard and metric units of measure.

During some of the procedures there will be references to headings in other chapters or sections of the manual. When a specific heading is called out it in a step it will be *italicized* as it appears in the man-

ual. If a sub-heading is indicated as being "in this section" it is located within the same main heading. For example, the sub-heading *Handling Gasoline Safely* is located within the main heading *SAFETY*.

This chapter provides general information on shop safety, tools and their usage, service fundamentals and shop supplies. **Tables 1-9** at the end of the chapter provide general motorcycle specifications and information, and general shop data.

Chapter Two covers methods for diagnosing problems. Troubleshooting procedures present typical symptoms and logic methods to pinpoint the problem.

Chapter Three explains routine maintenance, tune-up and lubrication procedures.

Subsequent chapters describe specific systems such as engine, transmission, clutch, drive system, fuel system, suspension, brakes, body and exhaust components. Each procedure is explained in step-by-step from.

WARNINGS, CAUTIONS AND NOTES

The terms WARNING, CAUTION and NOTE have specific meanings in this manual.

A WARNING emphasizes areas where injury or even death could result from negligence. Mechanical damage may also occur. WARNINGS *are to be taken seriously.*

A CAUTION emphasizes areas where equipment damage could result. Disregarding a CAUTION could cause permanent mechanical damage, though injury is unlikely.

A NOTE provides additional information to make a step or procedure easier or clearer. Disregarding a NOTE could cause inconvenience, but would not cause equipment damage or personal injury.

SAFETY

Professional mechanics can work for years and never sustain an injury or mishap. Follow these guidelines and practice common sense to safely service the motorcycle:

1. Do not operate the motorcycle in an enclosed area. The exhaust gasses contain carbon monoxide, an odorless, colorless and tasteless poisonous gas. Carbon monoxide levels build quickly in small enclosed areas and can cause unconsciousness and death in a short time. Make sure the work area is properly ventilated, or operate the motorcycle outside.

2. *Never* use gasoline or any extremely flammable liquid to clean parts. Refer to *Cleaning Parts* and *Handling Gasoline Safely* in this chapter.

3. *Never* smoke or use a torch in the vicinity of flammable liquids, such as gasoline or cleaning solvent.

4. If welding or brazing on the motorcycle, remove the fuel tank, fuel body and shocks to at least 15 m (50 ft.) away.

5. Use the correct type and size of tools to avoid damaging fasteners.

6. Keep tools clean and in good condition. Replace or repair worn or damaged equipment.

7. When loosening a tight fastener, be guided by what would happen if the tool slipped.

8. When replacing fasteners, make sure the new fasteners are of the same size and strength as the original ones.

9. Keep the work area clean and organized.

10. Wear eye protection *any time* the safety of the eyes is in question. This includes procedures involving drilling, grinding, hammering, compressed air and chemicals.

11. Wear the correct clothing for the job. Tie up or cover long hair so it cannot catch in moving equipment.

12. Do not carry sharp tools in clothing pockets.

13. Always have an approved fire extinguisher available. Make sure it is rated for gasoline (Class B) and electrical (Class C) fires.

14. Do not use compressed air to clean clothes, the motorcycle or the work area. Debris may be blown into the eyes or skin. *Never* direct compressed air at anyone. Do not allow children to use or play with any compressed air equipment.

15. When using compressed air to dry rotating parts, hold the part so it cannot rotate. Do not allow the force of the air to spin the part. The air jet is capable of rotating parts at an extreme speed. The part may be damaged or disintegrate, causing serious injury.

16. Do not inhale the dust created by brake pad and clutch wear. These particles may contain asbestos. In addition, some types of insulating materials and gaskets may contain asbestos. Inhaling asbestos particles is hazardous to health.

17. Never work on the motorcycle while someone is working under it.

18. When placing the motorcycle on a stand, make sure it is secure before walking away.

Handling Gasoline Safely

Gasoline is a volatile flammable liquid and is one of the most dangerous items in the shop. Because gasoline is used so often, many people forget it is hazardous. Only use gasoline as fuel for gasoline internal combustion engines. When working on a motorcycle, keep in mind that gasoline is always present in the fuel tank, fuel line and fuel body. To

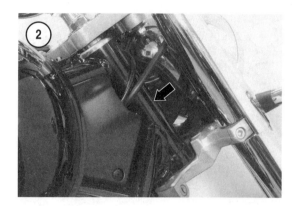

avoid a disastrous accident when working around the fuel system, carefully observe the following precautions:

1. *Never* use gasoline to clean parts. Refer to *Cleaning Parts* in this chapter.

2. When working on the fuel system, work outside or in a well-ventilated area.

3. Do not add fuel to the fuel tank or service the fuel system while the motorcycle is near open flames, sparks or where someone is smoking. Gasoline vapor is heavier than air, it collects in low areas and is more easily ignited than liquid gasoline.

4. Allow the engine to cool completely before working on any fuel system component.

5. Do not store gasoline in glass containers. If the glass breaks, an explosion or fire may occur.

6. Immediately wipe up spilled gasoline with rags. Store the rags in a metal container with a lid until they can be properly disposed of, or place them outside in a safe place for the fuel to evaporate.

7. Do not pour water onto a gasoline fire. Water spreads the fire and makes it more difficult to put out. Use a class B, BC or ABC fire extinguisher to extinguish the fire.

8. Always turn off the engine before refueling. Do not spill fuel onto the engine or exhaust system. Do not overfill the fuel tank. Leave an air space at the top of the tank to allow room for the fuel to expand because of temperature fluctuations.

Cleaning Parts

Cleaning parts is one of the more tedious and difficult service jobs performed in the home garage. Many types of chemical cleaners and solvents are available for shop use. Most are poisonous and extremely flammable. To prevent chemical exposure,

vapor buildup, fire and injury, observe each product warning label and note the following:

1. Read and observe the entire product label before using any chemical. Always know what type of chemical is being used and whether it is poisonous and/or flammable.

2. Do not use more than one type of cleaning solvent at a time. If mixing chemicals is called for, measure the proper amounts according to the manufacturer.

3. Work in a well-ventilated area.

4. Wear chemical-resistant gloves.

5. Wear safety glasses.

6. Wear a vapor respirator if the instructions call for it.

7. Wash hands and arms thoroughly after cleaning parts.

8. Keep chemical products away from children and pets.

9. Thoroughly clean all oil, grease and cleaner residue from any part that must be heated.

10. Use a nylon brush when cleaning parts. Metal brushes may cause a spark.

11. When using a parts washer, only use the solvent recommended by the manufacturer. Make sure the parts washer is equipped with a metal lid that lowers in case of fire.

Warning Labels

Most manufacturers attach information and warning labels to the motorcycle. These labels contain instructions important to personal safety when operating, servicing, transporting and storing the motorcycle. Refer to the owner's manual for the description and location of labels. Order replacement labels from the manufacturer if they are missing or damaged.

SERIAL NUMBERS

Serial numbers are stamped on various locations on the frame, engine, transmission and carburetor. Record these numbers in the *Quick Reference Data* section in the front of the book. Have these numbers available when ordering parts.

The VIN number label (**Figure 1**) is located on the left side of the steering head.

The frame serial number (**Figure 2**) is stamped on the right side of the steering head.

The engine serial number (**Figure 3**) is stamped on a raised pad on the right crankcase below the rear cylinder.

The carburetor identification number (**Figure 4**) is located on the intake side of the carburetor body.

The color label (**Figure 5**, typical) is attached to the tool bag holder behind the right side cover.

FASTENERS

Proper fastener selection and installation is important to ensure the motorcycle operates as designed and can be serviced efficiently. The choice of original equipment fasteners is not arrived at by chance. Make sure that replacement fasteners meet all the same requirements as the originals.

Threaded Fasteners

Threaded fasteners secure most of the components on the motorcycle. Most are tightened by turning them clockwise (right-hand threads). If the normal rotation of the component being tightened would loosen the fastener, it may have left-hand threads. If a left-hand threaded fastener is used, it is noted in the text.

Two dimensions are required to match the size of the fastener: the number of threads in a given distance and the outside diameter of the threads.

Two systems are currently used to specify threaded fastener dimensions: the U.S. Standard system and the metric system (**Figure 6**). Pay particular attention when working with unidentified fasteners; mismatching thread types can damage threads.

> *NOTE*
> *To ensure the fastener threads are not mismatched or cross-threaded, start all fasteners by hand. If a fastener is hard to start or turn, determine the cause before tightening with a wrench.*

The length (L, **Figure 7**), diameter (D) and distance between thread crests (pitch) (T) classify metric screws and bolts. A typical bolt may be identified by the numbers, 8—1.25 × 130. This indicates the bolt has diameter of 8 mm, the distance between thread crests is 1.25 mm and the length is 130 mm. Always measure bolt length as shown in

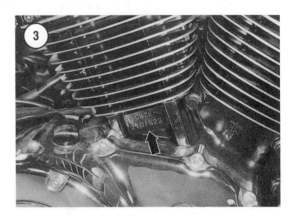

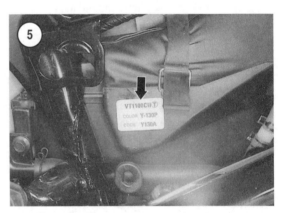

L, **Figure 7** to avoid purchasing replacements of the wrong length.

The numbers located on the top of the fastener (**Figure 7**) indicate the strength of metric screws and bolts. The higher the number, the stronger the fastener. Unnumbered fasteners are the weakest.

Many screws, bolts and studs are combined with nuts to secure particular components. To indicate the size of a nut, manufacturers specify the internal diameter and the thread pitch.

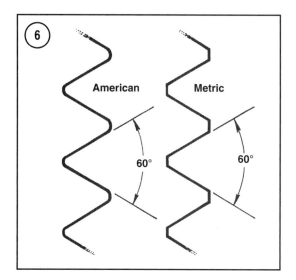

American   Metric

60°   60°

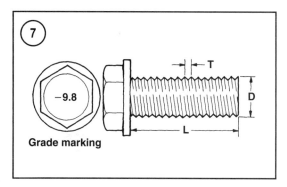

Grade marking

—9.8

T

D

L

Specifications for torque are provided in Newton-meters (N•m), foot-pounds (ft.-lb.) and inch-pounds (in.-lb.). Refer to **Table 7** for general torque specifications. To use **Table 7**, first determine the size of the fastener as described in *Fasteners* in this chapter. Torque specifications for specific components are at the end of the appropriate chapters. Torque wrenches are covered in the *Basic Tools* section.

Self-Locking Fasteners

Several types of bolts, screws and nuts incorporate a system that creates interference between the two fasteners. Interference is achieved in various ways. The most common type is the nylon insert nut and a dry adhesive coating on the threads of a bolt.

Self-locking fasteners offer greater holding strength than standard fasteners, which improves their resistance to vibration. Self-locking fasteners cannot be reused. The materials used to form the lock become distorted after the initial installation and removal. It is a good practice to discard and replace self-locking fasteners after their removal. Do not replace self-locking fasteners with standard fasteners.

The measurement across two flats on a nut or bolt indicates the wrench size.

> *WARNING*
> *Do not install fasteners with a strength classification lower than what was originally installed by the manufacturer. Doing so may cause equipment failure and/or damage.*

Washers

The two basic types of washers are flat washers and lockwashers. Flat washers are simple discs with a hole to fit a screw or bolt. Lockwashers are used to prevent a fastener from working loose. Washers can be used as spacers and seals or to help distribute fastener load and prevent the fastener from damaging the component.

As with fasteners, when replacing washers make sure the replacement washers are of the same design and quality.

Torque Specifications

The materials used in the manufacture of the motorcycle may be subjected to uneven stresses if the fasteners of the various subassemblies are not installed and tightened correctly. Fasteners that are improperly installed or work loose can cause extensive damage. It is essential to use an accurate torque wrench, described in this chapter, with the torque specifications in this manual.

Cotter Pins

A cotter pin is a split metal pin inserted into a hole or slot to prevent a fastener from loosening. In certain applications, such as the rear axle on an ATV or motorcycle, the fastener must be secured in this way. For these applications, a cotter pin and castellated (slotted) nut is used.

To use a cotter pin, first make sure the diameter is correct for the hole in the fastener. After correctly tightening the fastener and aligning the holes, insert the cotter pin through the hole and bend the ends over the fastener (**Figure 8**). Unless instructed to do so, never loosen a tightened fastener to align the holes. If the holes do not align, tighten the fastener just enough to achieve alignment.

Cotter pins are available in various diameters and lengths. Measure length from the bottom of the head to the tip of the shortest pin.

Snap Rings and E-clips

Snap rings (**Figure 9**) are circular-shaped metal retaining clips. They are required to secure parts and gears in place on parts such as shafts, pins or rods. External type snap rings are used to retain items on shafts. Internal type snap rings secure parts within housing bores. In some applications, in addition to securing the component(s), snap rings of varying thicknesses also determine endplay. These are usually called selective snap rings.

The two basic types of snap rings used are machined and stamped snap rings. Machined snap rings (**Figure 10**) can be installed in either direction because both faces have sharp edges. Stamped snap rings (**Figure 11**) are manufactured with a sharp edge and a round edge. When installing a stamped snap ring in a thrust application, install the sharp edge facing away from the part producing the thrust.

E-clips are used when it is not practical to use a snap ring. Remove E-clips with a flat blade screwdriver by prying between the shaft and E-clip. To install an E-clip, center it over the shaft groove and push or tap it into place.

Observe the following when installing snap rings:

1. Remove and install snap rings with snap ring pliers. Refer to *Snap Ring Pliers* in this chapter.

2. In some applications, it may be necessary to replace snap rings after removing them.

3. Compress or expand snap rings only enough to install them. If overly expanded, they lose their retaining ability.

4. After installing a snap ring, make sure it seats completely.

5. Wear eye protection when removing and installing snap rings.

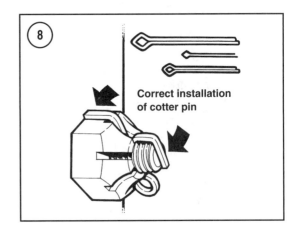

Correct installation of cotter pin

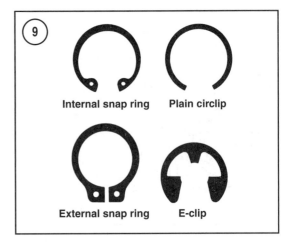

Internal snap ring   Plain circlip

External snap ring   E-clip

SHOP SUPPLIES

Lubricants and Fluids

Periodic lubrication helps ensure a long service life for any type of equipment. Using the correct type of lubricant is as important as performing the lubrication service, although in an emergency the wrong type is better than not using one. The following section describes the types of lubricants most often required. Make sure to follow the manufacturer's recommendations for lubricant types.

Engine oils

Engine oil for four-stroke motorcycle engine use is classified by the American Petroleum Institute (API) service classification, the Society of Automotive Engineers (SAE) viscosity rating and the Japanese Automobile Standards Organization (JASO) T 903 Standard rating.

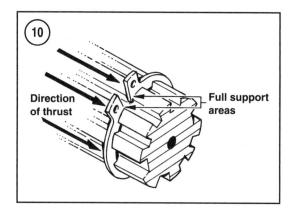

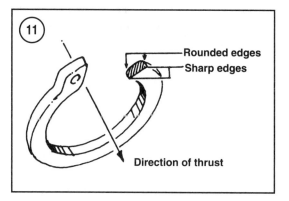

The API and SAE information is on all oil container labels. The JASO information is found on oil containers sold by the oil manufacturer specifically for motorcycle use. Two letters indicate the API service classification. The number or sequence of numbers and letter (10W-40 for example) is the oil's viscosity rating. The API service classification and the SAE viscosity index are not indications of oil quality. The JASO certification label identifies two separate oil classifications and a registration number to ensure the oil has passed all JASO certification standards for use in four-stroke motorcycle engines.

The API service classification indicates the oil meets specific lubrication standards. The first letter in the classification, *S*, indicates the oil is for gasoline engines. The second letter indicates the standard the oil satisfies.

The JASO certification label identifies two separate oil classifications and a registration number to ensure the oil has passed all JASO certification standards for use in four-stroke motorcycle engines. The classifications are MA (high friction applications) and MB (low friction applications). Only oil

that has passed JASO standards can carry the JASO certification label.

NOTE
*Refer to **Engine Oil and Filter** in Chapter Three for further information on API, SAE and JASO ratings.*

Always use an oil with a classification recommended by the manufacturer. Using an oil with a different classification can cause engine damage.

Viscosity is an indication of the oil's thickness. Thin oils have a lower number while thick oils have a higher number. Engine oils fall into the 5- to 50-weight range for single-grade oils.

Most manufacturers recommend multi-grade oil. These oils perform efficiently across a wide range of operating conditions. Multi-grade oils are identified by a *W* after the first number, which indicates the low-temperature viscosity.

Engine oils are most commonly mineral (petroleum) based; however, synthetic and semi-synthetic types are used more frequently. When selecting engine oil, follow the manufacturer's recommendation for type, classification and viscosity.

Greases

Grease is lubricating oil with thickening agents added to it. The National Lubricating Grease Institute (NLGI) grades grease. Grades range from No. 000 to No. 6, with No. 6 being the thickest. Typical multipurpose grease is NLGI No. 2. For specific applications, manufacturers may recommend water-resistant type grease or one with an additive such as molybdenum disulfide (MoS_2).

Brake fluid

Brake fluid is the hydraulic fluid used to transmit hydraulic pressure (force) to the wheel brakes. Brake fluid is classified by the Department of Transportation (DOT). Current designations for brake fluid are DOT 3, DOT 4 and DOT 5. This classification appears on the fluid container.

Each type of brake fluid has its own definite characteristics. Do not intermix different types of brake fluid because this may cause brake system failure. DOT 5 brake fluid is silicone based. DOT 5 is not compatible with other brake fluids or in systems for which it was not designed. Mixing DOT 5 fluid with other fluids may cause brake system failure. When adding brake fluid, *only* use the fluid recommended by the manufacturer.

Brake fluid damages any plastic, painted or plated surface it contacts. Use extreme care when working with brake fluids and remove any spills immediately with soap and water.

Hydraulic brake systems require clean and moisture-free brake fluid. Never reuse brake fluid. Keep containers and reservoirs properly sealed.

> **WARNING**
> *Never put a mineral-based (petroleum) oil into the brake system. Mineral oil causes rubber parts in the system to swell and break apart, causing complete brake failure.*

Coolant

Coolant is a mixture of water and antifreeze used to dissipate engine heat. Ethylene glycol is the most common form of antifreeze used. Check the motorcycle manufacturer's recommendations when selecting antifreeze; most require one specifically designed for use in aluminum engines. These types of antifreeze have additives that inhibit corrosion.

Only mix distilled water with antifreeze. Impurities in tap water may damage internal cooling system passages.

Final drive gear oil

Gear oil is a thick based oil specially formulated for final drive units. Always use a gear oil with a classification and viscosity recommended by the manufacturer. Do not use engine oil or transmission oil recommended for two-stroke engines or automobiles.

Cleaners, Degreasers and Solvents

Many chemicals are available to remove oil, grease and other residue from the motorcycle. Before using cleaning solvents, consider how they are used and disposed of, particularly if they are not water-soluble. Local ordinances may require special procedures for the disposal of many types of cleaning chemicals. Refer to *Safety and Cleaning Parts* in this chapter for more information on their uses.

Use brake parts cleaner to clean brake system components when contact with petroleum-based products damages seals. Brake parts cleaner leaves no residue. Use electrical contact cleaner to clean electrical connections and components without leaving any residue. Carburetor cleaner is a powerful solvent used to remove fuel deposits and varnish from fuel system components. Use this cleaner carefully because it may damage finishes.

Generally, degreasers are strong cleaners used to remove heavy accumulations of grease from engine and frame components.

Most solvents are designed to be used with a parts washing cabinet for individual component cleaning. For safety, use only nonflammable or high flash point solvents.

Gasket Sealant

Sealants are used in combination with a gasket or seal and are occasionally alone. Follow the manufacturer's recommendation when using sealants. Use extreme care when choosing a sealant different from the type originally recommended. Choose sealants based on their resistance to heat, various fluids and their sealing capabilities.

One of the most common sealants is RTV, or room temperature vulcanizing sealant. This sealant cures at room temperature over a specific time period. This allows the repositioning of components without damaging gaskets.

Moisture in the air causes the RTV sealant to cure. Always install the tube cap as soon as possible after applying RTV sealant. RTV sealant has a limited shelf life and does not cure properly if the shelf life has expired. Keep partial tubes sealed and discard them if they have surpassed the expiration date.

Applying RTV sealant

Clean all old gasket residue from the mating surfaces. Remove all gasket material from blind threaded holes; it can cause inaccurate bolt torque. Spray the mating surfaces with aerosol parts cleaner and wipe with a lint-free cloth. The area must be clean for the sealant to adhere.

Apply RTV sealant in a continuous bead 2-3 mm (0.08-0.12 in.) thick. Circle all the fastener holes unless otherwise specified. Do not allow any sealant to enter these holes. Assemble and tighten the fasteners to the specified torque within the time frame recommended by the RTV sealant manufacturer.

Gasket Remover

Aerosol gasket remover can help remove stubborn gaskets. This product can speed up the removal process and prevent damage to the mating surface that may be caused by using a scraping tool. Most of these types of products are very caustic. Follow the gasket remover manufacturer's instructions for use.

Threadlocking Compound

A threadlocking compound is a fluid applied to the threads of fasteners. After tightening the fastener, the fluid dries and becomes a solid filler between the threads. This makes it difficult for the fastener to work loose from vibration or heat expansion and contraction. Some threadlocking compounds also provide a seal against fluid leakage.

Before applying threadlocking compound, remove any old compound from both thread areas and clean them with aerosol parts cleaner. Use the compound sparingly. Excess fluid can run into adjoining parts.

> *CAUTION*
> *Threadlocking compounds are anaerobic and stress, crack and attack most plastic parts and surfaces. Use caution when using these products in areas where plastic components are located.*

Threadlocking compounds are available in different strengths. Follow the manufacturer's recommendations regarding compound selection. Two manufacturers of threadlocking compound are ThreeBond and Loctite. Both offer a wide range of compounds for various strengths, temperatures and repair applications.

BASIC TOOLS

Most of the procedures in this manual can be carried out with simple hand tools and test equipment familiar to the home mechanic. Always use the correct tools for the job at hand. Keep tools organized and clean. Store them in a tool chest with related tools organized together.

Quality tools are essential. The best are constructed of high-strength alloy steel. These tools are light, easy to use and resistant to wear. Their working surface is devoid of sharp edges and the tool is carefully polished. They have an easy-to-clean finish and are comfortable to use. Quality tools are a good investment.

When purchasing tools to perform the procedures covered in this manual, consider the tool's potential frequency of use. If a tool kit is just now being started, consider purchasing a basic tool set from a quality tool supplier. These sets are available in many tool combinations and offer substantial savings when compared to individually purchased tools. As work experience grows and tasks become more complicated, specialized tools can be added.

Some of the procedures in this manual specify special tools. In many cases the tool is illustrated in use. Those with a large tool kit may be able to use a suitable substitute or fabricate a suitable replacement. However, in some cases, the specialized equipment or expertise may make it impractical for the home mechanic to attempt the procedure. When necessary, such operations come with the recommendation to have a dealership or specialist perform the task. It may be less expensive to have a professional perform these jobs, especially when considering the cost of equipment.

If a tool part number is listed in the text, confirm this with a Honda dealership or tool supplier. The part number may have changed.

Screwdrivers

Screwdrivers of various lengths and types are mandatory for the simplest tool kit. The two basic types are the slotted tip (flat blade) and the Phillips tip. These are available in sets that often include an assortment of tip sizes and shaft lengths.

As with all tools, use a screwdriver designed for the job. Make sure the size of the tip conforms to the size and shape of the fastener. Use them only for driving screws. Never use a screwdriver for prying or chiseling metal. Repair or replace worn or damaged screwdrivers. A worn tip may damage the fastener, making it difficult to remove.

Phillips-head screws are often damaged by incorrectly fitting screwdrivers. Quality Phillips screwdrivers are manufactured with their crosshead tip machined to Phillips Screw Company specifications. Poor quality or damaged Phillips screwdrivers can back out (camout) and round over the screw head. In addition, weak or soft material screws can make removal difficult.

The best type of screwdriver to use on Phillips screws is the ACR Phillips II screwdriver, patented by the Phillips Screw Company. ACR stands for the horizontal anti-camout ribs found on the driving faces or flutes of the screwdrivers tip (**Figure 12**). ACR Phillips II screwdrivers were designed as part of a manufacturing drive system to be used with ACR Phillips II screws, but they work well on all common Phillips screws. A number of tool companies offer ACR Phillips II screwdrivers in different tip sizes and interchangeable bits to fit screwdriver bit holders.

NOTE
Another way to prevent camout and increase the grip of a Phillips screwdriver is to apply valve grinding compound or Permatex Screw & Socket Gripper onto the screwdriver tip. After loosening/tightening the screw, clean the screw recess to prevent engine oil contamination.

Wrenches

Open-end, box-end and combination wrenches (**Figure 13**) are available in a variety of types and sizes.

The number stamped on the wrench refers to the distance between the work areas. This size must match the size of the fastener head.

The box-end wrench is an excellent tool because it grips the fastener on all sides. This reduces the chance of the tool slipping. The box-end wrench is designed with either a 6 or 12-point opening. For stubborn or damaged fasteners, the 6-point provides superior holding ability by contacting the fastener across a wider area at all six edges. For general use, the 12-point works well. It allows the wrench to be removed and reinstalled without moving the handle over such a wide arc.

An open-end wrench is fast and works best in areas with limited overhead access. It contacts the fas-

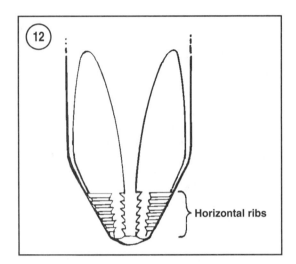

Horizontal ribs

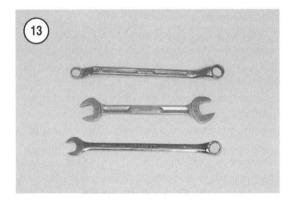

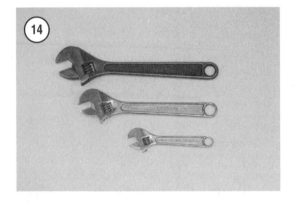

tener at only two points and is subject to slipping under heavy force or if the tool or fastener is worn. A box-end wrench is preferred in most instances, especially when breaking loose and applying the final tightness to a fastener.

The combination wrench has a box-end on one end and an open-end on the other. This combination makes it a convenient tool.

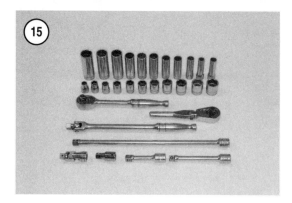

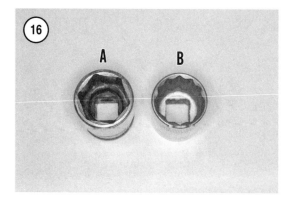

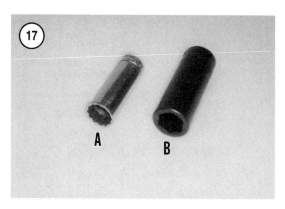

Adjustable Wrenches

An adjustable wrench (**Figure 14**) can fit nearly any nut or bolt head that has clear access around its entire perimeter. Adjustable wrenches are best used as a backup wrench to keep a large nut or bolt from turning while the other end is being loosened or tightened with a box-end or socket wrench.

Adjustable wrenches contact the fastener at only two points, which makes them more subject to slipping off the fastener. Because one jaw is adjustable and may loosen only aggravates this shortcoming.

Make certain the solid jaw is the one transmitting the force.

Socket Wrenches, Ratchets and Handles

Sockets that attach to a ratchet handle (**Figure 15**) are available with 6-point (A, **Figure 16**) or 12-point (B) openings and different drive sizes. The drive size indicates the size of the square hole that accepts the ratchet handle. The number stamped on the socket is the size of the work area and must match the fastener head.

As with wrenches, a 6-point socket provides superior-holding ability, while a 12-point socket needs to be moved only half as far to reposition it on the fastener.

Sockets are designated for either hand or impact use. Impact sockets are made of thicker material for more durability. Compare the size and wall thickness of a 19 mm hand socket (A, **Figure 17**) and the 19-mm impact socket (B). Use impact sockets when using an impact driver or air tools. Use hand sockets with hand-driven attachments.

> *WARNING*
> *Do not use hand sockets with air or impact tools because they may shatter and cause injury. Always wear eye protection when using impact or air tools.*

Various handles are available for sockets. The speed handle is used for fast operation. Flexible ratchet heads in varying lengths allow the socket to be turned with varying force and at odd angles. Extension bars allow the socket setup to reach difficult areas. The ratchet is the most versatile. It allows the user to install or remove the nut without removing the socket.

Sockets combined with any number of drivers make them undoubtedly the fastest, safest and most convenient tool for fastener removal and installation.

Impact Driver

An impact driver provides extra force for removing fasteners by converting the impact of a hammer into a turning motion. This makes it possible to remove stubborn fasteners without damaging them. Impact drivers and interchangeable bits (**Figure 18**) are available from most tool suppliers. When using a socket with an impact driver make sure the socket is designed for impact use. Refer to *Socket Wrenches, Ratchets and Handles* in this section.

> *WARNING*
> *Do not use hand sockets with air or impact tools because they may shatter and cause injury. Always wear eye protection when using impact or air tools.*

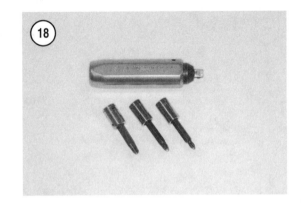

Allen Wrenches

Allen, or setscrew wrenches, (**Figure 19**) are used on fasteners with hexagonal recesses in the fastener head. These wrenches are available in L-shaped bar, socket and T-handle types. A metric set is required when working on most motorcycles. Allen bolts are sometimes called socket bolts.

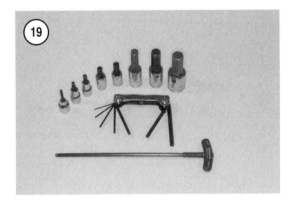

Torque Wrenches

A torque wrench is used with a socket, torque adapter or similar extension to tighten fastener to a measured torque. Torque wrenches come in several drive sizes (1/4, 3/8, 1/2 and 3/4) and have various methods of reading the torque value. The drive size indicates the size of the square drive that accepts the socket, adapter or extension. Common methods of reading the torque value are the reflecting beam, the dial indicator and the audible click (**Figure 20**). When choosing a torque rench, consider the torque range, drive size and accuracy. The torque specifications in this manual provide an indication of the range required. A torque wrench is a precision tool that must be properly cared for to remain accurate. Store torque wrenches in cases or separate padded drawers within toolbox. Follow the manufacturer's instructions for their care and calibration.

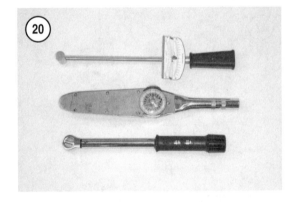

Torque Adapters

Torque adapters or extensions extend or reduce the reach of a torque wrench. The torque adapter shown in **Figure 21** is used to tighten a fastener that cannot be reached due to the size of the torque wrench head, drive and socket. If a torque adapter changes the effective lever length (**Figure 22**), the torque reading on the wrench does not equal the actual torque applied to the fastener. It is necessary to

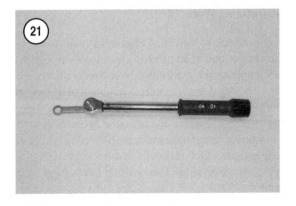

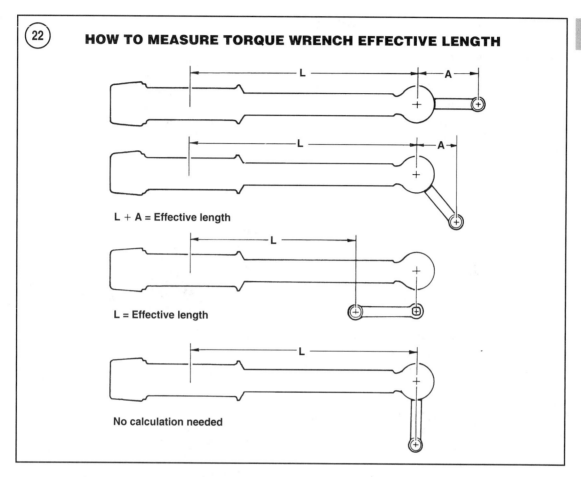

22   HOW TO MEASURE TORQUE WRENCH EFFECTIVE LENGTH

L + A = Effective length

L = Effective length

No calculation needed

recalibrate the torque setting on the wrench to compensate for the change of lever length. When a torque adapter is used at a right angle to the drive head, calibration is not required because the effective length has not changed.

To recalculate a torque reading when using a torque adapter, use the following formula, and refer to **Figure 22**:

$$TW = \frac{TA \times L}{L + A}$$

TW is the torque setting or dial reading on the wrench.

TA is the torque specification and the actual amount of torque that is applied to the fastener.

A is the amount that the adapter increases (or in some cases reduces) the effective lever length as measured along the centerline of the torque wrench (**Figure 22**).

L is the lever length of the wrench as measured from the center of the drive to the center of the grip.

The effective length is the sum of L and A (**Figure 22**).

Example:

TA = 20 ft.-lb.
A = 3 in.
L = 14 in.
$$TW = \frac{20 \times 14}{14 + 3} = \frac{280}{17} = 16.5 \text{ ft.-lb.}$$

In this example, the torque wrench would be set to the recalculated torque value (TW = 16.5 ft.-lb.). When using a beam-type wrench, tighten the fastener until the pointer aligns with 16.5 ft.-lb. In this example, although the torque wrench is preset to 16.5 ft.-lb., the actual torque is 20 ft.-lb.

Pliers

Pliers come in a wide range of types and sizes. Pliers are useful for holding, cutting, bending and crimping. Do not use them to turn fasteners. **Figure**

23 and **Figure 24** show several types of useful pliers. Each design has a specialized function. Slip-joint pliers are general-purpose pliers used for gripping and bending. Diagonal cutting pliers are needed to cut wire and can be used to remove cotter pins. Needlenose pliers are used to hold or bend small objects. Locking pliers (**Figure 24**) hold objects very tightly. They have many uses ranging from holding two parts together, to gripping the end of a broken stud. Use caution when using locking pliers because the sharp jaws damage the objects they hold.

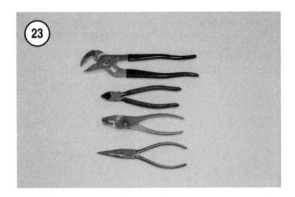

Snap Ring Pliers

Snap ring pliers are specialized pliers with tips that fit into the ends of snap rings to remove and install them.

Snap ring pliers (**Figure 25**) are available with a fixed action (either internal or external) or convertible (one tool works on both internal and external snap rings). They may have fixed tips or interchangeable ones of various sizes and angles. For general use, select a convertible type pliers with interchangeable tips (**Figure 25**).

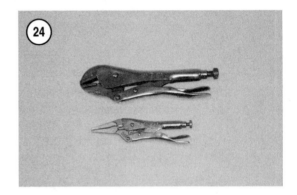

> *WARNING*
> *Snap rings can slip and fly off when removing and installing them. In addition, the snap ring pliers tips may break. Always wear eye protection when using snap ring pliers.*

Hammers

Various types of hammers are available to fit a number of applications. A ball-peen hammer is used to strike another tool, such as a punch or chisel. Soft-faced hammers are required when a metal object must be struck without damaging it. *Never* use a metal-faced hammer on engine and suspension components because damage occurs in most cases.

Always wear eye protection when using hammers. Make sure the hammer face is in good condition and the handle is not cracked. Select the correct hammer for the job and make sure to strike the object squarely. Do not use the handle or the side of the hammer to strike an object.

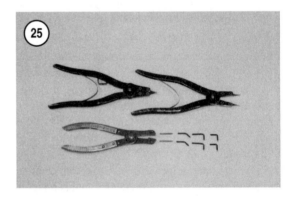

Ignition Grounding Tool

Some test procedures in this manual require turning the engine over without starting it. On the VT1100 engine, the easiest way to accomplish this is to remove the spark plug caps from the spark plugs. However, when doing so the ignition system should be grounded to prevent excessive resistance from damaging the ICM or other ignition system components.

Fabricate the grounding tool shown in **Figure 26** from a No. 6 screw, two washers and a length of wire with an alligator clip soldered on one end. To

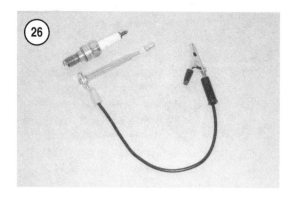

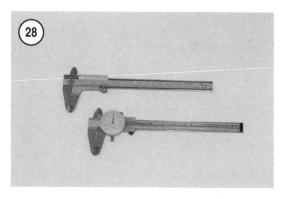

ground the ignition system, insert the tool into the spark plug cap and attach the alligator clip to a good engine ground. A separate grounding tool is required for each spark plug cap. Grounding tools are safer to use because there are no sparks firing across the end of the tool to potentially ignite fuel vapor spraying from an open spark plug hole or leaking carburetor.

PRECISION MEASURING TOOLS

The ability to accurately measure components is essential to successfully rebuild an engine. Equip-

ment is manufactured to close tolerances, and obtaining consistently accurate measurements is essential to determining which components require replacement or further service.

Each type of measuring instrument is designed to measure a dimension with a certain degree of accuracy and within a certain range. When selecting the measuring tool, make sure it is applicable to the task.

As with all tools, measuring tools provide the best results if cared for properly. Improper use can damage the tool and cause inaccurate results. If any measurement is questionable, verify the measurement using another tool. A standard gauge is usually provided with measuring tools to check accuracy and calibrate the tool if necessary.

Precision measurements can vary according to the experience of the person performing the procedure. Accurate results are only possible if the mechanic possesses a feel for using the tool. Heavy-handed use of measuring tools produces less accurate results. Hold the tool gently by the fingertips so the point at which the tool contacts the object is easily felt. This feel for the equipment produces more accurate measurements and reduces the risk of damaging the tool or component. Refer to the following sections for specific measuring tools.

Feeler Gauge

The feeler, or thickness gauge, (**Figure 27**) is used for measuring the distance between two surfaces.

A feeler gauge set consists of an assortment of steel strips of graduated thicknesses. Each blade is marked with its thickness. Blades can be of various lengths and angles for different procedures.

A common use for a feeler gauge is to measure valve clearance. Wire (round) type gauges are used to measure spark plug gap.

Calipers

Calipers (**Figure 28**) are excellent tools for obtaining inside, outside and depth measurements. Although not as precise as a micrometer, they allow reasonable precision, typically to within 0.05 mm (0.001 in.). Most calipers have a range up to 150 mm (6 in.).

Calipers are available in dial, vernier or digital versions. Dial calipers have a dial readout that provides convenient reading. Vernier calipers have marked scales that must be compared to determine the measurement. The digital caliper uses a LCD to show the measurement.

Properly maintain the measuring surfaces of the caliper. There must not be any dirt or burrs between the tool and the object being measured. Never force the caliper closed around an object; close the caliper around the highest point so it can be removed with a slight drag. Some calipers require calibration. Always refer to the manufacturer's instructions when using a new or unfamiliar caliper.

To read a vernier caliper refer to **Figure 29**. The fixed scale is marked in 1-mm increments. Ten individual lines on the fixed scale equal 1 cm. The moveable scale is marked in 0.05 mm (hundredth) increments. To obtain a reading, establish the first number by the location of the 0 line on the movable scale in relation to the first line to the left on the fixed scale. In this example, the number is 10 mm. To determine the next number, note which of the lines on the movable scale align with a mark on the fixed scale. A number of lines seem close, but only one aligns exactly. In this case, 0.50 mm is the reading to add to the first number. The result of adding 10 mm and 0.50 mm is a measurement of 10.50 mm.

Micrometers

A micrometer is an instrument designed for linear measurement using the decimal divisions of the inch or meter (**Figure 30**). While there are many types and styles of micrometers, most of the procedures in this manual call for an outside micrometer. The outside micrometer is used to measure the outside diameter of cylindrical forms and the thicknesses of materials.

A micrometer's size indicates the minimum and maximum size of a part that it can measure. The usual sizes (**Figure 31**) are 0-25 mm (0-1 in.), 25-50 mm (1-2 in.), 50-75 mm (2-3 in.) and 75-100 mm (3-4 in.).

Micrometers that cover a wider range of measurements are available. These use a large frame with interchangeable anvils of various lengths. This type of micrometer offers a cost savings; however, its overall size may make it less convenient.

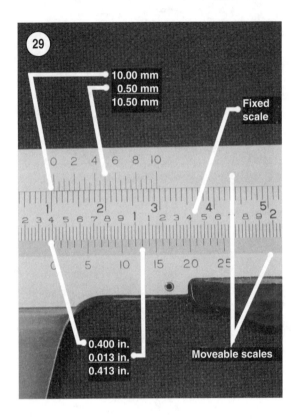

Reading

When reading a micrometer, numbers are taken from different scales and added together.

For accurate results, properly maintain the measuring surfaces of the micrometer. There cannot be any dirt or burrs between the tool and the measured object. Never force the micrometer closed around an object. Close the micrometer around the highest point so it can be removed with a slight drag. **Figure 32** shows the markings and parts of a standard metric micrometer. Be familiar with these terms before using a micrometer in the following sections.

The standard metric micrometer is accurate to one one-hundredth of a millimeter (0.01 mm). The sleeve line is graduated in millimeter and half millimeter increments. The marks on the upper half of the sleeve line equal 1.00 mm. Each fifth mark above the sleeve line is identified with a number. The number sequence depends on the size of the micrometer. A 0-25 mm micrometer, for example, has sleeve marks numbered 0 through 25 in 5 mm increments. This numbering sequence continues with larger micrometers. On all metric micrometers, each mark on the lower half of the sleeve equals 0.50 mm.

⑳

DECIMAL PLACE VALUES*

0.1	Indicates 1/10 (one tenth of an inch or millimeter)
0.010	Indicates 1/100 (one one-hundreth of an inch or millimeter)
0.001	Indicates 1/1000 (one one-thousandth of an inch or millimeter)

*This chart represents the values of figures placed to the right of the decimal point. Use it when reading decimals from one-tenth to one one-thousandth of an inch or millimeter. It is not a conversion chart (for example: 0.001 in. is not equal to 0.001 mm).

㉛

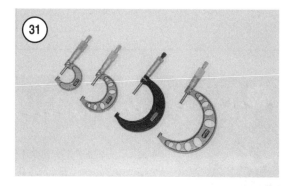

The tapered end of the thimble has 50 lines marked around it. Each mark equals 0.01 mm. One complete turn of the thimble aligns its 0 mark with the first line on the lower half of the sleeve line, or 0.50 mm.

When reading a metric micrometer, add the number of millimeters and half-millimeters on the sleeve line to the number of one one-hundredth millimeters on the thimble. Perform the following steps while referring to **Figure 33**:

1. Read the upper half of the sleeve line and count the number of lines visible. Each upper line equals 1 mm.

2. See if the half-millimeter line is visible on the lower sleeve line. If so, add 0.50 mm to the reading in Step 1.

3. Read the thimble mark that aligns with the sleeve line. Each thimble mark equals 0.01 mm.

NOTE
If a thimble mark does not align exactly with the sleeve line, estimate the amount between the lines. For accurate readings in two-thousandths of a millimeter (0.002 mm), use a metric vernier micrometer.

4. Add the readings from Steps 1-3.

Adjustment

Before using a micrometer, check its adjustment as follows:

1. Clean the anvil and spindle faces.

2A. To check a 0-1 in. or 0-25 mm micrometer:
   a. Turn the thimble until the spindle contacts the anvil. If the micrometer has a ratchet stop, use it to ensure the proper amount of pressure is applied.
   b. If the adjustment is correct, the 0 mark on the thimble aligns exactly with the 0 mark on the sleeve line. If the marks do not align, the micrometer is out of adjustment.
   c. Follow the manufacturer's instructions to adjust the micrometer.

2B. To check a micrometer larger than 1 in. or 25 mm use the standard gauge supplied by the manufacturer. A standard gauge is a steel block, disc or rod that is machined to an exact size.
   a. Place the standard gauge between the spindle and anvil, and measure its outside diameter or length. If the micrometer has a ratchet stop, use it to ensure the proper amount of pressure is applied.
   b. If the adjustment is correct, the 0 mark on the thimble aligns exactly with the 0 mark on the sleeve line. If the marks do not align, the micrometer is out of adjustment.
   c. Follow the manufacturer's instructions to adjust the micrometer.

Care

Micrometers are precision instruments. They must be used and maintained with great care. Note the following:

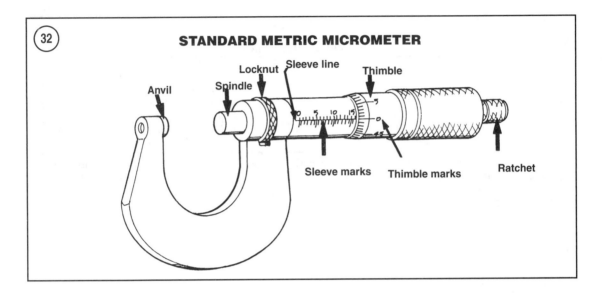

STANDARD METRIC MICROMETER

1. Store micrometers in protective cases or separate padded drawers in a toolbox.

2. When in storage, make sure the spindle and anvil faces do not contact each other or an other object. If they do, temperature changes and corrosion may damage the contact faces.

3. Do not clean a micrometer with compressed air. Dirt forced into the tool causes wear.

4. Lubricate micrometers with WD-40 to prevent corrosion.

Telescoping and Small Hole Gauges

Use telescoping gauges (**Figure 34**) and small hole gauges (**Figure 35**) to measure bores. Neither gauge has a scale for direct readings. An outside micrometer must be used to determine the reading.

To use a telescoping gauge, select the correct size gauge for the bore. Compress the movable post and carefully insert the gauge into the bore. Carefully move the gauge in the bore to make sure it is centered. Tighten the knurled end of the gauge to hold the movable post in position. Remove the gauge and measure the length of the posts. Telescoping gauges are typically used to measure cylinder bores.

To use a small hole gauge, select the correct size gauge for the bore. Carefully insert the gauge into the bore. Tighten the knurled end of the gauge to carefully expand the gauge fingers to the limit within the bore. Do not overtighten the gauge because there is no built-in release. Excessive tightening can damage the bore surface and damage the

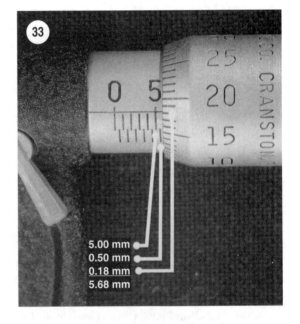

5.00 mm
0.50 mm
0.18 mm
5.68 mm

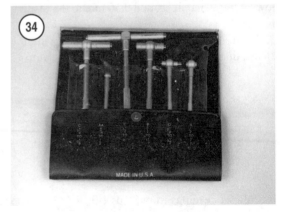

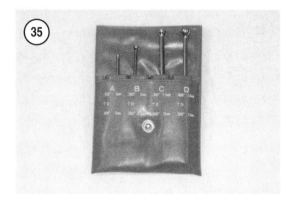

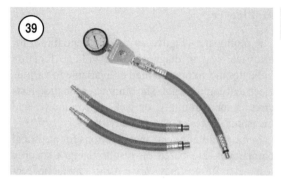

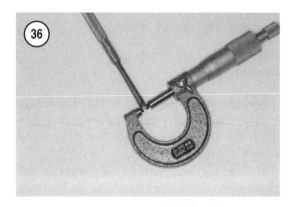

tool. Remove the gauge and measure the outside dimension (**Figure 36**). Small hole gauges are typically used to measure valve guides.

Dial Indicator

A dial indicator (**Figure 37**) is a gauge with a dial face and needle used to measure variations in dimensions and movements. Measuring brake rotor runout is a typical use for a dial indicator.

Dial indicators are available in various ranges and graduations and with three basic types of mounting bases: magnetic, clamp or screw-in stud. When purchasing a dial indicator, select the magnetic stand (**Figure 37**) type with a continuous dial.

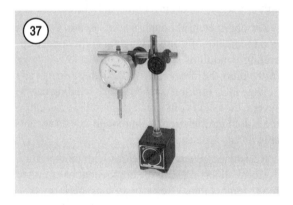

Cylinder Bore Gauge

A cylinder bore gauge is similar to a dial indicator. The gauge set shown in **Figure 38** consists of a dial indicator, handle and different length adapters (anvils) to fit the gauge to various bore sizes. The bore gauge is used to measure bore size, taper and out-of-round. When using a bore gauge, follow the manufacturer's instructions.

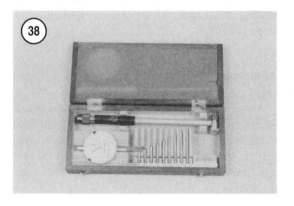

Compression Gauge

A compression gauge (**Figure 39**) measures combustion chamber (cylinder) pressure, usually in psi or kg/cm^2. The gauge adapter is either inserted or screwed into the spark plug hole to obtain the reading. Disable the engine so it does not start and hold the throttle in the wide-open position when performing a compression test. An engine that does not have adequate compression cannot be properly tuned. Refer to Chapter Three.

Multimeter

A multimeter (**Figure 40**) is an essential tool for electrical system diagnosis. The voltage function indicates the voltage applied or available to various electrical components. The ohmmeter function tests circuits for continuity, or lack of continuity, and measures the resistance of a circuit.

Some manufacturers' specifications for electrical components are based on results using a specific test meter. Results may vary if using a meter not recommend by the manufacturer is used. Such requirements are noted when applicable.

Ohmmeter (analog) calibration

Each time an analog ohmmeter is used or if the scale is changed, the ohmmeter must be calibrated.

Digital ohmmeters do not require calibration.

1. Make sure the meter battery is in good condition.
2. Make sure the meter probes are in good condition.
3. Touch the two probes together and observe the needle location on the ohms scale.
4. The needle must align with the 0 mark to obtain accurate measurements. If necessary, rotate the meter ohms adjust knob until the needle and 0 mark align.

ELECTRICAL SYSTEM FUNDAMENTALS

A thorough study of the many types of electrical systems used in today's motorcycles is beyond the scope of this manual. However, an understanding of electrical basics is necessary to perform simple diagnostic tests.

Refer to Chapter Two for general electrical testing and Chapter Nine for specific procedures.

Voltage

Voltage is the electrical potential or pressure in an electrical circuit and is expressed in volts. The more pressure (voltage) in a circuit, the more work that can be performed.

Direct current (DC) voltage means the electricity flows in one direction. All circuits powered by a battery are DC circuits.

Alternating current (AC) means that the electricity flows in one direction momentarily then switches to the opposite direction. Alternator output is an example of AC voltage. This voltage must be

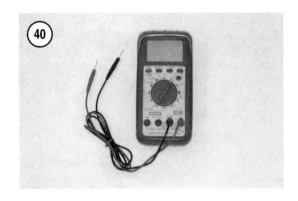

changed or rectified to direct current to operate in a battery powered system.

Resistance

Resistance is the opposition to the flow of electricity within a circuit or component and is measured in ohms. Resistance causes a reduction in available current and voltage.

Resistance is measured in an inactive circuit with an ohmmeter. The ohmmeter sends a small amount of current into the circuit and measures how difficult it is to push the current through the circuit.

An ohmmeter, although useful, is not always a good indicator of a circuit's actual ability under operating conditions. This is due to the low voltage (6-9 volts) the meter uses to test the circuit. The voltage in an ignition coil secondary winding can be several thousand volts. Such high voltage can cause the coil to malfunction, even though it tests acceptable during a resistance test.

Resistance generally increases with temperature. Perform all testing with the component or circuit at room temperature. Resistance tests performed at high temperatures may indicate false resistance readings and cause the unnecessary replacement of a component.

Amperage

Amperage is the unit of measure for the amount of current within a circuit. Current is the actual flow of electricity. The higher the current, the more work that can be performed up to a given point. If the current flow exceeds the circuit or component capacity, the system becomes damaged.

BASIC SERVICE METHODS

Most of the procedures in this manual are straightforward and can be performed by anyone reasonably competent with tools. However, consider personal capabilities carefully before attempting any operation involving major disassembly of the engine.

1. Front, in this manual, refers to the front of the motorcycle. The front of any component is the end closest to the front of the motorcycle. The left and right sides refer to the position of the parts as viewed by the rider sitting on the seat facing forward.

2. Whenever servicing an engine or suspension component, secure the motorcycle in a safe manner.

3. Tag all similar parts for location and mark all mating parts for position. Record the number and thickness of any shims as they are removed. Identify parts by placing them in sealed and labeled plastic sandwich bags.

4. Tag disconnected wires and connectors with masking tape and a marking pen. Do not rely on memory alone.

5. Protect finished surfaces from physical damage or corrosion. Keep gasoline and other chemicals off painted surfaces.

6. Use penetrating oil on frozen or tight bolts. Avoid using heat where possible. Heat can warp, melt or affect the temper of parts. Heat also damages the finish of paint and plastics.

7. When a part is a press fit or requires a special tool for removal, the information or type of tool is identified in the text. Otherwise, if a part is difficult to remove or install, determine the cause before proceeding.

8. To prevent objects or debris from falling into the engine, cover all openings.

9. Read each procedure thoroughly and compare the illustrations to the actual components before starting the procedure. Perform the procedure in sequence.

10. Recommendations are occasionally made to refer service to a dealership or specialist. In these cases, the work can be performed more economically by the specialist than by the home mechanic.

11. The term *replace* means to discard a defective part and replace it with a new part. *Overhaul* means to remove, disassemble, inspect, measure, repair and/or replace parts as required to recondition an assembly.

12. Some operations require the use of a hydraulic press. If a press is not available, have these operations performed by a shop equipped with the necessary equipment. Do not use makeshift equipment that may damage the motorcycle.

13. Repairs are much faster and easier if the motorcycle is clean before starting work. Degrease the motorcycle with a commercial degreaser; follow the directions on the container for the best results. Clean all parts with cleaning solvent as they are removed.

CAUTION
Do not direct high-pressure water at steering bearings, fuel body hoses, wheel bearings, suspension and electrical components. The water forces the grease out of the bearings and possibly damages the seals.

14. If special tools are required, have them available before starting the procedure. When special tools are required, they are described at the beginning of the procedure.

15. Make diagrams of similar-appearing parts. For instance, crankcase bolts are often not the same lengths. Do not rely on memory alone. It is possible for carefully laid out parts to become disturbed, making it difficult to reassemble the components correctly without a diagram.

16. Make sure all shims and washers are reinstalled in the same location and position.

17. Whenever rotating parts contact a stationary part, look for a shim or washer.

18. Use new gaskets if there is any doubt about the condition of old ones.

19. If self-locking fasteners are used, replace them with new ones. Do not install standard fasteners in place of self-locking ones.

20. Use grease to hold small parts in place if they tend to fall out during assembly. Do not apply grease to electrical or brake components.

Removing Frozen Fasteners

If a fastener cannot be removed, several methods may be used to loosen it. First, apply penetrating oil such as Liquid Wrench or WD-40. Apply it liberally and let it penetrate for 10-15 minutes. Rap the fastener several times with a small hammer. Do not hit

it hard enough to cause damage. Reapply the penetrating oil if necessary.

For frozen screws, apply penetrating oil as described, then insert a screwdriver in the slot and rap
the top of the screwdriver with a hammer. This loos-
ens the rust so the screw can be removed in the normal way. If the screw head is too damaged to use
this method, grip the head with locking pliers and
twist the screw out.

Avoid applying heat unless specifically instructed because it may melt, warp or remove the
temper from parts.

Removing Broken Fasteners

If the head breaks off a screw or bolt, several
methods are available for removing the remaining
portion. If a large portion of the remainder projects
out, try gripping it with locking pliers. If the pro-
jecting portion is too small, file it to fit a wrench or
cut a slot in it to fit a screwdriver (**Figure 41**).

If the head breaks off flush, use a screw extractor.
To do this, centerpunch the exact center of the re-
maining portion of the screw or bolt. Drill a small
hole in the screw and tap the extractor into the hole.
Back the screw out with a wrench on the extractor
(**Figure 42**).

Repairing Damaged Threads

Occasionally, threads are stripped through care-
lessness or impact damage. Often the threads can be
repaired by running a tap (for internal threads on
nuts) or die (for external threads on bolts) through
the threads (**Figure 43**). To clean or repair spark
plug threads, use a spark plug tap.

If an internal thread is damaged, it may be necessary to install a Helicoil or some other type of thread
insert. Follow the manufacturer's instructions when
installing the insert.

If it is necessary to drill and tap a hole, refer to
Table 9 for metric tap and drill sizes.

Stud Removal/Installation

A stud removal tool is available from most tool
suppliers. This tool makes the removal and installation of studs easier. If one is not available and the
threads on the stud are not damaged, thread two
nuts onto the stud and tighten them against each

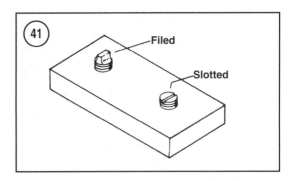

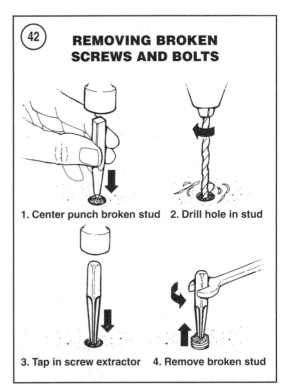

**REMOVING BROKEN
SCREWS AND BOLTS**

1. Center punch broken stud   2. Drill hole in stud

3. Tap in screw extractor   4. Remove broken stud

other. Remove the stud by turning the lower nut
(**Figure 44**).

1. Measure the height of the stud above the surface.

2. Thread the stud removal tool onto the stud and
tighten it, or thread two nuts onto the stud.

3. Remove the stud by turning the stud remover or
the lower nut.

4. Remove any threadlocking compound from the
threaded hole. Clean the threads with an aerosol
parts cleaner.

5. Install the stud removal tool onto the new stud,
or thread two nuts onto the stud.

6. Apply threadlocking compound to the threads of
the stud.

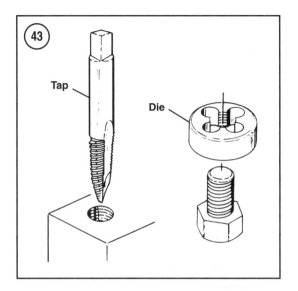

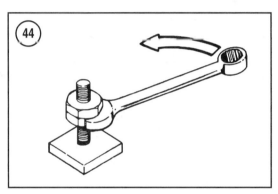

7. Install the stud and tighten with the stud removal tool or the top nut.

8. Install the stud to the height noted in Step 1 or its torque specification.

9. Remove the stud removal tool or the two nuts.

Removing Hoses

When removing stubborn hoses, do not exert excessive force on the hose or fitting. Remove the hose clamp and carefully insert a small screwdriver or similar blunt nose tool between the fitting and hose. Apply a spray lubricant under the hose and carefully twist the hose off the fitting. Clean the fitting of any corrosion or rubber hose material with a wire brush. Clean the inside of the hose thoroughly. Do not use any lubricant when installing the hose (new or old). The lubricant may allow the hose to come off the fitting, even with the clamp secure.

Bearings

Bearings are used in the engine and transmission assembly to reduce power loss, heat and noise resulting from friction. Because bearings are precision parts, they must be maintained with proper lubrication and maintenance. If a bearing is damaged, replace it immediately. When installing a new bearing, be sure not to damage it. Bearing replacement procedures are included in the individual chapters where applicable; however, use the following sections as a guideline.

NOTE
Unless otherwise specified, install bearings with the manufacturer's mark or number facing outward.

Removal

While bearings are normally removed only when damaged, there may be times when it is necessary to remove a bearing that is in good condition. However, improper bearing removal damages the bearing and maybe the shaft or case half.

1. Before removing the bearings, note the following:

   a. Refer to the bearing replacement procedure in the appropriate chapter for any special instructions.

   b. Remove any seals that interfere with bearing removal. Refer to *Seals* in this chapter.

   c. When removing more than one bearing, identify the bearings before removing them. Refer to the bearing manufacturer's numbers on the bearing.

   d. Note and record the direction in which the bearing numbers face for proper installation.

   e. Remove any set plates or bearing retainers before removing the bearings.

2. When using a puller to remove a bearing from a shaft, be sure the shaft is not damaged. Always place a piece of metal between the end of the shaft and the puller screw. In addition, place the puller arms next to the inner bearing race. Refer to **Figure 45**.

3. When using a hammer to remove a bearing from a shaft, do not strike the hammer directly against the shaft. Instead, use a brass or aluminum rod between the hammer and shaft (**Figure 46**) and make sure to

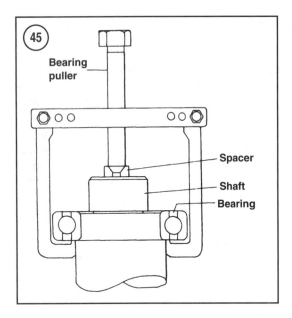

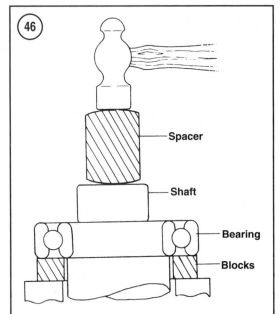

support both bearing races with wooden blocks as shown.

4. The ideal method of bearing removal is with a hydraulic press. Note the following when using a press:

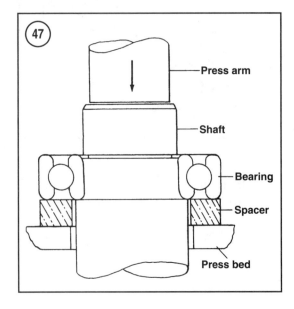

   a. Always support the inner and outer bearing races with a suitable size wooden or aluminum ring (**Figure 47**). If only the outer race is supported, pressure applied against the balls and/or the inner race damages them.

   b. Always make sure the press arm (**Figure 47**) aligns with the center of the shaft. If the arm is not centered, it may damage the bearing and/or shaft.

   c. The moment the shaft is free of the bearing, it drops to the floor. Secure or hold the shaft to prevent it from falling.

   d. When removing bearings from a housing, support the housing with 4 × 4 in. wooden blocks to prevent damage to gasket surfaces.

5. Use a blind bearing puller to remove bearings installed in blind holes (**Figure 48**).

Installation

1. When installing a bearing in a housing, apply pressure to the *outer* bearing race (**Figure 49**). When installing a bearing on a shaft, apply pressure to the *inner* bearing race (**Figure 50**).

2. When installing a bearing as described in Step 1, some type of driver is required. Never strike the

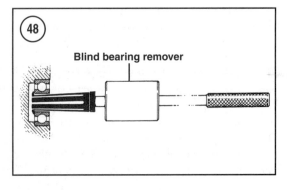

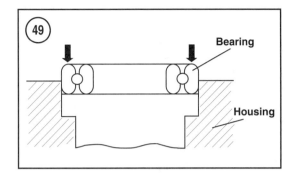

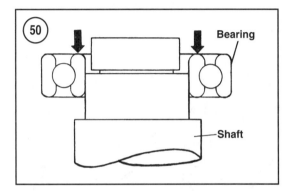

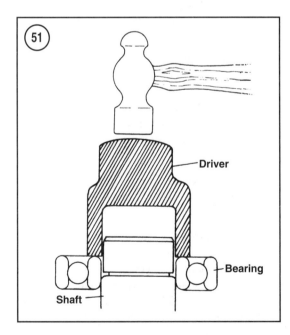

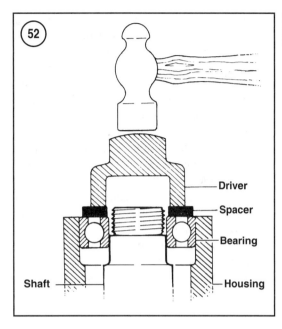

bearing directly with a hammer or the bearing becomes damaged. When installing a bearing, use a piece of pipe or a driver with a diameter that matches the bearing inner race. **Figure 51** shows the correct way to use a driver and hammer to install a bearing.

3. Step 1 describes how to install a bearing in a case half or over a shaft. However, when installing a bearing over a shaft and into the housing at the same time, a tight fit is required for both outer and inner bearing races. In this situation, install a spacer underneath the driver tool so that pressure is applied evenly across both races. Refer to **Figure 52**. If the outer race is not supported as shown in **Figure 52**, the balls push against the outer bearing race and damage it.

Interference fit

1. Follow this procedure when installing a bearing over a shaft. When a tight fit is required, the bearing inside diameter is smaller than the shaft. In this case, driving the bearing on the shaft using normal methods may cause bearing damage. Instead, heat the bearing before installation. Note the following:

    a. Secure the shaft so it is ready for bearing installation.

    b. Clean all residues from the bearing surface of the shaft. Remove burrs with a file.

    c. Fill a suitable pot or beaker with clean mineral oil. Place a thermometer rated above 120° C (248° F) in the oil. Support the thermometer so it does not rest on the bottom or side of the pot.

    d. Remove the bearing from its wrapper and secure it with a piece of heavy wire bent to hold it in the pot. Hang the bearing in the pot so it does not touch the bottom or sides of the pot.

e. Turn the heat on and monitor the thermometer. When the oil temperature rises to approximately 120° C (248° F), remove the bearing from the pot and quickly install it. If necessary, place a socket on the inner bearing race and tap the bearing into place. As the bearing chills, it tightens on the shaft, so installation must be done quickly. Make sure the bearing is installed completely.

2. Follow this step when installing a bearing in a housing. Bearings are generally installed in a housing with a slight interference fit. Driving the bearing into the housing using normal methods may damage the housing or cause bearing damage. Instead, heat the housing before the bearing is installed. Note the following:

> *CAUTION*
> *Before heating the housing in this procedure, wash the housing thoroughly with detergent and water. Rinse and rewash the cases as required to remove all traces of oil and other chemical deposits.*

a. Heat the housing to approximately 100° C (212° F) in an oven or on a hot plate. An easy way to check that it is the proper temperature is to place tiny drops of water on the housing; if they sizzle and evaporate immediately, the temperature is correct. Heat only one housing at a time.

> *CAUTION*
> *Do not heat the housing with a propane or acetylene torch. Never bring a flame into contact with the bearing or housing. The direct heat destroys the case hardening of the bearing and likely warps the housing.*

b. Remove the housing from the oven or hot plate, and hold onto the housing with welding gloves.

> *NOTE*
> *Remove and install the bearings with a suitable size socket and extension.*

c. Hold the housing with the bearing side down and tap the bearing out. Repeat for all bearings in the housing.

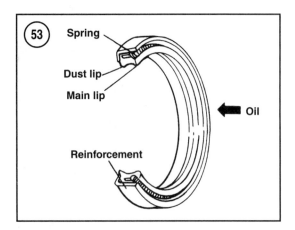

d. Before heating the bearing housing, place the new bearing in a freezer if possible. Chilling a bearing slightly reduces its outside diameter while the heated bearing housing assembly is slightly larger due to heat expansion. This makes bearing installation easier.

> *NOTE*
> *Always install bearings with the manufacturer's mark or number facing outward.*

e. While the housing is still hot, install the new bearing(s) into the housing. Install the bearings by hand, if possible. If necessary, lightly tap the bearing(s) into the housing with a socket placed on the outer bearing race (**Figure 49**). Do not install bearings by driving on the inner-bearing race. Install the bearing(s) until it seats completely.

Seal Replacement

Seals (**Figure 53**) are used to contain oil, water, grease or combustion gasses in a housing or shaft.

Improper removal of a seal can damage the housing or shaft. Improper installation of the seal can damage the seal. Note the following:

1. Prying is generally the easiest and most effective method of removing a seal from the housing. However, always place a rag underneath the pry tool (**Figure 54**) to prevent damage to the housing.
2. Pack waterproof grease in the seal lips before the seal is installed.
3. In most cases, install seals with the manufacturer's numbers or marks face out.
4. Install seals either by hand or with tools. Center the seal in its bore and attempt to install it by hand. If not, install the seal with a socket or bearing driver placed on the outside of the seal as shown in **Figure 55**. Drive the seal squarely into the housing until it is flush with its mounting bore. Never install a seal by hitting against the top of the seal with a hammer.

STORAGE

Several months of non-use can cause a general deterioration of the motorcycle. This is especially true in areas of extreme temperature variations. This deterioration can be minimized with careful preparation for storage. A properly stored motorcycle is much easier to return to service.

Storage Area Selection

When selecting a storage area, consider the following:

1. The storage area must be dry. A heated area is best, but not necessary. It should be insulated to minimize extreme temperature variations.
2. If the building has large window areas, mask them to keep sunlight off the motorcycle.

3. Avoid storage areas close to saltwater.
4. Consider the area's risk of fire, theft or vandalism. Check with an insurer regarding motorcycle coverage while in storage.

Preparing the Motorcycle for Storage

The amount of preparation a motorcycle should undergo before storage depends on the expected length of non-use, storage area conditions and personal preference. Consider the following list the minimum requirement:

1. Wash the motorcycle thoroughly. Make sure all dirt, mud and road debris are removed.
2. Start the engine and allow it to reach operating temperature. Drain the engine oil regardless of the riding time since the last service. Fill the engine with the recommended type and quantity of oil.
3. Fill the fuel tank completely.
4. Remove one spark plug from each cylinder head. Ground the spark plug caps to the engine. Refer to *Ignition Ground Tool* in this chapter. Pour a teaspoon (15-20 ml) of engine oil into the cylinders. Place a rag over the openings and slowly turn the engine over to distribute the oil. Reinstall the spark plugs.
5. Remove the battery and store it in a cool and dry location. Charge the battery once a month. Refer to *Battery* in Chapter Nine for information on battery charging and service.
6. Cover the exhaust and intake openings.
7. Apply a protective substance to the plastic and rubber components, including the tires. Make sure to follow the manufacturer's instructions for each type of product being used.
8. Rotate the front tire periodically to prevent a flat spot from developing and damaging the tire.
9. Cover the motorcycle with old bed sheets or something similar. Do not cover it with any plastic material that traps moisture.

Returning the Motorcycle to Service

The amount of service required when returning a motorcycle to service after storage depends on the length of non-use and storage conditions. In addition to performing the reverse of the above procedure, make sure the brakes, clutch, throttle and engine stop switch work properly before operating the motorcycle. Refer to Chapter Three and evaluate the service intervals to determine which areas require service.

Table 1 ENGINE AND FRAME SERIAL NUMBERS

Year/model	Engine serial number (start to end)	Frame serial number (start to end)
1995		
VT1100C2 (49-state)	SC32E-2000001-on	SC320-SA000001-on
VT1100C2 (Calif.)	SC32E-2000001-on	SC321-SA000001-on
1996		
VT1100C2 (49-state)	SC32E-2100001-on	SC320-TA100001-on
VT1100C2 (Calif.)	SC32E-2100001-on	SC321-TA100001-on
1997		
VT1100C (49-state)	SC18E-3000001-on	SC180-VA000001-on
VT1100C (Calif.)	SC18E-3000001-on	SC181-VA000001-on
VT1100C2 (49-state)	SC32E-2200001-on	SC320-VA200001-on
VT1100C2 (Calif.)	SC32E-2200001-on	SC321-VA200001-on
VT1100C2-2 (49-state)	SC32E-2240001-on	SC323-VA240001-on
VT1100C2-2 (Calif.)	SC32E-2240001-on	SC324-VA240001-on
1998		
VT1100C (49-state)	SC18E-3200001-on	SC180-WA200001-on
VT1100C (Calif.)	SC18E-3200001-on	SC181-WA200001-on
VT1100C2 (49-state)	SC32E-2240001-on	SC320-WA300001-on
VT1100C2 (Calif.)	SC32E-2240001-on	SC321-WA300001-on
VT1100C2-2 (49-state)	SC32E-2300001-on	SC322-WA300001-on
VT1100C2-2 (Calif.)	SC32E-2300001-on	SC323-WA300001-on
VT1100C3 (49-state)	SC39E-2000001-on	SC390-WA000001-on
VT1100C3 (Calif.)	SC39E-2000001-on	SC391-WA000001-on
VT1100T (49-state)	SC37E-2000001-on	SC370-WA000001-on
VT1100T (Calif.)	SC37E-2000001-on	SC371-WA000001-on
1999		
VT1100C (49-state)	SC18E-3300001-on	SC180-XA300001-on
VT1100C (Calif.)	SC18E-3300001-on	SC181-XA300001-on
VT1100C2 (49-state)	SC32E-2400001-on	SC320-XA400001-on
VT1100C2 (Calif.)	SC32E-2400001-on	SC321-XA400001-on
VT1100C3 (49-state)	SC39E-2100001-on	SC390-XA100001-on
VT1100C3 (Calif.)	SC39E-2100001-on	SC391-XA100001-on
VT1100D2 (49-state)	SC32E-2400001-on	SC323-XA400001-on
VT1100D2 (Calif.)	SC32E-2400001-on	SC324-XA400001-on
VT1100T (49-state)	SC37E-2200001-on	SC370-YA200001-on
VT1100T (Calif.)	SC37E-2200001-on	SC371-YA200001-on
2000		
VT1100C (49-state)	SC18E-3400001-on	SC180-YA400001-on
VT1100C (Calif.)	SC18E-3400001-on	SC181-YA400001-on
VT1100C2 (49-state)	SC43E-2000001-on	SC430-YA000001-on
VT1100C2 (Calif.)	SC43E-2000001-on	SC431-YA000001-on
VT1100C3 (49-state)	SC39E-2200001-on	SC390-YA200001-on
VT1100C3 (Calif.)	SC39E-2200001-on	SC391-YZ200001-on
VT1100T (49-state)	SC37E-2200001-on	SC371-YZ200001-on
VT1100T (Calif.)	SC37E-2200001-on	SC371-YZ200001-on
2001		
VT1100C (49-state)	SC18E-3500001-on	SC180-1A500001-on
VT1100C (Calif.)	SC18E-3500001-on	SC181-1A500001-on
VT1100C2 (49-state)	SC43E-2100001-on	SC430-1A100001-on
VT1100C2 (Calif.)	SC43E-2100001-on	SC431-1A100001-on
VT1100C3 (49-state)	SC39E-2300001-on	SC390-1A300001-on
VT1100C3 (Calif.)	SC39E-2300001-on	SC391-1A300001-on
2002		
VT1100C (49-state)	SC18E-3600001-on	SC180-2A600001-on
VT1100C (Calif.)	SC18E-3600001-on	SC181-2A600001-on
VT1100C2 (49-state)	SC43E-2200001-on	SC430-2A200001-on
VT1100C2 (Calif.)	SC43E-2200001-on	SC431-2A200001-on
(continued)		

Table 1 ENGINE AND FRAME SERIAL NUMBERS (continued)

Year/model	Engine serial number (start to end)	Frame serial number (start to end)
2002 (continued)		
VT1100C3 (49-state)	SC39E-2400001-on	SC390-2A400001-on
VT1100C3 (Calif.)	SC39E-2400001-on	SC391-2A400001-on
2003		
VT1100C (49-state)	SC18E-3700001-on	SC180-3A700001-on
VT1100C (Calif.)	SC18E-3700001-on	SC181-3A700001-on
VT1100C2 (49-state)	SC43E-2300001-on	SC430-3A300001-on
VT1100C2 (Calif.)	SC43E-2300001-on	SC431-3A300001-on
2004		
VT1100C (49-state)	SC18E-3800001-on	SC180-4A800001-on
VT1100C (Calif.)	SC18E-3800001-on	SC181-4A800001-on
VT1100C2 (49-state)	SC43E-2400001-on	SC430-4A400001-on
VT1100C2 (Calif.)	SC43E-2400001-on	SC431-4A400001-on
2005-on	NA	NA

Table 2 GENERAL DIMENSIONS

	mm	in.
Ground clearance		
VT1100C3	145	5.7
VT1100T	150	5.9
All other models	140	5.5
Overall height		
VT1100C	1220	48.0
VT1100C2		
ACE	1150	45.3
Shadow Sabre	1165	45.9
VT1100C3	1135	44.7
VT1100T	1430	56.3
Overall length		
VT1100C	2380	93.7
VT1100C2		
ACE	2435	95.9
Shadow Sabre	2490	98.0
VT1100C3	2540	100.0
VT1100T	2480	97.6
Overall width		
VT1100C	880	34.6
VT1100C2		
ACE	965	38.0
Shadow Sabre	920	36.2
VT1100C3	975	38.4
VT1100T	965	38.0
Seat height		
VT1100C	730	28.7
VT1100C2		
ACE	700	27.6
Shadow Sabre	690	27.2
VT1100C3	725	28.5
VT1100T	730	28.7
Wheelbase		
VT1100C	1650	65.0
VT1100C2		

(continued)

Table 2 GENERAL DIMENSIONS (continued)

	mm	in.
Wheelbase		
VT1100C2 (continued)		
ACE	1650	65.0
Shadow Sabre		
49-state	1640	64.5
Calif.	1642	64.6
VT1100C3	1680	66.1
VT1100T	1655	65.2

Table 3 VEHICLE WEIGHT SPECIFICATIONS

	kg	lb.
Curb weight		
VT1100C		
49-state/Canada	270	595
Calif.	271	597
VT1100C2		
49-state/Canada	279	615
Calif.	280	617
VT1100C3		
49-state/Canada	299	659
Calif.	300	661
VT1100T		
49-state/Canada	296	653
Calif.	297	655
Dry weight		
VT1100C		
49-state/Canada	251	553
Calif.	252	556
VT1100C2		
49-state/Canada	260	573
Calif.	261	575
VT1100C3		
49-state/Canada	279	615
Calif.	280	617
VT1100T		
49-state/Canada	284	626
Calif.	285	628
Maximum weight capacity		
VT1100C		
U.S.	164	362
Canada	168	370
VT1100C2		
ACE		
U.S.	169	373
Canada	173	381
Shadow Sabre		
U.S.	178	392
Canada	182	401
VT1100C3		
U.S.	174	384
Canada	178	392
VT1100T		
U.S.	173	381
Canada	177	390

Table 4 FUEL TANK CAPACITY

Fuel tank	
Total capacity	
VT1100C3	16.0 liters (4.23 U.S. gal.)
All other models	15.8 liters (4.17 U.S. gal.)
Reserve	
VT1100C3	4.2 liters (1.11 U.S. gal.)
All other models	2.2 liters (0.58 U.S. gal.)

Table 5 METRIC, INCH AND FRACTIONAL EQUIVALENTS

mm	in.	Nearest fraction	mm	in.	Nearest fraction
1	0.0394	1/32	26	1.0236	1 1/32
2	0.0787	3/32	27	1.0630	1 1/16
3	0.1181	1/8	28	1.1024	1 3/32
4	0.1575	5/32	29	1.1417	1 5/32
5	0.1969	3/16	30	1.1811	1 3/16
6	0.2362	1/4	31	1.2205	1 7/32
7	0.2756	9/32	32	1.2598	1 1/4
8	0.3150	5/16	33	1.2992	1 5/16
9	0.3543	11/32	34	1.3386	1 11/32
10	0.3937	13/32	35	1.3780	1 3/8
11	0.4331	7/16	36	1.4173	1 13/32
12	0.4724	15/32	37	1.4567	1 15/32
13	0.5118	1/2	38	1.4961	1 1/2
14	0.5512	9/16	39	1.5354	1 17/32
15	0.5906	19/32	40	1.5748	1 9/16
16	0.6299	5/8	41	1.6142	1 5/8
17	0.6693	21/32	42	1.6535	1 21/32
18	0.7087	23/32	43	1.6929	1 11/16
19	0.7480	3/4	44	1.7323	1 23/32
20	0.7874	25/32	45	1.7717	1 25/32
21	0.8268	13/16	46	1.8110	1 13/16
22	0.8661	7/8	47	1.8504	1 27/32
23	0.9055	29/32	48	1.8898	1 7/8
24	0.9449	15/16	49	1.9291	1 15/16
25	0.9843	31/32	50	1.9685	1 31/32

Table 6 CONVERSION FORMULAS

Multiply:	By:	To get the equivalent of:
Length		
Inches	25.4	Millimeter
Inches	2.54	Centimeter
Length (continued)		
Miles	1.609	Kilometer
Feet	0.3048	Meter
Millimeter	0.03937	Inches
Centimeter	0.3937	Inches
Kilometer	0.6214	Mile
Meter	3.281	Feet

(continued)

Table 6 CONVERSION FORMULAS (continued)

Multiply:	By:	To get the equivalent of:
Fluid volume		
U.S. quarts	0.9463	Liters
U.S. gallons	3.785	Liters
U.S. ounces	29.573529	Milliliters
Imperial gallons	4.54609	Liters
Imperial quarts	1.1365	Liters
Liters	0.2641721	U.S. gallons
Liters	1.0566882	U.S. quarts
Liters	33.814023	U.S. ounces
Liters	0.22	Imperial gallons
Liters	0.8799	Imperial quarts
Milliliters	0.033814	U.S. ounces
Milliliters	1.0	Cubic centimeters
Milliliters	0.001	Liters
Torque		
Foot-pounds	1.3558	Newton-meters
Foot-pounds	0.138255	Meters-kilograms
Inch-pounds	0.11299	Newton-meters
Newton-meters	0.7375622	Foot-pounds
Newton-meters	8.8507	Inch-pounds
Meters-kilograms	7.2330139	Foot-pounds
Volume		
Cubic inches	16.387064	Cubic centimeters
Cubic centimeters	0.0610237	Cubic inches
Temperature		
Fahrenheit	$(F - 32°) \times 0.556$	Centigrade
Centigrade	$(C \times 1.8) + 32°$	Fahrenheit
Weight		
Ounces	28.3495	Grams
Pounds	0.4535924	Kilograms
Grams	0.035274	Ounces
Kilograms	2.2046224	Pounds
Pressure		
Pounds per square inch	0.070307	Kilograms per square centimeter
Kilograms per square centimeter	14.223343	Pounds per square inch
Kilopascals	0.1450	Pounds per square inch
Pounds per square inch	6.895	Kilopascals
Speed		
Miles per hour	1.609344	Kilometers per hour
Kilometers per hour	0.6213712	Miles per hour

Table 7 GENERAL TORQUE SPECIFICATIONS

Fastener size or type	N•m	in.-lb.	ft.lb.
5 mm screw	4	35	–
5 mm bolt and nut	5	44	–
6 mm screw	9	80	–
6 mm bolt and nut	10	88	–
6 mm flange bolt (8 mm head, small flange)	9	80	–
6 mm flange bolt	12	106	–

(continued)

Table 7 GENERAL TORQUE SPECIFICATIONS (continued)

Fastener size or type	N•m	in.-lb.	ft.lb.
6 mm flange bolt (continued) (10 mm head) and nut			
8 mm bolt and nut	22	–	16
8 mm flange bolt and nut	27	–	20
10 mm bolt and nut	35	–	26
10 mm flange bolt and nut	40	–	29
12 mm bolt and nut	55	–	40

Table 8 TECHNICAL ABBREVIATIONS

ABDC	After bottom dead center
ATDC	After top dead center
API	American Petroleum Institute
BBDC	Before bottom dead center
BDC	Bottom dead center
BTDC	Before top dead center
C	Celsius (centigrade)
cc	Cubic centimeters
cid	Cubic inch displacement
CDI	Capacitor discharge ignition
cu. in.	Cubic inches
ECM	Engine control module
EVAP	Evaporative emission
EVAP CAV	EVAP carburetor air vent
F	Fahrenheit
ft.	Feet
ft.-lb.	Foot-pounds
gal.	Gallons
H/A	High altitude
hp	Horsepower
ICM	Ignition control module
in.	Inches
in.-lb.	Inch-pounds
I.D.	Inside diameter
JASO	Japanese Automobile Standards Organization
kg	Kilograms
kgm	Kilogram meters
km	Kilometer
kPa	Kilopascals
L	Liter
LED	Light emitting diode
m	Meter
mA	Milliampere
MAG	Magneto
ml	Milliliter
mm	Millimeter
N•m	Newton-meters
O.D.	Outside diameter
oz.	Ounces
PAIR	Pulsed secondary air injection system
psi	Pounds per square inch
PTO	Power take off
pt.	Pint
qt.	Quart
rpm	Revolutions per minute
RTV	Room temperature vulcanizing
SAE	Society of Automotive Engineers
TPS	Throttle position sensor

Table 9 METRIC TAP AND DRILL SIZES

Metric size	Drill equivalent	Decimal fraction	Nearest fraction
3 × 0.50	No. 39	0.0995	3/32
3 × 0.60	3/32	0.0937	3/32
4 × 0.70	No. 30	0.1285	1/8
4 × 0.75	1/8	0.125	1/8
5 × 0.80	No. 19	0.166	11/64
5 × 0.90	No. 20	0.161	5/32
6 × 1.00	No. 9	0.196	13/64
7 × 1.00	16/64	0.234	15/64
8 × 1.00	J	0.277	9/32
8 × 1.25	17/64	0.265	17/64
9 × 1.00	5/16	0.3125	5/16
9 × 1.25	5/16	0.3125	5/16
10 × 1.25	11/32	0.3437	11/32
10 × 1.50	R	0.339	11/32
11 × 1.50	3/8	0.375	3/8
12 × 1.50	13/32	0.406	13/32
12 × 1.75	13/32	0.406	13/32

CHAPTER TWO

TROUBLESHOOTING

The troubleshooting procedures described in this chapter provide typical symptoms and logical methods for isolating the cause(s). There may be several ways to solve a problem, but only a systematic approach is successful in avoiding wasted time and possibly unnecessary parts replacement.

Gather as much information as possible to aid in diagnosis. Never assume anything and do not overlook the obvious. Make sure the engine start switch is in the RUN position and there is fuel in the tank. Learning to recognize symptoms makes troubleshooting easier. In most cases, expensive and complicated test equipment is not needed to determine whether repairs can be performed at home. On the other hand, be realistic and do not start procedures that are beyond the experience and equipment available. If the motorcycle does require the attention of a professional, describe symptoms and conditions accurately and fully. The more information a technician has available, the easier it is to diagnose the problem.

Proper lubrication, maintenance and periodic tune-ups reduce the chance of problems occurring. However, even with the best of care the motorcycle may require troubleshooting.

ENGINE PRINCIPLES AND OPERATING REQUIREMENTS

An engine needs three basics to run properly: correct air/fuel mixture, compression and a spark at the right time. If one basic requirement is missing, the engine does not run. **Figure 1** explains basic four-stroke engine operation. This is helpful when troubleshooting the engine.

STARTING THE ENGINE

When experiencing engine-starting troubles, it is easy to work out of sequence and forget basic starting procedures. The following sections describe the recommended starting procedures for the VT1100.

Starting Notes

1. A sidestand ignition cutoff system is used on all models. The position of the sidestand can affect engine starting. Note the following:
   a. The engine cannot turn over when the sidestand is down and the transmission is in gear.

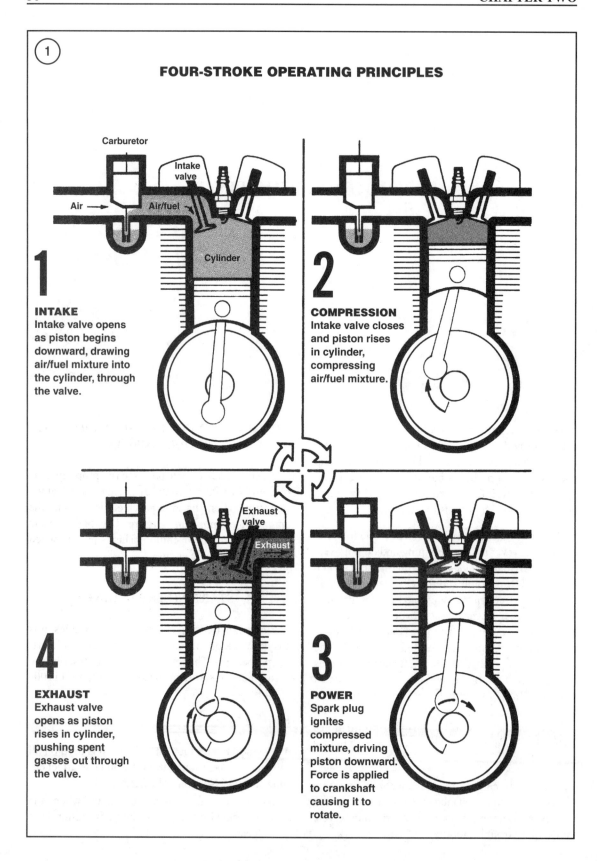

① FOUR-STROKE OPERATING PRINCIPLES

1 INTAKE
Intake valve opens as piston begins downward, drawing air/fuel mixture into the cylinder, through the valve.

2 COMPRESSION
Intake valve closes and piston rises in cylinder, compressing air/fuel mixture.

4 EXHAUST
Exhaust valve opens as piston rises in cylinder, pushing spent gasses out through the valve.

3 POWER
Spark plug ignites compressed mixture, driving piston downward. Force is applied to crankshaft causing it to rotate.

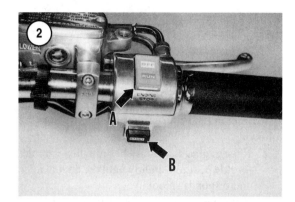

b. The engine can turn over when the sidestand is down and the transmission is in neutral. The engine stops when the transmission is shifted into gear with the sidestand down.

c. The engine can turn over when the sidestand is up and the transmission is in neutral, or in gear with the clutch lever pulled in.

2. Before starting the engine, shift the transmission into neutral and confirm the engine stop switch is in its RUN position (A, **Figure 2**).

3. Turn the ignition switch on and confirm the following:

   a. The neutral indicator light is on (when transmission is in neutral).

   b. The low oil pressure indicator is on. The indicator should go off a few seconds after the engine starts. If the light stays on, turn the engine off and check the oil level (Chapter Three).

NOTE
*The low oil pressure indicator comes on when the ignition switch is turned on to show the indicator is working correctly. If the indicator did not come on after turning on the ignition switch, refer to **Oil Pressure Indicator and Oil Pressure Switch** in Chapter Nine.*

4. Turn the fuel valve on (**Figure 3**, typical).

5. While not part of the starting procedure, the following information is useful in preventing component damage:

   a. Running the engine at a fast idle speed for more than 5 minutes and/or repeatedly snapping the throttle on and off at normal air temperature may cause the exhaust pipes to discolor.

   b. Excessive choke use can cause an excessively rich fuel mixture. This condition can wash oil off the piston and cylinder surfaces and cause piston and cylinder scuffing.

6. The engine is now ready to start. Refer to *Starting Procedure* in this section.

Starting Procedure

NOTE
Do not operate the starter for more than 5 seconds at a time. Wait approximately 10 seconds between starting attempts.

Cold engine with air temperature between 10-25° C (50-95° F)

1. Review *Starting Notes* in this section.
2. Place the engine stop switch (A, **Figure 2**) in the RUN position.
3. Turn the fuel valve on (**Figure 3**, typical).
4. Turn the ignition switch on.
5. Pull the choke lever (**Figure 4**) on.

6. Push the starter button (B, **Figure 2**) and start the engine. Do not open the throttle when pressing the starter button.

NOTE
Trying to start the engine with the throttle open and the choke on, causes a lean mixture and difficult starting.

7. With the engine running, operate the choke lever as required to keep the engine idling.
8. After approximately 30 seconds, push the choke lever off (**Figure 4**). If the idle is rough, open the throttle lightly until the engine warms up.

Cold engine with air temperature of 10° C (50° F) or lower

1. Review *Starting Notes* in this section.
2. Place the engine stop switch (A, **Figure 2**) in the RUN position.
3. Turn the fuel valve on (**Figure 3**).
4. Turn the ignition switch on.
5. Pull the choke lever (**Figure 4**) on.
6. Operate the starter button (B, **Figure 2**) and start the engine. Do not open the throttle when pressing the starter button.
7. Once the engine is running, open the throttle slightly to help warm the engine. Continue warming the engine until the choke can be turned off and the engine responds to the throttle cleanly.

Warm engine and/or high air temperature 35° C (95° F) or higher

1. Review *Starting Notes* in this section.
2. Place the engine stop switch (A, **Figure 2**) in the RUN position.
3. Turn the fuel valve on (**Figure 3**).
4. Turn the ignition switch on.
5. Open the throttle slightly and depress the starter button (B, **Figure 2**). Do not use the choke.

Engine flooded

If the engine does not start after a few attempts, it may be flooded. If a gasoline smell is present after attempting to start the engine, and the engine did not start, the engine is probably flooded. To start a flooded engine, perform the following:
1. Review *Starting Notes* in this section.

2. Place the engine stop switch (A, **Figure 2**) in the RUN position.
3. Turn the fuel valve on (**Figure 3**).
4. Turn the ignition switch on.
5. Push the choke (**Figure 4**) off.
6. Open the throttle completely and depress the starter button (B, **Figure 2**) for 5 seconds. Note the following:
   a. If the engine starts but idles roughly, vary the throttle position slightly until the engine idles and responds smoothly.
   b. If the engine does not start, turn the ignition switch off and wait approximately ten seconds. Then repeat the steps under the warm engine starting procedure in this section. If the engine still does not start, refer to *Engine Will Not Start* in this chapter.

ENGINE WILL NOT START

Identifying the Problem

Because so many things can cause a starting problem, it is important to narrow the possibilities by following a specific troubleshooting procedure—while never overlooking the obvious. Many times, the starting problem is simple, such as a disconnected or damaged wire, which can be found when troubleshooting in a specific order.

If the engine does not start, perform the following steps in order while remembering the *Engine Principals and Operating Requirements* described in this chapter. If the engine fails to start after performing these checks, refer to the troubleshooting procedures indicated in the steps. If the engine starts, but idles or runs roughly, refer to *Poor Engine Performance* in this chapter.

NOTE
An accidentally triggered anti-theft device can cutoff power to the ignition system or starter, depending on how it is wired into the circuit. If such a device is installed, check its operation for a short circuit.

1. Refer to *Starting the Engine* in this chapter to make sure all switch positions and starting procedures are correct.
2. If the starter does not turn over, perform these quick tests to isolate the starter problem:

a. Turn the ignition switch on and shift the transmission into neutral. If the headlight did not come on, check the main fuse and appropriate subfuse (Chapter Nine). If the fuses are good, check the battery cables for a loose or contaminated connection. If correct, check the battery (Chapter Nine).

b. If the headlight came on, push the starter button to start the engine. If the starter relay did not click, the problem is in the wiring to the starter relay, ignition switch or the starter relay is faulty.

c. If the starter relay did click but the starter did not turn the engine over, the problem may be due to excessive voltage drop in the starter circuit or the starter motor is damaged. This could be due to worn brushes or a shorted commutator. The problem can also be in the starter drive system or engine. Refer to *Starting System Troubleshooting* in Chapter Nine.

d. If the problem still exists, refer to the appropriate starter motor procedure in this section.

3. If the starter motor turns over, and the engine seems flooded, refer to *Engine Flooded* under *Starting The Engine* in this chapter. If the engine is not flooded, continue with Step 4.

4. Remove the cap from the fuel tank and make sure the fuel tank has a sufficient amount of fuel to start the engine.

5. If there is sufficient fuel in the fuel tank, remove one of the spark plugs immediately after attempting to start the engine. The plug's insulator should be wet, indicating fuel is reaching the engine. If the plug tip is dry, fuel is not reaching the engine. Confirm this condition by checking a spark plug from the other cylinder. A faulty fuel flow problem

causes this condition. Refer to *Fuel System* in this chapter. If there is fuel on each spark plug and the engine does not start, the engine may not have adequate spark. Continue with Step 6.

NOTE
It is important to note there can be too much fuel on the spark plugs, indicating a flooded condition. This condition can be caused by the following: choke valve stuck open, dirty air filter or flooded carburetor.

NOTE
When examining the spark plug caps in the following steps, check for the presence of water in the plug caps. Also, the plug caps (Figure 5) are permanently attached to the ignition coil secondary wires. Do not attempt to remove the caps from the secondary wires.

6. Make sure each spark plug wire is secure. Push the spark plug caps and slightly rotate them to clean the electrical connection between the cap and spark plug. If the engine does not start, continue with Step 7.

NOTE
Cracked or damaged spark plug caps and cables can cause intermittent problems that are difficult to diagnose. If the engine occasionally misfires or cuts out, use a spray bottle to wet the spark plug cables and caps while the engine is running. Water that enters a damaged cap or cable causes an arc through the insulating material, causing an engine misfire.

7. Perform the *Spark Test* in this section. If there is a strong spark at each plug, perform Step 8. If there is no spark at one coil group, or if the spark is very weak, refer to *Ignition System Troubleshooting* in Chapter Nine.

NOTE
Performing a spark test is the quickest way to isolate an ignition or fuel system problem. If a spark is recorded at each plug wire, there is sufficient voltage at each plug and the ignition system is working correctly. Refer to ***Fuel System*** *in this chapter.*

8. If the fuel and ignition systems are working correctly, perform a leakdown test (this chapter) and cylinder compression test (Chapter Three). If the leakdown test indicates a problem with a cylinder(s), or the compression is low, refer to *Low Engine Compression* under *Engine* in this chapter.

Spark Test

Perform a spark test to determine if the ignition system is producing adequate spark. This test should be performed with a spark tester. A spark tester looks like a spark plug with an adjustable gap between the center electrode and grounded base. Because the voltage required to jump the spark tester gap is sufficiently larger than that of a normally gapped spark plug, the test results are more accurate than with a spark plug. Do not assume that because a spark jumped across a spark plug gap, the ignition system is working correctly.

This test should be performed on a cold and hot engine, if possible. If the test results are positive for each test, the ignition system is considered to be working correctly.

NOTE
The spark tester used in this procedure is available from Motion Pro (part No. 08-0122) and can be purchased through motorcycle dealerships.

CAUTION
After removing the spark plug caps and before removing the spark plugs in Step 1, clean the area around each spark plug with compressed air. Dirt that falls into the cylinder causes rapid engine wear.

1. Disconnect the spark plug caps. Check for the presence of water in each plug cap.

2. Remove and visually inspect each spark plug for damage, then reinstall it.

3. Connect a spark tester to one of the spark plug caps. Ground the spark tester base (or spark plug) to the cylinder head (**Figure 6**). Position the spark tester or spark plug firing tip away from the open spark plug holes. Position the spark tester so the electrodes are visible.

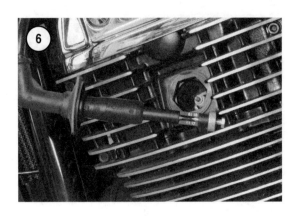

WARNING
If the spark plugs were removed from the cylinder heads, mount the spark tester and spark plugs away from the spark plug holes in the cylinder head so the spark plugs or tester cannot ignite the gasoline vapors in the cylinder. If the engine is flooded, do not perform this test. The firing of the spark plugs or spark tester can ignite fuel ejected through the spark plug holes.

4. Connect a separate grounding tool to each remaining spark plug cap to ground the ignition system.

NOTE
*For information on how to make a grounding tool, refer to **Ignition Grounding Tool** in Chapter One.*

5. With the transmission in neutral, turn the ignition system on and the engine stop switch to the RUN position (A, **Figure 2**).

WARNING
Do not hold the spark tester, spark plug or connector or a serious electrical shock may result.

6. Push the starter button to turn the engine over. A fat blue spark must be evident between the spark tester terminals. Repeat for each spark plug wire.

7. If there is a spark at each plug wire, the ignition system is functioning properly. Check for one or more of the following possible malfunctions:

   a. Faulty fuel system component.
   b. Flooded engine.
   c. Engine damage (low compression).

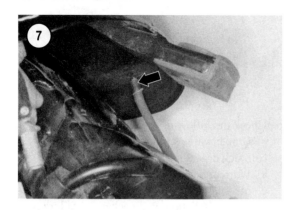

8. If the spark was weak or if there was no spark at one or more plugs, note the following:

 a. If there is no spark at all of the plugs, perform the peak voltage checks described under *Ignition System Troubleshooting* in Chapter Nine.

 b. If there is no spark at one spark plug only, and the plug is good, there is a problem with the spark plug wire or plug cap. Tighten the spark plug wire where it threads into the ignition coil and repeat the test. Refer to *Ignition Coil* in Chapter Nine for information on accessing the ignition coils.

 c. If there is no spark with one ignition group (two spark plugs, same ignition coil), switch the ignition coils and retest. If there is now spark (both spark plugs), the ignition coil is faulty.

Starter Does Not Turn Over

If the engine does not turn over, the battery or starting system is usually at fault. Check the following steps in order:

1. Refer to *Starting the Engine* in this chapter for proper switch and sidestand operation.

2. Check the condition of the main fuse and the ignition/starter subfuse (Chapter Nine).

3. Check for loose, contaminated or damaged battery cables. Check for damaged battery posts.

4. Discharged or damaged battery. Check the battery and battery cables as described in Chapter Nine.

5. Damaged sidestand switch (Chapter Nine).

6. Damaged starter, starter relay or starter switch. Test the starting circuit as described in Chapter Nine to isolate the problem.

7. Ignition system failure. Perform the peak voltage tests in Chapter Nine.

8. Engine damage.

Starter Turns Over Slowly

For the starter to work correctly, the battery must be 75 percent charged and the battery cables cleaned and in good condition. Inspect and test the battery as described in Chapter Nine.

Starter Turns Over Correctly, But Engine Will Not Start

If the starter turns over correctly, the battery and starting circuit are working correctly. Perform the *Spark Test* in this section to isolate the problem to the fuel or ignition system. If the ignition and fuel systems are working correctly, the engine may not have enough compression to start. Refer to *Low Engine Compression* under *Engine* in this chapter.

POOR ENGINE PERFORMANCE

If the engine runs, but performance or drivability is unsatisfactory, refer to the following section that best describes the symptoms.

Engine Starts But Stalls and is Difficult to Restart

Check for the following:

1. Incorrect choke operation. This can be due to improper use or the choke valve is stuck in the carburetor.

2. Open the fuel fill cap. If air is sucked into the tank, the fuel tank breather system is plugged. Note the following:

 a. On 49-state and Canada models, the fuel tank breather hose is connected onto the bottom of the fuel tank (**Figure 7**). Disconnect and clean the hose and the fitting on the fuel tank.

 b. On California models, check the Evaporative emission (EVAP) No. 1 hose. This hose is connected between the fuel tank (**Figure 7**) and the charcoal canister. Disconnect and clean both hose ends and hose fittings. Check the charcoal canister for gasoline.

3. When the ignition switch is turned on the fuel pump should run for approximately 2 seconds. Check for a faulty fuel pump or fuel pump system if the pump does not run when the ignition switch is turned on.

4. Plugged fuel feed hose or fuel filter.

5. Incorrect carburetor adjustment.

6. Incorrect float level adjustment.

7. Plugged carburetor jets.

NOTE
If a warm or hot engine starts with the choke on or if a cold engine starts and runs but shuts off when the choke is turned off, the pilot jets are probably plugged.

8. Contaminated or stale fuel.

9. Clogged air filter.

10. Intake air leak.

11. Plugged exhaust system. Check both mufflers, especially if the motorcycle was just returned from storage.

12. Emission control system (California models):
   a. Damaged EVAP CAV control valve.
   b. Damaged EVAP purge control valve.
   c. Plugged or disconnected emission control hose.

13. Faulty ignition system component.

Engine Backfires, Cuts Out or Misfires During Acceleration

A backfire occurs when fuel is burned or ignited in the exhaust system.

1. A lean air/fuel mixture can cause these engine performance problems. Check for the following conditions:
   a. Incorrect float level adjustment.
   b. Plugged pilot jets or pilot system.
   c. Vacuum leak.

2. Damaged air cutoff valve (installed in each carburetor).

3. Loose exhaust pipe-to-cylinder head connection.

4. Intake air leak.

5. Incorrect ignition timing or a damaged ignition system can cause these conditions. Perform the peak voltage tests in Chapter Nine to isolate the damaged ignition system component. Check the ignition timing as described in Chapter Three.

NOTE
The ignition timing is controlled by the ICM and cannot be adjusted. Checking the ignition timing is used as an aid to diagnose engine and drivability problems.

6. Check the following engine components:
   a. Broken valve springs.
   b. Stuck or leaking valves.
   c. Worn or damaged camshaft lobes.
   d. Incorrect valve timing due to incorrect camshaft installation or a mechanical failure.

Engine Backfires on Deceleration

If the engine backfires when the throttle is released, check the following:

1. Damaged air cutoff valve (installed in each carburetor).

2. Lean carburetor pilot system.

3. Loose exhaust pipe-to-cylinder head connection.

4. Damaged EVAP CAV control valve on California models.

5. On models so equipped, damaged pulse secondary air injection (PAIR) system.

6. Faulty ignition system component.

7. Check the following engine components:
   a. Broke valve springs.
   b. Stuck or leaking valves.
   c. Worn or damaged camshaft lobes.
   d. Incorrect valve timing due to incorrect camshaft installation or a mechanical failure.

Poor Fuel Mileage

1. Clogged fuel system.

2. Faulty thermostat.

3. Dirty or clogged air filter.

4. Incorrect ignition timing.

5. Vacuum leak.

6. Damaged EVAP CAV control valve on California models.

Engine Will Not Idle or Idles Roughly

1. Clogged air filter element.

2. Poor fuel flow resulting from a partially clogged fuel valve, fuel filter or fuel hose. A partially

clogged fuel tank breather hose (49-state and Canada) or evaporative emission hose (California) can also cause this problem.

3. Contaminated or stale fuel.
4. Incorrect carburetor adjustment.
5. Leaking head gasket(s) or vacuum leak.
6. Intake air leak.
7. Incorrect ignition timing (defective ICM or ignition pulse generator).
8. Low engine compression.
9. Tappet failure

Low Engine Power

1. Support the motorcycle on a stand with the rear wheel off the ground, then spin the rear wheel by hand. If the wheel spins freely, perform Step 2. If the wheel does not spin freely, check for the following conditions:
   a. Dragging brakes.

NOTE
After riding the motorcycle, come to a stop on a level surface (in a safe area away from all traffic). Turn the engine off and shift the transmission into neutral. Walk or push the motorcycle forward. If the motorcycle is harder to push than normal, check for dragging brakes.

   b. Damaged final drive gear assembly.
   c. Damaged wheel bearings.
2. Test ride the motorcycle and accelerate quickly from first to second gear. If the engine speed increased according to throttle position, perform Step 3. If the engine speed did not increase, check for one or more of the following problems:
   a. Slipping clutch.
   b. Warped clutch plates/discs.
   c. Worn clutch plates/discs.
   d. Weak or damaged clutch springs.
3. Test ride the motorcycle and accelerate lightly. If the engine speed increased according to throttle position, perform Step 4. If the engine speed did not increase, check for one or more of the following problems:
   a. Clogged air filter.
   b. Restricted fuel flow.

   c. Pinched or partially clogged fuel tank breather hose (49-state and Canada) or evaporative emission hose (California).
   d. Clogged or damaged muffler. Tap the mufflers with a rubber mallet to check for loose or broken baffles.

NOTE
A clogged muffler or exhaust system prevents some of the burned exhaust gasses from exiting the exhaust port at the end of the exhaust stroke. This condition affects the incoming air/fuel mixture on the intake stroke and reduces engine power.

4. Check for a retarded ignition timing as described in Chapter Three. A decrease in power results when the plugs fire later than normal.
5. Check for one or more of the following problems:
   a. Low engine compression.
   b. Hydraulic tappet failure. Refer to *Hydraulic Tappets* in this chapter.
   c. Worn spark plugs.
   d. Fouled spark plug(s).
   e. Incorrect spark plug heat range.
   f. Weak ignition coil(s).
   g. Incorrect ignition timing (defective ICM or ignition pulse generator).
   h. Plugged carburetor passages.
   i. Incorrect oil level (too high or too low).
   j. Contaminated oil.
   k. Worn or damaged valve train assembly.
   l. Engine overheating. Refer to *Engine Overheating* in this section.
6. If the engine knocks when it is accelerated or when running at high speed, check for one or more of the following possible malfunctions:
   a. Incorrect type of fuel.
   b. Lean fuel mixture.
   c. Advanced ignition timing (defective ICM).

NOTE
Other signs of advanced ignition timing are engine overheating and hard or uneven engine starting.

   d. Excessive carbon buildup in combustion chamber.
   e. Worn pistons and/or cylinder bores.

f. Hydraulic tappet failure. Refer to *Hydraulic Tappets* in this chapter.

Poor Idle or Low Speed Performance

1. Check for an incorrect pilot screw adjustment.
2. Check for damaged or loose intake manifold and air filter housing hose clamps. These conditions cause an air leak.
3. Perform the spark test in this chapter. Note the following:
   a. If the spark is good, go to Step 4.
   b. If the spark is weak, perform the *Peak Voltage Testing* described in Chapter Nine.
4. Check the ignition timing as described in Chapter Three. If ignition timing is correct, perform Step 5. If the timing is incorrect, perform the *Peak Voltage Testing* in Chapter Nine.
5. Check the fuel system as described under *Fuel System* in this chapter.
6. Hydraulic tappet failure. Refer to *Hydraulic Tappets* in this chapter.

Poor High Speed Performance

1. Check ignition timing as described in Chapter Three. If ignition timing is correct, perform Step 2. If the timing is incorrect, perform the peak voltage tests in Chapter Nine.
2. Check the fuel system as described under *Fuel System* in this chapter.
3. Hydraulic tappet failure. Refer to *Hydraulic Tappets* in this chapter.
4. Incorrect valve timing and worn or damaged valve springs can cause poor high-speed performance. If the camshafts were timed just before the motorcycle experienced this type of problem, the cam timing may be incorrect. If the cam timing was not set or changed and all of the other inspection procedures in this section failed to locate the problem, inspect the camshafts, hydraulic tappets and valve assembly.

FUEL SYSTEM

The following section isolates common fuel system problems under specific complaints. If the starter motor turns over and there is spark at each spark plug, poor fuel flow may be preventing the correct amount of fuel from being supplied to the spark plugs. Troubleshoot the fuel system as follows:

1. Open the fuel fill cap. If air is sucked into the tank, the fuel tank breather system is plugged. Note the following:
   a. On 49-state and Canada models, the fuel tank breather hose is connected onto the bottom of the fuel tank (**Figure 7**).
   b. On California models, check the Evaporative emission (EVAP) No. 1 hose. This hose is connected between the fuel tank (**Figure 7**) and the charcoal canister.
2. Check there is a sufficient amount of fuel in the tank.
3. After attempting to start the engine, remove one of the spark plugs (Chapter Three) and check for the presence of fuel on the plug tip. Note the following:
   a. If there is no fuel visible on the plug, remove a spark plug from the other cylinder. If there is no fuel on this plug, check for a clogged fuel filter or fuel line. If all of these are okay, continue with Step 4.
   b. If there is fuel present on the plug tip, and the engine has spark at all of the spark plugs, check for an excessive intake air leak, or the possibility of contaminated or stale fuel.

> *NOTE*
> *If the motorcycle was not used for some time and was not properly stored, the fuel may have gone stale where lighter parts of the fuel have evaporated. Depending on the condition of the fuel, a no-start condition can result.*

   c. If there is an excessive amount of fuel on the plug, check for a clogged air filter or flooded carburetor (incorrect float level).
4. Perform the *Fuel Pump System Test* in Chapter Eight.

Rich Mixture

The following conditions can cause a rich air/fuel mixture:
1. Clogged air filter.
2. Choke valve stuck open.
3. Float level too high.
4. Contaminated float valve seat.
5. Worn or damaged float valve and seat.

6. Leaking or damaged float.
7. Clogged carburetor jets.
8. Damaged vacuum piston/diagram.
9. Faulty EVAP purge control valve (California models).

Lean Mixture

The following conditions can cause a lean air/fuel mixture:
1. Intake air leak.
2. Float level too low.
3. Clogged fuel line.
4. Partially clogged fuel tank breather hose (49-state and Canada) or evaporative emission hose (California).
5. Damaged vacuum piston/diaphragm.
6. Plugged carburetor air vent hose.
7. Damaged float.
8. Damaged float valve.
9. Faulty PAIR control valve on models so equipped.

ENGINE

Engine Smoke

The color of engine smoke can help diagnose engine problems or operating conditions.

Black smoke

Black smoke is an indication of a rich air/fuel mixture where an excessive amount of fuel is being burned in the combustion chamber.

Blue smoke

Blue smoke indicates the engine is burning oil in the combustion chamber as it leaks past worn valve stem seals and piston rings. Excessive oil consumption is another indicator of an engine that is burning oil. Perform a compression test (Chapter Three) to isolate the problem.

White smoke or steam

It is normal to see white smoke or steam from the exhaust after first starting the engine in cold weather. This is actually condensed steam formed by the engine during combustion. If the motorcycle is ridden far enough, the water cannot collect in the crankcase and should not become a problem. Once the engine heats up to normal operating temperature, the water evaporates and exits the engine through the crankcase vent system. However, if the motorcycle is ridden for short trips or repeatedly started and stopped and allowed to cool off without the engine getting warm enough, water starts to collect in the crankcase. With each short run of the engine, more water collects. As this water mixes with the oil in the crankcase, sludge is produced. Water sludge can eventually cause engine damage as it circulates through the lubrication system and blocks off oil passages. Water draining from drain holes in exhaust pipes indicates water buildup.

Large amounts of steam can also be caused by a cracked cylinder head or cylinder block surface that allows coolant to leak into the combustion chamber. Perform a coolant pressure test as described in Chapter Ten.

Low Engine Compression

Problems with the engine top end affects engine performance and drivability. When the engine is suspect, perform the leakdown procedure in this chapter and make a compression test as described in Chapter Three. Interpret the results as described in each procedure to troubleshoot the suspect area. An engine can lose compression through the following areas:
1. Hydraulic tappets:
   a. Collapsed tappets.
   b. Tappets not properly bled during installation.
   c. Incorrect tappet adjustment during installation.
   d. Locked or damaged tappet(s).
2. Valves:
   a. Incorrect valve timing.
   b. Worn or damaged valve seats (valve and/or cylinder head).
   c. Bent valves.
   d. Weak or broken valve springs.
3. Cylinder head:
   a. Loose spark plug or damaged spark plug hole.
   b. Damaged cylinder head gasket.
   c. Warped or cracked cylinder head.
4. Worn pistons, piston rings and cylinder bore.

Engine Overheating
(Cooling System)

> *WARNING*
> *Do not remove the radiator cap, coolant drain plug or disconnect any coolant hose immediately after or during engine operation. Scalding fluid and steam may be blown out under pressure and cause serious injury. When the engine has been operated, the coolant is hot and under pressure. Attempting to remove the items when the engine is hot can cause the coolant to spray violently from the radiator, water pump or hose, causing excessive burns and injury on contact.*

1. Low coolant level.
2. Air in cooling system.
3. Clogged radiator, hose or engine coolant passages.
4. Thermostat stuck closed.
5. Worn or damaged radiator cap.
6. Open or short circuit in the cooling system wiring harness.
7. Damaged water pump.
8. Damaged coolant temperature indicator.
9. Radiator fan inoperative.
10. Damaged water pump.

Engine Overheating
(Engine)

1. Improper spark plug heat range.
2. Low oil level.
3. Oil not circulating properly.
4. Valves leaking.
5. Heavy engine carbon deposits in combustion chamber.
6. Dragging brake(s).
7. Clutch slipping.

Engine Temperature Too Low

1. Thermostat stuck open.
2. Thermostat removed.

Preignition

Preignition is the premature burning of fuel and is caused by hot spots in the combustion chambers. Glowing deposits in the combustion chambers, inadequate cooling or an overheated spark plug can all cause preignition. This is first noticed as a power loss but eventually causes damage to the internal parts of the engine because of higher combustion chamber temperatures.

Detonation

Commonly called spark knock or fuel knock, detonation is the violent explosion of fuel in the combustion chamber before the proper time of ignition. Excessive damage can result. Use of low octane gasoline is a common cause of detonation.

Even when using a high octane gasoline, detonation can still occur. Other causes are over-advanced ignition timing, lean air/fuel mixture at or near full throttle, inadequate engine cooling or the excessive accumulation of carbon deposits in the combustion chamber (cylinder head and piston crowns).

Power Loss

Refer to *Poor Engine Performance* in this chapter.

Engine Noises

Unusual noises are often the first indication of a developing problem. Investigate any new noises as soon as possible. Something that may be a minor problem, if corrected, could prevent the possibility of more extensive damage.

Use a mechanic's stethoscope or a small section of hose held near your ear (not directly on your ear) with the other end close to the source of the noise to isolate the location. Determining the exact cause of a noise can be difficult. If this is the case, consult with a professional mechanic to determine the cause. Do not disassemble major components until all other possibilities have been eliminated.

Consider the following when troubleshooting engine noises:

1. Knocking or pinging during acceleration is usually caused by using a lower octane fuel than recommended. It may also be caused by poor fuel.

Pinging can also be caused by an incorrect spark plug heat range or carbon build-up in the combustion chamber.

2. Slapping or rattling noises at low speed or during acceleration may be caused by excessive piston-to-cylinder wall clearance (piston slap).

NOTE
Piston slap is easier to detect when the engine is cold and before the pistons have expanded. Once the engine has warmed up, piston expansion reduces piston-to-cylinder clearance.

3. Knocking or rapping while decelerating is usually caused by excessive rod bearing clearance.

4. Persistent knocking and vibration occurring every crankshaft rotation is usually caused by worn rod or main bearing(s). It can also be caused by broken piston rings or damaged piston pins.

5. Rapid on-off squeal is because of a compression leak around the cylinder head gasket or spark plug(s).

6. If valve train noise, occurs, check for the following:

    a. Hydraulic tappets. Refer to *Hydraulic Tappets* in this chapter.

    b. Worn or damaged camshaft.

    c. Worn or damaged valve train components.

    d. Valve sticking in guide.

    e. Broken valve spring.

    f. Low oil pressure.

    g. Clogged oil hole or oil passage in tappet cylinder.

ENGINE LUBRICATION

An improperly operating engine lubrication system quickly leads to engine seizure. Check the engine oil level and oil pressure as described in Chapter Three. Oil pump service is described in Chapter Six.

High Oil Consumption or Excessive Exhaust Smoke

1. Worn valve guides.
2. Worn or damaged piston rings.

Low Oil Pressure

1. Low oil level.
2. Worn or damaged oil pump.
3. Clogged oil strainer screen.
4. Clogged oil filter.
5. Internal oil leakage.
6. Oil pressure relief valve stuck open.
7. Incorrect type of engine oil.

High Oil Pressure

1. Oil pressure relief valve stuck closed.
2. Clogged oil filter.
3. Clogged oil gallery or metering orifices.

No Oil Pressure

1. Low oil level.
2. Oil pressure relief valve stuck closed.
3. Damaged oil pump.
4. Damaged oil pump sprocket(s) or chain.
5. Incorrect oil pump installation.
6. Internal oil leak.

Oil Pressure Indicator Stays On

1. Low oil pressure.
2. No oil pressure.
3. Damaged oil pressure switch.
4. Short circuit in warning lamp circuit.

Oil Level Too Low

1. Oil level not maintained at correct level.
2. Worn piston rings.
3. Worn cylinder.
4. Worn valve guides.
5. Worn valve stem seals.
6. Piston rings incorrectly installed during engine overhaul.
7. External oil leaks.
8. Oil leaking into the cooling system.

Oil Contamination

1. Blown head gasket allowing the coolant to leak into the engine.
2. Coolant leak.

3. Oil and filter not changed at specified intervals or when operating conditions demand more frequent changes.
4. Damaged clutch friction plates.

HYDRAULIC TAPPETS

Noisy Tappet

1. If one or more tappets are noisy, check the oil level and bring to the correct level as required. Then ride the motorcycle for 5 minutes with the engine speed over 3000 rpm. Then stop and recheck the oil level. Note the following:
    a. If the oil level is correct, continue with Step 2.
    b. If the oil level is incorrect, check for a contaminated oil filter or contaminated oil.

> *NOTE*
> *If the oil level was initially low, air may have entered the tappet oil passage.*

2. Check the oil pressure as described in Chapter Three. Note the following:
    a. If the oil pressure reading is correct, continue with Step 3.
    b. If the oil pressure reading is incorrect, check for a clogged oil passage or oil hole leading to the cylinder head.
3. Remove the cylinder head covers (Chapter Four) and check the engine components for proper lubrication. Note the following:
    a. If it appears that the engine is being adequately lubricated, continue with Step 4.
    b. If the engine is not being adequately lubricated, check for a clogged oil pipe, a damaged O-ring or a damaged oil hole cap.
4. If a problem was not found, remove the hydraulic tappets (Chapter Four) and check them for the following conditions:
    a. Weak or damaged assist shaft spring.
    b. Damaged assist shaft.
    c. Sticking plunger.

> *NOTE*
> *The tappets are sealed units and cannot be rebuilt. The best way to troubleshoot suspect tappets is to remove and bleed them as described under* **Hydraulic Tappets** *in Chapter Four. Then try to compress the tappet as de-*

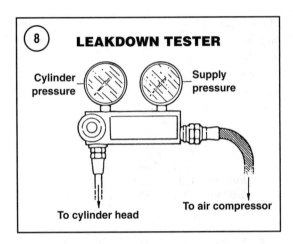

scribed in the procedure. If the tappet can be compressed by more than 0.2 mm (0.008 in.), bleed it once again. If the results are the same, replace the tappet.

Engine Lacks Power

A clogged oiling system or damaged tappet(s) can cause hard starting and reduced engine performance. To isolate this problem, perform the following steps:
1. Try to start the engine with the starter. Note the following.
    a. If the engine does not start, continue with Step 2.
    b. If the engine starts, the engine oil may be foaming from engine over-rev.
2. Check the oil pressure as described in Chapter Three. Note the following:
    a. If the oil pressure reading is correct, continue with Step 3.
    b. If the oil pressure reading is incorrect, check for a too low oil level. If the oil level is correct, check for a clogged oil control orifice, a clogged engine oil passage, contaminated oil or a contaminated oil filter.
3. Remove and inspect the tappets (Chapter Four).

CYLINDER LEAKDOWN TEST

A cylinder leakdown test is one of the best tests to perform when trying to determine engine condition. The test applies compressed air into the combustion chamber when the piston is set at TDC on its com-

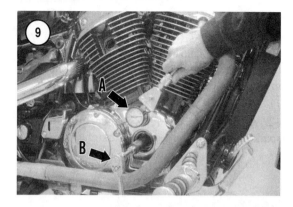

NOTE
*With the cylinder head covers installed on the engine, the camshafts cannot be viewed to ensure that the valves are closed when aligning the FT mark as described in Step 4. Because the spark plug hole is not accessible to check compression by hand, use this method to locate TDC. Thread a compression gauge (A, **Figure 9**) into the front cylinder spark plug hole. Then slowly turn the engine (B, **Figure 9**) clockwise while watching the compression gauge. When compression becomes available at the plug hole it starts to register on the gauge, indicating the piston is near TDC on its compression stroke. Continue turning the crankshaft and align the FT mark on the ignition pulse generator rotor with the right crankcase cover index mark. The front cylinder should now be at TDC on its compression stroke.*

5. To prevent the engine from turning over as compressed air is applied to the cylinder, shift the transmission into fifth gear and have an assistant apply the rear brake.

WARNING
Even with the steps made in Step 5, the crankshaft may turn when compressed air is applied to the cylinder. Do not put a socket on the primary drive gear bolt and try to hold the crankshaft by hand. The sudden application of air into the cylinder may turn the crankshaft unexpectedly and cause injury.

6. Thread the test adapter into the front cylinder spark plug hole. Connect the air compressor hose to the tester (**Figure 10**) following the manufacturer's instructions.

7. Apply compressed air to the leakage tester and make a cylinder leakage test following the manufacturer's instructions. Read the percent of leakage on the gauge, following the manufacturer's instructions. Record the reading and note the following:

NOTE
If the crankshaft did not move when air was applied to the cylinder, but

pression stroke. Because the valves are closed, there should be little air leaking from the cylinder. The leakdown tester, installed in the cylinder head spark plug hole, measures the percent of leakage. If the tester indicates excessive leakage, air blowing out through the worn or damaged part can be easily located. Both cylinders are checked separately in this manner. A cylinder leakdown tester (**Figure 8**) and an air compressor are required to perform this test.

Follow the tester manufacturer's directions along with the following information when performing a cylinder leakdown test:

1. Start and run the engine until it is warm. Turn the engine off.

2. Remove one of the front cylinder spark plugs as described under *Spark Plugs* in Chapter Three. Make sure the other spark plug is tight.

3. Remove the timing hole cap from the right crankcase cover.

4. Use a socket on the primary drive gear bolt, turn the crankshaft clockwise and align the FT mark on the ignition pulse generator rotor with the index mark on the right crankcase cover. Refer to *Cylinder Head Covers and Rocker Arms* in Chapter Four to view the timing marks.

there is an immediate high loss of air through the valves, the engine is not at TDC on its compression stroke. Because it is impossible to view the camshafts on an assembled VT1100 engine when setting the engine at TDC, the piston is probably moving through the exhaust stroke and the crankshaft is one turn off. Disconnect the air source entering the engine. Rotate the crankshaft clockwise one full turn and realign the FT mark on the ignition pulse generator with the index mark on the right crankcase cover. If there is a loss of air when the engine is at TDC on its compression stroke, the engine has probably suffered some type of major top end damage.

   a. For a new or rebuilt engine, a leakage rate of 0 to 5 percent per cylinder is desired. A leakage rate of 6 to 14 percent is acceptable and means the engine is in good condition.

   b. If testing a used engine, the critical rate is not the percent of leakage for each cylinder, but instead the difference between the cylinders. On a used engine, a leakage rate of 10 percent or less between cylinders is satisfactory.

   c. A leakage rate exceeding 10 percent between cylinders points to an engine that is in poor condition and requires further inspection and possible repair.

8. After checking the percent of leakage, and with air pressure still applied to the combustion chamber, listen for air escaping from the following areas. If necessary, use a mechanic's stethoscope to pinpoint the source.

   a. Air leaking through the exhaust pipe indicates a leaking exhaust valve.

   b. Air leaking through the carburetor or air filter indicates a leaking intake valve.

   c. Air leaking through the crankcase breather tube suggests worn piston rings or a worn cylinder bore.

   d. Air leaking into the cooling system causes the coolant to bubble in the radiator. When this condition is indicated, check for damaged cylinder head gaskets and warped cylinder head or cylinder block surfaces.

9. Remove the leakage tester and install it into one of the rear cylinder spark plug holes. Install the front cylinder spark plugs to help prevent the engine from turning over.

10. Turn the crankshaft clockwise and align the RT mark on the ignition pulse generator with the index mark on the right crankcase cover.

11. Repeat the leakdown test for the rear cylinder.

12. After testing the rear cylinder, reinstall the spark plug and reconnect the spark plug cap.

CLUTCH

This section lists basic clutch problems. Clutch service is covered in Chapter Six.

No Pressure at Clutch Lever

1. Incorrect clutch adjustment.
2. Broken clutch cable.
3. Damaged clutch release mechanism.

Clutch Lever Hard to Pull In

1. Dry, kinked or damaged clutch cable.
2. Incorrect clutch cable routing.
3. Damaged pressure plate.
4. Damaged clutch release mechanism.
5. Damaged clutch release bearing.

Rough Clutch Operation

1. Worn, grooved or damaged clutch hub and clutch housing slots.
2. Clutch system damage.

Clutch Slips

If the engine speed increases without an increase in motorcycle speed, the clutch is probably slipping. The main causes of clutch slippage are:

1. No clutch lever free play.
2. Worn clutch friction discs.
3. Weak clutch springs.
4. Sticking or damaged clutch release mechanism.
5. Clutch plates contaminated by engine oil additives.

Clutch Drag

If the clutch does not disengage or if the motorcycle creeps with the transmission in gear and the clutch disengaged, the clutch is dragging. Some main causes of clutch drag are:
1. Excessive clutch lever free play.
2. Warped clutch plates.
3. Damaged clutch release mechanism.
4. Loose clutch release mechanism.
5. High oil level.
6. Incorrect oil viscosity.
7. Engine oil additive being used.
8. Damaged clutch hub and clutch housing splines.

GEARSHIFT LINKAGE

The gearshift linkage assembly connects the shift pedal (external shift mechanism) to the shift drum (internal shift mechanism). Refer to Chapter Seven to identify the components called out in this section.

Transmission Jumps Out of Gear

1. Damaged stopper arm.
2. Damaged stopper arm spring.
3. Worn or damaged shift drum.
4. Damaged gearshift spindle B spring.
5. Loose or damaged cam plate.
6. Bent shift fork shaft(s).
7. Bent or damaged shift fork(s).
8. Worn gear dogs or slots.

Difficult Shifting

1. Incorrect clutch operation.
2. Incorrect oil viscosity.
3. Loose or damaged stopper arm assembly.
4. Bent shift fork shaft(s).
5. Bent or damaged shift fork(s).
6. Worn gear dogs or slots.
7. Damaged shift drum grooves.
8. Damaged gearshift spindle A or B.
9. Incorrect gearshift linkage installation.

Shift Pedal Does Not Return

1. Damaged shift pedal mechanism.
2. Bent gearshift spindle A.
3. Bent gearshift spindle B.

4. Weak or damaged gearshift spindle B return spring.
5. Gearshift spindle B incorrectly installed (return spring incorrectly indexed around pin).

Excessive Engine/Transmission Noise

1. Damaged primary drive and driven gears or bearing.
2. Damaged transmission bearings or gears.

TRANSMISSION

Transmission symptoms are sometimes difficult to distinguish from clutch symptoms. Basic transmission troubleshooting is listed below. Refer to Chapter Seven for transmission service procedures. Before working on the transmission, make sure the clutch and gearshift linkage assembly are not causing the problem.

Difficult Shifting

1. Incorrect clutch operation.
2. Bent shift fork(s).
3. Damaged shift fork guide pin(s).
4. Bent shift fork shaft(s).
5. Bent gearshift spindle A or B.
6. Damaged shift drum grooves.

Jumps Out of Gear

1. Loose or damaged stopper arm.
2. Bent or damaged shift fork(s).
3. Bent shift fork shaft(s).
4. Damaged shift drum grooves.
5. Worn gear dogs or slots.
6. Weak or damaged gearshift spindle B return spring.

Incorrect Shift Lever Operation

1. Bent shift pedal or linkage.
2. Stripped shift pedal splines.
3. Damaged shift linkage.
4. Damaged gearshift spindle A or B.

Excessive Gear Noise

1. Worn or damaged transmission bearings.
2. Worn or damaged gears.
3. Excessive gear backlash.

Excessive Output Gear Noise

The output gear assembly is mounted on the left crankcase. The output gear is mounted inside the engine.

1. Excessive output drive and driven gear backlash.
2. Excessively worn or damaged gearcase bearings.
3. Excessively worn or damaged output drive and driven gears.
4. Incorrect shim adjustment (due to worn gears or incorrect shim thickness installed after output gearcase reassembly).

FINAL DRIVE

Noise is usually the first indication of a final drive problem. However, trying to distinguish or trouble-shoot noises between the engine, output gear, drive shaft and final drive unit can be confusing. First, do not confuse tire and final drive noise. Test ride the motorcycle over different types of pavement and on both flat and curved roads and it becomes apparent how different road surfaces produce different sounds.

Consider the following when road testing and troubleshooting a final drive problem:

1. Check the final drive oil level (Chapter Three).
2. Check the tire pressure (Chapter Three).
3. Inspect the tires for an excessively worn or abnormal wear pattern that causes the tires to produce a growling or rumbling noise.
4. Because defective wheel bearings can produce a clicking or growling noise, check the wheel bearings as described in Chapter Eleven.
5. Support the motorcycle with the rear wheel off the ground. Shift the transmission into neutral and turn the rear wheel slowly. Check for any roughness or grabbing. A chipped gear or bearing often makes a clicking sound.
6. Ride the motorcycle long enough to bring the final drive oil up to normal operating temperature. Then road test the motorcycle under the following conditions and note any noise differences:
   a. Acceleration.

   b. Cruise. Here the motorcycle is being ridden at a constant speed.
   c. Coast. Accelerate the motorcycle, then release the throttle and let it coast in gear and under engine compression.
   d. A knocking or clicking noise usually results from a damaged gear or bearing.
   e. A whining or humming noise that varies during acceleration and deceleration indicates too little gear lash between the ring gear and pinion gear. If this condition continues, excessive wear eventually damages the gears.

Oil Inspection

Drain the final drive oil (Chapter Three) into a clean container. Wipe a small mount of oil on your fingers and then rub them together. Check for the presence of metal particles. While a small amount of particles in the oil is normal, a large amount indicates bearing or gear damage.

Oil Leak

1. Damaged oil seals.
2. Oil level too high.
3. Clogged breather.
4. Damaged housing or housing cover.

Excessive Noise

1. Oil level too low.
2. Excessive ring gear and pinion gear backlash.
3. Worn or damaged ring gear and pinion gears.
4. Worn or damaged ring gear or pinion gear bearing(s).
5. Worn or damaged drive pinion and splines.
6. Loose or damaged driven flange and wheel hub engagement.
7. Worn or damaged ring gear shaft and driven flange engagement.

Excessive Rear Wheel Backlash

1. Worn or damaged drive shaft splines.
2. Excessive ring gear and pinion gear backlash.
3. Worn or damaged universal joint bearing.
4. Worn or damaged ring gear shaft and driven flange engagement.

ELECTRICAL TESTING

This section describes basic electrical trouble-shooting and the use of test equipment. Refer to Chapter Nine for specific component testing.

Electrical troubleshooting can be time-consuming and frustrating without proper knowledge and a suitable plan. Refer to the color wiring diagrams at the end of the manual for component and connector identification. Use the wiring diagrams to determine how the circuit should work by tracing the current paths from the power source through the circuit components to ground. Also check any circuits that share the same fuse, ground or switch. If the other circuits work properly and the shared wiring is good, the cause must be in the wiring used only by the suspect circuit. If all related circuits are faulty at the same time, the probable cause is a poor ground connection or a blown fuse(s).

As with all troubleshooting procedures, analyze typical symptoms in a systematic manner. Never assume anything and do not overlook the obvious, such as a blown fuse or an electrical connector that has separated. Test the simplest and most obvious items first and try to make tests at easily accessible points on the motorcycle.

Electrical Component Replacement

Most motorcycle dealerships and parts suppliers do not accept the return of any electrical part. If you cannot determine the *exact* cause of any electrical system malfunction, have a Honda dealership retest that specific system to verify your test results. If you purchase a new electrical component(s), install it, and then find the system still does not work properly, you will probably be unable to return the unit for a refund.

Consider any test results carefully before replacing a component that tests only *slightly* out of specification, especially resistance. A number of variables can affect test results dramatically. These include the testing meter's internal circuitry, ambient temperature and conditions under which the machine has been operated. All instructions and specifications have been checked for accuracy; however, successful test results depend to a great degree upon individual accuracy.

Preliminary Checks and Precautions

Before starting any electrical troubleshooting, perform the following:

1. Check the main fuse (Chapter Nine). If the fuse is blown, replace it.
2. Check the subfuses mounted in the fuse box (Chapter Nine). Inspect the suspected fuse, and replace it if blown.
3. Inspect the battery. Make sure it is fully charged, and that the battery leads are clean and securely attached to the battery terminals. Refer to *Battery* in Chapter Nine.
4. Disconnect each electrical connector in the suspect circuit and make sure there are no bent terminals in the electrical connector. A bent terminal does not connect to the female terminal, causing an open circuit.
5. Make sure the terminals on the end of each wire are pushed all the way into the plastic housing. If not, carefully push them in with a narrow blade screwdriver.
6. Check all electrical wires where they enter the individual metal terminals in both the male and female plastic housings.
7. Make sure all electrical connectors within the housing are clean and free of corrosion. Check the connector for water contamination. Clean them, if necessary, and pack the connectors with dielectric grease.
8. Push the connector halves together. Make sure the connectors are fully engaged and locked together.
9. Never pull the electrical wires when disconnecting an electrical connector. Pull only on the connector plastic housing.

> *NOTE*
> *Always consider electrical connectors the weak link in the electrical system. Dirty, loose-fitting and corroded connectors cause numerous electrical related problems, especially on high-mileage motorcycles. When troubleshooting an electrical problem, carefully inspect the connectors and wiring harness.*

10. Never use a self-powered test light on circuits that contain solid-state devices. The solid-state devices may be damaged.

Intermittent Problems

Intermittent problems are problems that do not occur all the time and can be difficult to locate. For example, when a problem only occurs when the motorcycle is ridden over rough roads (vibration) or in wet conditions (water penetration), it is intermittent. To locate and repair intermittent problems, simulate the condition when testing the components. Note the following:

1. Vibration is a common problem with loose or damaged electrical connectors.

   a. Perform a continuity test as described in the appropriate service procedure or under *Continuity Test* in this chapter.

   b. Lightly pull or wiggle the connectors while repeating the test. Do the same when checking the wiring harness and individual components, especially where the wires enter a housing or connector.

   c. A change in meter readings indicates a poor connection. Find and repair the problem or replace the part. Check for wires with cracked or broken insulation.

NOTE
An analog ohmmeter is useful when making this type of test. Slight needle movements are visibly apparent to indicate a loose connection.

2. Heat is another common problem with connectors or plugs that have loose or poor connections. As these connections heat up, the connection or joint expands and separates, causing an open circuit. Other heat related problems occur when a component creates its own heat as it starts to fail or go bad.

   a. Troubleshoot the problem to help isolate the problem or area.

   b. To check a connector, perform a continuity test as described in the appropriate service procedure or under *Continuity Test* in this section. Then repeat the test while heating the connector with a heat gun or hair dryer. If the meter reading was normal (continuity) when the connector was cold, then fluctuated or read infinity when heat was applied, the connection is bad.

   c. To check a component, allow the engine to cool, then start and run the engine. Note oper-

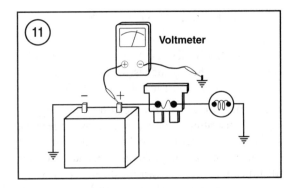

ational differences when the engine is cold and hot.

   d. If the engine does not start, isolate and remove the component. Test it at room temperature and retest after heating it with a hair dryer. A change in meter readings indicates a temperature problem.

CAUTION
A heat gun or hair dryer will quickly raise the heat of the component being tested. Do not apply heat directly to the ICM or use heat in excess of 60° C (140° F) on any electrical component. If available, monitor heat with an infrared thermometer.

3. When the problem occurs when riding in wet conditions or in areas with high humidity, start and run the engine in a dry area. Then, with the engine running, spray water onto the suspected component. Often times, water related problems repair themselves after the component becomes hot enough to dry itself, adding to the frustration.

Test Light or Voltmeter

A test light can be constructed from a 12-volt light bulb with a pair of test leads carefully soldered to the bulb. To check for battery voltage in a circuit, attach one lead to ground and the other lead to various points along the circuit. The bulb lights when battery voltage is present.

A voltmeter is used in the same manner as the test light to find out if battery voltage is present in any given circuit. The voltmeter, unlike the test light, also indicates how much voltage is present at each test point. When using a voltmeter, attach the positive lead to the component or wire to be checked

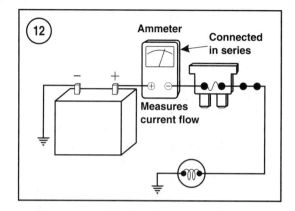

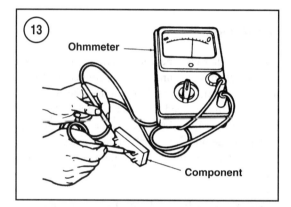

Use a self-powered test light as follows:

CAUTION
Do not use a self-powered test light with an incandescent bulb to test electronic equipment or circuits with solid-state devices. Because this type of test light uses a battery and applies voltage to the circuit during the test, the current draw can damage the component. Instead, use an LED test light or a digital multimeter with a minimum impedance of 10M ohms/DCV.

1. Touch the test leads together to make sure the light bulb goes on. If not, correct the problem before using it in a test procedure.
2. Disconnect the motorcycle's battery or remove the fuse(s) that protects the circuit to be tested.
3. Select two points within the circuit where there should be continuity.
4. Attach one lead of the self-powered test light to each point.
5. If there is continuity, the self-powered test light bulb comes on.
6. If there is no continuity, the self-powered test light bulb does not come on, indicating an open circuit.

Ohmmeter

An ohmmeter measures the resistance (in ohms) to current flow in a circuit or component. Like the self-powered test light, an ohmmeter contains its own power source and must not be connected to a live circuit.

Ohmmeters may be analog type (needle scale) or digital type (LCD or LED readout). Both types of ohmmeters have a switch that allows the user to select different ranges of resistance for accurate readings. The analog ohmmeter also has a set-adjust control which is used to zero or calibrate the meter (digital ohmmeters do not require calibration).

An ohmmeter is used by connecting its test leads to the terminals or leads of the circuit or component to be tested (**Figure 13**). If an analog meter is used, it must be calibrated by touching the test leads together and turning the set-adjust knob until the meter needle reads zero. When the meter does not zero properly, replace the battery in the meter and readjust. When the leads are uncrossed, the needle

and the negative lead to a good ground (**Figure 11**). When purchasing a digital voltmeter, select one with a minimum impedance of 10M ohms/DCV.

Ammeter

An ammeter measures the flow of current (amps) in a circuit (**Figure 12**). When connected in series in a circuit, the ammeter determines if current is flowing through the circuit and if that current flow is excessive because of a short in the circuit. Current flow is often referred to as current draw. Comparing actual current draw in the circuit or component to the manufacturer's specified current draw provides useful diagnostic information.

Self-powered Test Light (Continuity Tester)

A self-powered test light can be constructed from a 12-volt light bulb, a pair of test leads and a 12-volt battery. When the test leads are touched together the light bulb should go on.

should move to the other end of the scale indicating infinite resistance.

During a continuity test, a reading of infinity indicates there is an open in the circuit or component. A reading of zero indicates continuity, that is, there is no measurable resistance in the circuit or component being tested. If the meter needle falls between these two ends of the scale, this indicates the actual resistance to current flow that is present. To determine the resistance, multiply the meter reading by the ohmmeter scale. For example, a meter reading of 5 multiplied by the R × 1000 scale is 5000 ohms of resistance.

> *CAUTION*
> *Never connect an ohmmeter to a circuit which has power applied to it. Always disconnect the battery negative lead before using an ohmmeter.*

Jumper Wire

A jumper wire is a simple way to bypass a potential problem and isolate it to a particular point in a circuit. If a faulty circuit works properly with a jumper wire installed, an open exists between the two jumper points in the circuit.

To troubleshoot with a jumper wire, first use the wire to determine if the problem is on the ground side or the load side of a device. Test the ground by connecting a jumper between the lamp and a good ground. If the lamp comes on, the problem is the connection between the lamp and ground. If the lamp does not come on with the jumper installed, the lamp's connection to ground is good so the problem is between the lamp and the power source.

To isolate the problem, connect the jumper between the battery and the lamp. If it comes on, the problem is between these two points. Next connect the jumper between the battery and the fuse side of the switch. If the lamp comes on, the switch is good. By successively moving the jumper from one point to another, the problem can be isolated to a particular place in the circuit.

Pay attention to the following when using a jumper wire:

1. Make sure the jumper wire gauge (thickness) is the same as that used in the circuit being tested. Smaller gauge wire rapidly overheats and could melt.

2. Install insulated boots over alligator clips. This prevents accidental grounding, sparks or possible shock when working in cramped quarters.

3. Jumper wires are temporary test measures only. Do not leave a jumper wire installed as a permanent solution. This creates a severe fire hazard that could easily lead to complete loss of the motorcycle.

4. When using a jumper wire always install an inline fuse/fuse holder (available at most auto supply stores or electronic supply stores) to the jumper wire. Never use a jumper wire across any load (a component that is connected and turned on). This would cause a direct short and blow the fuse(s).

Voltage Testing

Unless otherwise specified, make all voltage tests with the electrical connectors still connected. Insert the test leads into the backside of the connector and make sure the test lead touches the electrical wire or metal terminal within the connector housing. Touching the wire insulation yields a false reading. If the meter is equipped with alligator clips, probe the connector with a paper clip, then attach the meter's clip.

Always check both sides of the connector as one side may be loose or corroded, thus preventing electrical flow through the connector. This type of test can be performed with a test light or a voltmeter. A voltmeter gives the best results.

1. Attach the voltmeter negative test lead to a good ground (bare metal). Make sure the part used for ground is not insulated with a rubber gasket or rubber grommet.

2. Attach the voltmeter positive test lead to the point (electrical connector, etc.) to be checked (**Figure 11**).

3. Turn the ignition switch on. If using a test light, the test light comes on if voltage is present. If using a voltmeter, note the voltage reading. The reading should be within 1 volt of battery voltage. If the voltage is less, there is a problem in the circuit.

Voltage Drop Test

The wires, cables, connectors and switches in an electrical circuit are designed to carry current with low resistance. This ensures current can flow through the circuit with a minimum loss of voltage. Voltage drop indicates there is resistance in a cir-

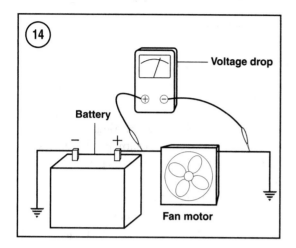

cuit. A higher-than-normal amount of resistance in a circuit decreases the flow of current and causes the voltage to drop between the source and destination in the circuit.

Because resistance causes voltage to drop, a volt meter can be used to determine resistance in an active circuit. This is called a voltage drop test. A voltage drop test measures the difference between the voltage at the beginning of the circuit and the available voltage at the end of the circuit while the circuit is operating. If the circuit has no resistance, there is no voltage drop so the voltmeter indicates 0 volts. The greater the resistance in a circuit, the greater the voltage drop reading.

To perform a voltage drop test:

NOTE
*To check the voltage drop in the starter circuit, refer to **Starter System Voltage Drop Test** under **Starter Troubleshooting** in Chapter Nine.*

1. Connect the positive meter test lead to the electrical source (where electricity is coming from [**Figure 14**]).

2. Connect the voltmeter negative test lead to the electrical load (where the electricity is going). Refer to **Figure 14**.

3. If necessary, activate the component(s) in the circuit. For example, if checking the voltage drop in the front brake light switch circuit, apply the front brake lever.

4. Read the voltage drop (difference in voltage between the source and destination) on the voltmeter. Note the following:

a. The voltmeter should indicate 0 volts. If there is a drop of 0.5 volts or more, there is a problem within the circuit. A voltage drop reading of 12 volts indicates an open in the circuit.

b. A voltage drop of 1 or more volts indicates that a circuit has excessive resistance.

c. For example, consider a starting problem where the battery is fully charged but the starter motor turns over slowly. Voltage drop would be the difference in the voltage at the battery (source) and the voltage at the starter (destination) as the engine is being started (current is flowing through the battery cables). A corroded battery cable would cause a high voltage drop (high resistance) and slow engine cranking.

d. Common sources of voltage drop are loose or contaminated connectors and poor ground connections.

Peak Voltage Test

Peak voltage tests check the voltage output of the ignition coil and ignition pulse generator at normal cranking speed. These tests make it possible to identify ignition system problems quickly and accurately.

Peak voltage tests require a peak voltage adapter or tester. Refer to *Ignition System Troubleshooting* in Chapter Nine.

Continuity Test

A continuity test is used to determine the integrity of a circuit, wire or component. A circuit has continuity if it forms a complete circuit; that is if there are no opens in either the electrical wires or components within the circuit. A circuit with an open, on the other hand, has no continuity.

This type of test can be performed with a self-powered test light or an ohmmeter. An ohmmeter gives the best results. If using an analog ohmmeter, calibrate the meter by touching the leads together and turning the calibration knob until the meter reads zero.

1. Disconnect the negative battery cable.

2. Attach one test lead (test light or ohmmeter) to one end of the part of the circuit to be tested.

3. Attach the other test lead to the other end of the part or the circuit to be tested.

4. The self-powered test light comes on if there is continuity. An ohmmeter reads 0 or very low resistance if there is continuity. A reading of infinite resistance indicates no continuity: the circuit is open.

Testing for a Short with a Self-powered Test Light or Ohmmeter

1. Disconnect the negative battery cable.
2. Remove the blown fuse from the fuse panel.
3. Connect one test lead of the test light or ohmmeter to the load side (battery side) of the fuse terminal in the fuse panel.
4. Connect the other test lead to a good ground (bare metal). Make sure the part used for a ground is not insulated with a rubber gasket or rubber grommet.
5. With the self-powered test light or ohmmeter attached to the fuse terminal and ground, wiggle the wiring harness relating to the suspect circuit at 15.2 cm (6 in.) intervals. Start next to the fuse panel, then work away from the fuse panel while watching the self-powered test light or ohmmeter.
6. If the test light blinks or the needle on the ohmmeter moves, there is a short-to-ground at that point in the harness.

Testing For a Short with a Test Light or Voltmeter

1. Remove the blown fuse from the fuse panel.
2. Connect the test light or voltmeter across the fuse terminals in the fuse panel. Turn the ignition switch on and check for battery voltage.
3. With the test light or voltmeter attached to the fuse terminals, wiggle the wiring harness relating to the suspect circuit at 15.2 cm (6 in.) intervals. Start next to the fuse panel and work systematically away from the panel while watching the test light or voltmeter.
4. If the test light blinks or if the needle on the voltmeter moves, there is a short-to-ground at that point in the harness.

FRONT STEERING AND SUSPENSION

Steering is Sluggish

1. Incorrect steering stem adjustment (too tight).
2. Damaged steering head bearings.
3. Tire pressure too low.

4. Damaged tire.

Motorcycle Steers to One Side

1. Bent axle.
2. Bent frame.
3. Worn or damaged wheel bearings.
4. Worn or damaged swing arm pivot bearings.
5. Damaged steering head bearings.
6. Bent swing arm.
7. Incorrectly installed wheels.
8. Front and rear wheels are not aligned.
9. Front fork legs positioned unevenly in steering stem.
10. Damaged tire.

Front Suspension Noise

1. Loose mounting fasteners.
2. Damaged fork(s).
3. Low fork oil capacity.

Front Wheel Wobble/Vibration

1. Loose front wheel axle.
2. Loose or damaged wheel bearing(s).
3. Damaged wheel rim(s).
4. Damaged tire(s).
5. Flat spot on tire.

NOTE
If the motorcycle is put in storage for a considerable amount of time, the weight placed on the front tire can cause the tire to flatten on the spot resting against the floor.

6. Unbalanced tire and wheel assembly.
7. Loose or damaged spokes (if so equipped).

Hard Suspension (Front Fork)

1. Excessive tire pressure.
2. Damaged steering head bearings.
3. Incorrect steering head bearing adjustment.
4. Bent fork tubes.
5. Binding slider.

NOTE
If a fork brace was installed onto the fork tubes, make sure it was installed correctly.

6. Incorrect weight fork oil.
7. Fork oil level too high.
8. Plugged fork oil passage.

Hard Suspension
(Rear Shock Absorber)

1. Excessive rear tire pressure.
2. Bent damper rod.
3. Incorrect shock adjustment.
4. Damaged shock absorber bushing(s).
5. Damaged shock absorber.
6. Damaged swing arm pivot bearings.

Soft Suspension
(Front Fork)

1. Insufficient tire pressure.
2. Insufficient fork oil level or fluid capacity.
3. Incorrect oil viscosity.
4. Weak or damaged fork springs.

Soft Suspension
(Rear Shock Absorber)

1. Insufficient rear tire pressure.
2. Weak or damaged shock absorber spring.
3. Damaged shock absorber.
4. Incorrect shock absorber adjustment.
5. Leaking damper unit.

BRAKE SYSTEM

The front and rear brake units are critical to riding performance and safety. Inspect the front and rear brakes frequently and repair any problem immediately. Use only DOT 4 brake fluid when replacing or refilling disc brake fluid. Refer to Chapter Three for additional information on brake fluid selection and routine brake inspection and service.

Always check front and rear brake operation before riding the motorcycle.

Disc Brake

Soft or spongy brake lever or pedal

Operate the front brake lever or rear brake pedal and check to see if the lever travel distance increases. If the lever travel does increase while being operated, or feels soft or spongy, there may be air in the brake line. In this condition, the brake system is not capable of producing sufficient brake force. When an increase in lever travel is noticed or when the brake feels soft or spongy, check the following :
1. Air in the system.

NOTE
If the brake level in the reservoir drops too low, air can enter the hydraulic system through the master cylinder. Air can also enter the system from loose or damaged hose fittings. Air in the hydraulic system causes a soft or spongy brake lever or pedal action. This condition is noticeable and reduces brake performance. When it is suspected that air has entered the hydraulic system, flush the brake system and bleed the brakes as described in Chapter Fourteen.

NOTE
If different handlebars were installed, an extreme bar angle may affect the brake fluid level in the reservoir. Check the fluid level with the handlebar in both left and right lock positions.

2. Low brake fluid level.

NOTE
As the brake pads wear, the brake fluid level in the master cylinder reservoir drops. Whenever adding brake fluid to the reservoir, visually check the brake pads for wear. If it does not appear there is an increase in pad wear, check the brake hoses, lines and banjo bolts for leaks.

3. Leak in the brake system.
4. Contaminated brake fluid.
5. Plugged brake fluid passages.
6. Damaged brake lever or pedal assembly.
7. Worn or damaged brake pads.
8. Worn or damaged brake disc.

9. Warped brake disc.
10. Contaminated brake pads and disc.

NOTE
A leaking fork seal can allow oil to contaminate the brake pads, caliper seals and disc.

11. Worn or damaged master cylinder cups and/or cylinder bore.
12. Worn or damaged brake caliper piston seals.
13. Contaminated master cylinder assembly.
14. Contaminated brake caliper assembly.
15. Brake caliper not sliding correctly on the slide pins.
16. Sticking master cylinder piston assembly.
17. Sticking brake caliper pistons.

Brake drag

When the brakes drag, the brake pads are not capable of moving away from the brake disc when the brake lever is released. Any of the following causes, if they occur, would prevent correct brake pad movement and cause brake drag.
1. Warped or damaged brake disc.
2. Brake caliper not sliding correctly on slide pins.
3. Sticking or damaged brake caliper pistons.
4. Worn or damaged brake caliper dust seal.
5. Contaminated brake pads and disc.
6. Plugged master cylinder port.
7. Contaminated brake fluid and hydraulic passages.
8. Restricted brake hose joint.
9. Loose brake disc mounting bolts.
10. Damaged or misaligned wheel.
11. Incorrect wheel alignment.
12. Incorrectly installed brake caliper.
13. Damaged wheel.

Hard brake lever or pedal operation

When the brakes are applied and there is sufficient brake performance, but the operation of brake lever or pedal feels excessively hard, check for the following:
1. Clogged brake hydraulic system.
2. Sticking caliper piston.
3. Sticking master cylinder piston.
4. Glazed or worn brake pads.
5. Mismatched brake pads.

6. Damaged front brake lever.
7. Damaged rear brake pedal.
8. Brake caliper not sliding correctly on slide pins.
9. Worn or damaged brake caliper seals.

Front or rear brake grabs

1. Damaged brake pad pin bolt. Look for steps or cracks along the pad pin bolt surface.
2. Contaminated brake pads and disc.
3. Incorrect wheel alignment.
4. Warped brake disc.
5. Loose brake disc mounting bolts.
6. Brake caliper not sliding correctly on slide pins.
7. Mismatched brake pads.
8. Damaged wheel bearings.

Brake squeal or chatter

1. Contaminated brake pads and disc.
2. Incorrectly installed brake caliper.
3. Warped brake disc.
4. Incorrect wheel alignment.
5. Mismatched brake pads.
6. Incorrectly installed brake pads.

Leaking brake caliper

1. Damaged dust and piston seals.
2. Damaged cylinder bore.
3. Loose banjo bolt.
4. Damaged banjo bolt washers.
5. Damaged banjo bolt threads in caliper body.

Leaking master cylinder

1. Damaged piston secondary seal.
2. Damaged piston circlip/circlip groove.
3. Worn or damaged master cylinder bore.
4. Loose banjo bolt.
5. Damaged banjo bolt washers.
6. Damaged banjo bolt threads in master cylinder body.
7. Loose or damaged reservoir cap.

Rear Drum Brake (VT1100C)

These models are equipped with a rear drum brake.

Poor brake performance

1. Incorrect brake adjustment.
2. Worn brake shoe linings or brake drum.
3. Contaminated brake drum and brake shoe linings.
4. Worn brake cam.
5. Brake panel cracked at brake cam operating area.
6. Brake arm and brake cam splines stripped or improperly indexed.
7. Bent or damaged brake rod.
8. Loose or missing parts at brake rod and brake pedal assembly.

Brake drag

1. Incorrect brake adjustment.
2. Contaminated brake drum and brake shoe linings.
3. Weak or damaged brake return springs.
4. Weak or damaged brake rod return spring.
5. Damaged brake shoes.
6. Warped brake drum.
7. Incorrect brake cam and brake arm alignment.

Brake grabs

1. Contaminated brake drum.
2. Contaminated brake shoe linings.
3. Weak or damaged brake return springs.

4. Warped brake drum.
5. Incorrect brake cam and brake arm alignment.

Brake squeals or chatters

1. Contaminated brake drum.
2. Contaminated brake linings.
3. Warped brake drum.
4. Damaged brake shoes.

NOTE
If the brake rod chatters when the motorcycle is rolled backward while the rear brake is applied, check the brake stopper arm where it is bolted onto the brake panel. If the stopper arm mounting bolt and nut are tight, check for excessive clearance between the stopper arm mounting bolt and its mounting bore in the brake panel.

Hard rear brake pedal operation or slow brake pedal return

1. Weak or damaged brake shoe return springs.
2. Contaminated brake drum.
3. Contaminated brake linings.
4. Incorrect brake adjustment.
5. Incorrect brake assembly.
6. Damaged brake cam or backing plate.
7. Damaged rear brake pedal assembly.
8. Damaged brake rod.

CHAPTER THREE

LUBRICATION, MAINTENANCE AND TUNE-UP

This chapter describes lubrication, maintenance and tune-up procedures required for the Honda VT1100 models.

To maximize the service life of the motorcycle and gain the utmost in safety and performance, it is necessary to perform periodic inspections and maintenance. Minor problems found during routine service can be corrected before they develop into major ones. A neglected motorcycle becomes unreliable and may be dangerous to ride.

Table 1 lists the recommended lubrication, maintenance and tune-up intervals. When operating the motorcycle in extreme conditions, it may be appropriate to reduce the time interval between some maintenance items.

For convenience, most of the services listed in **Table 1** are described in this chapter. Procedures that require more than minor disassembly or adjustment are covered in the appropriate chapter.

Before servicing the motorcycle, make sure the procedures and the required skills are thoroughly understood. If your experience and equipment are limited, start by performing basic procedures. Perform more involved tasks as you gain further experience and acquire the necessary tools.

Tables 1-9 are found at the end of the chapter.

FUEL TYPE

The VT1100 engine requires gasoline with a pump octane number of 86 or higher. Using a gasoline with a lower octane number can cause pinging or spark knock and lead to engine damage.

When choosing gasoline and filling the fuel tank, note the following:

1. When filling the tank, do not overfill it. There should be no fuel in the filler neck (tube located between the fuel cap and tank).

2. Because oxygenated fuels can damage plastic and paint, make sure not to spill fuel onto the fuel tank during filling. Wipe up spills with a soft cloth. If using oxygenated fuel, make sure it meets the minimum octane requirements.

3. An ethanol (ethyl or grain alcohol) gasoline that contains more than 10 percent ethanol by volume may cause engine starting and performance related problems. Gasoline containing ethanol may be sold under the name Gasohol.

4. A methanol (methyl or wood alcohol) gasoline that contains more than 5 percent methanol by volume may cause engine starting and performance related problems. Gasoline that contains methanol must have

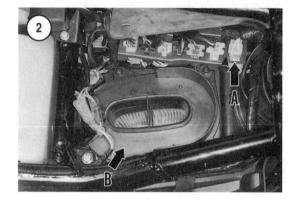

corrosion inhibitors to protect the metal, plastic and rubber parts in the fuel system from damage.

5. Gasoline that contains more than 15 percent MTBE (Methyl Tertiary Butyl Ether) should not be used.

TUNE-UP

A complete tune-up restores performance lost due to normal wear and deterioration of engine parts. Because engine wear occurs over a combined period of time and mileage, perform the engine tune-up procedures at the intervals specified in **Table 1**. More frequent tune-ups may be required if the motorcycle is operated primarily in stop-and-go traffic or in areas were there is a large amount of blowing dirt and dust.

The Motorcycle Emission Control Information label lists tune-up information. Refer to **Table 2** for tune-up specifications. On California models, the vacuum hose routing diagram is useful when identifying hoses used in the emission control system. Refer to Chapter Nine for the location of the decals on each model.

NOTE
If the specifications on the Motorcycle Emission Control Information label differ from those in ***Table 2***, *use those on the label.*

To perform a tune-up, service the following items as described in this chapter:
1. Air filter.
2. Spark plugs.
3. Engine compression.
4. Ignition timing.
5. Engine oil and filter.
6. Cooling system.
7. Final drive.
8. Wheels and tires.
9. Suspension components.
10. Brake system.
11. Fasteners.

CYLINDER IDENTIFICATION AND FIRING ORDER

Figure 1 identifies the cylinder numbers. The cylinder firing order is 2 (front) - 1 (rear).

AIR FILTER

The air filter removes dust and abrasive particles from the air before the air enters the engine. A clogged air filter decreases the efficiency and life of the engine. With a damaged air filter, very fine particles could enter the engine and cause rapid wear of the piston rings, cylinder and bearings. Never run the motorcycle without the air filter element installed.

Replace the air filter element at the service intervals specified in **Table 1**.

NOTE
The service intervals specified in ***Table 1*** *should be followed with general use. However, replace the air filter more often if dusty areas are frequently encountered.*

Replacement

1. Remove the seat (Chapter Fifteen).
2. On VT1100C2 ACE models, remove the bolt and move the connector block (A, **Figure 2**) away from the air filter cover.

3. Remove the bolts and the air filter cover (B, **Figure 2**).

4. Remove the air filter (**Figure 3**).

NOTE
*The air filter element contains a dust adhesive. Do not clean the filter element (**Figure 4**) with air or any type of chemical cleaner or water.*

5. Inspect the air filter element (**Figure 4**) for an excessive amount of dirt and possible damage. Check for holes or shredded filter seams. Do not run the motorcycle with a damaged air filter element or attempt to clean it. It may allow dirt to enter the engine. If the element is good, use it until the indicated time for replacement listed in **Table 1**.

6. Inspect the air box for dirt and debris that may have passed through the element. Wipe the inside of the air box and the air filter cover with a clean cloth.

7. Install the air filter element (**Figure 4**) and secure with the air filter cover and mounting screws.

8. Reverse Step 1 and Step 2.

CRANKCASE BREATHER INSPECTION

The engine is equipped with a crankcase emission control system to prevent fumes and gasses from being vented into the atmosphere. However, under various operating conditions, contaminants (water and blow-by gas) not burned in the combustion chamber collect in the air box. To remove these contaminants, the air box is equipped with a transparent drain tube (**Figure 5**). At the intervals specified in **Table 1**, inspect the drain tube for fluid, and if necessary, remove the cover from the end of the tube and drain the contaminants into a container. Reinstall the cover. Check the drain tube more frequently after riding the motorcycle in rain, after riding long distances under full-throttle, if the motorcycle is washed frequently, or after the motorcycle is dropped on its side.

ENGINE COMPRESSION TEST

A cranking compression test is one of the quickest ways to check the internal condition of the engine (piston rings, pistons, head gasket, valves and cylinders). It is a good idea to check compression at each tune-up, record it in the maintenance log at the back of the manual and compare it with the reading obtained at the next tune-up.

Use the spark plug tool included in the motorcycle's tool kit and a screw-in type compression gauge with a flexible adapter (**Figure 6**). Before using the gauge, check that the rubber gasket on the end of the adapter is not cracked or damaged; this gasket seals the cylinder to ensure accurate compression readings.

1. Make sure the battery is fully charged to ensure proper engine cranking speed (300 rpm).

2. Run the engine until it reaches normal operating temperature, then turn it off.

3. Disconnect all of the spark plug caps.

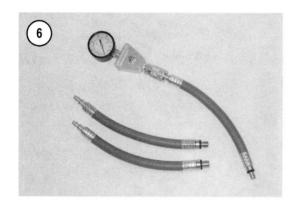

NOTE
If a cylinder requires a longer crank-
ing time to reach its maximum com-
pression reading, there is a problem
with that cylinder.

7. Install the spark plug.

8. Repeat for the rear cylinder.

9. When interpreting the results, also note the difference between the readings. **Table 2** lists the standard compression pressure reading. Low compression indicates worn or broken rings, leaking or sticky valves, blown head gasket or a combination of all three. Readings that are lower than normal, but are relatively even among both cylinders indicate piston, ring and cylinder wear. Note the following:

    a. If the compression readings do not differ between cylinders by more than 10 percent, the rings and valves are in good condition.

    b. If a low reading (10 percent or more) is obtained on one of the cylinders, it indicates valve or ring trouble. To determine which, perform a wet compression test. Pour about a teaspoon of engine oil into the spark plug hole. Repeat the compression test and record the reading. If the compression increases significantly, the valves are good but the rings are defective on that cylinder. If compression does not increase, the valves require servicing.

NOTE
An engine with low compression cannot
be tuned to maximum performance.

10. Reverse Steps 1-4 to complete installation. Reinstall the spark plugs and caps as described under *Spark Plugs* in this chapter.

SPARK PLUGS

Inspect and replace the spark plugs at the service intervals specified in **Table 1**.

Removal

Careful removal of the spark plug is important in preventing grit from entering the combustion chamber. It is also important to know how to remove a plug that is seized or is resistant to removal. Forcing

CAUTION
When the spark plug leads are discon-
nected, the electronic ignition produces
the highest voltage possible. This can
damage the ICM or other ignition com-
ponent. To protect the ignition system,
install a grounding tool in each spark
*plug cap. Refer to **Ignition Grounding***
***Tool** in Chapter One. Do not crank the*
engine more than necessary.

4. Remove one spark plug from the front cylinder.

5. Lubricate the threads of the compression gauge adapter with a *small* amount of antiseize compound and carefully thread the gauge into one of the spark plug holes. Tighten the hose by hand to form a good seal (**Figure 7**).

6. Move the engine stop switch to its RUN position, then turn the ignition switch on. *Open the throttle completely* and using the starter, crank the engine over while reading the compression gauge until there is no further rise in pressure. The compression reading should increase on each stroke. Maximum pressure is usually reached within 4-5 seconds of engine cranking. Record the reading.

a seized plug can destroy the threads in the cylinder head.

During removal, label each spark plug with its cylinder number (**Figure 1**) and position in the cylinder head.

1. Grasp the spark plug cap boot and twist it slightly to break it loose, then pull it from the spark plug.

CAUTION
Dirt that falls through the spark plug hole will cause engine wear and damage.

2. Blow any dirt that has accumulated around the spark plug hole.

3. Fit a spark plug wrench onto the spark plug, then remove it (**Figure 8**) by turning the wrench counterclockwise. If the plug is seized or drags excessively during removal, stop and try the following:

  a. Apply penetrating lubricant, such as Liquid Wrench or WD-40 and allow it to stand for about 15 minutes.

  b. If the plug is completely seized, apply moderate pressure in both directions with the wrench. Only break the seal so lubricant can penetrate under the spark plug and into the threads. If this does not work, and the engine can still be started, install the spark plug cap and start the engine. Allow to completely warm up. The heat of the engine may be enough to expand the parts and allow the plug to be removed.

  c. When a spark plug is loose, but drags excessively during removal, apply penetrating lubricant around the spark plug threads. Turn the plug in (clockwise) to help distribute the lubricant onto the threads. Slowly remove the plug, working it in and out of the cylinder head while continuing to add lubricant. Do no reuse the spark plug.

  d. Inspect the threads in the cylinder head for damage. Clean and true the threads with a spark plug thread-chaser. Apply a thick grease onto the thread-chaser threads before using it. The grease will help trap some of the debris cut from the threads to prevent it from falling into the engine.

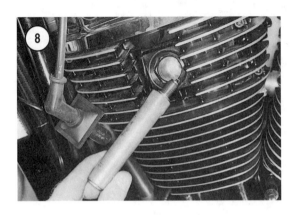

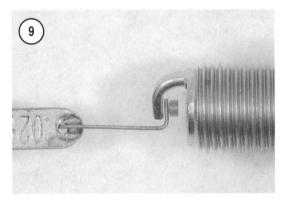

NOTE
Damaged spark plug threads will require removal of the cylinder head (Chapter Four) and repair.

4. Inspect the plug carefully. Look for a damaged porcelain cover, excessively eroded electrodes, and excessive carbon or oil fouling. Refer to *Reading/Inspection* in this section.

NOTE
The porcelain cover, found on the top of the spark plug, actually extends into the plug shell to prevent the spark from grounding through the plug shell and threads. The porcelain cover can be easily damaged from mishandling. Make sure the spark plug socket fits the plug fully before turning the plug.

5. Repeat for each spark plug.

Gap and Installation

Gap used and new spark plugs to ensure a reliable, consistent spark. Use a spark plug gapping

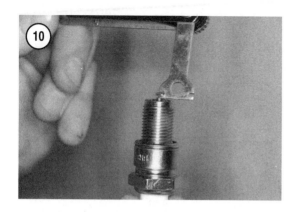

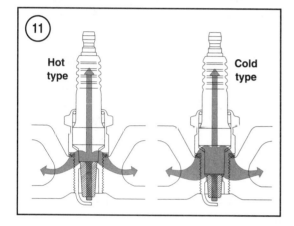

tool and a wire feeler gauge as described in this procedure.

1. Remove the new spark plug from the box. Remove the terminal nut installed onto the end of the plug.

2. Refer to the spark plug gap listed in **Table 2**. Then insert a wire feeler gauge between the center and side electrode (**Figure 9**). If there is a slight drag, the setting is correct. If the gap is too large or small, adjust the gap by bending the ground electrode with a gapping tool (**Figure 10**) to achieve the required gap.

> *NOTE*
> *Do not use a blade type feeler gauge to check the spark plug gap on a used spark plug or too large of a gap results.*

3. Wipe a *small* amount of antiseize compound to the plug threads before installing the spark plug. Do not allow the compound to get on the electrodes.

4. Screw the spark plug in by hand until it seats. Little effort should be required; if force is neces-

sary, the plug may be cross-threaded. Unscrew it and try again.

5. Tighten the spark plug to 14 N•m (124 in.-lb.) or use a spark plug wrench and tighten the plug an additional 1/4-1/2 turn after the gasket makes contact with the cylinder head. If installing an old, re-gapped spark plug and gasket, only tighten the plug an additional 1/8-1/4 turn.

> *NOTE*
> *Do not overtighten the spark plug. This may crush the gasket and cause a compression leak.*

6. Align and press the cap onto the spark plug.

> *CAUTION*
> *Position the spark plug wires so they do not contact the exhaust pipe.*

Selection

The proper spark plug is important to obtain maximum performance and reliability. The condition of a used spark plug can tell a trained mechanic or experienced rider a lot about engine condition and carburetion. **Table 2** lists the recommended spark plug.

Spark plugs are available in several heat ranges to accommodate the load and performance demands put on the engine. The standard spark plug recommended by the manufacturer is usually a medium heat-range plug that operates well over a wide range of engine speeds.

> *NOTE*
> *A hotter or cooler spark plug does not make a hotter or cooler spark. Heat range numbers determines how quickly a plug resists the transfer of heat into the cylinder head.*

Heat range is determined by the length, shape, thickness and chemical compound of a spark plugs lower insulator.

If the engine is run in hot climates, at high speed or under heavy loads for prolonged periods, a spark plug with a colder heat range may be required. A colder plug quickly transfers heat away from its firing tip and to the cylinder head. This is accomplished by a short path up the ceramic insulator and into the body of the spark plug (**Figure 11**). By transferring heat quickly, the plug remains cool enough to avoid overheating and preignition problems. If the engine is run slowly for prolonged periods, this type of plug fouls and causes poor performance. A colder plug does not cool down a hot engine.

If the engine is run in cold climates or at a slow speed for prolonged periods, a spark plug with a hotter heat range may be required. A hotter plug slowly transfers heat away from its firing tip and to the cylinder head. This is accomplished by a long path up the ceramic insulator and into the body of the plug (**Figure 11**). By transferring heat slowly, the plug remains hot enough to avoid fouling and buildup. If the engine is run in hot climates for fast or prolonged periods, this type of plug overheats, causes preignition problems and possibly melts the electrode. Damage to the piston and cylinder assembly is possible.

If the engine is unmodified, changing to a different heat range plug is normally not required. However, when operating a motorcycle with a modified engine, a different heat range play may be necessary. This type of change is usually based on a recommendation made by the engine builder. Experience in reading spark plugs is also required when trying to determine if a different heat range plug is required. When installing a different heat range plug, go *one step* hotter or colder from the recommended plug. Do not try to correct carburetor or ignition problems by using different spark plugs. This only compounds the existing problem(s) and possibly leads to engine damage.

The reach (length) of a plug is also important (**Figure 12**). A shorter-than-normal plug causes hard starting, reducing engine performance and carbon buildup on the exposed cylinder head threads. These same conditions can occur if the correct length plug is used without a gasket. Trying to thread a spark plug into threads with carbon buildup may damage the threads in the cylinder head.

Reading/Inspection

The spark plug is an excellent indicator of how the engine is operating. By correctly evaluating the condition of the plug, engine problems can be diagnosed. After removing the spark plug, compare the firing tip with the ones shown in **Figure 13**. The following sections provide a description, as well as common causes for each of the conditions.

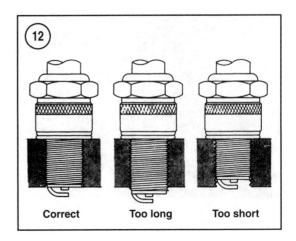

Correct   Too long   Too short

CAUTION
In all cases, when a spark plug is abnormal, find the cause of the problem before continuing engine operation. Engine damage is possible when abnormal plug readings are ignored.

Normal condition

The plug has light tan or gray deposits on the tip. No erosion of the electrodes or abnormal gap is evident. This indicates an engine that has properly adjusted carburetion, ignition timing and proper fuel mixture. This heat range of plug is appropriate for the conditions in which the engine has been operated. The plug can be reused.

Oil fouled

The plug is wet with black, oily deposits on the electrodes and insulator. The electrodes do not show wear.
1. Incorrect carburetor jetting.
2. Float level set too high.
3. Clogged air filter.
4. Faulty ignition component.
5. Spark plug heat range too cold.
6. Low engine compression.
7. Engine not properly broken in.

Carbon fouled

The plug is black with a dry, sooty deposit on the entire plug surface. This dry sooty deposit is conductive and can create electrical paths that bypass

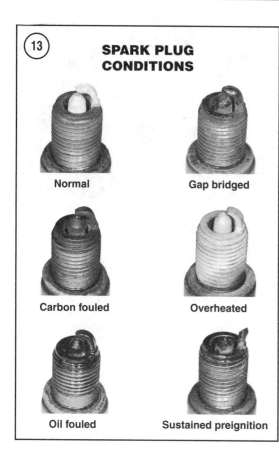

(13) **SPARK PLUG CONDITIONS**

Normal   Gap bridged

Carbon fouled   Overheated

Oil fouled   Sustained preignition

Gap bridging

The plug is clogged with deposits between the electrodes. The engine can run with a bridged spark plug, but will misfire.
1. Incorrect oil type.
2. Incorrect fuel or fuel contamination.
3. Excessive carbon deposits in combustion chamber.

Preignition

The plug electrodes are eroded or melted. This condition can lead to engine damage.
1. Faulty ignition system component.
2. Spark plug heat range too hot.
3. Air leak.
4. Excessive carbon deposits in combustion chamber.

Worn out

The plug electrodes are rounded from normal combustion. There is no indication of abnormal combustion or engine conditions. Replace the plug.

the electrode gap. This often causes misfiring of the plug.
1. Rich fuel mixture.
2. Spark plug heat range too cold.
3. Clogged air filter.
4. Faulty ignition component.
5. Low engine compression.
6. Prolonged idling.

Overheating

The plug is dry and the insulator has a white or light gray cast. The insulator may also appear blistered. The electrodes may have a burnt appearance.
1. Lean fuel mixture.
2. Spark plug heat range too hot.
3. Faulty ignition component.
4. Air leak.
5. Overtightened spark plug.
6. No crush washer on spark plug.
7. Spark plug heat range too hot.

IGNITION TIMING INSPECTION

The engine is equipped with a fully transistorized ignition system. Periodically check the timing to make sure all ignition components are operating correctly. Because of the solid state design, problems with the transistorized system are rare and adjusting the ignition timing is neither necessary nor possible. If there seems to be an ignition related problem, checking the ignition timing can confirm the condition of the ignition system or a related problem.

Incorrect ignition timing can cause a drastic loss of engine performance. It may also cause overheating.

WARNING
Do not start and run the motorcycle in an enclosed area. The exhaust gasses contain carbon monoxide, a colorless, odorless and poisonous gas. The carbon monoxide levels build quickly in an enclosed area and can cause unconsciousness and death in a short time.

1. Start the engine and let it reach normal operating temperature. Shut the engine off.

2. Remove the timing hole cap (**Figure 14**) and its O-ring to access the flywheel timing marks.

3. Connect a timing light to one of the rear cylinder's spark plug wires following the manufacturer's instructions.

4. Start the engine and set the idle speed as described in this chapter.

5. Aim the timing light at the timing hole and pull the trigger. The ignition timing is correct if the *F* timing mark on the ignition pulse generator rotor aligns with the index mark on the right crankcase cover. Refer to **Figure 15** or **Figure 16**.

6. Connect the timing light to one of the front cylinder's spark plug wires and repeat Step 5.

7. Turn the engine off and disconnect the timing light.

8. If the timing is incorrect, there is a problem with one or more ignition system components; refer to *Ignition System Troubleshooting* in Chapter Nine. There is no method of adjusting ignition timing.

9. Lubricate the timing hole cap threads and O-ring with grease and tighten to 18 N•m (159 in.-lb.).

CARBURETOR

Starting Enrichment Valve (Choke) Cable

Check and adjustment

Each carburetor is equipped with a manually operated starting enrichment (SE) valve assembly (choke) used to richen the air/fuel mixture when starting a cold engine. The system consists of a choke valve installed inside each carburetor, cables and a hand-operated choke lever (**Figure 17**) on the handlebar. With the choke lever moved all the way up, the choke valves are closed. Moving the choke lever all the way down opens the choke valves.

Choke valves that fail to open or close correctly can cause engine starting and drivability problems.

If the engine is difficult to start when cold but starts easily once it has warmed up, check for a choke valve that is not fully opening when the choke lever is moved all the way down. Move the choke lever down and check for any creeping. Check the cables for damage.

If the engine starts but idles or runs roughly, check for a choke valve that is not completely closed when the choke lever is move all the way up.

At the intervals specified in **Table 1**, check the choke operation and adjust if necessary:

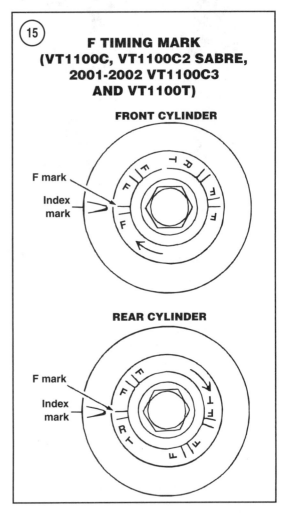

**F TIMING MARK
(VT1100C, VT1100C2 SABRE,
2001-2002 VT1100C3
AND VT1100T)**

FRONT CYLINDER

F mark

Index
mark

REAR CYLINDER

F mark

Index
mark

1. Remove the fuel tank (Chapter Eight).

2. Loosen the choke cable nut (**Figure 18**) and remove the choke valve (**Figure 19**) from each carburetor.

3. Push the choke lever (**Figure 17**) down to its fully closed position.

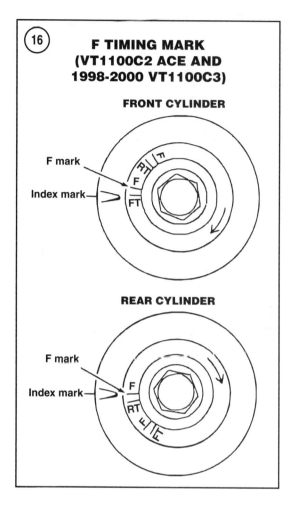

**F TIMING MARK
(VT1100C2 ACE AND
1998-2000 VT1100C3)**

FRONT CYLINDER

F mark

Index mark

REAR CYLINDER

F mark

Index mark

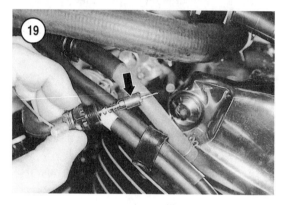

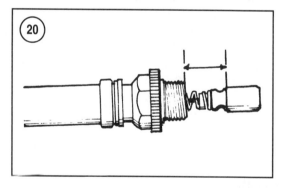

4. Measure the distance between the choke valve and the end of the cable nut threads as shown in **Figure 20**. The correct distance is 10-11 mm (0.39-0.43 in.). Note the following:

  a. To adjust the cable, continue with Step 5.

  b. If the cable adjustment is correct, go to Step 6.

5. Adjust the choke cable as follows:

  a. Turn the handlebar all the way to the right side.

  b. Loosen the choke cable locknut (A, **Figure 21**) and turn the choke cable elbow (B, **Figure 21**) until the correct valve adjustment (Step 4) is obtained.

  c. Tighten the choke cable locknut and recheck the adjustment.

6. Insert the choke valve (**Figure 19**) into the carburetor and tighten the cable nut (**Figure 18**) until it contacts the carburetor housing. Tighten the plunger an additional 1/4 turn.

7. Repeat for the other choke cable valve and carburetor.

8. Operate the choke lever and make sure the choke valves operate correctly. If the operation is incorrect or there is binding, check that the cable is routed and attached correctly.

9. Install the fuel tank (Chapter Eight).

Idle Mixture Adjustment

The idle mixture (pilot screw) is preset and should not be reset during engine tune-up. Do not adjust the pilot screws unless the carburetors have been overhauled. Refer to *Pilot Screw Adjustment* in Chapter Eight.

Idle Speed Adjustment

The engine idle speed is adjusted by turning the throttle stop screw (**Figure 22**) on the left side of the engine.

1. Start the engine and let it warm up approximately 2-3 minutes.

2. Support the motorcycle on its sidestand. Turn the engine off.

3. Connect a portable tachometer following the manufacturer's instructions.

4. Make sure the choke lever (**Figure 17**) is closed before adjusting the idle speed.

5. Restart the engine and set the idle speed by turning the throttle stop screw (**Figure 22**). **Table 2** lists the correct idle speed.

6. Open and close the throttle a couple times; check for variation in idle speed. Readjust if necessary.

> *WARNING*
> *With the engine idling, move the handlebar from side to side. If idle speed increases during this movement, the throttle cable needs adjusting or may be incorrectly routed through the frame. Correct this problem immediately. Do not ride the motorcycle in this unsafe condition.*

> *NOTE*
> *If the engine runs roughly at idle, first check for a dirty or contaminated air filter element. Then check the choke cable adjustment.*

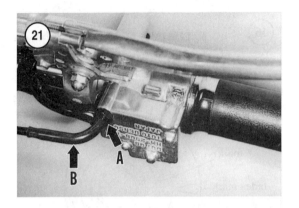

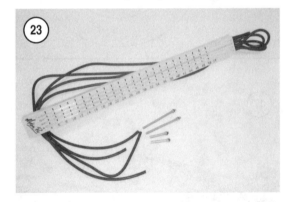

7. Turn the engine off and disconnect the portable tachometer.

Synchronization

Synchronizing adjusts the throttle plate in each carburetor so they open at the same time. This ensures that both carburetors deliver the same air/fuel mixture to both cylinders. A linkage assembly connects the throttle plates to each other. When this linkage goes out of adjustment, the throttle plates

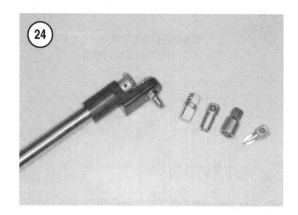

open at different intervals, resulting in poor engine idle, lack of throttle response (hesitation, stumble) and other driveability problems.

When the carburetors are properly synchronized, the engine warms up faster and there is an improvement in idle speed performance, throttle response and mileage.

A carburetor vacuum gauge tool: Motion Pro Deluxe Carb tuner (part No. 08-0009 [**Figure 23**]) and carburetor synchronization tool: Motion Pro 90-de-

gree 1/4 in. hex driver (part No. 08-02229 [**Figure 24**]) or equivalents are required to check and adjust carburetor synchronization.

NOTE
*For a description of Motion Pro tools, refer to **www.motionpro.com**.*

1. Start the engine and let it warm up to normal operating temperature. Turn the engine off.
2. Support the motorcycle on its sidestand.
3. Remove the fuel tank (Chapter Eight).
4. Remove the air filter housing (Chapter Eight).
5. Connect a remote fuel tank to the carburetor. Open the fuel valve to fill the fuel line. Repair any fuel leaks before starting the engine.
6. Remove the screw and washer from each cylinder head intake port (**Figure 25**, typical).
7. Install the vacuum gauge adapters into the intake ports (**Figure 26**, typical) and tighten securely.

WARNING
Mercury is poisonous. When using a mercury carburetor tuner, follow the manufacturer's handling instructions.

NOTE
When using a mercury carburetor tuner, do not increase the idle speed above 3500 rpm and/or drop the idle speed suddenly. The abrupt change in vacuum pressure may draw mercury into the engine. Refer to the manufacturer's instructions.

8. Start the engine and set the idle speed to 1000 (± 100) rpm with the throttle stop screw (**Figure 22**).

NOTE
With the fuel tank removed and the engine running at idle speed, listen for any hissing or other sounds indicating a disconnected or damaged vacuum hose. Reconnect or repair any damaged hoses before continuing.

9. With the engine running at idle speed, check the gauge readings following the manufacturer's instructions (**Figure 27**, typical). If the difference in analog gauge readings is 40 mm Hg (1.6 in. Hg) or less between the two cylinders, the carburetors are considered synchronized. Note the following:
   a. If the carburetors are not synchronized, continue with Step 10.

b. If the carburetors are synchronized, go to Step 12.

NOTE
Figure 28 shows the carburetor synchronization adjusting screw with the carburetor removed for clarity. The base carburetor is the No. 1 (rear) carburetor.

10. To access the synchronization screw, insert the hex driver between the lower throttle cable and the front cylinder head cover as shown in **Figure 29**. Use the hex driver and turn the synchronization adjusting screw (**Figure 30**) to adjust the carburetor so the gauge readings are as close to each other as possible (**Figure 27**, typical). Snap the throttle a few times to move the throttle linkage and make sure the adjustment stabilizes.

NOTE
If the synchronizing screw is hard to turn or is non-responsive, check the linkage assembly for a buildup of grit and rust. Spray the screw with a carburetor cleaner. If this does not help, check for damaged linkage components (springs, rods, clevis pins).

11. Slowly increase the engine speed to 3000 rpm. Both cylinder gauge readings should change but should still register nearly the same reading. If both cylinder gauge readings are close or nearly identical at idle speed but change unevenly when the engine speed is increased, a problem exists that is causing a change in the readings. Consider the following possible problems:
   a. Intake manifold air leak.
   b. Worn carburetor throttle valves or carburetor bores.
   c. Restricted exhaust system.
   d. Dirty air filter.
   e. Low engine compression.
   f. Poor vacuum line connection between the carburetor vacuum gauge and cylinder head.

12. Turn the engine off and remove the vacuum lines and adapters. Install the screws and washers into the vacuum ports in the cylinder heads. Make sure the screws are tight to prevent a vacuum leak. Replace any damaged washers.

13. Reverse these steps to install previously removed parts.

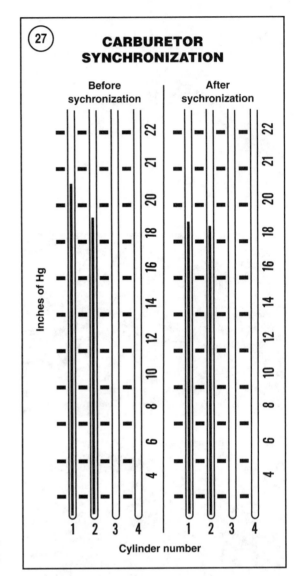

14. Start the engine and set the idle speed to 1000 (± 100) rpm with the throttle stop screw (**Figure 22**).

FUEL HOSE INSPECTION

Inspect the fuel hoses at the intervals specified in **Table 1**.

WARNING
Some fuel may spill from the hoses, fuel filter and fuel pump when disconnecting fuel hoses to check or replace them. Because gasoline is extremely flammable and explosive, perform

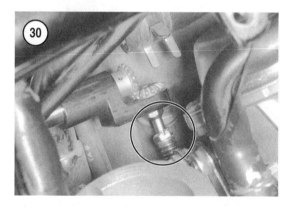

this procedure away from all open flames (including appliance pilot lights) and sparks. Do not smoke or allow someone to smoke in the work area. Always work in a well-venti-lated area. Wipe up any spills immedi-ately.

1. Remove the fuel tank (Chapter Eight).
2. Remove the left and right side covers (Chapter Fifteen).
3. Inspect the fuel hoses for leakage, hardness, age deterioration or other damage.
4. Replace damaged fuel hoses and weak or damaged hose clamps as required.

CAUTION
When replacing the fuel hoses, make sure to install the support springs over the hoses where used.

5. Reverse Step 1and Step 2.

THROTTLE CABLE

Throttle Operation

Check the throttle operation at the intervals specified in **Table 1**.

Check for smooth throttle operation from the fully closed to fully open positions. Check at various steering positions. The throttle grip must return to the fully closed position without any hesitation.

Check the throttle cables for damage, wear or deterioration.

If the throttle does not return to the fully closed position smoothly and the cables do not appear to be damaged, lubricate the throttle cables as described in this chapter. If the throttle still does not return properly, the cables are probably kinked or routed incorrectly. Replace damaged throttle cables.

Turn the throttle until resistance is felt. The distance the throttle moved is throttle cable free play (**Figure 31**). The correct throttle cable free play is 2-6 mm (1/8-1/4 in.). If adjustment is required, perform the following procedure.

Lubrication

Lubricate the throttle cables at the intervals specified in **Table 1** or whenever the throttle becomes stiff and sluggish and fails to snap back after releasing it.

The main cause of cable breakage or stiffness is improper lubrication. Periodic lubrication ensures long service life. Inspect the cables for fraying, and check the sheath for chafing. Replace defective cables.

CAUTION
When servicing aftermarket cables, follow the manufacturer's cable lubrication requirements.

1. Disconnect the upper throttle cable ends as follows:
   a. Remove the two screws (**Figure 32**) securing the lower throttle cable holder at the carburetor. Disconnect both cable ends from the carburetor throttle drum. Leave the lower part of the cables attached to the throttle cable holder.
   b. Remove the throttle housing and disconnect the upper throttle cable ends (**Figure 33**) as described under *Handlebar* in Chapter Twelve.

NOTE
When using an aerosol type lubricant, cover the area around the nozzle and tube with a plastic bag.

2. Lubricate the cables. **Figure 34** shows a cable lube tool. Lubricate each cable until fluid exits through the bottom of the cable. Wipe up all excess lube from the end of the cable.

CAUTION
Do not use chain lube to lubricate control cables unless it is also advertised as a cable lubricant.

3. Lightly lubricate the upper cable ends with grease.
4. Installation is the reverse of removal. Adjust the throttle cables by following the adjustment procedure described in this section.

WARNING
An improperly assembled and installed throttle grip assembly may cause the throttle to stick open. Failure to properly assemble and adjust the throttle cables and throttle grip could cause a loss of steering control. Do not start or ride the motorcycle until the throttle grip is correctly installed and snaps back when released.

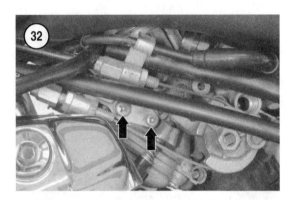

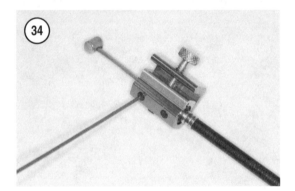

Adjustment

Cable adjusters are provided at both ends of the pull cable. Minor cable adjustment is made at the upper adjuster. If this does not provide enough adjustment, continue by adjusting the lower adjuster.

WARNING
If the idle speed increases when turning the handlebar, check the throttle cable routing. Correct this problem immediately. Do not ride the motorcycle in this unsafe condition.

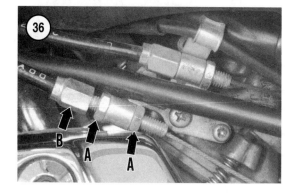

3. Operate the throttle a few times. The throttle grip should now be adjusted correctly. If not, the throttle cables may be stretched. Replace cables in this condition.

4. Reinstall all parts previously removed.

5. Open and release the throttle grip. Make sure it opens and closes (snaps back) without any binding or roughness. Then support the motorcycle and turn the handlebar from side to side, checking throttle operation at both steering lock positions.

6. Sit on the motorcycle and start the engine with the transmission in neutral. Turn the handlebars from lock-to-lock to check for idle speed variances due to improper cable adjustment, routing or damage.

WARNING
If idle speed increases when the handlebar is turned, recheck the throttle cable adjustment and routing. Do not ride the motorcycle in this unsafe condition.

7. Test ride the motorcycle, slowly at first, to make sure the throttle cables are operating correctly. Readjust if necessary.

1. Minor adjustment—Perform the following at the throttle grip:

 a. Loosen the locknut (A, **Figure 35**) and turn the upper adjuster (B) in or out to achieve 2-6 mm (3/32-1/4 in.) free play rotation.

 b. Tighten the locknut and recheck the adjustment. If there is not enough cable adjustment, turn the upper adjuster in (increase cable free play) and continue with Step 2.

WARNING
Do not turn the upper adjuster out so far that only a few threads are available for the adjuster and locknut. This could cause the adjuster to back out, lock the cable and cause the throttle to stick open.

2. Major adjustment—Perform the following:

 a. Loosen the cable locknuts (A, **Figure 36**) and turn the adjuster (B) to achieve proper free play rotation at the throttle grip (**Figure 34**). Tighten the locknuts securely.

 c. Recheck free play. If necessary, readjust the upper adjuster as described in Step 1 to obtain the optimum adjustment position for the upper and lower adjusters.

CLUTCH CABLE

Adjustment

Check frequently clutch lever free play. If necessary, adjust the free play to compensate for clutch cable stretching and clutch plate wear. Excessive clutch lever free play prevents the clutch from disengaging and causes clutch drag. Too little or no clutch lever free play does not allow the clutch to fully engage, causing clutch slippage. Both conditions cause unnecessary clutch wear. Transmission wear can also result from incorrect clutch adjustment.

1. Operate the clutch lever a few times. If the cable feels tight or dry, lubricate it as described in this chapter. If the clutch lever pivot bolt feels tight or dry, remove, clean and lubricate it with grease as described under *Clutch Cable Replacement* in Chapter Six.

2. With the engine turned off, pull the clutch lever until resistance is felt, then stop and measure free play at the end of the clutch lever (**Figure 37**). The clutch lever should have 10-20 mm (3/8-3/4 in.) free play.

3. Make minor adjustments at the clutch adjuster screw mounted at the clutch lever. Loosen the locknut (A, **Figure 38**) and turn the adjuster screw (B) as re-

quired to obtain the correct free play. Tighten the locknut and recheck the adjustment.

NOTE
If sufficient free play cannot be obtained at the hand lever or there is too much thread exposed on the clutch adjuster screw, use the adjuster at the opposite end of the clutch cable.

4. Remove the left crankcase rear cover (Chapter Fifteen).

5. Loosen the lower clutch cable adjuster locknut (A, **Figure 39**).

6. At the hand lever, loosen the locknut (A, **Figure 38**) and turn the adjuster screw (B) in to loosen the clutch cable all the way.

7. At the lower clutch cable adjuster, turn the adjuster (B, **Figure 39**) to adjust the cable. Tighten the locknut.

8. Now turn the handlebar adjuster screw (B, **Figure 38**) as described in Step 3 and adjust the clutch cable. Tighten the adjuster locknut (A).

9. Start the engine, then pull the clutch lever in and shift the transmission into first gear. Check that the clutch does not drag or the motorcycle does not stall. Slowly release the clutch lever while opening the throttle. The motorcycle should begin to move smoothly. If the clutch does not work correctly, turn the engine off and recheck the clutch adjustment. If the clutch does not work correctly, the clutch cable may be stretched or the friction discs are worn excessively.

Lubrication

1. Disconnect the upper clutch cable end.

2. Lubricate the cable end with a cable lubricating tool (**Figure 34**). Lubricate the cable until fluid exits through the bottom of the cable. Wipe up any excess cable lube.

3. Reattach the upper cable end and adjust the cable as described in this section.

SPEEDOMETER CABLE LUBRICATION (ALL MODELS EXCEPT VT1100C3)

Refer to *Speedometer Gear and Cable* in Chapter Eleven.

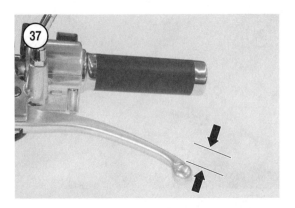

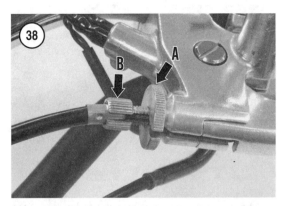

ENGINE OIL AND FILTER

Engine Oil Level Check

Check the engine oil level with the dipstick mounted in the right crankcase cover.

1. Support the motorcycle on a stand with the seat in a level position.

2. Start the engine and let it idle for 2-3 minutes.

3. Shut off the engine and let the oil settle for 2-3 minutes.

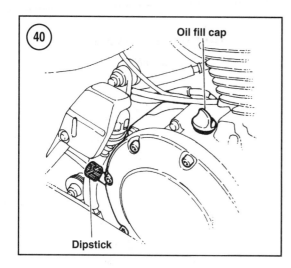

Oil fill cap

Dipstick

JASO CERTIFICATION LABEL

Sales oompany oil code number

M001XXXXXX

MA

OIL CLASSIFICATION
MA: Designed for high-friction applications
MB: Designed for low-friction applications

CAUTION
Do not check the oil level with the motorcycle on its sidestand; the oil flows away from the dipstick and causes a false reading.

4. Remove the dipstick (**Figure 40**), wipe the gauge and insert the dipstick *without* screwing it in.

5. Remove the dipstick. The oil level should be between the upper and lower level marks.

6. If the oil level is near or below the lower level mark, remove the oil fill cap (**Figure 40**) and add the

recommended oil (**Table 4**) to correct the level. Add oil slowly to avoid overfilling.

NOTE
*Refer to **Engine Oil and Selection** in this section for oil information.*

7. Inspect the O-rings on the oil fill cap and dipstick. Replace if starting to deteriorate or harden.
8. Install the oil fill cap and dipstick (**Figure 40**) and tighten securely.
9. If the oil level is too high, do the following:
   a. Remove the oil fill cap (**Figure 40**) and draw out the excess oil using a syringe or suitable pump.
   b. Recheck the oil level on the dipstick and adjust if necessary.
   c. Install the oil fill cap and dipstick and tighten securely.

Engine Oil and Selection

Regular oil and filter changes contribute more to engine longevity than any other maintenance. **Table 1** lists the recommended oil and filter change intervals. These intervals assume the motorcycle is operated in moderate climates. If the motorcycle is ridden infrequently, consider a time interval schedule for changing the oil. Combustion acids formed by gasoline and water vapors can collect as sludge and contaminate the oil if the motorcycle is not ridden regularly or is used for only short trips. If a motorcycle is operated under dusty conditions, the oil gets dirty quicker and should be changed more frequently than recommended.

Because the engine oil lubricates the engine, clutch and transmission components, oil requirements for motorcycle engines are more demanding than for automobile engines. Oils specifically designed for motorcycles contain special additives to prevent premature viscosity breakdown, protect the engine from oil oxidation resulting from higher engine operating temperatures and provide lubrication qualities designed for engines operating at higher rpm. Consider the following when selecting engine oil for the VT1100 engine:

1. Do not use oil with oil additives or oil with graphite or molybdenum additives. These may adversely affect clutch operation.
2. Do not use vegetable, non-detergent or castor based racing oils.

3. The Japanese Automobile Standards Organization (JASO) has established an oil classification for motorcycle engines. JASO motorcycle specific oils are identified by the *JASO T 903 Standard* label on the oil container. **Figure 41** shows the JASO label as it appears on the oil container and identifies its two separate motorcycle oil classifications—MA and MB. Honda recommends the MA-classification oil for the VT1100 engine. JASO classified oil also uses the Society of Automotive Engineers (SAE) viscosity grade ratings. For example, SAE 10W-40.

4. When selecting an American Petroleum Institute (API) oil, use only an oil with an SG classified or higher classification that does not display the term ENERGY CONSERVING on the oil container circular API service label. Refer to **Figure 42**.

5. Use SAE 10W-40 weight oil. Use a lighter viscosity oil (10W-30) in cool climates and a heavier viscosity oil (20W-50) in warm or hot climates. The classification is printed on the container.

NOTE
There are a number of ways to discard used oil safely. The easiest way is to pour it from the drain pan into a gallon plastic bleach, juice or milk container for disposal. Some service stations and oil retailers accept used oil for recycling. Do not discard oil in household trash or pour it onto the ground. Never add brake fluid, fork oil or any other type of petroleum-based fluid to any engine oil to be recycled. To locate a recycler, contact the American Petroleum Institute (API) at www.recycleoil.org.

Engine Oil and Filter Change

1. Start the engine and run it until it is at normal operating temperature, then turn it off.

NOTE
Warming the engine heats the oil so it flows freely and carries out contamination and sludge.

2. Support the motorcycle on its sidestand when draining the engine oil. This ensures complete draining.

CAUTION
The engine, exhaust pipes and oil are hot! Work carefully when removing the

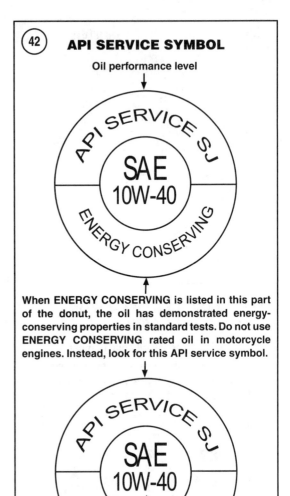

oil drain bolt and oil filter to avoid contacting the oil or hot engine parts.

3. Clean the area around the oil drain bolt and oil filter.

4. Place a clean drip pan under the crankcase and remove the oil drain bolt (**Figure 43**) and washer.

5. Remove the oil fill cap (**Figure 40**) to help speed up the flow of oil. Allow the oil to drain completely.

6. To replace the oil filter, perform the following:

a. Install a socket type oil filter wrench squarely onto the oil filter (**Figure 44**) and turn the filter counterclockwise until oil begins to run out, then remove the oil filter.

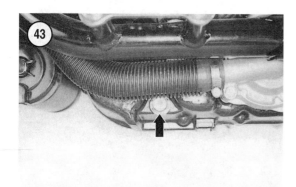

b. Hold the filter over the drain pan and pour out any remaining oil, then place the old filter in a plastic bag and discard it properly.

c. Carefully clean the oil filter sealing surface on the crankcase. Do not allow any dirt or other debris to enter the engine.

d. Lubricate the rubber seal on the new filter with clean engine oil.

e. Install the new oil filter onto the threaded fitting on the crankcase. Tighten the filter by hand until it contacts the crankcase. Then tighten an additional 3/4 turn. If using the oil filter socket, tighten the filter to 10 N•m (88 in.-lb.).

NOTE
Overtightening the filter causes it to leak.

7. Replace the drain bolt gasket if leaking or damaged.

8. Install the oil drain bolt (**Figure 43**) and gasket and tighten to 29 N•m (22 ft.-lb.).

9. Support the motorcycle on a stand with the seat in a level position.

10. Insert a funnel into the oil filler hole and fill the engine with the correct weight (**Table 4**) and quantity of oil (**Table 5**).

11. Remove the funnel and screw in the oil fill cap and its O-ring (**Figure 40**).

NOTE
*If servicing a rebuilt engine, check the engine oil pressure as described under **Engine Oil Pressure Test** in this section.*

12. Start the engine and let it idle.

NOTE
The oil pressure warning light should go out within 1-2 seconds. If it stays on, shut off the engine immediately and locate the problem. Do not run the engine with the oil pressure warning light on.

13. Check the oil filter and drain bolt for leaks.

14. Turn the engine off after 2-3 minutes and check the oil level as described in this chapter. Adjust the oil level if necessary.

WARNING
Prolonged contact with oil may cause skin cancer. Wash hands thoroughly with soap and water after contacting engine oil.

Engine Oil Pressure Test

Check the engine oil pressure after reassembling the engine or when troubleshooting the lubrication system.

An oil pressure gauge (Honda part No. 07506-3000000, or equivalent) and oil pressure adapter (07510-4220100, or equivalent) are required to test the oil pressure.

1. Check the oil level as described in this section. Add oil, if necessary, to correct the level.

2. Check the engine oil level as described in this section. Add oil if necessary.

3. Start the engine and allow it to reach normal operating temperature. Turn the engine off.

4. Support the motorcycle on a stand with the seat in a level position.

5. Remove the rubber boot and disconnect the wire (**Figure 45**) from the oil pressure switch. Then loosen and remove the oil pressure switch.

6. Assemble the oil pressure adapter and gauge. Thread the oil pressure gauge adapter into the engine

in place of the oil pressure switch. Make sure the fitting is tight to prevent leakage.

CAUTION
Keep the gauge hose away from the exhaust pipe during this test. If the hose contacts the exhaust pipe, it may melt and spray hot oil.

7. Start the engine and let it idle.

8. Increase engine speed to 5000 rpm and read the oil pressure on the gauge. The oil pressure should be as follows:

    a. VT1100C2 Sabre: 530 kPa (77 psi) when the oil temperature is 80° C (176° F).

    b. All other models: 441 kPa (64 psi) when the oil temperature is 80° C (176° F).

9. Allow the engine to return to idle, then shut it off and remove the test equipment.

10. If the oil pressure is lower or higher than specified, refer to *Engine Lubrication* in Chapter Two.

11. Install the oil pressure switch as follows:

    a. Clean the oil pressure switch and crankcase threads of all sealer and oil residue.

    b. Apply an RTV sealer to the oil pressure switch threads as shown in **Figure 46**. Do not apply sealer within 3-5 mm (0.1-0.2 in.) from the end of the switch threads.

NOTE
Allow the RTV sealer to set for 10-15 minutes before installing the oil pressure switch.

    c. Install the oil pressure switch and tighten to 12 N•m (106 in.-lb.).

    d. Reconnect the wire onto the switch and cover the switch with its rubber boot.

12. Follow the sealer manufacturer's recommendations for drying time, then start the engine and check for leaks.

NOTE
The oil pressure indicator should go out within 1-2 seconds. If it stays on, shut off the engine immediately and locate the problem. Do not run the engine with the oil pressure indicator on.

CAUTION
Do not overtighten the switch to correct an oil leak, as this may strip the crankcase threads. If oil leaks from the switch

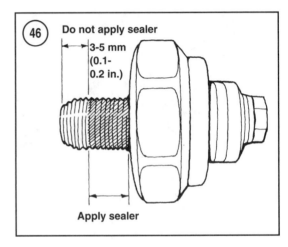

Do not apply sealer
3-5 mm
(0.1-
0.2 in.)

Apply sealer

after installing it, remove the switch and reclean the threads. Reseal and reinstall the switch.

13. Disconnect and remove the tachometer.

FINAL DRIVE

Final Drive Oil Level Check

1. Park the bike on a level surface and support it so it is upright.

CAUTION
Do not check the oil level with the bike resting on its sidestand. An incorrect reading results.

2. Wipe the area around the final drive oil filler cap and unscrew the oil filler cap (A, **Figure 47**).

3. The oil level must be up to the lower edge of the filler cap hole (**Figure 48**). If the oil level is low, add hypoid gear oil until the oil level is correct. Refer to **Table 4** for the correct oil viscosity.

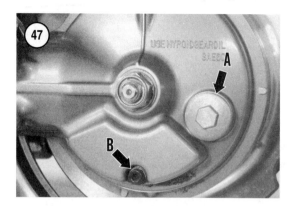

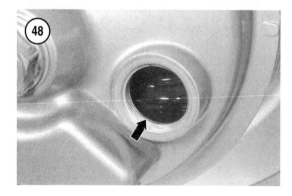

4. Inspect the oil filler cap O-ring for leaks or damage. Lubricate the O-ring with grease.

5. Install the final drive oil filler cap (A, **Figure 47**) and tighten to 12 N•m (106 in.-lb.).

6. Support the bike on its sidestand.

Final Drive Oil Change

The recommended oil change interval is listed in **Table 1**.

Discard the oil as described under *Engine Oil and Filter Change* in this chapter.

1. Ride the motorcycle until normal operating temperature is obtained.

2. Park the bike on a level surface and support it on a stand so the rear wheel just clears the ground.

3. Place a drain pan underneath the drain bolt.

4. Remove the oil filler cap (A, **Figure 47**) and drain bolt (B).

5. With the transmission in neutral, slowly turn the rear wheel to drain the oil from the final drive unit.

6. Install a new washer on the drain bolt, then install the drain bolt and tighten to 12 N•m (106 in.-lb.).

7. Add hypoid gear oil until the level is up to the lower edge of the filler cap hole (**Figure 48**). Refer to **Table 4** (oil type) and **Table 6** (oil quantity).

8. Inspect the oil filler cap O-ring for leaks or damage. Lubricate the O-ring with grease.

9. Install the final drive oil filler cap (A, **Figure 47**) and tighten to 12 N•m (106 in.-lb.).

10. Support the bike on its sidestand.

Front Fork Oil

Honda does not list an oil change interval for the front fork. However, it is good practice to change the fork oil once a year. On models that use sliders with drain bolts, replace the oil as described in the following section. Those without fork oil drain bolts require fork removal and partial disassembly to replace the fork oil. Refer to Chapter Twelve.

Front Fork Oil Change
(Fork With Oil Drain Bolts)

This procedure describes how to change the fork oil by using the oil drain bolts with the fork mounted on the motorcycle. For models without drain bolts, remove and partially disassemble the fork tubes as described under *Front Fork* in Chapter Twelve.

1. Cover both sides of the front wheel and tire to prevent fork oil from contacting the tire or brake caliper.

2. Sit on the motorcycle and have an assistant hold a drain pan underneath one of the fork tube drain bolts (**Figure 49**), then remove the drain bolt and allow the oil to drain out. When the oil flow starts to slow down, apply the front brake and pump the front forks up and down by applying pressure against the handlebars. Continue until the oil stops draining out of the hole.

3. Replace the drain bolt gasket if leaking or damaged.

4. Reinstall the fork tube drain bolt and gasket and tighten to 8 N•m (71 in.-lb.).

5. Repeat Steps 1-4 for the other fork tube.

> *WARNING*
> *Wipe up an oil that may have spilled onto the front tire or front brake caliper.*

6. Support the bike with a stand so the front wheel is off the ground.

7. Loosen the upper fork tube pinch bolt (A, **Figure 50**).

> *NOTE*
> *Place a plastic tie on the fork spring to identify its upper end.*

8. Remove the fork cap (B, **Figure 50**), spacer, spring seat and fork spring from the fork tube. Clean all parts, except the O-ring, in solvent. Refer to **Figure 51**.

9. Pour the specified type (**Table 4**) and quantity (**Table 7**) of fork oil into the fork tube.

10. Measure the fork spring free length as described under *Front Fork* in Chapter Twelve.

11. Lubricate fork cap O-ring and threads with fork oil.

12. Install original fork spring with their tighter wound coils (**Figure 51**) facing down. Remove the plastic tie from the fork spring, if used.

13. Install the spring seat, spacer and fork cap (**Figure 51**). Tighten the fork cap to the torque specification in Chapter Twelve.

14. Tighten the upper fork tube pinch bolt (B, **Figure 50**) to the torque specification in Chapter Twelve.

15. Repeat for the other fork tube.

COOLING SYSTEM

Service the cooling system at the intervals specified in **Table 1**.

> *WARNING*
> *When performing any service work on the engine or cooling system, never remove the radiator cap, coolant drain bolt or disconnect any coolant hose while the engine and radiator*

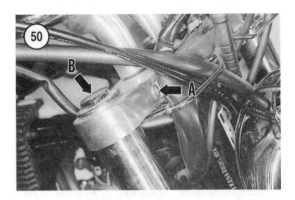

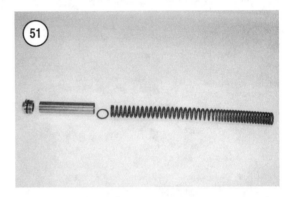

are hot. Scalding fluid and steam may be blown out under pressure and cause serious injury.

Coolant Selection

If adding coolant to the cooling system, use Pro Honda HP Coolant. This is a ready-to-use 50:50 antifreeze/purified, de-ionized water coolant blend. If mixing antifreeze and water, use a 50:50 mixture of distilled water and antifreeze that does not contain silicate inhibitors. Use only soft or distilled water. Never use tap or saltwater because this damages engine

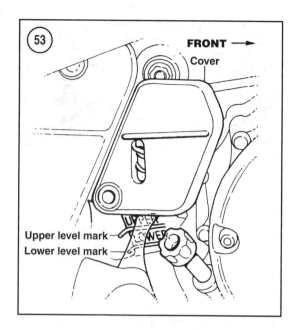

Upper level mark
Lower level mark

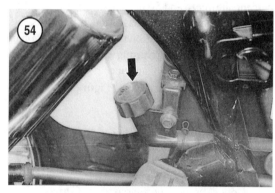

parts. Distilled (or purified) water can be purchased at supermarkets or drug stores in gallon containers. Never use alcohol-based antifreeze.

CAUTION
Many antifreeze solutions contain silicate inhibitors to protect aluminum parts from corrosion damage. However, these silicate inhibitors can cause premature wear to water pump seals. When selecting an antifreeze, make sure it does not contain silicate inhibitors.

Coolant Test

WARNING
*Never remove the radiator cap (**Figure 52**), coolant drain plugs or disconnect any coolant hose while the*

engine and radiator are hot. Scalding fluid and steam may be blown out under pressure and cause serious injury.

1. Remove the fuel tank (Chapter Eight).
2. Remove the right steering cover (Chapter Fifteen).
3. With the engine cold, remove the radiator cap (**Figure 52**).
4. Test the specific gravity of the coolant with an antifreeze tester to ensure adequate temperature and corrosion protection. A 50:50 mixture is recommended. Never allow the mixture become less than 40 percent antifreeze. Refer to *Coolant Selection* in this section.
5. Check the rubber washers on the radiator cap. Replace the cap if the washers show signs of deterioration, cracking or other damage.
6. Reinstall the radiator cap (**Figure 52**).
7. Reverse Step 1 and Step 2.

Coolant Level

The coolant reserve tank is mounted between the swing arm and the rear of the engine.
1. Support the motorcycle on a stand so the seat is level.
2. Start the engine and allow it to idle until it reaches normal operating temperature. The engine must be at normal operating temperature when checking the coolant level. Turn the engine off.
3. The coolant level should between the UPPER and LOWER level marks on the coolant reserve tank (**Figure 53**).
4. If necessary, add coolant as follows:
   a. Turn the engine off.
   b. Remove the coolant reserve tank cap (**Figure 54**) and add Pro Honda HP Coolant into the reserve tank (not the radiator) to bring the level to the upper mark. Refer to *Coolant Selection* in this section. Install the cap.
   c. Inspect the cooling system for leaks as described under *Cooling System Inspection* in Chapter Ten.

Coolant Change

Drain and refill the cooling system at the intervals listed in **Table 1**.

When it is necessary to drain the cooling system between service intervals, drain the coolant into a clean pan and store in a container for reuse.

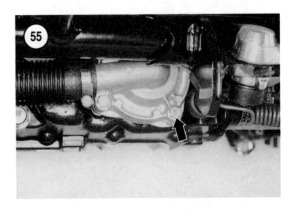

> *WARNING*
> *Waste antifreeze is toxic and may never be discharged into storm sewers, septic systems, waterway, or onto the ground. Place used antifreeze in the original container and dispose of it according to local regulations. Do not store coolant where it is accessible to children or pets.*

> *WARNING*
> *Do not remove the radiator cap (**Figure 52**) if the engine is hot. The coolant is very hot and is under pressure. Scalding results if hot coolant contacts skin.*

> *CAUTION*
> *Be careful not to spill antifreeze on painted surfaces because it damages the surface. Wash immediately with soapy water and rinse thoroughly.*

Perform the following procedure when the engine is *cold*.

1. Place the motorcycle on a stand so the seat is level.
2. Remove the fuel tank (Chapter Eight).
3. Remove the right steering cover (Chapter Fifteen).
4. Remove the radiator cap (**Figure 52**).

> *NOTE*
> *Cut the top part off a plastic gallon size milk container and use the bottom of the container to control the coolant as it drains from the water pump in Step 5.*

5. Place a drain pan under the coolant drain bolt. Remove the drain bolt (**Figure 55**) and washer and allow the coolant to drain into the pan. Discard the washer if damaged.
6. Reinstall the drain bolt and washer and tighten to 13 N•m (115 in.-lb.).
7. Disconnect the siphon tube from the bottom, right side of the coolant reserve tank and drain the coolant into the pan. Flush the tank with clean water and reconnect the siphon tube.

> *CAUTION*
> *Do not use a higher percentage of antifreeze-to-water solution than is recommended under **Coolant Selection** in this section. A higher concentration of coolant actually decreases the performance of the cooling system.*

8. Place a funnel in the radiator filler neck and slowly refill the radiator and engine with a mixture of 50 percent antifreeze and 50 percent distilled water. Add the mixture slowly so it expels as much air as possible from the cooling system. Refer to *Coolant Selection* in this section before purchasing and mixing coolant. **Table 8** lists engine coolant capacity.
9. Fill the coolant reserve tank (**Figure 53**) to its upper level line.

> *WARNING*
> *Do not start and run the motorcycle in an enclosed area. The exhaust gasses contain carbon monoxide, a colorless, odorless and poisonous gas. Carbon monoxide levels build quickly in an enclosed area and can cause unconsciousness and death in a short time.*

10. After filling the radiator, bleed the cooling system as follows:
   a. Start the engine and allow it to idle for 2 to 3 minutes.
   b. Snap the throttle a few times to bleed air from the cooling system. When the coolant level drops in the radiator, add coolant to bring the level to the bottom of the filler neck.
   c. When the radiator coolant level stabilizes, install the radiator cap (**Figure 52**).
11. Start the engine and let it run at idle speed until the engine reaches normal operating temperature. Make sure the coolant level in the coolant reserve tank stabilizes at the correct level. Add coolant to the coolant reserve tank as necessary.

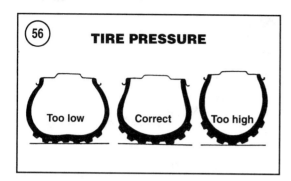

12. Test ride the motorcycle and readjust the coolant level in the coolant reserve tank as required. Check the coolant drain bolt for leakage.

EMISSION CONTROL SYSTEMS INSPECTION (CALIFORNIA MODELS)

California models and 2006-on 49 state/Canada models are equipped with emission control systems. At the intervals specified in **Table 1**, check all emission control hoses for deterioration, damage or loose connections. Replace any parts or hoses as required. Refer to the emission control sections in Chapter Eight for information on inspecting these systems.

TIRES AND WHEELS

Tire Pressure

Check and adjust the tire pressure to maintain the tire profile, good traction and handling and to get the maximum life out of the tire. Check tire pressure when the tires are *cold*. When the motorcycle is ridden, the tire temperature rises. Never release air pressure from a warm or hot tire to match the recommended tire pressure; doing so may cause the tire to be underinflated. Use an accurate tire pressure gauge. **Table 9** lists tire pressures for the original equipment tires.

NOTE
After checking and adjusting the air pressure, make sure to reinstall the air valve cap on each tire. The cap prevents dirt and debris from collecting in the valve stem, which could allow air leakage or result in an incorrect tire pressure reading.

NOTE
A loss of air pressure may be due to a loose or damaged valve core. Put a few drops of water on the top of the valve core. If the water bubbles, tighten the valve core and recheck. If air is still leaking from the valve after tightening it, replace the tube or valve stem.

Tire Inspection

Inspect the tires periodically for excessive wear and damage. Inspect the tires for the following:
1. Deep cuts and imbedded objects, such as nails and stones. If a nail or other object is in a tire, mark its location with a light crayon before removing it. Refer to Chapter Eleven for tire changing and repair information.
2. Flat spots. Storing the motorcycle with one or both wheels on the ground can cause flat spots.
3. Sidewall cracks and other visual damage.
4. Separating plies.
5. Bulges.
6. Improper tire centering on rim.
7. Damaged valve stem.

Tire Wear Analysis

Analyze abnormal tire wear to determine the cause. Common causes are:
1. Incorrect tire pressure. This is the biggest cause of abnormal tire wear. Compare the wear in the center of the contact patch with the wear at the edge of the contact patch (**Figure 56**). Check tire pressure and examine the tire tread. Note the following:
   a. If a tire shows excessive wear at the edge of the contact patch, but the wear at the center of the contact patch is normal, the tire has been underinflated. Underinflated tires causes the sidewalls to flex excessively, causing higher tire temperatures, hard or imprecise steering and abnormal tire wear on the tire edges.
   b. If a tire shows excessive wear in the center of the contact patch, but wear at the edge of the contact patch in normal, the tire has been overinflated. Overinflated tires causes the tire to bulge in the center of the tread, causing a hard ride and abnormal tire wear in the center of the tread. When a properly inflated tire hits a large bump in the road, it has a normal flex

or give and is capable of absorbing much of the shock. However, an overinflated tire cannot flex or give and the tire casing (cord material) takes the shock. This weakens and breaks the tire cords and eventually causes tire failure.

NOTE
Large amounts of high-speed riding on straight roads cause the tires to exhibit a similar wear pattern as described in substep b.

2. Overloading.
3. Incorrect wheel alignment.
4. Incorrect wheel balance.
5. Worn or damaged wheel bearings.

Tread Depth

Measure the tread depth (**Figure 57**) in the center of the tire using a small ruler or a tread depth gauge. Honda recommends replacing the original equipment tires before the center tread depth has worn to the following depth:
1. Front: 1.5 mm (0.06 in.).
2. Rear: 2.0 mm (0.08 in.).

Tires are also designed with tread wear indicators (**Figure 58**) that appear when a tire is worn out. When these are visible, the tire is no longer safe and must be replaced.

Wheel Bearing Inspection

Periodically inspect the wheel bearings.

Front wheel

1. Support the motorcycle with the front wheel off the ground.
2. Hold the caliper housing from the outside and push it toward its brake disc. This pushes the pistons into the caliper and away from the disc so the wheel can spin freely.
3. Spin the front wheel while listening for wheel bearing noise. The wheel should turn freely. If there is any roughness or catching, the wheel bearings may be worn or damaged.
4. Apply the front brake several times to reposition the caliper pistons and seat the brake pads against the disc.

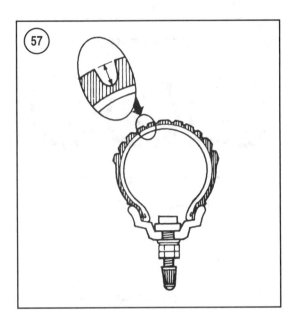

5. Have an assistant apply the front brake and then turn the handlebar to one side and hold securely in this position. Grasp the sides of the front tire 180° apart and try to move the tire from side to side. There should be no play. If play is detected, the wheel bearings may be worn.

6. Remove the stand from underneath the motorcycle. Sit on the motorcycle and apply the front brake. Pump the front forks while trying to detect any play at the wheel bearings. If play is detected, the wheel bearings may be worn.

NOTE
When performing Step 6, play detected at the steering stem indicates loose or damaged steering bearings. Check these bearings as described in this chapter.

7. If necessary, remove the front wheel and inspect the wheel bearings as described in Chapter Eleven.

Rear wheel

Because of the final drive unit, it is more difficult to detect worn or damaged rear wheel bearings when the wheel is mounted on the motorcycle. This procedure also checks the swing arm bearings.

1. Support the motorcycle with the rear wheel off the ground.

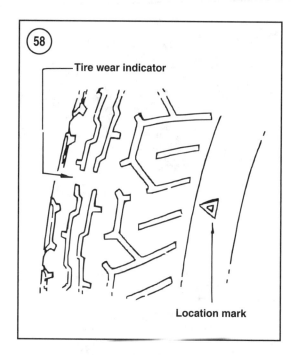

Tire wear indicator

Location mark

2A. Rear drum brake—Turn the rear brake adjuster counterclockwise to move the brake shoes away from the brake drum so the wheel can spin freely.

2B. Rear disc brake—Hold the caliper housing from the outside and push it toward its brake disc. This pushes the piston into the caliper and away from the disc so the wheel can spin freely.

3. Spin the rear wheel by hand. Listen for any excessive bearing noise that may indicate worn or damaged bearings.

4A. Rear drum brake—Readjust the rear brake as described in this chapter.

4B. Rear disc brake—Apply the rear brake pedal several times to reposition the caliper piston and seat the pads against the disc.

5. Have an assistant apply the rear brake while steadying the motorcycle. Then grasp the back of the rear tire and try to move it sideways (parallel to the swing arm). If play is detected, determine if it is from the rear wheel bearings, swing arm bearings or both.

6. If necessary, remove the rear wheel and inspect the wheel bearings as described in Chapter Eleven.

7. If there is any questionable swing arm play, service the swing arm bearings as described in Chapter Thirteen.

8. Install the swing arm (Chapter Thirteen) and rear wheel (Chapter Eleven) if removed.

Spokes and Rim Inspection

Check the spokes and wheel runout at the intervals specified in **Table 1**. Refer to Chapter Eleven.

STEERING BEARING INSPECTION

Periodically inspect the steering bearing adjustment.

1. Support the motorcycle on a stand with the front wheel off the ground.

2. Hold onto the handlebars and move them from side to side. Note any binding or roughness.

3. Support the motorcycle so both wheels are on the ground.

4. Sit on the motorcycle and hold onto the handlebars. Apply the front brake lever and try to push the front fork forward. Try to detect any movement in the steering head area. If so, the bearing adjustment is loose and requires adjustment.

5. If any roughness, binding or looseness was detected when performing Step 2 or Step 4, service the steering bearings as described in Chapter Twelve.

FRONT SUSPENSION INSPECTION

Inspect the front suspension at the intervals specified in **Table 1**.

1. Use a soft wet cloth to wipe the front fork tubes to remove any dirt, road tar and other debris. As this debris passes by the fork seals, it eventually damages the seals and causes them to leak oil.

2. Check both fork tubes for leaking oil seals.

3. Apply the front brake and pump the fork up and down as vigorously as possible. Check for smooth operation.

4. Make sure the upper and lower fork tube pinch bolts are tight.

5. Check that the handlebar mounting bolts are tight.

6. Make sure the front axle is tight.

CAUTION
If any of the previously mentioned fasteners are loose, refer to Chapter Twelve for procedures and torque specifications.

REAR SUSPENSION INSPECTION

Inspect the rear suspension at the intervals specified in **Table 1**.

1. With both wheels on the ground, check the shock absorbers by bouncing on the seat several times.

2. Check the swing arm bearings as described under *Wheel Bearings* in this chapter.

3. Check the shock absorbers for signs of oil leakage, loose mounting fasteners or other damage.

4. Check for loose or missing suspension fasteners.

5. Make sure the rear axle nut is tight.

6. To adjust the rear shock absorber, refer to Chapter Thirteen.

> *CAUTION*
> *If any of the previously mentioned bolts and nuts are loose, refer to Chapter Thirteen for procedures and torque specifications.*

BRAKES

All models are equipped with a front disc brake. VT1100C models are equipped with a rear drum brake. All other models are equipped with a rear disc brake. Check both brake assemblies at the intervals specified in **Table 1**. Immediately inspect the brake components when their operating condition has changed.

Bleeding disc brakes, servicing the brake components and replacing the brake pads and brake shoes are covered in Chapter Fourteen.

Brake System Inspection

Check the front and rear brake operation as follows:

1. Support the motorcycle on its sidestand.

2. Front and rear disc brake—Apply the front brake lever and rear brake pedal. Make sure it feels firm. If the lever or pedal feels soft or spongy, air has probably entered the system. Check the brake system and bleed the brake as described in Chapter Fourteen.

3. Rear drum brake—Support the motorcycle with the rear wheel off the ground. Spin the rear wheel and check for brake drag. Then apply the rear brake pedal. Make sure it feels firm. If necessary, check and adjust the rear brake as described in this section.

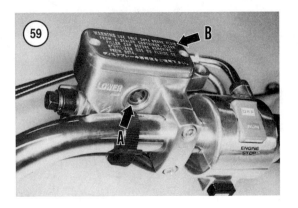

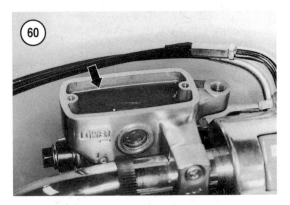

Brake Hose Inspection

Check the front and rear brake hoses between the master cylinder and brake caliper. If there is any leakage, tighten the bolt or hose and then bleed the brake as described in Chapter Fourteen. If this does not stop the leak or if a brake line is obviously damaged, cracked or chafed, replace the brake hose and bleed the system. Refer to Chapter Fourteen for brake system torque specifications.

Brake Fluid Selection

Use DOT 4 brake fluid in the front and rear master cylinder reservoirs.

> *WARNING*
> *Use brake fluid clearly marked DOT 4. Others may cause brake failure. Do not intermix different brands or types of brake fluid because they may not be compatible. Do not intermix silicone based (DOT 5) brake fluid because it can cause brake component damage leading to brake system failure.*

4. Add fresh DOT 4 brake fluid to fill the reservoir to the level mark located inside the reservoir (**Figure 60**).

5. Install the diaphragm, set plate and cover (B, **Figure 59**). Install and tighten the cover screws. Turn the handlebars so the master cylinder is sitting at an angle check for seepage around the cover, indicating the reservoir was overfilled.

6. If the brake fluid level was low, check the brake pads for excessive wear as described in this section.

Rear brake

1. Support the motorcycle on a stand so the seat is level.

2. The brake fluid level must be above the lower level line in the reservoir window (A, **Figure 61**). If the brake fluid level is at or below the lower level line, continue with Step 3.

3. Wipe off the master cylinder cover and remove the cover (B, **Figure 61**) and diaphragm. The diaphragm should come off with the cover. Do not remove the float.

> *WARNING*
> *If the reservoir is empty, air has entered the brake system. Bleed the front brake as described in Chapter Fourteen.*

4. Add fresh DOT 4 brake fluid to fill the reservoir to the upper level mark on the reservoir (A, **Figure 61**).

5. Install the diaphragm and cover and tighten securely.

6. If the brake fluid level was low, check the brake pads for excessive wear as described in this section.

Disc Brake Fluid Change

Every time the reservoir cap is removed, a small amount of dirt and moisture enters the brake fluid. The same thing happens if a leak occurs or when a brake hose is loosened. Dirt can clog the system and cause unnecessary wear. Water in the brake fluid vaporizes at high brake system temperatures, impairing the hydraulic action and reducing the brake's stopping ability. To maintain peak performance, change the brake fluid as specified in **Table 1** or whenever the caliper or master cylinder is over-

> *CAUTION*
> *Handle brake fluid carefully. Do not spill it on painted or plastic surfaces, because it damages the surface. Wash the area immediately with soap and water and thoroughly rinse it off.*

Brake Fluid Level Inspection

A low brake fluid level usually indicates brake pad wear. As the pads wear (become thinner), the caliper pistons automatically extend farther out of their bores. As the caliper pistons move outward, the brake fluid level drops in the system. However, if the brake fluid level is low and the brake pads are not worn excessively, check the brake hose for leaks.

Front brake

1. Park the motorcycle on its sidestand. Turn the handlebar and level the front master cylinder.

2. The brake fluid level must be above the lower level line in the master cylinder window (A, **Figure 59**). If the brake fluid level is at or below the lower level line, continue with Step 3.

3. Wipe off the master cylinder cover and remove the cover screws. Then remove the cover (B, **Figure 59**), set plate and diaphragm. Do not remove the float.

> *NOTE*
> *If the reservoir is empty, air has entered the brake system. Bleed the front brake as described in Chapter Fourteen.*

hauled. To change brake fluid, follow the brake bleeding procedure in Chapter Fourteen.

Brake Pad Wear Inspection

Inspect the brake pads for wear at the intervals specified in **Table 1**.

1. Use a flashlight and inspect the brake pads for uneven wear, oil contamination or other damage. Note the following:

   a. Binding or sticking caliper pistons or improper caliper bracket operation can cause uneven pad wear.

   b. A damaged fork oil seal allows oil to run down the fork tube and contaminate the front brake pads and caliper housing. Always check the pads for contamination when a leaking fork seal is detected and replace the seal immediately.

   c. If there is no visible brake pad damage or contamination, perform Step 2.

2. Replace the brake pads as a set if either pad is worn to the bottom of the wear limit groove (**Figure 62**, typical). Refer to Chapter Fourteen.

Front Brake Lever Adjustment

There is no adjustment for the front brake lever.

Front Brake Light Switch Adjustment

There is no adjustment for the front brake light switch.

Rear Brake Shoe Wear Inspection (VT1100C)

1. Support the motorcycle on its sidestand.

2. Apply the rear brake pedal and hold it in place.

3. Check the brake arm arrow position. If the arrow mark on the brake arm (A, **Figure 63**) aligns with the fixed index mark on the brake panel (B) when the rear brake is applied, the rear brake shoes are excessively worn and require replacement. Replace the rear brake shoes and measure the brake drum as described in Chapter Fourteen.

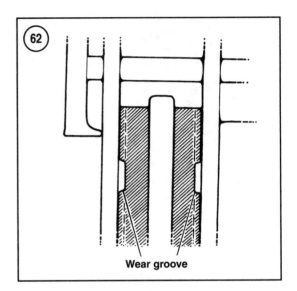

Wear groove

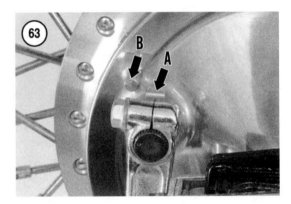

Rear Brake Pedal Adjustment (VT1100C)

Rear brake pedal height

Adjust the brake pedal height to suit rider preference.

1. Loosen the locknut (**Figure 64**) and turn the stopper bolt in or out until the preferred pedal height is reached. Tighten the locknut and recheck the pedal height.

2. If the pedal height adjustment was changed, check the rear brake pedal free play and the rear brake light switch adjustment as described in this section. Adjust if necessary.

Rear brake pedal free play

1. Support the motorcycle on its sidestand.

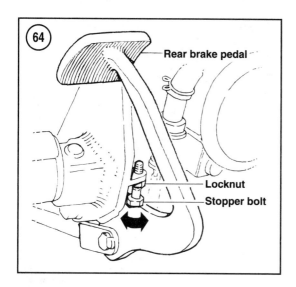

Rear brake pedal

Locknut

Stopper bolt

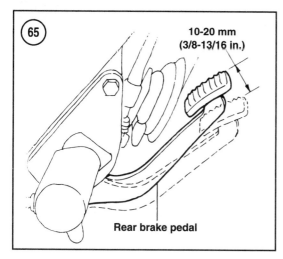

10-20 mm
(3/8-13/16 in.)

Rear brake pedal

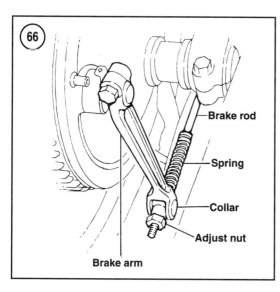

Brake rod

Spring

Collar

Adjust nut

Brake arm

2. Before checking and adjusting the free play, check the brake rod and brake arm assemblies for missing parts or damage.

3. Depress the brake pedal (**Figure 65**) until resistance is felt at the pedal. The distance the brake pedal moved is rear brake free play. The correct free play measurement is 10-20 mm (3/8-13/16 in.). If out of specification, continue with Step 4.

4. Turn the rear brake rod adjust nut (**Figure 66**) to adjust the rear brake free play. After turning the adjust nut, make sure the notch in the nut seats against the brake arm collar.

5. Apply the rear brake a few times, and recheck the free play. Then support the motorcycle with its rear wheel off the ground and spin the wheel, making sure it rotates freely. If there is any noticeable brake drag, the rear brake is adjusted too tightly. Readjust the brake pedal free play to the specifications in Step 3.

NOTE
If the rear brake pedal free play cannot be adjusted so there is no brake drag, the brake shoe linings and the brake drum area may be contaminated. Check and service the rear brake as described in Chapter Fourteen.

6. Check the rear brake light switch adjustment as described in the following section.

Rear Brake Light Switch Adjustment (All Models)

Check the rear brake light switch adjustment at the intervals specified in **Table 1**.

NOTE
*On VT1100C models, perform the **Rear Brake Pedal Height** and **Rear Brake Pedal Free Play** adjustments before checking and adjusting the rear brake light switch in this section.*

1. Turn the ignition switch on.

2. Depress the brake pedal. The brake light should come on just before the brake begins to work.

3. If the brake light comes on too late, continue with Step 4.

CAUTION
Do not turn the switch body when adjusting the rear brake light switch.

This damages the wires at the top of the switch. Hold the switch body and turn the adjust nut.

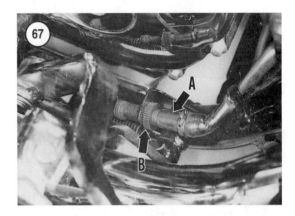

4. Hold the brake light switch body (A, **Figure 67**) and turn the adjust nut (B) as required to make the brake light come on earlier.

5. Recheck the rear brake light switch adjustment. Verify the rear brake light does not stay on when the rear brake pedal is released.

6. Turn the ignition switch off.

LIGHTS AND HORN

Check the headlight aim at the intervals specified in **Table 1**. Refer to *Headlight* in Chapter Nine.

With the engine running, check the following.

1. Pull the front brake lever and check that the brake light comes on.

2. Push the rear brake pedal and check that the brake light comes on.

3. Move the dimmer switch up and down between the high and low positions, and check to see that both headlight elements are working.

4. Move the turn signal switch to the left position and then to the right position and check that all of the turn signal lights are working.

5. Operate the horn button and make sure that both horns sound loudly.

6. If the horn or any light failed to work properly, refer to Chapter Nine.

SIDESTAND AND IGNITION CUTOFF SWITCH INSPECTION

Check the sidestand and the ignition cutoff system operation at the intervals specified in **Table 1**.

1. Operate the sidestand to check its movement and spring tension. Replace the spring if it is weak or damaged.

2. Lubricate the sidestand pivot bolt if necessary.

3. Check the sidestand ignition cutoff system as follows:

   a. Sit on the motorcycle and raise the sidestand.

   b. Shift the transmission into neutral.

   c. Start the engine, then squeeze the clutch lever and shift the transmission into gear.

   d. With the engine in gear and the clutch lever released, move the sidestand (**Figure 68**) down. When doing so, the engine should

stop. This indicates that the sidestand switch is working correctly.

   e. If the engine did not stop as the sidestand was lowered, test the sidestand switch as described in Chapter Nine.

WARNING
Do not ride the motorcycle until the sidestand switch operates correctly. Riding the motorcycle with the sidestand down causes the rider to lose control when the sidestand contacts the ground.

FASTENER INSPECTION

Constant vibration can loosen many fasteners on a motorcycle. Periodically inspect the fasteners.

1. Check the tightness of all exposed fasteners. Refer to the appropriate chapter for torque specifications.

2. Check that all hose clamps, cable stays and safety clips are properly installed. Replace missing or damaged items.

Table 1 MAINTENANCE AND LUBRICATION SCHEDULE[1]

Weekly/gas stop
  Check tire pressure cold; adjust to suit load and speed
  Check condition of tires
  Check brake fluid level; if low, check brakes for excessive wear
  Check brake operation
  Check throttle grip for smooth operation and return
  Check for smooth but not loose steering
  Check axle, suspension and controls; tighten if necessary
  Check engine oil level; add oil if necessary
  Check lights and horn operation, especially brake light
  Check stop switch operation
  Check coolant level
  Check for any abnormal engine noise and leaks
At 600 miles (1000 km)
  Replace engine oil and filter
  Check engine idle speed; adjust if necessary
  Check carburetor synchronization; adjust if necessary
  Check brake system
  Check clutch adjustment; adjust if necessary
  Check steering adjustment
  Check tightness of exposed chassis and engine fasteners
  Check tire and wheel condition
Every 4000 miles (6400 km)
  Check battery water level on standard type batteries
  Check crankcase breather and clean if necessary[2]
  Check spark plugs, replace if necessary
  Check engine idle speed; adjust if necessary
  Check clutch adjustment; adjust if necessary
  Inspect clutch cable and lubricate if necessary
  Check brake fluid level
  Check front and rear brake pads for wear; replace if necessary
  Check rear brake linings on VT1100C for wear; replace if necessary
  Check tire and wheel condition
At 8000 miles (12,800 km); thereafter every 8000 miles (12,800 km)
  Check fuel line; replace if leaking or damaged
  Check choke operation; readjust cable if necessary or replace cable if damaged
  Replace spark plugs
  Replace engine oil and filter[3]
  Check final drive oil level
  Inspect throttle cables and lubricate if necessary
  Check throttle cable adjustment; adjust if necessary
  Check carburetor synchronization; adjust if necessary
  Check secondary air supply system (models so equipped)
  Check coolant for contamination
  Check radiator and all coolant hoses for leaks.
  Check weep hole in bottom of water pump for coolant leakage; replace water pump if necessary
  Check front and rear brake system
  Check brake light switch operation
  Check headlight aim; adjust if necessary
  Check side stand operation and fastener tightness
  Check side stand ignition cutoff system operation; replace the side stand switch if necessary
Every 12,000 miles (19,200 km)
  Inspect the evaporative emission control system (California models)
  Replace the air filter[4]
Every 24,000 miles (38,400 km) or every two years, whichever comes first:
  Replace brake fluid
  Replace coolant
  Replace final drive gear oil

1. Consider this maintenance schedule a guide to general maintenance and lubrication intervals. Harder than
   normal use and exposure to mud, water, and high humidity will require more frequent attention.
2. Increase service intervals when riding at full throttle or in rain.
3. Or every 12 months on 2006-on models.
4. Service more often when riding in wet or dusty conditions.

Table 2 TUNE-UP SPECIFICATIONS

Carburetor synchronization	
Base carburetor	No. 1 (rear carburetor)
Maximum vacuum difference	40 mm Hg (1.6 in. Hg)
Choke valve adjustment distance	10-11 mm (0.39-0.43 in.)
Clutch lever free play	10-20 mm (3/8-3/4 in.)
Cylinder number	No. 1 (rear)
	No. 2 (front)
Engine compression	1275 ± 196 kPa (185 ± 28 psi) @ 300 rpm
Engine firing order	
VT1100C2 ACE	
Front	315°
Rear	405°
VT1100C3	
1998-2000	
Front	315°
Rear	405°
2001-2002	
Front	225°
Rear	495°
All other models	
Front	495°
Rear	225°
Engine idle speed	1000 ± 100 rpm
Ignition timing	
F mark	
VT1100C and VT1100T	12° BTDC @ 1000 rpm
VT1100C2	
ACE	6.5° BTDC @ 1000 rpm
Shadow Sabre	11.5° BTDC @ 1000 rpm
VT1100C3	6.5° BTDC @ 1000 rpm
Spark plug gap	0.8-0.9 (0.031-0.035 in.)
Spark plug type	
NGK	
Standard	DPR7EA-9
Cold climate*	DPR6EA-9
Extended high speed riding	DPR8EA-9
Denso	
Standard	X22EPR-U9
Cold climate*	X20EPR-U9
Extended high speed riding	X24EPR-U9
Throttle grip free play	2-6 mm (5/64-1/4 in.)

* Ambient temperature below 5° C (41° F).

Table 3 MAINTENANCE TORQUE SPECIFICATIONS

	N•m	in.-lb.	ft.-lb.
Clutch cable locknut	10	88	–
Coolant drain bolt	13	115	–
Engine oil drain bolt	29	–	22
Final drive oil drain bolt	12	106	–
Final drive oil filler cap	12	106	–
Fork drain bolt	8	71	–
Oil filter cartridge[1]	10	88	–
Oil pressure switch[2]	12	106	–
Spark plug	14	124	–
Timing hole cap[3]	18	159	–

1. Lubricate threads and O-ring with engine oil.
2. Apply silicone sealant to switch threads as described in text. Do not tighten further if leakage occurs.
3. Lubricate threads with grease.

Table 4 RECOMMENDED LUBRICANTS AND FUEL

Brake fluid	DOT 4 brake fluid
Control cables	Cable lubricant
Cooling system	Honda HP Coolant or equivalent[1]
Engine oil[2]	
Classification	
JASO T 903 standard rating	MA
API classification	SG or higher[3]
Viscosity rating	
1995-2006	SAE 10W-40
2007-on	SAE 10W-30
Final drive unit	Hypoid gear oil, SAE No. 80
Fork oil	Pro Honda Suspension Fluid SS-8 or equivalent 10 wt fork oil
Fuel	Unleaded gasoline with a pump octane number of 86 or higher

1. Coolant must not contain silicate inhibitors as they can cause premature wear to the water pump seals. Refer to text for further information.
2. Do not use oil with molybdenum additives.
3. API SG or higher classified oils not specified as ENERGY CONSERVING can be used. Refer to text for additional information.

Table 5 ENGINE OIL CAPACITY

	Liters	U.S. qt.
Engine oil change only		
VT1100C2 ACE and	3.3	3.5
VT1100C3		
1998-2000	3.3	3.5
2001-2002	2.9	3.1
All other models	2.9	3.1
Engine oil and filter change		
VT1100C2 ACE	3.5	3.7
VT1100C3		
1998-2000	3.5	3.7
2001-2002	3.1	3.3
All other models	3.1	3.3
After engine disassembly		
VT1100C2	4.2	4.4
VT1100C3		
1998-2000	4.2	4.4
2001-2002	3.8	4.0
All other models	3.8	4.0

Table 6 FINAL DRIVE UNIT OIL CAPACITY

	MI	U.S. oz.
Oil change	130	4.4
After drive unit disassembly	150	5.1

Table 7 FRONT FORK OIL SPECIFICATIONS

Fork oil capacity	
VT1100C	449 ml (15.2 U.S. oz.)
VT1100C2	
ACE	
1995-1998	482 ml (16.3 U.S. oz.)
1999	495 ml (16.7 U.S. oz.)
Sabre	538 ml (18.2 U.S. oz.)
VT1100C3	488 ml (16.5 U.S. oz.)
VT1100T	497 ml (16.8 U.S. oz.)
Fork oil level	
VT1100C	173 mm (6.8 in.)
VT1100C2	
ACE	
1995-1998	151 mm (5.9 in.)
1999	139 mm (5.5 in.)
Sabre	108 mm (4.3 in.)
VT1100C3	151 mm (5.9 in.)
VT1100T	140 mm (5.5 in.)
Fork oil type	Pro-Honda Suspension Fluid SS-8 or 10 wt. fork oil

Table 8 COOLANT CAPACITY

	Liters	U.S. qt.
Radiator and engine	2.0	2.1
Reserve tank	0.39	0.41

Table 9 TIRE INFLATION PRESSURE[1]

	Front psi (kPa)	Rear psi (kPa)
Up to 90 kg (200 lb.) load		
VT1100C	33 (225)	33 (225)
VT1100C2		
ACE		
1995-1996	33 (225)	33 (225)
1997-on	29 (200)	33 (225)
Shadow Sabre	29 (200)	33 (225)
VT1100C3	29 (200)	29 (200)
VT1100T	33 (225)	33 (225)
From 90 kg (200 lb.) load to the maximum weight limit[2]		
VT1100C	33 (225)	41 (280)
VT1100C2		
ACE	33 (225)	41 (280)
Shadow Sabre	29 (200)	41 (280)
VT1100C3	29 (200)	41 (280)
VT1100T	33 (225)	36 (250)

1. Tire inflation pressure for original equipment tires. Refer to Table 1 in Chapter Eleven for OEM tire brands and tire sizes. Aftermarket tires may require different inflation pressures. Refer to tire manufacturer's specifications.
2. Refer to Table 3 (Vehicle Weight Specifications) in Chapter One for the maximum weight limit for each model.

ENGINE TOP END

4

The engine is a V-twin liquid-cooled, 4-stroke design. The cylinders are offset and set at a 45° angle; the cylinders fire on alternate crankshaft rotations. Each cylinder is equipped with a single camshaft and three valves.

Both engine and transmission share a common case and the same wet sump oil supply. The clutch is a wet-type located on the right side of the engine. Refer to Chapter Five for service to the engine bottom end components. Refer to Chapter Six for clutch service.

This chapter provides complete service and overhaul procedures, including information for disassembly, removal, inspection, service and reassembly of the engine top end components. These include the cylinder head covers, hydraulic lifters, rocker arms, camshafts, cylinder heads, valves, cylinders, pistons and piston rings.

Before starting any work, review the service hints in Chapter One.

The engine must be removed from the frame before servicing any of the components in this chapter. This procedure is described in Chapter Five.

Before removing and servicing the engine, perform an engine compression test (Chapter Three) and an engine leakdown test (Chapter Two). Record the results from each test and compare them with the tests made after servicing the engine.

Table 1 lists general engine specifications and **Tables 2-4** lists engine service specifications. **Tables 1-5** are at the end of the chapter.

CYLINDER HEAD COVERS AND ROCKER ARMS

Each cylinder head cover (**Figure 1**) is machined with integral bearing surfaces for the camshaft. Each cover is also equipped with three rocker arms and shafts and three assist springs and assist shafts that are part of the hydraulic tappet assembly. A semi-drying gasket sealer seals the cylinder head covers to the cylinder heads.

Removal

1. Remove the engine from the frame (Chapter Five).
2. Plug the opening of each intake manifold.
3. Before removing the cylinder head cover, check for any oil leaks that may indicate a damaged gasket surface. If a leak is found, mark the area for inspection. Check the water pipes for coolant leakage.

NOTE
When removing the cylinder head cover nuts and bolts in Step 5, do not

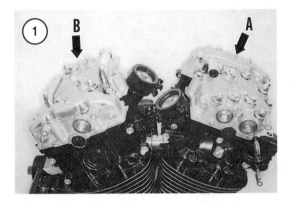

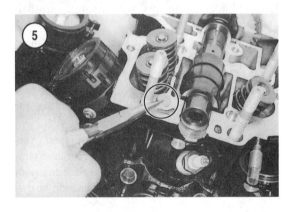

loosen the three assist shaft caps (A,
Figure 2).

4. Loosen the 8-mm and 10-mm cap nuts, and the
8-mm cylinder head cover bolts.

5. Remove the nuts, bolts and water pipe (B, **Figure 2**) from the cylinder head cover.

> *NOTE*
> *Tilting the engine as described in Step
> 6 prevents the hydraulic tappets and
> shims from falling into the lower
> crankcase when the front cylinder
> head cover is being removed.*

6A. Front cylinder head cover (A, **Figure 2**)—Tilt
the engine 45° to its right side and support it with
wooden blocks. Tap the cylinder head cover and
carefully remove it from the cylinder head.

6B. Rear cylinder head cover (B, **Figure 2**)—Tilt the
engine 45° toward its left side and support it with
wooden blocks. Then tap the cylinder head cover and
carefully remove it from the cylinder head.

7. Remove the camshaft plugs (**Figure 3**) from the
grooves in the cylinder head.

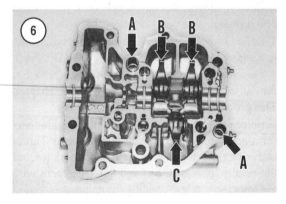

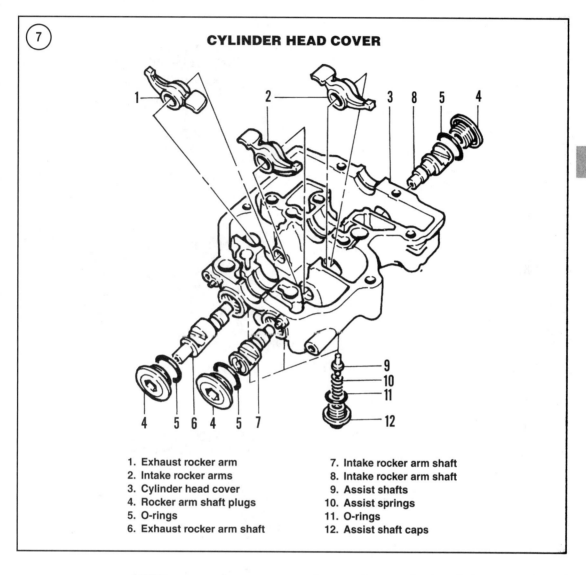

CYLINDER HEAD COVER

1. Exhaust rocker arm
2. Intake rocker arms
3. Cylinder head cover
4. Rocker arm shaft plugs
5. O-rings
6. Exhaust rocker arm shaft
7. Intake rocker arm shaft
8. Intake rocker arm shaft
9. Assist shafts
10. Assist springs
11. O-rings
12. Assist shaft caps

NOTE

The hydraulic tappets and shims must be kept in their respective pairs and in their original mounting positions. If a hydraulic tappet and shim(s) pulls out of its hole in the cylinder head, reinstall them into their original mounting positions. If two or more tappets and shims come out and their original mounting positions cannot be identified, perform the **Tappet Shim Measurement and Adjustment** *under* **Hydraulic Tappets** *before reinstalling the cylinder head cover.*

8. Remove the hydraulic tappets (**Figure 4**) and shims (**Figure 5**) and store them in a divided con-tainer so they can be installed in their original mounting positions. Be sure no shims are left in the cylinder head.

9. Locate the two cylinder head cover dowel pins (A, **Figure 6**). Remove them if necessary.

10. Repeat for the other cylinder head cover.

Disassembly

This procedure describes removal of the rocker arms and shafts from the cylinder head cover. Refer to **Figure 7**.

1. Remove the assist shaft caps (A, **Figure 8**) and O-rings, assist springs (**Figure 9**) and assist shafts (**Figure 10**).

2. Remove the two rocker arm shaft plugs (B, **Figure 8**) and O-rings.

> *NOTE*
> *Store each rocker arm and its shaft in a divided container so they can be reinstalled in their original operating positions.*

3. Using a rubber mallet, tap on the end of the cylinder head cover to work the intake rocker arm shafts (7 and 8, **Figure 7**) partially out of the cover. Then remove the intake rocker arm shafts and rocker arms (B, **Figure 6**).

4. Thread a 6-mm screw into the exhaust rocker arm shaft and remove the shaft (**Figure 11**) and rocker arm (C, **Figure 6**).

Cylinder Head Cover
Cleaning and Inspection

1. Before cleaning the cylinder head cover, inspect the oil lubrication holes for contamination. Small passages and holes in the cover provide lubrication for the cover, camshaft and cylinder head journals. Make sure these passages and holes are clean and open.

> *NOTE*
> *Infrequent oil and filter changes may be indicated if the cover passages are dirty. Contaminated oil passages can result in camshaft and journal failure.*

2. Remove all sealer residue from the cylinder head cover and cylinder head gasket surfaces.

3. Clean the cylinder head cover in solvent, and then dry thoroughly. Clean and dry the cylinder head cover oil passages with compressed air.

4. Inspect the camshaft bearing surfaces (**Figure 12**) in the cylinder head cover for grooves, cracks or wear.

> *NOTE*
> *If the cylinder head cover bearing surfaces are excessively worn or damaged, inspect the camshaft and cylinder head bearing surfaces for the same conditions. Refer to **Camshaft Inspection** in this chapter.*

5. Replace the cap O-rings if leaking or damaged.

6. Measure camshaft oil clearance as described under *Camshaft* in this chapter.

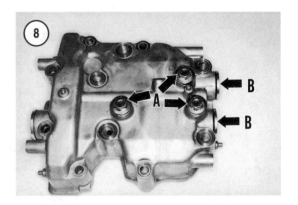

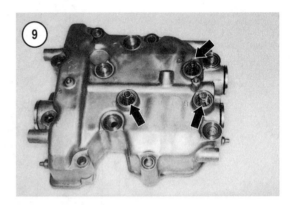

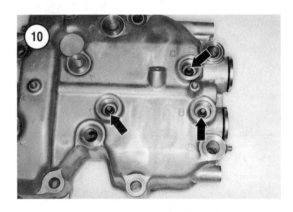

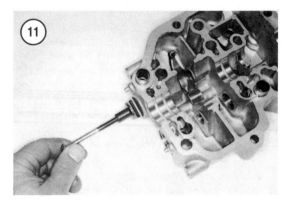

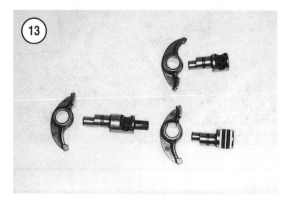

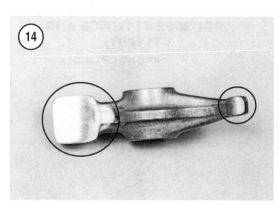

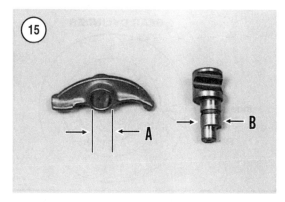

7. Replace the cylinder head cover if damaged.

Rocker Arms and Shafts
Cleaning and Inspection

When measuring the rocker arm components in this section, compare the actual measurements to the new and service limit specifications in **Table 2**. Replace parts that are out of specification or show signs of excessive wear, cracks, seizure or other damage.

1. Clean all parts (**Figure 13**) in solvent and dry with compressed air.

2. Clean the rocker arm and rocker arm shaft oil holes with compressed air.

3. Inspect both rocker arm contact surfaces (**Figure 14**) for cracks, flat spots, uneven wear and scoring.

4. Inspect the rocker arm shafts for scoring, cracks or other damage.

5. Measure the rocker arm bore inside diameter (A, **Figure 15**).

6. Measure the rocker arm shaft outside diameter (B, **Figure 15**).

7. Calculate the rocker arm-to-rocker arm shaft clearance as follows:

   a. Subtract the rocker arm shaft outside diameter (Step 6) from the rocker arm bore inside diameter (Step 5).

   b. Replace the rocker arm and shaft if the clearance is too large (**Table 2**).

8. Repeat for the other rocker arm and shaft assemblies.

Assist Springs and Shafts

Inspection

1. Clean and dry the assist springs and shafts (**Figure 16**).

2. Inspect each assist shaft (**Figure 16**) for wear or bending. Replace if necessary.

3. Measure the free length of each assist spring (**Figure 17**) and compare to the service limit in **Table 2**. Replace the spring if it is too short.

4. Refer to *Hydraulic Tappets* in this chapter to service the hydraulic tappets.

Assembly

All parts must be clean and dry.

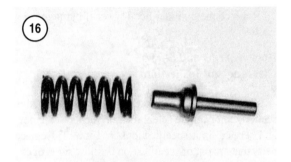

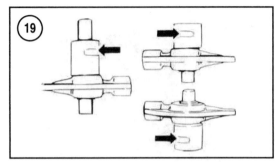

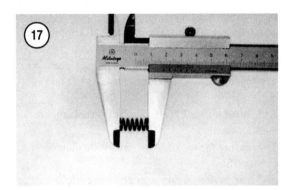

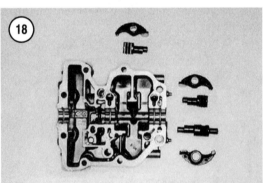

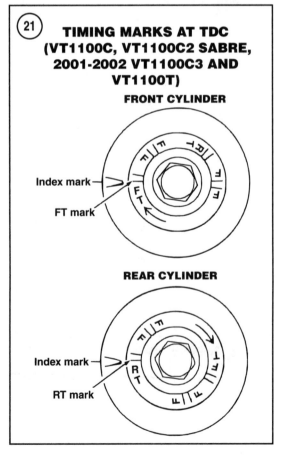

TIMING MARKS AT TDC (VT1100C, VT1100C2 SABRE, 2001-2002 VT1100C3 AND VT1100T)

FRONT CYLINDER

Index mark

FT mark

REAR CYLINDER

Index mark

RT mark

1. Lubricate the rocker arm shafts and rocker arm bores with molybdenum oil solution (50:50 mixture of engine oil and molybdenum disulfide grease).

2. Install the rocker arm shafts and rocker arms (**Figure 18**) in their original locations. Position each rocker arm with its notch (**Figure 19**) facing toward the assist shaft hole in the cylinder head cover. Refer to **Figure 6**.

3. Use a screwdriver on the end of the rocker arm shafts and rotate each rocker arm shaft so the arms move in toward the *center* of the cover.

4. Do not install the assist shafts and springs until after the cylinder head cover has been installed and tightened onto the cylinder head.

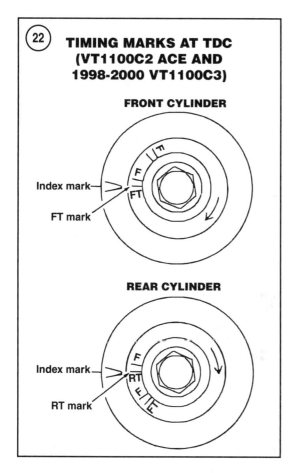

(22) **TIMING MARKS AT TDC
(VT1100C2 ACE AND
1998-2000 VT1100C3)**

FRONT CYLINDER

Index mark

FT mark

REAR CYLINDER

Index mark

RT mark

(23)

Installation

1. Bleed the hydraulic tappets as described under *Hydraulic Tappets* in this chapter.

2. Adjust the hydraulic tappets if the tappet and shims were not identified during removal, the valve seats were refaced, or one of the following parts were replaced; refer to *Hydraulic Tappets* in this chapter:

(24)

a. Cylinder head cover.

b. Rocker arms and rocker arm shafts.

c. Camshaft.

d. Valves and valve guides.

e. Cylinder head.

f. Hydraulic tappet.

3. Remove the timing hole cap from the right side of the engine. Turn the crankshaft (**Figure 20**) clockwise and align the *FT* (front cylinder) or *RT* (rear cylinder) timing marks with the index mark on the right crankcase cover. Refer to **Figure 21** or **Figure 22**. Check that the camshaft lobes for the cylinder being worked on are facing down (A, **Figure 23**).

CAUTION
If the cam lobes are not facing down, turn the crankshaft clockwise 360° and realign the timing marks.

4. Install the correct number of shims (B, **Figure 23**) into each tappet hole in the cylinder head.

5. Install the hydraulic tappets (**Figure 24**) into the cylinder head tappet holes with their rocker arm contact ends facing up.

6. Fill the cylinder head oil pockets with engine oil to cover the cam lobes.

7. Clean the cylinder head and cylinder head cover mating surfaces of all oil and grease residue.

NOTE
Use a semi-drying liquid gasket sealer (ThreeBond Liquid Gasket 1104, Yamabond 4 or equivalent) when gasket sealer is called for in the following steps.

8. Apply gasket sealer to the camshaft plugs where they contact the cylinder head, then install them into the cylinder head. **Figure 3** shows one of the plugs.

> *CAUTION*
> *Do not apply gasket sealant around the three hydraulic tappet holes identified in **Figure 25**. The sealant could cause hydraulic tappet failure.*

9. Apply a thin, even coat of gasket sealer onto the cylinder head cover mating surface (except for the three areas identified in **Figure 25**).

10. If removed, install the two dowel pins into the cylinder head.

11. Install the cylinder head cover (**Figure 26**) and press it into position. Note the following:

   a. Make sure the cylinder head cover engaged the two dowel pins.

   b. Make sure the two camshaft plugs (A, **Figure 27**) seat squarely between the cylinder head cover and cylinder head mating surfaces.

12. With the cylinder head cover seating firmly against the cylinder head, check that the slots in the exhaust and intake rocker arm shafts (B, **Figure 27**) fall within the limits shown in **Figure 28**. If not, remove the cylinder head cover and check the position of the camshaft lobes. They must face down as described in Step 3. If the rocker arm slot positions are correct, continue with Step 13.

13. On all models except the VT1100C2 ACE and VT1100C3, lubricate the cylinder head cover mounting bolt, nut threads and flange surfaces with engine oil.

14. Install the cylinder head cover mounting bolts, nuts, water pipe and copper washers. Install the copper washers onto the bolts whose holes are marked with a triangle (**Figure 29**).

15. Tighten the cylinder head cover mounting bolts and nuts in a crossing pattern to the torque specifications in **Table 5**.

16. Install an assist shaft with the long end facing down (**Figure 30**) into each cylinder head cover hole. Move each shaft to check for binding.

17. Install an assist spring (**Figure 31**) over each assist shaft.

18. Lubricate the assist shaft cap O-rings with oil, then install and tighten the caps (12, **Figure 7**) to 22 N•m (16 ft.-lb.).

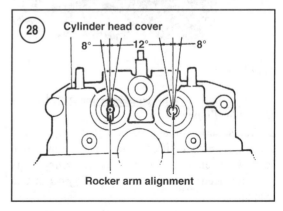

Cylinder head cover

8° 12° 8°

Rocker arm alignment

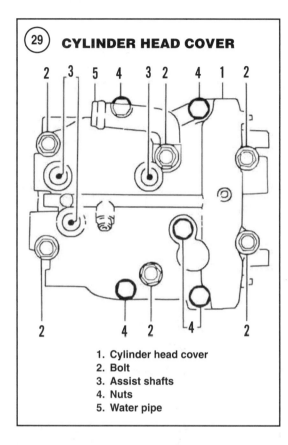

CYLINDER HEAD COVER

2 3 5 4 3 2 4 1 2

2 4 2 4 2

1. Cylinder head cover
2. Bolt
3. Assist shafts
4. Nuts
5. Water pipe

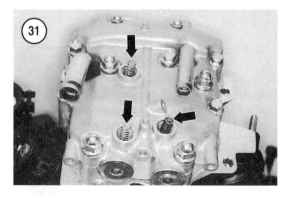

19. Lubricate the rocker arm shaft plug O-rings with oil, then install and tighten the plugs (4, **Figure 7**) to 39 N•m (29 ft.-lb.).

20. Install and tighten the timing hole cap.

21. Install the engine in the frame as described in Chapter Five.

HYDRAULIC TAPPETS

The hydraulic valve adjuster system is designed to create an automatic zero valve clearance setting throughout the engine's rpm range, thus eliminating any routine valve adjustment. Valve clearance remains the same when the engine is cold or hot. The system is basically a tensioning system and does not contain hydraulic valve lifters like those used in many automobile engines.

Each rocker arm is installed on an eccentric rocker arm shaft. The rocker arm shaft has a notch on top of it where an assist shaft and spring are positioned. There is also a notch on the bottom of the rocker arm shaft that accepts the hydraulic tappet. The hydraulic tappets are supplied with air-bled engine oil from the defoaming chambers in the cylinder head cover. The combined effect maintains zero valve clearance.

Refer to **Figure 32** for the following description of the system:

1. When there is no cam lift on the rocker arm, the hydraulic tappet, assist shaft and spring are in the at-rest position (A, **Figure 32**).

2. As the cam lobe starts to lift the rocker arm, the eccentric rocker arm shaft also moves and begins to compress the hydraulic tappet, assist shaft and spring.

3. When the hydraulic tappet is compressed, the oil pressure in the tappet's high-pressure chamber increases and moves the check valve onto its seat and to the closed position.

4. When the cam lobe reaches its maximum lift, the oil pressure within the tappet high-pressure chamber is very high and keeps the check valve closed.

5. As the rocker arm is pressing on the tappet, some of the oil within the high pressure chamber is forced out. This allows the plunger in the tappet to absorb some of the load when the cam lobe is at its maximum lift (B, **Figure 32**).

6. As the cam lobe moves past its maximum lift, the valve springs apply force on the other end of the rocker arm and move the rocker arm back in the other direction.

7. As the rocker arm shaft moves back in the other direction, the springs within the tappet push the plunger upward (C, **Figure 32**).

8. The oil pressure within the high-pressure chamber has now decreased, allowing the check valve to leave its seat. This allows oil to re-enter the high-pressure chamber.

9. The sequence starts over.

Inspection

The tappets are permanently sealed. Do not attempt to disassemble them.

1. Remove the tappets as described under *Cylinder Head Cover and Rocker Arms* in this chapter.

2. Inspect the exterior of the tappet (**Figure 33**) for excessive wear, scoring or damage. Replace if necessary.

3. Make sure the oil holes in the tappet are open and free of any oil sludge.

4. If the tappet is in good condition, bleed it before installing it into the cylinder head.

Bleeding

For proper operation, the hydraulic tappets must be free of air in the high-pressure chamber. The Honda Hydraulic Tappet Bleeder (part No. 07973-MJ00000 [**Figure 34**]) or an improvised tool setup may be used for this procedure. A transparent container filled with kerosene, dial indicator and magnetic stand are also required.

> *CAUTION*
> *Note the location in the cylinder head from which the tappet and shim(s) were removed.*

1. Remove the tappet and shim(s) from the cylinder head as described under *Cylinder Head Cover and Rocker Arms* in this chapter.

2. Fill a transparent jar with new kerosene. Fill the jar with enough kerosene to completely submerge the tappet.

> *CAUTION*
> *Keep the tappet submerged and upright during this procedure.*

3A. To bleed the tappets with the Honda Hydraulic Tappet Bleeder (**Figure 34**), perform the following:

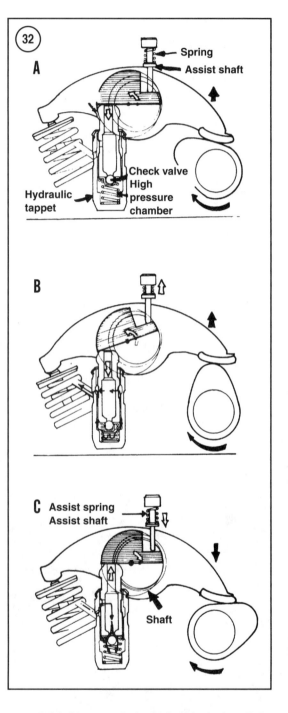

a. With the tappet facing right side up, install the tool's bleed shaft into the tappet's oil hole.

b. Place the tool and tappet into the jar filled with kerosene (**Figure 35**).

c. Hold the tappet and tool upright, then push down on the tool and pump the tappet as shown in **Figure 35**.

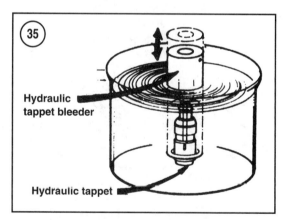

Hydraulic
tappet bleeder

Hydraulic tappet

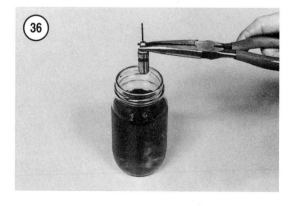

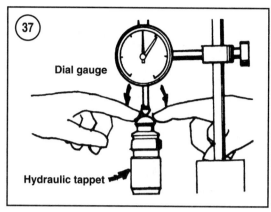

Dial gauge

Hydraulic tappet

4

d. Continue pumping the tappet until air bubbles stop coming from the high pressure chamber in the tappet.

e. Remove the tappet and set it upright onto the workbench.

3B. If the special tool is not available, perform the following:

a. Insert a 1/16 in. drill bit into the oil hole in the top of the tappet (**Figure 36**).

b. Place the tappet and drill bit into a jar filled with kerosene.

c. Hold the tappet upright, then push down on the drill bit with a piece of metal or a wooden dowel and pump the tappet (**Figure 36**).

d. Continue to pump until air bubbles stop coming from the high pressure chamber in the tappet.

e. Remove the tappet and set it upright on the workbench.

NOTE
After removing the tappet from the jar filled with kerosene, keep the tappet upright. If the tappet is laid down at an angle or on its side, air enters the high pressure chamber and the tappet has to be bled again.

NOTE
The small amount of kerosene left in the tappet's high pressure chamber does not contaminate the engine's oil.

4. With the tappet sitting on a flat surface and facing right side up, try to quickly compress the tappet with your fingers. Any compression felt must be minimal. To confirm, place the tappet underneath a dial indicator (**Figure 37**) and compress the tappet with your fingers while watching the dial gauge. If

the tappet can be compressed by more than 0.20 mm (0.008 in.), it must be bled again. If the tappet cannot be bled so its compression stroke is less than this limit, replace the tappet.

5. Reinstall the tappet and shim(s) into the correct cylinder head tappet holes as described under *Cylinder Head Cover and Rocker Arms* in this chapter.

6. Repeat this procedure for each tappet.

**Tappet Shim Measurement
and Adjustment**

To achieve zero clearance in the valve train, the tappet must provide the correct amount of pressure on the rocker arm (**Figure 32**). To compensate for manufacturing tolerances in various parts, one or more shims are installed underneath each tappet (B, **Figure 23**).

1. Determine the correct number of shims if the tappet and shims were not identified or any of the following components were serviced or replaced:

    a. Valve seats refaced.

    b. Cylinder head cover.

    c. Rocker arms and rocker arm shafts.

    d. Camshaft.

    e. Valves and valve guides.

    f. Cylinder head.

    g. Hydraulic tappet.

2. If removed, install the cylinder head and camshaft as described in this chapter.

3. Bleed the tappets as described in this chapter.

4. Install the tappets (without shims) and cylinder head cover as described under *Cylinder Head Cover and Rocker Arms* in this chapter. Do not apply sealer to the cylinder head cover.

5. Install the assist shafts and their springs as described under *Cylinder Head Cover and Rocker Arms* in this chapter.

6. Mount a dial indicator onto the cylinder head cover. Then center the indicator's plunger against the top of one assist shaft (**Figure 38**). Zero the dial on the dial indicator.

7. Have an assistant rotate the crankshaft clockwise two times (**Figure 20**).

8. Record the assist shaft's stroke movement during these two revolutions.

9. Determine the number of shim(s) required for that tappet by referring to the stroke movement specifications in **Table 3**.

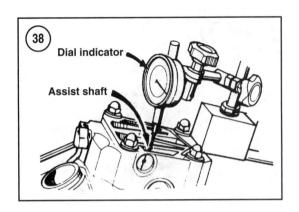

(38) Dial indicator
Assist shaft

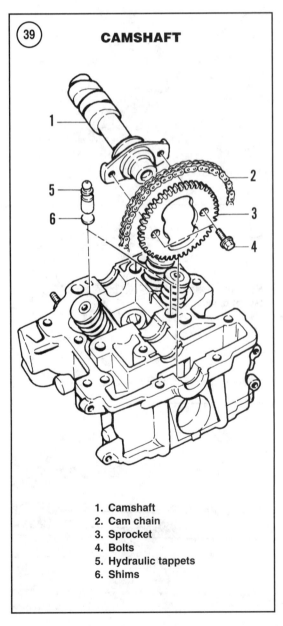

(39) **CAMSHAFT**

1. Camshaft
2. Cam chain
3. Sprocket
4. Bolts
5. Hydraulic tappets
6. Shims

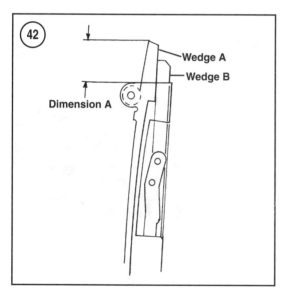

Wedge A
Wedge B
Dimension A

NOTE
Additional shims can be purchased from a Honda dealership.

10. Repeat this procedure for all tappets affected by replaced parts or services.

11. After replacing the shims and installing the tappets into the cylinder head, repeat this procedure (with shims in place) and make sure the stroke movement for each tappet is within the 0-1.20 mm (0-0.047 in.) range.

12. Remove the dial indicator.

CAMSHAFTS

Refer to **Figure 39**.

Removal

This section describes removal of both camshafts. If it is only necessary to remove one camshaft, it is still necessary to remove both cylinder head covers to view the camshaft timing marks.

1. Remove the engine as described in Chapter Five.

2. Remove the spark plugs as described in Chapter Three.

3. Remove the spark plug sleeve with the Honda fork tube holder attachment (part No. 07930- KA50100 [**Figure 40**]) or a bolt that is 27 mm (1 1/16 in.) across the flats of the head. Refer to **Figure 41**. Cover the spark plug openings to prevent small items from falling into the engine.

4. Remove the timing hole cap from the right crankcase cover. The right crankcase cover must be installed on the engine when viewing the ignition pulse generator rotor timing marks.

NOTE
*Always turn the crankshaft clockwise, as viewed from the right side of the motorcycle, in the following steps (unless otherwise specified). Use a socket through the right crankcase cover to engage the crankshaft bolt (**Figure 20**).*

5. Remove the cylinder head covers, hydraulic tappets and shims as described under *Cylinder Head Cover and Rocker Arms* in this chapter.

6. Before removing the camshaft, measure cam chain wear as follows:

   a. Measure the exposed height of cam chain tensioner wedge A (**Figure 42**).

   b. If the measurement exceeds 9.0 mm (0.35 in.), the cam chain is excessively worn and must be replaced.

NOTE
It is helpful to rotate the engine and check the front and rear camshaft and

ignition pulse generator rotor timing marks a few times before actually removing the camshafts. Doing so is important because it confirms the timing marks and camshaft positions are correct. This is an important step to make when troubleshooting a camshaft, cam chain or valve timing problem.

7. Release the cam chain tensioner spring tension against the cam chain as follows:

    a. Cover the area around the cam chain tensioner to prevent small parts from falling into the engine.

    b. At the chain tensioner, pull wedge A up with pliers, then push wedge B down with a screwdriver to expose the hole in wedge A (**Figure 43**).

    c. Install a 2 mm (5/64 in.) pin through the hole in wedge A (**Figure 44**), then release wedge B.

NOTE
Leave the pin in place until after the camshaft and its sprocket have been reinstalled.

8. Remove the exposed cam sprocket bolt (**Figure 45**).

9. Rotate the engine 360° clockwise and remove the other sprocket bolt.

CAUTION
When rotating the crankshaft in the following steps, pull up on the cam chain(s) so it properly engages the crankshaft drive sprocket(s). Otherwise, the cam chain could bind against the sprocket and damage both the chain and sprocket.

10. Rotate the engine clockwise until the cam sprocket opening is positioned as shown in **Figure 46**. This eases camshaft removal from the sprocket.

11. Slide the cam sprocket and cam chain off the shoulder on the camshaft, then remove the camshaft (**Figure 47**).

12. Tie a piece of wire to the cam chain and remove the cam sprocket.

13. Repeat these steps to remove the opposite camshaft.

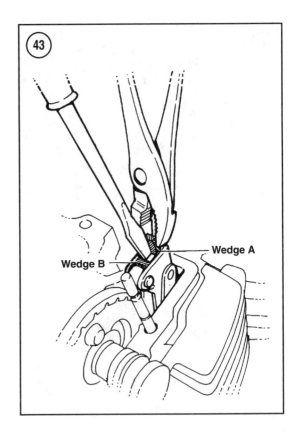

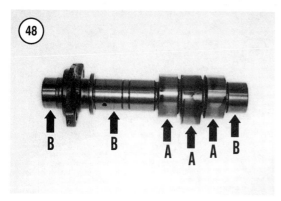

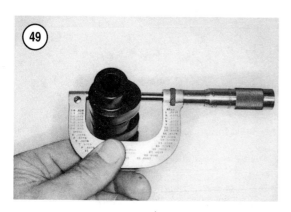

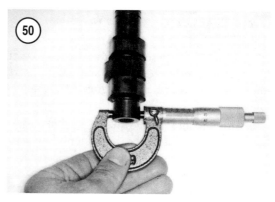

Camshaft Inspection

When measuring the camshafts, compare the actual measurements to the specifications in **Table 2**. Replace worn or damaged parts as described in this section.

1. Before cleaning the camshafts, inspect the oil lubrication holes for contamination. Make sure these holes are clean and open.

2. Clean the camshafts in solvent and dry thoroughly. Flush the camshaft oil passages with solvent and compressed air.

3. Clean the camshaft and cam sprocket bolt threads of all threadlock residue.

4. Check the cam lobes (A, **Figure 48**) for wear. The lobes should not be scored and the edges should be square. Replace the camshaft if the lobes are scored, worn or damaged.

5. Check the camshaft bearing journals (B, **Figure 48**) for wear or scoring. Replace the camshaft if the journals are scored, worn or damaged.

6. If the camshaft lobes or journals are excessively worn or damaged, check the journal surfaces in the cylinder head and in the camshaft cover. Refer to *Camshaft Holder and Rocker Arms* in this chapter.

7. Measure each cam lobe height (**Figure 49**) with a micrometer.

8. Measure each cam journal outside diameter (**Figure 50**) with a micrometer at the points marked A, B and C in **Figure 51** and check against the corresponding A, B and C specifications in **Table 2**.

9. Check the cam bearing journal surfaces in the cylinder head cover and cylinder for wear and scoring. The journal surfaces must be smooth with no visible damage areas. If excessive wear is noted, replace the cylinder head cover and cylinder head as a set. To measure bearing journal wear, perform the

Camshaft Oil Clearance Measurement in this section.

10. Support the camshaft journals on a set of V-blocks or crankshaft truing stand and measure runout with a dial indicator (**Figure 52**). Note the following:

a. If the runout is excessive, replace the camshaft and measure the camshaft oil clearance as described in this section. If the clearance is still out of specification, the cylinder head cover and cylinder head cam bearing journals were damaged from a bent camshaft.

b. If the camshaft was replaced, inspect it and remeasure the camshaft oil clearance with the new camshaft.

11. Inspect the camshaft sprockets (**Figure 53**) for broken or chipped teeth. Also inspect the cam chains and timing sprockets mounted on the crankshaft.

Camshaft Oil Clearance Measurement

This section describes how to measure the clearance between the camshaft and the camshaft journals using Plastigage (**Figure 54**). Plastigage is a soft material that flattens when pressure is applied to it. The marked bands on the envelope are then used to measure the width of the flattened Plastigage. The camshaft and cylinder head cover must be installed on the cylinder head when performing this procedure.

Plastigage is available from automotive parts stores in different clearance ranges. Refer to the camshaft oil clearance specifications in **Table 2**.

1. Wipe all oil residue from each cam bearing journal (camshaft, cylinder head cover and cylinder head). These surfaces must be clean and dry.

2. Identify the camshafts by the *F* (front) and *R* (rear) cast marks indicated in **Figure 55**. Disregard all other camshaft marks.

3. Install the camshaft into the cylinder head with its lobes facing down so the valves are not pressed open by the cylinder head cover/rocker arm assembly. Refer to *Camshaft Installation* in this chapter.

4. Place a strip of Plastigage material on top of each camshaft bearing journal, parallel to the camshaft (**Figure 56**).

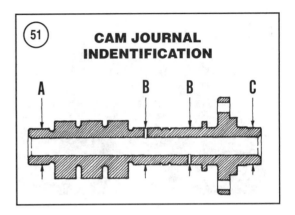

51

CAM JOURNAL INDENTIFICATION

A   B   B   C

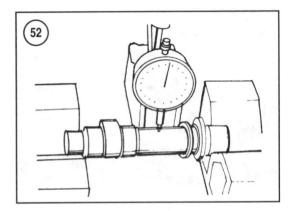

52

53

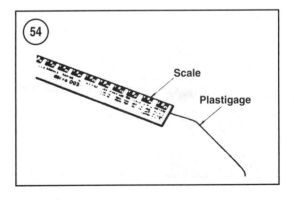

54

Scale

Plastigage

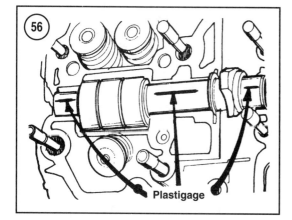

Plastigage

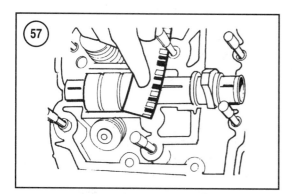

NOTE
The rocker arms and shafts do not have to be installed in the cylinder head cover when performing this procedure.

5. Install and tighten the cylinder head cover as described under *Cylinder Head Cover and Rocker Arms* in this chapter. Note the following:
   a. Do not apply a sealer to the gasket surface. These surfaces can be left dry.
   b. Position the cam chain and its holding wire so they do not interfere with the camshaft, cylinder head or cylinder head cover.

CAUTION
Do not rotate the camshafts with the Plastigage in place.

6. Remove the cylinder head cover as described under *Cylinder Head Cover and Rocker Arms* in this chapter. Make sure the camshaft does not rotate. Do not drop the dowel pins into the engine.

7. Measure the widest portion of the flattened Plastigage according to the manufacturer's instructions (**Figure 57**). Compare each Plastigage measurement point (A, B and C in **Figure 51**) with the A, B and C camshaft oil clearance specifications in **Table 2**. Note the following:
   a. If all the measurements are within specification, the cylinder head, camshaft and cylinder head cover can be reused.
   b. If any measurement exceeds the service limit, replace the camshaft and recheck the oil clearance.
   c. If the new measurement exceeds the service limit with the new camshaft, replace the cylinder head cover and cylinder head as a set.

8. Remove all Plastigage material from the camshaft, cylinder head cover and cylinder head.

Camshaft Installation

Before installing the camshaft(s), note the following:

1. Rotate the engine with a socket on the crankshaft mounting bolt (**Figure 58**).

2. Rotating the crankshaft 360° (1 turn) rotates the camshafts 180° (1/2 turn).

3. Identify the camshafts by the *F* (front) and *R* (rear) flange marks identified in **Figure 55**. Disregard all other marks.

4. The camshaft identification marks (**Figure 55**) are also used as the camshaft TDC (top dead center) timing marks. When the camshaft identification marks are facing up, the cam lobes are facing down.

5. The crankshaft timing marks are on the ignition pulse generator rotor, which is mounted on the right side of the crankshaft. In this procedure, this part is referred to as the rotor.

6. If both camshafts were removed, install the *front* camshaft first, then the rear camshaft.

7. If only one camshaft was removed, remove the opposite cylinder head cover so the installed camshaft timing marks can be viewed.

8. Clean the camshaft sprocket bolts and camshaft threaded holes of all threadlock residue and oil. These threads must be clean and dry.

9. Two different sets of crankshaft timing marks, each identifying different models or model years, are referenced during crankshaft installation. Confirm the correct timing mark and procedural step before setting the crankshaft position.

> *CAUTION*
> *When rotating the crankshaft in the following steps, pull both cam chains outward to prevent them from jamming against the crankshaft drive sprockets. Doing so could damage the chains and sprockets.*

Front camshaft

1. Read the information under *Camshaft Installation* at the beginning of this section.

2. Lubricate the camshaft journal surfaces in the cylinder head with molybdenum oil solution (50:50 mixture of engine oil and molybdenum disulfide grease).

3A. If both camshafts were removed, turn the crankshaft (**Figure 58**) clockwise and align the *FT* mark on the rotor with the index mark on the crankcase cover. Refer to **Figure 59** or **Figure 60**. Check that the front piston is at TDC. If not, turn the crankshaft one full turn (360°) and realign the *FT* mark.

3B. If the rear camshaft was not removed, turn the crankshaft clockwise and align the *RT* mark on the rotor with the index mark on the crankcase cover. Refer to **Figure 59** or **Figure 60**. Check the position of the *R* mark on the rear camshaft (**Figure 61**) and note the following:

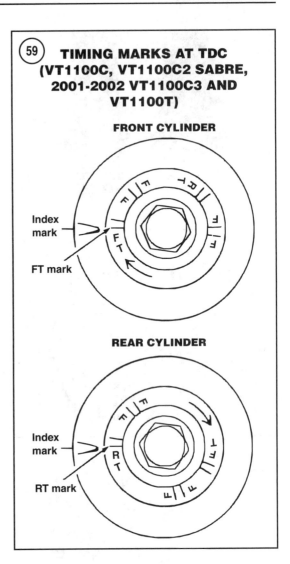

59   **TIMING MARKS AT TDC (VT1100C, VT1100C2 SABRE, 2001-2002 VT1100C3 AND VT1100T)**

FRONT CYLINDER

Index mark

FT mark

REAR CYLINDER

Index mark

RT mark

a. If the *R* mark faces up on VT1100C, VT1100C2 Sabre, 2001-2002 VT100C3 and VT1100T models, turn the crankshaft clockwise 1 3/8 turn (495°) and align the *FT* mark on the rotor with the index mark on the crankcase cover (**Figure 59**).

b. If the *R* mark faces down (mark cannot be seen) on VT1100C, VT1100C2 Sabre, 2001-2002 VT100C3 and VT1100T models, turn the crankshaft clockwise 3/8 turn (135°) and align the *FT* mark on the rotor (**Figure 59**) with the index mark on the crankcase cover.

c. If the *R* mark faces up on VT1100C2 ACE and 1998-2000 VT1100C3 models, turn the crankshaft clockwise 1 1/8 turn (405°) and align the *FT* mark on the rotor with the index mark on the crankcase cover (**Figure 60**).

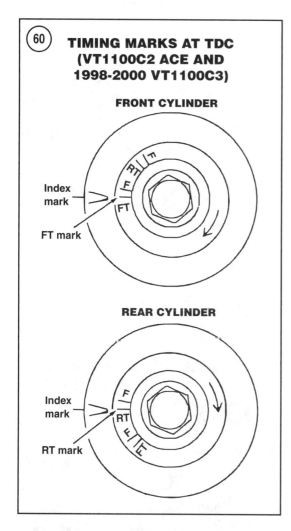

TIMING MARKS AT TDC (VT1100C2 ACE AND 1998-2000 VT1100C3)

FRONT CYLINDER

Index mark

FT mark

REAR CYLINDER

Index mark

RT mark

d. If the *R* mark faces down (mark cannot be seen) on VT1100C2 ACE and 1998-2000 VT1100C3 models, turn the crankshaft 1/8 turn (45°) clockwise and align the *FT* mark on the rotor with the index mark on the crankcase cover (**Figure 60**).

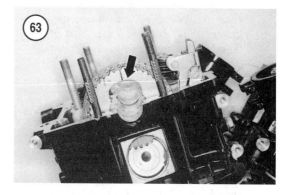

4. Pull the cam chain up to mesh it with the crankshaft drive sprocket. Install the cam sprocket with its index marks (**Figure 53**) facing out and aligned with the cylinder head gasket surface as shown in A, **Figure 62**. The *ME9* mark on the cam sprocket must be facing up (B, **Figure 62**).

NOTE
Positioning the cam sprocket as described in Step 5 makes it easier to install the camshaft through the sprocket.

5. Hold the sprocket so it remains meshed with the cam chain, then turn the crankshaft 1/2 turn (180°) clockwise to position the cam sprocket opening as shown in **Figure 63**.

6. Install the front camshaft (**Figure 55**) into the cylinder head and through the sprocket opening (**Figure 64**).

7. Hold the sprocket so it remains meshed with the cam chain and turn the crankshaft 1/2 turn (180°) counterclockwise and realign the two sprocket index marks with the cylinder head gasket surface (A, **Figure 65**). The *ME9* sprocket mark (B, **Figure 65**) should be facing up. Then check that the FT mark

on the rotor aligns with the index mark on the crank-case cover. Refer to **Figure 59** or **Figure 60**.

8. Turn the camshaft so its F mark faces up (**Figure 66**), then slide the sprocket onto the camshaft's shoulder. Recheck the timing mark alignment made in Step 7. If incorrect, correct it at this time.

NOTE
If there is not enough chain slack for the cam sprocket to slide onto the camshaft, it is necessary to straighten the guide on the chain tensioner to loosen the chain. Do this by perform-ing one of two methods: (1) press the chain tensioner's guide with a screw-driver; or (2) hold the lower part of the cam chain tensioner guide against its engine guide with an adjustable wrench (Figure 67). To access the lower part of the cam chain tensioned as shown in Figure 67, remove the starter clutch as described in Chapter Nine.

NOTE
The camshaft threads and the cam sprocket mounting bolt threads must be clean and dry.

9. Apply a medium strength threadlock to the cam-shaft sprocket bolt threads.
10. Install the first sprocket bolt (A, **Figure 68**) hand-tight.
11. Turn the crankshaft clockwise one turn (360°) and install the second sprocket bolt. Tighten this bolt to 18 N•m (159 in.-lb.).
12. Turn the crankshaft clockwise one turn (360°) and align the *FT* mark on the rotor with the index mark on the crankcase cover (**Figure 59** or **Figure 60**). Then check that the sprocket index marks (B, **Figure 68**) align with the cylinder head gasket sur-face. If the camshaft timing is correct, continue with Step 13. If not, retime the camshaft.
13. Tighten the first sprocket bolt (A, **Figure 68**) to 18 N•m (159 in.-lb.).
14. Remove the 2-mm pin (C, **Figure 68**) installed through the cam chain tensioner. Turn the engine clockwise again and recheck the timing marks.

CAUTION
The timing marks must align correctly at this time or the camshaft timing is incorrect. Do not proceed if the cam-

shaft sprocket timing marks are positioned incorrectly.

15. Lubricate the spark plug sleeve threads and both O-rings (**Figure 41**) with molybdenum oil so-lution (50:50 mixture of engine oil and molybde-num disulfide grease). Then install and tighten the sleeve (**Figure 40**) to 13 N•m (115 in.-lb.).

16A. Install the rear camshaft as described in the following procedure.

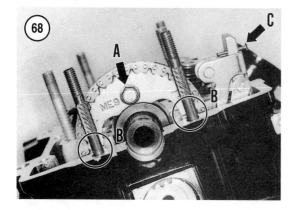

16B. If the rear camshaft is already installed, perform the following steps to complete engine assembly.

    a. Install the shims, hydraulic lifters and cylinder head covers as described in this chapter.

    b. Install the engine in the frame (Chapter Five).

Rear camshaft

1. Read the information under *Camshaft Installation* at the beginning of this section.

2. Lubricate the camshaft journal surfaces in the cylinder head with molybdenum oil solution (50:50 mixture of engine oil and molybdenum disulfide grease).

3. Remove the timing hole cap from the right crankcase cover.

4. If removed, install the front camshaft (**Figure 69**) before installing the rear camshaft. Refer *Front Camshaft* in this section.

CAUTION
When rotating the crankshaft in the following steps, keep the rear cam chain taut and meshed with the timing sprocket on the crankshaft; otherwise, the chain may bind against the crankshaft sprocket, possibly damaging the chain and crankshaft sprocket.

5. Perform the following:

    a. If installed on the engine, remove the front cylinder head cover as described in this chapter.

    b. Turn the crankshaft clockwise (**Figure 58**) and align the *FT* mark on the rotor with the index mark on the crankcase cover. Refer to **Figure 59** or **Figure 60**. Check the position of the *F* mark on the front camshaft (**Figure 66**).

    c. If the *F* mark faces up on VT1100C, VT1100C2 Sabre, 2001-2002 VT1100C3 and VT1100T models, turn the crankshaft clockwise 5/8 turn (225°) and align the *RT* mark on the rotor with the index mark on the crankcase cover. See **Figure 59**.

    d. If the *F* mark faces down (mark cannot be seen) on VT1100C, VT1100C2 Sabre, 2001-2002 VT1100C3 and VT1100T models, turn the crankshaft 1 5/8 turn (585°) clockwise and align the *RT* mark on the rotor with the index mark on the crankcase cover. Refer to **Figure 59**.

    e. If the *F* mark faces up on VT1100C2 ACE and 1998-2000 VT1100C3 models, turn the crankshaft clockwise 7/8 turn (315°) and align the *RT* mark on the rotor with the index mark on the crankcase cover. Refer to **Figure 60**.

    f. If the *F* mark faces down (mark cannot be seen) on VT1100C2 ACE and 1998-2000 VT1100C3 models, turn the crankshaft 1 7/8 turn (675°) clockwise and align the *RT* mark on the rotor with the index mark on the crank-case cover. Refer to **Figure 60**.

6. Pull the cam chain up to mesh it with the crankshaft drive sprocket. Install the cam sprocket with its index marks (**Figure 53**) facing out and aligned with the cylinder head gasket surface as shown in A, **Figure 70**. The *ME9* mark on the camshaft (B, **Figure 70**) must be facing up.

NOTE
Positioning the cam sprocket as described in Step 7 makes it easier to install the camshaft through the sprocket.

7. Hold the sprocket so it remains meshed with the cam chain, then turn the crankshaft 1/2 turn (180°) clockwise to position the cam sprocket opening as shown in **Figure 71**.

8. Install the rear camshaft (**Figure 55**) into the cylinder head and through the sprocket opening (**Figure 72**).

9. Hold the sprocket so it remains meshed with the cam chain and turn the crankshaft 1/2 turn (180°) counterclockwise and realign the two sprocket index marks with the cylinder head gasket surface (A, **Figure 73**). The *ME9* sprocket mark (B, **Figure 73**) mark should be facing up. Then check that the *RT* mark on the rotor aligns with the index mark on the crankcase cover. Refer to **Figure 59** or **Figure 60**.

10. Turn the camshaft so its *R* mark faces up (**Figure 61**), then slide the sprocket onto the camshaft's shoulder. Recheck the timing mark alignment made in Step 9. If incorrect, correct it at this time.

NOTE
The camshaft threads and the cam sprocket mounting bolt threads must be clean and dry.

11. Apply a medium strength threadlock to the camshaft sprocket bolt threads.

12. Install the first sprocket bolt (A, **Figure 74**) hand-tight.

13. Turn the crankshaft clockwise 1 turn (360°) and install the second sprocket bolt. Tighten this bolt to 18 N•m (159 in.-lb.).

14. Turn the crankshaft clockwise 1 turn (360°) and align the *RT* mark on the rotor with the index mark on the crankcase cover (**Figure 59** or **Figure 60**). Then check that the sprocket index marks (B, **Figure 74**) align with the cylinder head gasket sur-

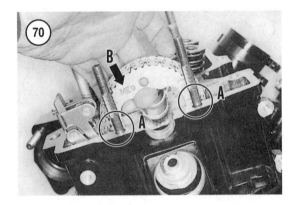

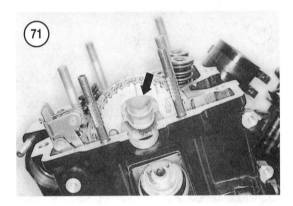

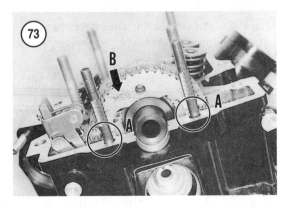

face. If the camshaft timing is correct, continue with Step 15. If not, correct it at this time.

15. Tighten the first sprocket bolt (A, **Figure 74**) to 18 N•m (159 in.-lb.).

16. Remove the 2-mm pin (C, **Figure 74**) installed through the chain tensioner. Turn the engine clockwise again and recheck the timing marks.

> *CAUTION*
> *The timing marks must align correctly at this time or camshaft timing is incorrect. Do not proceed if the camshaft sprocket timing marks are positioned incorrectly.*

17. Lubricate the spark plug sleeve threads and both O-rings (**Figure 41**) with molybdenum oil solution (50:50 mixture of engine oil and molybdenum disulfide grease). Then install and tighten the sleeve (**Figure 40**) to 13 N•m (115 in.-lb.).

18. Install the shims, hydraulic lifters and cylinder head covers as described in this chapter.

19. Install the engine in the frame (Chapter Five).

CAM CHAIN TENSIONER AND CAM CHAIN REPLACEMENT

The engine is equipped with a cam chain tensioner, a fixed chain guide and cam chain for each cylinder (**Figure 75**). The chain tensioner is mounted at the rear of each cylinder. The fixed chain guide is mounted at the front of each cylinder. The engine must be removed from the frame to service these components.

A damaged or inoperative cam chain tensioner (3, **Figure 75**) increases cam chain free play. Depending on the looseness of the cam chain, it may jump teeth on the sprockets and change the valve opening and closing times in relation to piston position. This phasing error may allow the valves to hit the top of the pistons, causing excessive engine damage. Always replace suspect cam chain tensioners, chain guides and cam chains.

Cam Chain Tensioner Removal/Inspection/Installation

The front and rear cylinder cam chain tensioners and service procedures are identical. The cam chain tensioner spring (4, **Figure 75**) can be replaced separately.

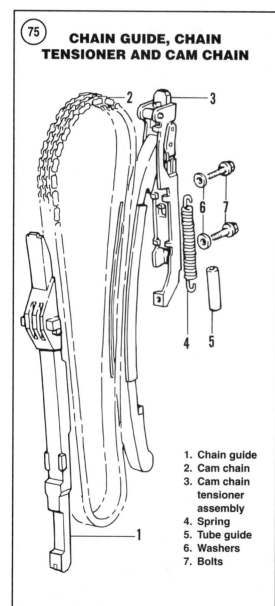

CHAIN GUIDE, CHAIN TENSIONER AND CAM CHAIN

1. Chain guide
2. Cam chain
3. Cam chain tensioner assembly
4. Spring
5. Tube guide
6. Washers
7. Bolts

1. Remove the camshaft as described in this chapter.

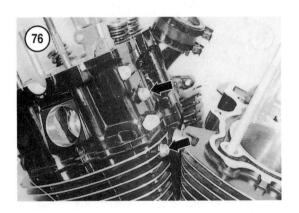

NOTE
*Unless the text procedure specifies otherwise, do not remove the pin (C, **Figure 74**) when removing and inspecting the cam chain tensioner.*

2. Remove the cam chain tensioner mounting bolts (**Figure 76**), washers and tensioner (**Figure 77**). Discard the washers.

3. Clean and dry all parts.

4. Inspect the chain tensioner spring (A, **Figure 78**) for weakness, cracked or broken coils and other damage. Inspect the tube guide (B, **Figure 78**) for damage.

5. To replace the chain tensioner spring (A, **Figure 78**) or tube guide (B):

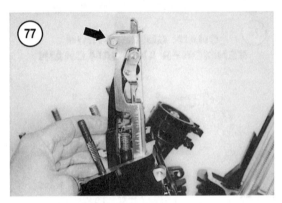

   a. Remove the 2-mm pin installed through the chain tensioner during camshaft removal.

   b. Disconnect the spring from the two points on the tensioner housing. Slide the spring tube off the spring.

   c. Inspect the spring attachment points on the tensioner housing for cracks, hole elongation or other damage. Replace the cam chain tensioner if there is wear at these points.

   d. Install and center the tube guide over the spring and reconnect the spring as shown in A, **Figure 78**.

6. Inspect the chain guide surface (C, **Figure 78**) for excessive wear or places along the guide that have chipped or broken off. Replace the chain tensioner assembly if there is any wear or damage. The tensioner chain guide (C, **Figure 78**) cannot be replaced separately.

7. Make sure the cam chain is properly meshed with the timing sprocket on the crankshaft (**Figure 79**, typical).

8. Install the cam chain tensioner (**Figure 77**) into position. Make sure the bottom of the tensioner seats into the lower pocket in the crankcase.

9. Install a new sealing washer (6, **Figure 75**) onto each chain tensioner mounting bolt (**Figure 76**) and tighten to 12 N•m (106 in.-lb.).

NOTE
The sealing washers prevent oil from leaking past the chain tensioner mounting bolts.

10. Install the camshaft as described in this chapter.

Cam Chain Replacement

Continuous cam chains are used on all models. Do not cut the chains; replacement link components are not available.

NOTE
*Before removing the camshaft in Step 1, make sure to measure the cam chain tensioner exposed wedge as described under **Camshaft Removal** in this chapter. Replace the cam chain if the measurement indicates a worn chain.*

NOTE
If the cam chains are being replaced due to excessive wear, replace both cam chain tensioner springs at the same time.

1. Remove the camshaft as described in this chapter.

2. Remove the cam chain tensioner as described in this section.

3. Drain the engine oil as described in Chapter Three.

4. To replace the front cam chain, remove the starter clutch (Chapter Nine).

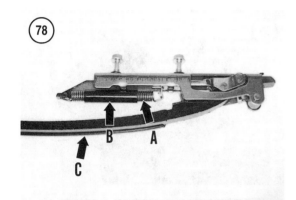

5. To replace the rear cam chain, remove the primary drive gear (Chapter Six).

6. Move the chain guide away from the drive sprocket and remove the cam chain from the sprocket (**Figure 79**, typical). Pull the cam chain up through the chain tunnel and remove the chain.

NOTE
*If there is not enough clearance to remove the chain from the sprocket, remove the chain guide (1, **Figure 75**) as*

*described under **Cylinder Head** in this section.*

7. Install the cam chain by reversing these steps. Refill the engine with oil as described in Chapter Three.

Inspection

If the cam chain or chain guides are excessively worn, the cam chain tensioner may not be working properly. Inspect the cam chain tensioner as described in this section.

1. Clean and dry the chain.
2. Inspect the cam chain for:
    a. Worn or damaged pins and rollers.
    b. Cracked or damaged side plates.
3. If the cam chain is excessively worn or damaged, inspect the drive (crankshaft) and driven (camshaft) sprockets for the same wear conditions. The driven sprockets can be replaced separately. The right side drive sprocket can be replaced separately. The left side drive sprocket is an integral part of the crankshaft. Crankshaft replacement is required if the left drive sprocket is damaged.

Chain Guide

Refer to *Cylinder Head* in this chapter to service the chain guide (1, **Figure 75**).

CYLINDER HEAD

The engine must be removed from the frame to service the cylinder heads.

Removal

1. Remove the engine from the frame (Chapter Five).
2. Remove the Allen bolts and the cylinder head fins.
3. Remove the camshaft as described in this chapter.
4. Remove the cam chain tensioner as described in this chapter.
5. Before removing the cylinder head, inspect the mating surfaces between the cylinder head and cylinder for any oil leakage or blow-by. If leakage is present, mark the area for further inspection.

6. Remove the cylinder head mounting bolts.

7. Insert a screwdriver between the cylinder head and cylinder pry points (**Figure 80**), then lift the screwdriver to break the head gasket seal. Do not use excessive force.

CAUTION
Do not pry between any gasket surface or permanent damage may result to the cylinder head and cylinder mating surfaces.

8. Remove the cylinder head (**Figure 81**).

9. Place the cylinder head on wooden blocks to avoid damaging the gasket surfaces.

10. Remove the cylinder head gasket and the two dowel pins (**Figure 82**). Discard the head gasket.

NOTE
If the dowel pins are tight, do not remove them unless necessary. Stuck or rusted dowel pins are easily damaged during removal.

NOTE
After removing the cylinder head, check the top and bottom gasket surfaces for any indications of leakage. Also check the head and base gaskets for signs of leakage. A blown gasket could indicate possible cylinder head or cylinder block warp or other damage.

11. Remove the chain guide (**Figure 83**).

12. Cover the cylinder and chain tunnel with a clean shop cloth.

Solvent Test for Valve Seat Seal

Before removing the valves from the cylinder head, perform a solvent test to check the valve face-to-valve seat seal.

1. Remove the cylinder head as described in this chapter.

2. Examine the valve seating in the cylinder head. Each valve must appear to seat flush against its seat. If there is a gap between a valve face and its seat, the valve is bent.

3. Support the cylinder head with the exhaust port facing up (**Figure 84**, typical). Then pour solvent or kerosene into the port. Check the combustion chamber (**Figure 85**) for solvent leaking past the exhaust valve.

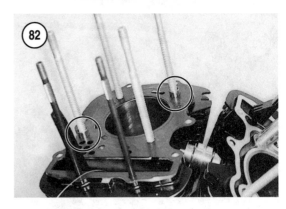

4. Repeat Step 3 for the intake valves.

5. If there is a leak past a valve, the combustion chamber appears wet, indicating that the valve is not seating correctly. The following conditions cause poor valve seating:
   a. A bent valve stem.
   b. A worn or damaged valve seat.
   c. A worn or damaged valve face.
   d. A crack in the combustion chamber.

6. Service the valves and valve seats as described in this chapter.

Cylinder Head Inspection

1. Perform the *Solvent Test* before cleaning or servicing the cylinder head.

2. Remove the spark plugs.

3. Remove all traces of gasket residue from the cylinder head (**Figure 85**) and cylinder block gasket surfaces. Do not scratch the gasket surface. If the gasket residue is difficult to remove, place a solvent-soaked rag across the cylinder head gasket surface to soften the deposits.

4. Before removing the valves, remove all carbon deposits from the combustion chambers (**Figure 85**)

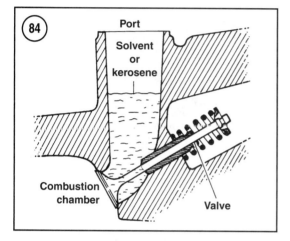

Port

Solvent
or
kerosene

Combustion
chamber

Valve

with a small wire brush mounted in a drill. Support the cylinder head on wooden blocks and work carefully, making sure not to damage the head's gasket surface, valves or spark plug threads.

CAUTION
Cleaning the combustion chambers with the valves removed can damage the valve seat surfaces. A damaged or even slightly scratched valve seat causes poor valve seating.

5. Examine the spark plug threads in the cylinder head for damage. If damage is minor or if the threads are contaminated with carbon, use a spark plug thread tap to clean the threads following the manufacturer's instructions. If thread damage is excessive, repair the head by installing a steel thread insert. Thread insert kits can be purchased at automotive supply stores or have the inserts installed by a Honda dealership or machine shop.

NOTE
When using a tap to clean spark plug threads, lubricate the tap with an aluminum tap cutting fluid or kerosene.

NOTE
Aluminum spark plug threads are commonly damaged due to galling, cross threading and overtightening. To prevent galling, apply an antiseize compound on the plug threads before installation and do not overtighten. Do not lubricate the spark plug threads with engine oil.

6. Clean the entire head in solvent. Make sure the coolant passageways are clear.

NOTE
If the cylinder head was bead blasted, grit in small crevices can be difficult to remove. Any residual grit left in the engine contaminates the oil and causes premature wear. Repeatedly wash the cylinder head in a solution of hot soap and water and use compressed air to remove the debris.

7. Check for cracks in the combustion chamber (**Figure 85**) and exhaust port. A cracked head must be replaced.
8. Examine the piston crown. The crown should show no signs of wear or damage. If the crown appears pecked or spongy-looking, check the spark plug, valves and combustion chamber for aluminum deposits. If these deposits are found, the cylinder is overheating.

CAUTION
Do not clean the piston crown while the piston is installed in the cylinder. Carbon scraped from the top of the piston may fall between the cylinder wall and piston and onto the piston rings. Be-

*cause carbon grit is abrasive, prema-
ture cylinder, piston and ring wear
occurs. If the piston crowns have heavy
deposits of carbon, remove them as described in this chapter to clean them
properly. Excessive carbon buildup on
the piston crowns reduces piston cooling, raises engine compression and
causes overheating.*

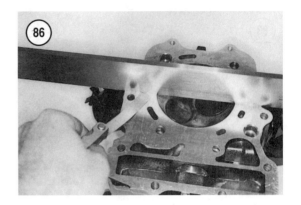

9. Place a straightedge across the gasket surface at
several points (**Figure 86**). Measure warp by inserting a feeler gauge between the straightedge and cylinder head at each location. Maximum allowable
warp is listed in **Table 2**. If the warp exceeds this
limit, the cylinder head must be resurfaced or replaced. Distortion or nicks in the cylinder head surface could cause an air leak and cause overheating.

10. Check the exhaust pipe studs for looseness or
thread damage. Slight thread damage can be repaired with a thread file or die. If thread damage is
excessive, replace the damaged stud(s) as described
in Chapter One.

11. Service the intake tube (**Figure 87**) as follows:

   a. Inspect the intake tube for cracks or other
   damage that would allow unfiltered air to enter the engine. On high mileage vehicles, it is
   common to see surface cracks along the side
   of the tube. Make sure the cracks do not pass
   through the tube.

   b. If necessary, loosen the hose clamp and remove
   the intake tube.

   c. Install the intake tube by aligning the notch in
   the tube with the vacuum port plug on the cylinder head. Tighten the hose clamp to 2 N•m
   (17 in.-lb.).

12. Inspect the camshaft bearing journals in the
cylinder head (**Figure 88**) for cracks, seizure marks
or other damage. Measure bearing journal wear as
described under *Cylinder Head Cover and Rocker
Arms* in this chapter.

13. Check the valves and valve guides as described under *Valves and Valve Components* in this
chapter.

Chain Guide Inspection

Any visible wear or damage to the chain guide may
indicate excessive cam chain wear or a damaged cam
chain tensioner.

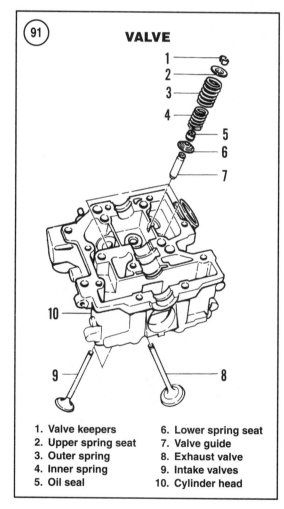

VALVE

1. Valve keepers
2. Upper spring seat
3. Outer spring
4. Inner spring
5. Oil seal
6. Lower spring seat
7. Valve guide
8. Exhaust valve
9. Intake valves
10. Cylinder head

1. Inspect the chain guide (1, **Figure 75**) for excessive wear or places along the guide that have chipped or broken off. Replace the chain guide if there is any wear or damage.

2. Inspect the cam chain tensioner (3, **Figure 75**) as described in this chapter.

Installation

Identify each cylinder head by its F (front) or R (rear) cast mark (**Figure 89**). Install the cylinder heads in their correct positions. The cylinder head and cylinder block basket surfaces must be clean.

1. Install the chain guide:
   a. Lift the cam chain so it is properly meshed with the timing sprocket on the crankshaft (**Figure 79**, typical).
   b. Install the chain guide by aligning its tabs with the slots in the cylinder (**Figure 90**). Make sure the end of the chain guide seats into the pocket in the crankcase (**Figure 79**, typical).

2. Position the cam chain and its holding wire inside the chain tunnel so they do not interfere with cylinder head installation.

3. If removed, install the two dowel pins (**Figure 82**).

4. Install a *new* cylinder head gasket (**Figure 82**) over the dowel pins and against the cylinder block. Make sure all holes align.

5. Install the cylinder head over the dowel pins and against the head gasket. Check that the cylinder head is sitting flush against the head gasket.

6. Install and tighten the two cylinder head mounting bolts.

7. Pull on the cam chain and make sure it is properly engaged with the drive sprocket on the crankshaft.

8. Install the cam chain tensioner as described in this chapter.

9. Install the camshaft as described in this chapter.

10. Install the engine in the frame (Chapter Five).

VALVES AND VALVE COMPONENTS

Because of the number of special tools and the skills required to use them, it is a general practice by those who do their own service to remove the cylinder heads and refer valve service to a dealership or machine shop.

Service Tools

A valve spring compressor is required to remove and install the valves in this section.

Valve Removal

Refer to **Figure 91**.

1. Remove the cylinder head as described in this chapter.

2. Install a valve spring compressor (**Figure 92**) squarely over the upper retainer with the other end of the tool placed against the valve head.

3. Tighten the valve spring compressor until the valve keepers separate. Lift the valve keepers out through the valve spring compressor with needlenose pliers or tweezers.

4. Gradually loosen the valve spring compressor and remove it from the head. Remove the upper spring seat.

5. Remove the valve springs.

> *CAUTION*
> *Remove any burrs from the valve stem groove (**Figure 93**) before removing the valve; otherwise, the valve guide becomes damaged as the valve stem passes through it.*

6. Remove the valve from its guide while rotating it slightly.

> *NOTE*
> *If a valve is difficult to remove, it may be bent, causing it to stick in its valve guide. This condition requires valve and valve guide replacement.*

7. Pull the oil seal (**Figure 94**) off the valve guide and discard it.

8. Remove the lower spring seat.

9. Identify the parts because they must be reinstalled in their original position. Refer to **Figure 91** for the intake and exhaust valve parts.

10. Repeat for the remaining intake and exhaust valves.

> *NOTE*
> *Do not remove the valve guides unless they require replacement.*

Inspection

Refer to the troubleshooting chart in **Figure 95** when performing valve inspection procedures in this section. When measuring the valves and valve components, compare the actual measurements to the specifications in **Table 2**. Replace parts that are damaged or out of specification as described in this section. Maintain the alignment of the valve components because they must be reinstalled in their original position.

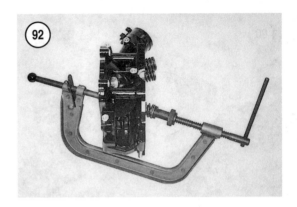

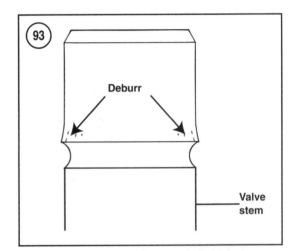

1. Clean the valve components in solvent. Do not damage the valve seating surface.

2. Inspect the valve face (**Figure 96**) for burning, pitting or other signs of wear. Unevenness of the valve face is an indication the valve is not serviceable. If the wear on a valve is too extensive to be corrected by hand-lapping the valve into its seat, replace the valve. The face on the valve cannot be ground. Replace the valve if defective.

(95)

VALVE TROUBLESHOOTING

Valve deposits

Check:
- Worn valve guide
- Carbon buildup from incorrect tuning
- Carbon buildup from incorrect carburetor adjustment
- Dirty or gummed fuel
- Dirty engine oil

4

Valve sticking

Check:
- Worn valve guide
- Bent valve stem
- Deposits collected on valve stem
- Valve burning or overheating

Valve burning

Check:
- Valve sticking
- Cylinder head warped
- Valve seat distorted
- Valve clearance incorrect
- Incorrect valve spring
- Valve spring worn
- Worn valve seat
- Carbon buildup in engine
- Engine ignition and/or carburetor adjustments incorrect

Valve seat/face wear

Check:
- Valve burning
- Incorrect valve clearance
- Abrasive material on valve face and seat

Valve damage

Check:
- Valve burning
- Incorrectly installed or serviced valve guides
- Incorrect valve clearance
- Incorrect valve, spring seat and retainer assembly
- Detonation caused by incorrect ignition and/or carburetor adjustments

3. Inspect the valve stems for wear and roughness. Check the valve keeper grooves for damage.

4. Measure each valve stem outside diameter with a micrometer (**Figure 97**). Note the following:

   a. If a valve stem is out of specification, discard the valve.

   b. If a valve stem is within specification, record the measurement so it can be used to determine the valve stem-to-guide clearance in Step 7.

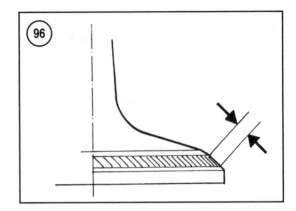

> *NOTE*
> *Honda recommends reaming the valve guides to remove any carbon buildup before checking and measuring the guides. For the home mechanic it is more practical to remove carbon and varnish from the valve guides with a stiff spiral wire brush. Then clean the valve guides with solvent to wash out all particles and dry with compressed air.*

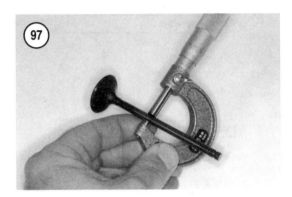

5. Insert each valve into its respective valve guide and move it up and down by hand. The valve should move smoothly.

6. Measure each valve guide inside diameter with a small hole gauge and record the measurements. Note the following:

> *NOTE*
> *Because valve guides wear unevenly (oval shape), measure each guide at different positions. Use the largest bore diameter measurement when determining its size.*

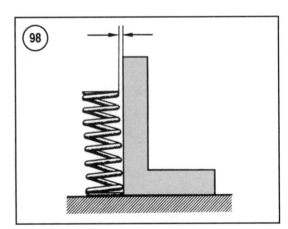

   a. If a valve guide is out of specification, replace it as described in this section.

   b. If a valve guide is within specification, record the measurement so it can be used to determine the valve stem-to-guide clearance in Step 7.

7. Subtract the measurement made in Step 4 from the measurement made in Step 6 to determine the valve stem-to-guide clearance. Note the following:

   a. If the clearance is out of specification, determine if a new guide would bring the clearance within specification.

   b. If the clearance would be out of specification with a new guide, replace the valve and guide as a set.

8. Inspect the valve springs as follows:

   a. Inspect each spring for any cracks or other visual damage.

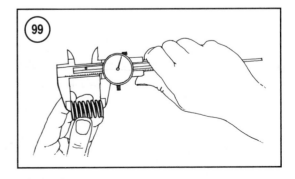

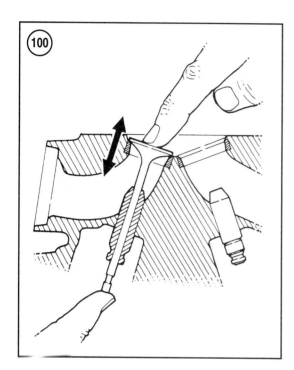

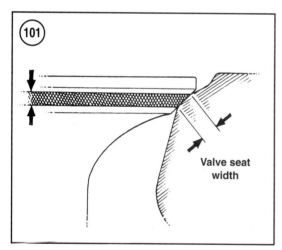

Valve seat
width

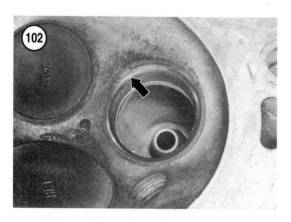

b. Use a square and check the spring for distortion or tilt (**Figure 98**).

c. Measure the free length of each valve spring with a vernier caliper (**Figure 99**).

d. Replace defective springs.

9. Check the valve keepers. If they are in good condition, they may be reused; replace in pairs as necessary.

10. Inspect the spring seats for damage.

11. Inspect the valve seats as described under *Valve Seat Inspection* in this chapter.

Valve Seat Inspection

The most accurate method for checking the valve seal is to use a marking compound (machinist's dye), available from auto parts and tool stores. Marking compound is used to locate high or irregular spots when checking or making close fits. Follow the manufacturer's directions.

NOTE
Because of the close operating tolerances within the valve assembly, the valve stem-to-guide clearance guide must be within specification; otherwise the inspection results will be inaccurate.

1. Remove, clean and inspect the valves as described in this chapter. The valve face must be in good condition for the inspection results to be accurate.

2. Clean the valve seat in the cylinder head and valve mating areas with contact cleaner.

3. Thoroughly clean all carbon deposits from the valve face with solvent and dry thoroughly.

4. Spread a thin layer of marking compound evenly on the valve face.

5. Slowly insert the valve into its guide and tap the valve against its seat several times (**Figure 100**) without spinning it.

6. Remove the valve and examine the impression left by the marking compound. If the impression (on the valve or in the cylinder head) is not even and continuous and the valve seat width (**Figure 101**) is not within the specified tolerance listed in **Table 2**, the valve seat in the cylinder head must be reconditioned.

7. Closely examine the valve seat in the cylinder head (**Figure 102**). It should be smooth and even with a polished seating surface.

8. If the valve seat is not in good condition, recondition the valve seat as described in this chapter.
9. Repeat for the other valves.

Valve Guide Replacement

Worn or damaged valve guides must be replaced. Special tools and considerable experience are required to properly replace the valve guides in the cylinder head. If these tools are unavailable, have a Honda dealership perform this procedure. Removing the cylinder head, and taking it to a dealership to have the valve guides replaced can save a considerable amount of money. When a valve guide is replaced, also replace the valve.

Read the entire procedure before attempting valve guide replacement. When using heat in the following steps, it is necessary to work quickly and have the correct tools on hand.

Tools

The following Honda tools (or equivalents) are required to remove and install the valve guides. Confirm part numbers with a Honda dealership before ordering them.
1. Honda 6.6 mm valve guide driver, part No. 07942-6570100.
2. Honda 6.6 mm valve guide reamer, part No. 07984-ZE2000D.

Procedure

1. Remove all the valves and valve guide seals from the cylinder head.
2. Place the new valve guides in the freezer for approximately one hour before heating the cylinder head. Chilling them slightly reduces the outside diameter, while the cylinder is slightly larger due to heat expansion. This makes valve guide installation much easier. Remove the guides one at a time, as needed.

> *NOTE*
> *Flangeless valve guides are used. Step 3 confirms that the original guides were installed to the correct valve guide projection height specified in **Table 2**. If the projection height measurement is incorrect, the valve guide bore(s) in the cylinder head*

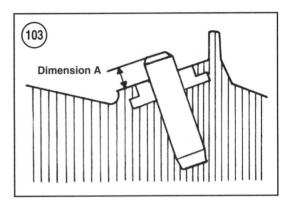

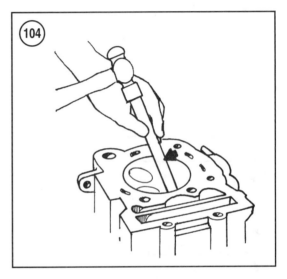

may have widened, allowing the guide to move.

3. Measure the valve guide projection height above the cylinder head surface with a vernier caliper (**Figure 103**) and record for each valve guide. Compare to the valve guide projection height specification in **Table 2**.
4. Place the cylinder head on a hot plate and heat to 130-140° C (275-290° F). Do not exceed 150° C (300° F). Monitor the temperature with heat sticks, available at welding supply stores, or use an infrared thermometer.

> *CAUTION*
> *Do not heat the cylinder head with a torch; never bring a flame into contact with the cylinder head or valve guide. The direct heat destroys the case hardening of the valve guide and may warp the cylinder head.*

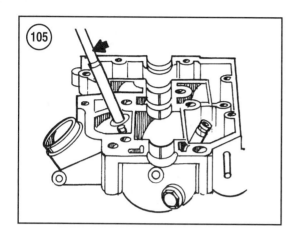

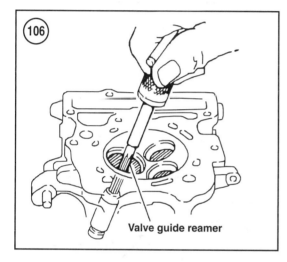

Valve guide reamer

WARNING
Wear welding gloves or similar insulated gloves when handling the head. The cylinder head is very hot.

5. Remove the cylinder head from the hot plate and place on wooden blocks with the combustion chamber facing *up*.

6. From the combustion chamber side of the head, drive out the valve guide with the valve guide remover (**Figure 104**). Quickly repeat this step for each guide to be replaced. Reheat the head as required. Discard the valve guides after removing them.

CAUTION
Because the valve guides are installed with an interference fit, do not remove them if the cylinder head is not hot enough. Doing so may damage (widen) the valve guide bore in the

cylinder head and require replacement of the head.

7. Allow the cylinder head to cool.

8. Inspect and clean the valve guide bores. Check for cracks or any scoring along the bore wall.

9. Reheat the cylinder head as described in Step 4, then place onto wooden blocks with the valve spring side facing *up*.

10. Remove one new valve guide, either intake or exhaust, from the freezer.

11. Align the valve guide in the bore. Using the valve guide driver tool and a hammer, drive in the valve guide (**Figure 105**) into the cylinder head until the valve guide projection height is within the specification in **Table 2** (**Figure 103**).

12. Repeat to install the remaining valve guides.

13. Allow the cylinder head to cool to room temperature.

14. Ream each valve guide as follows:

  a. Place the cylinder head on wooden blocks with the combustion chamber facing *up*. The guides are reamed from this side.

  b. Coat the valve guide and valve guide reamer with cutting oil.

CAUTION
*Always rotate the reamer **clockwise** through the entire length of the guide, both when reaming the guide and when removing the reamer. Rotating the reamer counterclockwise reverses the cut and damages (enlarges) the valve guide bore.*

CAUTION
Do not allow the reamer to tilt. Keep the tool square to the hole and apply even pressure and twisting motion during the entire operation.

  c. Rotate the reamer clockwise into the valve guide (**Figure 106**).

  d. Slowly rotate the reamer through the guide, while periodically adding cutting oil.

  e. As the end of the reamer passes through the valve guide, maintain the clockwise motion and work the reamer back out of the guide while continuing to add cutting oil.

  f. Clean the reamer of all chips and relubricate with cutting oil before starting on the next guide. Repeat for each guide as required.

4

15. Thoroughly clean the cylinder head and all valve components in solvent, then with detergent and hot water to remove all cutting residue. Rinse in cold water. Dry with compressed air.

16. Measure the valve guide inside diameter with a small hole gauge. The measurement must be within the specification listed in **Table 2**.

17. Apply engine oil to the valve guides to prevent rust.

18. Lubricate a valve stem with engine oil and pass it through its valve guide, verifying it moves without any roughness or binding. Repeat for each valve and guide.

19. Reface the valve seats as described under *Valve Seat Reconditioning* in this chapter.

Valve Seat Reconditioning

Before reconditioning the valve seats, inspect and measure them as described under *Valve Seat Inspection* in this chapter.

Tools

To cut the cylinder head valve seats the following tools are required:

1. Valve seat cutters (**Figure 107**). Refer to a Honda dealership.
2. A vernier caliper.
3. Gear-marking compound.
4. Valve lapping tool.

Procedure

> *NOTE*
> *Follow the manufacturer's instructions when using valve facing equipment.*

1. Carefully rotate and insert the solid pilot into the valve guide. Be sure the pilot is correctly seated.
2. Install the 45° cutter and cutter holder onto the solid pilot.

> *CAUTION*
> *Work slowly and make light cuts during reconditioning. Overcutting the valve seats recedes the valves into the cylinder head, reducing the valve adjustment range. If cutting is excessive, the ability to set the valve adjustment*

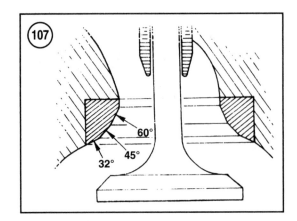

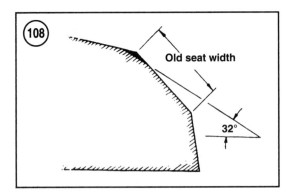

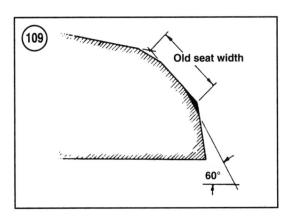

may be lost. This condition requires cylinder head replacement.

3. Using the 45° cutter, de-scale and clean the valve seat with one or two turns.

4. If the seat is still pitted or burned, turn the 45° cutter additional turns until the surface is clean.

5. Measure the valve seat with a vernier caliper (**Figure 101**). Record the measurement to use as a reference point when performing the following.

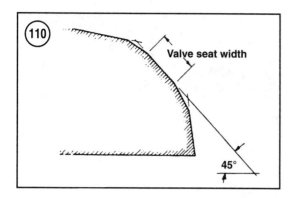

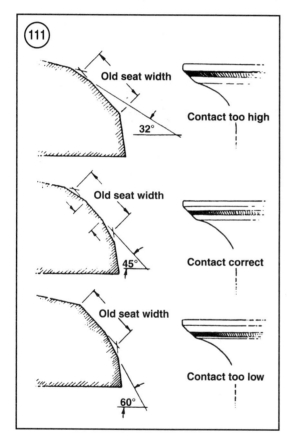

CAUTION
The 32° cutter removes material quickly. Work carefully and check the progress often.

6. Install the 32° cutter onto the solid pilot and lightly cut the seat to remove 1/4 of the existing valve seat (**Figure 108**).

7. Install the 60° cutter onto the solid pilot and lightly cut the seat to remove 1/4 of the existing valve seat (**Figure 109**).

8. Measure the valve seat with a vernier caliper (**Figure 101**). Then fit the 45° cutter onto the solid pilot and cut the valve seat to the specified width (**Figure 110**) listed in **Table 2**.

9. When the valve seat width is correct, check valve seating as follows:

    a. Clean the valve seat with contact cleaner.

    b. Spread a thin layer of marking compound evenly on the valve face.

    c. Slowly insert the valve into its guide.

    d. Support the valve with two fingers (**Figure 100**) and tap the valve up and down in the cylinder head several times. Do not rotate the valve or a false reading results.

    e. Remove the valve and examine the impression left by the marking compound (**Figure 111**).

    f. Measure the valve seat width as shown in **Figure 101**. Refer to **Figure 2** for specified valve width.

    g. The valve contact should be approximately in the center of the valve seat area (**Figure 111**).

10. If the contact area is too high on the valve or if it is too wide, use the 32° cutter and remove a portion of the top area of the valve seat material to lower and narrow the contact area on the valve (**Figure 111**).

11. If the contact area is too low on the valve or too wide, use the 60° cutter and remove a portion of the lower area of the valve seat material to raise and narrow the contact area on the valve (**Figure 111**).

12. After the desired valve seat position and width is obtained, use the 45° cutter to lightly clean off any burrs that may have been caused by previous cuts.

13. When the contact area is correct, lap the valve as described in this chapter.

14. Repeat Steps 1-13 for all remaining valve seats.

15. Thoroughly clean the cylinder head and all valve components in solvent, then with detergent and hot water. Rinse in cold water and dry with compressed air. Apply a light coat of clean engine oil to all non-aluminum surfaces to prevent rust.

Valve Lapping

Valve lapping can restore the valve seat without machining if the amount of wear or distortion is not too great.

Perform this procedure after determining that the valve seat width and outside diameter are within specifications. A valve lapping tool and compound are required.

1. Smear a light coating of fine grade valve lapping compound on the valve face seating surface.

2. Insert the valve into the head.

3. Wet the suction cup of the lapping stick and stick it onto the head of the valve. Spin the tool in both directions, while pressing it against the valve seat and lap the valve to the seat. Every 5 to 10 seconds, lift and rotate the valve 180° in the valve seat. Continue until the gasket surfaces on the valve and seat are smooth and equal in size.

4. Closely examine the valve seat in the cylinder head (**Figure 101**). It should be smooth and even with a smooth, polished seating ring.

5. Repeat Steps 1-4 for the other valves.

6. Thoroughly clean the cylinder head and all valve components in solvent, then with detergent and hot water. Rinse in cold water and dry with compressed air. Apply a light coat of clean engine oil to all non-aluminum surfaces to prevent rust.

CAUTION
Any compound left on the valves or in the cylinder head causes excessive wear to the engine components.

7. Install the valve assemblies as described in this chapter.

8. After the lapping is completed and the valves are reinstalled in the head, perform the *Solvent Test* under *Cylinder Head* in this chapter. There should be no leakage past the seat. If leakage occurs, the combustion chamber appears wet. If fluid leaks past any of the seats, disassemble the valve assembly and repeat the lapping procedure until there is no leakage.

9. If the cylinder head and valve components are cleaned in detergent and hot water, apply a light coat of engine oil to all bare metal surfaces to prevent rust formation.

Valve Installation

Install the valves in their original locations. Refer to **Figure 91**.

1. Install the lower spring seat with its shoulder facing up.

2. Lubricate the inside of a *new* oil seal with engine oil. Then push the seal straight down the valve guide until it snaps into the groove in the top of the guide (**Figure 112**). Check that the oil seal is centered

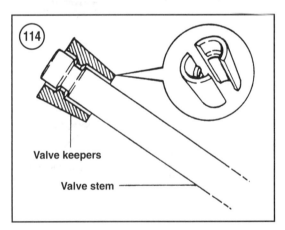

Valve keepers

Valve stem

and seats squarely on top of the guide. If the seal is cocked to one side, oil will leak past the seal during engine operation.

NOTE
The oil seals must be replaced whenever the valves are removed. Also, if a new seal was installed and then removed, do not reuse it.

3. Install the valve as follows:

CAUTION
To avoid loss of spring tension, do not compress the spring any more than necessary when installing the valve keepers.

6. Compress the valve spring with a valve spring compressor tool and install the valve keepers. Make sure the keepers fit into the rounded groove in the valve stem (**Figure 114**).
7. Gently tap the upper retainer with a plastic hammer to ensure that the keepers (**Figure 115**) are properly seated.
8. Repeat Steps 1-7 for the remaining valves.

CYLINDER

Each alloy cylinder (**Figure 116**) has a pressed-in cast iron cylinder liner. Oversize pistons and ring sizes are available through Honda dealerships in 0.25 mm and 0.50 mm sizes.
Service procedures for the front and rear cylinders are the same.

Removal

Identify each part with its cylinder (front or rear). All used parts must be reinstalled in their original operating position.

CAUTION
When it is necessary to rotate the crankshaft, pull up the cam chains so they cannot bind internally.

1. Remove the engine from the frame (Chapter Five).
2. Remove the cylinder head as described in this chapter.
3. Remove the bolts and disconnect the water hose joint (**Figure 117**) from the rear cylinder.
4. Remove the two clips (**Figure 118**) from the water pipe.
5. Slide the water pipe either toward the front or rear cylinder (**Figure 119**).
6. Loosen the cylinder by tapping around the perimeter with a rubber or plastic mallet.
7. Pull the cylinder straight up the studs for a short distance, then stop. Install a clean shop rag or paper towels underneath the piston to prevent any broken piston rings from falling into the crankcase. Remove the cylinder from the crankcase.

a. Coat a valve stem with molybdenum oil solution (50:50 mixture of engine oil and molybdenum disulfide grease).
b. Install the valve partway into its guide. Then slowly turn the valve as it enters the valve stem seal and continue turning it until the valve is installed all the way.
c. Make sure the valve moves up and down smoothly.
4. Install the valve springs with their closer wound coils (**Figure 113**) facing the cylinder head.
5. Install the upper spring seat on top of the valve spring.

8. Remove the base gasket and two dowel pins. Discard the gasket.

9. Slide a length of plastic hose down the cylinder studs and rest the piston and rings against them (**Figure 120**).

10. Cover the piston and crankcase opening.

11. Remove the water pipe (A, **Figure 121**) and discard the O-ring (B) from each cylinder.

Inspection

When measuring the cylinder in this section, compare the actual measurements to the specifications in **Table 4**. Service the cylinder if it is out of specification or shows damage as described in this section.

1. Soak the cylinder surfaces in solvent, then carefully remove gasket material from the top and bottom mating surfaces with a scraper. Do not nick or gouge the gasket surfaces or leaks occur.

2. Wash the cylinder block in solvent. Dry with compressed air.

3. Check the dowel pin holes for cracks or other damage.

4. Place a straight edge across the upper cylinder block surface. Insert a flat feeler gauge between the straight edge and the cylinder block at different locations and check for warp (**Figure 122**).

5. Measure the cylinder bore with a bore gauge or inside micrometer at the points shown in **Figure 123**. Measure in line with the piston pin and 90° to the pin. Use the largest measurement to determine cylinder bore. If the taper or out-of-round is greater than specifications, bore the cylinder oversize and install a new piston and rings.

6. Determine piston-to-cylinder clearance as described in *Piston Clearance* in this chapter.

7. If the cylinder is not worn past the service limit, check the bore for scratches or gouges. The bore still may require boring and reconditioning.

8. After the cylinder has been serviced, clean the cylinder as follows:

> *CAUTION*
> *A combination of soap and hot water is the only solution that completely cleans cylinder walls. Solvent and kerosene cannot wash fine grit out of cylinder crevices. Any grit left in the cylinder acts as a grinding compound and causes premature wear to the new rings.*

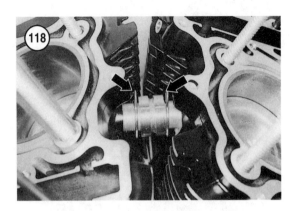

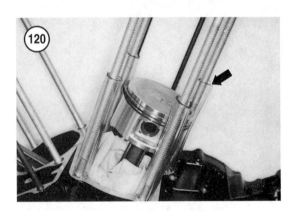

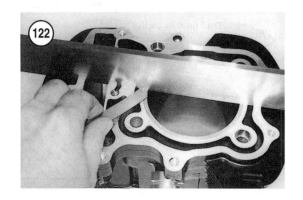

a. Wash the cylinder bore in hot soapy water.
b. Also wash out any fine grit material from the cooling passages surrounding the cylinder.
c. After washing the cylinder, wipe the cylinder wall with a clean white cloth. It should *not* show any traces of grit or debris. If the rag is the slightest bit dirty, the wall is not thoroughly cleaned and must be washed again.
d. When the cylinder is clean, lubricate the liner with clean engine oil to prevent rust.

Installation

Identify the cylinders following the marks made before removal.

CAUTION
When rotating the crankshaft, pull up the cam chains so they cannot bind internally.

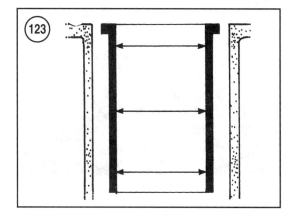

1. Make sure all crankcase and cylinder block gasket surfaces are clean and dry.
2. If removed, install the piston as described in this chapter.

CAUTION
Make sure to install and secure the piston pin circlips when installing the pistons.

3. Lubricate new water pipe O-rings with coolant and install them into the pipe grooves as shown in B, **Figure 121**.
4. Lubricate the water pipe (A, **Figure 121**) inner bore with coolant, then slide it all the way onto one cylinder (**Figure 124**). It does not matter which cylinder.

NOTE
The water pipe cannot be installed onto a cylinder when both cylinders are installed on the engine.

5. Install the dowel pins (**Figure 125**) into the crankcase.
6. Install a new base gasket. Make sure all holes align.
7. Install a piston holding fixture (**Figure 126**) under the piston.
8. Lubricate the cylinder wall, piston and rings with engine oil. Liberally lubricate the oil control rings to fill the spacer with oil.

9. Stagger the piston ring end gaps evenly around the piston circumference. They must not align.

NOTE
The cylinder can be installed with or without a piston ring compressor (Figure 127).

10A. Without a piston ring compressor, align the cylinder with the cylinder studs and lower it onto the piston. Compress each piston ring by hand as it enters the cylinder. Push the cylinder down until it bottoms on the piston holding fixture.

10B. With a piston ring compressor, lubricate the part of the piston ring compressor that contacts the piston rings with clean engine oil. Install the compressor so it covers all three rings (**Figure 127**). Tap the top of the cylinder evenly to push the cylinder over the rings and piston. Push the cylinder down until the ring compressor bottoms on the piston holding fixture. Remove the ring compressor.

11. Remove the piston holding fixture and push the cylinder down into place over the dowel pins and against the base gasket.

12. Install a length of hose over one of the cylinder studs and secure it with a nut (**Figure 128**). The hose holds the cylinder in place to prevent it from sliding up and off the piston rings when the crankshaft is turned over in the following steps.

13. Have an assistant pull up on both cam chains, then rotate the crankshaft clockwise. The piston must move up and down in the bore with no binding or roughness. If there is any interference, a piston ring may have broken during cylinder installation.

14. Make sure the water pipe (**Figure 124**) is installed on one of the cylinders.

15. Repeat these steps to install the other cylinder.

16. Slide the water pipe (**Figure 119**) into the opposite cylinder and secure with the two clips (**Figure 118**). Make sure the clips seat in the grooves completely.

17. Install the cylinder heads, camshafts and cylinder head covers as described in this chapter.

18. Install the engine into the frame (Chapter Five).

PISTON AND PISTON RINGS

Refer to **Figure 129** when servicing the piston and rings in the following section. Procedures for the front and rear piston and rings are the same.

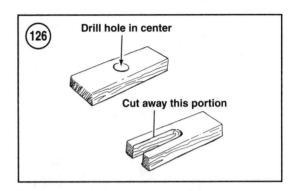

Drill hole in center

Cut away this portion

Piston

Removal

Identify each part with its cylinder (front or rear). All used parts must be reinstalled in their original positions.

CAUTION
When it is necessary to rotate the crankshaft, pull up the cam chains so they cannot bind internally. Protect the pistons so their skirts do not catch and bind against the crankcase.

1. Remove the cylinder as described in this chapter.

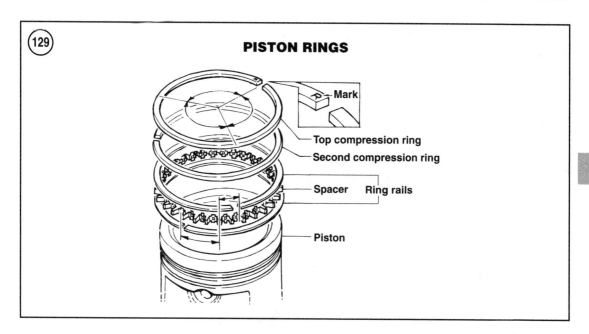

PISTON RINGS

- Mark
- Top compression ring
- Second compression ring
- Spacer   Ring rails
- Piston

4

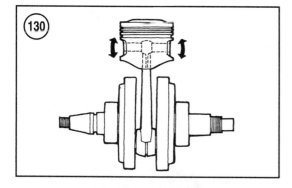

4. Before removing the piston, hold the rod and rock the piston (**Figure 130**). Any rocking motion (do not confuse with the normal sliding motion) indicates wear on the piston pin, rod bushing, pin bore or a combination of all three.

5. Support the piston with a piston holder fixture, then install two plastic hoses over the cylinder studs to protect the piston rings (**Figure 120**) when removing the circlips and piston pin.

6. Remove the piston circlips (**Figure 131**).

NOTE
The operating clearance between the piston pin and pin bore is such that the piston pin can be removed and installed by hand. However, problems such as varnish on the piston pin, a burred pin bore or circlip groove or a damaged piston can make it difficult to remove the piston pin.

7. Push the piston pin (**Figure 132**) out of the piston by hand. If the pin is tight, use a homemade tool (**Figure 133**) to remove it. Do not drive the piston pin out as this action may damage the piston pin, connecting rod or piston. Heat can also be used to ease removal. Heat the piston crown (not the side of the piston) with a heat gun.

8. Lift the piston off the connecting rod.

9. Remove and clean the oil jet installed in the top of the crankcase as described in this chapter.

10. Inspect the piston as described in this chapter.

2. Mark the top of the piston with an identification letter (F or R) and a directional arrow pointing toward the front of the engine.

3. Block off the crankcase below the piston with a clean shop cloth to prevent the piston pin circlips from falling into the crankcase.

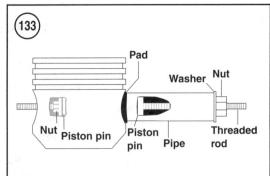

Pad, Washer, Nut, Nut, Piston pin, Piston pin, Pipe, Threaded rod

Inspection

1. Remove the piston rings as described in this chapter.

2. Soak the piston in solvent to soften the carbon deposits.

3. Clean the carbon from the piston crown (**Figure 134**) with a soft scraper or wire wheel mounted in a drill. A thick carbon buildup reduces piston cooling and causes detonation and piston damage. Relabel the piston crown after cleaning it.

CAUTION
Do not wire brush the piston skirt.

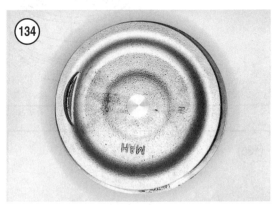

4. After cleaning the piston, examine the crown. The crown must show no signs of wear or damage. If the crown appears pecked or spongy-looking, also check the spark plug, valves and combustion chamber for aluminum deposits. If these deposits are found, the engine is overheating.

5. Examine each ring groove (A, **Figure 135**) for burrs, dented edges or other damage. Pay particular attention to the top compression ring groove because it usually wears more than the others. Because the oil rings are bathed in oiled, these rings and grooves wear little compared to compression rings and their grooves. If there is evidence of oil ring groove wear or if the oil ring is tight and difficult to remove, the piston skirt may have collapsed due to excessive heat. Replace the piston.

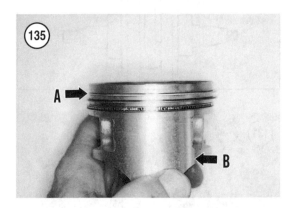

6. Clean the oil control holes (**Figure 136**) in the piston.

7. Check the piston skirt (B, **Figure 135**) for cracks or other damage. If the piston shows signs of partial seizure (bits of aluminum built up on the piston skirt), replace the piston.

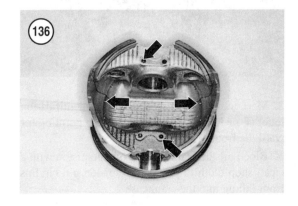

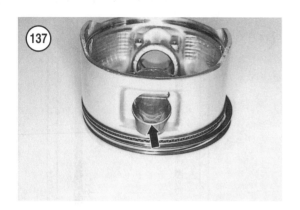

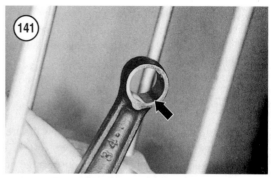

4

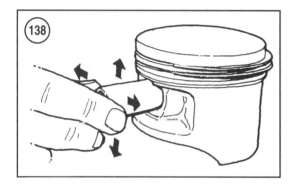

NOTE
If the piston skirt is worn or scuffed unevenly from side-to-side, the connecting rod may be bent or twisted.

8. Check the piston circlip grooves (**Figure 137**) for wear, cracks or other damage.
9. Measure piston-to-cylinder clearance as described under *Piston Clearance* in this chapter.

Piston Pin Inspection

When measuring the piston pin in this section, compare the actual measurements to the specifications in **Table 4**. Replace the piston pin if out of specification or if it shows damage as described in this section.
1. Clean and dry the piston pin.
2. Inspect the piston pin for chrome flaking or cracks.
3. Lubricate the piston pin and install it in the piston. Slowly rotate the piston pin and check for tightness or excessive play (**Figure 138**).

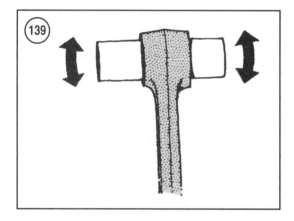

4. Lubricate the piston pin and install it (**Figure 139**) in the connecting rod. Slowly rotate the piston pin and check for radial play.
5. Measure the piston pin bore inside diameter (A, **Figure 140**).
6. Measure the piston pin outside diameter (B, **Figure 140**).
7. Subtract the measurement made in Step 6 from the measurement made in Step 5. The difference is the piston-to-piston pin clearance.

Connecting Rod
Small End Inspection

1. Inspect the connecting rod small end (**Figure 141**) for cracks or heat damage.

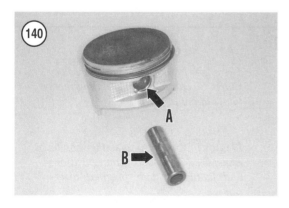

2. Measure the connecting rod small end inside diameter check against the dimension in **Table 4**. If out of specification, replace the crankshaft as described in Chapter Five.

Piston Clearance

1. Make sure the piston skirt and cylinder walls are clean and dry.
2. Measure the cylinder bore with a bore gauge or inside micrometer at the points shown in **Figure 142**. Measure in line with the piston pin and 90° to the pin. Use the largest measurement to determine cylinder bore diameter. If the cylinder bore is out of specification, replace the piston and bore the cylinder oversize. If the cylinder bore is within specification, continue with Step 3.
3. Measure the piston diameter with a micrometer at a right angle to the piston pin bore. Measure up 10 mm (0.4 in.) from the bottom edge of the piston skirt (**Figure 143**).
4. Subtract the piston diameter from the largest bore diameter. The difference is piston-to-cylinder clearance. If clearance exceeds the service limit in **Table 4**, determine if the piston, cylinder or both are worn. If necessary, take the cylinder to a dealership that can rebore the cylinder to accept an oversize piston.

Piston Ring

Inspection and removal

A three-ring type piston and ring assembly is used (**Figure 129**). The top and second rings are compression rings. The lower ring is an oil control ring assembly (consisting of two side rails and a spacer).

When measuring the piston rings in this section, compare the actual measurements to the specifications in **Table 4**. Replace the piston rings as a set if out of specification.

1. Measure the side clearance of each ring in its groove with a flat feeler gauge (**Figure 144**):
   a. If the clearance is greater than specified, replace the rings. If the clearance is still excessive with new rings, replace the piston.
   b. If the clearance is too small, check the ring and ring groove for carbon and oil residue. Carefully clean the ring without removing any metal from its surface. Clean the piston ring groove as described in this section.

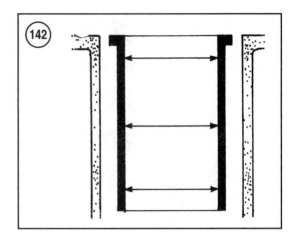

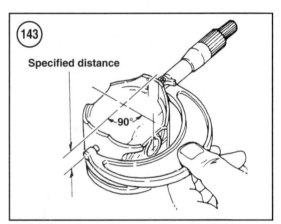

Specified distance

90°

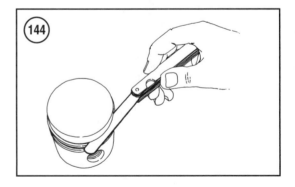

WARNING
The edges of all piston rings are very sharp. Be careful when handling them to avoid cut fingers.

NOTE
Identify the piston rings so they can be reinstalled in their original positions and facing in their original directions.

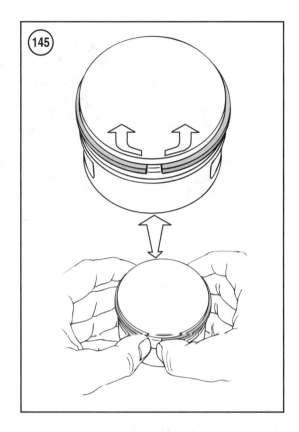

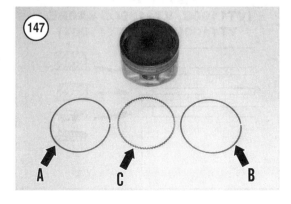

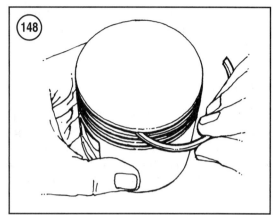

2. Remove the compression rings (1 and 2, **Figure 129**) with a ring expander tool or spread the ring ends by hand (**Figure 145**).

3. Remove the oil ring assembly (**Figure 146**) by first removing the upper (A, **Figure 147**) and lower (B) side rails. Then remove the expander spacer (C, **Figure 147**).

NOTE
Soak the piston in solvent to soften the carbon before attempting to clean the ring grooves in Step 4.

4. Remove carbon and oil buildup in the piston ring grooves with a broken piston ring (**Figure 148**). Do not remove aluminum material from the ring grooves as this will increase the side clearance.

5. Inspect the ring grooves for burrs, nicks or broken or cracked lands. Replace the piston if necessary.

6. Check the end gap of each ring. Insert the ring into the bottom of the cylinder bore and square it with the cylinder wall by tapping it with the piston. Measure the end gap with a feeler gauge (**Figure 149**). Replace the rings if the gap is too large. If the gap on the new ring is smaller than specified, hold a small file in a vise. Then grip the ends of the ring and slowly enlarge the gap.

NOTE
*When measuring the oil control ring end gap, measure the upper and lower side rail (A and B, **Figure 147**) end gaps only. Do not measure the spacer (C, **Figure 147**).*

7. Roll each compression ring around its piston groove (**Figure 150**) to check for binding. Repair minor binding with a fine-cut file.

Installation

1. Before installing new piston rings, hone or deglaze the cylinder wall. This helps the new rings seat in the cylinder. If necessary, refer this service to a Honda dealership. After honing, measure the end gap of each ring and compare to the dimensions in **Table 4**.

> *NOTE*
> *If the cylinder was honed or deglazed, clean the cylinder as described under* **Cylinder Inspection** *in this chapter.*

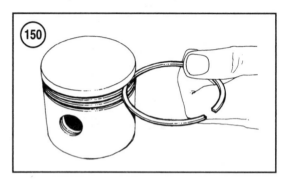

2. Clean and dry the piston and rings.
3. Identify the piston rings as follows:
   a. Refer to **Figure 151** or **Figure 152** to identify the shape of the piston rings.
   b. The top and second compression rings are different. The top ring is chrome-coated and the second ring is black (not coated).
   c. The piston rings have a mark on one side. Install the rings with their marks facing toward the top of the piston. When installing used piston rings, these marks may not be visible. Refer to the marks made during ring removal.

4. Install the oil ring assembly into the bottom ring groove. Install the spacer (C, **Figure 147**) first, and then the top (A) and bottom (B) side rails. Make sure the ends of the expander spacer butt together (**Figure 153**). They must not overlap. If reassembling used parts, install the side rails in their original positions.

5. Install the second compression ring, then the top compression ring.

6. Make sure the rings are seated completely in their grooves all the way around the piston.

7. If new parts were installed, follow the *Engine Break-In* procedure in Chapter Five.

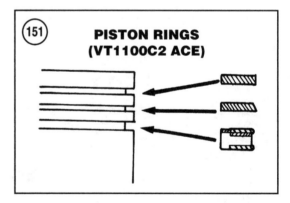

PISTON RINGS
(VT1100C2 ACE)

Piston Installation

> *CAUTION*
> *When it is necessary to rotate the crankshaft, pull the cam chains so they cannot bind internally. Protect*

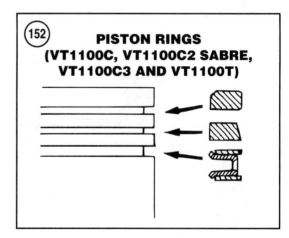

PISTON RINGS
(VT1100C, VT1100C2 SABRE, VT1100C3 AND VT1100T)

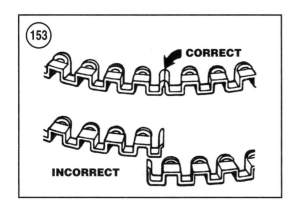

CORRECT

INCORRECT

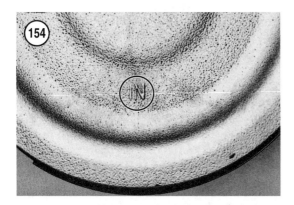

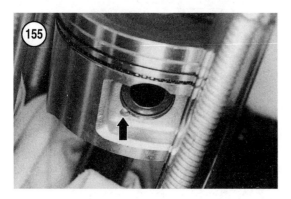

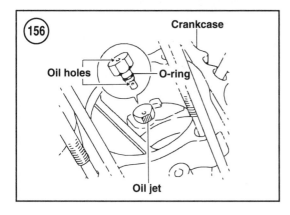

Crankcase

Oil holes

O-ring

Oil jet

the pistons so they are not damaged
when retracting into the crankcase.

1. Make sure the crankcase gasket surface is clean.

2. Install the oil jet as described in this chapter.

3. Install the piston rings onto the piston as described in this chapter.

4. Coat the connecting rod small end, piston pin and piston with engine oil.

5. Use the plastic hoses and piston fixture to support the piston and protect the piston rings as described under *Piston Removal*.

6. Slide the piston pin into the piston until its end is flush with the piston pin boss.

7. Place the piston over the connecting rod so the IN mark (**Figure 154**) on the piston crown faces toward the intake side of the cylinder head.

8. Line up the piston pin with the hole in the connecting rod. Push the piston pin (**Figure 132**) through the connecting rod and into the other side of the piston. Center the piston pin in the piston.

9. Block off the crankcase below the piston with a clean shop cloth to prevent the piston pin circlips from falling into the crankcase.

10. Install *new* piston pin circlips (**Figure 131**) in both ends of the piston pin boss. Make sure they seat in the piston grooves completely.

CAUTION
Do not align the piston pin circlip end
*gap with the notch (**Figure 155**) in the*
piston.

11. Install the cylinder as described in this chapter.

OIL JET

An oil jet is installed in the top of each crankcase bore and is accessible after removing the piston.

Removal/Inspection/Installation

The oil jets are directional and must be installed correctly or the oil spray will lubricate the parts. The oil hole in the side of the oil jet (**Figure 156**) must face toward the connecting rod. Mark the oil jet's installed position in the crankcase before removing it.

1. Remove the piston as described in this chapter.

2. Remove the oil jet (**Figure 156**, typical) and its O-ring from the crankcase. Discard the O-ring.

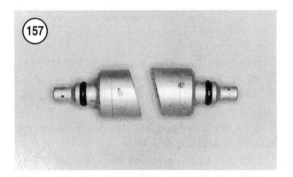

3. Inspect the oil jet (**Figure 157**) for any debris that may be clogging the oil holes. If the engine suffered any type of lubrication failure, it is safer to replace the oil jets than attempting to clean and reuse them.

4. Lubricate a new O-ring (**Figure 157**) and install it in the oil jet groove. Store the oil jet in a plastic bag until installation.

5. Lubricate the O-ring with clean engine oil and install the oil jet into the crankcase (**Figure 156**) until it bottoms.

CYLINDER STUD REPLACEMENT

Three different length cylinder studs (**Figure 158**) are used. The cylinder studs can be serviced without splitting the crankcase.

1. Remove the cylinder as described in this chapter. Cover the crankcase opening with clean rags.

2. Check for loose, bent or damaged studs. Retighten or replace damaged studs as described in the following steps.

3. Remove the stud as described under *Basic Service Methods* in Chapter One.

4. Clean the threaded hole in the crankcase. Check for any debris or damaged threads.

5. Install the studs (**Figure 158**) to the dimension shown in **Figure 159**.

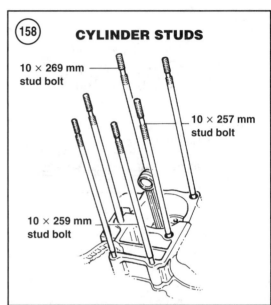

CYLINDER STUDS

10 × 269 mm stud bolt
10 × 257 mm stud bolt
10 × 259 mm stud bolt

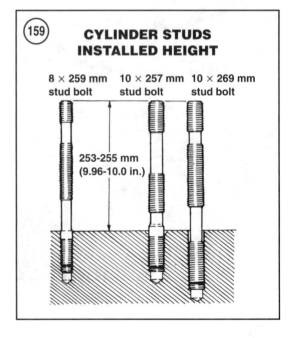

CYLINDER STUDS INSTALLED HEIGHT

8 × 259 mm stud bolt   10 × 257 mm stud bolt   10 × 269 mm stud bolt

253-255 mm (9.96-10.0 in.)

Table 1 GENERAL ENGINE SPECIFICATIONS

Bore and stroke	87.5 × 91.4 mm (3.44 × 3.60 in.)
Compression ratio	8.0:1
Cylinder alignment	2 cylinder 45° V transverse
Displacement	1099 cc (67.0 cu.-in.)
Engine firing order	
VT1100C2 ACE	
Front	315°
Rear	405°
VT1100C3	
1998-2000	
Front	315°
Rear	405°
2001-2002	
Front	225°
Rear	495°
All other models	
Front	495°
Rear	225°
Valve timing	
Front cylinder	
Intake valve	
Opens	5° BTDC @ 1 mm (0.04 in.) lift
Closes	30° ABDC @ 1 mm (0.4 in.) lift
Exhaust valve	
Opens	30° BBDC @ 1 mm (0.04 in.) lift
Closes	5° ATDC @ 1 mm (0.04 in.) lift
Rear cylinder	
Intake valve	
Opens	2° BTDC @ 1 mm (0.04 in.) lift
Closes	33° ABDC @ 1 mm (0.4 in.) lift
Exhaust valve	
Opens	37° BBDC @ 1 mm (0.04 in.) lift
Closes	-2° ATDC @ 1 mm (0.04 in.) lift
Valve train	Silent, multi-link cam chain, OHC with rocker arms and hydraulic lifters

4

Table 2 CYLINDER HEAD AND VALVES SERVICE SPECIFICATIONS

	New mm (in.)	Service limit mm (in.)
Cylinder head warp limit	–	0.05 (0.002)
Camshaft		
Lobe height		
Intake	38.021-38.181 (1.4969-1.5032)	37.99 (1.496)
Exhaust	38.027-38.187 (1.4971-1.5034)	38.00 (1.496)
Journal outside diameter		
A/B	23.949-23.970 (0.9429-0.9437)	23.92 (0.942)
	(continued)	

Table 2 CYLINDER HEAD AND VALVES SERVICE SPECIFICATIONS (continued)

	New mm (in.)	Service limit mm (in.)
Camshaft (continued)		
Journal outside diameter		
C	23.934-23.955	23.90
	(0.9423-0.9431)	(0.941)
Oil clearance		
A/B	0.050-0.111	0.130
	(0.0020-0.0044)	(0.005)
C	0.065-0.126	0.145
	(0.0026-0.0050)	(0.006)
Runout	–	0.05
		(0.002)
Rocker arm and shaft		
Rocker arm bore inside diameter	13.750-13.768	13.778
	(0.5413-0.5420)	(0.5424)
Rocker arm shaft outside diameter	13.716-13.734	13.706
	(0.5400-0.5407)	(0.5396)
Rocker arm-to-rocker arm shaft clearance	0.016-0.052	0.072
	(0.0006-0.0020)	(0.0028)
Tappet		
Assist spring free length	18.57	17.80
	(0.731)	(0.701)
Tappet adjuster compression stroke*	–	0.2
		(0.008)
Valve		
Valve stem outside diameter		
Intake	6.575-6.590	6.57
	(0.2589-0.2594)	(0.259)
Exhaust	6.555-6.570	6.54
	(0.2580-0.2587)	(0.257)
Valve guide inside diameter		
Intake and exhaust	6.600-6.615	6.635
	(0.2598-0.2604)	(0.2612)
Valve stem-to-guide clearance		
Intake	0.010-0.040	0.08
	(0.0004-0.0016)	(0.003)
Exhaust	0.030-0.060	0.12
	(0.12-0.0024)	(0.005)
Valve guide projection height above cylinder head		
Intake	14.5	–
	(0.57)	
Exhaust	15.5	–
	(0.61)	
Valve seat width	0.90-1.10	1.50
	(0.035-0.043)	(0.059)
Valve spring free length		
Inner		
Intake and exhaust	41.37	39.9
	(1.629)	(1.57)
Outer		
Intake	45.70	43.90
	(1.799)	(1.728)
Exhaust	43.50	41.80
	(1.713)	(1.646)

* This step performed with kerosene. See text for instructions.

Table 3 HYDRAULIC TAPPET SHIM SELECTION

Assist shaft stroke	Number of 0.5 mm (0.02 in.) shims required
0-1.20 mm (0-0.047 in.)	0
1.20-1.50 mm (0.047-0.059 in.)	1
1.50-1.80 mm (0.059-0.070 in.)	2
1.80-2.10 mm (0.070-0.083 in.)	3
2.10-2.40 mm (0.083-0.094 in.)	4
2.40-2.70 mm (0.094-0.106 in.)	5

Table 4 PISTON, RINGS AND BORE SPECIFICATIONS

	New mm (in.)	Service limit mm (in.)
Connecting rod small end inside diameter	22.020-22.041 (0.8669-0.8678)	21.051 (0.8681)
Connecting rod-to-piston pin clearance	0.020-0.047 (0.0008-0.0019)	0.07 (0.003)
Cylinder		
Bore inside diameter	87.500-87.515 (3.4449-3.4455)	87.545 (3.4466)
Block warpage limit	–	0.05 (0.002)
Out-of-round	–	0.05 (0.002)
Taper	–	0.05 (0.002)
Piston-to-cylinder clearance	0.010-0.045 (0.0004-0.0018)	0.32 (0.013)
Piston		
Outside diameter*	87.470-87.490 (3.4437-3.4445)	87.41 (3.441)
Piston pin bore inside diameter	22.002-22.008 (0.8662-0.8665)	22.018 (0.8668)
Piston pin outside diameter	21.994-22.000 (0.8659-0.8661)	21.984 (0.8655)
Piston-to-piston pin clearance	0.002-0.014 (0.0001-0.0006)	0.034 (0.0013)
Piston rings		
Ring-to-groove clearance		
Top ring	0.020-0.050 (0.0008-0.0020)	0.25 (0.010)
Second ring	0.015-0.045 (0.006-0.0018)	0.20 (0.008)
Piston ring end gap		
Top and second ring	0.20-0.35 (0.008-0.014)	0.50 (0.020)
Oil ring (side rails)	0.30-0.90 (0.012-0.035)	1.1 (0.04)

*See text for piston measuring point.

Table 5 ENGINE TOP END TORQUE SPECIFICATIONS

	N•m	in.-lb.	ft.-lb.
Assist shaft cap	22	–	16
Cam chain tensioner bolt	12	106	–

(continued)

Table 5 ENGINE TOP END TORQUE SPECIFICATIONS (continued)

	N•m	in.-lb.	ft.-lb.
Cam sprocket bolt[1]	18	159	–
Cylinder head cover[2]			
8 mm	27	–	20
10 mm			
VT1100C2 ACE	40	–	30
All other models	43	–	32
Cylinder head cover shroud bolt			
VT1100C2 ACE	12	106	–
VT1100C3	9	80	–
All other models	8.8	78	–
Intake tube hose clamp	2	17	–
Rocker arm shaft plug	39	–	29
Spark plug sleeve[3]	13	115	–
Spark plug	14	124	–

1. Apply a medium strength threadlock to bolt threads.
2. On all models except VT1100C2 ACE and VT1100C3, lubricate fastener threads and flange surfaces with engine oil.
3. Apply molybdenum oil solution to threads.

CHAPTER FIVE

ENGINE LOWER END

This chapter describes service procedures for lower end engine components and the output gearcase assembly. Engine removal and installation procedures are also described.

Throughout the text, there is frequent mention of the left and right side of the engine. This refers to the engine as it sits in the frame, not as it sits on the workbench.

Tables 1-9 are at the end of the chapter.

SERVICING ENGINE IN FRAME

Many engine components can be serviced with the engine mounted in the frame:

1. Oil pump.

2. Clutch.

3. Gearshift linkage.

4. Alternator.

5. Starter clutch and flywheel.

6. Starter motor.

7. Ignition pulse generator.

SUBFRAME

Refer to **Figure 1**, typical, when removing the subframe in this section.

Removal

1. Support the motorcycle on its sidestand, or use a scissors type jack.
2. Cover the front fender with a heavy blanket.
3. Remove the exhaust system (Chapter Fifteen).
4. Remove the rear brake pedal as described in Chapter Fourteen.
5. On models with a rear disc brake, remove the rear master cylinder assembly as described in Chapter Fourteen.
6. On California models, remove the EVAP canister (Chapter Eight).
7. Disconnect the horn connectors at the horn (A, **Figure 2**).
8. Remove the rear brake light switch and its wiring harness from the subframe (B, **Figure 2**).
9. Remove the front lower engine mounting nut and rubber washer (**Figure 3**).
10. Remove the front lower engine mounting bolt (A, **Figure 4**), spacers and rubber washer.

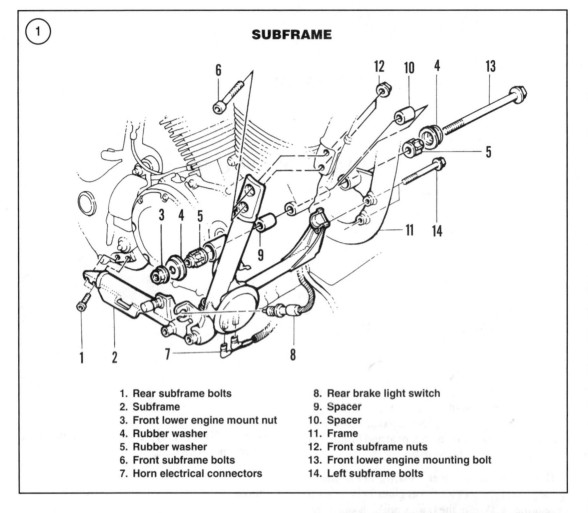

SUBFRAME

1. Rear subframe bolts
2. Subframe
3. Front lower engine mount nut
4. Rubber washer
5. Rubber washer
6. Front subframe bolts
7. Horn electrical connectors
8. Rear brake light switch
9. Spacer
10. Spacer
11. Frame
12. Front subframe nuts
13. Front lower engine mounting bolt
14. Left subframe bolts

11. Remove the two left side subframe bolts (B, **Figure 4**). On VT1100C and VT1100C2 Sabre models, the upper bolt is installed through the footpeg mounting bracket.

12. Loosen the front subframe mounting bolts and nuts (**Figure 5**).

13. Loosen the rear subframe mounting bolts (**Figure 6**).

14. Hold the subframe in place and remove the nuts and bolts loosened in Step 12 and Step 13. Then remove the subframe after releasing the radiator from the subframe. Refer to **Figure 7**.

Inspection

1. Clean and inspect the fasteners.
2. Inspect the subframe for cracks or other damage.
3. Remove the rubber damper from the subframe (**Figure 8**) and engine mounts, if used.

4. Replace the rubber dampers and rubber washers if deteriorated or damaged.

5. Install the rubber damper, shoulder side facing out (**Figure 8**), into the subframe and frame mounts, if used.

5

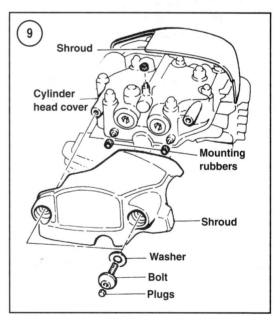

Shroud

Cylinder
head cover

Mounting
rubbers

Shroud

Washer

Bolt

Plugs

Installation

CAUTION
To avoid cross-threading the
subframe mounting bolts, install all of

the bolts finger-tight during installation.

1. Install the subframe onto the frame while aligning the radiator mounting stays (on the subframe) with the radiator mounting dampers. Then hold the subframe in place against the frame.

2. Install the front subframe mounting bolts (**Figure 5**) as follows:

   a. Lubricate the bolt threads and seating surfaces with engine oil.

   b. The upper bolt is longer than the lower bolt.

   c. Install both bolts. Do not install the nuts at this time.

3. Install the rear subframe mounting bolts (**Figure 6**).

4. Install the two left-side subframe bolts (B, **Figure 4**).

5. Lubricate the front subframe mounting nuts with engine oil, and then install them onto the two bolts (**Figure 5**).

6. Install the front lower engine mount bolt from the left side with its rubber washer (if used) and both spacers (A, **Figure 4**).

7. Tighten all of the subframe mounting bolts and nuts in two or three stages to make sure the subframe seats squarely against the frame, then tighten the fasteners in the following order to the torque specification listed in **Table 9**:

   a. Front lower engine mounting nut (**Figure 3**).

   b. Front subframe bolts and nuts (**Figure 5**).

   c. Rear subframe bolts (**Figure 6**).

   d. Left subframe bolts (B, **Figure 4**).

8. Install the rear brake light switch and its wiring harness (B, **Figure 2**) onto the subframe.

9. Reconnect the horn connectors at the horn.

10. On California models, install the EVAP canister (Chapter Eight).

11. On models with a rear disc brake, install the rear master cylinder (Chapter Fourteen).

12. Install the rear brake pedal (Chapter Fourteen).

13. Install the exhaust pipe and muffler (Chapter Fifteen).

14. Adjust the rear brake light switch (Chapter Three).

ENGINE REMOVAL

1. Park the motorcycle on a level surface.

2. Remove the fuel tank (Chapter Nine).

3. Before disassembling the engine, perform a compression test (Chapter Two) and leakdown test (Chapter Three). Record the readings for future use.

4. Drain the engine oil (Chapter Three).

5. Drain the coolant (Chapter Three).

6. Support the motorcycle frame with a jack or centerstand. Do not support the subframe.

7. Remove the right side cover (Chapter Fifteen).

8. Remove the battery and battery holder (Chapter Nine).

9. Remove the carburetor (Chapter Eight).

10. Remove the radiator (Chapter Ten).

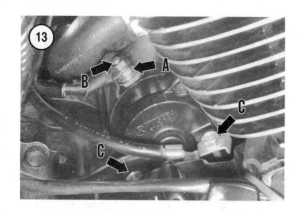

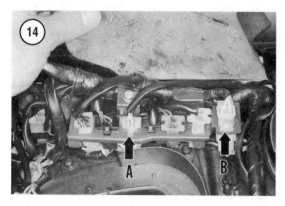

11. On models with a rear disc brake, remove the rear master cylinder reservoir (Chapter Fourteen).

12. Remove the left crankcase rear cover as described in Chapter Fifteen.

13. Remove the spark plug caps and tie them out of the way.

14. Remove the subframe as described in this chapter.

15. On VT1100C models, remove the right side lower cover (Chapter Fifteen).

16. On 2004 California models, disconnect the No. 16 hose from the PAIR reed valve cover mounted on each cylinder head cover. Refer to *Pulse Secondary Air Supply System* in Chapter Eight.

17. Remove the screw securing the cable clamp to the rear cylinder head fin.

18. Remove the head cover shrouds (**Figure 9**) as follows:
   a. Identify each shroud for installation.
   b. Remove the rubber plug from each shroud bolt.
   c. Remove the shroud bolts, washer and shroud.
   d. Remove the mounting rubbers installed behind each shroud.

19. Disconnect the coolant hoses at the cylinder head covers.

20. Remove the water pump cover stud bolt (**Figure 10**) as follows:
   a. Thread two nuts onto the stud bolt and lock them together.
   b. Turn the inner nut to loosen and remove the stud bolt (**Figure 11**).

21A. On VT1100C and VT1100C2 Sabre models, remove the pinch bolt and disconnect the shift pedal from the shift shaft.

21B. On VT1100C2 ACE and VT1100T models, perform the following:
   a. Remove the bolts and the left footpeg.
   b. Remove the pinch bolt and disconnect the shift pedal from the shift shaft.

21C. On VT1100C3 models, perform the following:
   a. Remove the bolts and the left footrest assembly.
   b. Remove the pinch bolt and disconnect the shift pedal from the shift shaft.

22. On VT1100C2 ACE and 1998-2000 VT1100C3 models, remove the bolts and disconnect the breather joint (**Figure 12**) from the left crankcase cover. Note the O-ring installed in the breather joint.

NOTE
Holding the inner starter terminal nut (Step 23) prevents the terminal bolt from turning and damaging the insulator installed inside the starter.

23. To prevent damaging the starter insulators, hold the inner starter terminal nut (A, **Figure 13**) with a wrench, then loosen and remove the starter cable nut (B) and disconnect the cable.

24. Remove the bolt and disconnect the ground cable at the engine (C, **Figure 13**).

25A On VT1100C2 ACE models, disconnect the following electrical connectors :
   a. White ignition pulse generator 4-pin connector (A, **Figure 14**).
   b. White alternator 3-pin connector (B, **Figure 14**).

25B. On all other models, disconnect the following electrical connectors from the connector pouch located next to the air filter (**Figure 15**):
   a. White ignition pulse generator 2-pin connector.
   b. White alternator 3-pin connector.

5

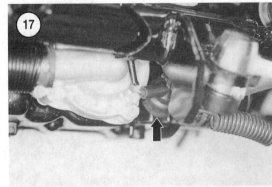

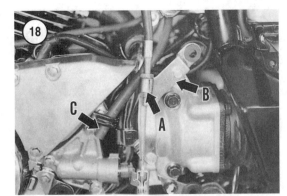

c. On VT1100C3 models, white 3-pin speed sensor connector.

26A. When removing an assembled engine, disconnect the oil pressure and neutral switch electrical connectors from the group of connectors on the left side of the engine, between the ignition switch and battery.

26B. If the left crankcase cover has been removed, perform the following:

   a. Disconnect the neutral switch electrical connector at the switch (**Figure 16**).

   b. Disconnect the oil pressure switch connector at the switch (**Figure 17**).

27. Disconnect the clutch cable (A, **Figure 18**) at the engine. Then disconnect the cable from its holder on the rear cylinder head.

28. Remove the bolts and the clutch cable holder (B, **Figure 18**).

29. On California models, remove the EVAP CAV control air vent tube (C, **Figure 18**) from the clamp.

30. Remove the crankcase breather tube from the clamp at the front of the engine.

31. Install a rubber hose over the cylinder head exhaust pipe studs (**Figure 19**) to protect them when removing the engine from the frame.

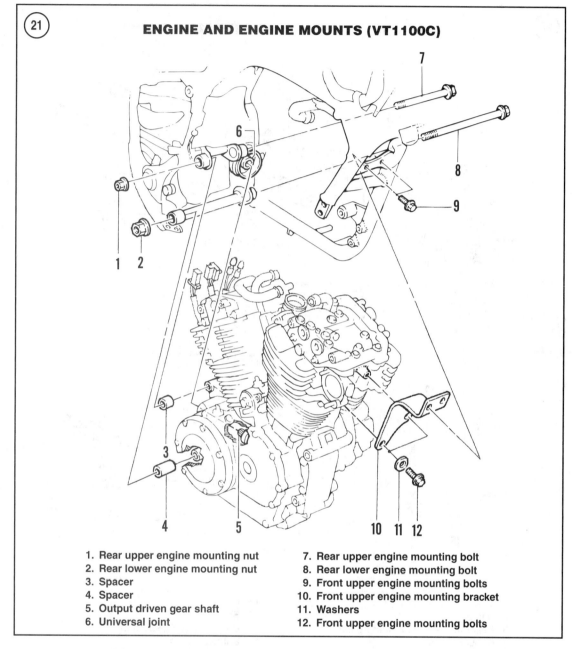

ENGINE AND ENGINE MOUNTS (VT1100C)

1. Rear upper engine mounting nut
2. Rear lower engine mounting nut
3. Spacer
4. Spacer
5. Output driven gear shaft
6. Universal joint
7. Rear upper engine mounting bolt
8. Rear lower engine mounting bolt
9. Front upper engine mounting bolts
10. Front upper engine mounting bracket
11. Washers
12. Front upper engine mounting bolts

32. Wrap the exposed frame tubes around the engine with pieces of rubber cut from an inner tube (**Figure 19**) to protect them from scratches and other damage when removing the engine.

33. Check the engine to make sure all hoses, cables and wires have been either disconnected or removed.

34. Place a jack under the crankcase (**Figure 20**). Place a piece of wood between the jack pad and the engine to protect the crankcase.

NOTE
Apply a slight amount of jack pressure up on the engine as the engine mounting bolts are loosened and removed in the following steps.

35. Refer to appropriate engine mount illustration when removing the engine mount fasteners in the following steps:

    a. **Figure 21**—VT1100C.

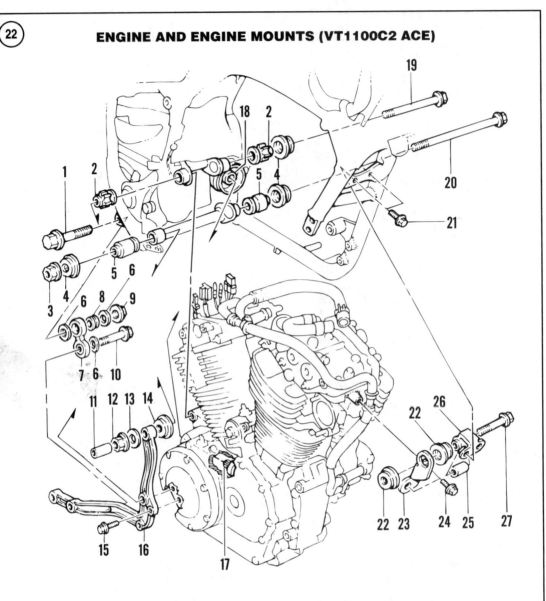

22 **ENGINE AND ENGINE MOUNTS (VT1100C2 ACE)**

1. Bolt
2. Damper
3. Rear lower engine mounting nut
4. Rubber washer
5. Damper
6. Washer
7. Bracket
8. Damper
9. Nut
10. Bolt
11. Collar
12. Rear upper engine mounting nut
13. Washer
14. Rubber washer

15. Bolt
16. Bracket
17. Output driven gear shaft
18. Universal joint
19. Rear upper engine mounting bolt
20. Rear lower engine mounting bolt
21. Front upper engine mounting bolt
22. Rubber washer
23. Front upper engine mounting bracket
24. Bolt
25. Collar
26. Bracket
27. Front upper engine mounting bolt

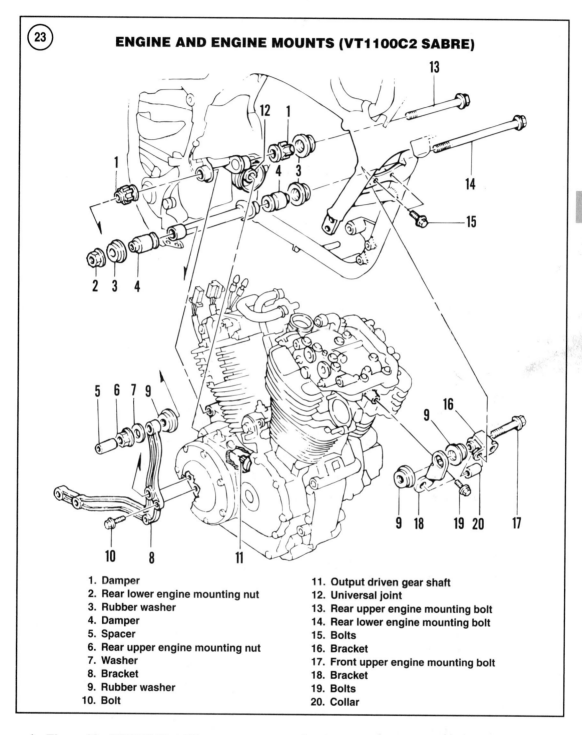

(23) ENGINE AND ENGINE MOUNTS (VT1100C2 SABRE)

1. Damper
2. Rear lower engine mounting nut
3. Rubber washer
4. Damper
5. Spacer
6. Rear upper engine mounting nut
7. Washer
8. Bracket
9. Rubber washer
10. Bolt
11. Output driven gear shaft
12. Universal joint
13. Rear upper engine mounting bolt
14. Rear lower engine mounting bolt
15. Bolts
16. Bracket
17. Front upper engine mounting bolt
18. Bracket
19. Bolts
20. Collar

b. **Figure 22**—VT1100C2 ACE.

c. **Figure 23**—VT1100 C2 Sabre.

d. **Figure 24**—VT1100C3.

e. **Figure 25**—VT1100T.

36A. On VT1100C models, remove the bolts and washers securing the front upper engine mounting bracket to the engine. Then remove the bolts securing the bracket to the frame and remove the bracket.

36B. On all other models, remove the front upper engine mounting bolts, brackets and rubber washers.

37. Remove the muffler bracket, if so equipped.

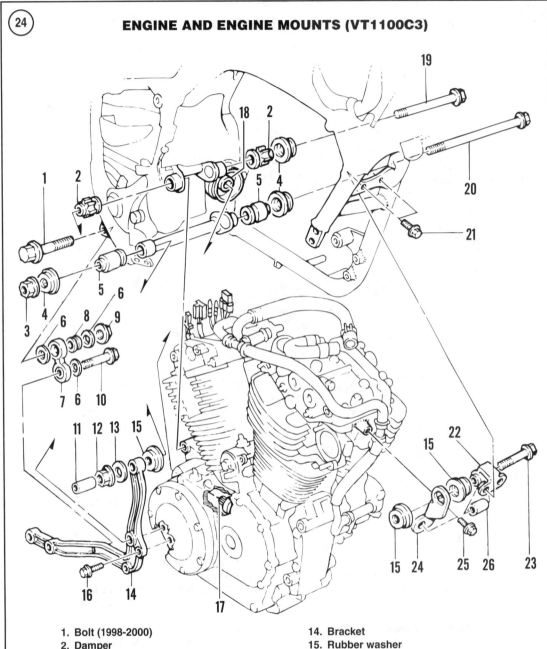

ENGINE AND ENGINE MOUNTS (VT1100C3)

1. Bolt (1998-2000)
2. Damper
3. Rear lower engine mounting nut
4. Rubber washer
5. Damper
6. Washer (1998-2000)
7. Bracket (1998-2000)
8. Damper (1998-2000)
9. Nut (1998-2000)
10. Bolt (1998-2000)
11. Spacer
12. Rear upper engine mounting nut
13. Washer
14. Bracket
15. Rubber washer
16. Bolt
17. Output driven gear shaft
18. Universal joint
19. Rear upper engine mounting bolt
20. Rear lower engine mounting bolt
21. Bolts
22. Bracket
23. Front upper engine mounting bolt
24. Bracket
25. Bolts
26. Collar

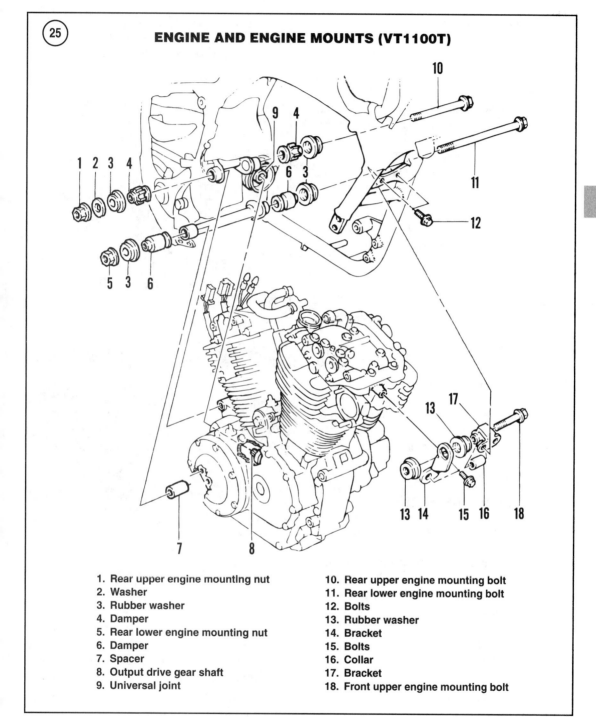

25 **ENGINE AND ENGINE MOUNTS (VT1100T)**

1. Rear upper engine mounting nut
2. Washer
3. Rubber washer
4. Damper
5. Rear lower engine mounting nut
6. Damper
7. Spacer
8. Output drive gear shaft
9. Universal joint
10. Rear upper engine mounting bolt
11. Rear lower engine mounting bolt
12. Bolts
13. Rubber washer
14. Bracket
15. Bolts
16. Collar
17. Bracket
18. Front upper engine mounting bolt

38A. On VT1100C models, remove the rear lower engine mounting nut, bolt and spacer.

38B. On all other models, remove the rear lower engine mounting nut and rubber washer, then remove the mounting bolt and the other rubber washer.

CAUTION
The rear upper mounting bolt (removed in the next step) is the last bolt holding the engine to the frame. Steps 39-43 requires a minimum of two, preferably three people to safely re-

move the engine from the frame and carry it to a workbench. An assembled engine weighs approximately 96 kg (212 lbs.).

39. With the engine supported on the jack and an assistant steadying the engine, remove the nut, steel washer and rubber washer (if used) from the rear upper engine mounting bolt. Then remove the bolt and rubber washer (if used). On VT1100C models, remove the spacer. The engine is now resting on the jack.

> *CAUTION*
> *There is little clearance between the engine and the frame. Take your time and be careful not to drop the engine out of the frame.*

40. Slowly pull the jack and engine forward to disconnect the engine's output driven gear shaft from the universal joint in the swing arm.

41. Carefully and slowly pivot the engine (on the jack) out of the right side of the frame. Move it far enough so everyone can get a good hand-hold on the engine.

42. Slide the engine out of the open frame area on the right side.

43. Take the engine to a workbench for further service.

ENGINE INSTALLATION

1. Inspect the engine for any cracks or damage.
2. Repair or replace any damaged wires or hoses.
3. Clean and inspect all the engine mounting fasteners.
4. Inspect all the engine mount rubber dampers and washers and replace if excessively worn or damaged.
5. Apply 1 g. (0.04 oz.) of molybdenum disulfide grease to the engine's output driven gear shaft splines.

> *CAUTION*
> *Installing the engine in the frame requires a minimum of two, preferably three people. An assembled engine weighs approximately 96 kg (212 lbs.).*

6. Place the engine on a jack, then position the engine in the frame. Insert the output driven gear shaft into the universal joint in the swing arm.

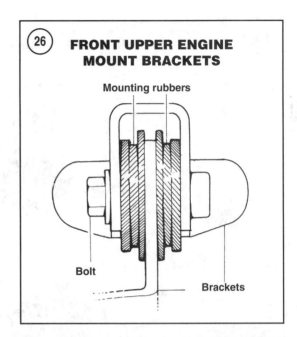

FRONT UPPER ENGINE MOUNT BRACKETS

Mounting rubbers

Bolt

Brackets

> *NOTE*
> *Tighten the engine mount fasteners finger-tight when installing them in the following steps.*

7. Refer to appropriate engine and engine mount illustration when assembling and installing the engine mount fasteners in the following steps:
  a. **Figure 21**—VT1100C.
  b. **Figure 22**—VT1100C2 ACE.
  c. **Figure 23**—VT1100C2 Sabre.
  d. **Figure 24**—VT1100C3.
  e. **Figure 25**—VT1100T.

8. Align the engine and frame mounting bolt holes, then install the rear upper mounting bolt assembly from the left side. On VT1100C models, install the spacer.

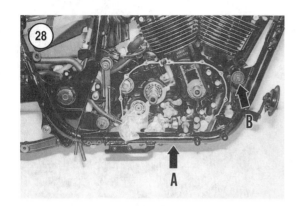

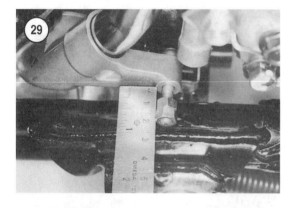

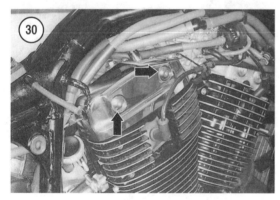

9. Install the rear lower mounting bolt assembly from the left side. On VT1100C and VT1100T models, install the spacer.

10. Install the muffler bracket, if used.

11A. On VT1100C models, mount the front upper engine mounting bracket onto the frame using the two mounting bolts and against the engine using the bolts and washers.

110B. On all other models, assemble the front upper engine mounting brackets, rubber washers and center bolt (**Figure 26**). Then install the mounting bracket in place and secure with its mounting bolts.

12. Pull the rubber boot over the output gearcase shoulder (**Figure 27**).

13. Install the subframe (A, **Figure 28**) and tighten all its mounting bolts and nuts, except the front lower engine mounting nut (B), as described under *Subframe* in this chapter.

14A. On VT1100C models, tighten the engine mounting fasteners to the following torque specifications:

    a. Front lower engine mounting nut: Lubricate the threads and seating surface with engine oil and tighten to 27 N•m (20 ft.-lb.).

    b. Front upper engine mounting bolt: 26 N•m (19 ft.-lb.).

    c. Rear lower engine mounting nut: Lubricate the threads and seating surface with engine oil and tighten to 64 N•m (47 ft.-lb.).

    d. Rear upper engine mounting nut: 52 N•m (38 ft.-lb.).

14B. On all other models, tighten the engine mounting fasteners to the following torque specifications:

    a. Front lower engine mounting nut: 40 N•m (30 ft.-lb.).

    b. Front upper engine mounting bolt: 27 N•m (20 ft.-lb.).

    c. Rear lower engine mounting nut: 55 N•m (41 ft.-lb.).

    d. Rear upper engine mounting nut: 55 N•m (41 ft.-lb.).

    e. Muffler bracket engine attaching bolt (if used): 27 N•m (20 ft.-lb.).

15. Install the water pump cover stud bolt (**Figure 11**) as follows:

    a. Clean the stud bolt and water pump cover threads with contact cleaner.

    b. Install the bolt until the distance from the bolt head to the water pump cover is 19-21 mm (0.76-0.84 in.). Refer to **Figure 29**.

    c. Remove the two locknuts.

16. Remove the rubber hose over each exhaust pipe stud and the covers installed around the frame tubes.

17. Reverse Steps 1-30 of *Engine Removal* to complete engine installation. Tighten the cylinder head cover shroud bolts (**Figure 30**) to the torque specifications in **Table 8**.

18. On models with a rear disc brake, bleed the rear brake (Chapter Fourteen).

19. Perform the following as described in Chapter Three:

5

a. Refill the engine with oil.

b. Adjust the rear brake light switch.

c. Check and adjust the clutch.

d. Adjust the throttle cables.

e. Adjust the choke cable.

f. Refill the engine with coolant.

20. Start the engine and check for leaks.

CRANKCASE AND CRANKSHAFT

The crankcase is made in two halves of precision diecast aluminum alloy. To avoid damage to the crankcase, do not hammer or pry on any of the interior or exterior projected walls. These areas are easily damaged. A gasket sealer seals the crankcase halves while dowel pins align the crankcase halves when they are bolted together.

The procedure that follows is presented as a complete, step-by-step major lower end overhaul.

References to the left and right side of the engine, as used in the text, refers to the engine as it sits in the frame, not as it sits on a workbench.

Special Tools

The tool requirements vary depending on the type of work to be performed. The engine can be disassembled and the crankshaft removed and installed without special tools. Special tools are required when replacing the crankcase bearings and when removing and installing the output gear assembly. To protect the case halves during the service procedures, support them on wooden blocks and thick pieces of rubber (old car floor mats) placed across the workbench.

Crankcase Disassembly

This procedure describes disassembly of the crankcase halves and removal of the crankshaft, transmission and internal shift mechanism.

1. With the engine mounted in the frame, remove the following components as described in Chapter Six:

a. Clutch.

b. Primary drive gear.

c. Gearshift linkage.

d. Oil pump.

2. With the engine mounted in the frame, remove the following components as described in Chapter Nine:

a. Left side crankcase cover.

b. Flywheel.

c. Starter clutch assembly.

3. Remove the engine from the frame as described in this chapter. Then remove the following components:

a. Cylinder heads (Chapter Four).

b. Cylinders and pistons (Chapter Four).

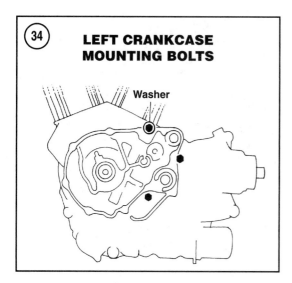

LEFT CRANKCASE MOUNTING BOLTS

Washer

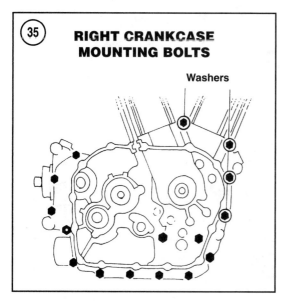

RIGHT CRANKCASE MOUNTING BOLTS

Washers

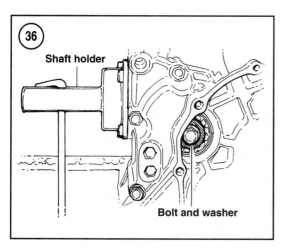

Shaft holder

Bolt and washer

c. Cam chain tensioners (Chapter Four).

d. Ignition pulse generators (Chapter Nine).

e. Water pump (Chapter Ten).

f. Starter motor (Chapter Nine).

4. Remove the front (**Figure 31**) and rear (**Figure 32**) cam chains.

5. Remove the rear cylinder cam chain drive sprocket (**Figure 33**).

6. Before removing the left and right side crankcase mounting bolts and washers, draw an outline of each crankcase on a piece of cardboard. Then punch holes along the outline for the placement of each mounting bolt. Refer to **Figure 34** (left crankcase) and **Figure 35** (right crankcase).

7. Remove the 6-mm bolt and the two 8-mm bolts (and washers) from the left crankcase (**Figure 34**). Place them in the corresponding holes in the cardboard.

8. Hold the output drive gear shaft with the Honda shaft holder (part No. 07923-6890101 or equivalent [**Figure 36**]). Then loosen and remove the output drive gear shaft bolt and washer (**Figure 36**).

9. Loosen the right side crankcase bolts (**Figure 35**) in a crossing pattern. Then remove all the bolts and washers and place them in the corresponding holes in the cardboard.

10. Place the engine on two wooden blocks with the left crankcase facing up.

NOTE
If the engine was experiencing shifting problems, examine the transmission assembly before removing it. Look for excessive wear or damaged parts. Spin the countershaft and turn the shift drum by hand to shift the transmission. Check the movement and operation of each shift fork and sliding gear. Look for hard shifting and incomplete gear dog engagement. Check also for seized gears and bushings.

NOTE
Because the crankshaft and transmission shafts slide through their respective bearings with a slip fit, the left crankcase should separate without the use of force. If the left crankcase will not separate as described in Step 11, check for an installed crankcase mounting bolt. Then check for a seized transmission shaft.

11. Lightly tap the left case half to separate it from the right case half. If necessary, use a screwdriver in the pry holes at the front and rear of the crankcase assembly. Do not pry between the gasket surfaces. Because the output gear assembly comes off with the left case half, it adds weight to the left case half. Locate the mainshaft washer, as it may have come off with the bearing in the left case half, and reinstall it (A, **Figure 37**).

12. Remove the two dowel pins (B, **Figure 37**).

13. Remove the remaining dowel pin and O-ring (C, **Figure 37**).

14. Remove the output gear and bushing (**Figure 38**). Then remove its thrust washer (**Figure 39**).

NOTE
Steps 15-17 describe removal of the internal shift mechanism and transmission assembly. Refer to Chapter Seven for service to these components.

NOTE
*The shift fork shaft shown in **Figure 40** has an exposed groove. On some models, the shift fork shaft does not use this groove.*

15. Remove the shift fork shaft (**Figure 40**).

16. Remove the shift drum and the three shift forks (**Figure 41**).

NOTE
The countershaft gears are free to fall off the end of the shaft when the countershaft is removed in the next step. Hold the countershaft's bottom gear when removing the transmission assembly.

17. Pull the mainshaft (A, **Figure 42**) and countershaft (B, **Figure 42**) straight up as an assembly and remove them (**Figure 43**).

NOTE
The mainshaft is equipped with an end washer on its left side. The countershaft is equipped with an end washer on its right side. Locate both washers and install them on their respective shafts.

18. Note the alignment of the front and rear connecting rods through the crankcase cylinder cut-

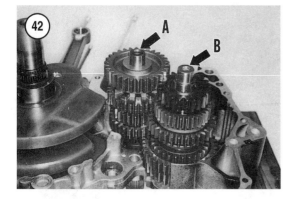

outs, then lift the crankshaft (B, **Figure 44**) and remove it from the crankcase.

> *CAUTION*
> *Use extreme care when servicing the crankshaft. Store the crankshaft in a manner that eliminates exposure to dirt and impact damage. Place the crankshaft on the workbench so it cannot roll off. If the crankshaft is damaged due to impact, it may affect the alignment and require service.*

19. Service the crankshaft and connecting rods as described under *Crankshaft* in this chapter.

20. Inspect the output gear as described under *Output Gear Assembly* in this chapter.

21. Service the transmission and internal shift mechanism as described in Chapter Seven.

Crankcase Inspection

> *CAUTION*
> *Do not pick up or hold the crankcase halves by their cylinder studs.*

1. Clean the gasket surfaces.
2. Clean the crankcase halves with solvent.
3. Using clean solvent, flush each bearing.
4. Dry the cases with compressed air.

> *WARNING*
> *When drying a bearing with compressed air, do not allow the inner bearing race to rotate. The air can spin the bearing at excessive speed, possibly causing the bearing to destruct.*

5. Blow through each oil passage with compressed air.

6. Lightly oil the engine bearings before inspecting their condition. A dry bearing exhibits more sound and looseness than a properly lubricated bearing.

7. Inspect the bearings for roughness, pitting, galling and play. Replace any bearing that is not in good condition. Always replace the opposite bearing (paired sets) at the same time. Refer to *Crankcase Bearing Replacement* in this chapter and *Bearings* in Chapter One for typical bearing replacement.

8. Inspect the case halves for fractures around all mounting and bearing bosses, stiffening ribs and threaded holes. If repair is required, have a dealer-

ship or machine shop that is experienced in the repairs of precision aluminum castings inspect the crankcase.

9. Check all threaded holes for damage or contamination. Clean threads with the correct size metric tap. Lubricate the tap with kerosene or aluminum tap fluid.

10. Retighten or replace the cylinder studs as described under *Cylinder Stud Replacement* in Chapter Four.

Crankcase Assembly

> *NOTE*
> *Molybdenum oil solution referred to in this procedure is a 50:50 mixture of engine oil and molybdenum disulfide grease.*

1. Check the mainshaft and countershaft as described in Chapter Seven. Check that all washers and snap rings are in their correct positions. Then set each shaft aside until reassembly.

2. If removed, install the output gear assembly into the left crankcase as described under *Output Gear Assembly* in this chapter.

3. Lubricate the main bearing inserts with molybdenum oil solution.

4. Lubricate the transmission bearing surfaces with engine oil.

5. Clean both crankcase surfaces with electrical contact cleaner.

6. Support the right crankcase half (**Figure 45**) on wooden blocks.

> *CAUTION*
> *Carefully guide the crankshaft into the bearing insert to prevent catching and damaging the insert.*

7. Install the crankshaft into the right crankcase half with the tapered (flywheel) end facing up (B, **Figure 44**). At the same time, position the connecting rods into their respective cylinder openings (**Figure 44**).

8. Install the transmission as follows:
   a. Check that the outer right side washer (**Figure 46**) is installed on the countershaft.
   b. Check that the outer left side washer (**Figure 47**) is installed on the mainshaft.

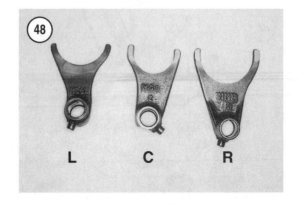

NOTE
A thin film of grease applied on the inside of the washers helps hold them in place.

  c. Mesh the countershaft and mainshaft together (**Figure 43**) and install them in the right crankcase (**Figure 42**). Check that the outer washer on the countershaft did not fall off.

9. Install the shift forks as follows:

  a. Identify each shift fork by its letter mark (**Figure 48**)—L (left shift fork), C (center shift fork) and R (right shift fork). Install each shift fork with its mark facing down (toward the right crankcase half).

  b. Install the R shift fork (**Figure 49**) into the countershaft third gear groove. Refer to A, **Figure 50**.

  c. Install the C shift fork (**Figure 51**) into the mainshaft second/fourth combination gear groove. Refer to B, **Figure 50**.

  d. Install the L shift fork (**Figure 52**) into the countershaft fifth gear groove. Refer to C, **Figure 50**.

10. Install the shift drum and mesh the shift forks as follows:

  a. Lubricate the shift drum's right side shoulder with engine oil and install into the right crankcase bearing (**Figure 53**).

  b. Engage the R shift fork pin into the bottom shift drum groove (A, **Figure 53**).

  c. Engage the C shift fork pin into the center shift drum groove (B, **Figure 53**).

  d. Engage the L shift fork pin into the upper shift drum groove (C, **Figure 53**).

11. Install the shift fork shaft as follows:

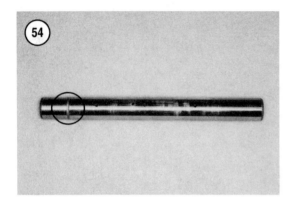

a. If the shift fork shaft has a groove on one end (**Figure 54**), install it with the groove end facing up.

b. If the shift fork shaft does not have a groove, install it with either end facing up.

c. Lubricate the shift fork shaft with molybdenum oil solution and install it through the three shift forks (**Figure 55**) until it bottoms solidly against the right crankcase. Make sure the pin on each shift fork engages the correct groove in the shift cam.

d. Spin the transmission shafts and turn the shift drum by hand to check transmission operation. Check that each shift fork travels through its operating groove in the shift drum and bottoms against both ends of the groove.

NOTE
It is difficult to identify the different gear positions when turning the shift drum without the stopper lever installed on the engine. Substep d shows whether the shift forks can or cannot move through their complete operational range.

12. Install the output gear assembly (**Figure 56**) as follows:

a. Lubricate the washer, bushing and gear bore with molybdenum oil solution.

b. Install the washer and center it against the right crankcase bearing (**Figure 57**).

c. Install the bushing into the gear, then install the gear into the right crankcase with its dog holes facing up (**Figure 58**). Align the gear and washer with the bearing bore.

13. Lubricate a new O-ring with oil and install it with its dowel pin (**Figure 59**).

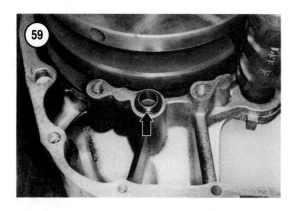

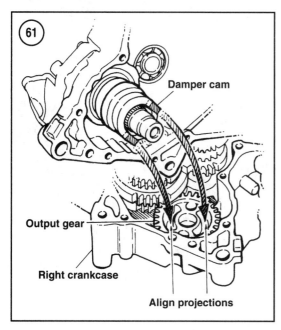

Damper cam

Output gear

Right crankcase

Align projections

16. Lubricate all of the shafts and gears with engine oil.

17. Clean both crankcase mating surfaces with an aerosol electrical contact cleaner. Allow the cleaner to evaporate before applying gasket sealant.

18. Apply a thin even coat of a nonhardening liquid gasket sealant to the right and left crankcase half mating surfaces. Observe the sealant manufacturer's instructions. Do not get any on the bearings or in the oil passages.

NOTE
Some acceptable sealants are: ThreeBond Liquid Gasket 1104 and Yamabond 4 (part No. ACC-YAMAB-ON-D4). Many sealants have a shelf life of one year, starting when a new tube is first opened. For best results, date the tube to avoid using old sealant.

19. Position the output gear (**Figure 58**) so its dog holes align with the two projections on the damper cam (**Figure 61**) when installing the left crankcase half in Step 20.

20. Install the left crankcase assembly over the right crankcase so the damper cam engages the output gear (**Figure 61**) and the output drive gear shaft is installed through the output gear, bushing and washer.

21. Lightly tap the left crankcase with a plastic mallet to seat it over the dowel pins and against the right crankcase.

CAUTION
The left crankcase should install without the use of force. If the crankcase halves do not fit together completely, do not pull them together with the crankcase screws. Remove the left crankcase and investigate the cause of the interference. Check that a transmission gear was not installed backward. Also make sure the output gear, bushing and washer are aligned and installed correctly.

22. Turn the transmission shafts, crankshaft and shift drum. Each component must turn freely with no binding. If everything turns okay, continue with Step 23.

14. Install the two dowel pins (A, **Figure 60**) into the right crankcase.
15. Make sure the washer (B, **Figure 60**) is installed on the mainshaft.

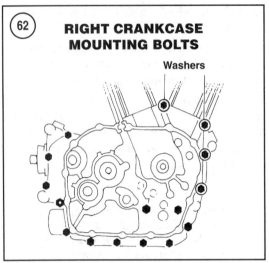

RIGHT CRANKCASE MOUNTING BOLTS

Washers

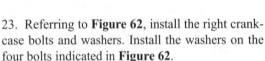

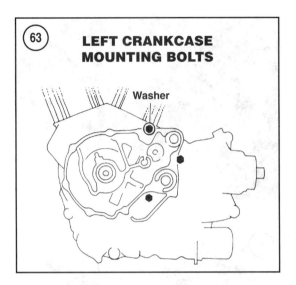

LEFT CRANKCASE MOUNTING BOLTS

Washer

23. Referring to **Figure 62**, install the right crankcase bolts and washers. Install the washers on the four bolts indicated in **Figure 62**.

24. Tighten the right crankcase bolts (**Figure 62**) in a crossing pattern in 2-3 steps to the following torque specifications:

    a. 6 mm: 12 N•m (106 in.-lb.).

    b. 8 mm: 27 N•m (20 ft.-lb.).

    c. 10 mm: 40 N•m (30 ft.-lb.).

25. Turn the engine over and install the left crankcase bolts and washer. Install the washer on the bolt indicated in **Figure 63**.

26. Tighten the left crankcase bolts (**Figure 63**) in a crossing pattern in 2-3 steps to the following torque specifications:

    a. 6 mm: 12 N•m (106 in.-lb.).

    b. 8 mm: 27 N•m (20 ft.-lb.).

27. Rotate the transmission shafts and crankshaft to ensure there is no binding. If there is any binding, remove the crankcase mounting bolts and the left crankcase and correct the problem.

28. Apply a medium strength threadlock onto the output drive gear shaft bolt threads. Then hold the output drive gear shaft with the Honda shaft holder (part No. 07923-689010 or equivalent [**Figure 64**]) and tighten the bolt 50 N•m (37 ft.-lb.).

29. Recheck the torque value of each crankcase mounting bolt.

30. Check shifting as follows:

    a. Temporarily install the cam plate and stopper arm (**Figure 65**) as described under *External Shift Mechanism* in Chapter Six.

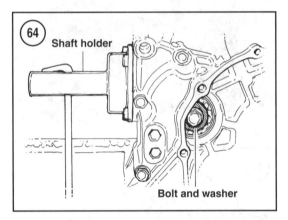

Shaft holder

Bolt and washer

    b. Shift the shift drum into neutral as shown in **Figure 65**. The raised ramp on the cam plate is the neutral position. Shift the transmission through each gear.

    c. If the transmission did not shift properly, disassemble the crankcase and inspect the trans-

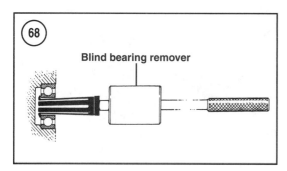

Blind bearing remover

5

CRANKCASE BEARING REPLACEMENT

This section services the transmission bearings installed in both crankcase halves. Refer to *Crankshaft* in this chapter to service the crankshaft main bearings installed in both crankcase halves. Refer to **Figure 66** and **Figure 67**.

1. Refer to *Basic Service Methods* in Chapter One for typical bearing removal and installation techniques. Also refer to *Interference Fit* if it is necessary to use heat for the removal and installation of the bearings in the crankcase halves.

2. When replacing crankcase bearings, note the following:

    a. Identify and record the size code of each bearing before it is removed from the case. This eliminates confusion when installing the bearings.

    b. Record the orientation of each bearing in its bore. Note if the size code faces toward the inside or outside of the case.

    c. Use a hydraulic press or a set of bearing drivers to remove and install bearings. Bearings can also be removed and installed using heat, as described in Chapter One.

    d. Remove bearings that are only accessible from one side of the case with a blind bearing puller (**Figure 68**). The puller is fitted through the bearing, then expanded to grip the back-side of the bearing.

3. Remove the bearing set plates (**Figure 69**) before replacing the transmission or shift drum bearings in the right crankcase. Install and tighten the setting plate fasteners as follows:

    a. Clean and dry the fastener and case half threads.

    b. Apply a medium strength threadlock onto the fastener threads.

mission for proper assembly or damaged parts.

31. Slide the rear cylinder cam chain drive sprocket (**Figure 33**) onto the crankshaft. Align the wide groove in the sprocket with the wide crankshaft tooth.

32. Install the front (**Figure 31**) and rear (**Figure 32**) cam chains.

33. Reverse Steps 1-3 under *Crankcase Disassembly* to complete installation.

34. Refill the engine with oil and coolant as described in Chapter Three.

35. Start the engine and check for leaks.

c. Tighten the bearing set plate screws to 9 N•m (80 in.-lb.).

d. Tighten the bearing set plate bolts to 12 N•m (106 in.-lb.).

CRANKSHAFT

Models are either equipped with a single pin or twin pin crankshaft (**Figure 70**). Service procedures for both crankshaft designs are identical.

1. The following models are equipped with the single pin crankshaft:

a. VT1100C2 ACE.

b. 1998-2000 VT1100C3.

2. The following models are equipped with the twin pin crankshaft:

a. VT1100C.

b. VT1100C2 Sabre.

c. 2001-2002 VT1100C3.

d. VT1100T.

Removal/Installation

Remove and install the crankshaft as described under *Crankcase* in this chapter.

Inspection

1. Clean the crankshaft and connecting rods thoroughly with solvent. Clean the crankshaft oil passageways with compressed air. Dry the crankshaft with compressed air, then lubricate all bearing surfaces with a light coat of engine oil.

2. Inspect each crankshaft main journal (**Figure 71**) for scratches, ridges, scoring, nicks or heat discoloration. Remove small nicks and scratches with crocus cloth. Anything more serious must be referred to a machine shop.

3. To determine main journal wear, perform the *Crankshaft Main Bearing Inspection* in this section.

4. Inspect the crankshaft splines, flywheel taper and drive gears for damage.

5. Measure crankshaft runout with the crankshaft mounted between centers (**Figure 72**). Rotate the crankshaft two full turns with a dial gauge contacting the main bearing journals. Replace the crankshaft if the runout exceeds the service limit in **Table 1**.

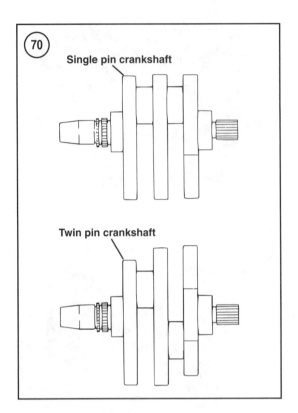

70

Single pin crankshaft

Twin pin crankshaft

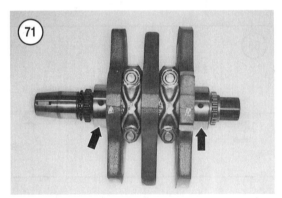

71

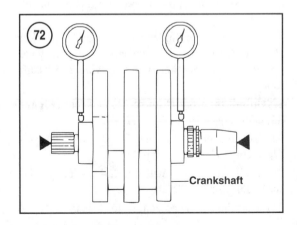

72

Crankshaft

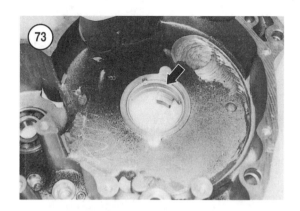

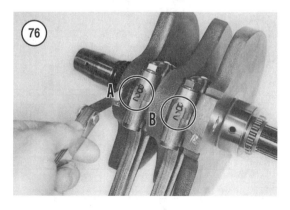

Crankshaft Main Bearing Inspection

Each crankcase is equipped with insert-type main bearings (**Figure 73**). These inserts cannot be replaced or serviced.

1. Inspect the inside surface of each bearing insert (**Figure 73**) for excessive wear, bluish or burned appearance, flaking and scoring. If the insert is questionable, replace the crankcase half.

NOTE
The left and right crankcase halves can be replaced separately.

2. Clean the crankshaft main bearing journal (**Figure 71**) and crankcase bearing insert (**Figure 73**) surfaces.

3. Measure the main bearing clearance by performing the following steps:

  a. Measure the inside diameter of the bearing insert with a bore gauge or inside micrometer (**Figure 74**).

  b. Measure the crankshaft main bearing journal outside diameter with a micrometer (**Figure 75**).

  c. Subtract the main bearing journal outside diameter from the bearing insert inside diameter to determine the main journal oil clearance. If the main bearing journal clearance exceeds the service limit in **Table 1**, replace the crankcase half.

CONNECTING RODS

Removal/Installation

1. Split the crankcase halves and remove the crankshaft assembly as described under *Crankcase* in this chapter.

2. Measure the connecting rod side clearance with a feeler gauge between the connecting rod and crankshaft machined surfaces (A, **Figure 76**). Compare to the connecting rod side clearance limit in **Table 1**. Measure each connecting rod. If the measurement is out of specification, replace the connecting rod as described in this chapter. Recheck the clearance with the new rod. If the clearance is excessive with the new rod, replace the crankshaft.

3. Remove the nuts securing the connecting rod caps and remove the caps (**Figure 77**).

4. Carefully remove the connecting rod from the crankshaft. Mark the rod, bearing and cap to show

its correct cylinder and crankpin position for reassembly (**Figure 78**).

5. Remove and identify each bearing insert (**Figure 79**) as to its upper or lower position.

6. Clean these parts and the crankshaft in solvent and dry with compressed air.

7. Inspect the connecting rods and bearings as described in this section.

8. If new bearing inserts are being installed, check the bearing clearance as described in this chapter.

9. Wipe off any oil from the bearing inserts, connecting rod and cap contact surfaces. These surfaces must be dry when installing the inserts.

10. Install the bearing inserts into each connecting rod and cap (**Figure 79**). Make sure they are locked in place correctly (**Figure 80**).

CAUTION
If the old bearing inserts are reused, they must be installed in their original positions (Step 4 and Step 5) or engine damage may occur.

11. Apply molybdenum oil solution to the bearing inserts and crank pin bearing thrust surfaces.

12. Install the connecting rod onto the crankshaft so it is facing in its original position, as noted during Step 4.

13. Match the code number on the end of the cap with the mark on the rod (B, **Figure 76**) and install the cap.

CAUTION
The fine threads used on the connecting rod studs and cap nuts are easily damaged. Start the nuts carefully by hand.

14. Lubricate the bearing cap nut threads and seating surfaces with engine oil and install the cap nuts (**Figure 77**). Tighten the connecting rod cap nuts in several steps to 60 N•m (44 ft.-lb.).

15. Rotate the connecting rod several times to check that there is no binding or roughness.

16. Repeat for the other connecting rod.

Connecting Rod Inspection

1. Remove and identify the connecting rods from the crankshaft as described in this section.

2. Clean the connecting rods and inserts in solvent and dry with compressed air.

3. Carefully inspect each rod journal on the crankshaft for scratches, ridges, scoring and other damage.

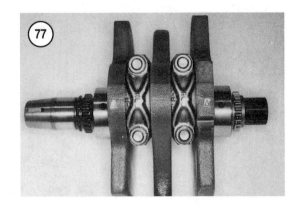

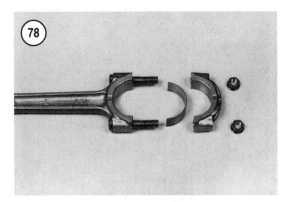

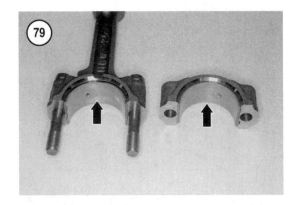

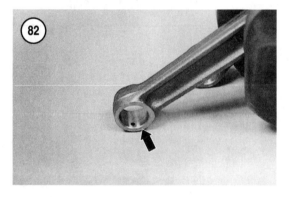

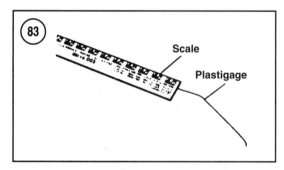

Scale

Plastigage

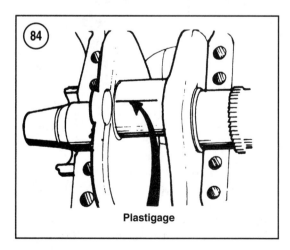

Plastigage

4. A bent or twisted connecting rod can be difficult to determine without a rod aligning fixture. Some signs of a damaged connecting rod are:
   a. The wear across a bearing insert is uneven.
   b. The piston skirt shows signs of unusual or uneven wear patterns.
   c. If any of these conditions are present, refer further inspection to a dealership.
5. Inspect each bearing insert (**Figure 79**) for evidence of wear, abrasion and scoring.
6. Measure the rod journal (**Figure 81**) with a micrometer and check for out-of-roundness and taper.
7. Check each connecting rod big end for signs of seizure, bearing or connecting rod damage.
8. Check each connecting rod small end (**Figure 82**) for signs of excessive heat (blue coloration) or other damage.
9. Measure the inside diameter of the small end of the connecting rod (**Figure 82**) with an inside micrometer or small hole gauge. Replace the connecting rod if the small end inside diameter exceeds the service limit specified in **Table 1**.
10. If all of the parts are within specification and do not show any type of visible damage, measure the connecting rod bearing oil clearance as described in this section.

Connecting Rod Bearing Oil Clearance

This section describes how to measure connecting rod bearing oil clearance using Plastigage (**Figure 83**). Plastigage is a soft material that flattens when pressure is applied to it. The marked bands on the envelope are then used to measure the width of the flattened Plastigage. The connecting rod and its bearing inserts must be installed on the crankshaft when performing this procedure.

Plastigage is available from automotive parts stores in different clearance ranges. Refer to the connecting rod bearing clearance specification in **Table 1**.

1. Clean any oil from the bearing insert and connecting rod journal surface.
2. Place a strip of Plastigage (**Figure 83**) over each journal parallel to the crankshaft as shown in **Figure 84**. Do not place the Plastigage material over an oil hole in the crankshaft.

> *NOTE*
> *Do not rotate the connecting rod while the Plastigage strip is in place.*

3. Install the bearing inserts into each connecting rod and cap. Make sure they are locked in place correctly (**Figure 80**).

NOTE
Make sure the bearing inserts are installed in their original mounting positions.

4. Install the connecting rod onto the crankshaft so it is facing in its original position.

5. Match the code number on the end of the cap with the mark on the rod (B, **Figure 76**) and install the cap.

6. Lubricate the bearing cap nut threads and seating surfaces with engine oil and install the cap nuts (**Figure 77**). Tighten the cap nuts in several steps to 60 N•m (44 ft.-lb.).

7. Remove the rod cap nuts and rod cap.

8. Measure the width of the flattened Plastigage (**Figure 85**) following the manufacturer's instructions. Measure both ends of the Plastigage strip.

   a. A difference of 0.025 mm (0.001 in.) or more indicates a tapered journal. Confirm the measurement using a micrometer.

   b. If the connecting rod bearing oil clearance exceeds the wear limit in **Table 1**, select new bearings as described in this section.

9. Remove all of the Plastigage material from the journals and connecting rod caps.

10. Repeat for the other rod.

Connecting Rod Bearing Selection

Connecting rod bearing inserts come in three standard sizes to compensate for manufacturing tolerances that result in different connecting rod journal outside diameters and connecting rod inside diameter sizes. There are no undersize bearing sizes. To determine the correct size bearing insert, a number and letter code system is used. A code *number* stamped on the side of each connecting rod and cap (**Figure 86**) identifies the connecting rod inside diameter. Half the number is stamped on the rod and the other half is stamped on the cap. A code *letter* stamped on each crankshaft web identifies the connecting rod journal outside diameter; refer to **Figure 87** (single pin) or **Figure 88** (twin pin).

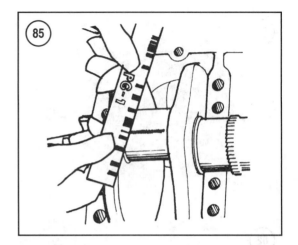

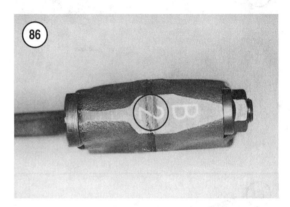

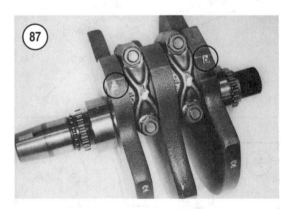

NOTE
If a code mark on either part is undecipherable, refer selection to a Honda dealership.

1. Record the journal outside diameter code letter (A or B) on the crankshaft web. Refer to **Figure 87** or **Figure 88**.

2. Measure the connecting rod journal outside diameter (**Figure 81**) with a micrometer. Compare the

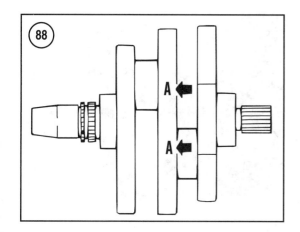

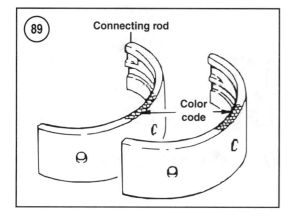

Connecting rod

Color code

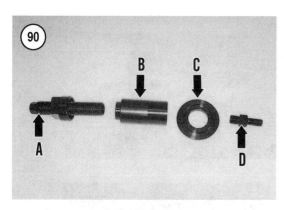

measurement with the connecting rod journal outside diameter code letter A or B measurement in **Table 2**. If the measurement for each journal is within tolerance, the new bearing can be selected by color code; continue with Step 3. If a measurement is out of specification, the crankshaft is worn; refer further inspection to a Honda dealership.

3. Record the connecting rod inside diameter code number (1 or 2) on the rod and cap (**Figure 86**).

4. Select new bearings by cross-referencing the connecting rod journal outside diameter code letter (**Figure 87** or **Figure 88**) in the vertical column of **Table 2** with the connecting rod inside diameter code number (**Figure 86**) in the horizontal column. Where the two columns intersect, the new bearing insert color is indicated. **Figure 89** and **Table 3** identify the different bearing colors and thicknesses. For *example*, if the connecting rod journal outside diameter code letter is B, and the connecting rod inside diameter code number is 2, the new bearing insert color is green.

5. After installing the new bearing inserts, recheck the bearing clearance as described in this section.

Connecting Rod Weight Selection

The front and rear connecting rods are matched according to weight. A code letter (A, B, C, D, or E) stamped on the side of each connecting rod cap (**Figure 86**) identifies the connecting rod weight.

Replace a connecting rod with the same weight code found on the original rod (**Figure 86**). If the same weight code is unavailable, match different weight codes as follows:

1. Record the connecting rod weight code letter (A, B, C, D, or E) on each rod cap (**Figure 86**).

2. Select a new connecting rod by cross-referencing the connecting rod code letters (**Figure 86**) in the vertical and horizontal columns of **Table 4**. Where the two columns intersect with a YES, a match is made and the rods can be used together.

OUTPUT GEAR ASSEMBLY

Special Tools

The following Honda tools (or equivalent) are required to service the damper spring assembly:

1. Assembly bolt (part No. 07965-1660200); A, **Figure 90**.

2. Assembly collar (part No. 07965-1660300); B, **Figure 90**.

3. Compressor seat (part No. 07967-9690200); C, **Figure 90**.

4. Threaded adapter (part No. 07965-KA30000); D, **Figure 90**.

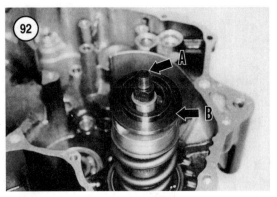

Removal

1. Disassemble the crankcase and remove the output gear, bushing and thrust washer assembly as described under *Crankcase Disassembly* in this chapter.

2. Place the left crankcase on two wooden blocks with the damper spring assembly facing up (**Figure 91**).

3. Thread the threaded adapter (A, **Figure 92**) into the output drive gear shaft.

4. Install the compressor seat, shoulder side facing up, over the output drive gear shaft and seat it against the damper cam (B, **Figure 92**).

5. Install the assembly bolt through the assembly collar, then screw the assembly bolt onto the threaded adapter (**Figure 93**).

> *WARNING*
> *Wear safety goggles during the following steps.*

> *CAUTION*
> *When applying pressure against the damper spring in Step 6, make sure the assembly collar is centered on the damper cam. If not, loosen the tool and reposition the assembly collar.*

6. Hold the assembly bolt and tighten the assembly collar nut (**Figure 94**) to compress the damper spring until the snap ring (**Figure 95**) installed on the output drive gear shaft is visible with enough room to remove it.

7. Using snap ring pliers, remove the snap ring from the output drive shaft groove and slide it up the shaft.

8. Loosen the assembly collar nut (**Figure 94**) to slowly release all of the tension from the damper spring. Then remove the tool assembly.

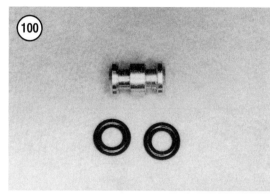

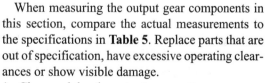

9. Remove the snap ring, damper cam and spring (**Figure 96**). Discard the snap ring as a new one must be installed.

10. Turn the left crankcase over so the output gear assembly faces up.

11. Remove the bolts (**Figure 97**) and the output gear assembly. Locate and remove the dowel pin (**Figure 98**).

12. Remove the oil jet (**Figure 99**) and its two O-rings from the left crankcase.

Inspection

When measuring the output gear components in this section, compare the actual measurements to the specifications in **Table 5**. Replace parts that are out of specification, have excessive operating clearances or show visible damage.

1. Clean and dry the output gear parts.

2. Clean the oil jet with compressed air (**Figure 100**).

3. Inspect the output gear and bushing (**Figure 101**) for excessive wear or damage.

4. Record the following measurements to determine wear and operating clearances:

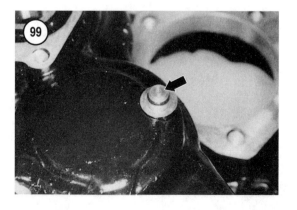

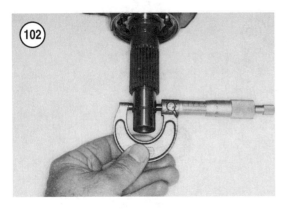

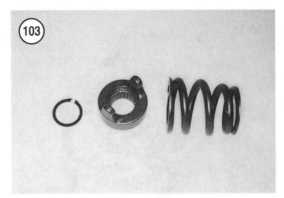

a. Measure the output gear bushing (A, **Figure 101**) outside diameter and inside diameter.

b. Measure the output gear (B, **Figure 101**) inside diameter.

c. Measure the output drive gear shaft outside diameter (**Figure 102**).

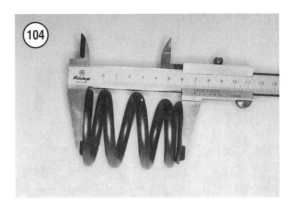

5. Subtract the bushing outside diameter measurement from the gear inside diameter to determine the gear-to-bushing clearance.

6. Subtract the shaft outside diameter from the bushing inside diameter to determine the bushing-to-shaft clearance.

7. Inspect the damper spring (**Figure 103**) for cracks and other damage. Measure the damper spring free length (**Figure 104**).

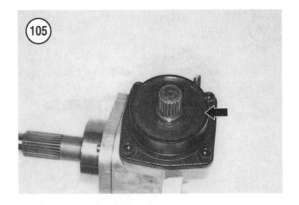

8. Inspect the damper cam ramps (**Figure 103**) for excessive wear or damage.

9. Inspect the oil seal (**Figure 105**) for oil leaks or other damage.

10. If the output drive gear shaft outside diameter is out of specification refer to *Output Gearcase Overhaul* in this chapter.

Installation

1. Lubricate two new O-rings with engine oil and install them onto the oil jet (**Figure 106**).

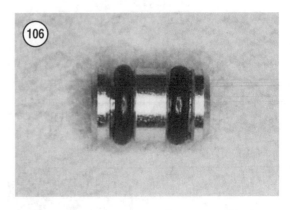

2. Install the oil jet into the crankcase (**Figure 99**) with its chamfered hole facing toward the crankcase. Refer to **Figure 107**.

3. Lubricate a new O-ring with engine oil and install it into the groove in the bearing holder (A, **Figure 108**).

4. Install the dowel pin (B, **Figure 108**) into the bearing holder.

5. Install the output gear assembly (**Figure 97**) onto the left crankcase. Make sure it engages the oil

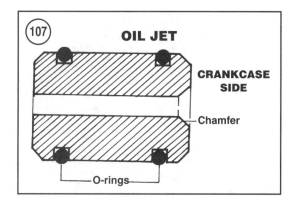

OIL JET

CRANKCASE SIDE

Chamfer

O-rings

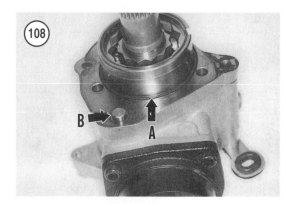

jet. Install and tighten the three bolts (**Figure 97**) hand-tight.

6. Turn the crankcase over so that the drive gear shaft (**Figure 109**) faces up.

7. Install the damper spring over the drive gear shaft with its closely wound spring end (**Figure 110**) facing down (toward left crankcase).

8. Install the damper cam (A, **Figure 111**) onto the damper spring.

9. Install a new snap ring (B, **Figure 111**) over the drive gear shaft.

10. Thread the threaded adapter (A, **Figure 92**) into the output drive gear shaft.

11. Install the compressor seat, shoulder side facing up, over the output drive gear shaft and seat it against the damper cam (B, **Figure 92**).

12. Install the assembly bolt through the assembly collar, then screw the assembly bolt onto the threaded adapter (**Figure 93**).

> *WARNING*
> *Wear safety goggles during the following steps.*

> *CAUTION*
> *When applying pressure against the damper spring in Step 13, make sure the assembly collar is centered on the damper cam. If not, loosen the tool and reposition the assembly collar.*

13. Hold the assembly bolt, then tighten the assembly collar nut (**Figure 94**) to compress the damper spring. Continue until the snap ring (**Figure 112**) groove on the output drive gear shaft is visible with enough room to install the snap ring.

14. Using snap ring pliers, install the new snap ring into the output drive shaft groove (**Figure 113**).

5

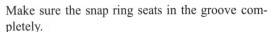

Make sure the snap ring seats in the groove completely.

15. Loosen the assembly collar nut (**Figure 94**) and allow the damper spring to unwind and for the damper cam to seat against the snap ring.

16. When all tension has been removed from the tool assembly, remove the tool assembly from the engine.

17. Tighten the output gearcase mounting bolts (**Figure 114**) to 32 N•m (24 ft.-lb.).

18. Install the output gear assembly and assemble the engine as described in this chapter.

OUTPUT GEARCASE OVERHAUL

This section describes service for the output gearcase components that includes the output drive gear, output driven gear, both bearing holders and bearings. The output drive and driven gears are beveled. The gearcase is lubricated with the same oil used to lubricate the engine. The output drive and driven gear assemblies can be removed and serviced separately. However, the gears are matched pairs and must be replaced as a set.

Service Notes

Before servicing the output gearcase assembly, note the following:

1. Refer to *Transmission* in Chapter Two to troubleshoot the output gearcase assembly. A new or rough sounding noise is usually the first indication of a problem with the gearcase assembly.

2. When checking bearings, they should turn freely and without any sign of roughness, catching or excessive noise. Always replace questionable bearings.

3. Refer to the general bearing removal and installation information found under *Basic Service Meth-*

ods in Chapter One before removing or installing bearings and seals in this section.

4. Use a heat gun or shop oven when necessary to heat the gearcase to replace its bearing. Do not use a torch because this heats the gearcase unevenly and may cause warp. Monitor heat with heat strips available from a welding supply store or use an infrared thermometer. The text lists the temperature required to remove and install the gearcase bearing.

5. The following tools are needed to service the gearcase assembly:
   a. Honda locknut wrench (part No. 07916-MB00002 or 07916-MB00001 or 07916-MB00000).
   b. Honda shaft holder (part No. 07923-6890101 or 07PAB-0010000).
   c. Hydraulic press.

6. Begin service by performing the *Backlash Measurement* procedure in this section.

Backlash Measurement

Backlash is the amount of play or clearance between the output drive and driven gears, measured

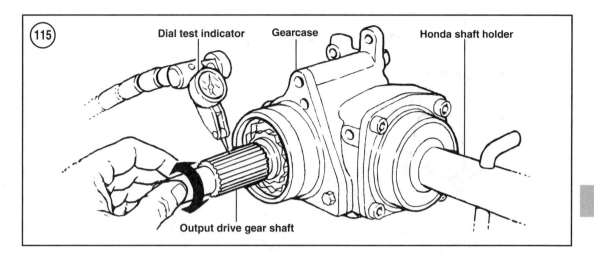

Dial test indicator **Gearcase** **Honda shaft holder**

Output drive gear shaft

in one-tenth of a millimeter. The output drive gear backlash measurement in this section determines gear wear, if the gears are running true or is used to troubleshoot a whining or howling gear noise. Always measure backlash before and after servicing the gearcase assembly.

1. Remove the output gearcase as described in this chapter.

2. Mount the gearcase in a vise with soft jaws.

3. Measure backlash with a dial test indicator mounted on a magnetic stand. Position the indicator so its stem is parallel to the output drive gear shaft and its tip contacts the side of one shaft tooth as shown in **Figure 115**.

4. Mount the Honda shaft holder onto the output driven gear shaft, then rotate the shaft holder to remove all gear slack when measuring backlash (**Figure 115**).

5. Turn the output drive gear shaft back and forth by hand (**Figure 115**). The reading on the dial indicator is the initial output drive gear backlash. Record the reading and perform the following:

   a. Remove the dial test indicator, then rotate the output drive gear shaft and take two additional backlash readings 120° from the original measuring point. If the difference between any two readings exceeds 0.10 mm (0.004 in.), the output drive gear shaft is running out of true. This can be caused by a damaged bearing or the bearing bore in the holder may be deformed. If the backlash measurement is being performed after the gearcase has been reassembled, the output drive gear

bearing (3, **Figure 116**) may have been installed incorrectly in its bore.

   b. If the initial backlash reading is out of specification, but the output drive gear shaft is running true, go to Step 6.

   c. If the backlash reading indicates that the output drive gear shaft is running out of true, remove the output drive gear shaft and inspect the shaft, bearing and bearing holder for damage.

6. To correct backlash, the output drive gear shaft is removed and the proper shim (8, **Figure 116**) installed. Note the following:

   a. Changing shim thickness by 0.10 mm (0.004 in.) changes backlash approximately 0.06-0.07 mm (0.002-0.003 in.).

   b. Refer to **Table 6** for output drive gear shim sizes.

   c. To replace the shim, remove the output drive gear and bearing holder as an assembly as described in this section.

7. After replacing the shim and reassembling the gearcase, perform the *Gear Mesh Pattern Check* in this section.

Output Drive Gear Removal/Installation

This procedure services the output drive gear, bearing, bearing holder and shim (**Figure 116**). Do not remove the bearing unless replacement is required. If the output drive gear is being removed for shim replacement only, do not remove the output drive gear from its bearing.

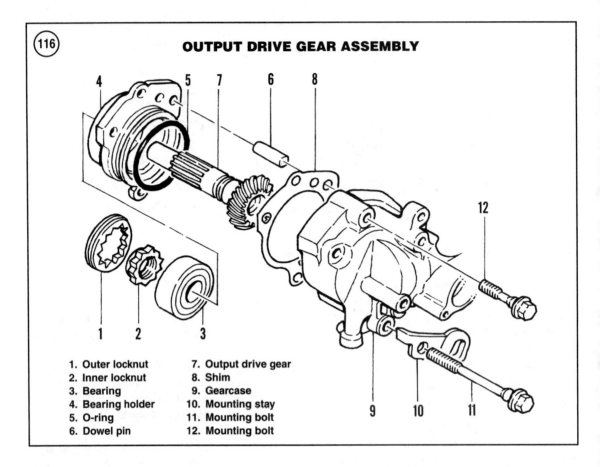

OUTPUT DRIVE GEAR ASSEMBLY

1. Outer locknut
2. Inner locknut
3. Bearing
4. Bearing holder
5. O-ring
6. Dowel pin
7. Output drive gear
8. Shim
9. Gearcase
10. Mounting stay
11. Mounting bolt
12. Mounting bolt

1. Review *Service Notes* in this section.

2. Perform the backlash measurement described in this section.

3. Support the gearcase in a vise with soft jaws.

4. Mount the Honda shaft holder onto the output driven gear shaft, then rotate the shaft holder and wedge its arm against the vise to lock the gears.

5. Use a grinder to unstake the inner locknut (**Figure 117**).

6. Remove the inner locknut (2, **Figure 116**) with the Honda locknut wrench. Discard the locknut.

7. Remove the Honda shaft holder from the output driven gear shaft.

8. Unstake the outer locknut (**Figure 117**).

9. Remove the outer locknut (1, **Figure 116**) with the Honda locknut wrench. Discard the locknut.

10. Remove the two gearcase assembly bolts (11 and 12, **Figure 116**) and the mounting stay (10).

11. Remove the bearing holder/output drive gear assembly from the gearcase.

12. Remove the O-ring (5, **Figure 116**) and dowel pin (6).

13. Remove the shim (8, **Figure 116**).

14. Support the bearing holder in a press. Make sure there is sufficient room for the output drive gear to clear the press as it is being pressed out of the bearing holder. Then press the output drive gear (7, **Figure 116**) out of the bearing holder.

15. Support the bearing holder in a press and press out the bearing (3, **Figure 116**). Discard the bearing.

16. Clean and dry all parts.

17. Inspect the output drive gear for damage. If it is necessary to replace the output drive gear, the output driven gear must be replaced at the same time. Both gears are purchased and installed as a matched set.

18. Inspect the bearing holder bore for any damage.

19. Install the correct size shim (8, **Figure 116**) as follows:

   a. If the unit was disassembled to correct the backlash measurement, install the correct size shim. Refer to *Backlash Measurement* in this section.

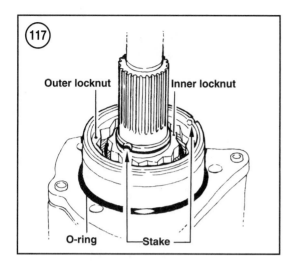

(117)

Outer locknut   Inner locknut

O-ring   Stake

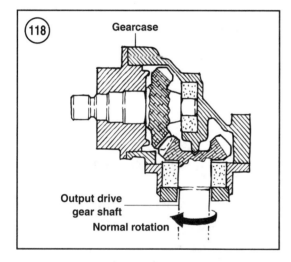

(118)   Gearcase

Output drive
gear shaft
Normal rotation

b. If the output drive gear, bearing, bearing holder or gearcase are being replaced, install a 0.50 mm (0.020 in.) shim (8, **Figure 116**) as a starting point.

20. Press a new bearing into the bearing holder. Make sure the bearing seats squarely in the bearing bore.

21. Support the bearing inner race in a press. Insert a pilot past the gear and into the end of the shaft and press the output drive gear into the bearing. Do not press against the gear. Turn the gear, making sure it turns smoothly.

22. Install the dowel pin.

23. Lubricate a new O-ring with engine oil and install it into the groove in the bearing holder.

24. Wipe the shim clean, then install it against the bearing holder. Align all holes. If installing the original shim, make sure it is in good condition.

25. Align and install the bearing holder into the gearcase. Make sure the dowel pin aligns with the shim.

26. Lubricate the output gearcase mounting bolt threads with engine oil and install them with the mounting stay. Tighten the bolts in a crossing pattern to 32 N•m (24 ft.-lb.).

27. Support the output gearcase in a vise with soft jaws and with the output drive gear shaft facing up.

NOTE
*In Step 28 and Step 30, mount the Honda locknut wrench onto the torque wrench so it forms a right angle as described under **Torque Adaptors** in Chapter One. Because this alignment does not change the effective length of the torque wrench, it is unnecessary to recalibrate the torque reading. However, if the Honda locknut wrench must be mounted so it increases the effective length of the torque wrench, recalculate the torque reading as described in Chapter One.*

28. Lubricate the threads on a new outer locknut (1, **Figure 116**) with engine oil and tighten to 100 N•m (74 ft.-lb.) with the Honda locknut wrench.

29. Mount the Honda shaft holder onto the output driven gear shaft, then rotate the shaft holder and wedge its arm against the vise to lock the shafts.

30. Lubricate the threads on a new inner locknut (2, **Figure 116**) with engine oil and tighten to 75 N•m (55 ft.-lb.).

31. Perform the *Backlash Check* described in this section.

32. Once the backlash is correctly set, stake the inner and outer locknuts as shown in **Figure 117**.

Gear Mesh Pattern Check

1. Remove the output drive gear as described in this section.

2. Clean and dry the output and driven gear teeth.

3. Apply a gear marking compound to the output driven gear teeth. Allow the compound to dry.

4. Reinstall the output drive gear and its adjustment shim as described in this section.

5. Turn the output drive gear in its normal operating direction (**Figure 118**) so a pattern is evident on the gear teeth.

5

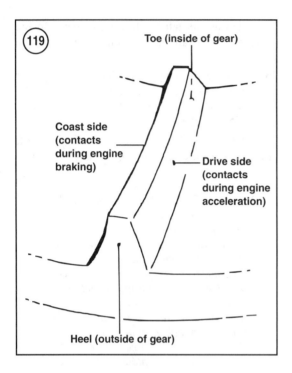

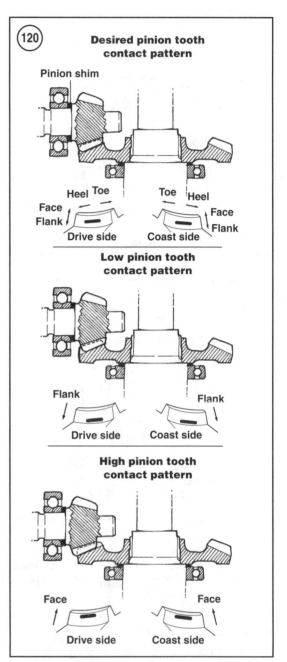

6. Remove the output drive gear as described in this section.

7. Examine the wear pattern on the gear teeth as follows:

    a. Refer to **Figure 119** to identify the parts of the gear teeth.

    b. The desired gear tooth wear pattern in **Figure 120** shows the pattern positioned approximately in the center of each tooth and slightly toward the toe side of the tooth.

    c. If the contact pattern is low (**Figure 120**), install a thicker shim (2, **Figure 121**).

    d. If the contact pattern is high (**Figure 120**), install a thinner shim.

    e. The output driven gear and bearing holder must be removed to replace the shim. Refer to *Output Driven Gear Removal/Installation* in this section.

    f. Changing shim thickness 0.10 mm (0.04 in.) moves the contact pattern approximately 1.5-2.0 mm (0.06-0.08 in.). Refer to **Table 7** for output driven gear shim sizes.

8. Reinstall the output driven gear assembly, if removed, as described in this section. After obtaining a satisfactory gear contact pattern, check the output drive gear backlash as described under *Backlash Measurement* in this section.

Output Driven Gear Removal/Installation

This procedure services the output driven gear, bearing, bearing holder and shim (**Figure 121**). Do not remove the bearing unless replacement is required. If the output driven gear is being removed for shim replacement only, do not remove the output driven gear from its bearing.

1. Review *Service Notes* in this section.

OUTPUT DRIVEN GEAR ASSEMBLY

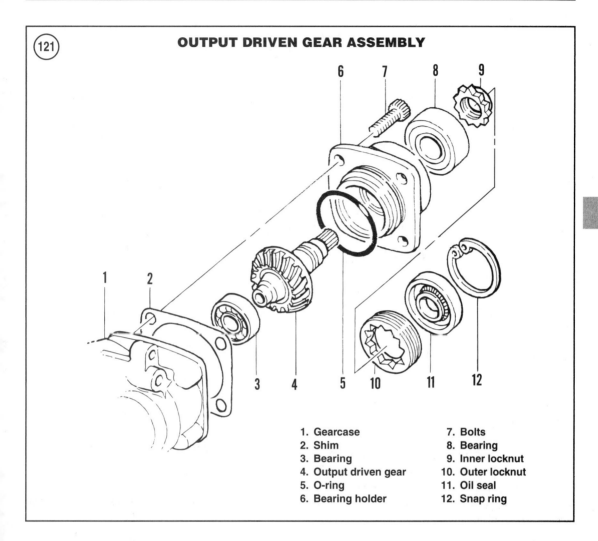

1. Gearcase
2. Shim
3. Bearing
4. Output driven gear
5. O-ring
6. Bearing holder
7. Bolts
8. Bearing
9. Inner locknut
10. Outer locknut
11. Oil seal
12. Snap ring

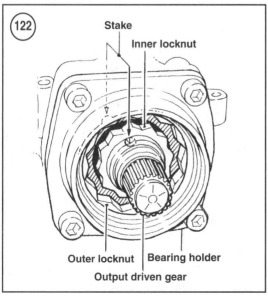

2. Perform the backlash measurement described in this section.

3. Support the gearcase in a vise with soft jaws.

4. Remove the snap ring (12, **Figure 121**).

5. Remove the oil seal from the bearing holder. Discard the seal.

6. Unstake the inner and outer locknuts (**Figure 122**) with a grinder.

7. Mount the Honda shaft holder onto the output driven gear shaft (**Figure 123**).

8. Remove the inner locknut (9, **Figure 121**) with the Honda locknut wrench (**Figure 123**). Discard the locknut.

9. Remove the bearing holder mounting bolts (7, **Figure 121**) and bearing holder (6) from the gearcase.

10. Remove the shim (2, **Figure 121**) and O-ring (5) from the bearing holder.

11. Support the bearing holder in a vise with soft jaws.

12. Remove the outer locknut with the Honda locknut wrench. Discard the locknut.

13. Support the bearing holder in a press and press the output driven gear (4, **Figure 121**) out of the bearing holder.

14. Support the bearing holder in a press and press the bearing (8, **Figure 121**) out of the bearing holder. Discard the bearing.

15. Clean and dry all parts.

16. Inspect the output driven gear for damage. If it is necessary to replace the output driven gear, the output drive gear must be replaced at the same time. Both gears are purchased and installed as a matched set.

17. Inspect the bearing holder bore for damage.

18. Inspect the gearcase bearing (3, **Figure 121**). If necessary, replace the bearing as described in this section.

19. Support the bearing holder and press a new bearing (8, **Figure 121**) into the holder. Make sure the bearing seats squarely in the bearing bore.

20. Install the output driven gear as follows:

    a. Support the bearing (8, **Figure 121**) inner race in a press (**Figure 124**).

    b. Insert a pilot into the end of the output driven gear and press the gear into the bearing. Do not press against the gear (**Figure 124**).

21. Support the bearing holder in a vise with soft jaws with the outside of the holder facing up.

NOTE
*In Step 22 and Step 27, mount the Honda locknut wrench onto the torque wrench so it forms a right angle as described under **Torque Adaptors** in Chapter One. Because the effective length of the torque wrench has not been changed, it is unnecessary to recalibrate the torque reading. However, if the Honda locknut wrench must be mounted so it increases the effective length of the torque wrench, recalculate the torque reading as described in Chapter One.*

22. Lubricate the threads on a new outer locknut (10, **Figure 121**) with engine oil and tighten to 100 N•m (74 ft.-lb.) with the Honda locknut wrench.

23. Lubricate a new O-ring with engine oil and install it into the groove in the bearing holder.

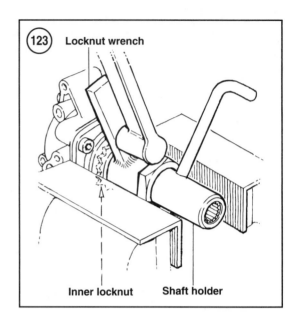

(123) **Locknut wrench**

Inner locknut   **Shaft holder**

24. Install the correct size shim (2, **Figure 121**) as follows:

    a. If the unit was disassembled to correct the gear mesh pattern, install the correct size shim. Refer to *Gear Mesh Pattern Check* in this section.

    b. If the output driven gear, bearing, bearing holder or gearcase are being replaced, install a 0.40 mm (0.016 in.) shim as a starting point.

    c. Wipe the shim clean, then install it against the bearing holder. Align all holes.

25. Align and install the bearing holder into the gearcase.

26. Lubricate the output driven gear bearing holder mounting bolt threads and seating surfaces with engine oil. Tighten the bolts in a crossing pattern to 32 N•m (24 ft.-lb.).

27. Lubricate the threads on a new inner locknut (9, **Figure 121**) with engine oil and install it finger-tight. Mount the Honda shaft holder onto the output driven gear shaft and tighten the inner locknut with the Honda locknut wrench to 75 N•m (55 ft.-lb.).

28. Lubricate the seal lips with grease and install the seal with its flat side facing out. Drive the seal until it is just clear of the snap ring groove in the bearing holder.

29. Install the snap ring into the bearing holder groove with its flat side facing out.

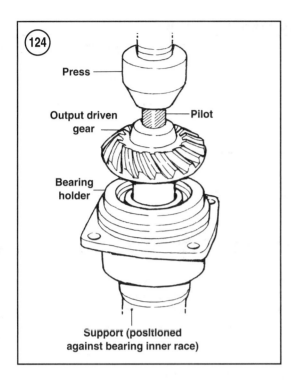

(124)

Press

Output driven gear — Pilot

Bearing holder

Support (positioned against bearing inner race)

Gearcase Bearing Replacement

Perform the following to replace the gearcase bearing (3, **Figure 121**).

1. Remove the output driven gear as described in this section.

2. Heat the housing to 80° C (176° F).

3. Tap the cover with a plastic hammer to remove the bearing. If the bearing does not fall out, remove it with a blind bearing puller.

4. Allow the housing to cool, then clean and dry the housing.

5. Reheat the gearcase and press bearing into gearcase bearing bore.

ENGINE BREAK-IN

5

If the rings were replaced, new pistons installed, the cylinders rebored or honed or major lower end work performed, break in the engine just as though it were new. The performance and service life of the engine depends greatly on a careful and sensible break-in.

Honda specifies the break-in range for the VT1100 engine at 300 miles. During this period, avoid full-throttle starts and hard acceleration.

During engine break-in, oil consumption may be higher than normal. It is therefore important to frequently check and correct the oil level. At no time during the break-in or later should the oil level be allowed to drop below the bottom line on the dipstick; if the oil level is low, the oil overheats and causes insufficient lubrication and increased wear.

Table 1 CRANKSHAFT SPECIFICATIONS

	New mm (in.)	Service limit mm (in.)
Crankshaft runout	–	0.05 (0.002)
Connecting rod bearing oil clearance measurement	0.038-0.062 (0.0015-0.0024)	0.070 (0.0028)
Connecting rod side clearance	0.10-0.25 (0.004-0.010)	0.28 (0.011)
Connecting rod small end inside diameter	22.020-22.041 (0.8669-0.8678)	22.051 (0.8681)
Main bearing journal oil clearance	0.030-0.046 (0.0012-0.0018)	0.060 (0.0024)

Table 2 CONNECTING ROD BEARING SELECTION

Connecton rod outside diameter code letter	Connecting rod inside diameter code number	
	No. 1 51.000-51.008 mm (2.0079-2.0082 in.)	No. 2 51.008-51.016mm (2.0082-2.0085 in.)
A 47.982-47.990 mm (1.8891-1.8894 in.)	Pink	Yellow
B 47.974-47.982 mm (1.8887-1-8891 in.)	Yellow	Green

Table 3 CONNECTING ROD BEARING INSERT THICKNESS

Color	mm	in.
Green	1.495-1.499	0.0589-0.0590
Yellow	1.491-1.495	0.0587-0.0589
Pink	1.487-1.491	0.0585-0.0587

Table 4 CONNECTING ROD WEIGHT SELECTION

Front rod code marking	Rear rod code marking				
	A	B	C	D	E
A	Yes	Yes			
B	Yes	Yes	Yes		
C		Yes	Yes	Yes	
D			Yes	Yes	Yes
E				Yes	Yes

Table 5 OUTPUT DRIVE TRAIN SERVICE SPECIFICATIONS

	New mm (in.)	Service limit mm (in.)
Backlash difference between measurements	–	0.10 (0.004)
Bushing to shaft clearance	0.020-0.062 (0.0008-0.0024)	0.082 (0.0032)
Gear to bushing clearance	0.020-0.062 (0.0008-0.0024)	0.082 (0.0032)
Output drive gear backlash	0.08-0.23 (0.003-0.009)	0.40 (0.016)
Output drive gear shaft outside diameter	21.979-22.000 (0.8653-0.8661)	21.969 (0.8649)
Output gear bushing outside diameter	24.959-24.980 (0.9826-0.9835)	24.949 (0.9822)

(continued)

Table 5 OUTPUT DRIVE TRAIN SERVICE SPECIFICATIONS (continued)

	New mm (in.)	Service limit mm (in.)
Output gear bushing (continued) Inside diameter	22.020-22.041 (0.8669-0.8678)	22.051 (0.8681)
Output gear damper spring free length	69.3 (2.73)	68.1 (2.68)
Output gear inside diameter	25.000-25.021 (0.9843-0.9851)	25.031 (0.9855)

Table 6 OUTPUT DRIVE GEAR SHIM SIZES

Output drive gear shim	Thickness mm (in.)
A	0.40 (0.016)
B	0.45 (0.018)
C (standard shim)	0.50 (0.020)
D	0.55 (0.022)
E	0.60 (0.024)

Table 7 OUTPUT DRIVEN GEAR SHIM SIZES

Output driven gear shim	Thickness mm (in.)
A	0.20 (0.008)
B	0.25 (0.010)
C	0.30 (0.012)
D	0.35 (0.014)
E (standard shim)	0.40 (0.016)
F	0.45 (0.018)
G	0.50 (0.020)
H	0.55 (0.022)
I	0.60 (0.024)

Table 8 ENGINE LOWER END TORQUE SPECIFICATIONS

	N•m	in.-lb.	ft.-lb.
Connecting rod cap nuts[1]	60	–	44
Cylinder head cover shroud bolt	8.8	78	–
Left crankcase bolts			
6 mm	12	106	–
8 mm	27	–	20
Output drive gear bearing holder bolts[1]	32	–	24
Output drive gear bearing locknut[1,2]			
Inner	75	–	55
Outer	100	–	74
(continued)			

Table 8   ENGINE LOWER END TORQUE SPECIFICATIONS (continued)

	N•m	in.-lb.	ft.-lb.
Output drive gear shaft bolt (right crankcase)[3]	50	–	37
Output driven gear bearing holder bolts[1]	32	–	24
Output driven gear bearing locknut[1,2]			
Inner	75	–	55
Outer	100	–	74
Output gearcase mounting bolts	32	–	24
Right crankcase bolts			
6 mm	12	106	–
8 mm	27	–	20
10 mm	40	–	30
Right crankcase bearing set plate[3]			
Screw	9	80	–
Bolt	12	106	–

1. Lubricate threads and seating surface with engine oil.
2. Stake nut after tightening to correct torque specification. See text.
3. Apply medium strength threadlock to fastener threads.

Table 9 ENGINE MOUNT TORQUE SPECIFICATIONS

	N•m	ft.-lb.
Muffler bracket engine attaching bolt	27	20
VT1100C		
Front lower engine mounting nut*	27	20
Front upper engine mounting bolt	26	19
Rear lower engine mounting nut*	64	47
Rear upper engine mounting nut	52	38
Subframe bolts and nuts		
Front*	64	47
Rear	39	29
Left	26	19
All other models		
Front lower engine mounting nut	40	30
Front upper engine mounting bolt	27	20
Rear lower engine mounting nut	55	41
Rear upper engine mounting nut	55	41
Subframe bolts and nuts		
Front*	65	48
Rear	40	30
Left	27	20

*Lubricate threads and seating surfaces with engine oil.

CHAPTER SIX

CLUTCH, PRIMARY DRIVE GEAR, GEARSHIFT LINKAGE AND OIL PUMP

This chapter describes service procedures for the following subassemblies mounted on the right side of the engine:
1. Clutch cable.
2. Clutch cover.
3. Clutch.
4. Right crankcase cover.
5. Primary drive gear.
6. Oil pump chain and sprockets.
7. Gearshift linkage.
8. Oil pump.

This chapter also describes service for the clutch release mechanism installed on the left side of the engine.

Read this chapter before attempting repairs to the clutch and other components in the right crankcase cover. Become familiar with the procedures to understand the skill and equipment required. Refer to Chapter One for tool usage and service methods.

Table 1 lists clutch service specifications. **Tables 1-3** are found at the end of the chapter.

The inspection procedures in this chapter help to detect parts that are excessively worn or damaged. However, inspect the parts during their removal and disassembly, especially when troubleshooting a problem area. Look for loose fasteners, incorrect adjustments, binding, rough turning and abnormal wear marks or patterns. Locating these types of problems can help to prevent future operating problems.

CLUTCH CABLE REPLACEMENT

1. Remove the fuel tank (Chapter Eight).
2. Remove the left crankcase rear cover (Chapter Fifteen).
3. Compare the new and old cables. Make sure the length of the new cable and both cable ends are correct.
4. Lubricate the new clutch cable as described in Chapter Three.
5. Loosen the clutch cable adjuster locknut (A, **Figure 1**) and adjuster (B) at the handlebar.
6. Loosen the clutch cable adjuster nuts (A, **Figure 2**) and disconnect the cable from the release arm (B).
7. Tie a piece of heavy string to the lower end of the old cable. Cut the string to a length longer than the new clutch cable.
8. Tie the lower end of the string to a frame or engine component.

NOTE
It may be necessary to detach cable clamps or guides when replacing the cable.

9. Remove the old clutch cable by pulling it from the top (upper cable end). Continue until the cable is removed from the frame, leaving the attached piece of string in its mounting position.

10. Untie the string from the old cable and discard the old cable.

11. Tie the string onto the bottom end of the new clutch cable.

12. Slowly pull the string and cable to install the cable along the path of the original clutch cable. Continue until the new cable is correctly routed beside the engine and through the frame. Untie and remove the string.

13. Visually check the entire length of the clutch cable. Make sure there are no kinks or sharp bends. Reroute the cable if necessary.

14. Lubricate the clutch hand lever bore and pivot bolt before attaching the cable:

   a. Remove the nut, clutch pivot bolt (C, **Figure 1**) and lever.

   b. Clean and dry the pivot bolt and clutch lever bore. Inspect the operating areas (**Figure 3**) for excessive wear or damage.

   c. Clean the recess in the clutch perch of all old grease.

   d. Lubricate the pivot bolt with grease and reinstall the lever, pivot bolt and nut. Tighten the pivot bolt. Then hold the pivot bolt and tighten the nut. Operate the clutch lever to make sure there is no binding.

15. Connect the upper cable end to the clutch lever (**Figure 1**).

16. Reattach the lower end of the clutch cable as shown in **Figure 2**.

17. Adjust the clutch cable as described in Chapter Three.

18. Install the left crankcase rear cover (Chapter Fifteen).

CLUTCH RELEASE LEVER

The clutch release lever operates in a holder (C, **Figure 2**) mounted on the left crankcase. The assembly consists of the clutch release lever (A, **Figure 4**), washer, return spring (B) and pushrod piece (C). The pushrod piece contacts the clutch pushrod installed through the mainshaft. The clutch cable and clutch lever at the handlebar are part of the system and are covered under *Clutch Cable* in this chapter.

Clutch disengagement is accomplished via the clutch release lever assembly. The clutch cable is attached between the clutch lever at the handlebar and the clutch release lever at the engine. Operating the clutch lever causes the release lever to rotate. This

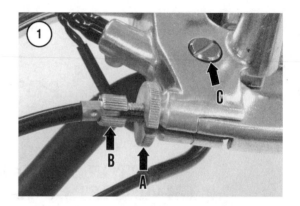

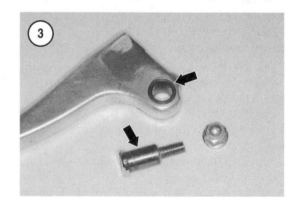
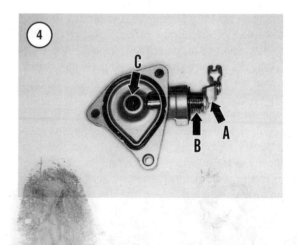

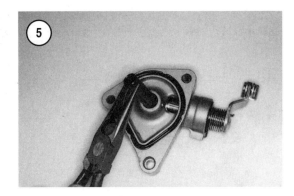

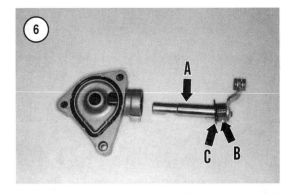

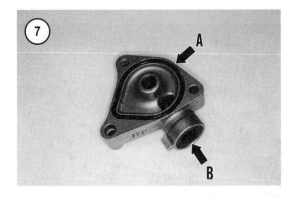

forces the pushrod against the pressure plate, thereby compressing the clutch springs and releasing the clutch plates where they can rotate freely. This system requires routine adjustment (Chapter Three) to compensate for cable stretch and clutch disc wear.

If the clutch lever (at the handlebar) does not return correctly and the clutch cable is okay, the clutch release lever may be damaged.

Removal

1. Remove the left crankcase rear cover (Chapter Fifteen).

2. Loosen the clutch cable adjuster locknuts (A, **Figure 2**) and disconnect the clutch cable from the release arm (B).
3. Remove the bolts and the clutch release holder assembly (C, **Figure 2**). Note the wiring harness clamp and wires mounted on the lower mounting bolt.
4. Remove the dowel pin.

Disassembly/Inspection/Assembly

During inspection, replace any parts that are damaged or worn.
1. Turn the release arm clockwise and remove the pushrod piece (**Figure 5**).
2. Remove the release arm, spring and washer (**Figure 6**).
3. Clean and dry the clutch release arm assembly.
4. Replace the O-ring (A, **Figure 7**) and oil seal (B) if leaking or damaged. Install the oil seal with its flat side facing out.
5. Inspect the washer and spring for damage. Check the spring coils and both spring ends for cracks.
6. Inspect the clutch release lever (A, **Figure 6**) operating areas as follows:
   a. Inspect the needle bearing operating areas for wear and damage.
   b. Inspect the pushrod piece contact area for roughness, wear and damage.
   c. If oil leaked past the seal, inspect the clutch release lever surface where it contacts the seal. Replace the lever if there is any noticeable wear.
7. Inspect the pushrod piece ends for damage. The sides of the pushrod piece must be smooth.
8. Inspect the pushrod piece bore in the holder for excessive wear, cracks or other damage.
9. Inspect the two needle bearings pressed in the release arm holder:
   a. Install the clutch release lever into the holder and turn it back and forth. If the release arm turns roughly or if there is any noticeable binding, one or both bearings are damaged.
   b. The needle bearings installed inside the holder cannot be replaced. If damaged, replace the release arm holder assembly.
10. Lubricate the needle bearings with engine oil.
11. Lubricate the oil seal lips (B, **Figure 7**) with grease.

12. Install the O-ring (A, **Figure 7**) into the holder groove.

13. Install the spring (B, **Figure 6**) and washer (C) onto the release arm.

14. Install the release arm assembly into the release arm holder. Hook the spring arms against the release arm and holder as shown in **Figure 8**.

15. Turn the release arm clockwise and align its notch with the release holder bore. Make sure spring pressure is applied against the release arm. Install the lifter piece (**Figure 5**) with the open side facing out through the bore and into the notch.

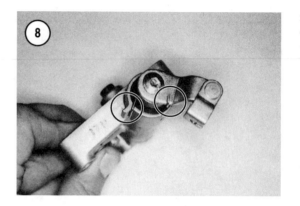

Installation

1. Lubricate the O-ring (A, **Figure 7**) with engine oil.

2. Install the dowel pin into the crankcase hole.

3. Install the release arm holder (C, **Figure 2**) by installing the pushrod piece over the clutch pushrod. Seat the holder over the dowel pin and against the crankcase. Check that the release arm holder seats flush against the crankcase.

4. Install and tighten the release arm holder mounting bolts as follows:

    a. Bolts A and B are longer than bolt C (**Figure 9**).

    b. Apply a medium strength threadlock onto the lower mounting bolt threads, then install the bolt and its clamp (A, **Figure 9**).

    c. Install bolts B and C, **Figure 9**.

    d. Tighten all bolts securely in a crossing pattern.

5. Route the neutral and oil pressure switch wiring harness through the lower mounting bolt clamp (A, **Figure 9**).

6. Reconnect the clutch cable (B, **Figure 2**) onto the release arm.

7. Adjust the clutch (Chapter Three).

8. Install the left crankcase rear cover (Chapter Fifteen).

CLUTCH COVER

The clutch cover is mounted on the right crankcase cover.

Removal/Installation

1. Drain the engine oil (Chapter Three).

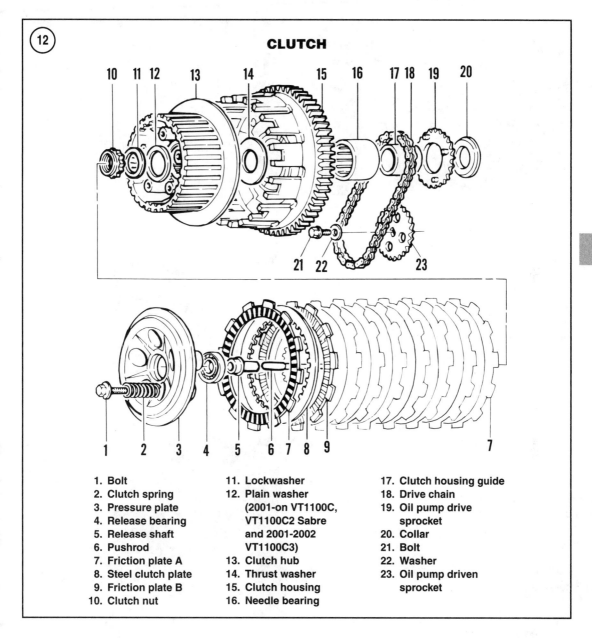

(12)

CLUTCH

1. Bolt
2. Clutch spring
3. Pressure plate
4. Release bearing
5. Release shaft
6. Pushrod
7. Friction plate A
8. Steel clutch plate
9. Friction plate B
10. Clutch nut
11. Lockwasher
12. Plain washer
    (2001-on VT1100C,
    VT1100C2 Sabre
    and 2001-2002
    VT1100C3)
13. Clutch hub
14. Thrust washer
15. Clutch housing
16. Needle bearing
17. Clutch housing guide
18. Drive chain
19. Oil pump drive
    sprocket
20. Collar
21. Bolt
22. Washer
23. Oil pump driven
    sprocket

2. Remove the exhaust system (Chapter Fifteen).

3. Remove the bolts that hold the clutch cover (**Figure 10**) to the right crankcase cover, then remove the clutch cover.

4. Remove the two dowel pins (**Figure 11**) and gasket.

5. Installation is the reverse of removal. Note the following:

a. Install a new clutch cover gasket.

b. Tighten the clutch cover mounting bolts to 12 N•m (106 in.-lb.).

c. Refill the engine with oil (Chapter Three).

d. If the clutch was serviced, check the clutch adjustment (Chapter Three).

e. Start the engine and check the cover for oil leaks.

CLUTCH

The clutch is a multi-plate type that operates immersed in the engine oil supply. The clutch assembly consists of a housing, pressure plate and clutch hub (**Figure 12**). A set of friction and steel clutch plates

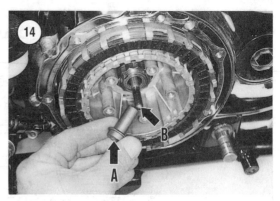

are alternately locked to the two parts. The gear-driven clutch housing is mounted on the transmission mainshaft. The housing receives power from the primary drive gear mounted on the crankshaft. The housing then transfers the power via the friction plates to the steel clutch plates locked to the clutch hub. The clutch hub is splined to the mainshaft and powers the transmission. The clutch plates are engaged by springs and disengaged by a cable-actuated release lever assembly.

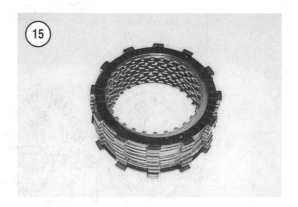

All clutch components, except the clutch housing, can be serviced through the clutch cover opening on the right crankcase cover.

1. Remove the clutch cover as described in this chapter.

2. Loosen the pressure plate bolts (A, **Figure 13**) 1/4 turn at a time in a crossing pattern. Then remove the bolts and springs.

3. Remove the pressure plate (B, **Figure 13**) and its bearing.

4. Remove the release shaft (A, **Figure 14**) and pushrod (B).

> *NOTE*
> *Before removing the clutch plates, note that two different sets of friction plates are used: friction plate A and friction plate B (**Figure 12**). During removal, place a plastic tie around friction plate A to identify them for reassembly.*

5. Remove the clutch plates (**Figure 15**).

6. Using a hand grinder with a small grinding stone, carefully grind the staked portion of the clutch nut (**Figure 16**) to *weaken* it. Do not grind through the nut or the mainshaft will be damaged.

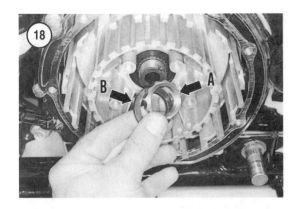

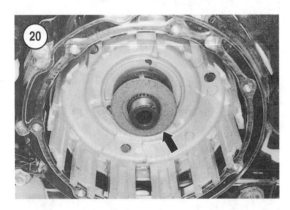

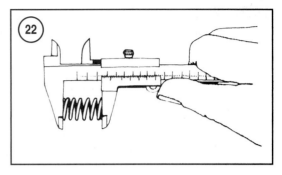

7. Hold the clutch center with a clutch holding tool (**Figure 17**), then loosen and remove the clutch locknut and lockwasher (**Figure 18**).

8. On 2001-on VT1100C, VT1100C2 Sabre and 2001-2002 VT1100C3 models, remove the plain washer (12, **Figure 12**).

9. Remove the clutch hub (**Figure 19**) and thrust washer (**Figure 20**).

NOTE
*Do not pull the clutch housing (**Figure 21**) outward in an attempt to remove it. Doing so causes it to disengage from the oil pump drive sprocket. This requires removal of the right side crankcase cover to properly reinstall the clutch housing.*

10. To remove the clutch housing (**Figure 21**), remove the right side crankcase cover as described in this chapter.

11. Inspect the clutch components as described in this chapter.

Inspection

Always replace steel clutch plates, friction plates or clutch springs as a set if individual components do not meet specifications (**Table 1**). If parts show other signs of wear or damage, replace them, regardless of their specifications. Individual parts that operate together or against each other must be inspected for the same wear and damage. When the damage on one part is more apparent than on the other part, replace both parts to prevent premature wear.

1. Clean and dry all parts.

2. Inspect the clutch springs for cracks and blue discoloration (heat damage).

3. Measure the free length of each clutch spring (**Figure 22**). To maintain even clutch pressure and

maximum performance, replace all springs as a set
if any one is not within the specified tolerance.

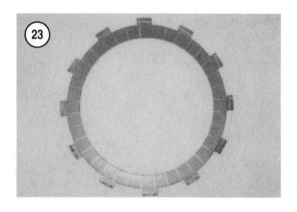

NOTE
A total of nine friction plates are used.
The first and last friction plates (Plate
*A [7, **Figure 12**]) are black and have*
a larger inside diameter than the re-
maining seven friction plates (Plate B
*[9, **Figure 12**]) used in the clutch.*
These seven inside friction plates are
brown. The thicknesses of the A and B
friction plates are the same.

4. Inspect each friction plate (**Figure 23**) as follows:

   a. The friction material on the friction plates is
      bonded to an aluminum plate for warp resis-
      tance and durability. Inspect the friction ma-
      terial for excessive or uneven wear, cracks
      and other damage.
   b. The tabs on the friction plates operate along
      the grooves in the clutch housing. Inspect the
      tabs for rough spots, notches or other damage.
      The tabs must slide smoothly in the clutch
      housing grooves or clutch drag results.
   c. Measure the thickness of each friction plate
      (**Figure 24**) at different locations around the
      plates.

5. Inspect each steel clutch plate (**Figure 25**) as follows:

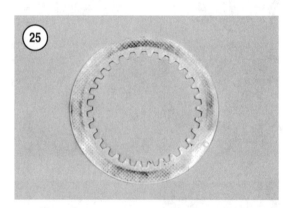

   a. Inspect the steel clutch plates for cracks, dam-
      age or color change. Overheated steel clutch
      plates have a blue discoloration.
   b. Check the steel clutch plates for an oil glaze
      buildup. Remove by lightly sanding both
      sides of each plate with 400-grit sandpaper
      placed on a surface plate or piece of glass.
   c. The steel clutch plate's inner teeth mesh with
      the clutch hub splines. Inspect the teeth for
      rough spots or other damage. The teeth must
      slide smoothly on the splines or clutch drag
      results.
   d. Place each steel clutch plate on a flat surface,
      such as a piece of glass, and check for warp
      with a feeler gauge (**Figure 26**). If any plate is
      warped more than specified, replace the en-
      tire set of steel clutch plates. Do not replace
      only one or two plates because clutch opera-
      tion will be unsatisfactory.

6. Inspect the clutch hub (**Figure 27**) as follows:

   a. Inspect the outer splines (A, **Figure 27**) for
      rough spots, grooves or other damage. Repair
      minor damage with a file or oil stone. If the
      damage is excessive, replace the clutch hub.
      The splines must smooth so the steel clutch
      plates can move smoothly when the clutch is
      released.
   b. Check the plate surface for cracks and other
      damage.

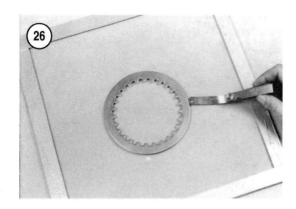

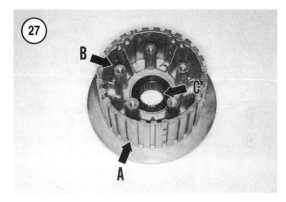

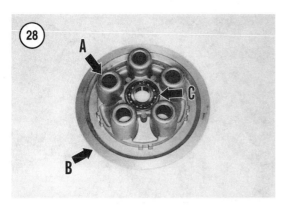

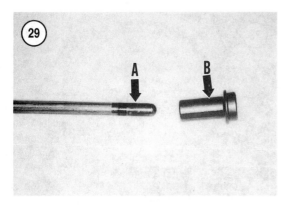

c. Inspect the spring towers (B, **Figure 27**) for damage.

d. Inspect the splines (C, **Figure 27**) for roughness and damage.

7. Check the pressure plate (**Figure 28**) as follows:

a. Inspect for damaged spring towers (A, **Figure 28**).

b. Inspect the plate surface (B, **Figure 28**) for cracks, grooves and other damage.

8. Inspect the pressure plate bearing (C, **Figure 28**) and bearing bore:

a. Turn the bearing inner race and check for any roughness, catching or binding. Replace the bearing if damage is noted.

b. The outer bearing race must fit in the plate bore without any play. If the bearing is loose, replace the bearing and pressure plate.

c. Replace the bearing with a press. Refer to *Bearings* in Chapter One.

9. Inspect the pushrod (A, **Figure 29**) and release shaft (B) for damage.

10. Without removing the clutch housing (**Figure 21**), inspect the clutch housing slots for notches, grooves or other damage. If damage is noted, remove and inspect the clutch housing as described in this chapter.

Assembly

Refer to **Figure 12**.

1A. If removed, install the clutch housing as described in this chapter.

1B. If the clutch housing was not removed, check that it is still engaged with the oil pump drive sprocket.

2. Lubricate the clutch plates with engine oil.

3. Install the thrust washer (**Figure 20**) and clutch hub (**Figure 19**).

4. On 2001-on VT1100C, VT1100C2 Sabre and 2001-2002 VT1100C3 models, install the plain washer (12, **Figure 12**) and seat it against the clutch hub.

5. Install the lockwasher (**Figure 18**) with its OUT mark facing out.

6. Lubricate the threads of a new clutch nut (**Figure 18**) with engine oil and thread it onto the mainshaft.

7. Hold the clutch hub with the same tool used during disassembly and tighten the clutch nut to the torque specification in **Table 3**.

8. Using a punch, stake the clutch locknut into the mainshaft groove (**Figure 16**).

9. Install the clutch plates (**Figure 15**) as follows:

NOTE
*A total of nine friction plates are used. The first and last friction plates (Plate A [7, **Figure 12**]) are black and have a larger inside diameter than the remaining seven friction plates (Plate B [9, **Figure 12**]). These seven inside friction plates are brown. Refer to **Figure 12** for clutch plate alignment.*

a. Install the first friction plate A.

b. Install the clutch plates and the seven inner friction plates (plate B), alternating between steel and friction plates (**Figure 12**).

c. Install the outer friction plate A by aligning its plate tabs with the grooves in the clutch housing (**Figure 30**). This is the only plate with its tabs aligned this way.

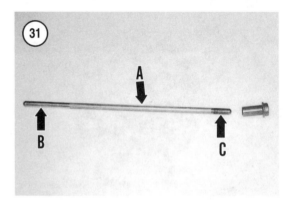

10. The pushrod (A, **Figure 31**) has one long (B) and one short (C) end. Install the pushrod with its short end (C, **Figure 31**) facing out of the engine. Refer to A, **Figure 32**.

11. Lubricate the release shaft with engine oil and install it over the pushrod. Refer to B, **Figure 32**.

12. Install the pressure plate (A, **Figure 33**) and its bearing. Make sure the release shaft seats in the pressure plate bearing as shown in B, **Figure 33**.

13. Install the clutch springs and bolts (**Figure 34**). Tighten the bolts in a crossing pattern in 2-3 steps to 12 N•m (106 in.-lb.).

14. Install the clutch cover as described in this chapter.

15. Check and adjust the clutch (Chapter Three).

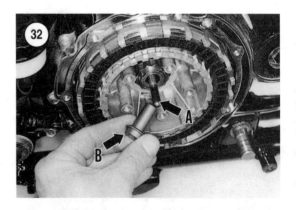

RIGHT CRANKCASE COVER

Removal/Installation

1. Drain the engine oil (Chapter Three).

2. Remove the exhaust system (Chapter Fifteen).

3. Remove the subframe (Chapter Five).

4. Remove the clutch cover as described in this chapter.

5. Before removing the right crankcase cover mounting bolts, draw an outline of the cover on a piece of cardboard (**Figure 35**). Then punch holes along the outline for the placement of each mounting bolt.

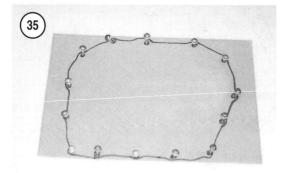

NOTE
*Two of the right crankcase cover mounting bolts (B, **Figure 36**) have a sealer applied to their threads and turn with more resistance during their removal.*

6. Remove the right crankcase cover mounting bolts and place them in the corresponding holes in the cardboard (**Figure 35**).

7. Remove the right crankcase cover (A, **Figure 36**).

8. Remove the two dowel pins (A, **Figure 37**) and gasket.

9. Remove all gasket residue from the crankcase and crankcase mating surfaces.

10. Clean the two bolts and the corresponding threaded holes in the crankcase of all sealer residue.

11. Installation is the reverse of removal. Note the following:

   a. Install a new gasket.

   b. Apply a sealer to the threads of the two bolts identified in B, **Figure 36**. Do not use a sealer on the other mounting bolt threads.

   c. Install the right crankcase cover (**Figure 36**) and secure it with its mounting bolts. Install and tighten the mounting bolts securely.

   d. Refill the engine with oil (Chapter Three).

   e. Start the engine and check for oil leaks.

CLUTCH HOUSING

Refer to **Figure 38**.

Removal

1. Remove the clutch as described in this chapter.

2. Remove the right crankcase cover as described in this chapter.

3. Install, but do not tighten, a 6 × 20 mm Allen bolt into the primary drive gear as shown in **Figure 39**.

4. Insert a wide-blade screwdriver (A, **Figure 40**) between the clutch housing and primary drive gear teeth, then pry the subgear to align it with the primary drive gear. Tighten the Allen bolt (B, **Figure 40**) to hold the subgear in alignment.

5. Turn the primary drive gear to move all of the ignition pulse generator rotor tips (A, **Figure 41**) away from the clutch housing gear teeth (B).

6. Remove the clutch housing (**Figure 42**).

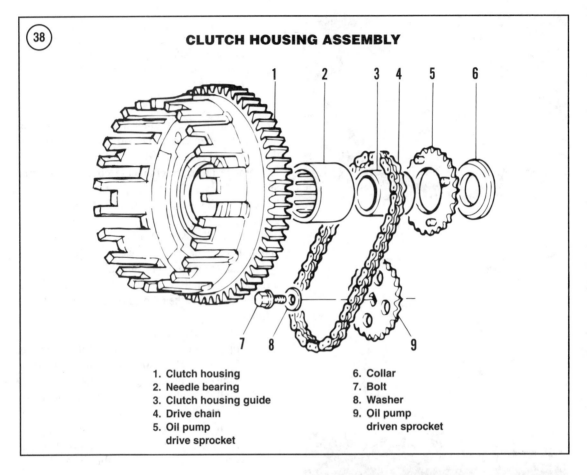

CLUTCH HOUSING ASSEMBLY

1. Clutch housing
2. Needle bearing
3. Clutch housing guide
4. Drive chain
5. Oil pump
   drive sprocket
6. Collar
7. Bolt
8. Washer
9. Oil pump
   driven sprocket

7. Remove the needle bearing (**Figure 43**) and the clutch housing guide (**Figure 44**).

Inspection

1. Clean and dry all parts.
2. Check the clutch housing (**Figure 45**) as follows:

    a. Check the primary driven gear (A, **Figure 45**) for excessive wear, pitting, chipped gear teeth or other damage.

    b. Hold the clutch housing and turn the primary driven gear (A, **Figure 45**). Replace the clutch housing if there is any free play.

    c. Check the clutch housing bore (B, **Figure 45**) for cracks, deep scoring, excessive wear or heat discoloration.

    d. Inspect the clutch housing slots (C, **Figure 45**) for notches, grooves or other damage. Repair minor damage with a file. If damage is excessive, replace the clutch housing. The

slots must be smooth so the friction plates can move without interference when the clutch is released.

> *NOTE*
> *Filing the clutch housing slots is only a temporary fix because removing metal from the sides of the slots provides more room for the plates to*

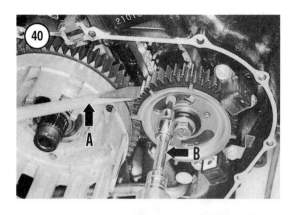

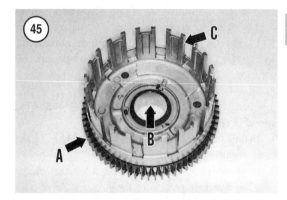

move around and start wearing new grooves.

   e. Inspect the pin holes (**Figure 46**) in which the oil pump drive sprocket pins operate. Replace the clutch housing if these holes are cracked, enlarged or damaged. Check the oil pump drive gear pins for damage.

3. Check the needle bearing (A, **Figure 47**) for damage.

4. Check the clutch housing guide (B, **Figure 47**) for excessive wear, cracks or other damage. Then

measure the clutch housing guide inside diameter and replace if out of specification (**Table 1**).

5. Measure the mainshaft outside diameter (**Figure 48**) and replace if out of specification (**Table 1**).

> *NOTE*
> *The engine has to be disassembled to replace the mainshaft. Refer to Chapter Five and Chapter Seven.*

Installation

The molybdenum oil solution called out in this section is a 50:50 mixture of engine oil and molybdenum disulfide grease.

1. Lubricate the clutch housing guide outside diameter (B, **Figure 47**) with a molybdenum oil solution.

2. Install the clutch housing guide over the mainshaft and slide it through the oil pump drive sprocket (**Figure 44**).

3. Install the needle bearing (**Figure 43**) over the clutch housing guide.

4. If the crankshaft was turned after the clutch housing was removed, turn the primary drive gear to move all of the ignition pulse generator rotor tips away from the clutch housing. Refer to *Removal* in this section.

5. Lubricate the clutch housing bore (B, **Figure 45**) with a molybdenum oil solution.

6. Align the four holes in the clutch housing (**Figure 46**) with the four pins on the oil pump drive sprocket (**Figure 49**) and install the clutch housing. Refer to **Figure 42**.

7. Check that the clutch housing gear teeth are flush with the subgear as shown in **Figure 50**. If not, remove the clutch housing and reinstall it.

8. Remove the Allen bolt (**Figure 39**) installed in the primary drive gear. This releases the subgear and allows it to turn and apply pressure against the clutch housing gear teeth.

9. Install the right crankcase cover as described in this chapter.

10. Install the clutch as described in this chapter.

OIL PUMP CHAIN AND SPROCKETS

Refer to **Figure 38**.

Removal

1. Remove the clutch as described in this chapter.

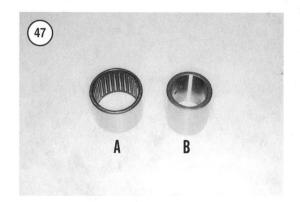

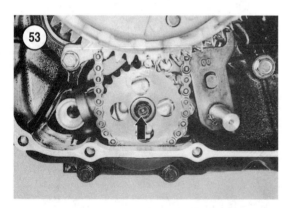

2. Remove the right crankcase cover as described in this chapter.

NOTE
Do not remove the clutch housing until after the oil pump driven sprocket mounting bolt is loosened.

3. Remove the oil pipe (**Figure 51**) and both O-rings. Discard the O-rings.

4. Lock the clutch and primary drive gears with a separate gear (**Figure 52**).

5. Loosen the bolt (**Figure 53**) securing the oil pump driven sprocket to the oil pump.

6. Remove the clutch housing as described in this chapter.

7. Remove the bolt and washer (**Figure 53**) loosened in Step 5.

8. Remove the oil pump sprockets and chain (**Figure 54**) as a set.

9. Remove the collar (**Figure 55**) from the mainshaft.

Inspection

Replace excessively worn or damaged parts as described in this section.

1. Clean and dry all parts. Remove all threadlock residue from the oil pump driven sprocket mounting bolt threads.

2. Flush the oil pipe with solvent and dry with compressed air. Make sure there is no solvent remaining inside the pipe.

3. Inspect the sprockets (**Figure 56**) for chipped or missing teeth.

4. Inspect the bore in the center of the driven sprocket (A, **Figure 56**) for elongation, cracks or other damage.

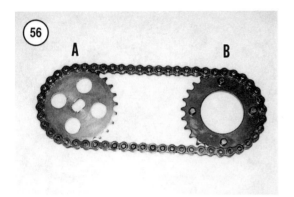

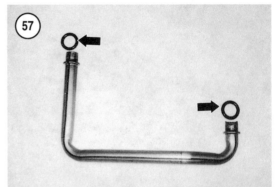

5. Inspect the pins on the driven sprocket (B, **Figure 56**) for damage.

6. Inspect the drive chain for damaged pins and other visible wear.

NOTE
If wear or damaged is indicated to one part, replace both sprockets and the chain as a set.

7. Inspect the distance collar for damage.

Installation

1. Install the distance collar with the shoulder side facing out over the mainshaft. Refer to **Figure 55**.

2. Mesh the oil pump drive and driven sprockets with the drive chain (**Figure 56**), then install the drive sprocket over the mainshaft with its pins facing out (**Figure 54**).

3. Install the drive sprocket against the distance collar and align the flat surfaces of the driven sprocket hole with the oil pump shaft.

4. Install a medium strength threadlock onto the oil pump sprocket bolt, then install the bolt and washer (**Figure 53**) and tighten finger-tight at this time.

5. Install the clutch housing as described in this chapter.

6. Lock the clutch and primary drive gears with a separate gear (**Figure 52**).

7. Tighten the oil pump sprocket bolt (**Figure 53**) securely. Remove the holding gear.

8. Coat two new O-rings (**Figure 57**) with engine oil and install them onto the oil pipe.

9. Install the oil pipe (**Figure 51**) into the crankcase oil ports.

10. Install the right crankcase cover as described in this chapter.

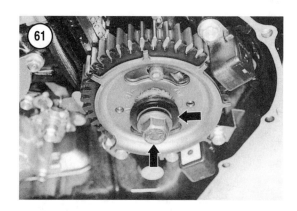

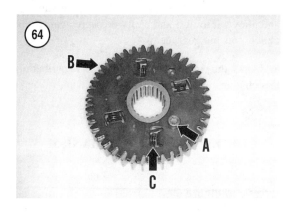

11. Install the clutch as described in this chapter.

PRIMARY DRIVE GEAR

The primary drive gear is mounted on the crankshaft and positioned behind the ignition pulse generator rotor. The primary drive gear assembly is an antibacklash type consisting of a fixed primary drive gear (inner gear) and a spring-loaded subgear (outer gear).

Removal

1. Remove the right crankcase cover as described in this chapter.
2. Install, but do not tighten, a 6 × 20 mm Allen bolt into the primary drive gear as shown in **Figure 58**.
3. Insert a wide-blade screwdriver (A, **Figure 59**) between the clutch housing and primary drive gear teeth, then pry the subgear to align it with the primary drive gear. Tighten the Allen bolt (B, **Figure 59**) to hold the subgear in alignment.
4. To prevent crankshaft rotation when loosening the primary drive gear bolt, lock the clutch and primary gears together with a separate gear (**Figure 52**).
5. Loosen the primary drive gear bolt (**Figure 60**).
6. Remove the primary drive gear bolt and washer (**Figure 61**).
7. Remove the ignition pulse generator rotor (**Figure 62**).
8. Remove the primary drive gear assembly (**Figure 63**).
9. Remove the Allen bolt (A, **Figure 64**) and remove the subgear (A, **Figure 65**) from the primary drive gear (B, **Figure 65**). Note the springs (C, **Figure 65**) installed in the primary drive gear.

Inspection

1. Clean and dry all parts.
2. Inspect the subgear (A, **Figure 65**) for:
   a. Missing, broken or chipped teeth.
   b. Damaged arms.
3. Inspect the primary drive gear (B, **Figure 65**) for:
   a. Missing, broken or chipped teeth.
   b. Worn or damaged splines.
   c. Weak, damaged or missing springs (C, **Figure 65**).

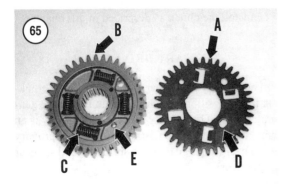

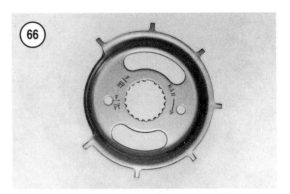

4. Inspect the ignition pulse generator rotor (**Figure 66**) for:
   a. Damaged splines.
   b. Damaged rotor tips.
5. Replace excessively worn or damaged parts.

Installation

1. Assemble the subgear and primary drive gear assembly:
   a. Install the springs into the primary drive gear grooves (C, **Figure 65**).
   b. Align the oblong hole in the subgear (D, **Figure 65**) with the threaded hole in the primary drive gear (E, **Figure 65**) and install the subgear (B, **Figure 64**) into the primary drive gear. Check that the tabs on the subgear fit in front of each spring as shown in C, **Figure 64**.
   c. Pry the gear teeth with a wide-blade screwdriver to align them, then install and tighten the Allen bolt (A, **Figure 64**).
2. Install the primary drive gear (**Figure 63**) by aligning the wide gear groove with the wide crankshaft tooth (**Figure 67**).
3. Install the ignition pulse generator rotor (**Figure 66**) by aligning the wide gear groove with the wide crankshaft tooth (**Figure 68**).
4. Lubricate the primary drive gear bolt threads with engine oil.
5. Install the primary drive gear bolt and washer (**Figure 61**) and tighten hand-tight. Check that the clutch housing gear teeth are flush with the subgear as shown in **Figure 50**.
6. Use the same tool to hold the clutch and primary drive gears and tighten the primary drive gear bolt (**Figure 60**) to the torque specification in **Table 3**. Remove the holding tool.

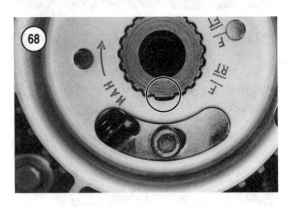

7. Remove the Allen bolt (**Figure 58**) installed in the primary drive gear. This releases the subgear and allows it to turn and apply pressure against the clutch housing gear teeth.

8. Install the right crankcase cover as described in this chapter.

EXTERNAL SHIFT MECHANISM

Refer to **Figure 69**.

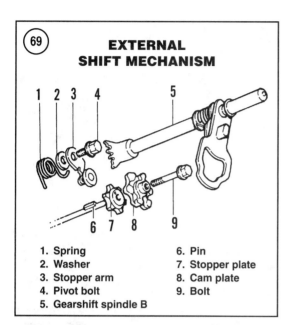

EXTERNAL SHIFT MECHANISM

1. Spring
2. Washer
3. Stopper arm
4. Pivot bolt
5. Gearshift spindle B
6. Pin
7. Stopper plate
8. Cam plate
9. Bolt

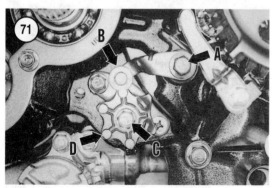

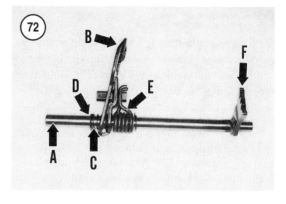

Removal

1. Shift the transmission into neutral.

2. Remove the following components as described in this chapter.

   a. Right crankcase housing.

   b. Clutch.

   c. Oil pump chain and sprockets.

3. Remove gearshift spindle B (**Figure 70**) from the crankcase.

4. Remove the pivot bolt (A, **Figure 71**) washer, return spring and the stopper arm (B).

5. Remove the bolt (C, **Figure 71**), cam plate (D), stopper plate and dowel pin.

6. To remove gearshift spindle A installed on the left side of the engine, refer to *Flywheel, Starter Clutch, Starter Reduction Gears and Gearshift Spindle A* in Chapter Nine.

Inspection

1. Clean and dry all parts.

2. Inspect gearshift spindle B for:

   a. Bent shaft (A, **Figure 72**).

   b. Damaged gearshift plate (B, **Figure 72**) and spring (C). The gearshift plate and spring can be replaced separately. Make sure the snap ring (D, **Figure 72**) seats in the groove completely.

   c. Damaged return spring (E, **Figure 72**). Make sure the return spring arms are centered around the extended arm on the gearshift spindle. The return spring is not available separately. If damaged, do not attempt to remove it. Replace gearshift spindle B as an assembly.

   d. Damaged engagement teeth (F, **Figure 72**). If excessive wear or damaged is noted, check gearshift spindle A for the same conditions.

3. Inspect the shift drum stopper arm assembly for excessive wear and damage.

4. Inspect the cam plate and stopper plate detents for excessive wear and damage.

Installation

1. Assemble the spring, washer, stopper arm and pivot bolt as shown in **Figure 69**, then install the assembly into the crankcase (**Figure 73**). Tighten the stopper arm pivot bolt to 10 N•m (88 in.-lb.).

> *NOTE*
> *After tightening the pivot bolt, move the stopper arm with a screwdriver (A, **Figure 74**). If the stopper arm does not move, it is not centered correctly on the pivot bolt.*

2. Install the dowel pin (B, **Figure 74**) into the shift drum hole.
3. Align the hole in the stopper plate with the dowel pin and install the stopper plate (**Figure 75**).
4. Align the hole in the cam plate with the dowel pin and install the cam plate (**Figure 76**).
5. Apply a medium strength threadlock onto the cam plate mounting bolt threads, then install and tighten the bolt (C, **Figure 71**) securely.
6. Shift the transmission into neutral as shown in A, **Figure 77**.

> *NOTE*
> *The cam plate's raised ramp surface (A, **Figure 77**) is its neutral position.*

7. Install gearshift spindle B (A, **Figure 78**) by performing the following steps at the same time:
    a. Mesh gearshift spindle B with gearshift spindle A (**Figure 79**).
    b. Center the return spring (B, **Figure 78**) around the crankcase lug (B, **Figure 77**).

> *NOTE*
> *Figure 70 shows gearshift spindle A properly installed. Refer to **Flywheel, Starter Clutch, Starter Reductions Gears and Gearshift Spindle A** in Chapter Nine for additional information on meshing gearshift spindle A and gearshift spindle B. **Figure 80** shows how the gear teeth must mesh.*

8. Fabricate a plate to prevent the spindle from backing out of the crankcase when shifting the transmission by hand. Bolt the plate to the crankcase so it rests against the exposed end of the gearshift spindle A (**Figure 70**). If the engine is out of the frame, turn the mainshaft by hand and shift the transmission with the shift pedal. If the engine is in

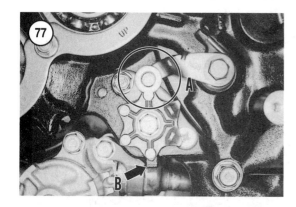

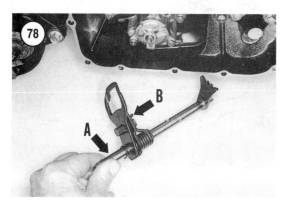

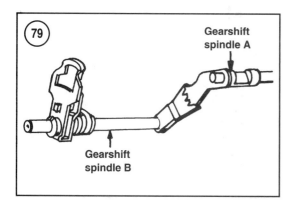

Gearshift
spindle A

Gearshift
spindle B

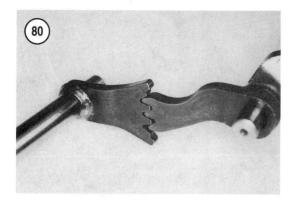

the frame and connected to the driveshaft and rear wheel, turn the rear wheel and shift the transmission with the shift pedal. The transmission should shift in and out of each gear and neutral correctly. If not, recheck the installation of gearshift spindle A. When the shifting is correct, remove the plate from the crankcase.

9. Install the following components as described in this chapter.

    a. Oil pump chain and sprockets.

    b. Clutch center.

    c. Right crankcase housing.

OIL PUMP

The oil pump (**Figure 81**) can be serviced with the engine mounted in the frame.

Removal

1. Remove the external shift mechanism as described in this chapter.

2. Remove the oil pump and relief pipe mounting bolts (A, **Figure 82**). Remove the relief pipe (B, **Figure 82**) from the oil pump.

3. Remove the oil pump (**Figure 83**) from the crankcase.

4. Remove the relief pipe (**Figure 84**).

5. Remove the large dowel pin and O-ring (A, **Figure 85**).

6. Remove the small dowel pin (B, **Figure 85**).

7. Turn the oil pump shaft by hand. The shaft should turn without any binding or roughness. If the shaft does not turn properly, disassemble and inspect the oil pump as described in this section.

8. If the oil pump is not going to be serviced, store in a plastic bag until installation.

Disassembly

1. Pull the relief valve (**Figure 86**) out of the oil pump.

2. Remove the oil strainer and seal (**Figure 87**) from the oil pump body. Discard the seal.

3. Remove the bolts (**Figure 88**) and disassemble the oil pump assembly. Refer to **Figure 89**.

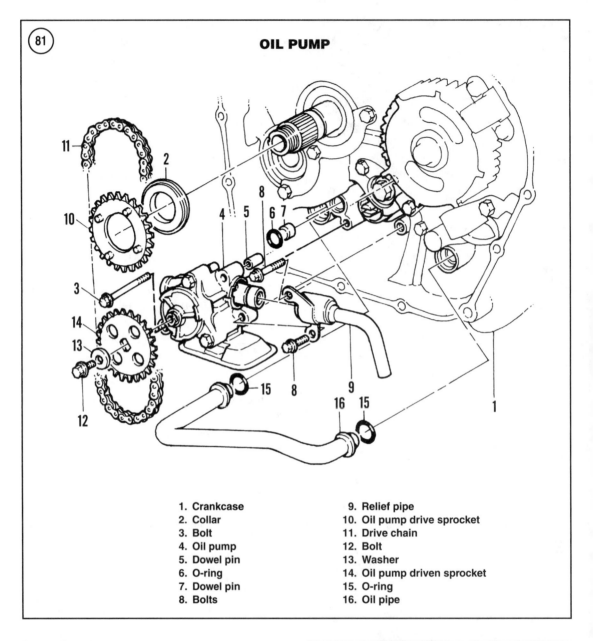

81 **OIL PUMP**

1. Crankcase	9. Relief pipe
2. Collar	10. Oil pump drive sprocket
3. Bolt	11. Drive chain
4. Oil pump	12. Bolt
5. Dowel pin	13. Washer
6. O-ring	14. Oil pump driven sprocket
7. Dowel pin	15. O-ring
8. Bolts	16. Oil pipe

Inspection

Measure the oil pump components and compare the measurements to the specifications in **Table 2**. If any measurement is out of specification or if any component shows visual damage, replace the oil pump assembly.

1. Clean and dry all parts.

2. Inspect the outer cover and body for cracks.

3. Check the inner and outer rotors and the body (**Figure 90**) for deep scratches and excessive wear.

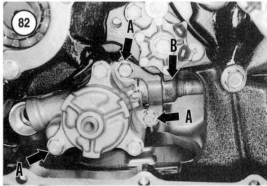

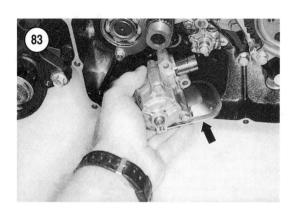

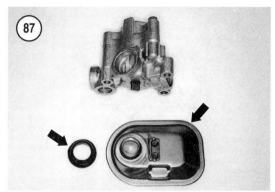

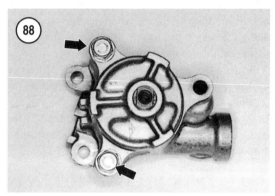

6

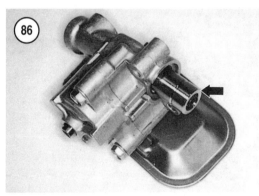

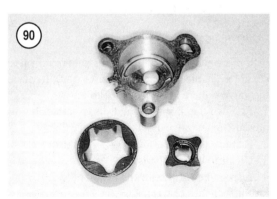

4. Inspect the strainer screen (**Figure 91**) for broken areas. Inspect the metal frame for separation along the seams and against the screen. Replace if damaged. Do not repair the strainer screen.

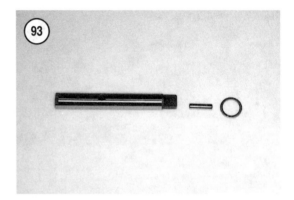

5. Inspect the relief pipe (**Figure 92**) for loose or broken joints. Check the mounting bracket for looseness.

6. Inspect the shaft, pin and shim (**Figure 93**) for cracks or other damage. The shaft surface must be smooth.

7. Install outer rotor into the pump body with its punch mark facing out (A, **Figure 94**).

8. Install the inner rotor into the pump body with its pin groove facing out (B, **Figure 94**).

9. Measure the rotor end clearance with a straightedge and flat feeler gauge (**Figure 95**).

10. Install the pin into the shaft and install the shaft and pin into the inner rotor (**Figure 96**).

11. Measure the tip clearance between the inner tip and outer rotor with a flat feeler gauge (**Figure 96**).

12. Measure the body clearance between the outer rotor and body with a flat feeler gauge (**Figure 97**).

13. Inspect the oil pressure relief valve as described in this section.

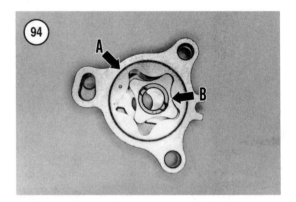

Oil Pressure Relief Valve

Inspection

Replacement parts for the oil pressure relief valve are not available (except the outer O-ring). Replace the valve is there is any questionable part.

1. Remove the snap ring and disassemble the oil pressure relief valve assembly (**Figure 98**).

2. Remove and discard the O-ring (**Figure 99**).

3. Clean and dry all parts.

4. Inspect the valve bore and piston outside diameter for scratches or wear.

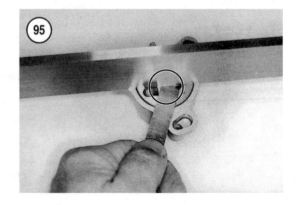

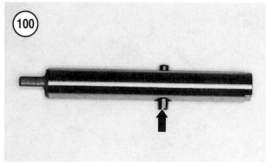

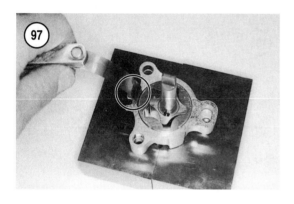

6

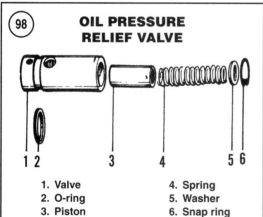

OIL PRESSURE RELIEF VALVE

1 2   3   4   5 6

1. Valve
2. O-ring
3. Piston
4. Spring
5. Washer
6. Snap ring

5. Inspect the spring for cracks, distortion or other damage. The spring coils must appear uniform in shape.

6. Make sure the holes in the valve body are not clogged.

7. Install the piston, spring, washer and snap ring. Make sure the snap ring seats in the groove completely.

8. Install a new O-ring (**Figure 99**) into the valve body groove.

Assembly

1. Lubricate the rotors, shaft and shim with engine oil, then place the parts on a clean, lint-free cloth until reassembly.

2. Install the outer rotor into the pump body with its dot mark facing out (A, **Figure 94**).

3. Install the inner rotor into the pump body with its pin groove facing out (B, **Figure 94**).

4. Install the pin into the shaft (**Figure 100**), then install the shaft and pin into the inner rotor (**Figure 101**).

5. Install the shim (**Figure 102**) over the shaft and seat it against the inner rotor.

6. Install the two dowel pins into the body (**Figure 103**).

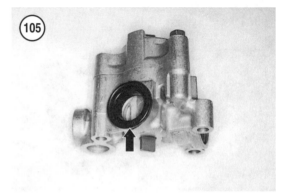

7. Lubricate the shaft with engine oil.

8. Install the pump body onto the cover (**Figure 104**).

9. Install and tighten the oil pump body bolts (**Figure 88**) to 13 N•m (115 in.-lb.).

10. Turn the shaft to make sure the oil pump turns freely. Disassemble and inspect the oil pump if there is any binding or roughness.

11. Lubricate a new seal with engine oil and install it into the groove in the oil pump (**Figure 105**).

12. Install the oil strainer through the seal and seat against the oil pump (A, **Figure 106**).

13. Install the oil pressure relief valve with the O-ring end first into the oil pump (**Figure 86**).

14. Install the oil pump as described in this chapter.

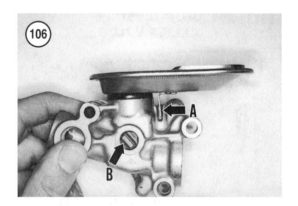

Installation

Refer to **Figure 81**.

1. Lubricate a new O-ring with engine oil and install it and its dowel pin (A, **Figure 107**) into the crankcase.

2. Install the small dowel pin (B, **Figure 107**).

3. Install the relief pipe (**Figure 108**) into the crankcase.

4. Align the oil pump shaft (B, **Figure 106**) with the notch in the end of the water pump shaft (C, **Figure 107**) and install the oil pump into the crankcase.

5. Connect the relief pipe (A, **Figure 109**) over the oil pressure relief valve.

6. Check that the oil screen is positioned against the raised crankcase boss as shown in **Figure 110**.

7. Install the oil pump mounting bolts (B, **Figure 109**) and tighten to 12 N•m (106 in.-lb.).

8. Install the external shift mechanism as described in this chapter.

Table 1 CLUTCH SERVICE SPECIFICATIONS

	New mm (in.)	Service limit mm (in.)
Clutch spring free length	44.0 (1.73)	42.5 (1.67)
Clutch friction plate thickness	3.72-3.88 (0.146-0.153)	3.1 (0.12)
Clutch housing guide inside diameter	27.955-28.012 (1.1022-1.1028)	28.08 (1.106)
Clutch plate (steel) warp limit	–	0.30 (0.012)
Mainshaft outside diameter (at clutch housing guide position)	27.980-27.993 (1.1016-1.1021)	27.93 (1.100)

Table 2 OIL PUMP SERVICE SPECIFICATIONS

	New mm (in.)	Service limit mm (in.)
Body clearance	0.15-0.22 (0.006-0.009)	0.35 (0.014)
Rotor end clearance	0.02-0.07 (0.001-0.003)	0.10 (0.004)
Tip clearance	0.15 (0.006)	0.20 (0.008)

Table 3 CLUTCH TORQUE SPECIFICATIONS

	N•m	in.-lb.	ft.-lb.
Clutch cover mounting bolts	12	106	–
Clutch lifter arm holder bolt			
VT1100C2 Sabre	12	106	–
All other models[3]	–		
Clutch spring bolts	12	106	–
Clutch nut[1,2]			
VT1100C			
1997-2000	98	–	72
2001-on	127	–	94
VT1100C2			
ACE	100	–	74
Shadow Sabre	127	–	94
VT1100C3			
1998-2000	98	–	72
2001-2002	127	–	94
VT1100T	98	–	72
Left crankcase rear cover nut	12	106	–
Oil pump body bolts	13	115	–
Oil pump mounting bolts	12	106	–
Primary drive gear bolt[1]			
VT1100C2 ACE	100	–	74
All other models	98	–	72
Right crankcase cover mounting bolt	12	106	–
Stopper arm pivot bolt	10	88	–

1. Lubricate threads and flange surface with engine oil.
2. Stake nut as described in text.
3. Specification not provided by manufacturer.

CHAPTER SEVEN

TRANSMISSION AND INTERNAL SHIFT MECHANISM

This chapter describes disassembly and reassembly of the transmission shafts and internal shift mechanism. Remove the engine and separate the crankcase halves to service these components as described in Chapter Five.

Table 1 lists transmission gear ratios. Service specifications are listed in **Tables 2-4**. **Tables 1-4** are at the end of the chapter.

TRANSMISSION OPERATION

The engine is equipped with a 5-speed constant-mesh transmission. The gears on the mainshaft (A, **Figure 1**) are meshed with the gears on the countershaft (B). Each pair of meshed gears represents one gear ratio. For each pair of gears, one of the gears is splined to its shaft, while the other gear freewheels on its shaft.

Next to each freewheeling gear is a gear that is splined to the shaft. Each splined gear can slide on the shaft and lock onto the freewheeling gear, making that gear ratio active. Any time the transmission is in gear, one pair of meshed gears are locked to their shafts, and that gear ratio is selected. All other meshed gears are freewheeling, making those ratios inoperative.

To engage and disengage the various gear ratios, the splined gears are moved by shift forks (C, **Figure 1**). The shift forks are guided by grooves in the shift drum (D, **Figure 1**), which is operated by a shift pedal and linkage assembly. As the transmission is upshifted and downshifted, the shift drum rotates and guides the forks to engage and disengage pairs of gears on the transmission shafts.

TRANSMISSION TROUBLESHOOTING

Refer to *Transmission* in Chapter Two.

TRANSMISSION SERVICE

1. Before disassembling the transmission shafts, check the gears for visual damage. Check sliding gears for excessive play. If excessive play is noted, check the snap ring installation in the shaft grooves. A snap ring may be worn or damaged or the transmission groove may be damaged. Check spinning gears for roughness, indicating possible heat damage. Note damage for further inspection and troubleshooting. Measure parts after disassembly to determine excessive operating clearances.

2. Clean and dry the transmission shafts and gears before disassembling them.

3. As the transmission shafts are disassembled, store the individual parts in a divided container, or make an identification mark on each part to indicate orientation.

> *NOTE*
> *Heavy duty marking pens, such as those made by Speedry, work well when marking and identifying gears and other metal parts. These pens can be purchased in different colors at tool and bearing supply stores.*

4. Install *new* snap rings during reassembly. The snap rings fatigue and distort when removed. Do not reuse them, although they may appear to be in good condition.

5. To install new snap rings without distorting them, use the following installation technique. Open the new snap ring with a pair of snap ring pliers while holding the back of the snap ring with a pair of pliers (**Figure 2**). Then slide the snap ring down the shaft and seat it into its correct groove. This technique can also be used to remove the snap rings from a shaft.

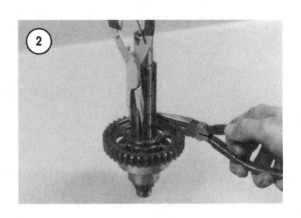

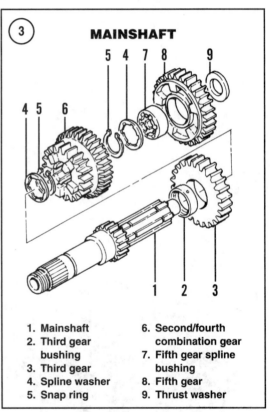

MAINSHAFT

1. Mainshaft
2. Third gear bushing
3. Third gear
4. Spline washer
5. Snap ring
6. Second/fourth combination gear
7. Fifth gear spline bushing
8. Fifth gear
9. Thrust washer

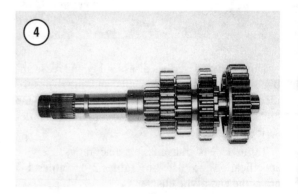

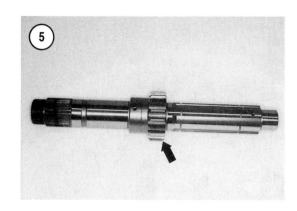

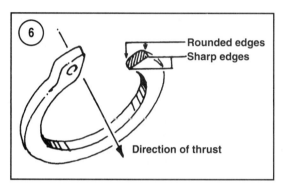

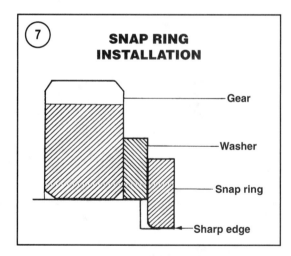

MAINSHAFT

Refer to **Figure 3**.

Disassembly

Remove the parts from the mainshaft (**Figure 4**) in the following order:

1. Thrust washer.

2. Fifth gear and fifth gear bushing.
3. Spline washer and snap ring.
4. Second/fourth combination gear.
5. Snap ring and spline washer.
6. Third gear and third gear bushing.

> *NOTE*
> *First gear is an integral part of the mainshaft.*

7. Inspect the mainshaft assembly as described under *Transmission Inspection* in this chapter.

Mainshaft Assembly

Before beginning assembly, have two *new* snap rings on hand. Throughout the procedure, the orientation of parts is made in relationship to first gear (**Figure 5**), which is part of the mainshaft.

> *CAUTION*
> *The snap rings and washers used on the transmission shafts are stamped types. One edge is rounded, while the other is sharp. The side with the sharp edge, referred to as the flat side, must be installed so the flat side always faces away from the part producing the thrust (**Figure 6**). The sharp edge prevents the snap ring from rolling out of its groove when thrust is applied (**Figure 7** and **Figure 8**).*

1. Clean and dry all parts before assembly. Use contact cleaner to remove all solvent residue from inside the shaft. Lubricate all parts with engine oil.
2. Install the third gear bushing (**Figure 9**) and seat it against first gear.
3. Install third gear (**Figure 10**) so the gear dogs face *away* from first gear.
4. Install the spline washer (A, **Figure 11**) and a *new* snap ring (B) onto the shaft. The flat side of both parts must face *away* from first gear. The snap ring must seat in the groove in the shaft.

> *CAUTION*
> *Install the snap ring so its ends align with a groove in the splines (**Figure 12** and **Figure 13**).*

5. Install the second/fourth combination gear (**Figure 14**) with the smaller gear facing toward first

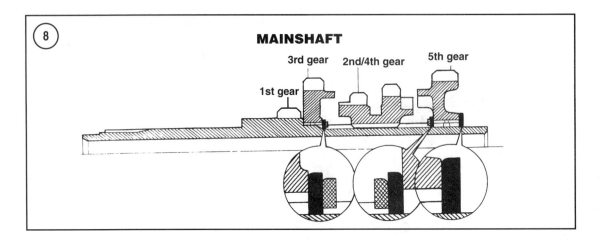

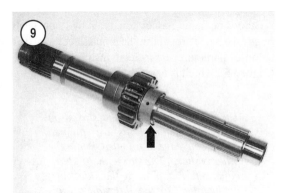

gear. Align the oil hole in the gear with the oil hole in the shaft, if so equipped.

6. Install a *new* snap ring (A, **Figure 15**) and spline washer (B) onto the shaft. The flat sides of both parts must face *toward* first gear. The snap ring must seat in the groove in the shaft (**Figure 16**).

CAUTION
*Install the snap ring so its ends align with a groove in the splines (**Figure 13**).*

7. Install the fifth gear spline bushing (**Figure 17**) and seat it against the spline washer. Align the oil hole in the bushing with the oil hole in the shaft.

8. Install fifth gear (**Figure 18**) so the gear dogs face *toward* first gear. Refer to A, **Figure 19**.

9. Install the thrust washer (B, **Figure 19**) and seat against fifth gear.

10. Refer to **Figure 4** for the correct placement of the mainshaft gears.

11. Wrap a heavy rubber band around the end of the shaft to prevent parts from sliding off the shaft.

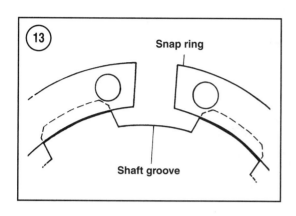

7

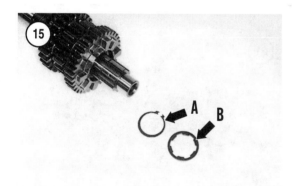

Wrap and store the assembly until it is ready for installation into the crankcase.

COUNTERSHAFT

Refer to **Figure 20**.

Disassembly

Remove the parts from the countershaft (**Figure 21**) in the following order:

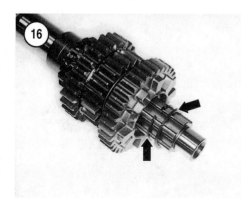

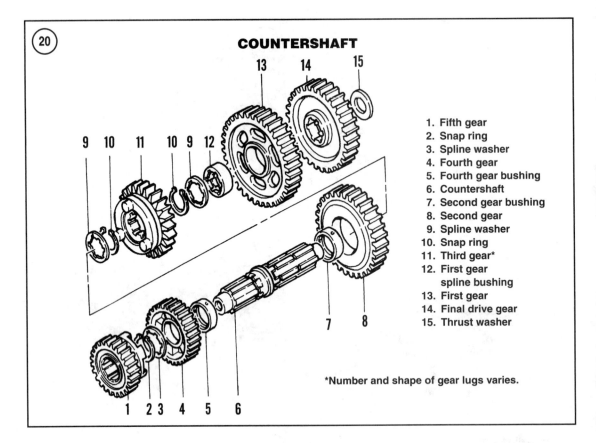

COUNTERSHAFT

13 14 15

9 10 11 10 9 12

1 2 3 4 5 6

7 8

1. Fifth gear
2. Snap ring
3. Spline washer
4. Fourth gear
5. Fourth gear bushing
6. Countershaft
7. Second gear bushing
8. Second gear
9. Spline washer
10. Snap ring
11. Third gear*
12. First gear
    spline bushing
13. First gear
14. Final drive gear
15. Thrust washer

*Number and shape of gear lugs varies.

1. Fifth gear.
2. Snap ring and spline washer.
3. Fourth gear and fourth gear bushing.
4. Thrust washer.

> *NOTE*
> *The final drive gear (14, **Figure 20**) is symmetrical and can be installed facing either direction on the shaft. However, it is best to mark the gear and reinstall it facing in its original direction.*

5. Final drive gear.
6. First gear and first gear bushing.
7. Spline washer and snap ring.
8. Third gear.
9. Snap ring and spline washer.
10. Second gear and second gear bushing.

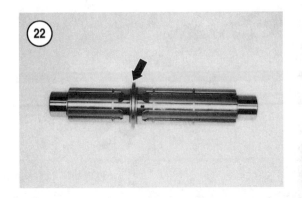

Assembly

Before beginning assembly, have three *new* snap rings on hand. Throughout the procedure, the orien-

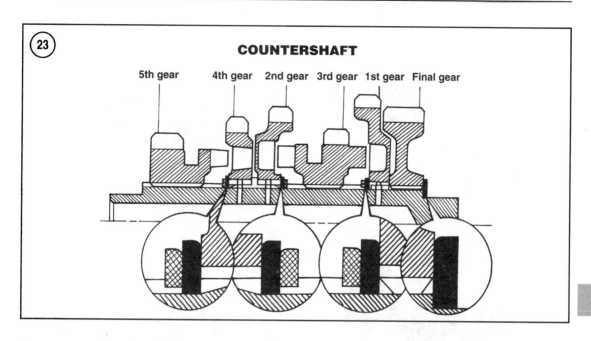

COUNTERSHAFT

5th gear   4th gear   2nd gear   3rd gear   1st gear   Final gear

7

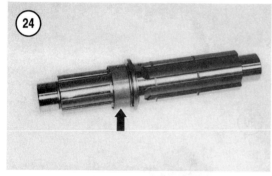

other is sharp. The side with the sharp edge, referred to as the flat side, must be installed so the flat side always faces away from the part producing the thrust (**Figure 6**). The sharp edge prevents the snap ring from rolling out of its groove when thrust is applied (**Figure 7** and **Figure 23**).

NOTE
A number of updates have been made to some of the countershaft gears. Confirm the engine's model year and engine number when ordering new gears.

1. Clean and dry all parts before assembly. Use contact cleaner to remove all solvent residue from inside the shaft. Lubricate all parts with engine oil.
2. Install the fourth gear bushing (**Figure 24**) and seat it against the shaft shoulder on the left side of the countershaft.
3. Install fourth gear so the side with the gear dogs (**Figure 25**) faces *away* from the shoulder.
4. Install the spline washer (A, **Figure 26**) and a *new* snap ring (B) onto the shaft. The flat sides of both parts must face *away* from the shoulder (**Figure 23**). The snap ring must seat in the groove in the shaft.

tation of many parts is made in relationship to the shoulder on the countershaft (**Figure 22**).

CAUTION
The snap rings and washers used on the transmission shafts are stamped types. One edge is rounded, while the

CAUTION
*Install the snap ring so its ends align with a groove in the splines (**Figure 27**).*

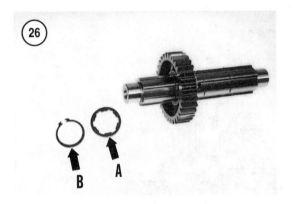

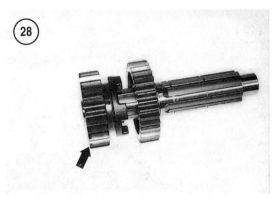

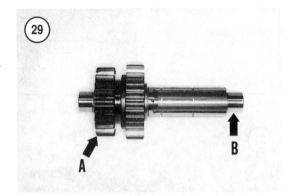

5. Install fifth gear (**Figure 28**) so the gear dogs face *toward* the shoulder.

> *NOTE*
> *This completes assembly of the left side of the countershaft (A, **Figure 29**). Steps 6-14 assemble the gears on the right side of the countershaft (B, **Figure 29**).*

6. Install the second gear bushing (**Figure 30**) and seat it against the shoulder.

7. Install second gear over its bushing (**Figure 31**) so the gear dogs face *away* from the shoulder.

8. Install the spline washer (A, **Figure 32**) and a *new* snap ring (B) onto the shaft. The flat sides of both parts must face *away* from the shoulder (**Figure 23**). The snap ring must seat in the groove in the shaft.

> *CAUTION*
> *Install the snap ring so its ends align with a groove in the splines (**Figure 33**).*

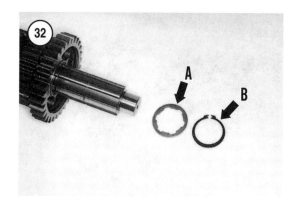

9. Install third gear (**Figure 34**) so its slider groove faces *toward* the shoulder.

10. Install a *new* snap ring (A, **Figure 35**) and spline washer (B) onto the shaft. The flat sides of both parts must face *toward* the shoulder (**Figure 23**). The snap ring must seat in the groove (**Figure 36**) in the shaft.

> *CAUTION*
> *Install the snap ring so its ends align with a groove in the splines (**Figure 13**).*

11. Install the first gear bushing (**Figure 37**) and seat it against the spline washer. Align the oil hole in the bushing with the oil hole in the shaft.

12. Install first gear (**Figure 38**) so its shoulder recess faces toward the shoulder on the countershaft. Refer to **Figure 39**.

13. Install the final drive gear (A, **Figure 40**) and seat it against fifth gear. Both sides of the final drive gear are symmetrical and can be installed either way. If the gear was marked before removal, install it facing in its original position.

14. Install the thrust washer (B, **Figure 40**) and seat against first gear. The flat side of the washer must face *away* from the shoulder.

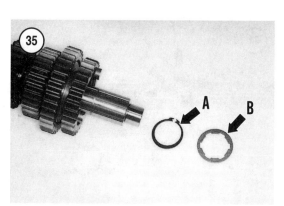

15. Refer to **Figure 21** for the correct placement of the countershaft gears.

16. Wrap a heavy rubber band around both ends of the shaft to prevent parts from sliding off the shaft. Wrap and store the assembly until it is ready for installation into the crankcase.

TRANSMISSION INSPECTION

Measure the transmission components and compare the actual measurements to the specifications in **Table 2** (mainshaft) or **Table 3** (countershaft). Replace worn or damaged parts.

NOTE
Maintain the alignment of the transmission components when cleaning and inspecting the parts in this section. If the gears were identified with a marking pen, the solvent may wash the pen markings off the gears.

1. Inspect the mainshaft (**Figure 41**) and countershaft (**Figure 42**) for:

  a. Worn or damaged splines.

  b. Missing, broken or chipped mainshaft first gear teeth (A, **Figure 41**).

  c. Worn or damaged bearing surfaces.

  d. Cracked or rounded-off snap ring grooves.

2. Measure the mainshaft outside diameter at its third gear operating position (B, **Figure 41**).

3. Measure the countershaft outside diameter at its second (A, **Figure 42**) and fourth (B) gear operating positions.

4. Check each gear for excessive wear, burrs, pitting or chipped or missing teeth. Check the splines on sliding gears and the bore on stationary gears for excessive wear or damage.

5. To check stationary gears for wear, install them and their bushings on their correct shafts and in their original operating positions. If necessary, use the old snap rings to secure them in place. Then spin the gears by hand. The gears should turn smoothly. A rough turning gear indicates heat damage. Check for a dark blue color or galling on the operating surfaces. Rocking indicates excessive wear, either to the gear, bushing or shaft.

6. To check the sliding gears, install them on their correct shafts and in their original operating positions. The gears should slide back and forth without any binding or excessive play.

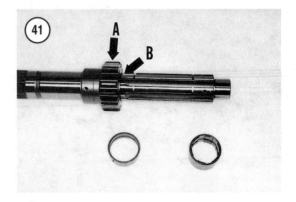

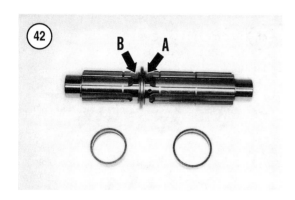

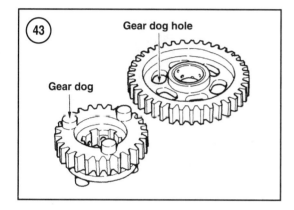

Gear dog hole

Gear dog

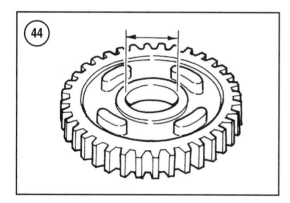

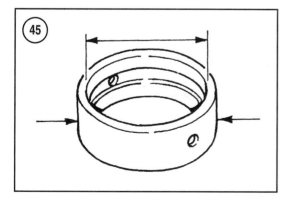

7. Check the dogs and dog slots (**Figure 43**) on the gears for excessive wear, rounding, cracks or other damage. Any wear on the engagement side of the dogs and mating recesses should be uniform. If the dogs are not worn evenly, the remaining dogs are overstressed and could possibly fail.

8. Check engaging gears by installing both gears on their respective shafts and in their original operating positions, then twist the gears together to engage the dogs. Check for positive engagement in both directions. If damage is evident, also inspect the condition of the shift forks, as described in this chapter.

NOTE
The side of the gear dogs that carries the engine load wears and eventually becomes rounded. The unloaded side of the dogs remains unworn. Rounded dogs cause the transmission to jump out of gear.

9. Check for worn or damaged shift fork grooves. Check the gear groove and its mating shift fork.

10. Measure the mainshaft third and fifth gear inside diameters. Refer to **Figure 44**.

11. Measure the countershaft first, second and fourth gear inside diameters. Refer to **Figure 44**.

12. Check the bushings for:
   a. Excessively worn or damaged bearing surface.
   b. Worn or damaged splines.
   c. Cracked or scored gear bore.

13. Measure the mainshaft third and fifth gear bushing outside diameters. Also measure the third gear bushing inside diameter (**Figure 45**).

14. Measure the countershaft first, second and fourth gear bushing outside diameters. Also measure the second and fourth gear bushing inside diameters (**Figure 45**).

15. Using the measurements recorded in the previous steps, determine the bushing-to-shaft and gear-to-bushing clearances specified in **Table 2** (mainshaft) and **Table 3** (countershaft). Replace worn parts to correct any clearance not within specification.

NOTE
Replace defective gears and their mating gear at the same time, though they may not show equal wear or damage. This helps to prevent exces-

*sive gear noise and prevent wear to
the new gear.*

16. Inspect the spline washers. The teeth in the washer should be uniform, and the washers should not be loose on the shaft.

17. Inspect the thrust washers. The washers should be smooth and show no signs of wear or heat damage (bluing).

INTERNAL SHIFT MECHANISM

As the transmission is upshifted and downshifted, the shift drum and fork assembly engages and disengages pairs of gears on the transmission shafts. Gear shifting is controlled by the shift forks, which are guided by cam grooves in the shift drum.

It is important that the shift drum grooves, shift forks and mating gear grooves be in good condition. Too much wear between the parts causes unreliable and poor engagement of the gears. This can lead to premature wear of the gear dogs and other parts.

Shift Drum
Inspection

1. Clean and dry the shift drum.
2. Check the shift drum (**Figure 46**) for wear and damage as follows:
    a. The shift drum grooves should be a uniform width. Worn grooves can prevent complete gear engagement, which can cause rough shifting and allow the transmission to disengage.
    b. Check both journal ends. These surfaces must not be worn or show overheating discoloration due to lack of lubrication. Then measure the shift drum left journal end outside diameter **Figure 47**. Replace the shift drum if the measurement is equal to or less than the service limit in **Table 4**.

Shift Fork and Shaft
Inspection

Table 4 lists new and service limit specifications for the shift forks and shift fork shaft. Replace the shift forks and shaft if out of specification or if they show damage as described in this section.

1. Inspect each shift fork (**Figure 48**) for signs of wear or damage. Examine the shift forks where they

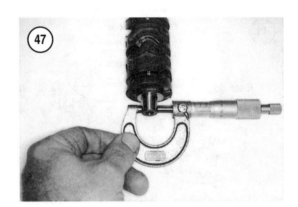

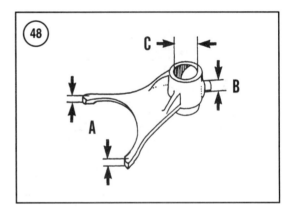

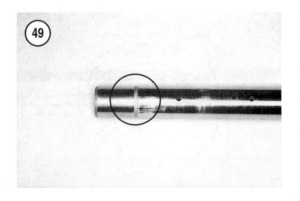

contact the slider gear (A, **Figure 48**). These surfaces must be smooth with no signs of excessive wear, bending, cracks, heat discoloration or other damage.

2. Check each shift fork for arc-shaped wear or burn marks. These marks indicate a bent shift fork.

3. The guide pin (B, **Figure 48**) should be symmetrical. Replace if there are any flat spots on the side of the pin.

4. Measure the thickness of each shift fork claw (A, **Figure 48**).

5. Measure the inside diameter (C, **Figure 48**) of each shift fork.

6. Slide each shift fork along the shaft and check for any binding or roughness. If damage is noted, check for a bent shaft.

7. Inspect the shift fork shaft for wear and damage. Measure the shaft diameter(s) as follows:

   a. On VT1100C2 ACE models, its shift shaft uses a stepped end (**Figure 49**). Measure both shaft diameters and compare to the specifications in **Table 4**.

   b. On all other models, their shaft is one size. Measure the shift fork shaft at each of the three shift fork operating areas and compare to **Table 4**.

Shift Shaft and Shift Drum Journal Inside Diameter Measurement

Using a bore gauge or inside micrometer, measure the following journal inside diameters and compare to the specifications in **Table 4**. Replace one or both crankcase halves if any measurement is out of specification.

1. On all models, measure the shift drum journal inside diameter in the left crankcase (A, **Figure 50**).

2. On VT1100C2 ACE models, measure the shift shaft journal inside diameters in the left (B, **Figure 50**) and right (**Figure 51**) crankcase halves.

Table 1 TRANSMISSION GENERAL SPECIFICATIONS

Final reduction ratio	3.091 (34/11)
Primary reduction ratio	
VT1100C	0.806 (29/36)
VT1100C2 ACE	1.692 (66/39)
VT1100C2 Sabre	0.939 (31/33)
VT1100C3	1.692 (66/39)
VT1100T	1.692 (66/39)
Secondary reduction ratio	
VT1100C	0.806 (29/36)
VT1100C2	
ACE	0.806 (29/36
Sabre	0.939 (31/33)
	(continued)

Table 1 TRANSMISSION GENERAL SPECIFICATIONS (continued)

Secondary reduction ratio (continued)	
VT1100C3	
1998-2000	0.806 (29/36)
2001-2002	0.939 (31/33)
VT1100T	0.939 (31/33)
Shift pattern	1-N-2-3-4-5
Third reduction ratio (output drive reduction)	1.059 (18/17)
Transmission	Constant mesh, 5-speed
Transmission gear ratios	
First gear	
VT1100C2 ACE	2.235 (38/17)
All other models	2.375 (38/16)
Second gear	1.391 (32/23)
Third gear	1.037 (28/27)
Fourth gear	0.888 (32/36)
Fifth gear	
VT1100C3	
1998-2000	0.800 (24/30)
2001-2002	0.766 (23/30)
All other models	0.766 (23/30)

Table 2 MAINSHAFT SERVICE SPECIFICATIONS

	New mm (in.)	Service limit mm (in.)
Gear bushing inside diameter		
Third gear	28.000-28.021 (1.1024-1.1032)	28.04 (1.104)
Gear bushing outside diameter		
Third gear	30.970-30.995 (1.2193-1.2203)	30.94 (1.218)
Fifth gear	30.950-30.975 (1.2185-1.2195)	30.94 (1.218)
Gear bushing-to-shaft clearance	0.020-0.062 (0.0008-0.0024)	0.082 (0.0032)
Gear inside diameter		
Third and fifth gears	31.000-31.025 (1.2205-1.2215)	31.035 (1.2218)
Gear-to-bushing clearance		
Third gear	0.005-0.055 (0.0002-0.0022)	0.075 (0.0030)
Fifth gear	0.025-0.075 (0.0010-0.0030)	0.095 (0.0037)
Mainshaft outside diameter at third gear position	27.959-27.980 (1.1007-1.1016)	27.94 (1.100)

Table 3 COUNTERSHAFT SERVICE SPECIFICATIONS

	New mm (in.)	Service limit mm (in.)
Countershaft outside diameter		
At second gear	29.950-29.975 (1.1791-1.1801)	29.94 (1.179)
	(continued)	

Table 3 COUNTERSHAFT SERVICE SPECIFICATIONS (continued)

	New mm (in.)	Service limit mm (in.)
Countershaft outside diameter (continued)		
At fourth gear	27.967-27.980	27.95
	(1.1011-1.1016)	(1.100)
Gear bushing inside diameter		
Second gear	29.985-30.006	30.03
	(1.1805-1.1813)	(1.182)
Fourth gear	28.000-28.021	28.04
	(1.1024-1.1032)	(1.104)
Gear bushing outside diameter		
First gear	32.950-32.975	32.94
	(1.2972-1.2982)	(1.297)
Second gear	32.955-32.980	32.94
	(1.2974-1.2984)	(1.297)
Fourth gear	30.970-30.995	30.94
	(1.2193-1.2203)	(1.218)
Gear bushing-to-shaft clearance		
Second gear	0.005-0.056	0.076
	(0.0002-0.0022)	(0.0030)
Fourth gear	0.020-0.054	0.074
	(0.0008 0.0021)	(0.0029)
Gear inside diameter		
First and second gears	33.000-33.025	33.035
	(1.2992-1.3002)	(1.3006)
Fourth gear	31.000-31.025	31.035
	(1.2205-1.2215)	(1.2218)
Gear-to-bushing clearance		
First gear	0.025-0.075	0.095
	(0.0010-0.0030)	(0.0037)
Second gear	0.020-0.070	0.090
	(0.0008-0.0028)	(0.0035)
Fourth gear	0.005-0.055	0.075
	(0.0002-0.0022)	(0.0030)

Table 4 SHIFT FORK AND SHIFT DRUM SERVICE SPECIFICATIONS

	New mm (in.)	Service limit mm (in.)
Shift drum journal inside diameter		
at left crankcase	14.000-14.018	14.028
	(0.5512-0.5519)	(0.5523)
Shift drum outside diameter at left end	13.966-13.984	13.956
	(0.5498-0.5506)	(0.5494)
Shift fork claw thickness		
VT1100C		
1997-2000		
Left	5.93-6.00	5.83
	(0.233-0.236)	(0.230)
Center and right	6.43-6.50	6.33
	(0.253-0.256)	(0.249)
2001-2002		
All shift forks	5.93-6.00	5.83
	(0.233-0.236)	(0.230)
(continued)		

Table 4 SHIFT FORK AND SHIFT DRUM SERVICE SPECIFICATIONS (continued)

	New mm (in.)	Service limit mm (in.)
VT1100C2 ACE and VT1100T		
Left	5.93-6.00 (0.233-0.236)	5.83 (0.230)
Center and right	6.43-6.50 (0.253-0.256)	6.33 (0.249)
VT1100C2 Sabre		
All shift forks	5.93-6.00 (0.233-0.236)	5.83 (0.230)
VT1100C3		
1998-2000		
Left	5.93-6.00 (0.233-0.236)	5.83 (0.230)
Center and right	6.43-6.50 (0.253-0.256)	6.33 (0.249)
2001-2002		
All shift forks	5.93-6.00 (0.233-0.236)	5.83 (0.230)
Shift fork inside diameter		
VT1100C2 ACE	–	
All other models	14.000-14.021 (0.5512-0.5520)	14.04 (0.553)
Shift shaft journal inside diameter		
VT1100C2 ACE		
Left side crankcase	13.500-13.527 (0.5315-0.5326)	13.537 (0.5330)
Right side crankcase	14.000-14.027 (0.5512-0.5522)	14.037 (0.5526)
All other models	–	
Shift fork shaft outside diameter		
VT1100C2		
Left end	13.466-13.484 (0.5302-0.5309)	13.456 (0.5289)
Right end	13.966-13.984 (0.5498-0.5506)	13.956 (0.5494)
All other models	13.966-13.984 (0.5498-0.5506)	13.956 (0.5494)

FUEL AND EMISSION CONTROL SYSTEMS

The carburetor fuel system consists of a fuel tank, shutoff valve, fuel pump, fuel filter, two Keihin constant velocity carburetors and air filter.

This chapter includes service procedures for all parts of the fuel and emission control systems. Refer to Chapter Three for air filter service.

Carburetor specifications are listed in **Table 1**. **Tables 1-3** are at the end of this chapter.

FUEL SYSTEM PRECAUTIONS

WARNING
Because of the explosive and flammable conditions that exist around gasoline, always observe the following:

1. Disconnect the negative battery cable before working on the fuel system.
2. Gasoline dripping onto a hot engine component may cause a fire. Always allow the engine to cool completely before working on any fuel system component.
3. Wipe up spilled gasoline immediately with dry rags. Store the rags in a suitable metal container.
4. Do not service any fuel system component while in the vicinity of open flames, sparks or while anyone is smoking next to the motorcycle.

5. Always have a fire extinguisher nearby when working on the fuel system.

FUEL HOSE IDENTIFICATION

The fuel system uses a number of fuel and vacuum hoses. To allow easier reassembly, develop a system to identify the hoses before disconnecting them. Make tags with strips of masking tape and a fine point permanent-marking pen. Use a permanent marking pen as most ink marks, as well as lead pencil marks, fade on tape. There are also a number of reusable aftermarket hose identification kits, which can be purchased at automotive parts stores.

CARBURETOR OPERATION

Understanding the function of each of the carburetor components and their relationships to one another is a valuable aid for pinpointing carburetor trouble.

The carburetor's purpose is to supply and atomize fuel and mix it in correct proportions with air that is drawn in through the air intake. At the primary throttle opening (idle), a small amount of fuel is siphoned through the pilot jet by the incoming air. As the throttle is opened further, the air stream begins to siphon fuel through the main jet and needle jet. The tapered needle increases the effective flow capacity of the needle jet as it is lifted, in that it occupies less of the area of the jet.

At full throttle, the carburetor venturi is fully open and the needle is lifted far enough to permit the main jet to flow at full capacity.

The choke circuit is a bystarter system in which the choke lever opens a choke valve and needle rather than closing a butterfly in the venturi area as on many carburetors. In the open position, the pilot jet discharges a stream of fuel into the carburetor venturi, enriching the mixture when the engine is cold.

CARBURETOR SERVICE

The rear cylinder carburetor (No. 1) is mounted on the left side of the motorcycle; the front cylinder carburetor (No. 2) is mounted on the right side.

Removal/Installation

1. Read the information listed under *Fuel Hose Identification* in this chapter.
2. Remove the fuel tank as described in this chapter.
3. Connect a hose (A, **Figure 1**) to the drain channel on the left carburetor. Loosen the drain screw (B, **Figure 1**) and drain the carburetor. Tighten the screw and remove the hose.
4. Repeat Step 3 for the right carburetor.
5. Remove the bolt (A, **Figure 2**) from the crankcase breather storage tank. Then disconnect the two hoses (B, **Figure 2**) from the tank and remove the tank from the frame. B, **Figure 2** shows one of the two hoses.
6. Loosen the three hose clamps securing the connecting tube (**Figure 3**) to the frame and both carburetors. Remove the connecting tube as an assembly.

> *NOTE*
> *If the connecting tube is going to be disassembled, locate and identify the tube alignment marks so the tube can be reassembled correctly.*

7. Disconnect the hose band from the left side of the frame, if used.
8. On all models except VT1100C2 ACE, disconnect the sub-air filter hose (A, **Figure 4**) from each carburetor, then remove the sub-air filter assembly

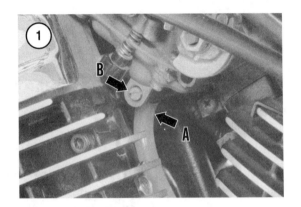

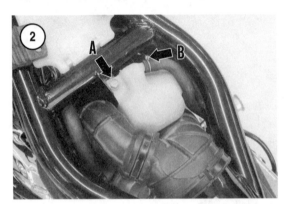

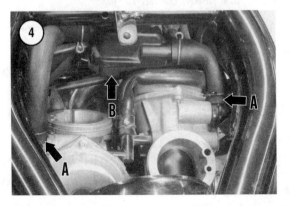

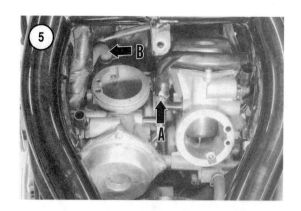

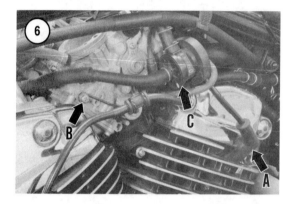

(B) with both hoses attached. Clean the sub-air filter with compressed air. Replace the element if damaged.

9A. On 49-state and Canada models, disconnect the carburetor air vent hose (A, **Figure 5**) from the nozzle in the middle of the carburetors.

9B. On California models, disconnect the No. 6 hose (A, **Figure 5**) from the nozzle in the middle of the carburetors.

10. Disconnect the fuel hose from each carburetor (B, **Figure 5**, typical).

NOTE
Steps 11-14 service the front (right side) carburetor.

11. Disconnect the right rear spark plug cap (A, **Figure 6**). Then remove the screw and cable bracket (B, **Figure 6**) from the rear carburetor. Reinstall the screw to prevent its loss.

12. On California models, disconnect the hoses connected to the EVAP CAV control valve (C, **Figure 6**). Then pull the valve off its mounting bracket. Do not disconnect the No. 6 hose at the valve unless necessary.

13. Loosen and remove the choke cable (A, **Figure 7**) at the front carburetor (right side). Disconnect the spring and valve (**Figure 8**) from the cable to prevent their loss.

14. On California models, disconnect the No. 5 hose (B, **Figure 7**) from the front cylinder carburetor.

NOTE
Steps 15-19 service the rear carburetor.

15. Disconnect the left rear spark plug cap (A, **Figure 9**) and remove it from the clutch cable holder (B).

16. Disconnect the No. 5 hose (A, **Figure 10**) from the rear carburetor.

17. Loosen and remove the choke cable (B, **Figure 10**). Disconnect the spring and valve from the cable to prevent their loss (**Figure 8**, typical).

18. Remove the choke cable from the speedometer cable bracket (A, **Figure 11**).

19. Remove the throttle cable bracket and disconnect the throttle cables as follows:

NOTE
Note the clutch cable routing on the left side of the motorcycle before disconnecting the throttle cables.

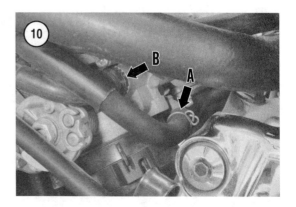

   a. Remove the two screws (B and C, **Figure 11**) securing the throttle cable bracket to the carburetor.

   b. After the screws are removed, push the cable bracket rearward to provide slack in the lower cable. Then disconnect the lower cable from the carburetor.

   c. Disconnect the upper cable from the carburetor.

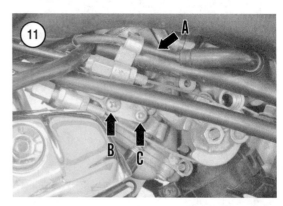

20. Loosen each upper carburetor hose clamp. **Figure 12** shows the rear (left side) carburetor hose clamps and manifold. **Figure 13** shows the front (right side) carburetor. Do not loosen the lower clamps that secure the intake manifolds to the cylinder heads.

21. Remove the carburetor assembly:

   a. Carefully pry the carburetors from the manifolds.

   b. When the carburetors are free, cover the manifold openings with clean shop rags.

   c. Tilt the rear carburetor up and remove the carburetors through the opening in the center of the frame (A, **Figure 14**).

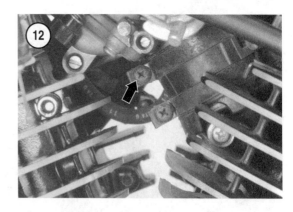

   d. On California models, disconnect the No. 11 hose from the rear carburetor (B, **Figure 14**).

   e. Remove the carburetors.

   f. Remove the rags and plug each manifold opening with a rubber plug.

22. Check the intake manifold installation and alignment. Tighten the lower hose clamp screws securely.

23. Installation is the reverse of removal. Note the following:

   a. After installing the choke valves into the carburetors, tighten choke cable nuts (A, **Figure**

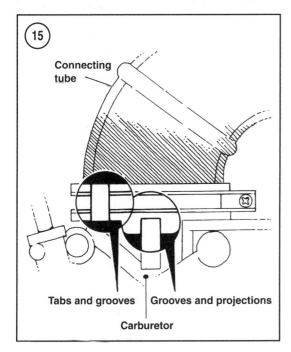

Connecting tube

Tabs and grooves | Grooves and projections

Carburetor

7) until they contact the carburetor. Then tighten an additional 1/4 turn.

b. Install the connecting tube assembly through the frame tubes and connect it to each carburetor and to the large frame tube. Align the notch in each connecting tube with the projection tab on each carburetor (**Figure 15**).

c. Adjust the throttle cables (Chapter Three).

d. Adjust the choke and check choke cable operation (Chapter Three).

e. Check and adjust carburetor idle speed and synchronization (Chapter Three).

f. After installing the fuel tank and turning on the fuel valve, check the carburetors for any fuel

leaks. Repair any leak before starting the engine.

WARNING
Do not ride the motorcycle until the throttle cables are adjusted properly.

Air Cutoff Valve
Removal/Installation

When the throttle is released during deceleration, the fuel mixture becomes lean, a condition that can cause backfiring and popping in the exhaust pipe. To prevent this, a vacuum operated air cutoff valve is mounted in each carburetor. Each valve assembly contains a spring-loaded diaphragm that is installed inside a sealed chamber. The shaft on the end of the diaphragm operates in the carburetor pilot air passageway. A separate carburetor passageway aligns with the hole in the diaphragm cover to supply vacuum to operate the valve.

When the throttle is released, vacuum in the air cut off valve chamber increases enough to overcome the spring pressure applied against the diaphragm. This allows the diaphragm's shaft to move outward and close the pilot jet air passageway and richen the air/fuel mixture. During acceleration, the vacuum decreases and the spring pressure once again operates against the diaphragm to open the pilot air passageway.

The air cutoff valves can be removed without separating or disassembling the carburetors. Refer to **Figure 16**.

1. Remove the carburetor assembly (**Figure 16**) as described in this chapter.

NOTE
The air cutoff valve cover is under spring pressure. Hold the cover in place when removing its screws.

2. Remove the air cutoff valve cover screws, retainer (A, **Figure 17**) and cover (B). The retainer is not used on all models.

3. Remove the spring (A, **Figure 18**), diaphragm (B) and O-ring (C).

4. Inspect the spring (**Figure 19**) for corrosion, weakness or damage.

5. Inspect the cover (**Figure 19**) for corrosion or damage. Clean the cover passageway with compressed air.

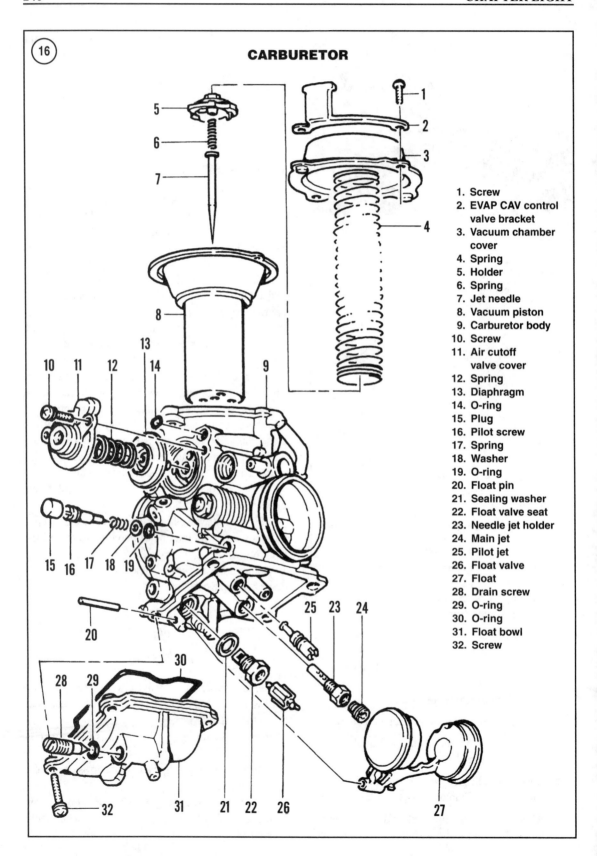

CARBURETOR

1. Screw
2. EVAP CAV control valve bracket
3. Vacuum chamber cover
4. Spring
5. Holder
6. Spring
7. Jet needle
8. Vacuum piston
9. Carburetor body
10. Screw
11. Air cutoff valve cover
12. Spring
13. Diaphragm
14. O-ring
15. Plug
16. Pilot screw
17. Spring
18. Washer
19. O-ring
20. Float pin
21. Sealing washer
22. Float valve seat
23. Needle jet holder
24. Main jet
25. Pilot jet
26. Float valve
27. Float
28. Drain screw
29. O-ring
30. O-ring
31. Float bowl
32. Screw

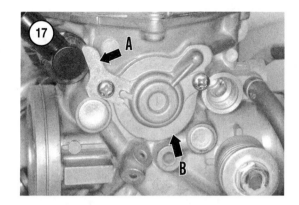

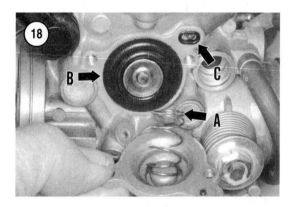

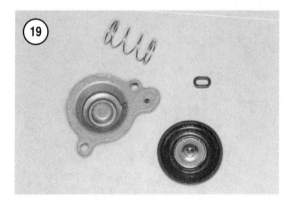

6. Inspect the diaphragm (**Figure 19**) for soft spots, deterioration or other damage.

7. Inspect the diaphragm shaft (**Figure 19**) for grooves, wear or damage.

8. Replace the O-ring (**Figure 19**) if deteriorated or damaged.

9. Check the vacuum passageways in the carburetor (**Figure 20**) for dirt and other debris.

10. Install the O-ring (C, **Figure 18**) with its flat side facing toward the carburetor body.

11. Install the diaphragm and seat it into the carburetor groove as shown in B, **Figure 18**.

12. Install the spring and seat it into the cover (A, **Figure 18**), then install the cover (B, **Figure 17**) and retainer (A, **Figure 17**) and secure with the mounting screws.

13. Repeat these steps for the other carburetor air cutoff valve assembly.

Carburetor Disassembly

The carburetors are joined together. All internal carburetor parts can be serviced without separating the carburetors. To clean the carburetor internally or replace the hose joints or O-rings, separate the carburetors as described in this section.

Refer to **Figure 16**.

NOTE
Do not interchange parts between the front and rear carburetors. Keep both carburetors and their parts separate when servicing them.

1. If hoses are still connected to the carburetors, identify the hoses first, then disconnect them.

2. Remove the air cutoff valve as described in this chapter.

NOTE
Before removing the vacuum chamber cover, lift the vacuum piston with a finger, then release it. It should move up the bore smoothly and then drop slowly with no binding or roughness. If there is any noticeable drag, check for a damaged or incorrectly installed vacuum chamber spring or damaged diaphragm.

8

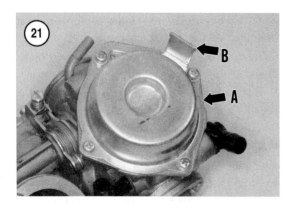

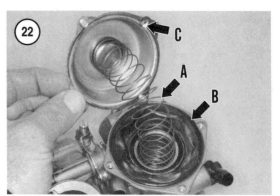

3. Remove the vacuum chamber cover screws and cover (A, **Figure 21**). Remove the EVAP CAV control valve mounting bracket (B, **Figure 21**), if used.

4. Remove the spring (A, **Figure 22**) and the vacuum piston (B).

5. To remove the jet needle (A, **Figure 23**) from the vacuum piston, perform the following:

   a. Insert a Phillips screwdriver into the vacuum piston cavity and turn the holder (**Figure 24**) counterclockwise to unlock it from the tangs within the piston cavity.

   b. Remove the holder, spring and jet needle (**Figure 25**).

> *NOTE*
> *Compare the jet needle assembly with the parts in **Figure 25**. Any additional shims or spacers installed underneath the jet needle indicate that an aftermarket jet kit was installed by a previous owner.*

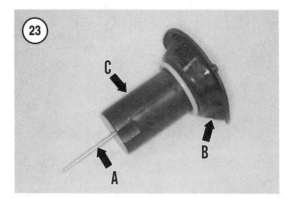

6. Remove the float bowl mounting screws, float bowl (**Figure 26**) and O-ring. Inspect the float bowl for dirt and other contamination.

> *NOTE*
> *If necessary, measure the float height as described in this chapter.*

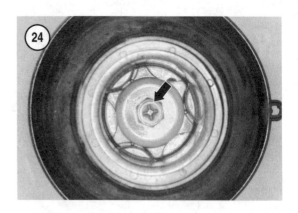

7. Remove the float pin, float (**Figure 27**) and float valve (**Figure 28**).

> *NOTE*
> *If troubleshooting a rich air/fuel mixture or carburetor flooding, check for debris in the float valve seat and/or a loose float valve seat or damaged gasket.*

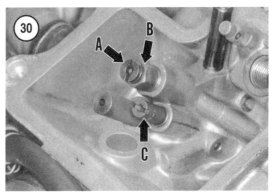

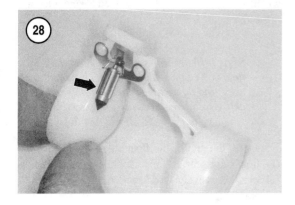

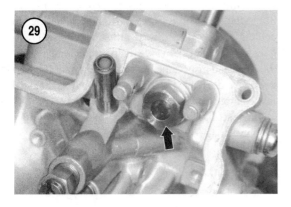

8. Remove the float valve seat and gasket (**Figure 29**).

9. Remove the main jet (A, **Figure 30**) and the needle jet holder (B).

NOTE
The needle jet is pressed into place and cannot be removed.

10. Remove the pilot jet (C, **Figure 30**).

11. For complete cleaning of the carburetors, separate the carburetor assemblies as described in this chapter

NOTE
Further disassembly is not recommended. If the throttle plate and shaft are damaged, the carburetor body must be replaced.

Carburetor
Cleaning and Inspection

The following procedure list step-by-step cleaning and inspection procedures for both carburetors.

WARNING
Wear safety goggles when cleaning the carburetors.

1. A gasket kit is available from Honda and includes the following replacement parts identified in **Figure 16**: No. 14, 19, 21, 29 and 30. The two O-rings installed on the air vent joint connected to both carburetors are also included in the kit. A separate gasket kit will be required for each carburetor.

NOTE
Replace all O-rings upon assembly. O-rings tend to become hardened after

prolonged use and exposure to heat and lose their ability to seal properly.

2. Before cleaning the parts in a dip-type carburetor cleaner or with an aerosol carburetor cleaner, note the following:

    a. Remove the drain screw and O-ring from the float bowl.

    b. Remove the pilot screws as described in this chapter.

    c. All parts, except the carburetor housing, rubber and plastic parts, can be cleaned with carburetor cleaner.

NOTE
When using a dip-type carburetor cleaner, the parts are placed in a small basket and immersed in the container. Follow the manufacturer's directions for immersion time.

3. After soaking the parts, rinse them in warm water and blow dry with compressed air. Blow out the jets with compressed air.

4. Visually inspect the main jet, pilot jet and needle jet bores for plugging or contamination. Hold the part with pliers and blow out the bore with compressed air. If the bore is still plugged, soak the part in a carburetor cleaner, then dry and clean again with compressed air. If the bore is still plugged, either replace the part or try to clean it with a piece of wire or a drill bit. The pilot jet is the most difficult part to clean because its bore is the smallest. Before starting, examine the same part in the other carburetor. If its bore is not plugged, find a cleaning tool that can pass through it. The K&L Carb Cleaner Wire Set (part No. 35-3498 [**Figure 31**]) includes a number of different size probes designed for cleaning jets and passageways.

CAUTION
When using a carburetor cleaning tool, wire or drill bit to clean jets and other carburetor passages, work carefully to avoid gouging or enlarging the bore. Doing so can alter flow rate and change the air/fuel mixture.

5. Clean the carburetor housing with compressed air. Operate the throttle shaft to check for binding or damage. Then try to move the throttle shaft back and forth. If there is any play, the throttle shaft and shaft bores are worn. This requires replacement of the carburetor body.

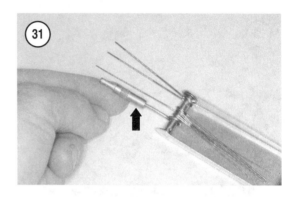

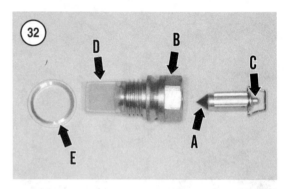

6. Make sure all openings in the carburetor housing are clear. Clean them if plugged, then clean with compressed air.

NOTE
*Steps 7-10 describes how to inspect the float valve and seat. If any part is damaged, the float valve seat must be purchased and replaced as an assembly (**Figure 16**: parts No. 21, 22 and 26).*

7. Inspect the end of the float valve (A, **Figure 32**) and float valve seat (B) for wear or damage. If the float valve is excessively worn or damaged, replace the valve and seat.

8. Lightly press on the spring-loaded pin (C, **Figure 32**) in the float valve. The pin should easily move in and out of the valve. If it is varnished with fuel residue, replace the float valve and seat assembly.

9. Clean and inspect the float valve seat filter (D, **Figure 32**) and replace if damaged. The filter is included in the carburetor gasket kit.

10. Inspect the float valve sealing gasket (E, **Figure 32**) for damage that would allow it to leak.

NOTE
A worn float valve and seat assembly cause engine flooding. If there is any

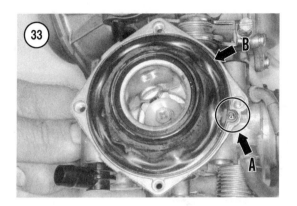

doubt about the condition of these parts, replace them as a set.

11. Inspect the main jet, needle jet holder and pilot jet for thread damage.

12. Inspect the jet needle (A, **Figure 23**) for excessive wear at the tip or other damage on the needle.

13. Check the diaphragm (B, **Figure 23**) for tearing, soft spots, pin holes, age deterioration or other damage.

14. Check the vacuum piston (C, **Figure 23**) for nicks, scoring or damage. Install the vacuum piston/diaphragm into the carburetor body and move it up and down in the bore. The vacuum piston should move smoothly with no binding or excessive play.

15. Inspect the jet needle spring and holder (**Figure 25**) for corrosion or damage.

16. Submerge the float in water and check for leakage. Replace the float if water or fuel is detected inside the float.

Assembly

1. If the pilot screw was removed, install as described under *Pilot Screw and Plug Removal/Installation* in this section.

2. Install and tighten the pilot jet (C, **Figure 30**).

3. Install and tighten the needle jet holder (B, **Figure 30**).

4. Hold the needle jet holder, then install and tighten the main jet (A, **Figure 30**).

5. Install the sealing gasket (E, **Figure 32**) onto the float valve seat (B), then install and tighten the seat (**Figure 29**).

6. Hook the float valve onto the float (**Figure 28**), then install the float and secure with the float pin (**Figure 27**).

7. Measure the float height as described under *Carburetor Adjustment* in this chapter.

8. If removed, install the O-ring into the float bowl groove.

9. Align the float bowl with the carburetor body and install the float bowl (**Figure 26**). Install and tighten the float bowl mounting screws securely.

10. Install the needle jet assembly (**Figure 25**) as follows:

   a. Install the needle jet into the vacuum piston.

   b. Install the spring onto the holder, then install the holder into the vacuum piston.

   c. Press and turn the holder (**Figure 24**) 1/4 turn clockwise to lock it in place.

11. Install the vacuum piston into the carburetor. Align the diaphragm tab with the cavity in the carburetor housing (A, **Figure 33**).

12. Lift the vacuum piston (from the bottom) and seat the diaphragm lip (B, **Figure 33**) into the groove in the top of the carburetor housing.

13. Install the spring (A, **Figure 22**) into the vacuum piston.

14. Align the shoulder on the inside of the vacuum chamber cover with the spring, then install the cover (A, **Figure 21**). Align the concave part of the cover (C, **Figure 22**) with the diaphragm tab (A, **Figure 33**).

15. Install the bracket (B, **Figure 21**), if used, and tighten the vacuum chamber cover screws securely.

NOTE
*Lift the vacuum piston with a finger, then release it. If the piston moves roughly, the spring (4, **Figure 16**) was incorrectly installed.*

16. If the carburetors were separated, assemble them as described in this chapter.

17. Referring to the notes made during disassembly, install the fuel and vacuum hoses onto the carburetors.

18. Install the air cutoff valves as described in this chapter.

Carburetor Separation/Assembly

The carburetors are joined together by two screws. All internal carburetor parts can be replaced without separating the carburetors. If the carburetors must be cleaned internally or the synchronization springs replaced, separate the carburetors.

Refer to **Figure 34**.

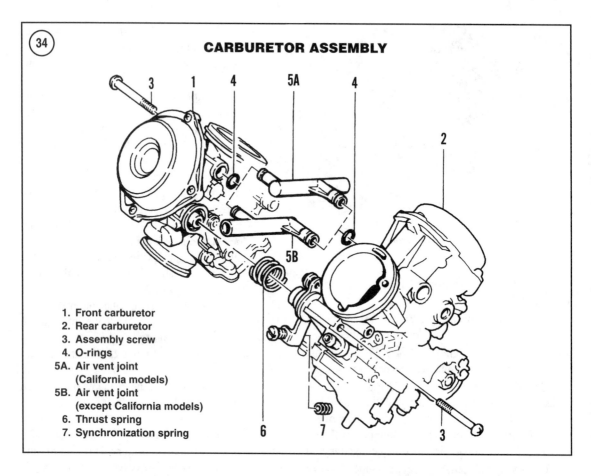

CARBURETOR ASSEMBLY

1. Front carburetor
2. Rear carburetor
3. Assembly screw
4. O-rings
5A. Air vent joint
    (California models)
5B. Air vent joint
    (except California models)
6. Thrust spring
7. Synchronization spring

1. Loosen the synchronization screw (**Figure 35**) to remove all tension from the screw.

> *NOTE*
> *The carburetor assembly screws are secured tightly. Wrap the carburetors with a thick towel. Then loosen the screws with a hand impact driver and the correct size Phillips bit.*

2. Loosen, then remove the two carburetor assembly screws (**Figure 34**).

3. Separate the carburetors while removing the thrust spring, synchronization spring (**Figure 34**), air vent joint (**Figure 36**) and both O-rings.

4. Service the carburetors as described in this chapter.

5. Clean the two springs in solvent. Check the springs for cracks, flat spots and other damage. Replace if necessary.

6. Assemble by reversing these disassembly steps, while noting the following.

7. Replace the air vent joint O-rings (4, **Figure 34**) if worn or damaged.

8. Install the thrust spring and synchronization spring and join the two carburetors as shown in **Figure 34**.

9. Check that there is no clearance or gap where the two carburetor housings join together, then install and tighten the assembly screws gradually, first one screw and then the other until they are both tight.

10. Open the throttle with the throttle drum and release it. The throttle should return smoothly with no drag.

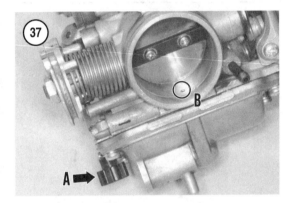

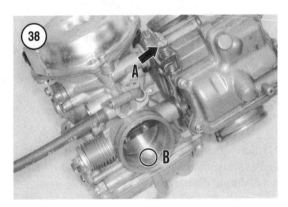

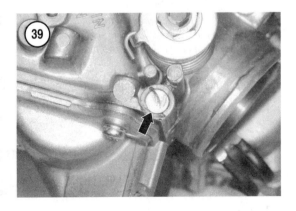

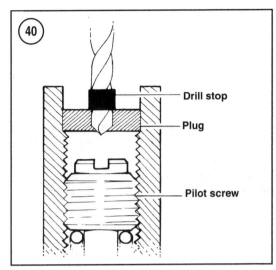

Drill stop

Plug

Pilot screw

11. Turn the throttle stop screw (A, **Figure 37**) to align the throttle valve with the edge of the by-pass hole (B, **Figure 37**) in the No. 1 (rear) carburetor.

12. Turn the synchronization screw (A, **Figure 38**) to align the throttle valve with the edge of the by-pass hole (**Figure 38**) in the No. 2 (front) carburetor.

13. Rotate the throttle drum to make sure each throttle valve opens and closes correctly.

14. If the throttle drum does not move smoothly or return properly, recheck all previous steps until the problem is solved.

15. Adjust carburetor synchronization after installing the carburetors onto the motorcycle (Chapter Three).

Pilot Screw and Plug
Removal/Installation

The pilot screw bores are sealed with an aluminum plug (**Figure 39**) to prevent routine pilot screw adjustment. The pilot screws do not require adjustment unless the carburetors are overhauled, the pilot screws are incorrectly adjusted, the pilot screws require replacement or to adjust them when installing a jet kit. The following procedure describes how to remove and install the plugs and pilot screws.

1. Use a small center punch and hammer and center punch the middle of the plug (**Figure 39**).

2. Install a drill stop 3 mm (1/8 in.) from the end of a 5/32 inch drill bit (**Figure 40**).

NOTE
If tape is used as a drill stop, use it as a visual guide only. The tape does not

stop the drill bit from drilling deeper into the plug.

3. Drill a hole into the plug until the drill stop contacts the plug (**Figure 40**). If a drill stop is not used, do not drill too deeply. The pilot screw is difficult to remove if the head is damaged.

4. Thread a sheet metal screw into the drilled hole. Continue to turn the screw until the plug starts to turn with the screw.

5. Remove the plug and screw with a pair of pliers (**Figure 41**) and blow away all metal shavings from the area.

> ### CAUTION
> *The pointed end of the pilot screw can break off if the screw is tightened against the carburetor seat. Seat the screw as described in Step 6.*

> ### NOTE
> *If the pilot screw uses a D-shaped head, a D-shaped driver head tool is required to remove and install the screw. An inexpensive tool can be assembled by mounting a Motion Pro D-shaped 1/4 inch hex drive bit (part No. 08-0242 [A, **Figure 42**]) on any standard driver (B) that can accept 1/4 inch hex-shaped bits. Honda also sells a D-shaped pilot screw wrench (part No. 07KMA-MS60101 (C, **Figure 42**).*

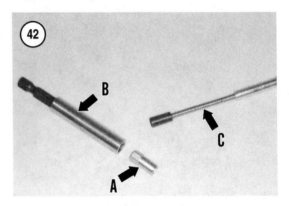

6. Screw the pilot screw in until it *lightly* seats while counting and recording the number of turns. Reinstall the pilot screw to the same position during assembly.

> ### NOTE
> *Identify the pilot screws so they can be reinstalled in their original carburetor.*

7. Remove the pilot screw, spring, washer and O-ring.

8. Inspect the pilot screw for an excessively worn or damaged tip. Replace if damaged.

> ### NOTE
> *If one pilot screw is damaged, both pilot screws must be replaced at the same time.*

9. Replace the O-ring if cracked or damaged.

10. Slide the spring, washer and O-ring onto the pilot screw.

> ### NOTE
> *Install used pilot screws into their original carburetor.*

11. Screw the pilot screw into the carburetor until it *lightly* seats, then back it out the number of turns noted during disassembly.

> ### NOTE
> *Do not install new plugs until after the carburetor has been installed on the motorcycle and the carburetor adjusted.*

12. Repeat these steps for the other carburetor.

13. If new pilot screws were installed, perform the pilot screw adjustment as described under *Carburetor Adjustment* in this chapter.

14. Drive in new pilot screw plugs (**Figure 39**) until their outer surface is recessed 1 mm (0.04 in.) into the pilot screw bore.

CARBURETOR ADJUSTMENT

Float Level Adjustment

The carburetors must be removed and partially disassembled for this adjustment.

1. Remove the carburetors as described in this chapter.

2. Remove the screws securing the float bowls to the main bodies.

3. Hold the carburetor assembly so the float arm is just touching the float needle and not compressing its plunger tip. Use a float level gauge (Honda part No. 07401-0010001 or equivalent) and measure the distance from the carburetor body to the float arm (**Figure 43**). Position the measurement tool in line with the main jet. The correct float level is 9.2 mm (0.36 in.). If the measurement is incorrect, note the following:

   a. On some floats, the float arm lip is not adjustable. If the float level is incorrect on this type of float, replace the float.

   b. If the float arm lip is adjustable, bend it to correct the float level. Install the float and recheck the float level adjustment.

NOTE
If the float level is too high, the result is a rich air/fuel mixture. If it is too low, the mixture is too lean.

4. Install the float bowl as described under *Carburetor Assembly* in this chapter.

5. Reassemble and install the carburetors as described in this chapter.

Jet Needle Adjustment

The jet needle is non-adjustable on all models.

Pilot Screw Adjustment
(Idle Drop Procedure)

1. The pilot screws are preset. Adjustment is not necessary except under the following conditions:

   a. The carburetors have been overhauled.

   b. The pilot screws were replaced.

   c. The carburetor is being adjusted for high altitude (see procedure in following section).

   d. An aftermarket jet kit is being installed.

2. Check the air filter and replace if necessary (Chapter Three).

3. Check carburetor synchronization and adjust if necessary (Chapter Three).

4. Remove the pilot screw plugs (**Figure 39**) as described in this chapter.

CAUTION
Seat the pilot screw lightly in Step 5 or the screw tip can break off into the pilot screw bore.

NOTE
*If the pilot screws use D-shaped heads, a D-shaped driver head tool is required. An inexpensive tool can be assembled by mounting a Motion Pro D-shaped 1/4 inch hex drive bit (part No. 08-0242 [A, **Figure 42**]) on any standard driver (B) that can accept 1/4 inch hex-shaped bits. Honda also sells a D-shaped pilot screw wrench (part No. 07KMA-MS60101 (C, **Figure 42**).*

5. Carefully turn the pilot screw on each carburetor (A, **Figure 44**) in until it *lightly* seats and then back it out the number of turns listed under *Idle Drop Procedure* in **Table 1**.

8

6. Start the engine and let it reach normal operating temperature. Approximately 10-15 minutes of stop-and-go riding is sufficient.

7. Turn the engine off and support it on its sidestand.

8. Connect a portable tachometer (that can register a change of 50 rpm or less) to the engine following the manufacturer's instructions.

9. On 2004 California models, locate the No. 10 hose at the PAIR control valve (**Figure 45**). Trace the hose from this point and disconnect it from its tee-connection. Plug the tee-connection hose joint. Then connect a vacuum pump to the No. 10 hose and apply more than 230 mm HG (9.06 in. HG) vacuum with the pump.

10. Start the engine and turn the throttle stop screw (B, **Figure 44**) in or out to achieve the idle speed listed in **Table 1**.

11. Read the tachometer scale and turn each pilot screw (A, **Figure 44**) out 1/2 turn from the initial setting in Step 5. If the engine speed increases by 50 rpm or more, turn each pilot screw out by an additional 1/2 turn at a time until the engine speed does not increase.

12. Turn the throttle stop screw (B, **Figure 44**) in or out to achieve the idle speed listed in **Table 1**.

13. Turn the rear cylinder pilot screw clockwise until the engine speed drops 50 rpm.

14. Turn the pilot screw on the rear cylinder counterclockwise 3/4 turn from the position obtained in Step 13.

15. Turn the throttle stop screw (B, **Figure 44**) in or out to achieve the idle speed listed in **Table 1**.

16. Repeat Steps 13-15 for the front cylinder carburetor pilot screw.

17. Turn the engine off and disconnect the portable tachometer.

18. On 2004 California models, disconnect the vacuum pump and reconnect the No. 10 hose onto its tee-connection.

19. Test ride the motorcycle. Throttle response from idle should be rapid and without any hesitation.

20. Drive in new pilot screw plugs until their outer surface is recessed 1 mm (0.04 in.) into the pilot screw bore.

High Elevation Adjustment

If the motorcycle is going to be ridden for any sustained period at high elevation (2000 m/6500 ft. and above), the carburetors should be readjusted to improve performance and decrease emissions.

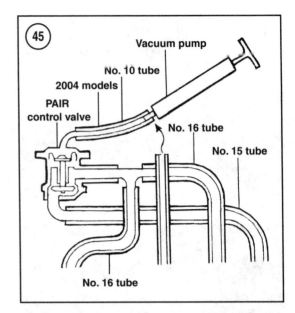

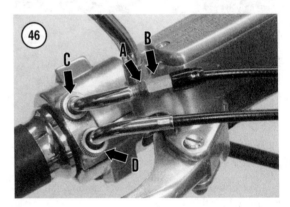

NOTE
Honda technicians place a Vehicle Emission Control Information update label on the inside of the left side cover or on the left side of the frame when the carburetors have been adjusted for high altitude. Before adjusting the carburetors on an unfamiliar motorcycle, check for this label.

1. Remove each pilot screw plug (A, **Figure 44**) as described in this section.

2. Start the engine and let it reach normal operating temperature. Approximately 10-15 minutes of stop-and-go riding is sufficient.

NOTE
If the pilot screws use D-shaped heads, a D-shaped driver head tool is re-

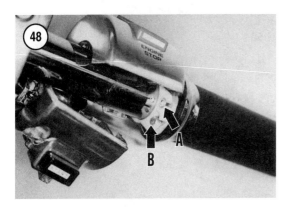

*quired. An inexpensive tool can be assembled by mounting a Motion Pro D-shaped 1/4 inch hex drive bit (part No. 08-0242 [A, **Figure 42**]) on any standard driver (B) that can accept 1/4 inch hex-shaped bits. Honda also sells a D-shaped pilot screw wrench (part No. 07KMA-MS60101 (C, **Figure 42**).*

3. Turn each pilot screw (A, **Figure 44**) *clockwise* 1/2 turn.

4. Turn the throttle stop screw (B, **Figure 44**) in or out again to achieve the idle speed listed in **Table 1**.

5. Drive in new limiter caps until their outer surface is recessed 1 mm (0.04 in.) into the pilot screw bore.

6. When the motorcycle is returned to elevations below 2000 (6500 ft.), adjust the pilot screws to their original positions and reset the idle speed to the rpm specified in **Table 1**. Make sure to make these adjustments with the motorcycle at a lower altitude and with the engine at its normal operating temperature.

WARNING
Adjust the carburetors for the elevation that the motorcycle is primarily operated in. Operating the motorcycle at al-

titudes lower than 1500 m (5000 ft.) with the carburetors adjusted for high altitude may cause the engine to idle roughly and stall in traffic. Overheating may also cause engine damage.

THROTTLE CABLE REPLACEMENT

NOTE
There are two throttle cables. One is the pull cable (accelerate) and the other is the return cable (decelerate). These cables must be reinstalled in the correct position on the carburetor and connected to the correct position on the throttle sleeve pulley.

1. Lubricate the new cables (Chapter Three) and set them aside until installation.

2. Remove the fuel tank as described in this chapter.

3. Note the routing of both cables from the throttle grip to the carburetors. Record this information on a piece of paper for proper installation. Then identify each cable's mounting position at the handlebar and carburetor for proper installation.

4. At the throttle grip, loosen the locknut (A, **Figure 46**) and turn the adjuster (B) all the way in to obtain maximum slack in the pull cable.

5. Loosen the pull (C, **Figure 46**) and return (D) cable nuts at the throttle housing.

6. Loosen the pull cable (A, **Figure 47**) and return cable (B) locknuts at the carburetor. Then disconnect the cables from the throttle drum.

7. Remove the two handlebar switch/throttle housing screws and separate the switch housing from around the handlebar.

8. Disconnect the pull (A, **Figure 48**) and return (B) cable ends from the throttle sleeve. Then remove the pull and return cables from the throttle housing.

9. Remove any cable clamps or plastic ties from the cables.

10. Tie a piece of heavy string to the lower end of both cables. Cut the string to a length that is longer than the new cables.

11. Tie the lower end of both strings to a frame or engine component.

12. Remove one cable by pulling it from the top (upper cable end). Continue until the cable is removed from the frame, leaving the attached piece of string in its mounting position.

13. Repeat to remove the other cable.

8

14. Untie the string from the old cable and discard the old cable.

15. Tie the string onto the bottom end of the new cable.

16. Slowly pull the string and cable to install the cable along the path of the original cable. Continue until the new cable is correctly routed beside the engine and through the frame. Untie and remove the string.

17. Repeat to install the other cable.

18. Visually check the entire length of both cables. Make sure there are no kinks or sharp bends. Reroute the cables if necessary.

19. Connect the pull throttle cable as follows:
   a. Connect the pull throttle cable into the upper hole (C, **Figure 46**) in the throttle housing and into the upper hole in the throttle sleeve (A, **Figure 48**).
   b. Attach the pull throttle cable into the lower portion of the throttle drum (A, **Figure 47**).

20. Connect the return throttle cable as follows:
   a. Connect the return throttle cable into the lower hole (D, **Figure 46**) in the throttle housing and into the lower hole in the throttle sleeve (B, **Figure 48**).
   b. Attach the return throttle cable into the upper portion of the throttle drum (B, **Figure 47**).

21. Install and tighten the right side switch housing as follows:
   a. Align the switch housing locating pin (**Figure 49**) with the hole in the handlebar and close the switch halves around the handlebar. Try to twist the switch; it must not turn.
   b. Install the front and rear switch housing screws and tighten securely.

22. Secure the throttle cables with the cable clamps or plastic ties in their original positions.

23. Install the fuel tank as described in this chapter.

24. Operate the throttle grip and make sure the carburetor linkage is operating correctly with no binding. If operation is incorrect or if there is binding, carefully check that the cables are attached correctly and that there are no tight bends in the cables.

25. Adjust the throttle cables as described in Chapter Three.

> *WARNING*
> *Improperly adjusted or incorrectly routed throttle cables can cause the throttle to hang open This could cause loss of control. Do not ride the*

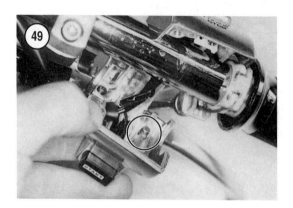

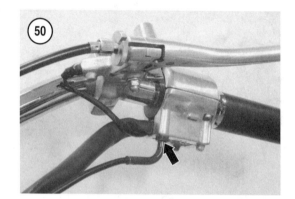

motorcycle until throttle cable operation is correct.

26. Start the engine and let it idle. Turn the handlebar from side to side and listen to the engine speed. Make sure the idle speed does not increase. If it does, the throttle cables are adjusted incorrectly or the throttle cables are improperly routed. Find and correct the source of the problem before riding.

27. Test ride the motorcycle slowly at first and make sure the throttle is operating correctly.

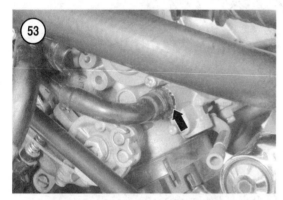

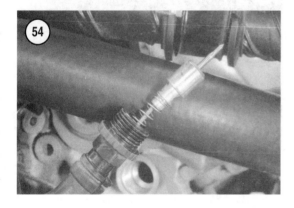

CHOKE CABLE REPLACEMENT

1. Remove the fuel tank as described in this chapter.

2. Remove the right steering cover (Chapter Fifteen).

3. Draw a diagram of the choke cable routing, from the choke lever on the handlebar to where the cable separates at its junction housing and connects to both carburetors.

4. Perform the following at the left handlebar switch housing:

    a. Remove the mirror.

b. Loosen the choke cable nut at the switch housing (**Figure 50**).

c. Remove the two screws and separate the left handlebar switch housing.

d. Disconnect the choke cable from the lever (**Figure 51**).

5. Remove the bolt securing the choke cable junction housing to the frame (**Figure 52**).

6. Loosen the choke cable locknut (**Figure 53**) and remove the choke valve assembly from the carburetor. Remove the valve, spring (**Figure 54**) and cap from the end of the cable.

7. Repeat Step 6 at the other carburetor.

8. Remove the choke cable assembly.

9. Install the new choke cable assembly, following the original path recorded in Step 3.

10. Reconnect the choke cable at the lever (**Figure 50**) and assemble the switch housing. Operate the choke lever. If okay, continue with Step 11

11. Reconnect the choke cables to the carburetors as follows:

    a. Install the choke cable locknut, spring and choke valve onto the cable (**Figure 54**).

    b. Insert the choke valve into the carburetor and tighten the choke cable locknut until it contacts the carburetor housing, then tighten 1/4 turn.

    c. Repeat for the other cable end and carburetor.

12. Operate the choke lever and make sure the choke valves operate correctly. If the operation is incorrect or there is binding, check the cables and choke valve before continuing. Make sure the cables work correctly before adjusting the choke.

13. Reverse Step 1 and Step 2.

14. Adjust the choke cable as described in Chapter Three.

FUEL FILTER

The fuel filter is connected into the fuel line between the fuel tank and fuel pump. A restricted fuel filter lowers the fuel pressure and causes hard starting, engine hesitation during acceleration and surging at high speed. While there is no recommended fuel filter replacement interval, inspect the fuel filter at the same time the fuel hoses are inspected (refer to intervals in Chapter Three). Because the fuel filter is plastic, contaminants are not always visible. If a restricted fuel filter is suspected, check the fuel pump discharge volume as described in this chapter.

8

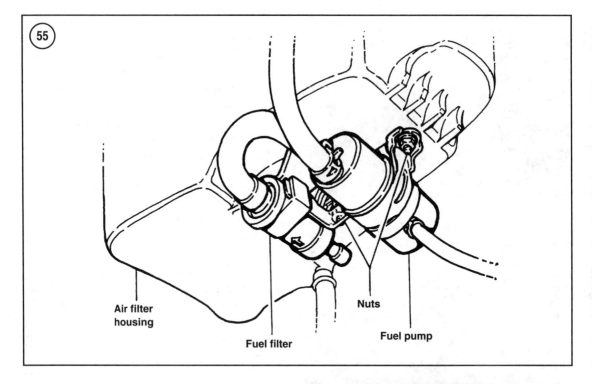

Air filter housing

Fuel filter

Nuts

Fuel pump

Removal/Installation

The fuel filter is mounted on the bottom of the air box and behind the fuel pump (**Figure 55**). This procedure describes how to access the fuel filter by disconnecting both shock absorbers from the swing arm, then raising the motorcycle away from the swing arm.

1. Read the *Fuel System Precautions* at the beginning of this chapter before removing the fuel filter.
2. Turn the fuel valve off.
3. Remove the battery holder (Chapter Nine).
4. Support the motorcycle with an adjustable wide platform jack as described under *Motorcycle Lift* in Chapter Eleven. Do not use a narrow scissors jack because it does not provide sufficient support. Block the front wheel so the motorcycle cannot roll forward or backward. If the motorcycle is mounted on a motorcycle lift, lock the front wheel in a wheel vise.
5. Remove the right side shock absorber (Chapter Thirteen).
6. Remove the lower mounting bolt from the left shock absorber.
7. Raise the motorcycle with the jack to provide clearance between the top of the swing arm and left side of the fuel filter.

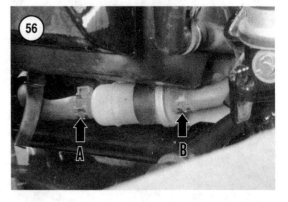

NOTE
If there is not enough clearance to safely replace the fuel filter, remove the swing arm as described in Chapter Thirteen.

8. Working through the left side of the motorcycle, disconnect the hose from the left side of the fuel filter (A, **Figure 56**).

9. Working through the right side of the motorcycle and above the swing arm, pull the fuel hose and its rubber mount off the mounting bracket. Then disconnect the hose from the right side of the fuel filter (B, **Figure 56**) and remove the filter.

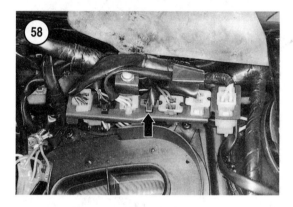

10. Clean the hose ends before installing the new filter. Replace weak or damaged hose clamps.

11. Replace the fuel filter so the arrow mark on the new filter faces as shown in **Figure 55**. Push each hose end fully onto the filter and secure with a hose clamp (**Figure 56**).

12. Installation is the reverse of removal. Note the following:

    a. Check for fuel leaks.

    b. Install the right side shock absorber and tighten the lower left side shock absorber mounting bolt as specified in Chapter Thirteen.

FUEL SYSTEM TESTING

This section tests the fuel pump and fuel cutoff relay.

Fuel Pump
System Test

1. Before testing the fuel pump system, check if the fuel pump runs:

    a. Remove the left side cover (Chapter Fifteen).

    b. Turn the engine stop switch to its RUN position.

    c. Turn the ignition switch on but do not start the engine. You should hear the fuel pump run for 2 seconds. If the fuel pump ran, perform the *Fuel Pump Flow Test* in this section. If the fuel pump did not run, test the fuel pump electrical system as described in this section.

NOTE
A timer function in the fuel cutoff relay allows it to run for 2 seconds when the ignition switch is turned on. This allows the fuel pump to fill the carburetor float bowls with fuel.

NOTE
The ignition system primary circuit controls the fuel cutoff relay. When performing voltage tests with the ignition switch turned on in this section, set the engine stop switch in its RUN position.

2. Turn the ignition switch off.

3. Remove the seat (Chapter Fifteen).

4. Disconnect the three-pin fuel cutoff relay connector at the relay (**Figure 57**).

5. Turn the ignition switch on and measure voltage between the fuel cutoff relay harness side connector black terminal and engine ground. The voltmeter should read battery voltage. Turn the ignition switch off.

    a. If there is no battery voltage, check the black wire for an open circuit or a contaminated or damaged connector. If okay, check the ignition system sub-fuse, fuse contacts and the ignition switch (Chapter Nine).

    b. If battery voltage is present, go to Step 6.

6. Check for continuity on the black/blue wire between the three-pin fuel cutoff relay harness side connector and ground. There should be no continuity.

    a. If there is continuity, the fuel cutoff relay is faulty. Replace the relay and retest.

    b. If there is no continuity, go to Step 7.

7. Disconnect the two-pin fuel pump connector. Refer to **Figure 58** (VT1100C2 ACE) or **Figure 59** (all other models).

8. Connect a jumper wire between the three-pin fuel cutoff relay harness side connector black and

8

black/blue terminals (**Figure 59**). Turn the ignition switch on and measure voltage between the two-pin fuel pump harness side connector green and black/blue terminals. There should be battery voltage. Turn the ignition switch off and disconnect the jumper wire.

    a. If there is no battery voltage, check the black/blue and green wires for an open circuit or a contaminated or damaged connector.

    b. If battery voltage is present, replace the fuel pump as described in this chapter.

9. Reconnect the fuel pump and fuel cutoff relay connector terminals.

10. Install the seat (Chapter Fifteen).

Fuel Cutoff Relay Replacement

1. Remove the seat (Chapter Fifteen).
2. Disconnect the electrical connector from the fuel cutoff relay (**Figure 57**).
3. Remove the fuel cutoff relay and replace it.
4. Install by reversing these removal steps.

Fuel Pump Flow Test

1. Because gasoline is flowing into an open container during this procedure, read *Fuel System Precautions* at the beginning of this chapter.
2. Remove the seat (Chapter Fifteen).

> *NOTE*
> *Make sure the hose disconnected in Step 3 was originally connected to the outlet nozzle at the fuel pump.*

3A. On VT1100C, VT1100C2 Sabre and VT1100T models, perform the following:

    a. Remove the fuel tank mounting bolts.

    b. Raise the fuel tank and support it with wooden blocks.

    c. Disconnect the fuel hose from the hose joint (**Figure 60**). Place the hose into a plastic graduated beaker (**Figure 60**).

3B. On VT1100C2 ACE and VT1100C3 models, perform the following:

    a. Remove the right side cover (Chapter Fifteen).

    b. Disconnect the fuel hose from the hose joint (**Figure 61**). Place the hose into a plastic graduated beaker (**Figure 61**).

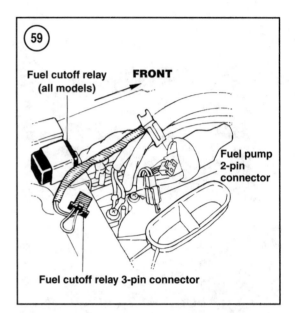

59

Fuel cutoff relay (all models)   **FRONT**

Fuel pump 2-pin connector

Fuel cutoff relay 3-pin connector

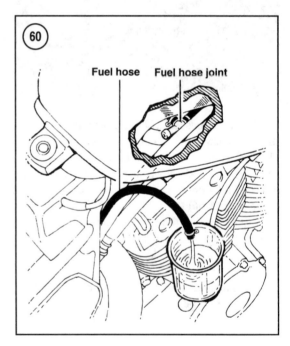

60

Fuel hose   Fuel hose joint

4. Disconnect the 3-pin fuel cutoff relay connector (**Figure 57**). Connect a jumper wire between the harness side connector black and black/blue terminals (**Figure 59**).

5. Turn the fuel valve on.

6. Have an assistant turn the ignition switch to the ON position and allow fuel to run out of the fuel hose and into the graduated beaker for 5 seconds, then turn the ignition switch off.

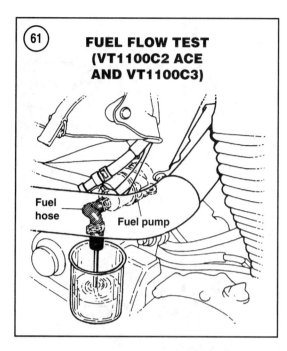

(61)

**FUEL FLOW TEST
(VT1100C2 ACE
AND VT1100C3)**

Fuel
hose

Fuel pump

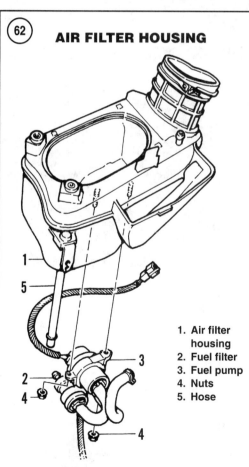

(62)

AIR FILTER HOUSING

1. Air filter
   housing
2. Fuel filter
3. Fuel pump
4. Nuts
5. Hose

7. Multiply the amount of fuel in the beaker by 12 (12 × 5 = 60 seconds). This gives the fuel pump flow capacity for 1 minute.

8. Refer to **Table 2** for the correct fuel flow capacity for one minute.

9. If the fuel pump does not flow the minimum specified amount of fuel in 1 minute, replace the fuel pump as described in this chapter.

10. Pour the fuel from the beaker back into the fuel tank.

11. Reconnect the fuel outlet hose to the hose joint. Secure the hose with its clamp.

12. Disconnect the jumper wire, then reconnect the fuel cutoff relay connector at the relay.

13. Start the engine and allow it to idle. Inspect the fuel hose for leaks.

WARNING
Repair any fuel leaks before riding the motorcycle.

14. Install all previously removed parts.

AIR FILTER HOUSING AND FUEL PUMP

The fuel pump is mounted on the bottom of the air filter housing (**Figure 55** and **Figure 62**). The air filter housing must be removed to replace the fuel pump.

Removal/Installation

1. Read *Fuel System Precautions* at the beginning of this chapter.

2. Remove the battery holder (Chapter Nine).

3. Remove the right side cover (Chapter Fifteen).

4. Remove the rear swing arm (Chapter Thirteen).

5. Disconnect the crankcase breather hose from the air filter housing.

6. Disconnect the rubber strap securing the tool kit to the side of the air box.

7. Disconnect the 2-pin fuel pump connector. Refer to **Figure 58** (VT1100C2 ACE) or **Figure 59** (all other models). Then disconnect the clamp securing the fuel pump wiring harness to the frame.

8. Disconnect the breather hose (A, **Figure 63**) at the fuel pump.

9. Disconnect the fuel filter hose (B, **Figure 63**).

10. Disconnect the hose at the fuel pump hose joint (**Figure 64**).

11. Disconnect the air box drain hose from the air box.

12. Remove the bolts securing the coolant filler neck to the right side of the air box.

13. Remove the two mounting bolts (**Figure 65**) and ground terminal from the top of the air filter housing.

14. Loosen the hose clamp that is securing the air filter housing connecting hose to the frame.

15. Remove the air filter housing from the frame.

16. Remove the two nuts and the fuel pump and fuel filter from the bottom of the air box (**Figure 55**).

17. Installation is the reverse of removal. Note the following:

 a. Inspect the fuel hoses and the breather hose for cracks, soft spots or other damage, and replace if necessary.

 b. Replace weak or damaged hose clamps.

 c. Clean the hose ends before reconnecting them.

CAUTION
Some fuel remains in the old fuel pump. Properly store the pump until it can be discarded.

 d. If the connecting hose was removed from the air filter housing, apply Gasgacinch to the mating surfaces before reconnecting the hose. Install the hose by aligning the groove in the air filter housing with the tab on the hose.

 e. When installing the ground terminal onto the top of the air filter housing (**Figure 65**), position it against the frame stopper, then tighten its mounting bolt.

 f. Turn the fuel valve on. Then turn the engine stop switch to RUN and turn the ignition switch on. The pump should run for approximately 2 seconds then stop. Check for fuel leaks at all hose connections.

FUEL TANK

Removal/Installation

Refer to **Figure 66**.

1. Read *Fuel System Precautions* at the beginning of this chapter.

2. Disconnect the battery negative cable as described in Chapter Nine.

3. Turn the fuel valve off and disconnect the fuel hose. Plug the end of the hose.

4. Remove the fuel tank mounting bolts, washer and collars.

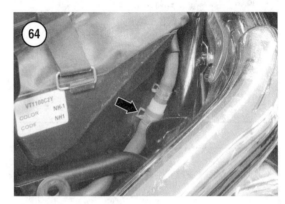

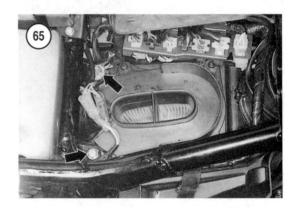

5. Perform the following:

 a. Lift the rear of the tank and secure it with a wooden block.

 b. On 49-state and Canada models, disconnect the fuel tank breather hose (**Figure 67**) from the bottom of the fuel tank.

 c. On California models, disconnect the Evaporative Emission (EVAP) No. 1 (**Figure 67**) hose from the bottom of the fuel tank.

6. Remove the fuel tank.

7. Installation is the reverse of removal. Note the following:

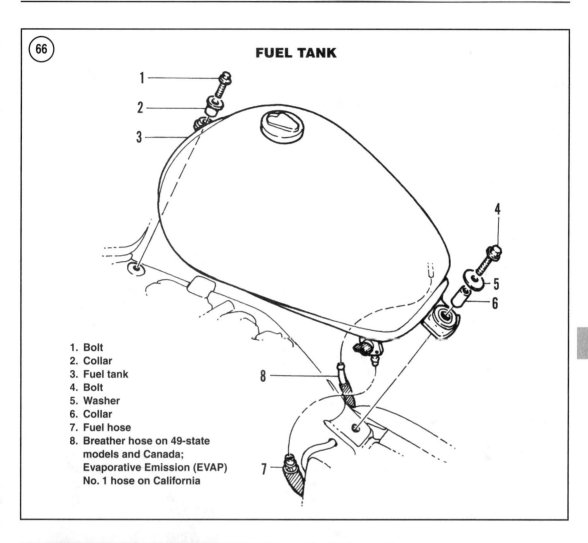

FUEL TANK

1. Bolt
2. Collar
3. Fuel tank
4. Bolt
5. Washer
6. Collar
7. Fuel hose
8. Breather hose on 49-state models and Canada; Evaporative Emission (EVAP) No. 1 hose on California

8

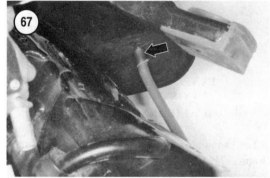

a. Replace missing or damaged fuel tank dampers.

b. Tighten the 6 mm bolt to 12 N•m (106 in.-lb.) and the 8 mm bolt to 26 N•m (19 ft.-lb.).

c. After completing installation, turn the fuel valve on and check for leaks.

Fuel Valve and Screen Replacement

Refer to **Figure 68**.

1. Read *Fuel System Precautions* at the beginning of this chapter.

2. Disconnect the battery negative cable as described in Chapter Nine.

3. Turn the fuel valve off and disconnect the fuel hose (7, **Figure 66**).

4. Connect a separate hose onto the fuel valve and insert the other end of the hose in a container suitable for gasoline storage. Turn the fuel valve on and drain the tank. Then turn the fuel valve off and disconnect the hose.

5. Remove the fuel tank as described in this section.

6. Place the fuel tank on a blanket with the fuel valve facing up.

7. Loosen the fuel valve nut and remove the fuel valve.

8. Remove the fuel strainer and O-ring from the fuel valve. Discard the O-ring.

9. Clean the fuel strainer. Replace the fuel strainer if it cannot be cleaned.

10. Installation is the reverse of removal. Note the following:

   a. Install a new O-ring.

   b. Tighten the fuel valve nut to 34 N•m (25 ft.-lb.).

   c. Pour a small amount of fuel into the tank and check for leaks. Do not overtighten the fuel valve nut to stop a leak.

EMISSION CONTROL LABELS

Emission control labels are attached to either the the left side cover, the left side of the swing arm or the rear fender. The motorcycle emission control information label (A, **Figure 69**) lists tune-up information. The vacuum hose routing diagram label (B, **Figure 69**) shows a schematic of the emission control system. This decal is useful when identifying hoses used in the emission control system.

Emission control system hoses are labeled with identification numbers that correspond with the numbers listed on the vacuum hose routing diagram label (B, **Figure 69**). If these identification numbers have deteriorated or the original hose was replaced, identify the hoses and their fittings for proper installation. Refer to *Fuel Hose Identification* in this chapter for tips on how to identify hoses.

A Vehicle Emission Control Information Update label is used when the carburetors have been adjusted for high altitude operation. Refer to *High Elevation Adjustment* in this chapter.

CRANKCASE BREATHER SYSTEM

The engine is equipped with a closed crankcase breather system (**Figure 70**). The system draws blow-by gasses from the crankcase and recirculates them into the combustion chamber to be burned.

Liquid residues collect in the crankcase breather drain tube. These must be emptied at periodic intervals. Refer to *Crankcase Breather Inspection* in Chapter Three for service intervals and procedures.

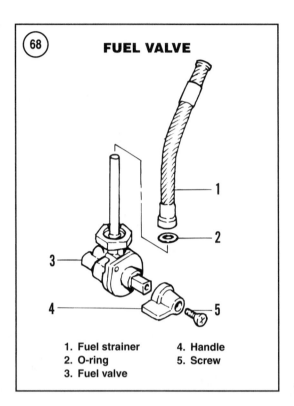

68 **FUEL VALVE**

1. Fuel strainer   4. Handle
2. O-ring   5. Screw
3. Fuel valve

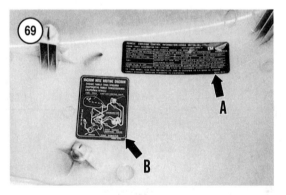

69

A

B

EVAPORATIVE EMISSION CONTROL SYSTEM (CALIFORNIA MODELS)

The evaporative emission control (EVAP) system (**Figure 71**) captures fuel system vapors and stores them in the charcoal canister so they cannot be released into the atmosphere. When the engine is started, the stored vapors are drawn from the canister. They pass through the purge control valve, flow into the carburetors and then into the engine where they are burned. At the same time, the carburetor air vent control valve (EVAP CAV) opens so air is drawn into the carburetors.

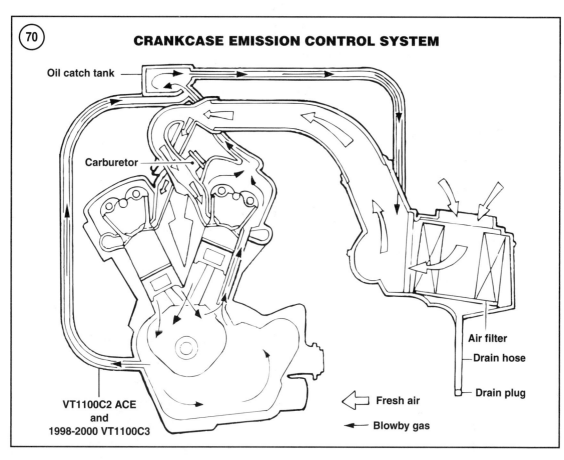

CRANKCASE EMISSION CONTROL SYSTEM

Oil catch tank

Carburetor

Air filter

Drain hose

Drain plug

VT1100C2 ACE
and
1998-2000 VT1100C3

Fresh air

Blowby gas

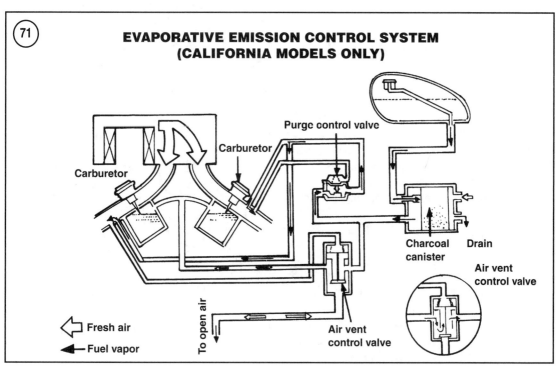

**EVAPORATIVE EMISSION CONTROL SYSTEM
(CALIFORNIA MODELS ONLY)**

Purge control valve

Carburetor

Carburetor

Charcoal
canister

Drain

Air vent
control valve

To open air

Fresh air

Fuel vapor

Air vent
control valve

Make sure all hoses are correctly routed, properly attached to the different components and all hose clamps are tight. Check all hoses for deterioration, and replace them as necessary.

Charcoal Canister
Removal/Installation

The charcoal canister is mounted below the radiator (**Figure 72**).
1. Disconnect the No. 1 hose and No. 4 hose from the canister.
2. Remove the mounting bolts and the charcoal canister.
3. Installation is the reverse of these steps.

Evaporative Emission (EVAP)
Purge Control Valve

Removal/installation

Refer to **Figure 73**.
1. Remove the fuel tank as described in this chapter.
2. Pull the EVAP purge control valve off its mounting stay.
3. Disconnect the following hoses from the EVAP purge control valve:
   a. No. 4 hose.
   b. No. 5 hose.
   c. No. 11 hose.
4. Reverse these steps to install the EVAP purge control valve.

Testing

If the engine is difficult to restart when hot, test the EVAP purge control valve as follows. Refer to **Figure 73** and **Figure 74** to identify the hose fittings called out in this procedure.

A hand-operated vacuum pump and pressure pump are required.
1. Remove the EVAP purge control valve as described in this chapter.
2. Connect a vacuum pump to the No. 5 hose fitting and apply 33 kPa (9.8 in.) HG of vacuum. The vacuum should hold. If the vacuum does not hold, replace the EVAP purge control valve.
3. Disconnect the vacuum pump.
4. Connect the vacuum pump to the No. 11 hose fitting and apply 33 kPa (9.8 in.) HG of vacuum. The

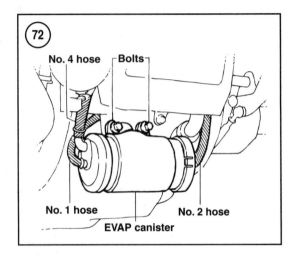

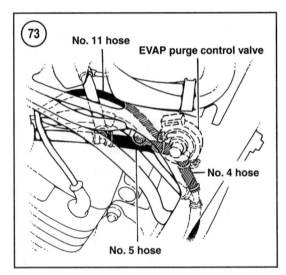

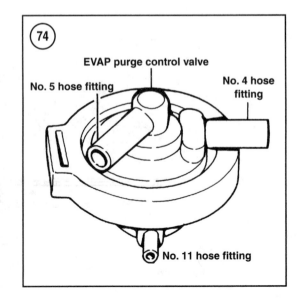

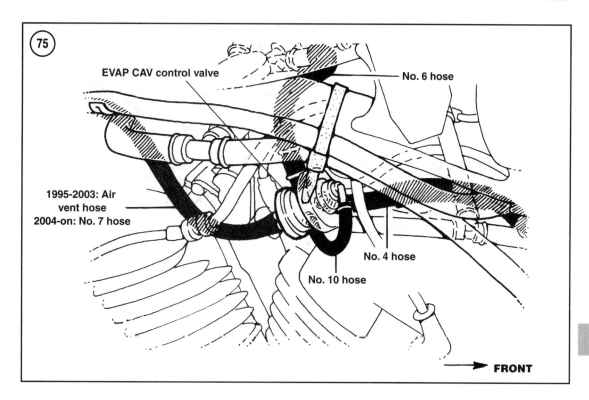

75

EVAP CAV control valve

No. 6 hose

1995-2003: Air
vent hose
2004-on: No. 7 hose

No. 4 hose

No. 10 hose

FRONT

vacuum should hold. If the vacuum does not hold, re-place the EVAP purge control valve. If the vacuum held, leave the vacuum pump connected to the No. 11 hose fitting and continue with Step 5.

5. Connect a pressure pump to the No. 4 hose fitting.

CAUTION
Use only a hand-operated pressure pump. Using air from a high-pressure source will damage the EVAP purge control valve.

6. Apply 33 kPa (9.8 in.) HG of vacuum to the No. 11 hose fitting, then pump air through the No. 4 hose fit-ting. When doing so, air should flow through the No. 5 hose fitting. If air did not flow through the No. 5 hose fitting, replace the EVAP purge control valve.

7. Disconnect the vacuum and pressure pumps.

8. Install the EVAP purge control valve as described in this chapter.

Evaporative Emission Carburetor Air Vent (EVAP CAV) Control Valve

Removal/installation

Refer to **Figure 75**.

1. Remove the fuel tank as described in this chapter.

2. Pull the EVAP CAV control valve off its mounting stay.

3. Disconnect the following hoses from the EVAP CAV control valve:

   a. No. 4 hose.
   b. No. 6 hose.
   c. No. 10 hose.
   d. 1995-2003—Air vent hose.
   e. 2004—No. 7 hose.

4. Reverse these steps to install the EVAP CAV con-trol valve.

Testing

Refer to **Figure 75** and **Figure 76**.

A hand-operated vacuum pump and pressure pump are required.

1. Remove the EVAP CAV control valve as described in this chapter.

2. Connect a vacuum pump to the No. 10 hose fitting and apply 33 kPa (9.8 in.) HG of vacuum. The vac-uum should hold. If the vacuum does not hold, replace the EVAP CAV control valve.

3. Disconnect the vacuum pump.

4. Connect the vacuum pump to the air vent hose/No. 7 hose fitting and apply 33 kPa (9.8 in.) HG of vac-

uum. The vacuum should hold. If the vacuum does not hold, replace the EVAP CAV control valve.

> *CAUTION*
> *Use only a hand-operated pressure pump. Using air from a high-pressure source in Step 5 damages the EVAP CAV control valve.*

5. Remove the vacuum pump and reconnect it to the No. 10 hose fitting. Connect a pressure pump to the air vent hose/No. 7 hose fitting.

6. Apply vacuum to the No. 10 hose fitting, then pump air through the air vent hose/No. 7 hose fitting. Air must flow through the valve and exit through the No. 6 hose fitting.

7. Plug the No. 6 hose fitting. Then apply vacuum to the No. 10 hose fitting while pumping air through the air vent hose fitting. The air pressure pumped through the air vent hose/No. 7 hose fitting should hold steady.

8. Disconnect the vacuum and pressure pumps.

9. Replace the EVAP CAV control valve if it failed any one of these tests.

10. Install the EVAP CAV control valve as described in this chapter.

PULSE SECONDARY AIR INJECTION (PAIR) SYSTEM (MODELS SO EQUIPPED)

The PAIR system lowers emission output by using vacuum pulses from the carburetor to introduce secondary air into the exhaust ports (**Figure 77**). The additional air raises the exhaust temperature, which consumes some of the unburned fuel in the exhaust. Reed valves installed in the cylinder head cover prevent a reverse flow of air through the system. The PAIR control valve prevents air from entering the engine during deceleration, thus preventing backfiring in the exhaust system.

System Inspection

> *NOTE*
> *Refer to the vacuum hose routing diagram mounted on the motorcycle and **Figure** 77 when disconnecting and reconnecting the hoses.*

1. Start the engine and warm to normal operating temperature. Turn the engine off.

2. Remove the air filter element (Chapter Three).

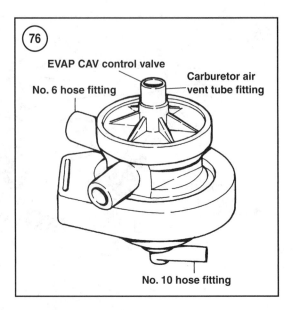

No. 6 hose fitting — EVAP CAV control valve — Carburetor air vent tube fitting

No. 10 hose fitting

3. Check that the secondary air injection port, located inside the air filter housing, is clean and free of carbon deposits. If the port is clogged or partially blocked by carbon, remove and inspect the PAIR reed valves as described in this section.

4. Locate the No. 10 hose at the PAIR control valve (**Figure 77**). Trace the hose from this point and disconnect it from its tee-connection. Plug the tee-connection hose joint to prevent a vacuum leak. Then connect a vacuum pump to the No. 10 hose.

5. Disconnect the No. 15 hose at the air filter housing secondary air intake port (**Figure 77**).

6. Start the engine and slightly open the throttle. Check that air is being drawn through the No. 15 hose. If not, check for a clogged or damaged No. 15 hose.

7. With the engine running, apply 230 mm (9.06 in.) HG of vacuum to the PAIR control valve with the vacuum pump. With vacuum applied, check that the No. 15 hose stops drawing air. Then check that the vacuum does not bleed off.

8. If air is drawn in or if the specified vacuum is not maintained, the PAIR control valve is defective and must be replaced.

9. Turn the engine off.

10. If backfiring occurs on deceleration and the secondary air supply system tests correctly, the air cutoff valve on one or both carburetors may be defective. Refer to *Air Cutoff Valve Removal/Installation* in this chapter.

11. Remove the vacuum pump and reconnect the No. 15 and No. 10 hoses.

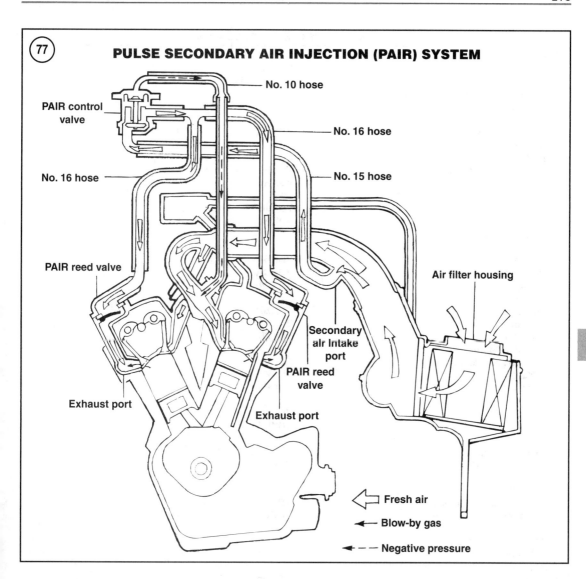

(77) **PULSE SECONDARY AIR INJECTION (PAIR) SYSTEM**

No. 10 hose

PAIR control valve

No. 16 hose

No. 16 hose

No. 15 hose

PAIR reed valve

Air filter housing

Secondary air intake port

PAIR reed valve

Exhaust port

Exhaust port

Fresh air

Blow-by gas

Negative pressure

8

12. Install the air filter (Chapter Three).

PAIR Control Valve
Removal/Installation

1. Remove the fuel tank as described in this chapter.
2. Label and then disconnect the hoses at the PAIR control valve (**Figure 77**).
3. Remove the PAIR control valve.
4. Installation is the reverse of removal.

PAIR Reed Valves
Removal/Installation

1. Remove the fuel tank as described in this chapter.

2. Disconnect the No. 16 hose from the PAIR reed valve cover on the cylinder head cover.
3. Remove the bolts, cover and reed valve.
4. Inspect each reed valve for fatigue, damage or carbon buildup. Inspect the rubber seat on the reed valve for cracks, flat spots, deterioration or other damage. Replace the reed valve if necessary.

NOTE
Do not service or disassemble the reed valves. Do not bend the stopper. If part of the valve is damaged, the valve assembly must be replaced.

5. Install the reed valve into the cylinder head cover. Install and tighten the PAIR reed valve cover bolts to 5 N•m (44 in.-lb.).

Table 1 CARBURETOR SPECIFICATIONS

Carburetor	
Manufacturer	Keihin
Throttle bore	36 mm (1.4 in.)
Carburetor identification number	
VT1100C	
1997-2003	
49-state and Canada	VDKHA
California	VDKJA
2004-2005	
49-state and Canada	VDKHB
California	VDKHC
2006-on	
49-state and Canada	VDKJB
California	VDKHC
VT1100C2 ACE	
1995	
49-state	VDKBA
California	VDKCA
Canada	VDK2A
1996-on	
49-state	VDKBB
California	VDKCB
Canada	VDK2B
VT1100C2 Sabre	
49-state and Canada	
2000-2005	VDKED
2006-on	VDKEK
California	
2000-2003	VDKEE
2004	VDKEJ
VT1100C3	
1998-2000	
49-state and Canada	VDKKA
California	VDKLA
2001-2002	
49-state and Canada	VDKED
California	VDKEE
VT1100T	
49-state and Canada	VDKFA
California	VDKGA
Engine idle speed	1000 ± 100 rpm
Float level	9.2 mm (0.36 in.)
Idle drop procedure	
Pilot screw initial adjustment	
VT1100C	2 turns out
VT1100C2 ACE	
1995	1 3/4 turns out
1996-1999	1 1/2 turns out
VT1100C2 Sabre	2 1/2 turns out
VT1100C3	2 1/2 turns out
VT1100T	2 1/2 turns out
Pilot jet	42
Main jet	
VT1100C	
1997-2003	178
2004	
Front carburetor	178
Rear carburetor	
49-state and Canada	185
California	190
(continued)	

Table 1 CARBURETOR SPECIFICATIONS (continued)

Main jet (continued)	
VT1100C2 ACE	
Front carburetor	
1995	180
1996-on	175
VT1100C2 ACE	
Rear carburetor	
1995	185
1996-on	180
VT1100C2 Sabre	
Front carburetor	175
Rear carburetor	180
VT1100C3	
Front carburetor	
1998-2000	180
2001-2002	175
Rear carburetor	
1998-2000	185
2001-2002	180
VT1100T	
Front carburetor	175
Rear carburetor	180

8

Table 2 FUEL PUMP SPECIFICATIONS

VT1100C2 ACE	
1995	Minimum 650 ml (22.0 U.S. oz.) per minute
1996-1999	Minimum 800 ml (27.1 U.S. oz.) per minute
All other models	Minimum 800 ml (27.1 U.S. oz.) per minute

Table 3 FUEL SYSTEM TORQUE SPECIFICATIONS

	N•m	in.-lb.	ft.-lb.
Fuel tank mounting bolts			
6 mm	12	106	–
8 mm	26	–	19
Fuel valve nut	34	–	25
PAIR reed valve cover			
2004 California models	5.0	44	–

CHAPTER NINE

ELECTRICAL SYSTEM

This chapter contains service and test procedures for the following components:

1. Battery.
2. Charging system.
3. Ignition system.
4. Starting system.
5. Lighting system.
6. Electrical components.
7. Switches.
8. Fuses.

Tables 1-12 are at the end of this chapter.

ELECTRICAL COMPONENT REPLACEMENT

Most motorcycle dealerships and parts suppliers do not accept the return of any electrical part. If you cannot determine the exact cause of any electrical system malfunction, have a Honda dealership retest that specific system to verify your test results. If you purchase a new electrical component(s), install it, and then find that the system still does not work properly, you probably cannot return the unit for a refund.

Consider any test result carefully before replacing a component that tests only *slightly* out of speci-

fication, especially resistance. A number of variables can affect test results dramatically. These include the testing meter's internal circuitry, ambient temperatures and conditions under which the motorcycle has been operated. All instructions and specifications have been checked for accuracy; however, successful test results depend largely upon individual accuracy.

ELECTRICAL CONNECTORS

The Honda VT1100 is equipped with numerous electrical components, connectors and wiring harnesses. Corrosion-causing moisture can enter these electrical connectors and cause poor electrical connections leading to component failure. Troubleshooting an electrical circuit with one or more corroded electrical connectors can be time-consuming and frustrating.

When reconnecting electrical connectors, pack them in a dielectric grease compound. Dielectric grease is especially formulated for sealing and waterproofing electrical connections without interfering with current flow. Use only this compound or an equivalent designed for this specific purpose. Do not use a substitute that may interfere with the cur-

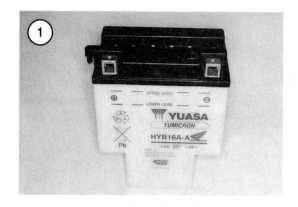

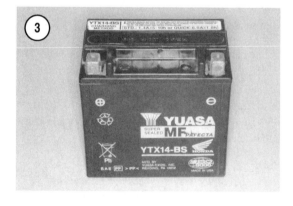

BATTERY

Most no-start problems and electrical system problems can be traced to battery neglect. To keep the battery in good condition, inspect, clean and test the battery at the service intervals specified in Chapter Three.

The VT1100 models covered in this manual are equipped with either a conventional or maintenance-free battery. Refer to **Table 1** and **Table 2** for applications.

Conventional batteries (**Figure 1**) are equipped with removable breather caps (**Figure 2**) for maintaining the fluid level and testing with a hydrometer. Internal battery pressure and gasses are vented through an open nozzle on one side of the battery. A breather hose is connected to the nozzle and routed to prevent the discharged gasses from contacting the motorcycle. This battery requires periodic electrolyte inspection and refilling with distilled water when the level is low. Refer to **Table 1** for battery specifications.

A maintenance-free battery (**Figure 3**) is permanently sealed after its initial service and does not require periodic electrolyte inspection or refilling. Never remove the sealing cap from the top of the battery because the battery electrolyte must not be serviced. Internal battery pressure is controlled by a safety relief valve and an external vent. However, no vent tube is used. Always replace a sealed battery with the same type of battery; do not install a conventional or non-sealed battery. Refer to **Table 2** for battery specifications.

To prevent accidental shorts that could blow a fuse when working on the electrical system, always disconnect the negative battery cable from the battery before starting service.

On all models covered in this manual, the negative side is ground. When removing the battery, disconnect the negative cable first, then the positive cable. This minimizes the chance of a tool shorting to ground when disconnecting the battery positive cable.

Safety Precautions

Use extreme care to avoid spilling or splashing the electrolyte when working with conventional batteries. Also observe caution when working with sealed batteries; a cracked or damaged battery case

rent flow within the electrical connector. Do not use silicone sealant.

After cleaning both the male and female connectors, make sure they are thoroughly dry. Apply dielectric grease to the interior of one of the connectors before connecting the two connector halves. After the connector is fully packed, wipe the exterior of all excessive compound.

Get into the practice of cleaning and sealing all electrical connectors every time they are unplugged. This may prevent a breakdown on the road, and save time when troubleshooting a circuit.

9

can leak electrolyte. This solution contains sulfuric acid, which can ruin clothing and cause serious chemical burns. If any electrolyte is spilled or splashed on clothing or skin, immediately neutralize with a solution of baking soda and water, then flush with an abundance of clean water.

WARNING
Protect your eyes, skin and clothing when working with batteries; sulfuric acid, an active ingredient in electrolyte, is corrosive and can cause severe burns and permanent injury. If electrolyte gets into your eyes, flush your eyes thoroughly with clean, running water and get immediate medical attention. Always wear safety goggles when servicing the battery. This also applies when working with maintenance-free or sealed batteries because the battery case may be cracked and leaking electrolyte.

WARNING
While batteries are being charged, highly explosive hydrogen gas forms in each cell. Some of this gas escapes through a vent opening and may form an explosive atmosphere in and around the battery. This condition can persist for several hours. Sparks, an open flame or a lighted cigarette can ignite the gas, causing an internal battery explosion and possible serious injury.

Note the following when handling and servicing batteries:

1. Always wear safety goggles or a face shield when servicing and testing batteries.

2. Wear rubber gloves to protect hands and arms from acid burns when handling batteries.

3. Wear a shop apron or similar protective clothing to protect clothes from acid damage.

4. If electrolyte is spilled or splashed onto any surface, neutralize it immediately with a baking soda and water solution and then rinse with clean water.

5. Keep children and pets away from battery and charging equipment.

6. If the motorcycle is in an accident, check for battery damage and electrolyte leakage.

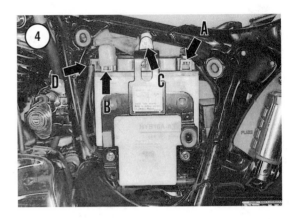

7. Do not smoke or permit any open flame near any battery being charged or which has been recently charged.

8. Do not disconnect live circuits at battery terminals since a spark usually occurs when a live circuit is broken.

9. Take care when connecting or disconnecting any battery charger. Make sure the power switch is off before making or breaking connections. Poor connections are a common cause of electrical arcs, which cause explosions.

Removal/Installation

The battery is mounted behind the left side cover.

1. Read *Safety Precautions* in this section.

2. Turn the ignition switch off.

3. Remove the left side cover (Chapter Fifteen).

4. Visually inspect the battery for any visible damage or electrolyte leaks.

NOTE
If electrolyte is on top of a conventional battery, check for loose or damaged filler caps. If the caps are tight, an excessive charging rate may be causing the electrolyte spray from around the cap seals and through their vents. You may also notice the strong presence of electrolyte fumes immediately after removing the side cover.

5A. Conventional battery:
   a. Disconnect the negative battery cable from the battery. Refer to A, **Figure 4**.
   b. Disconnect the positive battery cable from the battery. Refer to B, **Figure 4**.

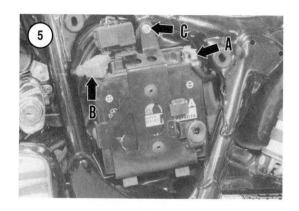

c. Remove the battery mounting holder bolt or nut (C, **Figure 4**) and pivot the holder away from the battery.

d. Disconnect the breather hose (D, **Figure 4**) from the battery.

5B. Maintenance-free battery:

a. Disconnect the negative battery cable from the battery. Refer to A, **Figure 5**.

b Disconnect the positive battery cable from the battery. Refer to B, **Figure 5**.

c. Remove the battery mounting holder bolt or nut (C, **Figure 5**) and pivot the holder away from the battery.

6. Remove the battery.

CAUTION
Be careful not to spill battery electro-lyte on painted or polished surfaces. The liquid is highly corrosive and damages the finish. If spilled, wash it off immediately with soapy water and thoroughly rinse with clean water.

7. Installation is the reverse of removal. Note the following:

NOTE
Recycle the old battery. When replacing the battery, be sure to turn in the old battery at that time. The lead plates and the plastic case can be recycled. Most motorcycle dealerships accept old batteries in trade when purchasing a new one. Never place an old battery in household trash; it is illegal in most states to place any acid or lead (heavy metal) contents in landfills.

a. Make sure the top of the battery is clean and dry. This is especially critical on conventional

batteries where it is normal for electrolyte to seep around the battery vent caps when the battery is charging. Dirt and other residue on top of the battery mixes with the electrolyte and can cause the battery to discharge. Clean the battery as described under *Cleaning and Inspection* in this section.

b. Install the battery with its terminals facing in their original position.

c. For a conventional battery, reconnect the battery breather hose (D, **Figure 4**). If installing a new battery, install the new breather hose equipped with the battery. Refer to the battery breather hose routing decal mounted on the battery holder (**Figure 4**).

WARNING
After installing a conventional battery, make sure the breather hose is routed properly and vented to the atmosphere. A pinched or kinked hose allows high pressure to accumulate in the battery. If the hose does not blow off, pressure builds inside the battery and causes the case to crack or explode. If the hose blows off, gasses discharged from the battery damages parts on contact.

d. Always connect the positive cable first, then the negative cable.

CAUTION
Be sure the battery cables are connected to their proper terminals. Connecting the battery backward reverses the polarity and damages components in the electrical system. When installing a replacement battery, confirm the positions of the positive and negative battery terminals.

e. Coat the battery leads with dielectric grease or petroleum jelly.

Cleaning and Inspection

1. Read *Safety Precautions* in this section.

2. Remove the battery from the motorcycle as described in this section. Do not clean the battery while it is mounted in the motorcycle.

3A. Before cleaning a conventional battery, turn each battery breather cap (**Figure 2**) to make sure it is tight. This prevents the cleaning solution from entering the cells and neutralizing the acid.

> *CAUTION*
> *Keep cleaning solution out of the battery cells or the electrolyte level will be seriously weakened.*

3B. On a maintenance-free battery, electrolyte level cannot be serviced. *Never* remove the sealing bar cap from the top of the battery (**Figure 3**). The battery does not require periodic electrolyte inspection or refilling.

4. Clean the battery case (**Figure 6**) with a solution of warm water and baking soda. Rinse thoroughly with clean water.

5. Inspect the physical condition of the battery. Look for bulges or cracks in the case, leaking electrolyte or corrosion buildup.

6. Check the battery terminal bolts, spacers and nuts for corrosion and damage. Clean parts with a solution of baking soda and water, and rinse thoroughly. Replace if damaged.

7. Check the battery cable clamps for corrosion and damage. If corrosion is minor, clean the battery cable clamps with a stiff brush. Replace excessively worn or damaged cables.

> *CAUTION*
> *Do not overfill the battery cells in Step 8. Electrolyte expands due to heat from charging and will overflow if the level is above the upper level line.*

8. Conventional battery:

> *CAUTION*
> *Check the battery periodically for electrolyte level, state of charge and corrosion. During hot weather periods, frequent checks are recommended. If the electrolyte level is below the bottom of the vent well in one or more cells, add distilled water as required. To assure proper mixing of the water and acid, operate the engine immediately after adding water. Never add battery acid instead of water because this shortens the battery's life.*

   a. Place the battery on a level surface and check the fluid level through the translucent case, or remove the battery vent caps (**Figure 2**). If

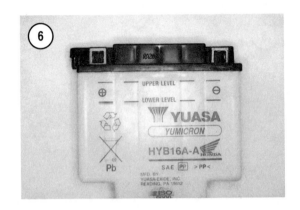

the electrolyte level is low, add distilled water to bring the level within the upper and lower level lines on the battery case (**Figure 6**).

   b. Install and tighten the battery breather caps. Do not overtighten.

Battery Testing

Depending on the type of battery tester used, battery testing determines either a battery's state of charge, capacity or both. The battery tests described in this section are described below:

1. Hydrometer testing: This test uses a hydrometer to test the specific gravity of the electrolyte to determine a conventional battery's state of charge. Specific gravity is the weight of the electrolyte compared to the weight of pure water. The test results do not indicate if a battery has enough current to operate the starter motor or other electrical systems on the motorcycle.

2. Open-circuit voltage test: This test uses a digital voltmeter to measure battery voltage without discharging current from the battery. This is the most common test performed on maintenance-free batteries. The voltage reading is only an indicator of a battery's state of charge. It does not indicate if a battery has enough current to operate the starter motor or other electrical systems on the motorcycle.

3. Low load battery test: This test is performed with a digital voltmeter while the headlights are on. This test is performed to approximate battery capacity when a high load battery tester is not available.

4. High load battery test: This test is performed with a battery load tester to determine a battery's capacity. The battery must be at least 75 percent charged before making the test. This is the best test

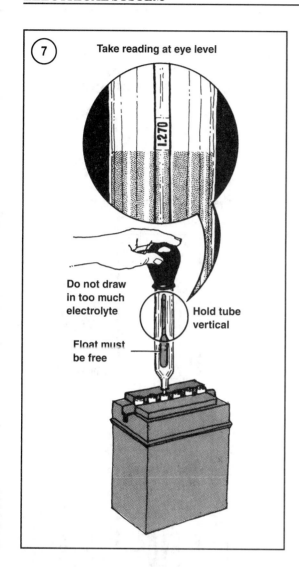

⑦ **Take reading at eye level**

L.270

**Do not draw
in too much
electrolyte**

**Hold tube
vertical**

**Float must
be free**

tions from 1.100 to 1.300 rather than one with just color-coded bands or floating balls.

> *CAUTION*
> *This test can only be performed on conventional batteries.*

1. Remove the battery as described in this section.
2. Clean and dry the top of the battery as described under *Cleaning and Inspection* in this section.
3. Remove the breather caps from the top of the battery.
4. Examine the fluid level in each cell. If a cell is low, add distilled water to correct the level. Then charge the battery for 15-20 minutes to ensure the water and electrolyte are mixed thoroughly.

> *NOTE*
> *Do not test a battery with a hydrometer immediately after adding water to the cells. Because the cells are diluted with water, a lower specific gravity reading results.*

5. Squeeze the rubber ball and insert the tip of the hydrometer into the battery cell next to the positive battery post. Slowly release the ball (**Figure 7**) to suck electrolyte into the tube. Draw enough electrolyte to float the weighted float inside the hydrometer. When using a temperature-compensated hydrometer, release the electrolyte and repeat this process several times to make sure the thermometer has adjusted to the electrolyte temperature before taking the reading.

> *NOTE*
> *If a temperature-compensated hydrometer is not used, temperature corrections can be made as described in Step 11.*

6. Hold the hydrometer vertically at eye-level and note the number in line with the surface of the electrolyte (**Figure 7**). This is the specific gravity for this cell. Make sure the float is not dragging against the inside of the hydrometer.
7. If a temperature-compensated hydrometer is being used, note the temperature on the thermometer.
8. Slowly squeeze the bulb to return the electrolyte to the cell from which it came.
9. Record the specific gravity reading and repeat these steps for each battery cell.

available to determine a battery's capacity and internal condition.

5. Battery conductance test: This test is performed with a battery conductance tester. The battery does not have to be fully charged. The test results are a good indicator of a battery's state of charge and internal cell condition.

**Hydrometer Testing
(Conventional Battery)**

The hydrometer tests the specific gravity of the battery electrolyte and is the best way to check the condition of a conventional battery. Use a temperature corrected hydrometer with numbered gradua-

10. The specific gravity of the electrolyte in each battery cell is an excellent indication of that cell's condition (**Table 3**). A fully charged cell reads 1.260-1.280 while a cell in good condition reads from 1.230-1.250. A specific gravity difference of 0.050 or more between cells indicates that the battery is approaching the end of its operating life.

11. Because the specific gravity of electrolyte changes with temperature, hydrometers are temperature calibrated at 27° C (80° F). At colder temperatures, electrolyte thickens and its specific gravity raises (gaining gravity). At higher temperatures, electrolyte thins and its specific gravity lowers (loses gravity). If a temperature-compensated hydrometer is not used, add 0.004 to the specific gravity reading for every 10° above 27° C (80° F). For every 10° below 27° C (80° F), subtract 0.004. Refer to the temperature correction chart in **Figure 8**.

12. Reinstall the battery breather caps.

Open-Circuit Voltage Test

An open-circuit voltage test checks battery voltage by connecting the leads from a digital voltmeter across the battery terminals. This is an unloaded or stabilized test because there is no load placed on the battery (the ignition switch is off). If the engine was just turned off, allow the voltage to stabilize for 10 minutes before testing. If the battery was recently charged, turn the headlights on for 15 seconds to remove the surface charge from the battery. Refer to **Table 3** or **Table 4** for battery voltage specifications.

1. Read *Safety Precautions* in this section.

> *NOTE*
> *To prevent false test readings, do not test the battery if the battery terminals are corroded. Remove and clean the battery and terminals as described in this chapter, then reinstall it.*

2A. On a conventional battery, connect a digital voltmeter between the battery negative and positive leads (**Figure 9**). Then locate the voltage reading in **Table 3** to determine the battery state of charge. Note the following:

   a. If the battery voltage is 12.6 volts or higher, the battery is fully charged.

   b. If the battery voltage is below 12.4 volts, the battery is undercharged and requires charging.

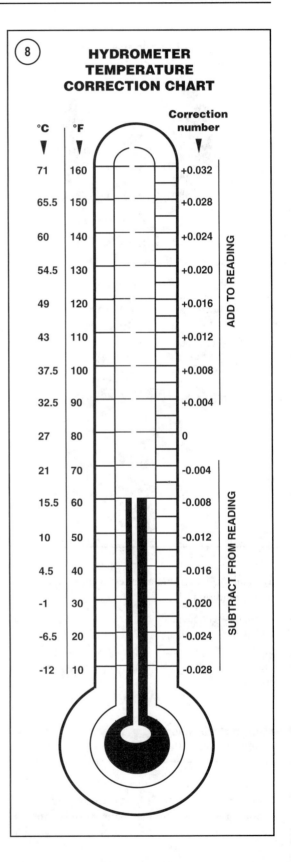

⑧ HYDROMETER TEMPERATURE CORRECTION CHART

°C	°F	Correction number
71	160	+0.032
65.5	150	+0.028
60	140	+0.024
54.5	130	+0.020
49	120	+0.016
43	110	+0.012
37.5	100	+0.008
32.5	90	+0.004
27	80	0
21	70	-0.004
15.5	60	-0.008
10	50	-0.012
4.5	40	-0.016
-1	30	-0.020
-6.5	20	-0.024
-12	10	-0.028

ADD TO READING

SUBTRACT FROM READING

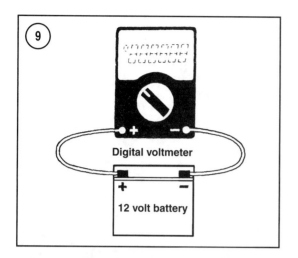

Digital voltmeter

12 volt battery

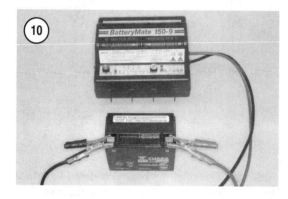

2B. On a maintenance-free battery, connect a digital voltmeter between the battery negative and positive leads (**Figure 9**). Then locate the voltage reading in **Table 4** to determine the battery state of charge. Note the following:

a. If the battery voltage is 12.8-13.0 volts, the battery is fully charged.

b. If the battery voltage is below 12.3-12.5 volts, the battery is undercharged and requires charging. Refer to **Table 4** for charge time required.

3. If the battery is undercharged, recharge it as described in this section.

4. If the battery charge is good, but does not operate the starter motor, perform the *High Load Battery Test* in this section.

Low Load Battery Test

A low-load test places a small load on the battery while measuring battery voltage with a digital voltmeter.

1. Connect a digital voltmeter between the battery negative and positive leads (**Figure 9**).

2. Turn the ignition switch on and make sure the headlight is on. Read the voltmeter and note the following:

a. If the voltage reading is 11.5 minimum, the battery charge is good.

b. If the voltage reading is less than 11.5 volts, the battery requires charging. Recharge the battery as described in this section.

High Load Battery Test

A high load battery test is the most accurate way to determine battery condition. This is an independent test where a battery load tester checks a battery's performance under full current load. A battery load tester places an electrical load on the battery to determine if it can provide current while maintaining the minimum required voltage. A load test may also be called a battery capacity test. **Figure 10** shows the TestMate battery load tester sold by Motion Pro.

A battery load test procedure varies depending on the type of tester. A battery must be at least 75 percent charged before making a load test. Use the following guidelines to supplement the manufacturer's instructions:

1. Remove the battery as described in this section.

2. Inspect the battery case for any leaks or damage. Do not test the battery if the case is damaged.

3. Clean the battery terminals.

4A. Conventional battery:

a. Test the specific gravity of the battery. Charge the battery if the reading is below 1.260.

b. Make sure the breather caps are installed and tightened securely.

4B. On a maintenance-free battery, perform the *Battery Voltage Test* in this section. Charge the battery if the reading is below 12.4 volts.

5. Connect the load tester to the battery terminals with the red lead to the positive terminal and the black lead to the negative terminal.

6. Determine the correct amount of load to apply to the battery. Refer to the manufacturer's instructions, plus the following:

a. Refer to **Table 1** or **Table 2** for battery capacity.

b. The amount of load to use is determined by the original capacity of the battery. This is measured in cold cranking amperes (CCA) or in the amp/hour rating. The correct load to apply is 1/2 the CCA rating or three times the amp/hour rating.

7. Test the battery and determine the results following the manufacturer's instructions.

8. It the battery fails the load test, recharge the battery and retest. If the battery fails the load test again, replace the battery.

Battery Conductance Test

This test measures a battery's ability to produce current rather than testing a battery while operating under a load (load test). The test also detects shorts, open circuits and cell damage that reduces a battery's ability to deliver current. A battery conductance tester is required for this test. **Figure 11** shows the TestMate conductance battery tester sold by Motion Pro.

The following procedure lists a typical procedure for making a conductance test. Refer to the tester's instruction manual for programming and operating the tester.

1. Disconnect the battery cables at the battery as described in this section. The battery can remain in the motorcycle during the test.

2. Inspect the battery case for any leaks or damage. Do not test the battery if the case is damaged.

3. Clean the battery terminals.

4. Conventional battery: Make sure the breather caps are installed and tightened securely.

5. Connect the load tester to the battery terminals with the red lead to the positive terminal and the black lead to the negative terminal.

6. Test the battery and determine the results (**Figure 12**) following the manufacturer's instructions. On testers of this type, the results can be read immediately on the tester's display. Typical results provided by the tester are:

   a. Good & Pass.
   b. Good & Recharge.
   c. Recharge & Retest.
   d. Bad cell & Replace.
   e. Bad & Replace.

Routine Battery Charging

Refer to *New Battery Setup* in this section if the battery is new.

The battery should only self-discharge approximately 1 percent of its given capacity each day. If a battery is not in use and loses its charge within one

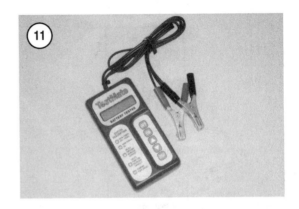

week after charging, the battery is defective. Make sure the battery does not have any parasitic loads connected to it.

If the motorcycle is not used for long periods, an automatic battery charger with variable voltage and amperage outputs is recommended for optimum battery service life.

WARNING
During the charging process, highly explosive hydrogen gas is released from the battery. Charge the battery only in a well-ventilated area away from any open flames (including pilot lights on home gas appliances). Do not allow any smoking in the area. Never check the charge of the battery by connecting screwdriver blades or other metal objects between the terminals; the resulting spark can ignite the hydrogen gas.

CAUTION
Always remove the battery from the motorcycle before connecting the battery charger. Never recharge a battery in the

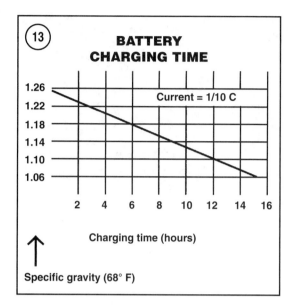

frame; corrosive gasses emitted during the charging process damage surfaces.

Conventional battery

1. Remove the battery as described in this section.
2. Connect the positive charger lead to the positive battery terminal and the negative charger lead to the negative battery terminal.
3. Remove all breather caps (**Figure 2**) from the battery, set the charger at 12 volts and switch it on. Normally, a battery should be charged at a slow charge rate of 1/10 its given capacity. Refer to *Charging Current* in **Table 1**.

> *CAUTION*
> *When using an adjustable battery charger, follow the manufacturer's instructions. Do not use a larger output*

battery charger or increase the charge rate on an adjustable battery charger to reduce charging time. Doing so can cause permanent battery damage.

> *CAUTION*
> *The electrolyte level must be maintained at the upper level during the charging cycle; check and refill with distilled water as necessary.*

4. The charging time depends on the discharged condition of the battery. Perform the *Hydrometer Test* described in this section, then refer to the chart in **Figure 13** to determine approximate charging times at different specific gravity readings. For example, if the specific gravity of the battery is 1.180, the approximate charging time would be 6 hours.

> *NOTE*
> *During charging, the cells show signs of gassing or bubbling. If one cell has no gas bubbles or if its specific gravity is low, the cell is probably shorted. Replace the battery.*

5. If the battery becomes hot to the touch during charging, turn the charger off and allow the battery to cool. Then resume charging.
6. After charging the battery for the pre-determined time, turn the charger off and disconnect the leads. All of the cells must be gassing. Check the battery's specific gravity or voltage as described in this section. For a fully charged battery, the specific gravity reading for each cell should read at least 1.265. A voltmeter should read at least 12.60 volts. If the readings are correct and remain stable for 1 hour, the battery is fully charged.

Maintenance-free battery

To recharge a maintenance-free battery, a digital voltmeter and a charger (**Figure 14**) with an adjustable or automatically variable amperage output are required. Excessive voltage and amperage from an unregulated charger can damage the battery and shorten service life.

1. Remove the battery as described in this section.
2. Measure the battery voltage as described under *Open-Circuit Voltage Test* in this section. Locate the voltage reading in **Table 4** to determine the battery's state of charge and the amount of charge time re-

quired. For example, if the voltage reading is 12.3 volts, the battery state of charge is between 50 and 75 percent. Using the information in **Table 4**, the battery needs to be charged for approximately 5-11 hours.

NOTE
*If the voltage reading is 11.5 volts or less, internal resistance in the battery may prevent it from recovering when following normal charging attempts. When a battery's state of charge is 25 percent or less (**Table 4**), it is necessary to increase the charging voltage of the battery by applying a low current rate to allow the battery to recover. This requires an adjustable battery charger with a separate amp and volt meter. However, some battery chargers can do this automatically. The OptiMate III Battery Optimiser (**Figure 14**) can automatically diagnose and recover deep-discharged batteries. The OptiMate III can also be used to charge and maintain batteries during all normal battery service without overcharging or overheating the battery. Refer to the battery charger manufacturer's instructions and specifications for making this test.*

3. Clean the battery terminals and case.
4. Connect the positive (+) charger lead to the positive battery terminal and the negative (−) charger lead to the negative battery terminal.
5. Charge the battery following the manufacturer's instructions. Set the charger at 12 volts and switch it on. Charge the battery at a slow charge rate of 1/10 its given capacity. To determine the current output in amps, divide the battery amp hour capacity by 10. Refer to *Charging Current* in **Table 2**.

CAUTION
When using an adjustable battery charger, follow the manufacturer's instructions. Do not use a larger output battery charger or increase the charge rate on an adjustable battery charger to reduce charging time. Doing so can cause permanent battery damage.

6. After the battery has been charged for 4-5 hours, turn the charger off, disconnect the leads and allow the battery to set for a minimum of 30 minutes. Then check the battery with a digital voltmeter. A

fully charged battery reads 12.8 volts or higher 30 minutes after taken off the charger. If the battery reading is between 12.5 and 12.8 volts, it may require charging again.

New Battery Setup

Follow the battery manufacturer's instructions while observing the following guidelines when activating a new battery:

WARNING
Safety goggles must be worn when servicing and handling the battery in this section.

CAUTION
A new battery must be fully charged before installation. Failure to do so reduces the life of the battery. Using a new battery without an initial charge causes permanent battery damage. That is, the battery never is able to hold more than an 80 percent charge. Charging a new battery after it has been used does not bring its charge to 100 percent. When purchasing a new battery from a dealership or parts store, verify its charge status. If necessary, have them perform the initial or booster charge before accepting the battery.

1. Use the electrolyte that comes with the battery. Do not use electrolyte from a common container.
2. Fill the battery using all the electrolyte included with the battery kit.
3. Allow the battery to sit for 1 hour. This allows the plates to absorb the electrolyte for optimum performance.

4. Do not install filler caps or sealing caps.

5. Charge the battery following the manufacturer's instructions. Wait 30 minutes and test the battery as described under *Open-Circuit Voltage Test* in this section. If the battery charge is 12.6 volts (conventional battery), 12.8 volts (maintenance-free battery) or higher, the battery is considered fully charged. If the battery charge reads less than this amount, repeat the charging process. When the battery charge reading is correct 30 minutes after charging, go to Step 6.

6A. On a conventional battery, install the filler caps tightly.

6B. On a maintenance-free battery, press the sealing cap firmly to seal each of the battery fill holes. Make sure the cap seats flush into the battery.

Battery Storage

When the motorcycle is ridden infrequently or put in storage for an extended amount of time, the battery must be periodically charged to ensure it is capable of working correctly when returned to service. Use an automatic battery charger with variable voltage and amperage outputs (**Figure 14**).

1. Remove the battery as described in this chapter.

2. Clean the battery and terminals with a solution of baking soda and water.

3. Inspect the battery case for any cracks, leaks or bulging. Replace the battery if the case is leaking or damaged.

4. Clean the battery box in the motorcycle.

5A. Temporary storage: If the motorcycle is used infrequently, install the battery into the motorcycle but do not connect the battery terminals. Check the battery every two weeks and charge as necessary.

5B. Extended storage: When storing the motorcycle longer than one month, charge the battery to 100

percent. Then store the battery in a cool dry place. Continue to charge the battery once a month when stored in temperatures below 16°C (60° F) and every two weeks when stored in temperatures above 16° C (60° F).

BATTERY HOLDER

The battery holder is mounted behind the left side cover.

Removal/Installation

1. Remove the seat (Chapter Fifteen).

2. Remove the battery as described in this chapter.

3A. On VT1100C2 ACE models, remove the fuse box cover. Then remove the two bolts and the fuse box from the frame.

3B. On all other models, remove the fuse box from the battery holder.

4. Remove the clips securing the starter cable and ground cable to the bottom of the battery holder (if so mounted).

5A. On VT1100C2 ACE models, remove the ICM unit mounted on the battery holder.

NOTE
If it is difficult to disconnect the ICM connector in Step 5B, remove the battery holder first and then disconnect the connector. Protect the ICM wiring harness from damage.

5B. On all other models, disconnect the ICM connector (**Figure 15**) at the ICM unit mounted on the lower, right side of the battery box. Cover the ICM connector with a small plastic bag to prevent contamination.

CAUTION
The battery holder fits tightly in the frame. Remove it carefully to prevent scratching the frame.

6. Remove the fasteners securing the battery holder (**Figure 16**) to the frame, and remove it with the ICM unit.

7. Inspect the battery box holder and cover assembly for acid damage. Scrape, clean and repaint the assembly if necessary.

8. Replace any missing or damaged rubber plugs installed in the battery box holder assembly. These plugs hold the battery securely in place during motorcycle

operation. Missing or damaged plugs allow the battery to vibrate or slide in the holder. This condition eventually causes battery plate damage and requires battery replacement.

9. Installation is the reverse of removal. Note the following:

    a. Connect the ICM connector firmly onto the ICM unit.

    b. Check the routing of all wiring.

CHARGING SYSTEM

The charging system supplies power to operate the engine and electrical system components and keeps the battery charged. The charging system consists of the battery, alternator and a voltage regulator/rectifier. A 30-amp fuse protects the circuit. Refer to the appropriate wiring diagram at the end of this manual.

Alternating current generated by the alternator is rectified to direct current. The voltage regulator maintains constant voltage to the battery and additional electrical loads (such as lights or ignition) despite variations in engine speed and load.

Troubleshooting

Because the charging system is not equipped with an indicator system (light or gauge), slow cranking or short bulb life may be the first indicator of a charging system problem.

1. A fully charged battery is required to accurately test the charging system. Perform the battery load test as described under *Battery* in this chapter. If the battery is damaged or worn out, the charging system may not be at fault.

2. Use the correct wiring diagram at the end of this manual to identify and locate the appropriate connectors.

3. Once a repair has been made, repeat the *Charging Voltage Test* described in this section to confirm the charging system is working correctly.

Battery discharging

If the battery is dead or the regulated voltage readings recorded in the *Charging Voltage Test* described in this section were too low, perform the steps in the order listed below:

1. Check all of the electrical connections. Make sure they are tight and free of corrosion.

2. Perform the *Charging Voltage Test* described in this section and note the following:

    a. If the reading is correct, go to Step 3.

    b. If the regulated voltage is too low, go to Step 5.

    c. If the regulated voltage is too high, refer to *Battery Overcharging* described in this section.

3. Perform the *Current Leakage Draw Test* as described in section and note the following:

    a. If the reading is correct, the battery is probably faulty. Perform the battery load test as described under *Battery* in this chapter.

    b. If the reading is incorrect, continue with Step 4.

4. Disconnect the regulator/rectifier connectors and repeat the *Current Leakage Draw Test* described in Step 3 and note the following:

    a. If the reading is correct, the regulator/rectifier is faulty. Replace the regulator/rectifier as described in this section and retest.

    b. If the reading is incorrect, a short in the wiring may cause the problem or the ignition switch is faulty. Check for a short circuit in the charging system by disconnecting the connectors one at a time while repeating the current leakage test performed in Step 3. Then reconnect the connector and continue with the next connector. If the current leakage returns to normal when a connector is disconnected, the circuit is shorting to ground. If a short circuit cannot be located, test the ignition switch as described in this chapter.

5. Check the battery charge line as described under *Wiring Harness Test* in this section and note the following:

    a. If there is battery voltage, go to Step 6.

    b. If there is no battery voltage, check the red/white wire between the starter relay switch and regulator/rectifier for an open circuit. Then check the circuit connectors for dirty or damaged terminals.

6. Check the charge coil circuit and stator coil resistance as described under *Left Crankcase Cover and Stator Coil* in this chapter and note the following:

    a. If the readings are correct, replace the regulator/rectifier as described in this section.

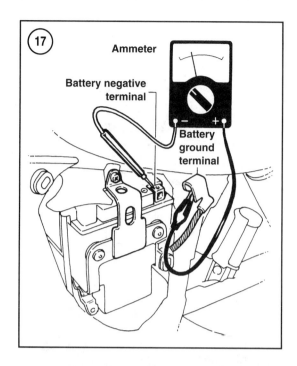

(17)

Ammeter

Battery negative terminal

Battery ground terminal

b. If one or both readings are incorrect, check the yellow wires between the alternator and regulator/rectifier for an open circuit. Then check the connectors for dirty or damaged terminals.

Battery overcharging

If the regulated voltage is too high, perform this test in the order listed below:

1. Perform the *Charging Voltage Test* described in this section and note the following:

   a. If the regulated voltage is correct, replace the battery and retest.

   b. If the regulated voltage is too high, go to Step 2.

2. Test the ground circuit as described under *Wiring Harness Test* in this section and note the following:

   a. If there is no continuity, check for dirty or loose-fitting terminals. Then check for an open circuit in the wiring harness.

   b. If there is continuity, check the regulator/rectifier connector for dirty or loose-fitting terminals. If the battery continues to overcharge after cleaning or repairing these connectors, replace the regulator/rectifier.

Current Leakage Draw Test

A short circuit increases current draw and drains the battery. Perform this test before troubleshooting the charging system or performing the charging voltage test to determine if the current leakage is normal or excessive. If the battery discharges because of a short, the charging system may not be at fault.

> *NOTE*
> *When installing electrical accessories, do not wire them into a live circuit where they stay on all the time. Refer to the manufacturer's instructions.*

1. Turn the ignition switch off.

2. Disconnect the negative battery cable as described under *Battery, Removal/Installation* in this chapter.

> *CAUTION*
> *Before connecting the ammeter into the circuit, set the meter to its highest amperage scale. This prevents a large current flow from damaging the meter or blowing the meter's fuse.*

3. Connect an ammeter between the negative battery cable and the negative battery terminal (**Figure 17**). Do *not* turn the ignition switch on once this connection is made.

4. Switch the ammeter to its lowest scale and note the reading. Refer to the current draw specification in **Table 1** or **Table 2**. The cause of an excessive current draw must be found and repaired.

5. If the current draw exceeds the specification in **Table 1** or **Table 2**, consider the following probable causes:

   a. Damaged battery.

   b. Faulty voltage regulator/rectifier.

   c. Short circuit in the system.

   d. Loose, dirty or faulty electrical connectors.

   e. Aftermarket electrical accessories added to the electrical system.

> *NOTE*
> *After installing an aftermarket electrical accessory, perform the **Charging Voltage Test** in this section so see if the charging system is capable of powering the accessory.*

9

6. To find the short circuit that is causing the excessive current draw, refer to the appropriate wiring diagram at the end of this manual. Then disconnect different electrical connectors one by one while monitoring the ammeter. Then reconnect the connector and continue with the next connector. If any aftermarket electrical products were installed into the system, check them first. If the current draw returns to an acceptable level after disconnecting a connector, the faulty circuit is indicated. Test the circuit further to find the problem.

7. Disconnect the ammeter.

8. Reconnect the negative battery cable.

Charging Voltage Test (Regulated Voltage)

This procedure tests charging system operation. To obtain accurate test results, the battery must be fully charged (**Table 1** or **Table 2**).

1. Start and run the engine until it reaches normal operating temperature, then turn the engine off.

2. Connect a digital voltmeter to the battery terminals as shown in **Figure 18**. To prevent a short, make sure the voltmeter leads attach firmly to the battery terminals. Record the minimum or measured battery voltage reading on the voltmeter.

> *CAUTION*
> *Do not disconnect either battery cable when making this test. Doing so may damage the voltmeter or electrical accessories.*

3. Start the engine and allow it to idle. Turn the headlight to HI beam. Gradually increase engine speed to 5000 rpm and read the voltage indicated on the voltmeter. The voltmeter should show a reading greater than the minimum or measured battery voltage recorded in Step 2 and less than 15.5 volts.

> *NOTE*
> *If the battery is often discharged, but the charging voltage tested normal during Step 3, the battery may be damaged. Perform a battery load-test as described under **Battery** in this chapter.*

4. If the voltage reading is incorrect, perform the *Wiring Harness Test* in this section, while noting the following:

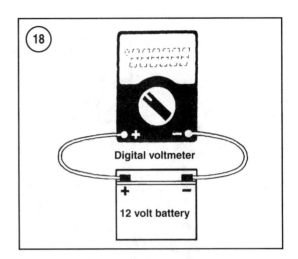

Digital voltmeter

12 volt battery

a. If the charging voltage is too low, check for an open or short circuit in the charging system wiring harness, an open or short in the alternator, high resistance in the battery cable or a damaged regulator/rectifier.

b. If the charging voltage is too high, check for a poor regulator/rectifier ground, damaged regulator/rectifier or a damaged battery.

Wiring Harness Test

This procedure tests the integrity of the wires and connectors attached to the regulator/rectifier. Refer to the appropriate wiring diagram at the end of this · manual to identify the three regulator/rectifier connectors and wiring harness color codes called out in this procedure.

1. Remove the seat (Chapter Fifteen).

2A. On VT1100C2 ACE models, disconnect the three regulator/rectifier connectors from the connector block mounted beside the air filter housing:

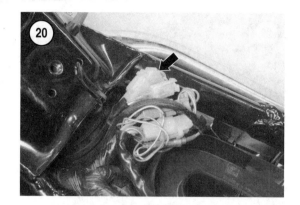

a. Green 2-pin connector (A, **Figure 19**).

b. White 2-pin connector (B, **Figure 19**).

c. White 3-pin connector (C, **Figure 19**).

2B. On all other models, disconnect the three regulator/rectifier connectors inside the connector pouch mounted beside and in front of the air filter housing (**Figure 20**, typical).

3. Check for loose or corroded terminals in the regulator/rectifier and wiring harness side connectors.

NOTE
Make all of the tests on the wiring harness connector side, not on the regulator/rectifier connector side.

4. Check the battery charge line as follows:

a. Connect a voltmeter between the red/white wire and a good engine ground.

b. The voltmeter should read battery voltage at all times (ignition switch on or off).

c. If there is no voltage, check the red/white wire for an open circuit.

d. Disconnect the voltmeter leads.

5. Check the ground circuit as follows:

a. Connect the ohmmeter between the green wire and a good engine ground.

b. The ohmmeter should read continuity.

c. If there is no continuity, check the green wire for an open circuit.

6. Check the charge coil circuit and stator coil resistance as described under *Left Crankcase Cover and Stator Coil* in this chapter.

7. Reverse Step 1 and Step 2.

**Regulator/Rectifier
Removal/Installation**

The regulator/rectifier unit is mounted on the left side of the frame and behind the oil filter. Refer to the appropriate wiring diagram at the end of this manual to identify the three regulator/rectifier connectors.

1. Remove the seat and the left side cover (Chapter Fifteen).

2. Disconnect the negative battery cable at the battery.

3A. On VT1100C2 ACE models, disconnect the three regulator/rectifier connectors from the connector block mounted beside the air filter housing:

a. Green 2-pin connector (A, **Figure 19**).

b. White 2-pin connector (B, **Figure 19**).

c. White 3-pin connector (C, **Figure 19**).

3B. On all other models:

a. Remove the battery as described in this chapter.

b. Remove the battery holder as described in this chapter.

c. Disconnect the three regulator/rectifier connectors from the connector pouch mounted beside and in front of the air filter housing (**Figure 20**, typical).

4. Disconnect any bands securing the wiring harness to the frame.

5. Remove the bolts and the regulator/rectifier unit (**Figure 21**) from the frame. On VT1100C2 ACE models, if the wires and connectors cannot pass by the battery holder, remove the battery and battery holder as described in this chapter.

6. Installation is the reverse of removal.

9

LEFT CRANKCASE COVER
AND STATOR COIL

The stator coil is mounted inside the left crank-case cover.

Left Crankcase Cover
Removal/Installation

1. Remove the seat and the left side cover (Chapter Fifteen).
2. Remove the battery and battery holder as described in this chapter.
3. Drain the engine oil (Chapter Three).
4. Remove the clutch lifter arm holder as described in Chapter Six.
5. Remove the starter drive gear and torque limiter as described in this chapter.
6A. On VT1100C and VT1100C2 Sabre models, remove the pinch bolt and disconnect the shift pedal from the shift shaft.
6B. On VT1100C2 ACE and VT1100T models, perform the following:
   a. Remove the bolts and the left footpeg.
   b. Remove the pinch bolt and disconnect the shift pedal from the shift shaft.
6C. VT1100C3—Perform the following:
   a. Remove the bolts and the left footrest assembly.
   b. Remove the pinch bolt and disconnect the shift pedal from the shift shaft.
7A. On VT1100C2 ACE models, unhook and fold back the rubber cover protecting the electrical connector block mounted beside the air filter housing. Then disconnect the alternator 3-pin white connector (C, **Figure 19**).
7B. On all other models, disconnect the alternator 3-pin connector located in the connector pouch beside the air filter housing (**Figure 20**, typical).
8. On VT1100C2 ACE and 1998-2000 VT1100C3 models, remove the bolts that hold the breather joint (**Figure 22**) to the crankcase. Then remove the breather joint and its O-ring (**Figure 23**).
9. Before removing the left crankcase cover mounting bolts, draw an outline of the cover on a piece of cardboard (**Figure 24**). Then punch holes along the outline for the placement of each mounting bolt.

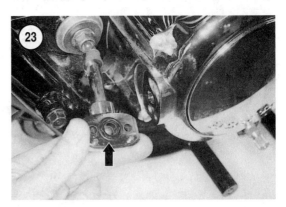

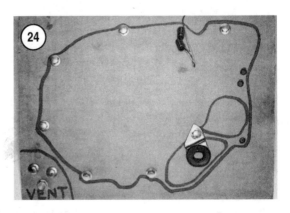

10. Remove the left crankcase cover mounting bolts and cover stay and place them in the corresponding holes in the cardboard (**Figure 24**).
11. Remove the left crankcase cover (A, **Figure 25**) and gasket.

NOTE
*The bolt identified in B, **Figure 25** has a sealer applied to its threads and turns with more resistance during removal.*

12. Remove the two dowel pins (**Figure 26**).

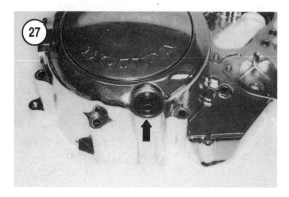

Inspection

1. Clean the left crankcase cover and crankcase gasket surfaces.

2. Check the shift shaft oil seal (**Figure 27**) for oil leaks or damage. If necessary, replace the oil seal as follows:

    a. Pry the oil seal out of the cover with a seal remover or wide-blade screwdriver.

    b. Clean the oil seal bore.

    c. Pack the new oil seal lips with grease.

    d. Press the new seal into the crankcase cover with its flat side facing out.

3. If necessary, service the star in this section.

Installation

1. Install the two dowel pins (**Figure 26**) and a new gasket.

2. Install the left crankcase cover (A, **Figure 25**) and secure it with its mounting bolts. Install the cover stay at the lower mounting position shown in **Figure 24**.

3. Apply an RTV sealer onto the left crankcase cover mounting bolt identified in B, **Figure 25**. Do not apply sealer to any of the other mounting bolt threads.

4. Tighten the mounting bolts securely.

5. On VT1100C2 ACE and 1998-2000 VT1100C3 models, lubricate a new the O-ring with engine oil and install it into the breather cover groove (**Figure 23**). Install the breather cover (**Figure 22**) and tighten its mounting bolts securely.

6. Route the alternator connector and its wiring harness through the frame along its original path. Reconnect the alternator 3-pin connector.

7A. On VT100C and VT1100C2 Sabre models, align the slit in the shift pedal with the punch mark on the shift shaft and install the shift pedal. Tighten the pinch bolt to 26 N•m (19 ft.-lb.).

7B. On VT1100C2 ACE and VT1100T models, perform the following:

    a. Align the slit in the shift pedal with the punch mark on the shift shaft and install the shift pedal. Tighten the pinch bolt to 23 N•m (17 ft.-lb.).

    b. Install the left footpeg and tighten the mounting bolts to 26 N•m (19 ft.-lb.).

7C. On VT1100C3 models, perform the following:

    a. Align the slit in the shift pedal with the punch mark on the shift shaft and install the shift pedal. Tighten the pinch bolt to 23 N•m (17 ft.-lb.).

    b. Install the left footrest and tighten the mounting bolts to 39 N•m (29 ft.-lb.).

8. Install the starter drive gear and torque limiter as described in this chapter.

9. Install the clutch lifter arm holder as described in Chapter Six.

10. Refill the engine with the correct type and quantity of oil (Chapter Three).

9

11. Install the battery holder and battery as described in this chapter.

12. Install the left side cover and seat (Chapter Fifteen).

13. Start the engine and check for leaks.

Stator Charge Coil Resistance Test

The stator coil is mounted inside the left crankcase side cover (**Figure 28**). The stator coil can be tested while mounted on the engine.

1. Remove the seat (Chapter Fifteen).

NOTE
The connector disconnected in Step 2 has three yellow wires.

2A. On VT1100C2 ACE models, unhook and fold back the rubber cover protecting the electrical connector block mounted beside the air filter housing. Then disconnect the alternator 3-pin white connector (C, **Figure 19**).

2B. On all other models, disconnect the alternator 3-pin connector located in the connector pouch beside the air filter housing (**Figure 20**, typical).

NOTE
The engine must be cold when measuring the charging coil resistance.

3. Measure resistance between each yellow wire on the alternator side of the connector. **Table 5** lists the specified stator coil resistance.

4. Replace the stator coil if any resistance reading is incorrect.

5. Check continuity from each yellow stator wire to ground. Replace the stator coil if any yellow terminal has continuity to ground. Continuity indicates a short within the stator coil winding.

NOTE
Before replacing the stator assembly, check the electrical wires to and within the electrical connector for any opens or poor connections.

6. If the stator coil (A, **Figure 28**) fails either of these tests, replace it as described in this section.

7. Make sure the electrical connector is secure and corrosion free, then reconnect the connectors.

8. Install thc scat (Chapter Fifteen).

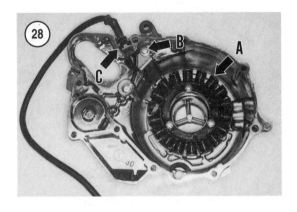

Stator Coil Removal/Installation

1. Remove the left crankcase cover as described in this section.

2. Remove the clamp bolt and clamp (B, **Figure 28**).

3. Pull the rubber plug (C, **Figure 28**) out of the cover.

4. Remove the stator coil mounting bolts and remove the stator coil (A, **Figure 28**).

5. Remove all threadlock residue from the mounting bolts and housing threads.

6. Clean and dry the left crankcase cover.

7. Installation is the reverse of removal. Note the following:
   a. Apply a medium strength threadlock to the stator coil mounting bolts and tighten the bolts securely.
   b. Apply Gasgacinch or a silicone sealer to the wiring harness rubber plug, then insert the plug into the cover notch (C, **Figure 28**).
   c. Install the clamp and its mounting bolt (B, **Figure 28**). Tighten the bolt securely.

FLYWHEEL, STARTER CLUTCH, STARTER REDUCTION GEARS AND GEARSHIFT SPINDLE A

The flywheel (alternator rotor) is mounted on the left end of the crankshaft. The starter clutch is mounted on the back of the flywheel (**Figure 29**).

Special Tools

The following special tools or their equivalents are required to remove the flywheel:

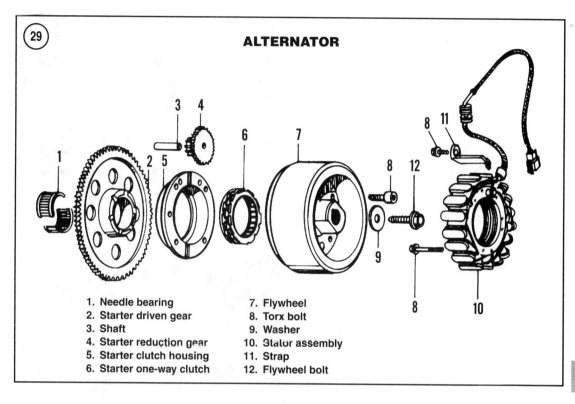

ALTERNATOR

1. Needle bearing
2. Starter driven gear
3. Shaft
4. Starter reduction gear
5. Starter clutch housing
6. Starter one-way clutch
7. Flywheel
8. Torx bolt
9. Washer
10. Stator assembly
11. Strap
12. Flywheel bolt

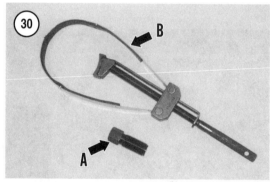

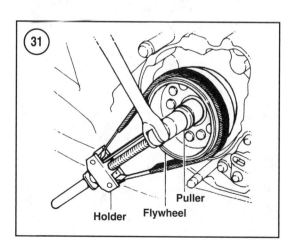

Puller
Holder Flywheel

1. Flywheel puller, Motion Pro part No. 08-074 (A, **Figure 30**) or Honda part No. 07733-002001 or 07933-329001.

2. Honda flywheel holder, Honda part No. 07725-0040000 (B, **Figure 30**) or equivalent. This tool is also required to hold the flywheel when tightening the flywheel bolt.

Removal

1. Remove the left crankcase cover as described in this chapter.

CAUTION
*The flywheel mounting bolt has **left-hand** threads.*

2. Hold the flywheel with a flywheel tool (**Figure 31**) and turn the flywheel bolt *clockwise* to loosen it. Remove the flywheel bolt and washer (**Figure 32**).

3. Screw the flywheel puller (A, **Figure 33**) into the flywheel.

CAUTION
Do not try to remove the flywheel without a puller. Any attempt to do so

ultimately leads to some form of damage to the crankshaft and flywheel.

> *CAUTION*
> *If normal flywheel removal attempts fail, do not force the puller. Excessive force strips the flywheel threads, causing damage. Take the engine to a dealership for flywheel removal.*

4. Hold the flywheel with the flywheel holder (**Figure 31**) and gradually tighten the flywheel puller until the flywheel (B, **Figure 33**) pops off the crankshaft taper. The starter clutch remains on the crankshaft.
5. Remove the puller from the flywheel.
6. If necessary, remove the Woodruff key (A, **Figure 34**) from the crankshaft.

> *NOTE*
> *Steps 7-12 describe removal of the starter reduction gear, starter driven gear and gearshift spindle A.*

7. Remove the starter reduction gear (B, **Figure 34**) and shaft (C).
8. Remove the neutral switch rubber plug (**Figure 35**) from the crankcase.
9. Use a screwdriver and pry the gearshift spindle guide plug (**Figure 36**) from the crankcase.
10. Pull gearshift spindle A outward to release it from gearshift spindle B.
11. Remove the starter driven gear (A, **Figure 37**) and its needle bearing.
12. Remove gearshift spindle A (B, **Figure 37**) from the crankcase.
13. If necessary, service the starter clutch as described in this section.

Inspection

1. Clean the flywheel/starter clutch assembly and the starter gears in solvent and dry with compressed air.
2. Check the flywheel for cracks or breaks.

> *WARNING*
> *Replace a cracked or chipped flywheel. A damaged flywheel can fly apart at high engine speeds, throwing metal fragments into the engine. Do not repair a damaged flywheel.*

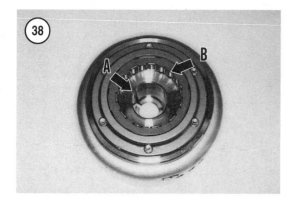

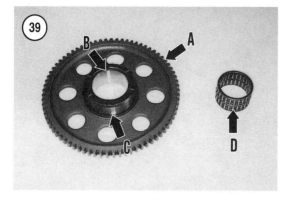

3. Check the flywheel tapered bore and the crankshaft taper for pitting and other damage.

4. Inspect the flywheel keyway (A, **Figure 38**) for damage.

5. Inspect the starter clutch assembly as follows:

   a. Inspect the one-way clutch roller cage (B, **Figure 38**) for overheating, pitting or flat areas. If damaged, replace the starter clutch as described in this section.

   b. Inspect the starter reduction gear for damaged gear teeth (A, **Figure 39**). Then inspect the needle bearing (B, **Figure 39**) and starter clutch (C) operating surfaces for cracks, pitting and other damage.

   c. Measure the starter driven gear outside diameter (C, **Figure 39**) and compare to the specification in **Table 6**. Replace the gear if the measurement is out of specification.

   d. Inspect the needle bearing (D, **Figure 39**) for damage. Check the cage for cracks or areas where the needles have fallen out. Check the needles for flat spots, pitting and other damage.

   e. Inspect the spring installed in the one-way clutch grooves. If any part of the spring has pulled out of the clutch, replace the one-way clutch as described under *Starter Clutch Disassembly/Assembly* in this section. Do not attempt to reinstall the spring and reuse the one-way clutch.

   f. If there is no visible damage, perform Step 6 to check the starter clutch operation.

6. Insert the starter driven gear (**Figure 40**) into the starter clutch. Hold the flywheel and try to turn the gear clockwise and then counterclockwise. The gear should only turn *counterclockwise* (**Figure 40**). If the gear turns clockwise, replace the one-way clutch as described under *Starter Clutch Disassembly/Assembly* in this section.

7. Inspect the starter reduction gear and shaft (**Figure 41**) for:

    a. Broken or chipped gear teeth.

    b. Worn or scored gear bores.

    c. Pitted or damaged shaft surfaces.

8. Inspect the flywheel mounting bolt and washer for damage. Both parts are made of hardened material. Replace only with Honda parts.

9. Inspect gearshift spindle A for the following:

    a. Excessively worn or damaged gear teeth (A, **Figure 42**).

    b. Damaged splines (B, **Figure 42**).

    c. Bent spindle shaft (C, **Figure 42**).

10. Inspect the spindle guide plug (**Figure 43**) for damage along its sealing edge that would cause an oil leak. Discard the O-ring.

Starter Clutch

Disassembly/assembly

The starter clutch assembly (**Figure 29**) is mounted onto the flywheel and consists of the one-way clutch and starter clutch housing. The starter clutch can be inspected while assembled and installed on the flywheel. Do not disassemble the starter clutch unless replacement is necessary.

1. Inspect the starter clutch as described under *Inspection* in this section. If the starter clutch is damaged or if the spring installed in the one-way clutch grooves has pulled out of the clutch, continue with Step 2.

2. Secure the flywheel with the flywheel holder tool (A, **Figure 44**). Then remove the Torx bolts (B, **Figure 44**) securing the starter clutch assembly to the flywheel. Remove the starter clutch housing (**Figure 45**) from the flywheel.

3. Remove the one-way clutch (**Figure 45**) from the starter clutch housing and discard it.

4. Clean and dry all parts. Remove all thread sealer residue from the Torx bolts and starter clutch housing threads.

5. Measure the starter clutch housing inside diameter (**Figure 46**) and compare to the dimensions in **Table 6**. Replace the starter clutch housing if the bore is too large.

> *NOTE*
> *Handle the one-way clutch carefully to prevent its spring from slipping out of the clutch grooves.*

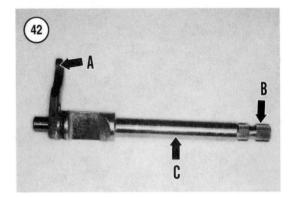

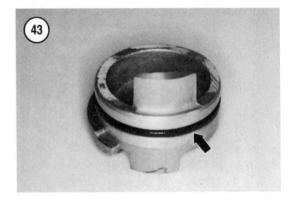

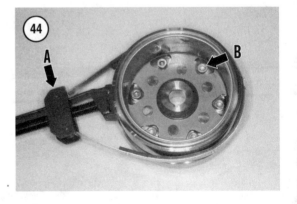

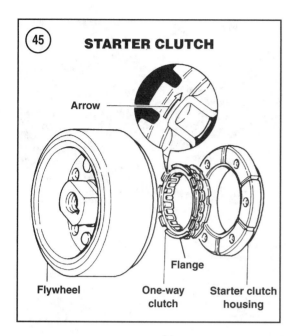

STARTER CLUTCH

Arrow

Flywheel

One-way clutch

Flange

Starter clutch housing

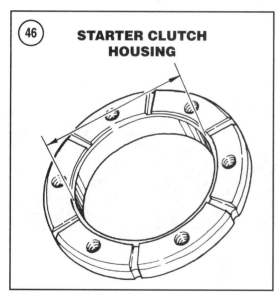

STARTER CLUTCH HOUSING

6A. On VT1100C2 ACE models, install the one-way clutch into the clutch housing with its arrow mark facing toward the flywheel (**Figure 45**).

6B. On all other models, install the one-way clutch into the clutch housing with its flange side facing toward the flywheel (**Figure 45**).

7. Install the starter clutch housing onto the flywheel (**Figure 45**).

8. Apply a medium strength threadlock onto the threads of each starter clutch housing Torx bolt and tighten to 23 N•m (17 ft.-lb.).

9

Installation

NOTE
If other engine service was performed and the camshafts are not installed on the engine, install them before installing the starter clutch. This allows the front cam chain tensioner to be repositioned if additional cam chain slack is needed when installing the front cam sprocket.

1. Install gearshift spindle A (**Figure 47**) but do not mesh it with gearshift spindle B.

2. Lubricate the needle bearing, crankshaft and driven gear inside diameter with engine oil.

3. Install the driven gear (A, **Figure 48**) with the shoulder side facing out over the crankshaft. Then install the needle bearing (B, **Figure 48**) over the crankshaft and through the driven gear. Push the driven gear and needle bearing on all the way.

4. Mesh gearshift spindle A with gearshift spindle B (**Figure 49**).

NOTE
Figure 50 *shows how the spindle gear teeth must mesh together.*

5. Lubricate a new O-ring with engine oil and install it onto the spindle guide plug (**Figure 43**).

6. Install the spindle guide plug (**Figure 51**) into the crankshaft until the plug's flange contacts the crankcase evenly. Refer to **Figure 52**.

7. Reconnect the neutral switch electrical connector, then install its rubber plug (**Figure 35**) into the notch in the crankcase.

8. Lubricate the reduction gear shaft (**Figure 41**) with molybdenum oil solution.

> *NOTE*
> *Molybdenum oil solution is a 50:50 mixture of molybdenum grease and engine oil.*

9. Install the starter reduction gear (B, **Figure 34**) and shaft (C). The small gear on the starter reduction gear assembly must face inward (this gear meshes with the splines on the starter motor shaft).

10. Lubricate the driven gear shoulder (A, **Figure 53**) with engine oil.

11. Degrease the crankshaft outer taper (B, **Figure 53**) and the flywheel inner taper with an aerosol parts cleaner. Allow both tapers to dry before installing the flywheel.

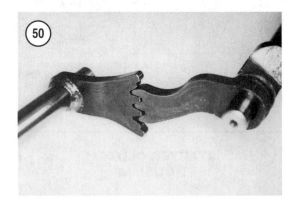

12. If removed, install the Woodruff key (C, **Figure 53**) into the crankshaft keyway.

13. Place a paint mark on the end of the crankshaft in-line with the crankshaft keyway (D, **Figure 53**). The paint mark serves as a visual aid to help align the flywheel keyway with the Woodruff key during installation.

14. Align the keyway in the flywheel (A, **Figure 54**) with the Woodruff key and install the flywheel while turning the starter driven gear (B) clockwise. Check that the paint mark on the crankshaft aligns with the flywheel keyway.

> *NOTE*
> *Shine a flashlight through the flywheel bore and check that the Woodruff key is installed in its keyway.*

> *NOTE*
> *The flywheel bolt uses **left-hand** threads.*

15. Lubricate the flywheel bolt threads and washer (**Figure 32**) with engine oil and thread into the crankshaft.

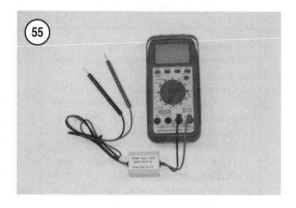

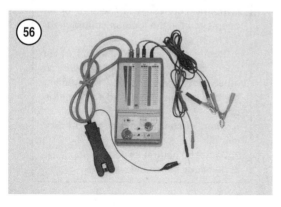

16. Hold the flywheel with the flywheel holder and tighten the flywheel bolt to 137 N•m (101 ft.-lb.).

17. Install the left crankcase cover as described in this chapter.

IGNITION SYSTEM TROUBLESHOOTING

All models are equipped with a digital ignition system.

Peak Voltage Tests and Equipment

> *WARNING*
> *High voltage is present during ignition system operation. Do not touch ignition components, wires or test leads while cranking or running the engine.*

Peak voltage tests check the voltage output of the ignition coils and pulse generator at normal cranking speed, thus making it possible to accurately test the voltage output under operating conditions.

The peak voltage specifications listed in **Table 7** are minimum values. If the measured voltage meets or exceeds the specification, the test results are satisfactory. In some cases, the voltage may greatly exceed the minimum specification.

A peak voltage tester is required. One of the following testers or an equivalent, can be used to perform peak voltage tests described in this section. Refer to the manufacturer's instructions when using these tools.

1. Honda Peak voltage adapter, part No. 07HGJ-0020100. This tool must be used in combination with a digital multimeter with a minimum impedance of 10M ohms/DCV. A meter with a lower impedance does not display accurate measurements. Refer to **Figure 55**.

2. Ignition Mate (Motion Pro part No. 08-0193). Refer to **Figure 56**.

Preliminary Checks

Before testing the ignition system, make the following checks:

1. Make sure the battery is fully charged and in good condition. A weak battery causes a slow engine cranking speed and low peak voltage readings.

IGNITION COIL PRIMARY PEAK VOLTAGE TROUBLESHOOTING

NOTE:
Initial voltage is the recorded battery voltage before cranking the engine with the starter motor.

| No peak voltage. | Check the following in order:
1. Damaged engine stop switch.
2. Open circuit in the black/white wire between the engine stop switch and ignition coil.
3. Poorly connected connectors or an open circuit in the ignition coil primary circuit.
4. Damaged ignition control module (ICM) when all of the above are normal. |

| Peak voltage reading is normal, but there is no spark. | Check the following in order:
1. Open circuit in the ignition coil ground or power circuits.
2. Damaged ignition coil.
3. Loose spark plug cap.
4. Damaged spark plug wire. |

| Initial voltage is normal, but drops to 2-4 volts when engine is cranked. | Check the following in order:
1. Incorrect peak voltage adapter connections.
2. Cranking speed is too low. Perform the starter motor voltage drop tests in this chapter to check for voltage drop when attempting to start engine.
3. No battery voltage between the black (+) ignition control module (ICM) connector and an engine ground (-). Check also for a loose or contaminated ICM connector.
4. Poorly connected connectors or an open circuit in the ignition control module (ICM) green wire.
5. Poorly connected connectors or an open circuit in the yellow/blue or blue/yellow wires between the ignition control module (ICM) and the ignition coils.
6. Short circuit in ignition coil primary circuit.
7. Damaged neutral switch.
8. Damaged sidestand switch. |

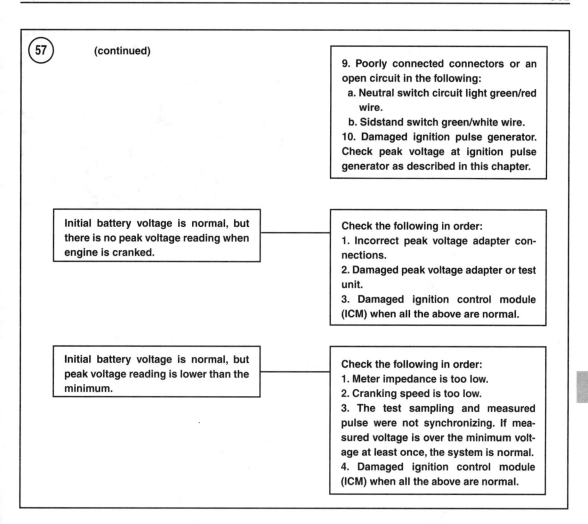

2. Perform the *Spark Test* in Chapter Two. If a crisp, blue spark is noted, the ignition system is working correctly. Test each spark plug and note the following:

   a. If there is no spark at all spark plugs, check for a disconnected or contaminated connector or a damaged ignition switch or engine stop switch. Test each switch as described in this chapter.

   b. If the spark test shows there is no spark at one coil group (front or rear cylinder), switch the ignition coils and repeat the spark test. If the inoperative cylinder now has spark, the original ignition coil is defective. Replace it and retest. However, if the inoperative cylinder still does not have spark, check the ignition coil wires for an open circuit.

   c. Also check for fouled or damaged spark plugs, loose spark plug caps or water in the spark plugs caps.

NOTE
The spark plug caps are an integral part of the plug wire and cannot be removed separately. Refer to **Ignition Coils** *in this chapter.*

3. If the problem has not been found and the spark plugs, plug caps and all electrical system connectors are in good working order, the problem is probably due to a defective switch or ignition system component. Perform the peak voltage tests in this section to locate the damaged component.

Ignition Coil Signal Peak Voltage Test

This test requires a peak voltage tester as described under *Peak Voltage Tests and Equipment* in this section. Refer to **Figure 57** for test results.

1. Check the battery to make sure it is fully charged and in good condition. A weak battery causes a slow engine cranking speed and inaccurate peak voltage tests results.

2. Remove the seat (Chapter Fifteen).

3. Remove the fuel tank (Chapter Eight).

4. Check engine compression as described in Chapter Three. If the compression is low in one or both cylinders, the test results will be inaccurate.

5. Check all of the ignition component electrical connectors and wiring harnesses. Check the electrical wires to and within the connector for any opens or poor connections. Make sure the connectors are clean and properly connected.

6. Disconnect each spark plug cap. Then connect a new spark plug to each plug cap and ground the plug against the cylinder head (**Figure 58**). Do not remove the spark plugs installed in the cylinder heads. These must remain in the cylinder heads to maintain engine compression.

7. If using the Honda peak voltage adapter, connect it to the multimeter as shown in **Figure 55**.

> *NOTE*
> *If using the Ignition Mate (**Figure 56**) tester or a similar peak voltage tester, follow its manufacturer's instructions for connecting the tester to the ignition coil.*

> *NOTE*
> *Do not disconnect the ignition coil primary connectors when performing Step 8.*

8. Refer to *Ignition Coils* in this chapter to locate and identify the ignition coils. Connect the peak voltage test leads to the ignition coil terminals (**Figure 59**) as follows:

   a. Front cylinder ignition coil: Connect the positive test lead to the blue/yellow terminal and the negative test lead to ground.

   b. Rear cylinder ignition coil: Connect the positive test lead to the yellow/blue connector terminal and the negative test lead to ground.

9. Shift the transmission into neutral.

10. Turn the ignition switch on and the engine stop switch to RUN. The voltmeter should read battery voltage. Note the following:

   a. If there is no battery voltage or the voltage reading is low, refer to the test results in **Fig-**

ure 57. Perform the steps in order to find the problem.

   b. If the battery voltage reading is correct, continue with Step 11.

> *WARNING*
> *High voltage is present during ignition system operation. Do not touch spark plugs, ignition components, connectors or test leads while cranking the engine.*

11. Press the starter button while reading the meter.

12. Release the starter button, then connect the test lead to the other ignition coil primary lead and repeat Step 11.

13. Turn the ignition switch off and interpret the test results as follows:

> *NOTE*
> *All peak voltage specifications in the text and **Table 7** are **minimum** voltages. As long as the measured voltage meets or exceeds the specification, consider the test results satisfactory. On some components, the voltage may greatly exceed the minimum specification.*

   a. The minimum ignition coil primary voltage reading is 100 volts minimum.

   b. The individual peak voltage reading recorded for each ignition coil can vary as long as the voltage readings are higher than the specified minimum value.

   c. If the peak voltage reading for one or both ignition coils is less than 100 volts, refer to the test results in **Figure 57**. Perform the steps in order to find the problem.

14. Disconnect the test leads.

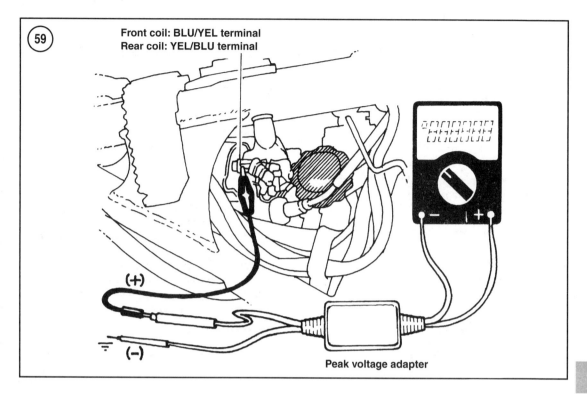

(59) Front coil: BLU/YEL terminal
Rear coil: YEL/BLU terminal

(+)

(−)

Peak voltage adapter

15. Remove the spark plugs from the plug caps, then reconnect the plug caps onto the spark plugs installed in the cylinder head.

16. Reverse Step 2 and Step 3 to complete installation.

Ignition Pulse Generator Peak Voltage Test

This test requires a peak voltage tester as described under *Peak Voltage Tests and Equipment* in this section. Refer to **Figure 60** for test results.

1. Check the battery to make sure it is fully charged and in good condition. A weak battery causes a slow engine cranking speed and inaccurate peak voltage tests results.

2. Check engine compression as described in Chapter Three. If the compression is low in one or both cylinders, the following test results are inaccurate.

3. Check all of the ignition component electrical connectors and wiring harnesses. Make sure the connectors are clean and properly connected.

4. Depending on model, refer to the appropriate test and perform the steps in order.

VT1100C2 ACE models

1. Remove the seat (Chapter Fifteen).

2. Unhook and fold back the rubber cover protecting the electrical connector block mounted beside the air filter housing. Then disconnect the white 4-pin pulse generator connector (**Figure 61**).

3. If using the Honda peak voltage adapter, connect it to the multimeter as shown in **Figure 55**.

> *WARNING*
> *High voltage is present during ignition system operation. Do not touch spark plugs, ignition components, connectors or test leads while cranking the engine.*

> *NOTE*
> *If using the Ignition Mate (**Figure 56**) tester or a similar peak voltage tester, follow its manufacturer's instructions for connecting the tester to the ignition coil.*

> *NOTE*
> *All peak voltage specifications in the text (Step 4 and Step 5) and **Table 7** are **minimum** voltages. If the measured voltage meets or exceeds the*

9

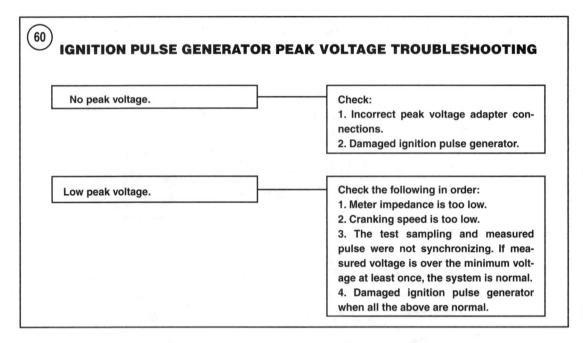

(60)

IGNITION PULSE GENERATOR PEAK VOLTAGE TROUBLESHOOTING

| No peak voltage. | Check:
1. Incorrect peak voltage adapter connections.
2. Damaged ignition pulse generator. |

| Low peak voltage. | Check the following in order:
1. Meter impedance is too low.
2. Cranking speed is too low.
3. The test sampling and measured pulse were not synchronizing. If measured voltage is over the minimum voltage at least once, the system is normal.
4. Damaged ignition pulse generator when all the above are normal. |

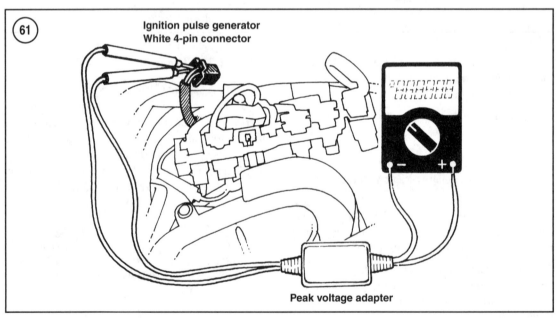

(61)

Ignition pulse generator
White 4-pin connector

Peak voltage adapter

specification, consider the test results satisfactory. On some components, the voltage may greatly exceed the minimum specification.

4. Perform the following test:
   a. Connect the peak voltage positive test lead to the pulse generator connector white/yellow terminal and the negative test lead to the yellow connector terminal (**Figure 61**).

b. Shift the transmission into neutral.
c. Turn the ignition switch on and the engine stop switch to RUN.
d. Press the starter button while reading the meter. The meter should indicate a minimum peak voltage reading of 0.7 volts DC.
e. Turn the ignition switch off and disconnect the test leads.

5. Perform the following test:

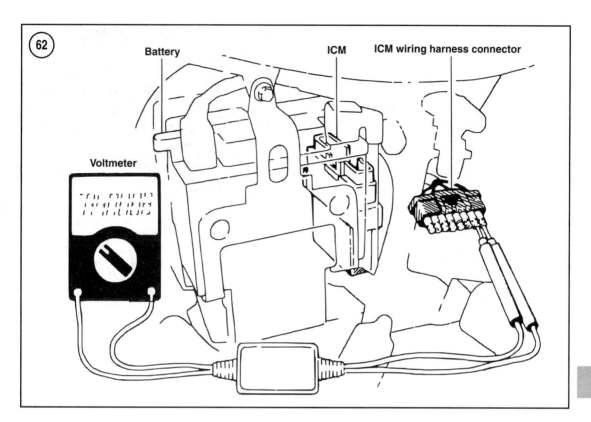

62

Battery   ICM   ICM wiring harness connector

Voltmeter

a. Connect the peak voltage positive test lead to the pulse generator connector white/blue terminal and the negative test lead to the blue connector terminal (**Figure 61**).

b. Shift the transmission into neutral.

c. Turn the ignition switch on and the engine stop switch to RUN.

d. Press the starter button while reading the meter. The meter should indicate a minimum peak voltage reading of 0.7 volts DC.

e. Turn the ignition switch off and disconnect the test leads.

6. If the voltage readings Step 4 and Step 5 were incorrect, refer to the test results in **Figure 60**. If the voltage reading in Step 4 or Step 5 was incorrect, check the affected wires in the wiring harness between the 4-pin connector and the ignition pulse generator for an open or short circuit. At the same time, check the connector for loose terminals or contamination. If the reading is still incorrect, refer to the test results in **Figure 60**.

7. Install the previously removed parts to complete assembly.

All other models

1. Remove the left side cover (Chapter Fifteen).

2. Disconnect the ICM connector as described under *Ignition Control Module* in this chapter.

3. If using the Honda peak voltage adapter, connect it to the multimeter as shown in **Figure 55**.

NOTE
*If using the Ignition Mate (**Figure 56**) tester or a similar peak voltage tester, follow its manufacturer's instructions for connecting the tester to the ignition coil.*

4. Connect the peak voltage positive test lead to the ICM wiring harness connector white/blue terminal and the negative test lead to the blue connector terminal (**Figure 62**, typical).

5. Shift the transmission into neutral.

6. Turn the ignition switch on and the engine stop switch to RUN.

WARNING
High voltage is present during ignition system operation. Do not touch spark plugs, ignition components,

connectors or test leads while crank-
ing the engine.

NOTE
All peak voltage specifications in the
*text and **Table 7** are **minimum** volt-*
ages. If the measured voltage meets or
exceeds the specification, consider
the test results satisfactory. On some
components, the voltage may greatly
exceed the minimum specification.

7. Press the starter button while reading the meter. The meter should indicate a minimum peak voltage reading of 0.7 volts DC. If the reading is less than this, continue with Step 8.

8. Measure the peak voltage at the ignition pulse generator connector:

   a. Turn the ignition switch off.

   b. Remove the seat (Chapter Fifteen).

   c. Disconnect the ignition pulse generator 2-pin connector. Refer to *Ignition Pulse Generator* in this chapter to locate the connector.

   d. Connect the peak voltage positive test lead to the ignition pulse generator white/blue connector terminal and the negative test lead to the blue connector terminal.

NOTE
Connect the test leads to the ignition
pulse generator side connector termi-
nals, not to the wire harness connec-
tor terminals.

   e. Turn the ignition switch on and the engine stop switch to RUN.

   f. Press the starter button while reading the meter. The meter should indicate a minimum peak voltage reading of 0.7 volts DC. If the reading is now correct, check the wires between the ignition pulse generator and the ICM connector for an open or short circuit. Then check the wires between the ignition pulse generator and the ICM connector. At the same time, check the connectors for loose terminals or contamination. If the reading is still incorrect, refer to the test results in **Figure 60**.

9. Install the previously removed parts to complete assembly.

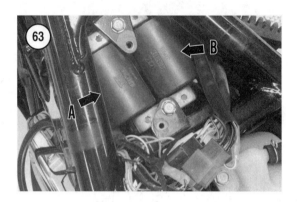

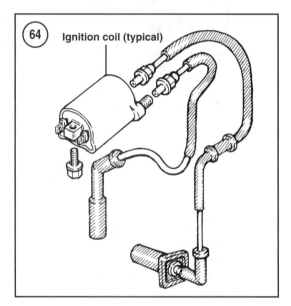

Ignition coil (typical)

IGNITION COILS

There are two ignition coils: the left coil (A, **Figure 63**) fires the plugs for the rear cylinder. The right coil (B, **Figure 63**) fires the plugs for the front cylinder. The ignition coils are identical (have the same part number).

The ignition coil is a form of transformer that develops the high voltage required to jump the spark plug gap. The only maintenance required is to keep the electrical connections clean and tight and occasionally check to see the coils are mounted securely.

Spark Plug Caps and Secondary Wire Replacement

Figure 64 shows how to replace the spark plug cap/secondary wire assembly. Identify each spark plug cap/secondary wire assembly before removing

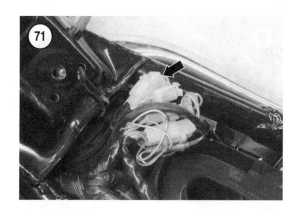

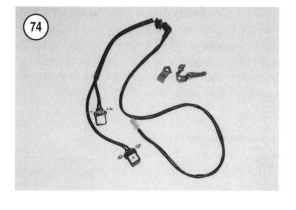

NOTE
The ignition pulse generator can be removed with the primary drive gear assembly installed on the crankshaft. The following photographs show the service performed with the primary drive gear assembly removed for clarity.

4. Remove the two wire clamp mounting bolts and clamps (A, **Figure 72**).

5. Pull the two wire grommets (**Figure 73**) out of the crankcase.

6. Remove the mounting bolts (B, **Figure 72**) and the two ignition pulse generators from the crankcase. Refer to **Figure 74**.

7. Remove all sealer residue from the crankcase and wire harness grommets.

8. Installation is the reverse of removal. Note the following:

   a. Apply a liquid sealant to the grommets before installing them into the crankcase notches.

   b. Lubricate the ignition pulse generator wire clamp bolt threads (A, **Figure 72**) with engine oil and tighten to 26 N•m (19 ft.-lb.).

   c. Tighten the pulse generator mounting bolts (B, **Figure 72**) securely.

   d. Route the ignition pulse generator wiring harness so it does not contact the primary drive gear or any moving part.

IGNITION CONTROL MODULE (ICM)

The ICM unit (**Figure 75**) is mounted on the battery holder. On VT1100C2 ACE models, the ICM is equipped with an integral wiring harness that plugs into the main wiring harness. On VT1100C3 models, the wiring harness connector plugs into the top of the ICM. On all other models, the wiring harness connector plugs into the bottom of the ICM.

Removal/Installation

1. Remove the seat and left side cover (Chapter Fifteen).
2. Remove the battery as described in this chapter.
3A. On VT1100C2 ACE models, perform the following:
   a. Remove the two screws and the fuse box cover.
   b. Remove the two screws (A, **Figure 76**) and fuse box (B).
   c. Disconnect the white 4-pin ignition pulse generator connector (A, **Figure 70**) and the black 6-pin ICM connector (B) from the connector block mounted beside the air filter housing.
   d. Remove the ICM unit from its rubber mount.
3B. On all other models, perform the following:
   a. Remove the fasteners securing the battery holder to the frame.
   b. Pull the battery holder partway out of the frame. Then hold the ICM and press the tab on the connector to disconnect the connector.
   c. Remove the ICM from the rubber holder.
4. Cover the wiring harness connector with a plastic bag to keep the connector clean and prevent pin damage while the ICM is disconnected from the circuit.
5. Installation is the reverse of these steps.

STARTING SYSTEM TROUBLESHOOTING

The starting system consists of the battery, starter switch, starter, starter relay, clutch switch, neutral switch, sidestand switch, engine stop switch, clutch diode, fuses, related wiring and the starter drive mechanism.

When the ignition switch is on and the start button is pushed, current is transmitted from the battery to the starter relay, causing its contacts to close. This is the click heard when the start button is pushed. The starter circuit is now closed, thus allowing battery power to activate the starter, which turns the crankshaft through engagement with the starter clutch mechanism. Failure of one or more electrical components in the starting system can cause a start-

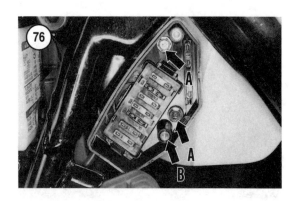

ing problem. Mechanical problems in the engine can also cause starting system failure. The *Engine Will Not Start* procedure in Chapter Two lists general troubleshooting procedures to help isolate starting problems. If the problem is traced to the starter circuit, perform the procedure in this section that matches the starting problem.

When troubleshooting a starting system problem, first make sure the battery can pass a load test and is fully charged. Refer to *High-Load Battery Test* under *Battery* in this chapter.

Starter Roadside Tests

If the starter does not turn over, perform these quick tests to isolate the starter problem:

1. Turn the ignition switch on and shift the transmission into neutral. If the headlight did not come on, check the main fuse and appropriate subfuse. Refer to *Fuses* in this chapter. If the fuses are good, check the battery.

2. If the headlight came on, push the starter button to start the engine. The starter relay should click. If not, the problem is in the wiring to the starter relay, ignition switch or the starter relay is faulty.

3. If the starter relay did click but the starter did not turn the engine over, the problem may be due to an excessive voltage drop in the starter circuit or the starter motor is damaged. This could be due to worn brushes or a shorted commutator. The problem can also be in the starter drive system or engine.

Troubleshooting Preparation

Before troubleshooting the starting system, check for the following:

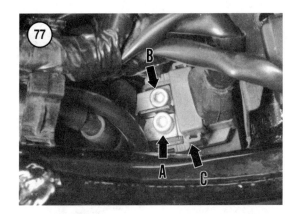

1. The battery is fully charged and passed a high-load battery test. Refer to *Battery* in this chapter.

2. Battery cables are the proper size and length. Replace damaged or undersized cables.

3. All electrical connections are clean and tight. High resistance caused from dirty or loose connections can affect voltage and current levels.

4. The wiring harness is in good condition with no worn or frayed insulation or lose harness sockets.

5. The fuel tank is filled with an adequate supply of fresh gasoline.

6. The spark plugs are in good condition and properly gapped.

7. The ignition system is working correctly.

Starter System
Voltage Drop Test

A voltage drop test measures the voltage drop (or difference in voltage) in a circuit between the power source and destination to locate poor electrical connections that may test normal during a resistance

test. Before performing the steps listed under *Starter Circuit Testing* in this section, perform the voltage drop tests in this procedure. These steps check the starting circuit from the battery to the starter motor to find dirty, loose or damaged connectors and wiring components that may be causing the problem.

A voltmeter that can read in millivolts (mV) (1/1000 of a volt) is required to test voltage drop.

NOTE
*To understand how a voltage drop test works, refer to **Voltage Drop Test** under **Basic Test Procedures** in Chapter Two.*

1. Remove the seat and the left side cover (Chapter Fifteen).

2. Turn the fuel valve off.

3. Disconnect the fuel pump electrical connector. Refer to *Fuel Pump* in Chapter Eight.

4. The starter relay is mounted underneath the seat. Slip the rubber cover off the top of the relay and identify the cable terminals called out in this procedure:

    a. Starter relay battery side terminal (A, **Figure 77**).

    b. Starter relay starter motor terminal (B, **Figure 77**).

5. While the engine must be turned over during these tests, it must not start. To prevent the engine from starting, disconnect each spark plug cap. Then ground the ignition system by installing a grounding tool into *each* spark plug cap as described under *Ignition Grounding Tool* in Chapter One. Do not remove the original spark plugs because they must remain in the cylinder head during the test.

CAUTION
When checking voltage drop, do not operate the starter for more than 5 seconds at a time. Wait approximately 10 seconds between starting attempts. Position the voltmeter so you can easily read it to reduce the amount of time the starter is actually used.

NOTE
*When connecting the voltmeter test lead to the starter motor terminal, connect it to the terminal bolt threads (**Figure 78**) and not to the cable or cable nut. When connecting the test*

*lead to a battery terminal, connect it to the battery terminal (**Figure 79**) and not to the end of the cable or the cable bolt. This allows the voltmeter readings to be taken directly off the starter and battery terminals to identify problems that may exist between the starter or battery terminal and its cable connection.*

6. For Test 1, test the positive side of the starter circuit (**Figure 80**) as follows:

   a. Connect the voltmeter positive lead across the battery positive terminal.

   b. Connect the voltmeter negative lead across the starter motor terminal. The voltmeter should read battery voltage.

   c. Turn the ignition switch on and press the starter button while reading the voltmeter. The voltmeter shows the difference in voltage between the two test points. The ideal voltage drop reading is 0 volts. A voltage drop of more than 0.5 volts indicates a faulty connection or excessive resistance in the starting circuit. A voltmeter reading of 12 volts indicates an open circuit. If the voltage drop exceeds 0.5 volts, continue with Step 7 to isolate the problem. If the voltage drop is 0.5 volts or less, go to Step 9 to check the negative (ground) side of the starter circuit.

7. For Test 2, test the voltage drop between the battery and the starter side of the relay as follows (**Figure 81**):

   a. Connect the voltmeter positive lead across the battery positive terminal.

   b. Connect the voltmeter negative lead across the starter relay starter motor side terminal. The voltmeter should read battery voltage.

   c. Turn the ignition switch on and press the starter button while reading the voltmeter. The voltmeter shows the difference in voltage between the two test points. A voltage drop of more than 0.2 volts indicates a faulty connection or excessive resistance between the battery terminal and the starter terminal on the relay switch.

   d. If the voltage drop is excessive, clean the terminals and wire connections between the two test points and retest.

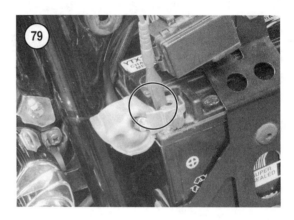

8. For Test 3, test the voltage drop between the battery and the battery side of the relay as follows (**Figure 82**):

   a. Connect the voltmeter positive lead across the battery positive terminal.

   b. Connect the voltmeter negative lead across the starter relay battery side terminal. The voltmeter should read approximately 0 volts.

   c. Turn the ignition switch on and press the starter button while reading the voltmeter. The voltmeter shows the difference in voltage between the two test points. A voltage drop of more than 0.2 volts indicates a faulty connection or excessive resistance between the battery terminal and the battery terminal on the relay switch.

   d. If the voltage drop is excessive, clean the terminals and wire connections between the two test points and retest.

9. For Test 4, test the negative (ground) side of the starter circuit (**Figure 83**) as follows:

   a. Connect the voltmeter negative lead across the battery negative terminal.

   b. Connect the voltmeter positive lead against a clean, unpainted part of the starter housing.

   c. With the voltmeter connected as described, it should read 0 volts.

   d. Turn the ignition switch on and press the starter button while reading the voltmeter. The voltmeter should read 0 volts. A voltage drop of more than 0.3 volts indicates high resistance in the ground circuit. If it does, check the ground connections between the meter leads. Then check the starter mounting bolts for looseness or contamination.

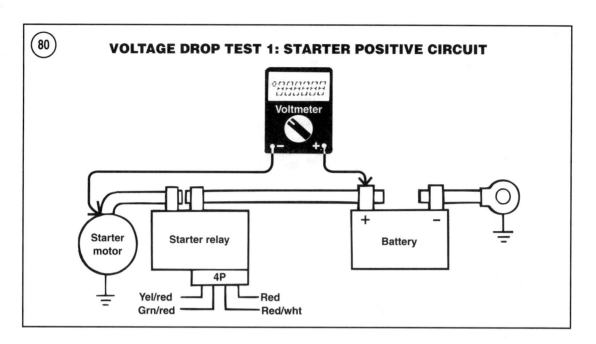

VOLTAGE DROP TEST 1: STARTER POSITIVE CIRCUIT

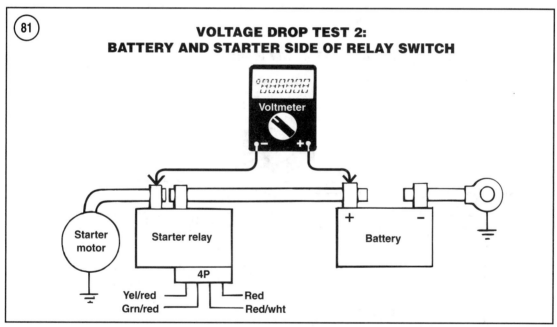

**VOLTAGE DROP TEST 2:
BATTERY AND STARTER SIDE OF RELAY SWITCH**

NOTE
Step 9 can be repeated to check any ground circuit in the starting circuit. Leave the negative lead connected to the battery and connect the positive lead to the ground in question.

10. If the problem is not found, refer to *Starter Circuit Testing* in this section.

11. Position the rubber cover over the starter relay switch.

12. Reconnect the fuel pump electrical connector.

13. Remove the grounding plugs and reconnect the spark plug caps.

Starter Circuit Testing

The basic starter-related troubles are:

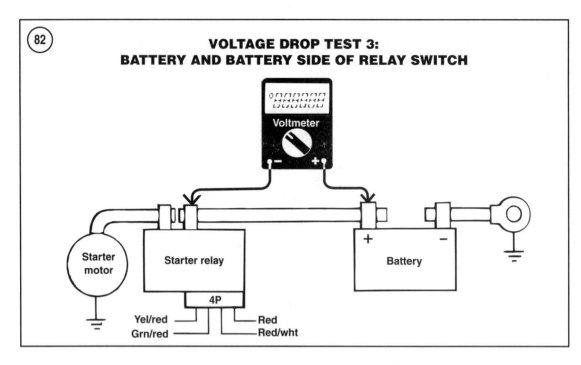

VOLTAGE DROP TEST 3:
BATTERY AND BATTERY SIDE OF RELAY SWITCH

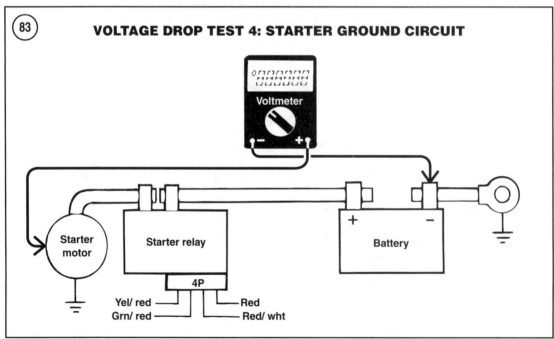

VOLTAGE DROP TEST 4: STARTER GROUND CIRCUIT

1. Starter spins slowly.

2. Starter relay clicks but the engine does not turn over.

3. Starter operates but the engine does not turn over.

4. Starter does not spin.

5. Starter spins with the transmission in neutral but does not turn with the transmission in gear with the clutch lever pulled in and the sidestand up.

CAUTION
Never operate the starter for more
than 5 seconds at a time. Allow the

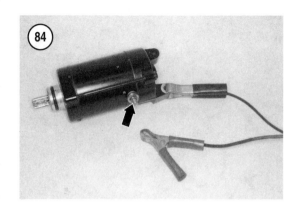

starter to cool 10 seconds before reusing it. Failing to allow the starter to cool after continuous starting attempts can damage the starter.

Starter spins slowly

If the starter operates but does not turn the engine over at normal speed, check the following:
1. Test the battery as described in this chapter.
2. Check for the following:
    a. Loose or corroded battery terminals.
    b. Loose or corroded battery ground cable.
    c. Loose starter motor cable.
3. If the battery is fully charged, passes a high-load test and the cables are in good condition, the starter motor may be faulty. Remove, disassemble and bench test the starter as described in this chapter.

Starter relay clicks but engine does not turn over

1. Test the battery as described in this chapter.
2. Perform the voltage drop tests described in this section. Confirm that all connections are clean and tight.
3. Damaged starter idle gear.
4. Damaged starter reduction gear.
5. Crankshaft cannot turn over because of mechanical failure.

Starter operates but engine does not turn over

1. If the starter was just overhauled, it may have been assembled incorrectly and is turning backward.

2. Check for a damaged starter clutch as described in this chapter.

Starter does not spin

1. Remove the seat.
2. Check for a blown main or subfuse as described in this chapter. If the fuses are good, continue with Step 3.
3. Check the starter cable for an open circuit or dirty or loose-fitting terminals. Perform the voltage drop tests as described in this section. Repair any dirty, loose fitting or damaged connectors or wiring.
4. Check the 4-pin starter relay connector (C, **Figure 77**) for dirty or loose-fitting terminals. Clean and repair as required. Reconnect the connector and continue with Step 5.
5. Check the starter relay as follows. Turn the ignition switch on and push the starter button while listening for a click at the starter relay. Turn the ignition switch off and note the following:
    a. If the starter relay clicks, continue with Step 6.
    b. If there was no click, go to Step 7.

CAUTION
Because of the large amount of current that flows from the battery to the starter in Step 6, use a large diameter cable when making the connection. To avoid damaging the starter, do not leave the battery connected for more than 5 seconds.

6. Remove the starter from the motorcycle as described this chapter. Using an auxiliary battery, apply battery voltage directly to the starter (**Figure 84**). The starter should turn when battery voltage is directly applied.
    a. If the starter did not turn, disassemble and inspect the starter as described in this chapter. Test the starter components and replace worn or damaged parts as required.
    b. If the starter turned, check for loose or damaged starter cables. If the cables are good, remove and test the starter relay switch as described in this chapter. Replace the starter relay switch if necessary.
    c. Reinstall the starter.
7. Check the starter relay ground line for continuity as described under *Starter Relay Switch Testing* in this chapter. There should be continuity.

9

a. If there is continuity, continue with Step 8.

b. If there is no continuity, check for a loose or damaged connector or an open circuit in the wiring harness. If these items are good, test the following items as described in this chapter: sidestand switch, neutral switch, clutch switch diode.

c. Reconnect the starter relay switch electrical connector.

8. Check the starter relay for voltage as described under *Starter Relay Testing* in this chapter. There should be voltage when the ignition switch is on and the starter button is pushed.

a. If there is battery voltage, continue with Step 9.

b. If there is no battery voltage, check for a blown main or subfuse. If the fuses are good, check for an open circuit in the wiring harness or for dirty or loose-fitting terminals. If the wiring and connectors are in good condition, check for a faulty ignition and/or starter switch as described in this chapter.

9. Perform the starter relay operational check as described under *Starter Relay Testing* in this chapter.

a. If the starter relay is normal, check for dirty or loose-fitting terminals in its connector block.

b. If the starter relay is faulty, replace it and retest.

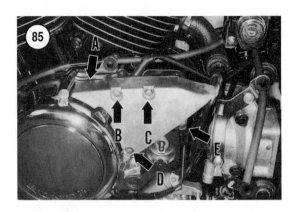

Starter works with the transmission in neutral but does not turn with the transmission in gear with the clutch lever pulled in and the sidestand up

1. Turn the ignition switch on and move the sidestand up and down while watching the sidestand switch indicator light (if so equipped).

a. If the indicator light works properly, continue with Step 2.

b. If the indicator light does not work, check for a blown bulb, damaged sidestand switch or an open circuit in the wiring harness.

2. Test the clutch switch as described in this chapter:

a. If the clutch switch is good, perform Step 3.

b. If the clutch switch is defective, replace the switch and retest.

3. Test the sidestand switch as described in this chapter.

a. If the sidestand switch is good, perform Step 4.

b. If the sidestand switch is defective, replace switch and retest.

4. Check for an open circuit in the wiring harness. Check for loose or damaged electrical connector.

WARNING
Before riding the motorcycle, make sure the sidestand switch and its indicator light (if so equipped) works properly. Riding the motorcycle with the sidestand down can cause loss of control.

STARTER DRIVE GEAR AND TORQUE LIMITER

The starter drive gear and torque limiter assembly are mounted on the left side of the engine.

Removal/Installation

1. Remove the left crankcase rear cover (Chapter Fifteen).

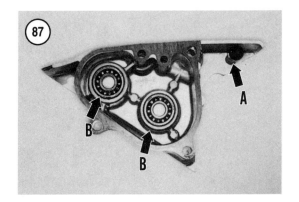

2. Remove the starter gear cover mounting bolts and remove the cover (A, **Figure 85**) and two dowel pins (A, **Figure 86**).

3. Remove the starter drive gear (B, **Figure 86**) and the starter torque limiter (C).

4. Refer to the *Inspection* procedure to clean and inspect all parts.

5. Installation is the reverse of removal. Note the following.

6. Install a new gasket during installation.

7. Make sure the rubber cap (A, **Figure 87**) is installed onto the cover.

8. The four starter gear cover mounting bolts are different lengths. Note the following for the length of each bolt:

    a. B, **Figure 85** (6 × 75 mm).
    b. C, **Figure 85** (6 × 40 mm).
    c. D, **Figure 85** (6 × 45 mm).
    d. E, **Figure 85** (6 × 32 mm).

9. Tighten each bolt securely.

Inspection

1. Remove the rubber plug (A, **Figure 87**) from the starter gear cover.

2. Remove all gasket residue from the starter gear cover and crankcase mating surfaces.

3. Clean the cover and flush the bearings using clean solvent. Dry the cover and bearings, then lightly oil the bearings before inspecting their condition.

4. Clean and dry the starter drive gear and torque limiter parts.

5. Check that the outer bearing races are secure in the cover. A bearing that has seized on a shaft may spin inside the case and damage the bearing bore. This requires starter gear cover replacement.

6. Inspect the bearings for roughness, catching, binding or excessive play. If necessary, replace the bearings as described in Step 7.

7. Replace the starter gear cover bearings (B, **Figure 87**) as follows:

> *NOTE*
> *Refer to **Bearings** in Chapter One for general information on bearing replacement and using a blind bearing puller.*

> *CAUTION*
> *The cover is heated during this procedure. Observe all safety and handling procedures when heating and handling the cover.*

    a. Chill the new bearings in a freezer before heating the cover.
    b. Support the cover so it can be held securely when removing the bearings with the puller.
    c. Heat the cover to approximately 80° C (176° F) with a heat gun. Monitor the temperature with heat sticks or an infrared thermometer to prevent overheating the cover.
    d. Remove both bearings with a blind bearing puller.
    e. Clean and inspect the cover bearing bores. Check for cracks and other damage.
    f. Reheat the cover to the same temperature.
    g. Press in the new bearings until they bottom out. Install both bearings with their manufacturer's marks facing out (away from cover).
    h. Allow the cover to cool.

8. Replace the starter gear cover rubber cap (A, **Figure 87**) if damaged.

9. Inspect the torque limiter (A, **Figure 88**) and starter drive gear (B, **Figure 88**) for damage. Replace if necessary.

STARTER

CAUTION
Do not operate the starter for more than 5 seconds at a time. Wait approximately 10 seconds between starting attempts.

Removal/Installation

1. Disconnect the negative battery cable at the battery as described in this chapter.
2. Remove the starter drive gear and torque limiter as described in this chapter.
3. Drain the engine coolant (Chapter Three).
4. Remove the bolts and disconnect the water hose joint (**Figure 89**) from the rear cylinder block.

NOTE
Holding the inner starter terminal nut (Step 5) prevents the terminal bolt from turning and damaging the insulator installed inside the starter. Because the insulator cannot be purchased separately, a damaged insulator requires a new starter or scavenging an insulator from a discarded starter.

5. Hold the inner starter terminal nut (A, **Figure 90**) with a wrench, then loosen and remove the starter motor cable nut (B) to disconnect the cable.
6. Remove the mounting bolts and ground cable (C, **Figure 90**).
7. Pull the starter toward the right side and remove it from the crankcase.
8. Installation is the reverse of removal. Note the following:
   a. Lubricate the starter O-ring (A, **Figure 91**) with engine oil.
   b. Remove all corrosion from the starter cables.
   c. Position the ground cable onto the front starter mounting bolt (C, **Figure 90**).
   d. Tighten the starter mounting bolts securely.
   e. Hold the inner starter terminal nut (A, **Figure 90**) and tighten the starter motor cable nut (B) securely.
   f. Fit the rubber cover securely over the starter cable. Replace the cover if damaged.
   g. Install a new O-ring onto the water hose joint. Tighten the hose joint bolts (**Figure 89**) securely.

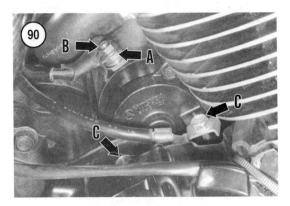
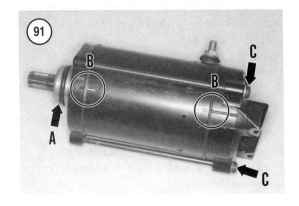

   h. Refill the cooling system (Chapter Three). Check the hose joint for leaks.
   i. Start the engine to make sure the starter works correctly.

Disassembly

Refer to **Figure 92**.

1. Find the alignment marks across the starter housing and both end covers. If necessary, scribe or paint the marks (B, **Figure 91**) to identify them.

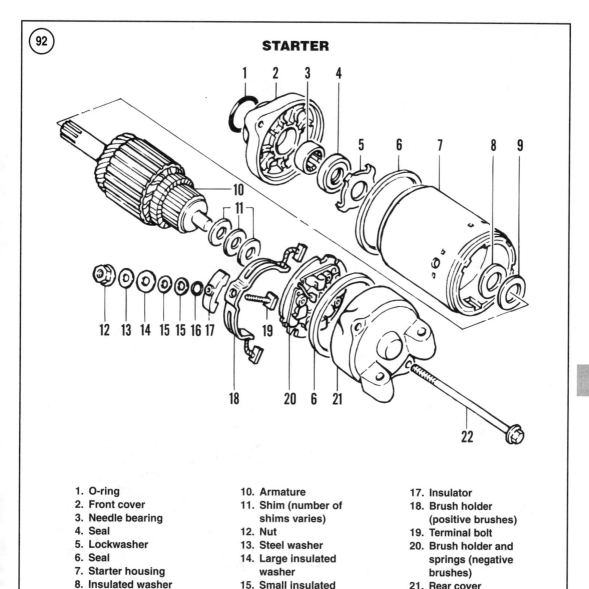

STARTER

1. O-ring
2. Front cover
3. Needle bearing
4. Seal
5. Lockwasher
6. Seal
7. Starter housing
8. Insulated washer
9. Shim (number of shims varies)
10. Armature
11. Shim (number of shims varies)
12. Nut
13. Steel washer
14. Large insulated washer
15. Small insulated washer
16. O-ring
17. Insulator
18. Brush holder (positive brushes)
19. Terminal bolt
20. Brush holder and springs (negative brushes)
21. Rear cover
22. Bolt

2. Remove the bolts (C, **Figure 91**).

NOTE
The number of shims used in each starter varies. The shims and washers must be reinstalled in their correct orders and numbers. Failing to install the correct number of shims and washers may increase armature end play and cause the starter to draw excessive current. Record the thickness

and alignment of each shim and washer removed during disassembly.

NOTE
If disassembling the starter to only check the brushes, remove only the rear cover. The brushes can be inspected and the cover installed if further disassembly is not required. When doing so, locate and reinstall the shims onto the armature shaft.

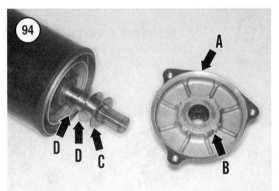

3. Remove the rear cover (A, **Figure 93**) and shims (B).

4. Remove the front cover (A, **Figure 94**) and the lockwasher (B).

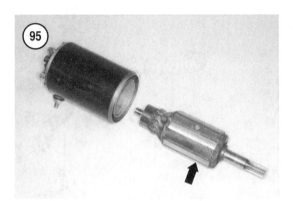

> *NOTE*
> *Do not remove the seal from the front cover. It is not available as a replacement part.*

5. Remove the insulated washer (C, **Figure 94**) and shim(s) (D).

6. Remove the armature (**Figure 95**) from the housing.

7. Before removing the brush holders, test the brushes, terminal bolt and brush holders as follows:

> *NOTE*
> *The positive brushes (A, **Figure 96**) have insulated leads. The negative brushes (B, **Figure 96**) do not.*

  a. Check for continuity between the starter motor terminal and each positive brush (**Figure 97**). There should be continuity. If there is no continuity, replace the positive brush holder (18, **Figure 92**) during reassembly.

  b. Check for continuity between the terminal bolt and starter housing (**Figure 98**). There should be no continuity. If there is continuity, check for damaged, missing or improperly installed insulators on the terminal bolt. Compare the alignment of the installed insulators with **Figure 92** when removing them.

  c. Check for continuity between the positive and negative brushes (**Figure 99**). There should be no continuity. If there is continuity, check the positive brush wires for damaged insulation sleeves. The insulation sleeves

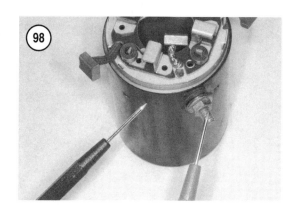

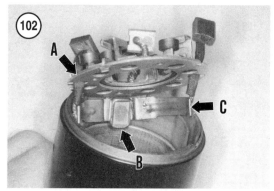

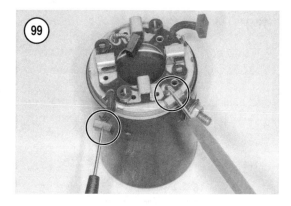

must be installed through the negative brush holder so the positive brush wires cannot short out.

d. Check for continuity between the positive and negative terminals on the negative brush holder (**Figure 100**). There should be no continuity. If there is continuity, replace the brush holder (20, **Figure 92**).

8. Remove the inner terminal nut and remove the steel washer, insulators and O-ring (**Figure 101**).

9. Remove the negative brush holder (A, **Figure 102**), terminal bolt (B) and positive brush holder (C).

10. Remove the insulator (17, **Figure 92**).

Inspection

If any starter component (other than O-rings and brush sets) is excessively worn or damaged, the starter motor must be replaced as an assembly. Individual replacement parts are not available.

NOTE
Before purchasing a new starter, try to find a replacement starter through a motorcycle wrecking yard. If you cannot locate an identical starter, look for a starter is similar in design. The internal part needed may be identical or similar enough to work.

1. The internal parts in a used starter are often contaminated with carbon and copper dust released from the brushes and commutator. Because a starter can be damaged from improper cleaning, note the following:

a. Clean all parts (except the armature, starter housing and insulated washers) in solvent.

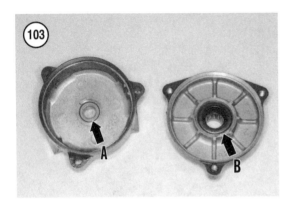

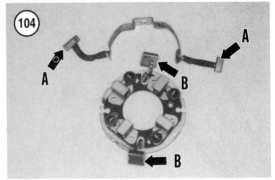

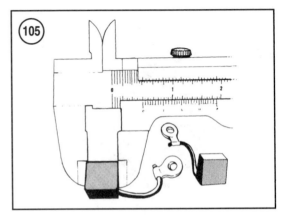

Use a rag lightly damped with solvent to wipe off the armature, insulated washers and the starter housing (inside and outside).

b. Use a fine grade sandpaper to clean the brushes. Do not use emery cloth as its fibers may insulate the brushes.

c. Use only crocus cloth to clean the commutator. Do not use emery cloth because it can leave metallic particles embedded in the commutator that may cause shorting, burning and rapid brush wear. Do not leave any debris on or between the commutator bars.

2. Replace the starter housing seals (6, **Figure 92**) if damaged.

3. Inspect the bushing (A, **Figure 103**) in the rear cover for wear or damage.

4. Inspect the seal and needle bearing (B, **Figure 103**) in the front cover for damage. Do not remove the seal to check the bearing.

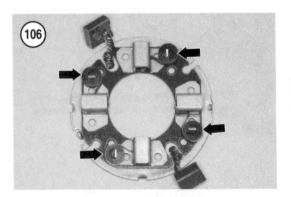

NOTE
The bushing, seal and bearing used in the end covers are not available separately.

5. Check the lockwasher, shims and insulated washers for damage.

6. Inspect the brushes (A and B, **Figure 104**) as follows:

a. Inspect each brush for cracks and other damage.

b. Inspect the insulation on the positive brushes (A, **Figure 104**) for tearing and other damage.

c. Check each brush where it is fixed to its holder (A or B, **Figure 104**).

d. Measure the length of each brush (**Figure 105**). If the length of any one brush is out of

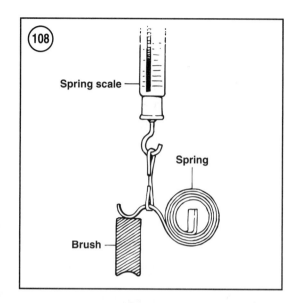

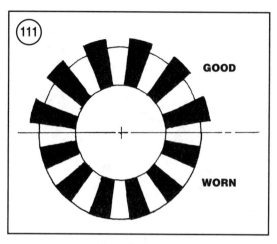

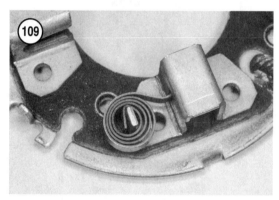

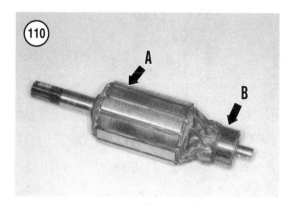

specification (**Table 8**), replace both brush holders (**Figure 104**) as a set. Replacement brushes are permanently fixed to the holders. Soldering is not required.

7. Inspect the brush springs (**Figure 106**) for weakness or damage. Even though a spring tension mea-

surement is not available, compare spring tension using a spring scale as follows:

    a. Assemble the negative brush holder, brushes and commutator as described under *Assembly*. Refer to **Figure 107**.

    b. Support the starter in a vise with soft jaws.

    c. Hook a spring scale to the exposed part of the spring as shown in **Figure 108**.

    d. Pull the spring scale and record the spring tension measurement the moment the spring lifts off the brush.

    e. Repeat for each spring. If there is any noticeable difference in tension measurements, replace the negative brush holder and springs as a set.

8. If removed, hook the brush springs around the brush holder as shown in **Figure 109**.

9. Inspect the armature (A, **Figure 110**):

    a. Inspect both shafts for scoring and other damage.

    b. Inspect the windings for obvious damage.

    c. To check the armature for a short circuit, have it tested on a growler. Refer this service to a Honda dealership or an automotive electrical repair shop.

10. Inspect the commutator (B, **Figure 110**):

    a. Inspect the commutator bars for visual damage.

    b. Clean the commutator surface as described in Step 1.

    c. The mica must be below the surface of the copper bars. On a worn commutator, the mica and copper bars may be worn to the same level (**Figure 111**).

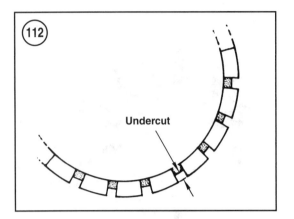

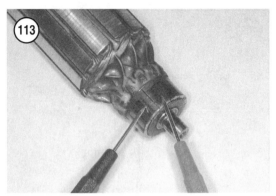

d. If the mica level is too high or if its shape is too narrow or V-shaped, undercut the mica with a hacksaw blade (**Figure 112**).

e. Inspect the commutator copper bars for discoloration. If a pair of bars are discolored, grounded armature coils are indicated.

f. Check for continuity across all adjacent pairs of commutator bars (**Figure 113**). There should be continuity across all pairs of bars. If an open circuit exists between a pair of bars, replace the starter.

g. Check for continuity between the armature shaft and each commutator bar (**Figure 114**). There should be no continuity. If there is continuity, replace the starter.

h. Check for continuity between the armature coil core and each commutator bar. There should be no continuity. If there is continuity, replace the starter.

11. Inspect the starter housing for cracks or other damage. Then inspect for loose, chipped or damaged magnets.

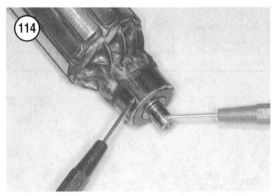

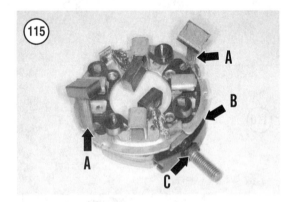

Assembly

1. Assemble the positive (A, **Figure 104**) and negative (B) brush holders as follows:

a. Install the insulated brush wires through the two notches in the negative brush holder as shown in A, **Figure 115**.

b. Install the terminal bolt through the brush holder, then install the insulator (B, **Figure 115**) and O-ring (C).

2. Install the terminal bolt through the hole in the starter housing (A, **Figure 116**) while aligning the tab on the negative brush holder with the notch in

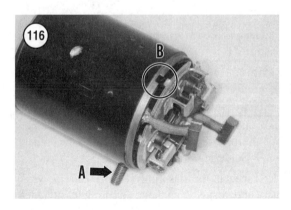

the starter housing (B). Align the insulator (17, **Figure 92**) with the notch in the starter housing bracket.

NOTE
In the next step, reinstall all parts in the order described. This is essential to insulate the positive brushes from the case.

3. Install the two small insulators (15, **Figure 92**), large insulator (14), steel washer (13) and nut (12) to secure the terminal bolt to the starter housing.

4. Perform the continuity checks described under *Disassembly* in Step 7 to check the positive brushes and terminal bolt for proper installation.

5. Install the brushes into their holders as follows:
   a. Cut a plastic tie into four separate pieces, each approximately 20 mm (0.80 in.) long.
   b. Hold the springs against their holders with the plastic strips (**Figure 117**). This allows the commutator to pass under the brushes with no tension placed against the brushes.
   c. Install the brushes into their holders (**Figure 118**).

NOTE
In Step 6, magnetic force pulls the armature against the coils inside the starter housing. Hold the armature tightly when installing it to avoid damaging the coils or brushes.

6. Install the armature into the starter housing. Then remove the plastic ties (**Figure 119**) to release the brush springs and allow them to push the brushes against the commutator. Check that each brush seats squarely against the commutator (**Figure 107**).

7. Install the shims (B, **Figure 93**) onto the armature shaft.

8. Install the O-ring onto the commutator side of the starter housing.

9. Apply a thin coat of grease onto the armature shaft.

10. Align the groove in the rear cover (A, **Figure 120**) with the raised tab on the negative brush holder (B) and install the rear cover.

11. Install the O-ring onto the front side of the starter housing.

12. Lubricate the front cover oil seal lips and bearing (B, **Figure 103**) with grease.

9

13. Refer to **Figure 94** and install the front cover as follows:

    a. Install the steel shims (D, **Figure 94**) onto the armature shaft. The number of shims on your starter may differ from the shims shown in **Figure 94**.

    b. Install the insulator (C, **Figure 94**) and seat against the shims.

    c. Install the lockwasher (B, **Figure 94**) onto the front cover.

    d. Align the front cover tabs with the lockwasher tabs and install the front cover. Then check that the index marks on the starter case and both covers align (B, **Figure 91**).

14. Install the starter bolts (C, **Figure 91**) and tighten securely.

> *NOTE*
> *If a bolt does not pass through the starter , the end covers and/or negative brush holder are installed incorrectly.*

15. Lubricate the O-ring with grease and install it into the front cover groove.

16. Hold the starter and turn the armature shaft by hand. The armature should turn with some resistance, but should not bind or lockup. If the armature does not turn properly, disassemble the starter motor and check the shim, insulated washer and lockwasher alignment.

17. Use an auxiliary battery and apply battery voltage directly to the starter (**Figure 121**). The starter should turn when battery voltage is directly applied. If the starter does not turn, disassemble and inspect the starter as described in this section.

STARTER RELAY

The starter relay (**Figure 122**) is mounted underneath the seat, behind the air filter housing. The 30 amp main fuse is located in the connector holder (**Figure 123**) plugged into the starter relay switch.

Starter Relay Testing

1. Refer to *Starter System Troubleshooting* in this chapter to test the starting circuit. If the problem has been isolated to the starter relay, perform the following test:

2. Remove the seat (Chapter Fifteen).

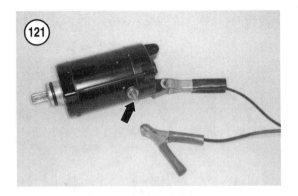

3. Shift the transmission into neutral.

4. Turn the ignition switch on and press the starter button. The starter relay should click.

    a. The starter relay is good if it clicked.

    b. If the starter relay did not click, continue with Step 5.

5. Disconnect the starter relay electrical connector (**Figure 123**). Repair any dirty, loose fitting or damaged terminals. If the wiring is in good condition, leave the connector disconnected and continue with Step 6.

6. Ground line connection test: Shift the transmission into neutral. Check for continuity between the starter relay connector green/red wire and ground. There should be continuity or a slight resistance reading.

> *NOTE*
> *Normally the ohmmeter reads 0 ohms when making a ground test. However, because of the diode placed in the circuit, it is normal for the ohmmeter to show a slight resistance reading.*

    a. If there is continuity, go to Step 7.

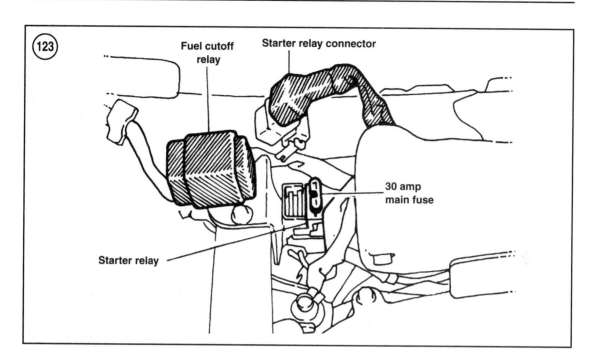

(123)

Fuel cutoff relay

Starter relay connector

30 amp main fuse

Starter relay

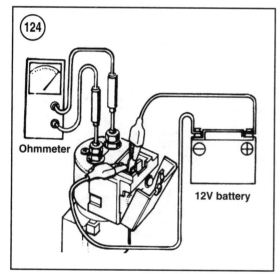

(124)

Ohmmeter

12V battery

b. If there is no continuity, repair the open circuit in the green/red wire between the starter relay connector and the left handlebar switch connector or diode.

7. Starter relay voltage check: Reconnect the starter relay electrical connector (**Figure 123**). Turn the ignition switch on and measure voltage between the starter relay yellow/red wire at the starter relay connector (**Figure 123**) and ground when pressing the starter button. There should be battery voltage.

   a. If there is battery voltage, go to Step 8.

b. If there is no battery voltage, repair the open in the yellow/red wire between the starter relay connector and the engine stop switch in the right-handlebar switch connector.

8. Bench test the starter relay as follows:

   a. Remove the starter relay as described in this section. Clean the relay electrical contacts.

   b. Connect the ohmmeter test leads across the two large leads on the starter relay (**Figure 124**). There should be no continuity.

   c. If there is continuity, replace the starter relay.

   d. If there is no continuity, leave the ohmmeter connected to the relay and continue with substep e.

   e. Connect the positive lead from a fully charged 12 volt battery to the starter relay yellow/red wire terminal and the negative battery lead to the green/red wire terminal (**Figure 124**). There should be continuity.

   f. If there is no continuity, replace the starter relay.

   g. If there is continuity, the starter relay is operational. Reinstall the starter relay and perform the *Starter System Voltage Drop Test* in this chapter to test the integrity of the wires and cables in the starting circuit.

9. Install all parts previously removed.

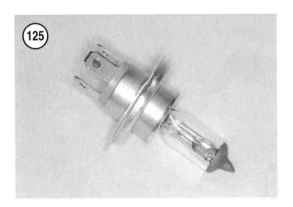

Removal/Installation

1. Remove the seat and left side cover.

2. Disconnect the negative battery lead at the battery as described in this chapter.

3. Disconnect the starter relay electrical connector (A, **Figure 122**) at the relay.

4. Disconnect the battery (B, **Figure 122**) and starter (C) cable leads at the starter relay.

5. Remove the starter relay from the frame.

6. Installation is the reverse of removal. Note the following:

   a. Clean the battery and starter cable leads before connecting them to the relay.

   b. Make sure to install the cover firmly over the two cable leads at the starter relay.

   c. Make sure the 30 amp fuse is installed in the fuse socket on the relay.

REPLACEMENT BULB

Refer to **Table 9** for bulb specifications. Always use the correct wattage bulb. Using the wrong size bulb gives a dim light or causes the bulb to burn out prematurely.

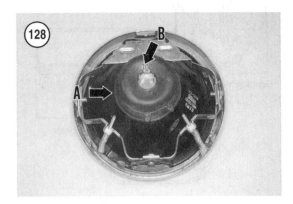

Headlight Lens Removal/Installation (Bulb Replacement)

A quartz-halogen bulb is installed inside the headlight lens assembly. The bulb and lens can be replaced separately.

> *WARNING*
> *If the headlight just burned out or it was just turned off it is hot! Do not touch the bulb until it cools off.*

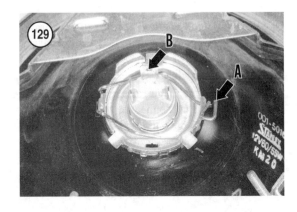

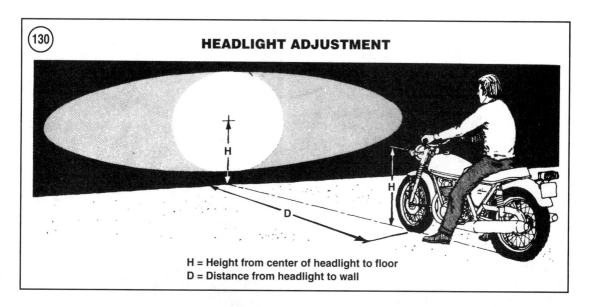

HEADLIGHT ADJUSTMENT

(130)

H = Height from center of headlight to floor
D = Distance from headlight to wall

CAUTION
All models use a quartz-halogen bulb
(Figure 125). Because traces of oil on
the glass reduces the life of the bulb,
do not touch the bulb glass. Clean any
oil or other chemicals from the bulb
glass with an alcohol-moistened
cloth.

1A. On VT1100C2 Sabre and VT1100C3 models, remove the headlight as follows:

   a. Remove the two bolts and collars (**Figure 126**).

   b. Without turning the headlight, slightly pull the bottom part of the headlight out of its housing, then lift the headlight and push its upper end into the headlight housing. Turn the headlight counterclockwise to release the tab on the headlight from the retainer on the housing and remove the headlight from the housing.

1B. On all other models remove the two outer bolts (**Figure 126**) and collars (if used) and remove the headlight from the housing.

2. Disconnect the electrical connector at the bulb (**Figure 127**) and remove the headlight assembly.

3. To replace the bulb:

   a. Remove the dust cover (A, **Figure 128**) from around the bulb.

   b. Unhook the bulb retainer (A, **Figure 129**) and remove the bulb (B).

   c. Align the tabs on the bulb with the notches in the bulb holder and install the bulb.

   d. Install the dust cover with its TOP mark (B, **Figure 128**) at the top of the housing. Make sure the dust cover fits tightly around the bulb and against the lens.

4. Installation is the reverse of removal. Note the following:

   a. Hook the tab at the top of the lens with the retainer at the top of the headlight housing, then pivot the lens into the housing and install the collars and two mounting bolts.

   b. Turn the ignition switch on and check the headlight operation. If necessary, perform the *Headlight Adjustment* in this section.

Headlight Adjustment

Adjust the headlight according to the motor vehicle regulations in your area, or use the following procedure as a guide:

1. Park the motorcycle on a level surface 7.6 m (25 ft.) from a wall.

2. Check tire inflation pressure (Chapter Three).

3. Draw a horizontal line on the wall the same height as the center of the headlight (**Figure 130**).

4. Have an assistant (with the same approximate weight as the primary rider) sit on the seat.

5. Turn the ignition switch on and the light switch to HIGH beam. Turn the handlebars so they point straight ahead and the beam is centered with the horizontal mark on the wall.

6. Check the headlight beam alignment. The broad, flat pattern of light (main beam of light) must be

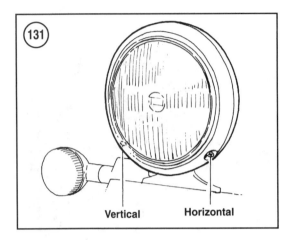

Vertical   Horizontal

centered on the horizontal light with an equal area of light above and below the line (**Figure 130**).

7. Check the headlight beam lateral alignment. With the front wheel pointed straight ahead, there should be an equal area of light to the left and right of center.

8. If the beam is incorrect, turn the screws on the right (vertical adjustment) or left side (horizontal adjustment) of the headlight (**Figure 131**, typical).

Brake Light/Taillight/Turn Signal Bulb Replacement

1. Remove the screws, lens and gasket.
2. Replace the gasket if damaged.
3. Push the bulb in and turn it counterclockwise to remove it (**Figure 132**, typical).
4. Install the new bulb and lens by reversing these steps. Do not overtighten the screws as the lens may crack.

License Plate Light Bulb Replacement

VT1100C

This model does not use a separate license plate bulb. License plate illumination is provided by the taillight bulb and its lens assembly.

VT1100C2 Sabre, VT1100C3 and VT1100T

1. Remove the screws from underneath the license light cover and remove the cover (**Figure 133**).
2. Remove the nuts (A, **Figure 134**), cover (B) and lens.

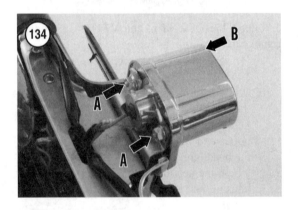

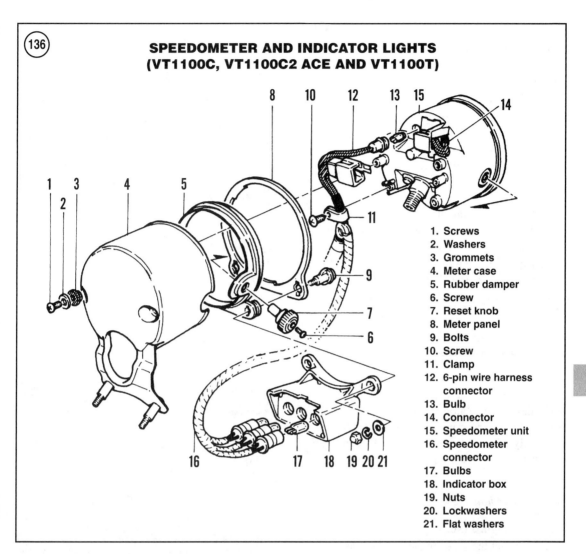

**SPEEDOMETER AND INDICATOR LIGHTS
(VT1100C, VT1100C2 ACE AND VT1100T)**

1. Screws
2. Washers
3. Grommets
4. Meter case
5. Rubber damper
6. Screw
7. Reset knob
8. Meter panel
9. Bolts
10. Screw
11. Clamp
12. 6-pin wire harness connector
13. Bulb
14. Connector
15. Speedometer unit
16. Speedometer connector
17. Bulbs
18. Indicator box
19. Nuts
20. Lockwashers
21. Flat washers

3. Push the bulb (**Figure 135**) in and turn it counterclockwise to remove it.

4. Install the new bulb and lens by reversing these steps.

VT1100C2 ACE

1. Remove the nuts bolts securing the license plate holder to the rear fender.

2. Disconnect the license light connectors.

3. Working from the backside of the license plate holder, remove the nuts securing the license light lens.

4. Push the bulb in and turn it counterclockwise to remove it.

5. Install the new bulb and lens by reversing these steps.

Indicator and Speedometer Housing Bulb Replacement (VT1100C, VT1100C2 ACE and VT1100T)

Indicator box bulbs

The neutral, high beam and turn signal indicators are mounted in the indicator box (**Figure 136**).

1. Remove the nuts and washers from the bottom side of the speedometer housing.

CAUTION
*The two bolts (A, **Figure 137**) have a lug that aligns with a groove in the indicator box mounting holes. Do not turn the bolts when removing them in Step 2 or they may damage the mounting holes.*

2. Push the two bolts (A, **Figure 137**) out of the housing and remove them.

3. Remove the speedometer housing (B, **Figure 137**) and the indicator box (C).

4. Pull the indicator box to the right side and out of the speedometer housing.

5. Remove the bulb holder from the indicator box and replace the blown bulb.

6. Reverse these steps to install the indicator box and speedometer housing, while noting the following:

   a. When installing the two bolts (A, **Figure 137**), align their lugs with the groove in the indicator box mounting holes.

   b. Do not turn the two bolts (A, **Figure 137**) to tighten the speedometer housing. Instead, hold the bolts and turn the lower nuts.

Coolant temperature, low oil pressure and sidestand indicators

An LED unit installed in the speedometer unit illuminates the coolant temperature, low oil pressure and sidestand indicators. The LED unit is an integral part of the speedometer and cannot be replaced separately. If an indicator does not light properly, test the indicator circuit as described in this chapter.

Speedometer housing bulb

Refer to **Figure 136**.

1. Disconnect the speedometer cable at the speedometer.

2. Remove the two screws, washers and grommets from the bottom of the speedometer meter case.

3. Lift the speedometer and pull the bulb socket out of the speedometer assembly.

4. Replace the bulb with a new one.

5. Reverse these steps to install reinstall the speedometer housing and reconnect the speedometer cable.

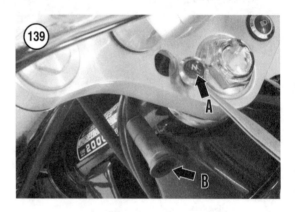

Indicator and Speedometer Housing Bulb Replacement (VT1100C2 Sabre)

Neutral, high beam and turn signal indicators

These bulbs are mounted in the upper steering bridge (**Figure 138**).

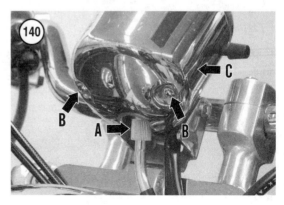

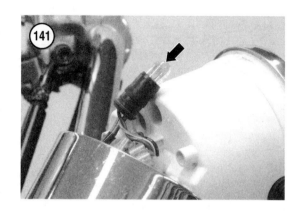

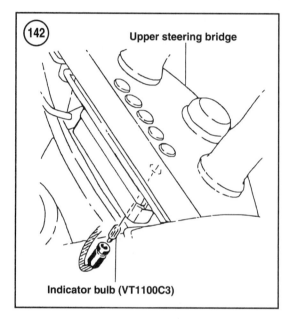

Indicator bulb (VT1100C3)

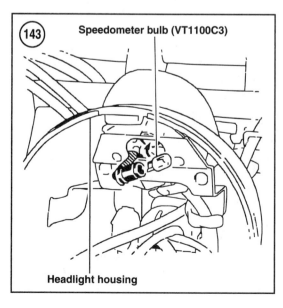

Speedometer bulb (VT1100C3)

Headlight housing

1. Remove the lens (A, **Figure 139**) from the socket and lower the socket (B) from the bridge.
2. Remove the bulb from the socket.
3. Installation is the reverse of removal.

Coolant temperature and oil pressure indicators

An LED unit installed in the speedometer unit illuminates the coolant temperature and low oil pressure indicators. The LED unit is an integral part of the speedometer and cannot be replaced separately. If an indicator does not light properly, test the indicator circuit as described in this chapter.

Speedometer housing bulb

The speedometer is equipped with a single bulb to light the speedometer unit.
1. Disconnect the speedometer cable (A, **Figure 140**) from the housing.
2. Remove the cover screws (B, **Figure 140**) and lower the cover (C) away from the housing.
3. Remove the holder and replace the bulb (**Figure 141**).
4. Installation is the reverse of removal.

Indicator and Speedometer Housing Bulb Replacement (VT1100C3)

Indicator bulbs

The high beam, neutral, low oil pressure, temperature and turn signal bulbs are mounted in the upper steering bridge.
1. Remove the socket and bulb from the bridge (**Figure 142**).
2. Remove the bulb (**Figure 142**) from the socket.
3. Installation is the reverse of removal.

Speedometer housing bulb

The speedometer is equipped with a single bulb to light the speedometer unit.
1. Remove the headlight lens as described in this chapter.
2. Remove the bulb (**Figure 143**) from the socket located inside the headlight housing.
3. Installation is the reverse of removal.

9

HEADLIGHT HOUSING

Removal/Installation

VT1100C

Refer to **Figure 144**.
1. Remove the headlight lens as described in this chapter.
2. Remove the two bolts, cable guides, collars and cover from the bottom of the steering stem.
3. Remove the two nuts and the headlight housing.
4. Installation is the reverse of removal. Note the following:
   a. Turn the ignition switch on and check the operation of all switches and indicators.
   b. Check the headlight adjustment as described in this chapter.

VT1100C2 ACE and VT1100T

1. Remove the headlight lens as described in this chapter.
2A. On VT1100C2 ACE models, remove the nuts (A, **Figure 145**) and bolts securing the headlight housing (B) to the steering stem and remove it.
2B. On VT1100T models, remove the front and lower (A, **Figure 145**) nuts securing the headlight housing to the steering stem and remove it.
3. Installation is the reverse of removal. Note the following:
   a. Turn the ignition switch on and check the operation of all switches and indicators.
   b. Check the headlight adjustment as described in this chapter.

VT1100C2 Sabre

1. Remove the headlight lens as described in this chapter.
2. Note how the wire harness clamps are installed and routed inside the headlight housing.
3. Disconnect the turn signal connectors (A, **Figure 146**) mounted inside the headlight housing. Pull the wires and connectors from the headlight housing.
4. Remove the bolts (B, **Figure 146**), wire clamps and collars inside the headlight housing and remove the housing.
5. Installation is the reverse of removal. Note the following:

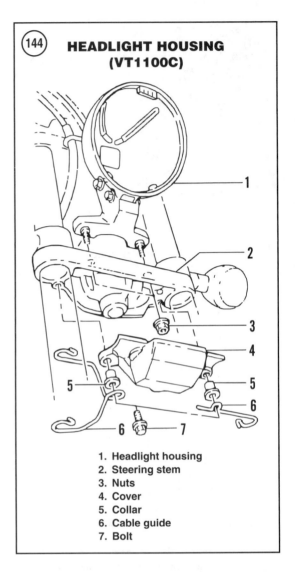

(144) **HEADLIGHT HOUSING (VT1100C)**

1. Headlight housing
2. Steering stem
3. Nuts
4. Cover
5. Collar
6. Cable guide
7. Bolt

   a. Turn the ignition switch on and check the operation of all switches and indicators.
   b. Check the headlight adjustment as described in this chapter.

VT1100C3

Refer to **Figure 147**.
1. Remove the headlight lens as described in this chapter.
2. Note how the wire harness clamps are installed and routed inside the headlight housing.
3. On 1998-2000 models, disconnect the coolant temperature indicator check unit (**Figure 148**) and remove it.

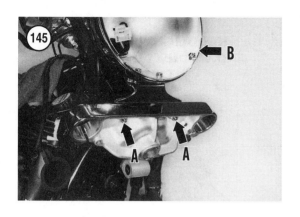

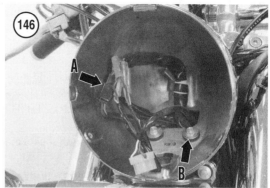

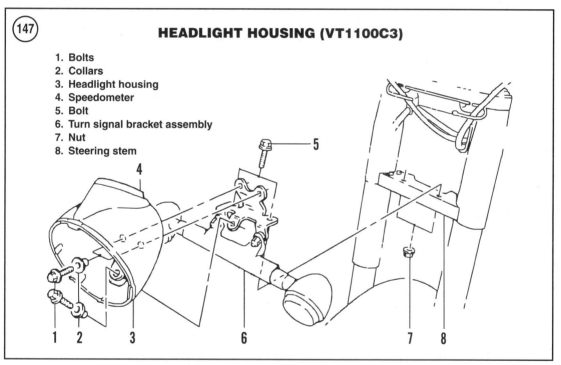

HEADLIGHT HOUSING (VT1100C3)

1. Bolts
2. Collars
3. Headlight housing
4. Speedometer
5. Bolt
6. Turn signal bracket assembly
7. Nut
8. Steering stem

4. Disconnect the following connectors located in the connector pouch (4, **Figure 148**):

   a. Front turn signal connectors.

   b. Trip meter reset switch connectors.

   c. Meter connector.

5. Disconnect the wire harness guide and free the wiring harnesses inside the housing.

6. Pull the wires and connectors from the headlight housing.

7. Remove the three bolts and collars and remove the headlight housing with the speedometer attached.

8. Installation is the reverse of removal. Note the following:

   a. Turn the ignition switch on and check the operation of all switches and indicators.

   b. Check the headlight adjustment as described in this chapter.

**SPEEDOMETER ASSEMBLY
(VT1100C, VT1100C2 ACE,
VT1100C2 SABRE AND VT1100T)**

Removal/Installation

VT1100C, VT1100C2 ACE and VT1100T

   Refer to **Figure 136**.

1. Remove the headlight lens as described in this chapter.
2. Disconnect the speedometer cable at the speedometer.
3. Remove the indicator box as described under *Indicator and Speedometer Housing Bulb Replacement* (VT1100C, VT1100C2 ACE and VT1100T) in this chapter.
4. Lift the speedometer and pull the bulb socket out of the speedometer assembly.
5. Remove the clamp (11, **Figure 136**) securing the 6-pin connector to the speedometer unit.
6. Remove the speedometer unit from its case.
7. Installation is the reverse of removal.

VT1100C2 Sabre

1. Remove the headlight lens as described in this chapter.
2. Disconnect the black 2-pin speedometer connector located inside the headlight housing (**Figure 146**).
3. Disconnect the speedometer cable (A, **Figure 140**).
4. Remove the nut (C, **Figure 140**), bolt, collar, dampers and the speedometer assembly with its wiring harness.
5. Installation is the reverse of removal.
6. Check all meter functions after installation.

SPEEDOMETER AND SPEED SENSOR ASSEMBLY (VT1100C3)

Troubleshooting

This section checks the integrity of the wires and terminals connected to the speedometer.

If the speedometer or tripmeter/odometer operates incorrectly, perform the troubleshooting steps in order.

Make all voltage checks on the wiring harness side connectors, not on the speedometer or speed sensor side connector.

When making a voltage test, do not turn the ignition switch on unless the procedures indicates to do so. If the ignition switch was turned on, turn it off after completing the voltage test.

1. Check the battery charge as described under *Battery* in this chapter. If the battery is good, continue with Step 2.

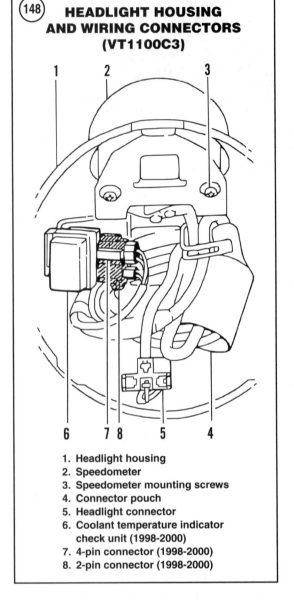

HEADLIGHT HOUSING AND WIRING CONNECTORS (VT1100C3)

1. Headlight housing
2. Speedometer
3. Speedometer mounting screws
4. Connector pouch
5. Headlight connector
6. Coolant temperature indicator check unit (1998-2000)
7. 4-pin connector (1998-2000)
8. 2-pin connector (1998-2000)

2. Check for a blown main or subfuse as described under *Fuses* in this chapter.
3. Access the wiring harness terminals mounted on the speedometer as follows:
   a. Remove the headlight lens as described in this chapter.
   b. Remove the speedometer mounting screws and rubber washers from inside the headlight housing (**Figure 148**).
   c. Pull the speedometer out of the headlight housing to access the wiring terminals (**Figure 149**).

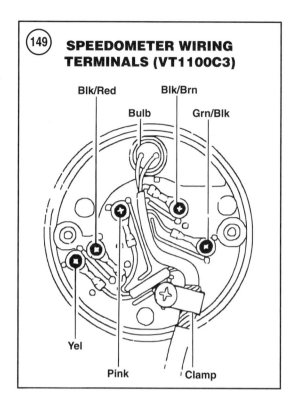

(149) SPEEDOMETER WIRING TERMINALS (VT1100C3)

Blk/Red

Blk/Brn

Bulb

Grn/Blk

Yel

Pink

Clamp

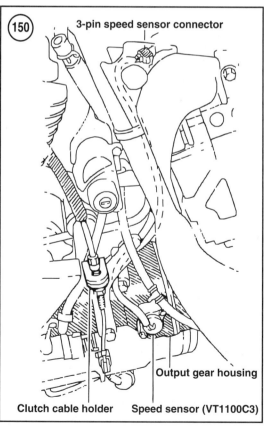

(150)

3-pin speed sensor connector

Output gear housing

Clutch cable holder   Speed sensor (VT1100C3)

4. Check the wiring terminals connected to the speedometer (**Figure 149**) for dirty, loose or damaged terminals and wires.

5. Check for continuity between the green/black speedometer terminal (**Figure 149**) and ground. There should be continuity.

   a. If there is no continuity, repair the open circuit in the green/black wire.

   b. If there is continuity, continue with Step 6.

6. Measure voltage between the pink and green/black speedometer terminals. There should be battery voltage at all times (ignition switch on or off).

   a. If there is no battery voltage, check for an open circuit in the pink wire.

   b. If there is battery voltage, continue with Step 7.

7. Turn the ignition switch on and measure voltage between the black/brown and green/black speedometer terminals. There should be battery voltage.

   a. If there is no battery voltage, check for an open circuit in the green/black wire between the speedometer and speed sensor. Then check for an open circuit in the black/brown wire between the speedometer and the speed sensor.

   b. If there is battery voltage, continue with Step 8.

8. Support the motorcycle with the rear wheel off the ground. Shift the transmission into neutral.

9. Turn the ignition switch on and measure voltage between the black/red and green/black terminals while slowly turning the rear wheel by hand. The voltmeter should read alternately between 0-5 volts. Note the following:

   a. If the reading is correct, test the speed sensor as described in this section.

   b. If the reading is incorrect, check for an open or short circuit in the black/red wire between the speedometer terminal (**Figure 149**) and the speedometer 9-pin connector. Then check the pink/black wire between the speedometer 9-pin connector and the speed sensor 3-pin connector.

10. Install all parts previously removed.

Speed Sensor
(Circuit Test)

This section tests just the speed sensor circuit.

1. Remove the seat (Chapter Fifteen).

2. Locate the speed sensor 3-pin connector (**Figure 150**) beside the air filter housing. It has three wires:

9

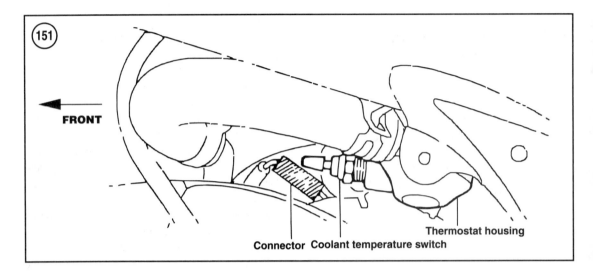

FRONT

Connector Coolant temperature switch Thermostat housing

green/black, pink/black and black/brown. Do not disconnect the connector.

3. Turn the ignition switch on and measure voltage between the black/brown and green/black wires in the speed sensor 3-pin connector. There should be battery voltage. Note the following:

    a. If there is no battery voltage, check for an open circuit in the green/black and black/brown wires.

    b. If there is battery voltage, continue with Step 4.

4. Turn the ignition switch on and measure voltage between the black/red and green/black terminals in the speedometer 9-pin connector while slowly turning the rear wheel by hand. The voltmeter should alternately read between 0-5 volts. Note the following:

    a. If the reading is correct, the speed sensor may be faulty.

    b. If the reading is incorrect, check for an open or short circuit in the black/red wire between the speedometer terminal (**Figure 149**) and the speedometer 9-pin connector. Then check the pink/black wire between the speedometer 9-pin connector and the speed sensor 3-pin connector.

5. Install all parts previously removed.

Speedometer
Removal/Installation

The speedometer is mounted inside the headlight housing.

1. Remove the headlight lens as described in this chapter.

2. Disconnect the connectors located inside the headlight housing (**Figure 148**).

3. Remove the speedometer mounting screws and rubber washers from inside the headlight housing (**Figure 148**).

4. Remove the speedometer from the headlight housing and perform the following (**Figure 149**):

    a. Remove the speedometer bulb socket.

    b. Remove the wire harness clamp.

    c. Remove the screws securing the wiring terminals to the speedometer.

    d. Remove the rubber seal from the speedometer.

5. Installation is the reverse of removal. Note the following:

    a. Refer to the color codes on the speedometer housing when reconnecting the wiring terminals.

    b. Check all meter functions.

Speed Sensor
Removal/Installation

The speed sensor (**Figure 150**) is mounted on the output gear housing.

1. Remove the seat (Chapter Fifteen).

2. Remove the battery holder as described in this chapter.

3. Remove the left crankcase rear cover (Chapter Fifteen).

4. Remove the bolts and the clutch cable holder.

5. Disconnect the 3-pin speed sensor connector.

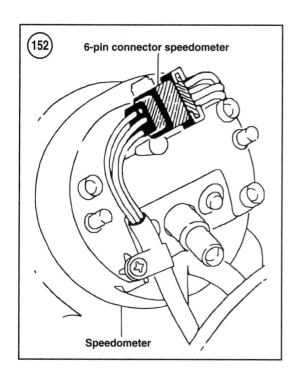

(152) 6-pin connector speedometer

Speedometer

6. Remove the two bolts and the speed sensor. Discard the O-ring.

7. Installation is the reverse of removal. Note the following:

a. Lubricate a new O-ring with engine oil and install it on the speed sensor.

b. Tighten the speed sensor mounting bolts securely.

COOLANT TEMPERATURE CIRCUIT TROUBLESHOOTING (VT1100C, VT1100C2 ACE, VT1100C2 SABRE AND VT1100T)

The coolant temperature switch is mounted in the thermostat housing (**Figure 151**).

NOTE
For models not equipped with a sidestand indicator, disregard all test references to the sidestand indicator.

Circuit Test

The coolant temperature indicator does not come on until the engine is overheating. To test the coolant temperature indicator circuit, perform the following test:

1. Park the motorcycle on its sidestand.

2. Turn the ignition switch on. The sidestand indicator and oil pressure indicator should come on. The coolant temperature indicator should not come on. Note the following:

a. If the sidestand and low oil pressure indicators did not come on, perform *Test 1* in this section.

b. If the sidestand and low oil pressure indicators came on, perform *Test 2* in this section.

c. If the coolant temperature indicator came on and stayed on, perform *Test 3* in this section.

3. Turn the ignition switch off.

Test 1

1. Turn the ignition switch on and lower the sidestand. The sidestand indicator and oil pressure indicator should come on. Note the following:

a. If both indicators came on, continue with Step 2.

b. If both indicators did not come on, check for a blown subfuse (meter). If the subfuse is okay, go to Step 2.

2A. On VT1100C, VT1100C2 ACE and VT1100T models, remove the speedometer from its case but do not disconnect the 6-pin speedometer electrical connector (**Figure 152**). Refer to *Speedometer* in this chapter.

2B. On VT1100C2 Sabre models, remove the headlight lens as described in this chapter. Disconnect the black 6-pin speedometer connector located inside the headlight housing (**Figure 146**).

3A. On VT1100C, VT1100C2 ACE and VT1100T models, turn the ignition switch on and measure voltage between the orange and green/black wires in the harness side of the 6-pin speedometer connector (**Figure 152**). Note the following:

a. If there is battery voltage, perform *Test 2* in this section.

b. If there is no battery voltage, check the wire harness for an open circuit in the orange and black/brown wire between the 6-pin speedometer connector and fuse box.

NOTE
The orange 6-pin speedometer connector wire changes to a black/brown wire. Review the appropriate wiring diagram and the end of the manual.

9

3B. On VT1100C2 Sabre models, turn the ignition switch on and measure voltage between the black/brown and green/black wires in the harness side of the 6-pin speedometer connector. Note the following:

 a. If there is battery voltage, perform *Test 2* in this section.

 b. If there is no battery voltage, check the wire harness for an open circuit in the black/brown wire between the 6-pin speedometer connector and fuse box.

Test 2

1. Remove the fuel tank (Chapter Eight).

2A. On VT1100C, VT1100C2 ACE and VT1100T models, remove the speedometer from its case but do not disconnect the 6-pin speedometer electrical connector (**Figure 152**). Refer to *Speedometer* in this chapter.

2B. On VT1100C2 Sabre models, remove the headlight lens as described in this chapter. Disconnect the black 6-pin speedometer connector located inside the headlight housing (**Figure 146**).

3. Disconnect the coolant temperature switch connector at the switch (**Figure 151**). Connect a jumper wire between the coolant temperature switch connector and ground. Turn the ignition switch on. The coolant temperature indicator should come on. Note the following:

 a. If the coolant temperature indicator came on, the coolant temperature indicator circuit is normal. The coolant temperature switch may be defective. Test the switch as described in this chapter.

 b. If the coolant temperature indicator did not come on, perform Step 4.

4. Ground the green/blue terminal at the speedometer 6-pin or 9-pin connector. Turn the ignition switch on and note if the coolant temperature indicator came on.

 a. If on VT1100C, VT1100C2 ACE and VT1100T models it came on, there is an open circuit in the green/blue wire between the speedometer and the coolant temperature switch. If the wire is okay, check the 6-pin speedometer and 9-pin wiring harness connectors for loose or dirty contacts.

 b. If on VT1100C2 Sabre models, it came on there is an open circuit in the green/blue wire

between the speedometer and the coolant temperature switch.

 c. If it did not come on, the speedometer is faulty. Replace the speedometer.

5. Install all parts previously removed.

Coolant Temperature Indicator Does Not Turn Off

1. Remove the fuel tank (Chapter Eight).

2. Disconnect the coolant temperature switch electrical connector (**Figure 151**).

3A. On VT1100C, VT1100C2 ACE and VT1100T models, remove the speedometer from its case and disconnect the 6-pin speedometer electrical connector (**Figure 151**). Refer to *Speedometer* in this chapter.

3B. On VT1100C2 Sabre models, remove the headlight lens as described in this chapter. Disconnect the black 6-pin speedometer connector located inside the headlight housing (**Figure 146**).

4. Check for continuity between the green/blue wire in the harness side of the 6-pin or 9-pin connector and ground. There should be continuity.

 a. If there is continuity, check for an open circuit in the green/blue wire between the connector and the coolant temperature switch.

 b. If there is no continuity, test the coolant temperature switch as described in this chapter. If the coolant temperature switch is okay, the speedometer is faulty.

COOLANT TEMPERATURE CIRCUIT TROUBLESHOOTING (VT1100C3)

The coolant temperature switch is mounted in the thermostat housing (**Figure 151**). On 1998-2000 models, a coolant temperature check unit (6, **Figure 148**) is mounted inside the headlight housing. On 2001-2002 models, the coolant temperature check unit circuit is built inside the ICM.

Circuit Test

1. Park the motorcycle on its sidestand.

2. Turn the ignition switch on. The coolant temperature indicator should light for a few seconds and then turn off. Note the following:

a. If the indicator worked correctly, the circuit is okay.

b. If the indicator did not come on, check for a blown bulb as described under *Replacement Bulbs* in this chapter. If the bulb is okay, refer to *Indicator Off* in this section.

c. If the indicator came on but did not turn off, refer to *Indicator Stays On* in this section.

Indicator off—1998-2000 models

1. Remove the headlight lens as described in this chapter.

2. Disconnect the white 4-pin connector from the coolant temperature indicator check unit (7, **Figure 148**). Short the light green/black and green/black connector terminals with a jumper wire. Then turn the ignition switch on and note if the coolant temperature indicator came on.

   a. No. Check for an open circuit in the light green/black, green/black and green/blue wires.

   NOTE
   The green/blue wire connects the coolant temperature indicator check unit to the coolant temperature switch.

   b. Yes. Go to Step 3.

3. Turn the ignition switch on and measure voltage between the black/brown and green/black wires in the harness side of the white 4-pin coolant temperature indicator check unit connector. Note the following:

   a. If there is battery voltage, replace the coolant temperature indicator check unit (**Figure 148**).

   b. If there is no battery voltage, check for an open circuit in the black/brown wire between the 4-pin connector and the speedometer.

4. Install all parts previously removed.

Indicator off—2001-2002 models

1. Disconnect the ignition control module connector. Refer to *Ignition Control Module (ICM)* in this chapter.

2. Connect a jumper wire between the light green/black wire in the black 22-pin ICM wiring harness connector and ground. Turn the ignition

switch on and note if the coolant temperature indicator came on.

   a. No. Check for an open circuit in the light green/black and green/blues wires between the indicator bulb and the ICM connector.

   b. Yes. The ICM may be faulty. Substitute a known good ICM and retest.

3. Install all parts previously removed.

Indicator stays on—1998-2000 models

1. Remove the fuel tank (Chapter Eight).

2. Disconnect the coolant temperature switch connector (**Figure 151**).

3. Remove the headlight lens as described in this chapter.

4. Disconnect the white 2-pin connector from the coolant temperature indicator check unit (8, **Figure 148**). Check for continuity between the 2-pin connector green/blue wire terminal and ground.

   a. If there is continuity, check for a short circuit in the green/blue wire.

   b. If there is no continuity, test the coolant temperature switch as described in this chapter. If the switch is okay, replace the coolant temperature indicator check unit (6, **Figure 148**).

5. Install all parts previously removed.

Indicator stays on—2001-2002 models

If the indicator stays on, check the following:

1. Disconnect the ignition control module connector. Refer to *Ignition Control Module (ICM)* in this chapter.

2. Remove the fuel tank (Chapter Eight).

3. Disconnect the coolant temperature switch connector (**Figure 151**).

4. Make the following wiring checks:

   a. Check for a short circuit in the green/blue and light green/black wires between the indicator bulb and the ICM.

   b. Check for a short circuit in the green/blue wire between the coolant temperature switch and the ICM.

5. If the wiring checks described in Step 4 are okay, test the coolant temperature switch as described in this chapter.

6. Install all parts previously removed.

COOLANT TEMPERATURE SWITCH TESTING AND REPLACEMENT

The coolant temperature switch threads into the thermostat housing (**Figure 151**) and controls current flow to the coolant temperature indicator according to coolant temperature.

> *CAUTION*
> *The coolant temperature switch can be damaged if dropped. Handle the switch carefully during service and testing.*

Removal/Installation

1. Remove the fuel tank (Chapter Eight).
2. Drain the engine coolant (Chapter Three).
3. Disconnect the coolant temperature switch connector at the switch and remove the switch (**Figure 151**).
4. Installation is the reverse of removal. Note the following:
   a. Clean the switch and thermostat housing threads of all sealant residue.
   b. Apply an electrically conductive water-resistant sealer to the threads on the switch. Do not apply sealant to the sensing element.
   c. Install the coolant temperature switch and tighten 10 N•m (88 in.-lb.).
   d. Allow the thread sealer to set before filling the radiator with coolant. Refer to the manufacturer's recommendations.
   e. Fill and bleed the cooling system (Chapter Three).

Testing

1. Remove the coolant temperature switch (**Figure 151**) from the thermostat housing as described in this section.
2. Fill a beaker or pan with 50/50 mixture of antifreeze and water, and place it on a stove or hot plate.
3. Position the switch so the temperature sensing element and the threaded portion of the switch body are submerged as shown in A, **Figure 153**. Maintain a distance of 40 mm (1.57 in.) from the switch threads to the bottom of the pan.

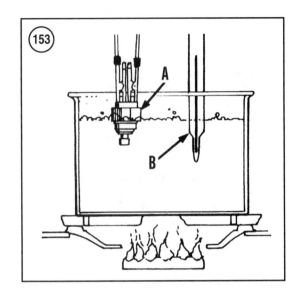

> *NOTE*
> *The switch and thermometer must not touch the container sides or bottom. If either does, it causes a false reading.*

4. Place a thermometer (B, **Figure 153**) in the pan (rated higher than the test temperatures).
5. Attach one ohmmeter lead to the switch lead and the other lead to the switch body (A, **Figure 153**). The ohmmeter should read infinity (switch off). If the ohmmeter reads continuity, the switch is shorted and must be replaced. If the switch reads infinity, continue with Step 6.
6. Test the switch as follows:
   a. Gradually heat the water.
   b. Monitor the temperature and record the resistance reading when the temperature reaches 80° C (176° F).
   c. Continue to heat the water and record the resistance reading when the temperature reaches 120° C (248° F).
7. Compare the recorded resistance readings with the temperature/resistance readings in **Table 10**. Replace the coolant temperature switch if a resistance reading at either temperature differs by more than 10 percent.
8. Install the switch as described in this section.

COOLANT TEMPERATURE INDICATOR CHECK UNIT (VT1100C3)

Refer to *Coolant Temperature Circuit Troubleshooting (VT1100C3)* in this chapter for testing and replacement.

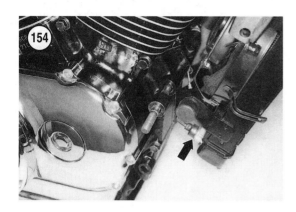

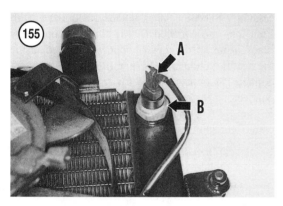

FAN MOTOR SWITCH

The fan motor switch is mounted on the bottom, right side of the radiator (**Figure 154**). It controls the radiator fan according to engine coolant temperature.

Testing

When troubleshooting the fan motor switch, first check the fan motor subfuse. Clean any rust or corrosion from the electrical terminals on the fan motor switch. If these items are good, refer to the appropriate section listed below:

Fan motor does not stop

1. Turn the ignition switch off and disconnect the fan motor switch connector (**Figure 154**), then turn the ignition switch on and note the operation of the fan motor.

2. If the fan motor stops, replace the fan motor switch as described in this section.

3. If the fan motor did not stop, check for a short circuit in the black wire between the fan motor switch and fan motor.

Fan motor does not start

1. Check for a blown fan subfuse. If the fuse is okay, continue with Step 2.

2. Start the engine and warm it up to normal operating temperature.

3. Disconnect the connector at the fan motor switch (**Figure 154**).

4. Connect a jumper wire between the fan motor switch connector and ground. Then turn the ignition switch on. The fan motor should run.

    a. If the fan motor runs, continue with Step 5.

    b. If the fan motor did not run, go to Step 6.

5. Check the connector at the fan motor switch for a dirty or loose fitting terminal. If the connector is okay, replace the fan motor switch and retest.

6. Remove the left steering side cover (Chapter Fifteen).

7. Disconnect the black 2-pin fan motor switch connector located in the connector pouch below the turn signal relay.

8. Turn the ignition switch on and measure voltage between blue/black and green wires in the harness side of the 2-pin connector. There should be battery voltage.

    a. If there is battery voltage, the fan motor is damaged. Replace the fan motor (Chapter Ten).

    b. If there is no battery voltage, check for an open circuit in the blue/black wire between the 2-pin connector and the fuse box. If the wire is good, continue with Step 9.

9. Check for the following conditions:

    a. Dirty or damaged wiring between the ignition switch and fuse box.

    b. Damaged ignition switch. Test the ignition switch as described in this chapter.

10. Install all parts previously removed.

Fan Motor Switch Replacement

1. Remove the radiator (Chapter Ten).

2. Disconnect the connector (A, **Figure 155**) and remove the fan motor switch (B) and O-ring.

3. Install a new O-ring onto the fan motor switch.

9

4. Install the fan motor switch and tighten to 18 N•m (159 in.-lb.).

OIL PRESSURE INDICATOR AND OIL PRESSURE SWITCH

The oil pressure switch (**Figure 156**) is mounted underneath the engine, next to the oil filter.

Troubleshooting

When the ignition switch is turned on, the oil pressure indicator comes on and remains on until the engine is started. When the engine is started, the oil pressure rises and the oil pressure indicator turns off (usually within 1-2 seconds). If the indicator fails to operate as specified, perform the test that matches the indicator's operating condition.

NOTE
Make sure the oil level (Chapter Three) is correct before making the following tests.

Oil pressure indicator does not come on when ignition switch is turned on

1. Check the engine oil level (Chapter Three).
2. Disconnect the wire at the oil pressure switch (**Figure 156**).
3. Ground the oil pressure switch wire with a jumper wire.
4. Turn the ignition switch on and note if the oil pressure indicator light came on.
   a. Yes. Replace the oil pressure switch and re-test.
   b. No. Go to Step 5.
5A. On VT1100C, VT1100C2 ACE and VT1100T models, remove the speedometer from its case but do not disconnect the 6-pin speedometer electrical connector (**Figure 152**). Refer to *Speedometer* in this chapter. Connect a jumper wire between the 6-pin connector blue/red terminal and ground. Turn the ignition switch on and note if the oil pressure indicator light came on.
   a. Yes. Check for an open circuit in the blue/red wire between the 6-pin connector terminal and the oil pressure switch. Check the connectors for loose or dirty terminals.
   b. No. Go to Step 6A.

5B. On VT1100C2 Sabre models, remove the headlight lens as described in this chapter. Locate the black 6-pin speedometer connector located inside the headlight housing (**Figure 146**), but do not disconnect it. Connect a jumper wire between the 6-pin connector blue/red terminal and ground. Turn the ignition switch on and note if the oil pressure indicator light came on.
   a. Yes. Check for an open circuit in the blue/red wire between the 6-pin connector terminal and the oil pressure switch. Check the connectors for loose or dirty terminals.
   b. No. Go to Step 6B.

5C. On VT1100C3 models, check for an open circuit in the blue/red wire between the indicator bulb and the oil pressure switch. Check the 9-pin indicator light connector terminals for loose or dirty terminals. This connector is located inside the connector box mounted underneath the fuel tank.

6A. On VT1100C, VT1100C2 ACE and VT1100T models, disconnect the 6-pin connector (**Figure 152**). Turn the ignition switch on and measure voltage between the orange and green/black wires in the harness side of the 6-pin connector (**Figure 152**).
   a. If there is battery voltage, the speedometer is faulty.
   b. If there is no battery voltage, check the wire harness for an open circuit in the orange and black/brown wire between the 6-pin speedometer connector and fuse box.

NOTE
The orange 6-pin speedometer connector wire changes to a black/brown wire. Review the appropriate wiring diagram and the end of the manual.

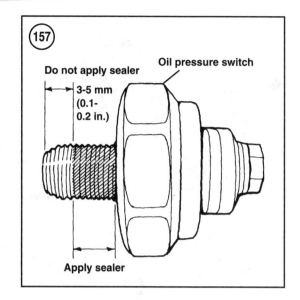

(157)

Do not apply sealer

Oil pressure switch

3-5 mm
(0.1-
0.2 in.)

Apply sealer

6B. On VT1100C2 Sabre models, turn the ignition switch on and measure voltage between the black/brown and green/black wires in the harness side of the 6-pin speedometer connector.

   a. If there is battery voltage, the speedometer is faulty.

   b. If there is no battery voltage, check the wire harness for an open circuit in the black/brown wire between the 6-pin speedometer connector and fuse box.

7. Install all previously removed parts.

Oil pressure indicator stays on when engine is running

1. Turn the engine off and check the engine oil level (Chapter Three).

2A. On VT1100C, VT1100C2 ACE and VT1100T models, remove the speedometer from its case and disconnect the 6-pin speedometer electrical connector (**Figure 152**). Refer to *Speedometer* in this chapter. Go to Step 3A.

2B. On VT1100C2 Sabre models, remove the headlight lens as described in this chapter. Locate and disconnect the black 6-pin speedometer connector located inside the headlight housing (**Figure 146**). Go to Step 3A.

2C. On VT1100C3 models, remove the low oil pressure indicator bulb as described under *Replacement Bulbs* in this chapter. Go to Step 3B.

NOTE
The ignition switch must be off when checking continuity in Step 3A and 3B.

3A. On VT1100C, VT1100C2 ACE, VT1100C2 Sabre and VT1100T models, check for continuity between the blue/red terminal in the harness side of the 6-pin connector and ground. There should be no continuity:

   a. If there is no continuity, check the oil pressure. Refert to *Engine Oil and Filter* in Chapter Three. If the oil pressure is normal, replace the oil pressure switch.

   b. If there is continuity, check for a short circuit in the blue/red wire between the speedometer and the oil pressure switch.

3B. On VT1100C3 models, check for continuity between the oil pressure switch wire and ground. There should be no continuity.

   a. If there is no continuity, check the oil pressure. Refer tp *Engine Oil and Filter* in Chapter Three. If the oil pressure is normal, replace the oil pressure switch.

   b. If there is continuity, check the blue/red wire between the oil pressure switch and speedometer for an open circuit.

CAUTION
Do not ride the motorcycle until the problem is corrected. Low oil pressure damages the engine.

4. Install all previously removed parts.

Oil Pressure Switch Replacement

1. Disconnect the wire at the oil pressure switch (**Figure 156**).

2. Loosen and remove the oil pressure switch (**Figure 156**).

3. Clean the oil pressure switch and crankcase threads of all sealer and oil residue.

4. Apply an RTV sealer to the oil pressure switch threads as shown in **Figure 157**. Do not apply sealer within 3-5 mm (0.1-0.2 in.) from the end of the switch threads.

NOTE
Allow the RTV sealer to set for 10-15 minutes before installing the oil pressure switch.

9

5. Install the oil pressure switch and tighten to 12 N•m (106 in.-lb.).

6. Reconnect the wire onto the switch and cover the switch with its rubber boot.

7. Follow the sealer manufacturer's recommendations for drying time, then start the engine and check for leaks.

> *NOTE*
> *The oil pressure indicator should go out within 1-2 seconds after starting the engine. If it stays on, shut off the engine immediately and locate the problem. Do not run the engine with the oil pressure indicator on.*

> *CAUTION*
> *Do not overtighten the switch to correct an oil leak because this may strip the crankcase threads. If oil leaks from the switch after installing it, remove the switch and reclean the threads. Reseal and reinstall the switch.*

NEUTRAL INDICATOR AND NEUTRAL SWITCH

The neutral switch (**Figure 158**) is mounted on the left crankcase, behind the left crankcase cover.

Circuit Test

1. Shift the transmission into neutral.

2. Turn the ignition switch on and note the following:

  a. If the neutral indicator came on, the system is normal.

  b. If the neutral indicator did not come on, go to Step 3.

3A. On 1997-2000 VT1100C, VT1100C2 ACE, 1998-2000 VT1100C3 and VT1100T models:

  a. Remove the battery holder as described in this chapter.

  b. Locate and disconnect the light green/red neutral switch connector in the connector pouch positioned next to the air filter.

3B. On 2001-on VT1100C, VT1100C2 Sabre, 2001-2002 VT1100C3 models:

  a. Remove the seat (Chapter Fifteen).

  b. Locate and disconnect the light green/red neutral switch connector positioned next to the ignition switch.

4. Check for continuity between the switch side of the light green/ red connector and ground. There should be continuity with the transmission in neutral and no continuity with the transmission in any gear.

  a. If the switch fails either of these tests, replace the neutral switch.

  b. If the switch is good, check for an open circuit in the light green/red wire.

5. Reverse Step 3 to complete installation.

Replacement

1. Remove the left crankcase cover as described in this chapter.

2. Disconnect the wire at the neutral switch (**Figure 158**).

3. Remove the neutral switch and sealing washer (**Figure 158**).

4. Install the neutral switch with a new sealing washer and tighten to 12 N•m (106 in.-lb.).

5. Installation is the reverse of these steps.

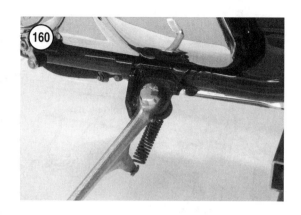

SIDESTAND SWITCH

The sidestand switch (**Figure 159**) is part of the ignition cutoff system. This is a safety system designed to prevent the motorcycle from being ridden when the sidestand is down. When the sidestand is down, the engine only starts when the transmission is in neutral. When the sidestand is up, the engine can be started in neutral or in gear when the clutch lever is pulled in. If the engine is started with the transmission in neutral and the sidestand down, the engine cuts off if the transmission is shifted into gear before the sidestand is raised.

Testing

A problem in the sidestand switch circuit can prevent the engine from starting or can cause the engine to cutout.

1A. On 1997-2000 VT1100C, VT1100C2 ACE, 1998-2000 VT1100C3 and VT1100T models:

   a. Remove the battery holder as described in this chapter.

   b. Locate and disconnect red 3-pin sidestand switch connector in the connector pouch positioned next to the air filter.

1B. On 2001-2004 VT1100C, VT1100C2 Sabre, 2001-2002 VT1100C3 models:

   a. Remove the seat (Chapter Fifteen).

   b. Locate and disconnect red 2-pin sidestand switch connector positioned next to the ignition switch.

NOTE
Perform Step 2 on the switch side of the connector, not on the harness side.

2A. On 1997-2000 VT1100C, VT1100C2 ACE, 1998-2000 VT1100C3 and VT1100T models, test the sidestand switch as follows:

   a. Check for continuity between the 3-pin connector yellow/black and green terminals. There should be continuity with the sidestand down (**Figure 160**) and no continuity with the sidestand up.

   b. Check for continuity between the 3-pin connector green/white and green terminals. There should be continuity with the sidestand up and no continuity with the sidestand down (**Figure 160**).

2B. On 2001-2004 VT1100C, VT1100C2 Sabre, 2001-2002 VT1100C3 models, test the sidestand switch as follows:

   a. Check for continuity between the 2-pin connector green/white and green terminals.

   b. There should be continuity with the sidestand up and no continuity with the sidestand down (**Figure 160**).

3. Replace the sidestand switch if it did not test as described in Step 2.

4. Reverse Step 1.

Replacement

The sidestand switch (**Figure 159**) is mounted on the sidestand mounting bracket.

1. Support the bike on a stand so the sidestand can be serviced.

NOTE
Note the sidestand switch wiring harness routing before removing the switch in this section.

2A. On 1997-2000 VT1100C, VT1100C2 ACE, 1998-2000 VT1100C3 and VT1100T models:

   a. Remove the battery holder as described in this chapter.

   b. Locate and disconnect red 3-pin sidestand switch connector in the connector pouch positioned next to the air filter.

2B. On 2001-2004 VT1100C, VT1100C2 Sabre, 2001-2002 VT1100C3 models:

   a. Remove the seat (Chapter Fifteen).

   b. Locate and disconnect red 2-pin sidestand switch connector positioned next to the ignition switch.

9

3. Remove the bolt and sidestand switch (**Figure 161**).

4. Clean the switch mounting area on the sidestand.

5. Install the sidestand switch by performing the following engagement steps (**Figure 161**):

    a. Align the pin on the switch with the hole in the sidestand.

    b. Align the switch groove with the return spring holding pin.

6. Install a *new* sidestand switch mounting bolt and tighten to 10 N•m (88 in.-lb.).

7. Reverse Step 2 to complete installation.

8. Remove the motorcycle from the stand. Shift the transmission into neutral and start the engine. Shift the transmission into first gear and lower the sidestand. The engine should turn off.

> *WARNING*
> *Do not ride the motorcycle until the sidestand switch and the ignition cutoff system is working correctly.*

CLUTCH SWITCH

The clutch switch is mounted inside the clutch lever housing.

Testing/Replacement

1. Disconnect the two electrical connectors at the clutch switch (**Figure 162**).

2. Connect the ohmmeter leads across the two clutch switch terminals (**Figure 163**).

3. Read the ohmmeter scale while operating the clutch lever. Note the following:

    a. There must be continuity with the clutch lever pulled in and no continuity with the lever released.

    b. Replace the clutch switch if it fails to operate as described.

4. Replace the clutch switch as follows:

    a. Disconnect the clutch cable from the clutch lever at the handlebar.

    b. Remove the nut, pivot bolt and clutch lever.

    c. Gently push the clutch switch out of the housing.

    d. Install the clutch switch by aligning the tab on the switch with the notch in the housing (**Figure 164**). Push the switch into the housing until it bottoms.

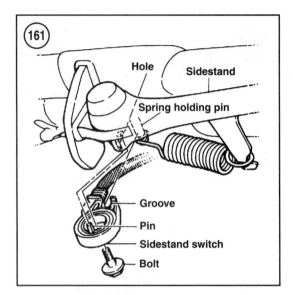

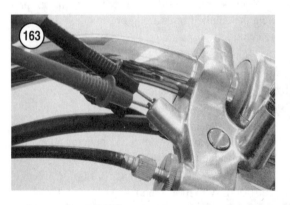

5. Clean the clutch lever pivot bolt and clutch lever bore, then lubricate with grease.

6. Install the clutch lever and pivot bolt. Tighten the pivot bolt securely, then the nut. Operate the clutch lever to make sure there is no binding.

7. Reconnect the clutch cable and adjust the clutch (Chapter Three).

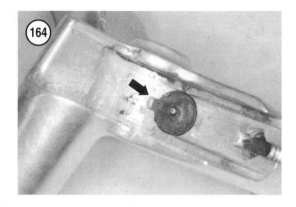

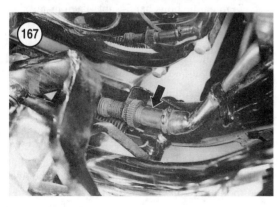

8. Reconnect the electrical connectors (**Figure 162**) at the switch.

FRONT BRAKE LIGHT SWITCH

The front brake light switch is mounted on the bottom of the front master cylinder.

Testing/Replacement

1. Disconnect the connectors from the switch terminals (**Figure 165**, typical).
2. Check for continuity between the switch terminals. There should be continuity with the brake lever applied and no continuity with the brake lever released. Replace the switch if faulty.
3. Replace the switch by removing the screw and switch.
4. Installation is the reverse of removal.
5. Make sure all connectors are plugged tightly into the switch.
6. Turn the ignition switch on and operate the front brake lever to check the rear brake light.

> *WARNING*
> *Do not ride the motorcycle until the rear brake light works correctly.*

REAR BRAKE LIGHT SWITCH

The rear brake light switch is mounted on the rear brake pedal assembly.

Testing/Replacement

1. Remove the left steering side cover (Chapter Fifteen).
2. Disconnect the white 2-pin rear brake light switch connector (**Figure 166**).
3. Check for continuity between the switch terminals. There should be no continuity with the brake pedal released and continuity with the brake pedal applied. Replace the switch if faulty.
4. To replace the switch:
   a. Disconnect the spring and remove the switch and spring (**Figure 167**, typical).
   b. Remove the spring and connect it onto the new switch.
   c. Install the switch onto its mounting bracket and reconnect the spring.

5. Installation is the reverse of removal.

6. Adjust the rear brake light switch (Chapter Three).

IGNITION SWITCH

The ignition switch is mounted on the left side of the motorcycle.

Testing/Replacement

NOTE
Note the ignition switch wiring harness routing before removing the switch in this section.

1A. On 1997-2000 VT1100C, VT1100C2 ACE, 1998-2000 VT1100C3 and VT1100T models:

   a. Remove the battery holder as described in this chapter.

   b. Locate and disconnect white 3-pin ignition switch connector in the connector pouch positioned next to the air filter.

1B. On 2001-on VT1100C, VT1100C2 Sabre, 2001-2002 VT1100C3 models:

   a. Remove the seat (Chapter Fifteen).

   b. Locate and disconnect white 3-pin ignition switch connector positioned next to the ignition switch.

2. Test the ignition switch as described under *Switch Continuity Test* in this chapter. Refer to the wiring diagram at the end of this manual for the ignition switch continuity diagram. Replace the switch if faulty.

NOTE
The ignition switch is secured with either break-off bolts, Allen bolts or Torx bolts. Identify the bolts and then refer to the appropriate procedure in Step 3A or Step 3B.

3A. Break-off bolts—Replace the ignition switch as follows:

NOTE
Order new ignition switch break-off bolts when ordering the switch.

   a. Disconnect the band from the ignition switch wiring harness.

   b. Remove the screw and switch cover, if used.

   c. Centerpunch the two break-off bolts. Then drill the bolt heads (**Figure 168**) off the bolt shanks with a hand drill. Remove the switch, collars (if used) and the rubber damper (if used).

   d. Remove the remaining threaded bolt shanks from the ignition switch mounting bracket and discard them.

   e. Secure the rubber damper (if used) and ignition switch with two new break-off bolts. Install the collars behind the ignition switch, if used.

   f. Tighten the bolts hand-tight. Then install the ignition key to make sure it turns freely.

   g. Tighten the bolt heads until they twist off.

3B. Allen and Torx bolts—Replace the ignition switch as follows:

   a. Disconnect the band from the ignition switch wiring harness.

   b. Remove the screw(s) and switch cover.

   c. Remove the Allen bolts or Torx bolts (A, **Figure 169**) and remove the switch (B).

   d. Install the ignition switch and tighten the two mounting bolts to 10 N•m (88 in.-lb.).

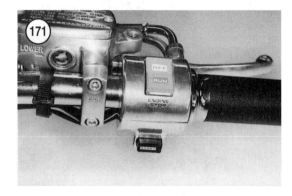

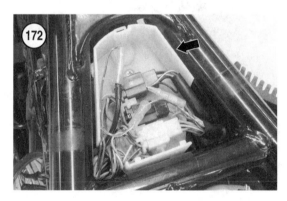

4. Record the new key number in the *Quick Reference Data* section at the front of this manual.

5. Reverse Step 1 to complete installation.

HANDLEBAR SWITCH

The left handlebar switch housing (**Figure 170**) includes the headlight dimmer switch, turn signal switch and horn button.

The right handlebar switch housing (**Figure 171**) includes the engine stop switch and the starter switch.

Testing/Replacement

1. Remove the fuel tank (Chapter Eight).
2. Remove the connector box cover.
3. Trace the switch wiring harness from the switch assembly to the connectors in the connector box (**Figure 172**) and disconnect them. Refer to the appropriate wiring diagram at the end of this manual to identify the connectors and wire colors for each switch.
4. Test the switch as described under *Switch Continuity Test* in this chapter. Note the following:
   a. If the continuity test shows a faulty switch, continue with Step 5 to replace the switch assembly.
   b. If the switch is okay, reconnect the connectors, install the connector box cover and fuel tank (Chapter Eight).
5. Note how the switch wiring harness is routed from the switch to the connector box. The carefully remove the wiring harness and connectors.
6. Remove the left (**Figure 170**) or right (**Figure 171**) side handlebar switches from the handlebars as described under *Handlebar* in Chapter Twelve.
7. Installation is the reverse of removal. Check each switch for proper operation.

WARNING
Do not ride the motorcycle until each switch works properly.

SWITCH CONTINUITY TEST

Test the switches for continuity using an ohmmeter (refer to Chapter One) or a self-powered test light at the switch connector by operating the switch in each of its operating positions. Compare the results with its switch continuity diagram. For example, **Figure 173** shows a continuity diagram for the dimmer switch. The horizontal line indicates which terminals should show continuity when the switch is in that position. Continuing with the example, in the LO position there should be continuity between the blue/white and white terminals. There should be no continuity between the blue/white and blue terminals, or between the white and blue terminals.

NOTE
*When testing the dimmer switch LO beam function, the white terminal indicated in **Figure 173** is located on*

*the white 3-pin headlight connector
(Figure 174). Remove the headlight
to access the 3-pin connector when
testing the white LO beam terminal.*

1. Refer to the appropriate switch procedure in this chapter to access the switch connectors. Some switches do not use a continuity diagram for testing. Instead, follow the test procedure in its appropriate section.

2. Check the subfuse as described under *Fuses* in this chapter.

3. Check the battery as described under *Battery* in this chapter. Charge the battery to the correct state of charge, if required.

4. Disconnect the negative battery cable at the battery if the switch connectors are not disconnected from the circuit.

CAUTION
Do not start the engine with the battery disconnected.

5. When separating two connectors, pull on the connector housings and not the wires.

6. After locating a defective circuit, check the connectors to make sure they are clean and properly connected. Check all wires going into a connector housing to make sure each wire is properly positioned and that the wire end is not loose.

7. Before disconnecting two connectors, check them for any locking tabs or arms that must be pushed or opened. If two connectors are difficult to separate, do not force them because damage may occur.

8. When reconnecting electrical connector halves, push them together until they click or snap into place.

9. If the switch is operating erratically, the contacts may be oily, dirty or corroded.

10. If a switch or button does not perform properly, replace the switch as described in its appropriate section.

TURN SIGNAL RELAY

The turn signal relay (**Figure 175**) is mounted below the upper frame rail and behind the steering neck.

DIMMER SWITCH			
	Blu/Wht	Wht	Blu
Lo	•——•		
N	•——•——•		
High	•——•——•		

Testing/Replacement

1. If both turn signals do not work, test the turn signal relay as described in this section. If only one bulb or individual side does not work, check for a blown bulb or a disconnected turn signal connector.

2. Remove the left steering side cover (Chapter Fifteen).

3. Disconnect the turn signal relay (**Figure 175**).

4. Check for loose, bent or corroded turn signal relay terminals. Then check the socket terminals in the connector or relay box for corrosion or damage.

5. Connect a jumper wire between the white/green wire and gray wire in the 3-pin turn signal relay

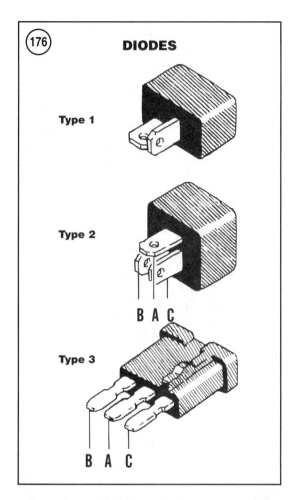

176 **DIODES**

Type 1

Type 2

B A C

Type 3

B A C

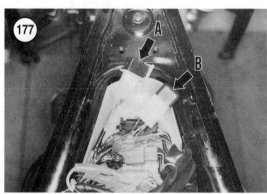

177

6. Check for continuity between the green terminal in the turn signal switch connector and a good body ground. There should be continuity.
   a. If there is no continuity, check the green wire for an open circuit.
   b. If there is continuity, replace the turn signal relay.
7. Installation is the reverse of removal. Install the turn signal relay, turn the ignition switch on and check the turn signal operation.

DIODES

Clutch Diode

Testing/replacement

The clutch diode is part of the starter motor circuit and is wired between the clutch switch and neutral switch. The diode prevents the starter from operating with the transmission in gear without pulling in the clutch lever.

1. When troubleshooting the clutch diode, note the following:
   a. The neutral indicator light should only come on when the transmission is in neutral. If the neutral light comes on when the transmission is in gear and the clutch is disengaged, suspect a faulty clutch diode.
   b. If the starter does not operate when the transmission is in neutral, check for dirty or loose clutch diode terminals connectors or a faulty diode.
   c. Three different type clutch diodes are used (**Figure 176**). Match the shape of the diode to the text descriptions in Step 3.
2A. On 2001-on VT1100C, VT1100C2 ACE, 1998-2000 VT1100C3 and VT1100T models, the diode is mounted underneath the fuel tank and inside the connector box:
   a. Remove the fuel tank (Chapter Eight).
   b. Remove the connector box cover.
   c. On VT1100C2 ACE models, disconnect the two terminal clutch diode (A, **Figure 177**) from the wiring harness. The three pin diode (B, **Figure 177**) is the sidestand diode.
   d. On all other models, disconnect the diode (A, **Figure 177**) from the wiring harness.
2B. On 1997-2000 VT1100C, VT1100C2 Sabre and 2001-2002 VT1100C3 models, the diode is mounted inside the fuse box:

connector. Turn the ignition switch on and operate the turn signal switch. The turn signal should light and stay on. Turn the turn signal off and the ignition switch off. Disconnect the jumper wire.
   a. If the light did not come on, check for an open circuit in the white/green and gray wires.
   b. If the light came on, continue with Step 6.

9

a. Remove the left side cover (Chapter Fifteen).

b. Open the fuse box and remove the diode (A, **Figure 178**).

3A. Type 1 diode test—Connect the ohmmeter leads across the two diode terminals (**Figure 176**) and note the reading. Reverse the test leads and note the reading. There must be continuity in one direction and no continuity with the leads reversed.

3B. Type 2 and Type 3 diode test—Connect an ohmmeter test lead to the A terminal (**Figure 176**). Then touch the opposite ohmmeter test lead to the B and then the C terminals and note the reading. Reverse the first test lead attached to the A terminal and check continuity in the opposite direction at the B, then the C terminals and note the reading. A good diode has two different readings: continuity in one direction and infinity with the test leads reversed. A damaged diode has the same reading in both directions.

4. Replace the diode if it fails this test.

5. Installation is the reverse of removal. Note the following:

a. Clean the diode terminals.

b. Install the Type 3 diode (A, **Figure 178**) by aligning the raised tab on the diode with the slot in the fuse box.

Sidestand Switch Diode (VT1100C2 ACE)

The sidestand switch diode (B, **Figure 177**) is mounted in the connector box located underneath the fuel tank.

1. Remove the fuel tank and unplug the diode (B, **Figure 177**).

2. Test the diode by connecting an ohmmeter test lead to the A terminal (**Figure 176**). Then touch the opposite ohmmeter test lead to the B and then the C terminals and note the reading. Reverse the first test lead attached to the A terminal and check continuity in the opposite direction at the B, then the C terminals and note the reading. A good diode has two different readings: continuity in one direction and infinity with the test leads reversed. A damaged diode has the same reading in both directions.

3. Replace the diode if it fails this test.

4. Installation is the reverse of removal. Note the following:

a. Clean the diode terminals.

b. Check the sidestand operation.

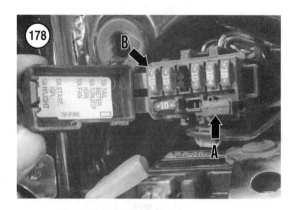

HORN

The horn is an important safety device and must be in working order.

Removal/Installation

1. Disconnect the electrical connectors from the horn (**Figure 179**, typical).

2. Remove the bolt and the horn assembly.

3. Install by reversing these removal steps. Make sure the electrical connections are secure and corrosion-free.

4. Check the horn operation. If the horn does not work properly, test the horn as described in this section.

> *WARNING*
> *Do not ride the bike until the horn works properly.*

Testing

1. Disconnect the electrical connectors from the horn.

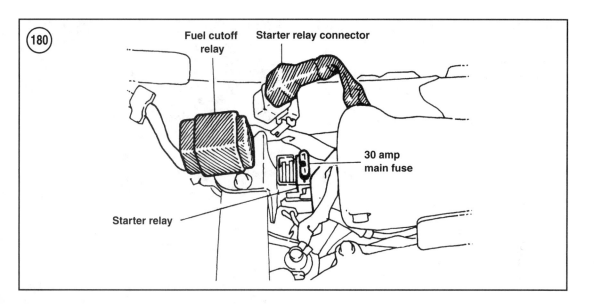

(180) Fuel cutoff relay   Starter relay connector

30 amp main fuse

Starter relay

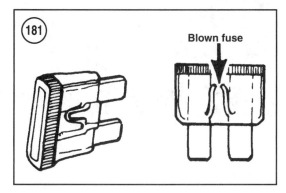

(181) Blown fuse

2. Connect a 12-volt battery across the horn terminals. The horn must sound loudly. If not, replace the horn.

FUSES

The plastic mini-fuses contain a strip of soft metal that melts (or blows) when the current flowing through the circuit exceeds its current rating. This opens the circuit before the wiring starts to smoke and burn. Fuses are rated by the maximum amount of amperage that can pass through them before melting. Never use a higher amperage fuse than specified on the fuse box or in **Table 11**.

When a fuse blows, check the circuit before replacing the fuse. Usually, the trouble is caused by a short to ground from a disconnected or damaged wire or a wire with worn-through insulation.

CAUTION
Never substitute any metal object for a fuse. Never use a higher amperage fuse than specified. An overload could cause a fire and the complete loss of the motorcycle.

9

Main Fuse

The main fuse is mounted on the starter relay switch (**Figure 180**). The starter relay switch is mounted underneath the seat. Perform the following to check or replace the main fuse:
1. Turn the ignition switch off.
2. Remove the seat (Chapter Fifteen).
3. Disconnect the electrical connector from the starter relay (**Figure 180**).
4. Remove the main fuse (**Figure 180**) and inspect it. Confirm that the proper rating fuse was used. Replace the fuse if blown (**Figure 181**).

NOTE
A spare 30-amp fuse is stored either in the fuse box (A, Figure 182) or on the battery holder (Figure 183).

5. Reconnect the starter relay connector.
6. Reinstall the seat (Chapter Fifteen).

Fuse Box (Subfuses)

All of the subfuses are mounted inside the fuse box located behind the left side cover. To identify an individual fuse and its amperage, refer to the printed information on the fuse box cover and **Table 11**.

1. Turn the ignition switch off.

2. Remove the left side cover (Chapter Fifteen).

3A. On 1997-2000 VT1100C, VT1100C2 ACE, 1998-2000 VT1100C3 and VT1100T models, remove the screws and the fuse box cover to access the fuses (B, **Figure 182**).

3B. On 2001-on VT1100C, VT1100C2 Sabre and 2001-2002 VT1100C3 models, push the tab and open the fuse box cover to access the fuses (B, **Figure 178**).

4. Remove and inspect the fuse. Confirm that the proper rating fuse was used. Replace the fuse if it has blown (**Figure 181**).

> *NOTE*
> *A spare 10-amp fuse is stored in the fuse box.*

5. Close and secure the fuse box cover.

6. Install the left side cover.

WIRING DIAGRAMS

Color wiring diagrams for all models are located at the end of this manual.

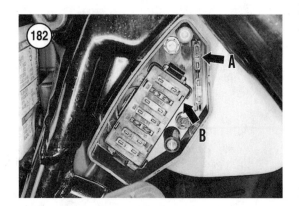

Table 1 BATTERY SPECIFICATIONS–CONVENTIONAL*	
Models	VT1100C (1997-2000)
	VT1100C2 ACE
	VT1100C3 (1998-2000)
	VT1100T
Capacity	12 volts, 16 amp hours
Charging current	1.6 amps maximum
Current draw	1 mA maximum
Specific gravity	
Fully charged	1.270-1.290
Needs charging	Below 1.260
*Conventional batteries require distilled water to maintain correct electrolyte levels.	

Table 2 BATTERY SPECIFICATIONS–MAINTENANCE-FREE*

Models	VT1100C (2000-on)
	VT1100C2 Shadow Sabre
	VT1100C3 (2001-2002)
Capacity	12 volts, 12 amp hour
Current draw	0.1 mA maximum
Voltage (at 20° C [68° F])	
Fully charged	12.8-13.0 volts
Needs charging	Below 12.3-12.5 volts
Charging current	
Normal	1.4 amps × 5-10 hours
Quick	6.0 amps × 1 hour

* This battery is sealed after activation and does not require periodic inspection for water level. Because this type of battery requires a high-voltage charging system, do not install a conventional type battery.

Table 3 CONVENTIONAL BATTERY STATE OF CHARGE

Hydrometer reading*	Voltage reading	State of Charge
1.265	12.60	100%
1.210	12.40	75%
1.160	12.10	50%
1.120	11.90	25%
Less than 1.100	Less than 11.80	0%

*Measured at 27° C (80° F).

Table 4 MAINTENANCE-FREE BATTERY STATE OF CHARGE

Voltage reading	State of charge	Charging Time*
12.8-13.0	100%	None
12.5-12.8	75-100%	3-6 hours
12.0-12.5	50-75%	5-11 hours
11.5-12.0	25-50%	Approximately 13 hours
11.5 volts or less	0-25%	20 hours

*Charging times can vary. Charging times listed in the table are for a constant current charger set at the stan dard amperage rating listed on the battery.

Table 5 ALTERNATOR AND CHARGING SYSTEM SPECIFICATIONS

Alternator type	Triple phase
Charging voltage test (regulated voltage)	See text for procedure and specification
Stator charge coil resistance*	0.3-0.5 ohms

* Test must be made at an ambient temperature of 20° C (68° F). Do not test when the engine or component is hot.

Table 6 STARTER CLUTCH SPECIFICATIONS

	New mm (in.)	Service limit mm (in.)
Starter clutch housing inside diameter	74.414-74.440 (2.9297-2.9307)	74.50 (2.933)
Starter driven gear outside diameter	57.749-57.768 (2.2735-2.2743)	57.639 (2.2692)

Table 7 IGNITION SYSTEM SPECIFICATIONS

Ignition coil resistance	
2001-on VT1100C, VT1100C2 Sabre and 2001-2002 VT1100C3	Not specified
1997-2000 VT1100C, VT1100C2 ACE, 1998-2000 VT1100C3 and VT1100T	
Primary coil resistance	2.1-2.7 ohms*
Secondary coil resistance	
Plug cap/secondary wire installed	24-32k ohms*
Plug cap/secondary wire removed	20-26k ohms*
Peak voltage	
Ignition coil primary peak voltage	100 volts minimum
Ignition pulse generator peak voltage	0.7 volts minimum

* Test must be made at an ambient temperature of 20° C (68° F). Do not test when the engine or component is hot.

Table 8 STARTING SYSTEM SPECIFICATIONS

Starter motor brush length	
New	12.5-13.0 mm (0.49-0.51 in.)
Service limit	6.5 mm (0.26 in.)

Table 9 REPLACEMENT BULBS

Item	Specification
Brake/taillight	32/3CP (21W/5CP [2006-on C2 Sabre])
Coolant temperature indicator	3.4W
Front turn signal/running light	
VT1100C2 Sabre	
2000-2003	21/5W
2004	32/3CP
All other models	32/3CP
Headlight (HI/low beam)	60/55W
High beam indicator	3.4W
License light	
VT1100C	–
All other models	4CP
Meter light	
VT1100C2 Sabre	3.4W
VT1100C3	1.7W
All other models	3W
Neutral indicator	3.4W
Oil pressure indicator	3.4W
Rear turn signal	
VT1100C2 Sabre	21W
All other models	32CP
Turn signal indicator	3.4W

Table 10 SENSOR TEST SPECIFICATIONS

Coolant temperature switch	
VT1100C3	
1998-2000	
80° C (176° F)	47-57 ohms
120° C (248° F)	14-18 ohms
2001-2002	
80° C (176° F)	2.5-3.1K ohms
120° C (248° F)	0.65-0.73K ohms
All other models	
80° C (176° F)	47-57 ohms
120° C (248° F)	14-18 ohms
Fan motor switch	
Starts to close (ON)	98-102° C (208-216° F)
Starts to open (OFF)	93-97° C (199-207° F)

Table 11 FUSE SPECIFICATIONS

Type	Specification
Main fuse	30A
Subfuses	10A (20A Fan [2006-on])

Table 12 ELECTRICAL SYSTEM TORQUE SPECIFICATIONS

	N•m	in.-lb.	ft.-lb.
Coolant temperature switch[1]	10	88	–
Fan motor switch	18	159	–
Flywheel bolt[2,3]	137	–	101
Headlight attaching bolt	4	35	–
Horn mounting bolt	21	186	–
Ignition pulse generator clamp bolt[2]	26	–	19
Ignition switch cover screw	2	17	–
Ignition switch mounting bolt	10	88	–
Left footpeg mounting bolt			
VT1100C2 ACE and VT1100T	26	–	19
Left footrest mounting bolts			
VT1100C3	39	–	29
Neutral switch	12	106	–
Oil pressure switch[1]	12	106	–
Shift pedal pinch bolt			
VT1100C and VT1100C2 Sabre	26	–	19
VT1100C2 ACE, VT1100C3 and VT1100T	23	–	17
Sidestand switch bolt	10	88	–
Starter clutch housing bolt[4]	23	–	17
Starter motor assembly bolt	5	44	–
Starter motor terminal nut	7	62	–
Timing hole cap[5]	18	159	–
Turn signal stopper bolt	9	80	–

1. Apply sealant to threads as described in text.
2. Lubricate bolt threads and flange surface with engine oil.
3. Left-hand threads.
4. Apply a medium strength threadlock onto fastener threads.
5. Lubricate threads and sealing surface with grease.

CHAPTER TEN

COOLING SYSTEM

This chapter describes repair and replacement of cooling system components. **Table 1** lists all the cooling system specifications. For routine maintenance of the system, refer to Chapter Three. The water pump requires no routine maintenance and is replaced as a complete unit if defective.

Table 1 and **Table 2** are at the end of the chapter.

> *WARNING*
> *Do not remove the radiator cap (**Figure 1**) or any cooling system component that is under pressure when the engine is hot. The coolant is very hot and under pressure. Scalding could result if the coolant touches skin. The cooling system must be cool before removing or disconnecting any system component.*

> *CAUTION*
> *Do not reuse the old coolant because it deteriorates with use. Do not operate the cooling system with only distilled water*

(even if freezing temperatures are not expected); the antifreeze inhibits internal engine corrosion and provides lubrication of moving parts in the water pump.

TEMPERATURE WARNING SYSTEM

A coolant temperature indicator is positioned in the top of the upper fork bridge (VT1100C3) or on the face of the speedometer (all other models). If the coolant temperature is above a preset level when the ignition switch is on, the indicator light illuminates.

During normal operation, the radiator fan does not operate constantly. It turns on when the temperature increases to a specified temperature. Problems in the cooling system can cause the engine to overheat. Conditions that do not have anything to do with the cooling system or engine can also cause overheating. These include riding in areas of high ambient temperatures, continuous stop-and-go traf-

fic and when climbing in foothill and mountain areas. Because the VT1100 is not equipped with a temperature gauge, the engine temperature cannot be monitored. The coolant temperature indicator coming on may be the first indicator that the engine is overheating. If this happens, park in a safe spot and turn the engine off. Steam coming from the engine or a part in the cooling system indicates a leak. Do not touch the engine or parts of the cooling system until the engine cools down. Determine the cause of the overheating before operating the motorcycle. Refer to *Engine Overheating* in Chapter Two for additional information.

COOLING SYSTEM INSPECTION

1. If steam is observed at a muffler after the engine has sufficiently warmed up, a head gasket might be damaged. If enough coolant leaks into a cylinder(s), the cylinder could hydrolock. This would prevent the engine from being turned over. Coolant may also be present in the engine oil. If the oil visible on the dipstick is foamy or milky-looking, there is coolant in the oil. If so, correct the problem before returning the motorcycle to service.

2. Refer to *Cooling System* in Chapter Three to check the coolant level.

3. Check the radiator for clogged or damaged fins.

4. Check the radiator for loose or missing mounting bolts.

5. Check all coolant hoses for cracks or damage. With the engine cold, squeeze the hoses by hand. If a hose collapses easily, it is damaged and must be replaced. Make sure the hose clamps are tight, but not so tight that they cut the hoses. Refer to *Hoses* in this chapter.

6. Make sure the overflow tube is c[...] radiator (next to the radiator cap) and [...] or damaged.

7. To check the cooling system for leak[...] [...]ure test it as described in this chapter.

HOSES

After removing any cooling system component, inspect the adjoining hose(s) to determine if replacement is necessary. Hoses deteriorate with age and should be inspected carefully for conditions that may cause them to fail. Loss of coolant causes the engine to overheat and spray from a leaking hose can injure the rider. A collapsed hose prevents coolant circulation and causes overheating. Observe the following when servicing hoses:

1. Refer to **Figure 2** for a diagram of the engine cooling hoses.

2. Make sure the cooling system is cool before removing any coolant hose or component.

3. Use original equipment replacement hoses; they are formed to a specific shape and dimension for correct fit.

4. Loosen the hose clamps on the hose that is to be replaced. Slide the clamps back off the component fittings.

5. Before disconnecting a formed hose, look for a paint mark on the end of the hose. This mark usually aligns with a raised boss on the connecting part to ensure the hose is properly installed.

> *CAUTION*
> *Do not use excessive force when removing a hose. Also use caution when loosening hoses with hose pliers. The aluminum radiator and water pump hose joints are easily damaged.*

6. Twist the hose to release it from the joint. If the hose is difficult to break loose, insert a small screwdriver between the hose and joint and spray WD-40 or a similar lubricant into the opening and carefully twist the hose to break it loose.

> *NOTE*
> *Remove all lubricant residue from the hose and hose fitting before reinstalling the hose.*

7. Examine the fittings for cracks or other damage. Repair or replace as necessary. If the fitting is good,

10

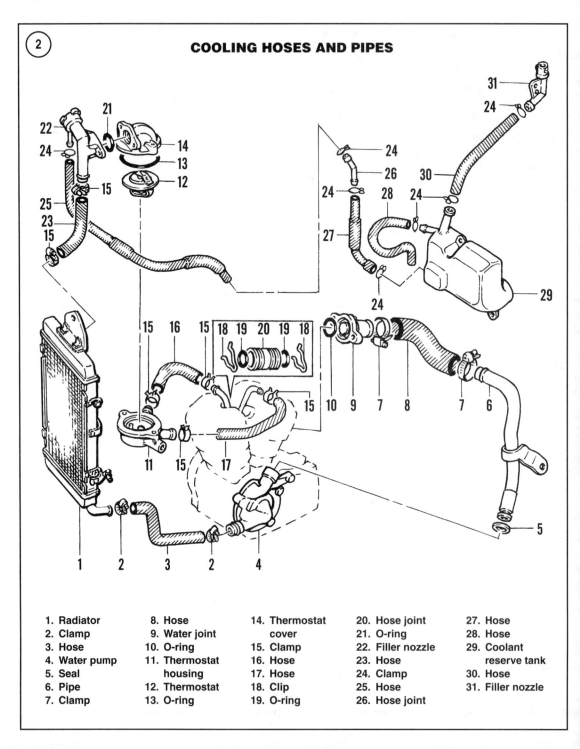

② **COOLING HOSES AND PIPES**

1. Radiator	8. Hose	14. Thermostat	20. Hose joint	27. Hose
2. Clamp	9. Water joint	cover	21. O-ring	28. Hose
3. Hose	10. O-ring	15. Clamp	22. Filler nozzle	29. Coolant
4. Water pump	11. Thermostat	16. Hose	23. Hose	reserve tank
5. Seal	housing	17. Hose	24. Clamp	30. Hose
6. Pipe	12. Thermostat	18. Clip	25. Hose	31. Filler nozzle
7. Clamp	13. O-ring	19. O-ring	26. Hose joint	

use a wire brush and clean off any hose residue that may have transferred to the fitting. Wipe clean with a cloth.

8. Inspect the hose clamps for rust and corrosion, and replace if necessary.

9. If a hose is difficult to install on the joint, soak the end in hot water to make it more pliable. Do not use any lubricant when installing hoses.

10. Formed hoses must be properly installed. Refer to Step 5.

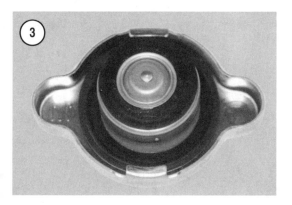

this test whenever troubleshooting the cooling system. The test is performed when the engine is cold. Use a hand pump tester to pressurize the system.

> *WARNING*
> *Never remove the radiator cap (**Figure 1**), coolant drain plugs or disconnect any coolant hose while the engine and radiator are hot. Scalding fluid and steam may be blown out under pressure and cause serious injury.*

1. Remove the fuel tank (Chapter Eight).
2. Remove the right side steering cover (Chapter Fifteen).
3. With the engine cold, remove the radiator cap (**Figure 1**).
4. Add coolant to the radiator to bring the level up to the filler neck.
5. Check the rubber washers on the radiator cap (**Figure 3**). Replace the cap if the washers show signs of deterioration, cracking or other damage. If the radiator cap is good, perform Step 6.

> *CAUTION*
> *Do not exceed 137 kPa (20 psi) or the cooling system components may be damaged.*

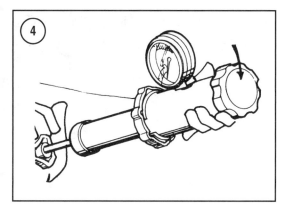

6. Lubricate the rubber washer on the bottom of the radiator cap with coolant and install it on a cooling system pressure tester (**Figure 4**). Apply 108-137 kPa (16-20 psi) and check for a pressure drop. Replace the cap if it cannot hold this pressure for 6 seconds.
7. Mount the pressure tester onto the thermostat housing filler neck (**Figure 5**) and pressure test the cooling system to 108-137 kPa (16-20 psi). If the system cannot hold this pressure for 6 seconds, check for a coolant leak:

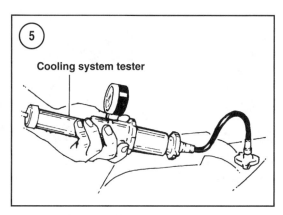

Cooling system tester

  a. Radiator cap. If the radiator cap passed the pressure test in Step 6, but the cooling system does not hold pressure, inspect the thermostat filler neck and cap mounting flange for damage.
  b. Leaking or damaged coolant hoses.
  c. Damaged or deteriorated O-rings installed in coolant hose connectors. Refer to **Figure 2**.
  d. Damaged water pump mechanical seal.
  e. Water pump leakage.
  f. Loose coolant drain bolt(s).

11. With the hose correctly installed, position and tighten the clamp securely. Position the clamp head so it is accessible for future removal and does not contact other parts.

PRESSURE TEST

This test simulates the integrity of the cooling system under engine running conditions by placing pressure on the hoses, gaskets and seals. Perform

g. Warped cylinder head or cylinder mating surfaces.

> *NOTE*
> *If the test pressure drops rapidly, but there are no visible coolant leaks, coolant may be leaking into one of the cylinder heads. Perform a compression test as described under* **Compression Test** *in Chapter Three.*

8. Check all cooling system hoses for damage or deterioration. Replace any questionable hose. Make sure all hose clamps are tight.

9. Remove the tester and install the radiator cap.

10. Reverse Step 1 and Step 2.

RADIATOR

A single radiator is mounted at the front of the engine. Refer to **Figure 2** for a diagram of the coolant hoses installed on the radiator.

Removal/Installation

1. Disconnect the negative battery cable (Chapter Nine).

2. Remove the fuel tank (Chapter Eight).

3. Remove the right side steering cover (Chapter Fifteen).

4. Drain the cooling system (Chapter Three).

5. Disconnect the fan motor switch connector (**Figure 6**) from the connector pouch on the left side of the frame.

6. Remove the radiator grille as follows:
   a. Remove the lower radiator mounting bolt (**Figure 7**).
   b. Lift the radiator grille (**Figure 8**) up to disconnect it from the tabs on top of the radiator, then remove it.

7. Disconnect the upper (A, **Figure 9**) and lower (**Figure 10**) hoses at the radiator.

8. On California models, disconnect the No. 4 tube from the clamp on the radiator. The No. 4 tube is mounted on the right side of the carbon canister.

9. Disconnect the horn and rear brake light switch wires from the clamps on the radiator.

10. Remove the upper radiator mounting bolt and collar (B, **Figure 9**), then lift the radiator to release it from the frame and remove it. Refer to **Figure 11**.

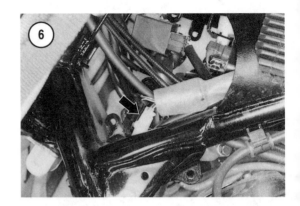
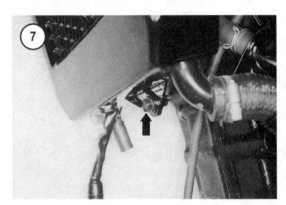

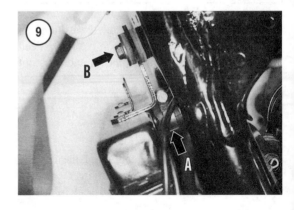

11. Installation is the reverse of removal. Note the following:

   a. Check the radiator hoses for damage that may have occurred during radiator removal.

   b. Replace missing or damaged rubber dampers.

   c. Hook the radiator grille slots over the radiator tabs (**Figure 12**).

   d. On California models, route the No. 4 tube on the left side of the carbon canister (**Figure 13**) between the radiator body and radiator grille. Make sure the hose is not bent.

   e. Refill and bleed the cooling system (Chapter Three).

   f. After starting the engine, check the coolant hoses for leaks.

   g. Turn the ignition switch on and operate the rear brake pedal to make sure the rear brake light works properly.

Inspection

1. Flush off the exterior of the radiator with a garden hose on low pressure. Spray the front and back sides to remove all debris. Remove dirt and bugs with a whisk broom or stiff paint brush.

> *CAUTION*
> *Do not press too hard or the cooling*
> *fins and tubes may be damaged.*

2. Carefully straighten out any bent cooling fins with a broad-tipped screwdriver or putty knife.

3. Check for cracks or leakage (usually a moss-green colored residue) at the filler neck, the inlet and outlet hose fittings and the upper and lower tank seams.

4. If paint has been worn off in any area of the radiator, repaint with a quality black spray paint. This helps prolong the radiator life by cutting down on oxidation from the outside. Do not apply too much paint to the cooling fin area because this cuts down on the cooling capabilities of the radiator.

5. Replace the lower mounting bracket rubber dampers if damaged.

6. Inspect the rubber seals on the radiator cap. Replace the cap if they are hardened or starting to deteriorate.

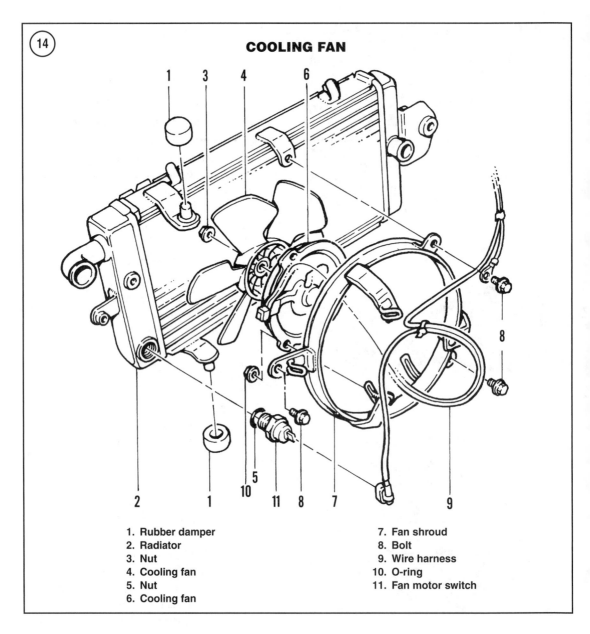

COOLING FAN

1 3 4 6
2 1 5 10 11 8 7 9

1. Rubber damper
2. Radiator
3. Nut
4. Cooling fan
5. Nut
6. Cooling fan
7. Fan shroud
8. Bolt
9. Wire harness
10. O-ring
11. Fan motor switch

COOLING FAN

The cooling fan is mounted onto the backside of the radiator.

Removal/Installation

Refer to **Figure 14**.

1. Remove the radiator as described in this chapter.
2. Disconnect the fan motor switch connector (A, **Figure 15**). Then remove the wire from the clamps on the radiator.

3. Remove the fan mounting bolts and ground wire (B, **Figure 15**), then remove the fan (C).
4. To separate the fan from the fan motor:
   a. Remove the nut and the cooling fan.
   b. Remove the bolts and the fan motor from the shroud.
5. Installation is the reverse of removal. Note the following:
   a. Install the cooling fan onto the fan motor shaft by aligning the flat surfaces. Install and tighten the fan motor nut securely.
   b. Check the wire harness routing.

THERMOSTAT

The thermostat is a temperature sensitive valve used to control the flow of coolant into the radiator. When the engine is cold, the thermostat is closed and coolant bypasses the radiator. This condition helps the engine to warm up quickly. When the engine reaches operating temperature, the thermostat opens and coolant flows between the engine and radiator. The thermostat can be removed without having to remove the thermostat housing or disconnect any coolant hoses. Refer to **Figure 17** when servicing the thermostat and thermostat housing in this section.

Thermostat Check

A stuck thermostat causes the engine to warm up slowly (when stuck open) or can cause overheating (stuck partially or fully closed). Check by starting the engine (when cold) and allow it to warm to normal operating temperature. During this time, carefully touch the top radiator hose (**Figure 2**). If the hose becomes hot quickly, the thermostat is probably stuck open. This condition causes the engine to run colder for a longer period. If the hose gradually warms and then becomes hot, the thermostat is probably opening correctly. However, if the upper hose and radiator do not feel hot after the engine has run long enough to warm to normal operating temperature, the thermostat is probably stuck closed and is blocking coolant flow through the radiator. This condition causes the engine to overheat.

Testing

Refer to *Fan Motor Switch* in Chapter Nine to test the fan motor and its related circuit.

COOLANT RESERVE TANK

The coolant reserve tank (**Figure 16**) is installed between the engine and swing arm.

Removal/Installation

1. Remove the swing arm (Chapter Thirteen).
2. Disconnect the hose from the bottom of the coolant reserve tank and drain the coolant from the tank.
3. Remove the coolant reserve tank mounting bolts.
4. Disconnect the filler hose from the coolant reserve tank.
5. Pull the coolant reserve tank to the rear of the motorcycle and remove it.
6. Flush and inspect the tank.
7. Installation is the reverse of removal. Fill the reserve tank with coolant as described under *Coolant Change* in Chapter Three.

Removal/Installation

The thermostat can be removed without having to remove the thermostat housing or disconnect any coolant hoses.
1. Drain the cooling system (Chapter Three).
2. Remove the fuel tank (Chapter Eight).
3. Remove the ignition coils (Chapter Nine).
4. Remove the thermostat filler neck bolts.
5. Remove the thermostat housing cover bolts, retainer and ground terminal.

NOTE
*Before removing the thermostat (10, **Figure 17**, find the hole (11A or 11B) in the thermostat flange and note its alignment position with the thermostat housing (12). On most models, the hole*

10

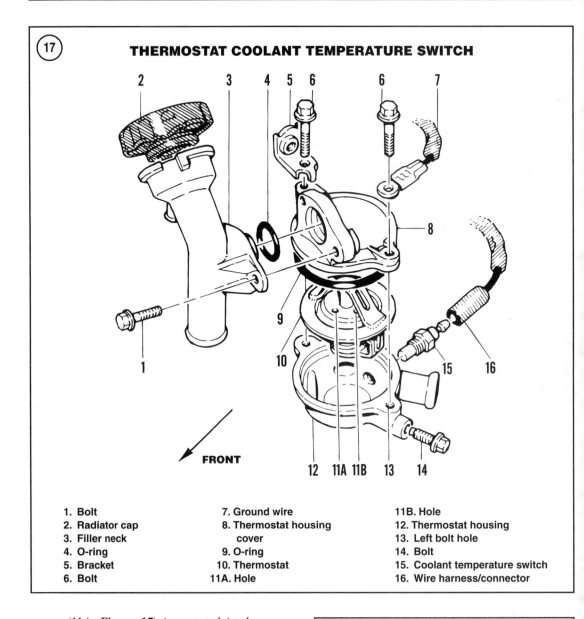

(17) THERMOSTAT COOLANT TEMPERATURE SWITCH

FRONT

1. Bolt	7. Ground wire	11B. Hole
2. Radiator cap	8. Thermostat housing	12. Thermostat housing
3. Filler neck	cover	13. Left bolt hole
4. O-ring	9. O-ring	14. Bolt
5. Bracket	10. Thermostat	15. Coolant temperature switch
6. Bolt	11A. Hole	16. Wire harness/connector

(11A, Figure 17) is mounted in the front of the thermostat and aligns with the front part of the thermostat housing. On some early VT1100C2 ACE models, the hole (11B, Figure 17) aligns with the flange running across the top of the thermostat. This thermostat is installed with its hole facing toward the thermostat housing's left mounting bolt hole (13, Figure 17).

6. Remove the thermostat from the housing.

7. To remove the thermostat housing, perform the following:

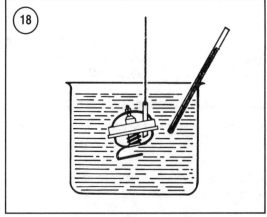

(18)

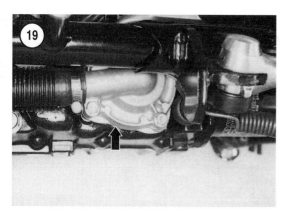

a. Disconnect the electrical connector to the coolant temperature switch.
b. Remove the cooling hoses from the housing.
c. Remove the housing.

8. Rinse the thermostat with clean water.

9. Inspect the thermostat for damage. Make sure the spring has not sagged or broken.

10. Inspect the thermostat valve and valve seat for any gaps, indicating a stuck thermostat.

11. If necessary, test the thermostat as described in this section.

12. Clean the thermostat housing, O-ring groove and all mating surfaces.

13. Installation is the reverse of removal. Note the following:

a. Install new O-rings on the filler neck and thermostat housing cover.
b. Locate the hole in the thermostat flange (11A or 11B, **Figure 17**). Install the thermostat so that its hole aligns with the thermostat housing as shown in **Figure 17**.
c. Make sure the thermostat outer flange sits flush in the housing and is even with the housing's upper surface.
d. Install the thermostat housing cover bolts and tighten securely.
f. Refill the cooling system with the recommended type and quantity of coolant (Chapter Three).

Testing

Test the thermostat to ensure proper operation. Replace the thermostat if it remains open at normal room temperature or stays closed after the specified temperature is reached during the test procedure.

Support the thermostat and a thermometer (rated higher than the test temperature) in a pan of water

(**Figure 18**). The thermostat and thermometer must not touch the sides or bottom of the pan or a false reading results. Gradually heat the water and continue to gently stir the water until it reaches 80-84° C (176-183° F). At this temperature, the thermostat valve should start to open. At 95° C (203° F), the thermostat should be fully open and the minimum valve lift should be 8 mm (0.31 in.).

NOTE
Valve operation is sometimes sluggish; it may take 3-5 minutes for the valve to operate properly.

If the valve fails to operate at the listed temperatures or if the valve lift is below minimum at the specified temperature, replace the thermostat. Always replace the thermostat with one of the same temperature rating.

COOLANT TEMPERATURE SWITCH

The coolant temperature switch (15, **Figure 17**) is mounted in the thermostat housing. Refer to *Coolant Temperature Switch Testing and Replacement* in Chapter Nine to test and service the switch.

10

WATER PUMP

The water pump is mounted on the bottom, left side of the engine (**Figure 19**). The engine must be removed from the frame to replace the water pump.

The water pump is sold as a complete unit only. If any component is damaged, the entire water pump assembly must be replaced. The water pump O-rings (**Figure 20**) can be replaced separately.

MECHANICAL SEAL INSPECTION

NOTE
Figure 21 shows the inspection hole with the water pump removed for clarity. The water pump is mounted on the bottom, left side of the engine (Figure 19).

An inspection or weep hole (**Figure 21**) is built into the bottom of the water pump. When coolant leaks from the hole, the mechanical seal in the water pump is damaged and the pump must be replaced. To view the inspection hole:

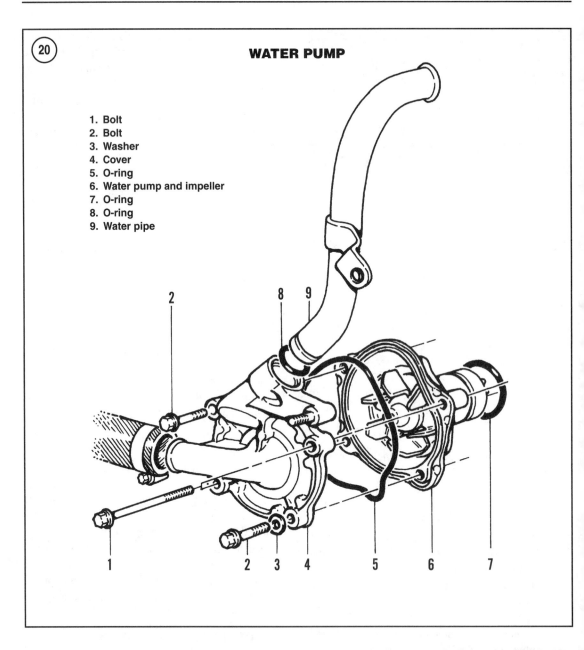

WATER PUMP

1. Bolt
2. Bolt
3. Washer
4. Cover
5. O-ring
6. Water pump and impeller
7. O-ring
8. O-ring
9. Water pipe

1. Check for signs of coolant or coolant stains on the bottom of the water pump. If there is coolant in this area, first check the condition of the hoses and hose clamps mounted on the water pump. Check the hose clamps for tightness.

> *NOTE*
> *Because the engine must be removed from the frame to replace the water pump, make sure the coolant leak is from the pump inspection hole and not from a leaking or damaged hose.*

2. Clean up any spilled coolant so it does not contact the rear tire.

Removal/Installation

Refer to **Figure 21**.

1. Remove the engine from the frame (Chapter Five).

2. Remove the water pipe clamp bolt (A, **Figure 22**).

3. Disconnect the cylinder hose (**Figure 23**) from the water pipe and remove the water pipe from the water pump. Install a new O-ring (8, **Figure 21**) onto the water pipe.

4. Remove the bolts and the water pump cover (B, **Figure 22**).

5. Remove the O-ring (A, **Figure 24**) from the water pump groove.

6. Remove the water pump (B, **Figure 24**) from the crankcase.

7. Inspect the water pump as described in this chapter.

8. Installation is the reverse of removal. Note the following:

   a. Install a new O-ring (A, **Figure 25**) on the pump body. Lubricate the O-ring with engine oil.

   b. When installing the water pump body into the engine, align the slot in the end of the water pump rotor shaft (B, **Figure 25**) with the notch in the end of the oil pump shaft (**Figure 26**).

   c. Install a new O-ring (A, **Figure 24**) into the water pump housing groove.

   d. Tighten the water pump cover mounting bolts 13 N•m (115 in.-lb.).

   e. Install the engine in the frame (Chapter Five).

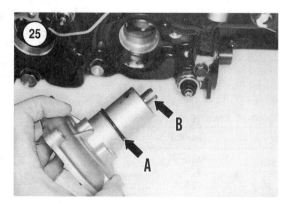

10

Inspection

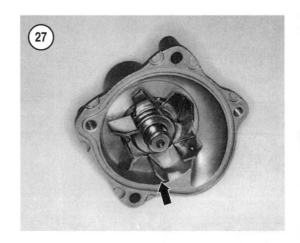

1. Replace the water pump if there is engine oil in the pump. This indicates the seal mounted over the pump shaft is damaged.

2. Check the impeller blades (**Figure 27**) for corrosion or damage. If the corrosion buildup on the blades is minor, clean the blades. If the corrosion is excessive or if the blades are cracked or broken, replace the water pump assembly.

3. Turn the impeller shaft and check the pump bearing for excessive noise or roughness. If the bearing operation is rough or abnormal, replace the water pump assembly.

Table 1 COOLING SYSTEM SPECIFICATIONS

Coolant	
Standard concentration	50% mixture coolant and purified water
Type	Honda HP coolant or an equivalent*
Coolant capacity	
Radiator and engine	
Radiator and engine	2.0L (2.1 U.S. qt.)
Reserve tank	0.39L (0.41 U.S. qt.)
Radiator cap relief pressure	108-137 kPa (16-20 psi)
Thermostat	
Begins to open	80-84° C (176-183° F)
Fully open	95° C (203° F)
Valve lift (minimum)	8 mm (0.3 in.)

* Use a high quality ethylene coolant that does not contain silicate inhibitors as they can cause premature wear to the water pump seals and block radiator passages.

Table 2 COOLING SYSTEM TORQUE SPECIFICATIONS

	N•m	in.-lb.	ft.-lb.
Coolant drain bolt	13	115	–
Fan motor switch	18	159	–
Water pump cover and mounting bolts	13	115	–

CHAPTER ELEVEN

WHEELS AND TIRES

This chapter describes service procedures for the wheels, hubs, spokes (VT1100C2 ACE and VT1100C3), wheel bearings and tires.

Tire and wheel specifications are listed in **Table 1**. **Tables 1-4** are at the end of the chapter.

MOTORCYCLE LIFT

Many procedures in this chapter require lifting either the front or rear wheel off the ground. Because the VT1100 is not equipped with a centerstand, a separate jack or lift stand is required. The K&L MC450 Center Jack is a scissors jack (**Figure 1**) that can be placed under the motorcycle to lift either the front or rear wheel. When using the MC450 center jack, have an assistant sit on the motorcycle to

support and center it upright. Place a wooden block across the jack and position the jack underneath the front part of the engine or the rear part of the frame. Operate the jack and lift the motorcycle until the front or rear wheel just clears the ground. The K&L Center Jack can be ordered through most motorcycle dealerships.

> *CAUTION*
> *Regardless of the type of jack or stand used to lift the motorcycle, make sure it is properly supported.*

FRONT WHEEL

Removal

> *CAUTION*
> *Use care when removing, handling and installing the front wheel. The brake disc can easily be damaged by side impacts due to its thin design. A disc that is not true causes brake pulsation. Protect the disc if the wheel is being transported for tire service.*

1. If the wheel is being removed to replace or service the tire or tube or balance the wheel, clean the tire and wheel assembly thoroughly.

2. Support the motorcycle securely with the front wheel off the ground.

3. On all models except the VT1100C3, remove the screw and disconnect the speedometer cable (**Figure 2**).

4. Remove the plastic covers from the axle pinch bolts, if used.

5. On the right fork tube, loosen the axle pinch bolts (A, **Figure 3**), then loosen and remove the front axle bolt (B).

6. On the left fork tube, loosen the axle pinch bolts (A, **Figure 4**) and remove the axle (B).

7A. On VT1100C3 models, pull the wheel forward and remove the collars from each side of the wheel (**Figure 5**).

7B. On all other models, pull the wheel forward and remove the speedometer gear housing (**Figure 6**) and collar (**Figure 7**).

NOTE
Do not operate the front brake lever while the wheel is removed. Insert a spacer block between the pads. This prevents the caliper pistons from extending if the lever is operated.

8. Inspect the front wheel as described in this chapter.

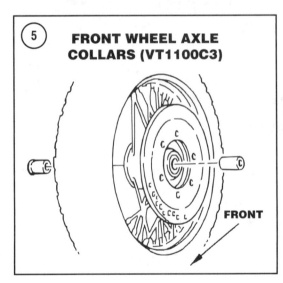

FRONT WHEEL AXLE
COLLARS (VT1100C3)

FRONT

Installation

1. Clean the front axle, collar(s) and axle bolt.

2. Check the axle bearing surfaces on both fork tubes and the axle for burrs and nicks. Smooth with a file.

3. Apply a light coat of grease to the axle and collar(s). Do not lubricate the axle threads. These threads must be free of all lubricants when the axle bolt is tightened.

4. Wipe each oil seal (A, **Figure 8**) with a rag to clean it. Apply a light coat of grease around the seal lip.

5. Remove the spacer block from between the brake pads.

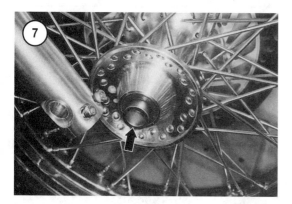

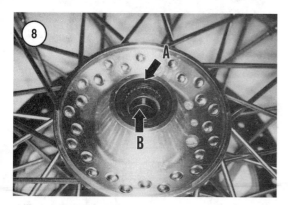

6A. On VT1100C3 models:

   a. Install the shouldered collar (**Figure 5**) into the right side of the wheel.

   b. Install the straight collar (**Figure 5**) into the left side of the wheel.

6B. On all other models:

   a. Install the collar (**Figure 7**) into the right side of the wheel. The shoulder side of the collar must face out.

   b. Install the speedometer gear housing by aligning the arms in the housing (A, **Figure 9**) with the slots in the retainer (B). Refer to **Figure 6**. The speedometer gear housing seats flush against the wheel bearing when properly installed.

7. Carefully insert the disc between the brake pads, then install the front axle (B, **Figure 4**) from the left side.

8. On all models except the VT1100C3, position the raised arm on the speedometer gear housing against the backside of the stopper on the left fork tube (**Figure 10**).

9. Clean any grease from the threaded end of the axle and install the axle bolt (B, **Figure 3**) finger-tight.

CAUTION
The front axle and pinch bolt tightening sequence in Steps 10-13 correctly seats the front axle so both sliders are positioned parallel with each other. Fork misalignment can cause premature seal and bushing wear, increases the wear against the slider and may cause steering problems.

NOTE
Figure 11 *shows the front axle groove called out in Step 10.*

11

10. Hold the axle and tighten the axle bolt to 59 N•m (43 ft.-lb.). Make sure the groove on the axle aligns with the outer edge of the fork tube axle bore as shown in C, **Figure 4**.

11. Pump the front brake lever to reposition the brake pads against the brake disc.

12. Remove the motorcycle from the stand so the front wheel is on the ground. Apply the front brake, then compress and release the front suspension several times to center the axle in the slider axle bores. Compress the forks as far as possible. Check that the fork legs are parallel.

13. Tighten the left (A, **Figure 4**) and right (A, **Figure 3**) side front axle pinch bolts to 22 N•m (16 ft.-lb.). Install the plastic caps into the axle pinch bolts, if used.

14. On all models except the VT1100C3, install the speedometer cable (**Figure 2**) by aligning the slot in the end of the cable with the tab in the speedometer gear housing (**Figure 12**). Install and tighten the screw securely.

Inspection

1. Inspect the seals (A, **Figure 8**) for wear, hardness, cracks or other damage. If necessary, replace the seals as described under *Front and Rear Hubs* in this chapter.

2. Inspect the bearings on both sides of the wheel for:

   a. Roughness. Turn each bearing inner race (B, **Figure 8**) by hand and check for smooth, quiet operation.

   b. Axial and radial play (**Figure 13**). Try to push the bearing in and out to check for axial play. Slight play is normal. Try to push the bearing up and down to check for radial play. Any radial play should be difficult to feel. If play is

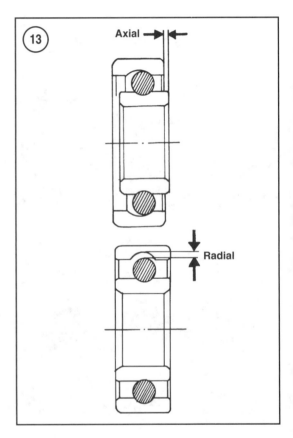

easily felt, the bearing is worn out. Always replace bearings as a set. Refer to *Front and Rear Hubs* in this chapter.

3. Clean the axle, axle bolt and collar(s) in solvent to remove all grease and dirt. Make sure the axle contact surfaces are clean.

4. On all models except the VT1100C3, service the speedometer gear housing as described in this chapter.

5. Check the axle for straightness with a set of V-blocks and dial indicator. Refer to **Table 2** for

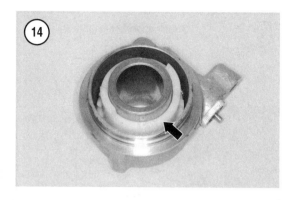

maximum axle runout. Actual runout is one-half of the gauge reading. Do not straighten a bent axle.

6. Check the brake disc bolts for tightness. To service the brake disc, refer to Chapter Fourteen.

7. For laced wheels, refer to *Wheel Service* in this chapter to inspect and true the rim.

SPEEDOMETER GEAR AND CABLE (ALL MODELS EXCEPT VT1100C3)

Periodically inspect and lubricate the speedometer drive gear and cable (if so equipped).

Speedometer Gear Inspection/Lubrication

1. Remove the front wheel as described in this chapter.
2. Remove the drive gear (**Figure 14**) and both washers (**Figure 15**) from the housing.
3. Clean and dry all parts.
4. Inspect the drive gear teeth for breakage or other damage. Check the slots on the top of the gear for cracks or other damage that would cause inaccurate speedometer readings. Replace the drive gear if necessary.

5. Check the washers for cracks, excessive thrust wear or other damage.
6. Check the gear shoulder in the speedometer housing for cracks or other damage.
7. Lubricate the gear and both washers with a high-temperature grease, then install the washers (**Figure 15**) and drive gear (**Figure 14**).
8. Inspect the retainer (B, **Figure 9**) in the left side of the front wheel that engages with the drive gear. Check the tabs for cracks or breakage. If necessary, replace the retainer as described under *Front and Rear Hubs* in this chapter.
9. Install the front wheel as described in this chapter.

Speedometer Cable Lubrication

1. Remove the screw (**Figure 2**) and disconnect the speedometer cable from the front wheel.
2. Pull the speedometer cable (**Figure 12**) out of is housing.
3. Wipe the cable with a rag soaked in solvent.
4. Inspect the cable for any broken cable strands or other damage. Check both cable ends for damage.
5. Lubricate the cable with a waterproof grease.
6. Install the cable into its housing, making sure its upper end engages with the square drive hole in the speedometer.
7. Lubricate the cable housing O-ring (**Figure 12**) with grease.
8. Reconnect the speedometer cable (**Figure 2**) at the front wheel and secure with the screw.

REAR WHEEL

Removal (VT1100C)

NOTE
The motorcycle must be raised considerably to provide clearance for removing and installing the rear wheel. Before beginning this procedure, make sure the jack can support the motorcycle at the required height. An alternative is to remove the rear fender as described in Chapter Fifteen.

1. If the wheel is being removed to replace or service the tire or tube or balance the wheel, clean the tire and wheel assembly thoroughly.

11

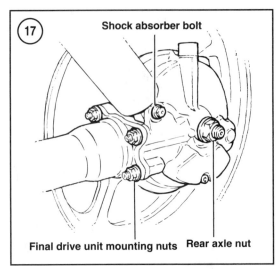

Final drive unit mounting nuts   Rear axle nut

2. Support the motorcycle with the rear wheel off the ground.

3. Remove the adjusting nut (A, **Figure 16**), collar and spring.

4. Remove the brake rod nut (B, **Figure 16**), flat washer and rubber cushion. Then remove the brake stopper arm pivot bolt.

5. Loosen and remove the rear axle nut (**Figure 17**).

6. Loosen the axle pinch bolt (**Figure 18**).

NOTE
The axle should slide out of the wheel without any excessive force. If the axle is tight, tap it out with an aluminum or brass rod. Do not use a steel rod or punch because it may damage the threads on the end of the axle.

7. Remove the rear axle and collar (**Figure 18**).

8. Move the wheel toward the right to separate it from the final drive unit, them remove from between the swing arm.

9. Remove the brake panel from the hub.

WARNING
When handling the rear brake assembly, do not inhale brake dust because it may contain asbestos, which can cause lung injury and cancer. Wear a disposable face mask and wash hands thoroughly after completing the work. Wet down the brake dust on brake components before storing or working on them. Secure and dispose of all brake dust and cleaning materials properly. Do not use compressed air to blow off brake parts.

10. If necessary, service the final driven flange (**Figure 19**) as described in this chapter.

11. Inspect the rear wheel as described in this chapter.

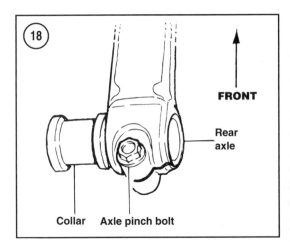

FRONT

Rear axle

Collar   Axle pinch bolt

Installation (VT1100C)

NOTE
If the final gearcase was removed, do not tighten its mounting nuts and the shock absorber bolt until after the rear wheel is installed and the rear axle tightened.

1. Clean the rear axle, collar and axle nut.

2. Apply a light coat of bearing grease to the axle and collar. Do not lubricate the axle threads. These threads must be free of oil and grease when the axle nut is tightened.

3. Check that the final driven flange and final drive unit splines are thoroughly lubricated with molybdenum disulfide paste. If not, lubricate them as follows:

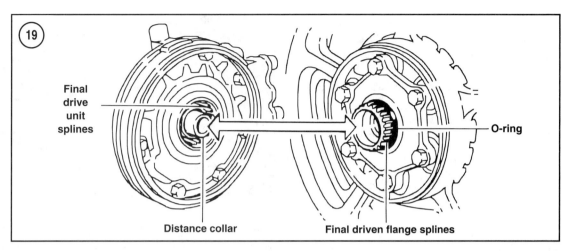

Final drive unit splines

O-ring

Distance collar

Final driven flange splines

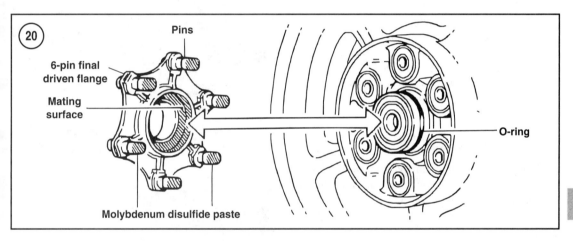

Pins

6-pin final driven flange

Mating surface

O-ring

Molybdenum disulfide paste

11

a. Remove the final driven flange and lubricate the flange hub and driven pin surfaces with molybdenum disulfide paste as shown in **Figure 20**. Reinstall the final driven flange into the hub.

b. Lubricate the final final drive unit and final driven flange splines (**Figure 19**) with molybdenum disulfide paste.

c. Lubricate the O-ring (**Figure 19**) installed on the final driven flange with molybdenum disulfide paste.

4. Install the brake panel into the brake drum.

5. Make sure the distance collar (**Figure 19**) is installed in the final drive unit.

6. Slide the wheel between the swing arm, then lift the wheel and engage the final driven flange and final drive unit splines (**Figure 19**). If using a scissors-jack, lower the motorcycle around the wheel to align the splines without lifting the wheel. Make sure the splines are fully engaged on both parts.

7. Align the wheel bearings with the swing arm and install the rear axle through the swing arm, collar (**Figure 18**), wheel and final drive unit until it bottoms .

8. Temporarily tighten the axle pinch bolt (**Figure 18**).

9. Install the bolt through the brake panel and install the brake arm over it. Then install the rubber cushion, flat washer and nut (**Figure 16**). Tighten the nut to 22 N•m (16 ft.-lb.). Install a new cotter pin through the bolt and bend its arms over to lock it.

10. Install the brake adjusting rod through the brake arm, then install the spring, collar and adjusting nut (**Figure 16**).

11. Tighten the rear axle nut (**Figure 17**) to 88 N•m (65 ft.-lb.).

12. If the final drive unit was removed, perform the following:

a. Tighten the nuts (**Figure 17**) in a crossing pattern to 64 N•m (47 ft.-lb.).

b. Tighten the shock absorber mounting bolt (**Figure 17**) to 23 N•m (17 ft.-lb.).

13. Tighten the axle pinch bolt (**Figure 18**) to 26 N•m (20 ft.-lb.).

14. Adjust the rear brake as described in Chapter Three.

15. After the wheel is completely installed, rotate it several times to make sure it rotates freely.

> *WARNING*
> *Do not ride the motorcycle until the brakes are operating properly.*

Removal (VT1100C2, VT1100C3 and VT1100T)

> *NOTE*
> *The motorcycle must be raised considerably to provide clearance for removing and installing the rear wheel. Before beginning this procedure, make sure the jack can support the motorcycle at the required height. An alternative is to remove the rear fender as described in Chapter Fifteen.*

1. If the wheel is being removed to replace or service the tire or tube or balance the wheel, clean the tire and wheel assembly thoroughly.

2. Support the motorcycle with the rear wheel off the ground.

3A. On VT1100C2 Sabre and VT1100C3 models, remove the exhaust system (Chapter Fifteen).

3B. On VT1100T models, perform the following:

　a. Remove both saddlebags (Chapter Fifteen).

　b. Remove the bolts, brackets and the rear saddlebag pipe assembly mounted behind the rear wheel.

　c. Remove the left and right mufflers (Chapter Fifteen).

4. Loosen and remove the rear axle nut (**Figure 21**).

5. Loosen and remove the rear caliper stopper pin bolt (A, **Figure 22**). If the exhaust pipe is installed, pull the pin bolt out until it contacts the pipe.

6. Loosen the rear axle pinch bolt (B, **Figure 22**).

7. Remove the axle (**Figure 23**) and its thrust washer (**Figure 24**).

> *NOTE*
> *The axle should slide out of the wheel without any excessive force. If the axle is tight, tap it out with an aluminum or*

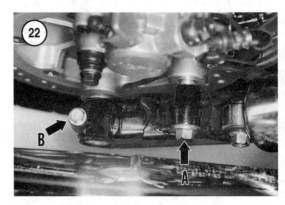

brass rod. Do not use a steel rod or punch because it may damage the threads on the end of the axle.

8. Lift the brake caliper and its holder off the brake disc (**Figure 25**) and support it with a wire hook.

9. Remove the collar (**Figure 26**).

10. Move the wheel toward the right to separate it from the final gearcase, then remove it from between the swing arm.

11. Insert a spacer block in the caliper between the brake pads.

NOTE
The spacer block installed in Step 11 prevents the piston from being forced out of its cylinder if the brake pedal is operated. If the piston is forced out too far, disassembly of the caliper is required to reseat the piston.

12. Remove and service the final driven flange as described in this chapter.

13. Inspect the rear wheel as described in this chapter.

Installation (VT1100C2, VT1100C3 and VT1100T)

1. Lubricate the rear axle and the right side oil seal lip with grease.

2A. On VT1100C2 ACE models, loosen the final drive unit mounting nuts (**Figure 27**). This helps ease axle installation while assuring correct final drive unit spline alignment.

2B. On all other models, if the final drive unit was removed, do not tighten its mounting nuts and the shock absorber bolt until after installing the rear wheel and tightening the rear axle.

3. Apply a light coat of bearing grease to the axle and collar. Do not lubricate the axle threads. These threads must be free of oil and grease when the axle nut is tightened.

4. Check that the final driven flange and final drive unit splines are thoroughly lubricated with molybdenum disulfide paste. If not, lubricate them as follows:

    a. Remove the final driven flange (A, **Figure 28**) and washer. Lubricate the hub surface, washer and driven flange mating surface (**Figure 29**) with molybdenum disulfide paste. Do *not* lubricate the pins on the final

11

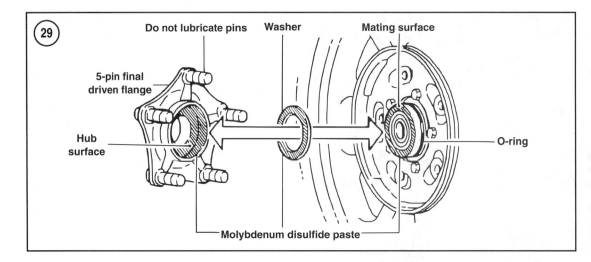

driven flange. Reinstall the washer and the final driven flange (A, **Figure 28**) into the hub.

b. Lubricate the final driven flange splines and O-ring (B, **Figure 28**) and the final drive unit splines (A, **Figure 30**) with molybdenum disulfide paste.

5. Make sure the distance collar (B, **Figure 30**) is installed in the final drive unit.

6. Slide the wheel between the swing arm and install the right side collar (**Figure 26**) with its shoulder facing out.

7. Remove the spacer block from between the brake pads.

8. Lift the wheel and engage the final driven flange and final drive unit splines. If using a scissors-jack, lower the motorcycle around the wheel and align the splines without lifting the wheel. Make sure the splines are fully engaged on both parts.

9. Remove the wire hook from the rear brake caliper bracket and install the rear brake caliper and bracket. Install the caliper pads over the brake disc and position the bottom of the caliper between the collar and swing arm (**Figure 31**).

10. Install the thrust washer between the swing arm and rear brake caliper bracket (**Figure 24**), then install the rear axle. Make sure the washer did not fall out.

disc, causing excessive wear and overheating.

CAUTION
The thrust washer must sit between the caliper bracket and swing arm. If the thrust washer sits between the collar and caliper bracket, the inner brake pad rides against the brake

11. Install a new rear caliper stopper pin bolt (A, **Figure 22**) and tighten finger-tight. If the old bolt cannot be removed because of the exhaust system, clean the threads and apply a medium strength threadlock before reinstalling the bolt.

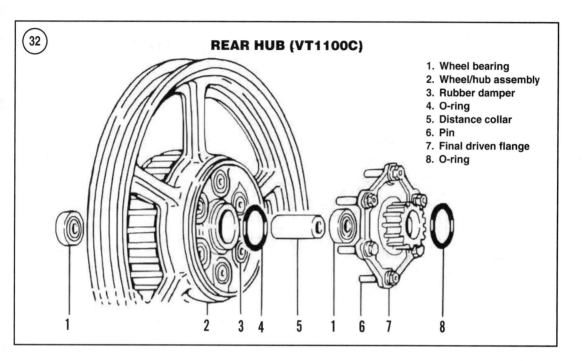

REAR HUB (VT1100C)

1. Wheel bearing
2. Wheel/hub assembly
3. Rubber damper
4. O-ring
5. Distance collar
6. Pin
7. Final driven flange
8. O-ring

12A. On VT1100C2 ACE models, perform the following:

  a. Install the rear axle nut (**Figure 21**) and hold the axle with a 17 mm hex socket and breaker bar. Tighten the rear axle nut (**Figure 21**) to 88 N•m (65 ft.-lb.).

  b. Tighten the final drive unit mounting nuts in a crossing pattern to (**Figure 27**) to 64 N•m (47 ft.-lb.). Then tighten the shock absorber lower mounting bolt (**Figure 27**) 23 N•m (17 ft.-lb.).

  c. Tighten the rear axle pinch bolt (B, **Figure 22**) to 26 N•m (19 ft.-lb.).

  d. Tighten the rear caliper stopper pin bolt (A, **Figure 22**) to 70 N•m (51 ft.-lb.).

12B. On all other models, perform the following:

  a. Temporarily tighten the axle pinch bolt (B, **Figure 22**).

  b. Install and tighten the rear axle nut (**Figure 21**) to 88 N•m (65 ft.-lb.).

  c. If the final drive unit was removed, tighten the nuts (**Figure 27**) in a crossing pattern to 64 N•m (47 ft.-lb.). Then tighten the shock absorber lower mounting bolt (**Figure 27**) to 23 N•m (17 ft.-lb.).

  d. Tighten the rear caliper stopper pin (A, **Figure 22**) bolt to 70 N•m (51 ft.-lb.).

  e. Tighten the axle pinch bolt (B, **Figure 22**) to 26 N•m (19 ft.-lb.).

13. Rotate the rear wheel several times while applying the rear brake to reposition the rear brake pads and to make sure the wheel rotates freely.

14A. On VT1100C Sabre and VT1100C3 models, install the exhaust system (Chapter Fifteen).

14B. On VT1100T models, perform the following:

  a. Install the mufflers (Chapter Fifteen).

  b. Install the rear saddlebag pipe assembly and secure it with its brackets and mounting bolts.

  c. Install the left and right saddlebags (Chapter Fifteen).

15. Remove the stand from the bike and lower the rear wheel onto the ground. Support the bike with its sidestand.

Inspection (All Models)

Refer to *Front Wheel* in this chapter.

FINAL DRIVEN FLANGE (VT1100C)

The 6-pin final driven flange connects the rear wheel to the final drive unit. Circular shaped rubber dampers pressed into the rear hub absorb some of the shock that results from torque changes during acceleration and braking.

Refer to **Figure 32**.

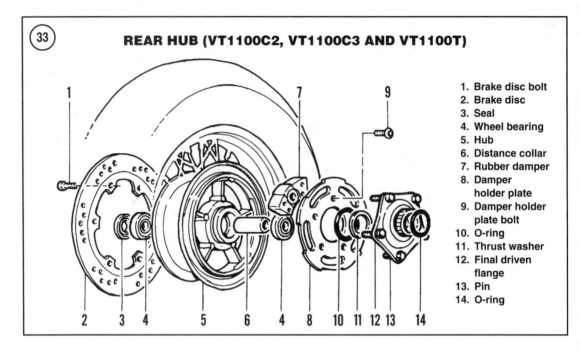

REAR HUB (VT1100C2, VT1100C3 AND VT1100T)

1. Brake disc bolt
2. Brake disc
3. Seal
4. Wheel bearing
5. Hub
6. Distance collar
7. Rubber damper
8. Damper holder plate
9. Damper holder plate bolt
10. O-ring
11. Thrust washer
12. Final driven flange
13. Pin
14. O-ring

Service Procedure

Inspect and lubricate the final driven flange whenever the rear wheel is removed from the motorcycle. Replacement parts, other than the two O-rings, are not available for the final driven flange assembly. Do not remove the pins (6, **Figure 32**) from the final driven flange or the rubber dampers (3) installed in the hub when performing the following steps.

WARNING
When handling the rear wheel and brake drum, do not inhale brake dust as it may contain asbestos, which can cause lung injury and cancer. Wear a disposable face mask and wash hands thoroughly after completing the work. Wet down the brake dust on brake components before storing or working on them. Secure and dispose of all brake dust and cleaning materials properly. Do not use compressed air to blow off brake parts.

1. Remove the rear wheel as described in this chapter.
2. Pull the final driven flange assembly (**Figure 20**) out of the wheel hub. Note whether or not the flange pins were previously lubricated. For proper operation and a normal service life, the pins must be lubricated. If the pins were not lubricated, check for wear as described in the following steps.

3. Remove the O-rings from the hub (4, **Figure 32**) and final driven flange (8) grooves. Replace the O-rings if stretched, deteriorated or damaged.
4. Clean the final driven flange assembly.
5. Clean the bores in the rubber dampers with a brush. Then inspect the rubber dampers for deterioration, looseness or damage. If one or more of the rubber dampers are unusable, replace the rear wheel assembly. The rubber dampers cannot be replaced separately.
6. Clean the brake drum of any grease and other residue resulting from when the rubber dampers and hub were cleaned.
7. Inspect the final driven flange (7, **Figure 32**) for:
    a. Cracked or damaged splines. If the splines are damaged, inspect the mating splines in the final drive housing for damage.
    b. Excessively worn or damaged pins. The pins must be tight.
    c. Cracks or other damage on the flange housing.
    d. If one or more pins are unusable or the flange is damaged, replace the final driven flange assembly.

NOTE
Use molybdenum disulfide paste when lubrication is called for in the following steps.

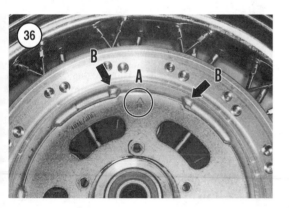

8. Lubricate both O-rings and install them in the hub and final driven flange grooves.

9. Lubricate the final flange driven surfaces identified in **Figure 20**.

10. Reinstall the final driven flange into the hub. The flange should fit snugly in the rubber dampers. Replace the wheel and flange assembly if there is any excessive looseness.

11. Lubricate the final driven flange splines (**Figure 19**).

12. Install the rear wheel as described in this chapter.

FINAL DRIVEN FLANGE (VT1100C2, VT1100C3 AND VT1100T)

The 5-pin final driven flange connects the rear wheel to the final drive unit. Wedge shaped rubber dampers installed into the rear hub absorb some of the shock that results from torque changes during acceleration and braking.

Refer to **Figure 33**.

Service Procedure

Inspect and lubricate the final driven flange whenever the rear wheel is removed from the motorcycle. Do not remove the pins (13, **Figure 33**) from the final driven flange when performing the following steps.

1. Remove the rear wheel as described in this chapter.

2. Pull the final driven flange assembly (A, **Figure 34**) up and out of the hub, then remove the thrust washer (B). Clean and dry both parts.

3. Remove the O-ring from the hub (10, **Figure 33**) and final driven flange (14) grooves. Replace the O-rings if stretched, deteriorated or damaged.

4. Remove the bolts (**Figure 35**) and turn the damper holder plate to align its arrow mark (A, **Figure 36**) between any two projection tabs (B) on the hub, then remove the damper holder plate. Discard the bolts.

5. Inspect the rubber dampers (**Figure 37**) for deterioration, cracks or other damage. If necessary, remove and replace all of the rubber dampers as a set. Install the rubber dampers with their OUTSIDE marks facing out.

6. Inspect the final driven flange (**Figure 38**) for:

    a. Cracked or damaged splines. If the splines are damaged, inspect the mating splines in the final drive housing for damage.

b. Excessively worn or damaged pins. The pins must be tight.

c. Cracks or other damage on the flange housing.

d. If one or more pins are unusable or the flange is damaged, replace the final driven flange assembly.

7. Inspect the damper holder plate for cracks, warp or other damage. Replace the plate if necessary.

8. Install the damper holder plate (8, **Figure 33**) as follows:

a. Install the damper holder plate with its OUTSIDE mark facing out.

b. Align the damper holder plate arrow between any two projection tabs on the hub (B, **Figure 36**) and install the plate onto the hub. Make sure the plate is sitting flush in the hub.

c. Turn the damper holder plate clockwise to align the bolt holes in the plate with the holes in the hub (**Figure 39**).

d. Install five new damper holder plate bolts (**Figure 35**) and tighten to 20 N•m (15 ft.-lb.).

NOTE
Use molybdenum disulfide paste when lubrication is called for in the following steps.

9. Lubricate both O-rings and install them in the hub and final driven flange grooves.

10. Lubricate and install the final driven flange assembly as follows:

a. Lubricate the wheel hub and thrust washer mating surfaces (**Figure 29**).

b. Install the thrust washer (B, **Figure 34**) onto the wheel hub surface.

c. Lubricate the final driven flange inner bore surface (**Figure 29**).

CAUTION
Do not lubricate the pins on the final driven flange. These pins must remain dry.

d. Reinstall the final driven flange into the hub (A, **Figure 28**). The flange should fit snugly in the rubber dampers. Replace the rubber dampers if there is any excessive looseness. If there is excessive looseness with new rubber dampers, replace the final driven flange assembly.

e. Lubricate the final driven flange splines (B, **Figure 28**).

11. Before installing the rear wheel, check the brake disc for any grease or moly paste. If necessary, clean the brake disc with a commercial brake cleaner.

12. Install the rear wheel as described in this chapter.

FRONT AND REAR HUBS

Each hub contains two wheel bearings and a distance collar. Seals are installed in both sides of the front hub. On the rear hub, a dust seal is installed on the brake drum or brake disc side. A brake disc is mounted onto the front hub and onto all rear hubs except the VT1100C. Refer to **Figure 40** (front) or **Figure 32** and **Figure 33** (rear) when servicing the front and rear hubs in this section.

Procedures for servicing the front and rear hubs are essentially the same. Where differences occur, they are described in the procedure.

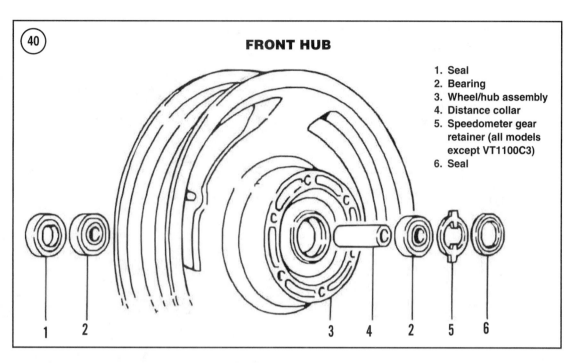

FRONT HUB

1. Seal
2. Bearing
3. Wheel/hub assembly
4. Distance collar
5. Speedometer gear retainer (all models except VT1100C3)
6. Seal

1 2   3   4   2   5   6

Inspection

CAUTION
Do not remove the wheel bearings to check their condition. If the bearings are removed, they must be replaced.

Initially inspect the bearings with the wheels installed on the motorcycle so leverage can be applied to the bearings when checking them for wear. In addition, the wheels can be spun to listen for roughness in the bearings. If the wheels must be removed, inspect the bearings as described under *Front Wheel* or *Rear Wheel* in this chapter.

1. Support the motorcycle with the wheel off the ground. The axle must be tight.

2. Grasp the wheel with both hands, 180° apart and have an assistant apply the brake. Rock the wheel up and down and side to side, to check for axial and axial play. If there is any noticeable play with the wheel locked, the bearings are worn and must be replaced.

3. Spin the wheel and listen for bearing noise. A grinding or catching noise indicates worn bearings.

4. If damage is evident, replace the bearings as a set. Always install new seals.

Seal Replacement

Seals protect the bearings from dirt and moisture contamination. Always install new seals when replacing bearings.

CAUTION
In the following procedure, do not allow the wheel to rest on the brake disc. Support the wheel on wooden blocks.

1. Rear wheel—Remove the final driven flange as described in this chapter.

2. Pry the seals out of the hub with a seal puller, tire iron or wide-blade screwdriver (**Figure 41**). Place a shop cloth under the tool to protect the hub from damage.

11

3. On all models except the VT1100C3, remove the speedometer gear retainer (**Figure 42**) from the left side of the front wheel.

NOTE
If necessary, replace the wheel bearings before installing the seals.

4. Clean the seal bore.

5. Inspect unshielded bearings for proper lubrication. If necessary, clean and repack the bearings while installed in the hub.

6. On all models except the VT1100C3, install the speedometer gear retainer by aligning its outer tabs with the two notches in the hub (**Figure 42**).

7. Pack grease into the lip of the new seal.

8. Place the seal in the bore with the closed side of the seal facing out. The seal must be square in the bore.

9. Use a seal driver or socket to install the seal in the bore. Install the seal until it is flush with the top of the hub bore surface (**Figure 43**, typical).

CAUTION
When installing the seals, the edge of the driver must fit at the perimeter of the seal. If the driver outside diameter is appreciably smaller than that of the seal, the driver presses against the center of the seal and damages it.

Wheel Bearing Tools

The wheel bearings are installed with a slight press fit and can be removed with or without special tools. The tools described in this section are inexpensive and prevent damage to the hub bore.

1. Motion Pro Bearing Remover Set (**Figure 44**)—This tool uses a remover head (split collet) that can be wedged against the inner bearing race. The bearing can then be driven from the hub using a driver rod (**Figure 45**). The set includes the following remover head sizes: 10, 12, 15, 17, 20 and 25 mm and two different size driver rods. The remover heads and driver rods can be purchased separately. To do so, select the 20 mm remover head and the large driver rod. The complete bearing remover set or the individual size tools can be ordered through most motorcycle dealerships.

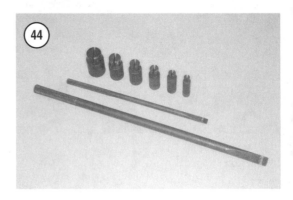

2. Wheel bearing removal with common shop tools—This method requires a propane torch, drift and hammer to remove the bearings.

Bearing Replacement

This section describes removal of the wheel bearings from the front and rear hubs. If the bearings are intact, one of the removal methods described in this section may be used. To remove a bearing where the inner race assembly has fallen out, refer to *Removing Damaged Bearings* in this section.

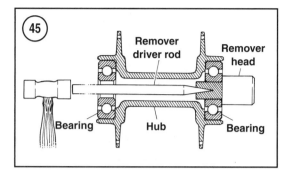

CAUTION
In the following procedure, do not al-
low the wheel to rest on the brake disc.
Support the wheel with wooden blocks.

1. Remove the seals as described in this section.
2. Examine the wheel bearings for excessive damage, especially the inner race. If the inner race of one bearing is damaged, remove the other bearing first. If both bearings are damaged, select the bearing with the least amount of damage and remove it first. On rusted and damaged bearings, applying pressure against the inner race can cause the inner race to pop out, leaving the outer race in the hub.

WARNING
Safety glasses must be worn when re-
moving the bearings in the following
steps.

NOTE
Step 3 describes two methods of re-
moving the wheel bearings. Step 3A
requires the use of the Motion Pro
Bearing Remover set. Step 3B de-
scribes steps on how to remove the
bearings with common hand tools.

3A. Remove the wheel bearings with the Motion Pro Bearing Remover set (**Figure 44**) as follows:

   a. Select the correct size remover head tool and insert it into one of the hub bearings (**Figure 46**).
   b. From the opposite side of the hub, insert the driver into the slot in the backside of the remover head. Position the hub with the remover head tool resting against a solid surface and strike the driver to wedge it firmly in the remover head (**Figure 45**).
   c. Position the hub so the remover head is free to move and the driver can be struck again.
   d. Strike the driver (**Figure 47**) as required to force the bearing (**Figure 48**) from the hub. Then release the driver from the remover head and remove the first bearing and distance collar.
   e. Repeat the procedure to remove the opposite bearing.

3B. Remove the wheel bearings with a hammer, drift and propane torch as follows:

CAUTION
This procedure requires the use of a
propane torch to heat the hub. Work in

11

a well-ventilated area away from combustible materials. Wear protective clothing, including eye protection and insulated gloves. For additional information, refer to **Interference Fit** *in Chapter One. Observe all safety and handling procedures when the hub is heated.*

a. Clean all lubricants from the hub.

b. Heat the hub around the bearing to be removed. Work the torch in a circular motion around the hub, making sure not to hold the torch in one area. Turn the wheel over and remove the bearing as described in the following steps.

c. Tilt the distance collar away from one side of the bearing with a long driver (**Figure 49**).

NOTE
Do not damage the distance collar when removing the bearing. If there is not enough room to tilt the distance collar away from the bearing, grind a clearance groove in the drift to allow it to contact the bearing while clearing the distance collar.

CAUTION
The bearing must be removed evenly to prevent it from binding into and damaging the hub bearing bore. Reheat the hub as required.

d. Tap around the inner bearing race to remove the bearing. Make several passes until the bearing is removed evenly from the hub. Do not allow the bearing to bind in the bore.

e. Remove the distance collar from the hub.

f. Turn the hub over and heat the opposite side.

g. Drive out the opposite bearing using a large socket or bearing driver placed on the bearing's outer race.

h. Inspect the distance collar for burrs created during removal. Remove burrs with a file.

Inspection

1. Clean and dry the interior of the hub.

2. Check the hub bearing bore for cracks or other damage. If a bearing fits loosely in the hub bore (no longer a press fit), replace the hub.

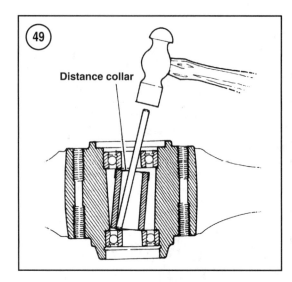

Distance collar

3. Clean the distance collar and inspect for corrosion and damage. Check the ends for cracks or other damage. Do not try to repair the distance collar by cutting or grinding its end surfaces because this shortens the distance collar. Replace the distance collar if one or both ends are damaged.

NOTE
The distance collar operates against both wheel bearing inner races to prevent them from moving inward when the axle is tightened. If the distance collar is too short or if it is not installed, the inner bearing races move inward and bind on the axle when the axle nut is tightened. This can damage the bearings and the bearing bores in the hub.

Assembly

1. Before installing the new bearings, note the following:

a. Install both bearings with their closed sides facing out. If a bearing is sealed on both sides, install the bearing with its manufacturer's marks facing out. If a shield is installed on one side of the bearing, the shield faces out.

b. Apply waterproof grease to the bearings that are not lubricated by the manufacturer or that are not sealed on both sides. Work the grease into the cavities between the balls and races.

c. Always support the bottom side of the hub, near the bore, when installing bearings.

CAUTION
*This procedure requires the use of a propane torch to heat the hub. Work in a well-ventilated area away from combustible materials. Wear protective clothing, including eye protection and insulated gloves. For additional information, refer to **Interference Fit** in Chapter One. Observe all safety and handling procedures when the hub is heated.*

2. Heat the hub around the bearing bore with a propane torch.

3. Place the first bearing squarely against the bore opening as described in Step 1.

4. Place a driver or socket over the bearing (**Figure 50**). The driver should seat against the bearing's outer race. Drive the bearing into the hub until it bottoms.

5. Turn the hub over and install the distance collar.

6. Position the opposite bearing squarely against the bore opening and drive the bearing partway into the bearing bore. Make sure the distance collar is centered in the hub. If not, install the axle through the hub to align the distance collar with the bearing. Then remove the axle and continue installing the bearing until it bottoms.

7. Insert the axle though the hub and turn it by hand. Check for any roughness or binding, indicating bearing damage.

NOTE
If the axle does not go in, the distance collar is not aligned correctly with one of the bearings.

8. Install the seals as previously described.

Removing Damaged Bearings

If damaged wheel bearings remain in use, the inner race can break apart, leaving the outer race pressed in the hub. Removal is difficult because only a small part of the race is accessible above the hub's shoulder, leaving little material to drive against. To remove a bearing's outer race under these conditions, first heat the hub evenly with a propane torch. Drive out the outer race with a drift and hammer. It may be necessary to grind a clearance tip on the end of the drift, to avoid damaging the hub bore. Check before heating the hub. Remove the race evenly by applying force at different points around the race. Do not allow the race to bind in its bore. After removing the race, inspect the hub mounting bore for cracks or other damage.

WHEEL SERVICE
(CAST WHEELS)

This section services the cast wheels installed on the following models:
1. VT1100C.
2. VT1100C2 Sabre.
3. VT1100T.

Rim Runout Check

1. Clean the wheel rim to remove all road grit and other debris. Any material left on the rim affects its runout. This includes any surface roughness caused by peeled or uneven paint and corrosion.

2. Inspect the wheel rim for dents, bending or cracks. Check the rim and rim sealing surface for scratches that could cause the tire to leak air.

NOTE
The runout check can be performed with the tire mounted on the rim.

3. Mount the wheel on a truing stand. Refer to **Figure 51** for the dial indicator inspection points.

4. Spin the wheel slowly by hand and measure the radial (up and down) runout with a dial indicator as shown in **Figure 51**. If the runout exceeds 2.0 mm (0.08 in.), go to Step 6.

5. Spin the wheel slowly by hand and measure the axial (side to side) runout with a dial indicator as shown in **Figure 51**. If the runout exceeds 2.0 mm (0.08 in.), go to Step 6.

11

6. If the runout is excessive, remove the wheel from the truing stand and turn each bearing inner race by hand. If necessary, remove the seal to check the bearings closely. Each bearing must turn smoothly and be a tight fit in its mounting bore. Some axial play, or end play, is normal, but radial play, or side play, must be negligible (**Figure 52**). Then check the bearing for visual damage. If a bearing turns roughly, replace both bearings as a set. If a bearing is loose in its mounting bore, the hub is probably damaged. Remove the bearings and check the mounting bore for any cracks, gouges or other damage. Refer to *Front and Rear Hubs* in this chapter. If the wheel bearings and hub are in good condition but the runout is out of specification, have the wheel inspected by a dealership for damage.

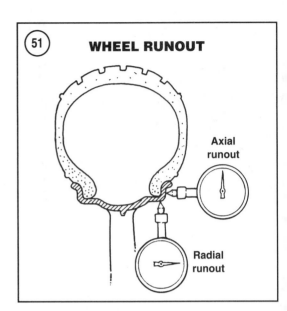

WHEEL SERVICE
(LACED WHEEL)

This section services the laced wheels found on the following models:
1. VT1100C2 ACE.
2. VT1100C3.

Component Condition

Inspect the wheels regularly for axial (side to side) and radial (up and down) runout, even spoke tension and visible rim damage. When a wheel has a noticeable wobble, it is out of true. This is usually caused by loose spokes, but it can be caused by a damaged hub or rim.

Truing a wheel corrects the axial and radial runout to bring the wheel back into specification. The condition of the individual wheel components determines if the wheel can be trued accurately. Note the following:

1. Spoke condition—Do not true a wheel by overtightening bent or damaged spokes. Doing so places an excessive amount of tension on the spokes, hub and rim. Replace damaged spokes before truing the wheel.

2. Nipple condition—When truing the wheels, the nipples must turn freely on the spoke. However, corroded and rusted spoke threads are common and difficult to adjust. Spray a penetrating liquid onto the nipple and allow sufficient time for it to penetrate before trying to turn the nipples. Turn the spoke wrench in both directions and continue to ap-

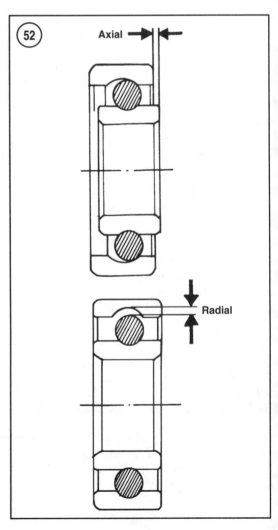

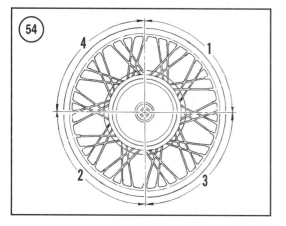

ply penetrating liquid. If the spoke wrench rounds off the nipple, it is necessary to remove the tire from the rim and cut the spoke(s) out of the wheel.

3. Rim condition—Minor rim runout can be corrected by truing the wheel. However, do not correct rim damage by overtightening the spokes. Inspect the rims for cracks, flat spots or dents. Check the spoke holes for cracks or elongation. Replace damaged rims and hubs.

Wheel Truing Preliminaries

Before checking the runout and truing the wheel, note the following:

1. Make sure the wheel bearings are in good condition.

2. Routine wheel runout checks can be made with the wheel mounted on the motorcycle by mounting a pointer against the fork or swing arm and slowly rotating the wheel. When truing a wheel that is out of adjustment, mount it on a truing or balance stand.

3. Use the correct size spoke wrench (**Figure 53**). Turning the spokes with the wrong tool may round

off the spoke nipples, making further adjustment difficult.

Tightening Loose Spokes

This section describes steps for checking and tightening a few loose spokes without affecting wheel runout. When many spokes are loose and the wheel is running out of true, refer to *Wheel Truing Procedure* in this section.

1. Support the wheel so it can turn freely.

2. Spokes can be checked for looseness in one of three ways:

   a. Spoke torque wrench: A number of different spoke torque wrenches are available on the aftermarket. When using a spoke torque wrench, the correct torque specification is 4.3 N•m (38 in.-lb.).

   b. Hand check: Grasp and squeeze two spokes where they cross. Loose spokes can be flexed by hand. Tight spokes feel stiff with little noticeable movement.

   c. Spoke tone: Tapping a spoke causes it to vibrate and produce sound waves. Loose and tight spokes produce different sounds or tones. A tight spoke rings. A loose spoke has a soft or dull ring. Tap each spoke with a spoke wrench or screwdriver to identify loose spokes.

3. Check the spokes using one of the methods described in Step 2. If there are loose spokes, spin the wheel and note the following:

   a. If the wheel is running true, continue with Step 4 to tighten the loose spokes.

   b. If the wheel is running out of true, go to *Wheel Truing Procedure* to measure runout and true the wheel.

4. Use tape and divide the rim into four equally spaced sections. Number the sections as shown in **Figure 54**.

5. Start by tightening the loose spokes in section 1, then in sections 2, 3 and 4. Do not turn each spoke more than 1/4 to 1/2 turn at a time. Doing so overtightens the spokes and brings the wheel out of true. Work slowly while checking spoke tightness. Continue until all the spokes are tightened evenly.

NOTE
If the spokes are hard to turn, spray penetrating oil into the top of the nipple. Wipe excess oil from the rim.

11

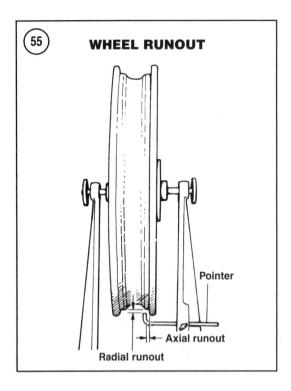

WHEEL RUNOUT

Pointer

Axial runout

Radial runout

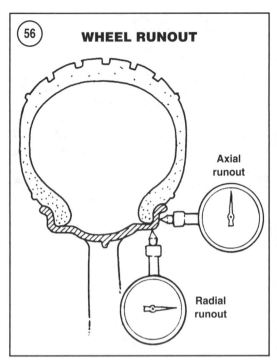

WHEEL RUNOUT

Axial runout

Radial runout

6. When all the spokes are tightened evenly, spin the wheel. If there is any noticeable runout, true the wheel as described in the following procedure.

Wheel Truing Procedure

Table 1 lists axial (side to side) and radial (up and down) runout specifications.

1. Clean the rim, spokes and nipples.

2. Position a pointer against the rim as shown in **Figure 55**. If the tire is mounted on the rim, position the pointer as shown in **Figure 56**.

3. Spin the wheel slowly and check the axial and radial runout. If the rim is out of adjustment, continue with Step 4.

> *NOTE*
> *It is normal for the rim to jump at the point where the rim was welded together. Small cuts and dings in the rim affect the runout reading, especially when using a dial indicator.*

4. Spray penetrating oil into the top of each nipple. Wipe excess oil from the rim.

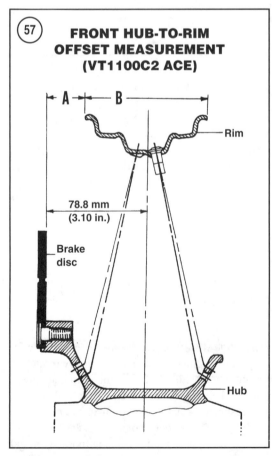

FRONT HUB-TO-RIM OFFSET MEASUREMENT (VT1100C2 ACE)

A B

Rim

78.8 mm (3.10 in.)

Brake disc

Hub

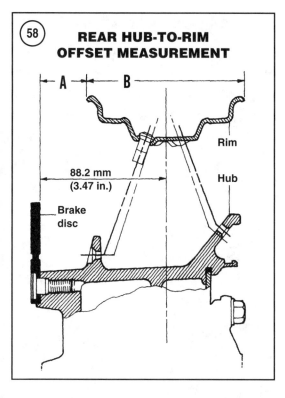

REAR HUB-TO-RIM OFFSET MEASUREMENT

A B

Rim

88.2 mm
(3.47 in.)

Hub

Brake disc

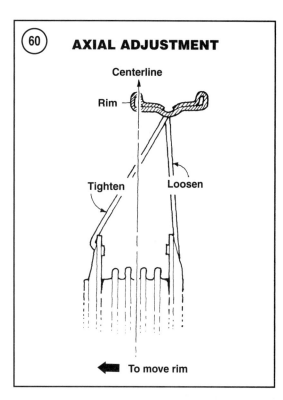

AXIAL ADJUSTMENT

Centerline

Rim

Tighten Loosen

To move rim

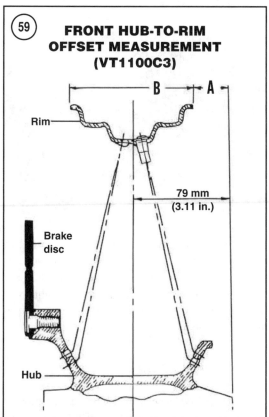

FRONT HUB-TO-RIM OFFSET MEASUREMENT (VT1100C3)

B A

Rim

79 mm
(3.11 in.)

Brake disc

Hub

NOTE
If the runout is minimal, the tire can be left on the rim. However, if the runout is excessive or if the rim must be centered with the hub (Step 5), remove the tire from the rim.

5. If there are a large number of loose spokes or if some or all of the spokes were replaced, measure the hub to rim offset. If necessary, reposition the hub:

   a. On VT1100C2 ACE models, **Figure 57** (front) and **Figure 58** (rear).

   b. On VT1100C3 models, **Figure 59** (front) and **Figure 58** (rear).

6. Axial runout adjustment—If the side-to-side runout is out of specification, adjust the wheel. For example, to pull the rim to the left side (**Figure 60**), loosen the spokes on the right side of the hub and tighten the adjacent spokes on the left side of the hub. Always loosen and tighten the spokes an equal number of turns.

NOTE
Determining the number of spokes to loosen and tighten depends on how far the runout is out of adjustment.

11

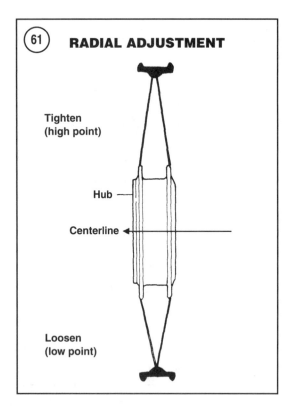

61 RADIAL ADJUSTMENT

Tighten
(high point)

Hub

Centerline

Loosen
(low point)

62

63

64

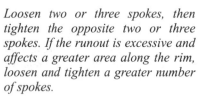

Loosen two or three spokes, then tighten the opposite two or three spokes. If the runout is excessive and affects a greater area along the rim, loosen and tighten a greater number of spokes.

7. Radial runout adjustment—If the up and down runout is out of specification, the hub is not centered in the rim. Draw the high point of the rim toward the centerline of the wheel by tightening the spokes in the area of the high point, and loosening the spokes on the side opposite the high point (**Figure 61**). Tighten the spokes in equal amounts to prevent distortion.

NOTE
Alternate between checking and adjusting axial and radial runout. Remember, changing spoke tension on one side of the rim affects the tension on the other side of the rim.

8. After truing the wheel, seat each spoke in the hub (**Figure 62**) by tapping it with a flat nose punch and hammer. Then recheck the spoke tension and

wheel runout. Readjust if necessary as described under *Tightening Loose Spokes* in this section.

9. Check the ends of the spokes where they are threaded in the nipples. Grind off any ends that protrude through the nipples to prevent them from puncturing the tube.

WHEEL BALANCE

An unbalanced wheel is unsafe because it seriously affects the steering and handling of the motorcycle.

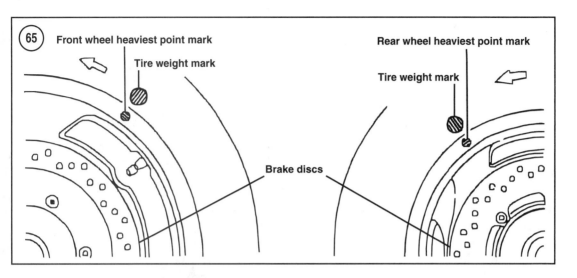

65

Front wheel heaviest point mark

Tire weight mark

Rear wheel heaviest point mark

Tire weight mark

Brake discs

66

Depending on the degree of unbalance and the speed of the motorcycle, anything from a mild vibration to a violent shimmy may occur, which may result in loss of control. An imbalanced wheel also causes abnormal tire wear.

Motorcycle wheels can be checked for balance either statically (single plane balance) or dynamically (dual plane balance). This section describes how to static balance the wheels using a wheel balancing stand. To obtain a higher degree of accuracy, take both wheels to a dealership and have them balanced with a two plane computer dynamic wheel balancer. This machine spins the wheel to accurately detect any imbalance.

Balance weights are used to balance the wheel and are attached to the spokes (**Figure 63**) on laced wheels and to the rim (**Figure 64**) on cast wheels. Weight kits are available from motorcycle dealerships.

The wheel must be able to rotate freely when checking wheel balance. Because excessively worn or dam-

aged wheel bearings affect the accuracy of this procedure, check the wheel bearings as described in this chapter.

1. Confirm that the tire balance mark (a paint mark on the tire) is positioned as follows:

   a. On the front tire of VT1100C2 Sabre models, the tire balance mark must align with the wheel mark on the brake disc side of the wheel (**Figure 65**).

   b. On the rear tire of VT1100C2 Sabre models, the tire balance mark must align with the wheel mark on the final driven flange side of the wheel (**Figure 65**).

   c. On all other models, the tire balance mark must align with the valve stem (**Figure 66**).

NOTE
Leave the brake disc mounted on the wheel when checking and adjusting wheel balance.

NOTE
To check the original balance of the wheel, leave the weights attached to the spokes or rim.

2. Remove the weights from the spokes or rim.

3. Clean the tire, rim and spokes. Remove any stones or pebbles stuck in the tire tread.

4. Remove the wheel as described in this chapter.

5. Clean the seals and inspect the wheel bearings as described in this chapter.

6. Mount the wheel with the brake disc attached (if used) on a balance stand (**Figure 67**).

11

7. Spin the wheel by hand and let it coast to a stop. Mark the tire at its bottom point with chalk.

8. Spin the wheel several more times. If the same spot on the tire stops at the bottom each time, the wheel is out of balance. This is the heaviest part of the tire. When an unbalanced wheel is spun, it always comes to rest with the heaviest spot at the bottom.

9A. Cast wheels—Tape a test weight to the upper or light side of the wheel.

9B. Laced wheels—Attach a test weight to the spoke at the upper or light side of the wheel.

10. Experiment with different weights until the wheel comes to a stop at a different position each time it is spun. When a wheel is correctly balanced, the weight of the tire and wheel assembly is distributed equally around the wheel.

11. Remove the test weight and install the correct size weight or weights to the rim. Crimp the weight tightly against the spoke and nipple (**Figure 63**) or against the center joint on the rim (**Figure 64**). If the weight must be placed beside a large spoke or arm on a cast wheel, use a stick-on wheel weight on each side of the rim.

NOTE
*Do not exceed the maximum wheel balance weight limit specified in **Table 1**. If a wheel requires an excessive amount of weight, make sure the tire balance mark on the tire is properly aligned.*

12. In the *NOTES* section at the back of this book, record the amount of weight and its position used on the wheel. If the motorcycle experiences a handling or vibration problem later, refer to your notes to check for any missing balance weights.

13. Install the wheel as described in this chapter.

TIRE SAFETY

Tire wear and performance is greatly affected by tire pressure. Have a good tire gauge on hand and make a habit of frequent pressure checks. Refer to Chapter Three.

Follow a sensible break-in period when running on new tires. New tires exhibit significantly less adhesion ability. Do not subject a new tire to hard corning, hard acceleration or hard braking for the first 100 miles (160 km). If possible, find a large, deserted parking area and scuff in the new tires without having to ride in traffic.

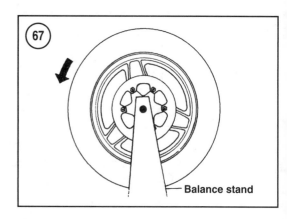
Balance stand

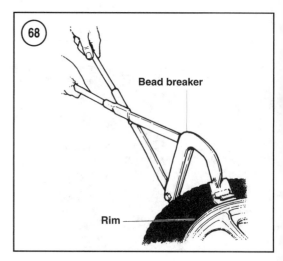
Bead breaker
Rim

TIRE CHANGING

The cast wheels can easily be damaged during tire removal. Take special care with the tire irons when changing a tire to avoid scratches and gouges to the outer rim surface. Insert rim protectors or scraps of leather between the tire iron and the rim to protect the rim from damage. All original equipment cast wheels are designed for use with tubeless tires only. All laced wheels use a tube and tire combination.

Removal

It is easier to change tires when the wheel is mounted on some type of raised platform. A popular item used by many home mechanics is a metal drum. Before placing the wheel on a drum, cover the drum edge with a length of garden hose, split lengthwise and secured in place with plastic ties. When changing the front tire at ground level, support the wheel on two

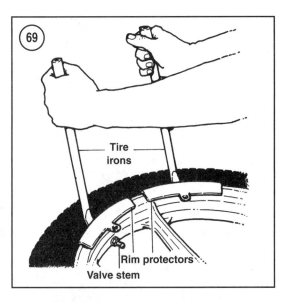

Tire irons

Rim protectors

Valve stem

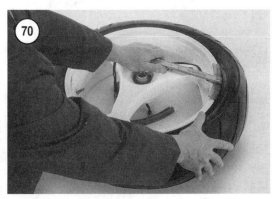

closed automobile. Place the new tire in the same location.

1. If remounting the tire, confirm that the tire balance mark (a paint mark on the tire) is positioned as follows:

    a. On the front tire of VT1100C2 Sabre models, the tire balance mark must align with the wheel mark on the brake disc side of the wheel (**Figure 65**).

    b. On the rear tire of VT1100C2 Sabre models, the tire balance mark must align with the wheel mark on the final driven flange side of the wheel (**Figure 65**).

    c. On all other models, the tire balance mark must align with the valve stem (**Figure 66**).

2. Remove the valve core and deflate the tire.

NOTE
*Removal of tubeless tires from their rims can be difficult because of the exceptionally tight tire bead-to-rim seal. Breaking the bead seal may require a special tool (**Figure 68**). If unable to break the seal loose, take the wheel to a motorcycle dealership and have the tire broken loose on a tire changing machine.*

CAUTION
The inner rim and tire bead areas are the sealing surfaces on the tubeless tire. Do not scratch the inside of the rim or damage the bead.

3. Press the entire bead on both sides of the tire into the center of the rim. Check that the beads are free on both sides of the rim.

4. Lubricate the beads on both sides of the tire with a tire lubricant or soapy water.

NOTE
*Use rim protectors or insert scraps of leather between the tire iron and the rim to protect the rim from damage (**Figure 69**).*

5. Insert the first tire iron under the bead on the opposite side of the valve stem. Force the bead into the center of the rim, then pry the bead over the rim with the tire iron (**Figure 70**).

6. Insert a second tire iron next to the first to hold the bead over the rim (**Figure 71**). While holding the tire with one tire iron, work around the tire with

wooden blocks to prevent the brake disc from contacting the floor.

NOTE
Warming the tire makes it softer and more pliable. Place the tire and wheel assembly in the sun or in a completely

11

the second tire iron, prying the tire over the rim and working in small bites of 1-2 inches at a time. On laced wheels, be careful not to pinch the inner tube with the tire irons.

> *NOTE*
> *If it is difficult to pry the bead over the rim with the second tire iron. Stop to make sure the bottom bead was broken from the rim. Excessive force splits and tears the tire bead and causes permanent tire damage.*

> *NOTE*
> *On laced wheels, if the tube is being removed to fix a flat, identify the tube's installed position in the tire immediately after removing it to help locate the foreign object in the tire.*

7. On laced wheels when the upper bead is free of the rim, remove the inner tube from the tire (**Figure 72**).

8. Stand the tire upright and pry the second tire bead (**Figure 73**) over the rim. Then peel the tire off the rim. If necessary, use a second tire iron.

Inspection

1. Inspect the tire for damage.

2. On laced wheels, if the tube was leaking air, pump air into it to locate the leak. Then place the tube on top of the tire, facing in its original position to help locate the object in the tire. Remove the object and check the tire for damage.

> *NOTE*
> *Cracks in the inner tire liner can pinch and damage the tube. If the tube is leaking air, but there are no foreign objects in the tire, spread the tire and check the inner liner for cracks.*

3. Run a rag through the inside of the tire to locate any protruding objects. Do not use bare hands.

> *WARNING*
> *Carefully consider whether a tire should be replaced. If there is any doubt about the condition of the existing tire, replace it with a new one. Do not take a chance on a tire failure at any speed.*

4. If any one of the following is observed, replace the tire:

    a. A noticeable puncture or split.

    b. A scratch or split on the sidewall or along the inner liner.

    c. Any type of ply separation.

    d. Tread separation or abnormal wear pattern.

    e. Tread depth of less than the minimum value specified in **Table 1** for original equipment tires. The minimum depth on aftermarket tires may vary. Refer to the tire manufacturer's information.

    f. Scratches on either sealing bead.

    g. The cord is cut in any place.

    h. Flat spots in the tread.

    i. Any abnormality in the inner liner.

5. If the tire can be reused, clean and dry the inside of the tire with compressed air.

6. Use a brush to clean dirt, rust and rubber from the inside of the rim.

7. On laced wheels, perform the following:

    a. Remove the rim strap from the center of the rim. Replace if damaged.

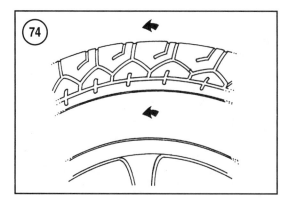

b. Inspect the spokes for rust and corrosion. Then check for any spoke ends that protrude above the nipple head and into the center of the rim. Grind or file the exposed part of the spoke flush with the nipple.

c. Check the valve stem hole in the rim for any roughness or cuts that could damage the valve stem. Remove any roughness with a file.

d. Mount the wheel onto a truing stand and check runout before mounting the tire.

e. If possible, install a new tube. If not, inflate the original tube to make sure it was not punctured during tire removal. Discard the tube if it has been previously patched or if it appears balancing liquids were introduced into the tube. Check the inner nut on the valve stem to make sure it is tight. Check the area around the valve stem for cracks and other weak spots.

8. On cast wheels, remove the old valve stem and discard it. Inspect the valve stem hole in the rim. Remove any dirt or corrosion from the hole and wipe it dry. Install a new valve stem and make sure it is properly seated in the rim.

Installation

NOTE
Installation is easier if the tire is pliable. This can be achieved by warming the tire in the sun or inside an enclosed automobile.

1. On laced wheels, install the rim band around the rim by aligning the hole in the band with the hole in the rim.

2. When installing the tire on the rim, make sure the correct tire, either front or rear, is installed on the correct wheel. Also install the tire with the direction arrow facing the normal direction of wheel rotation (**Figure 74**).

CAUTION
Use a tire lubricant when installing the tire over the rim and when seating the tire beads. Plain or soapy water can also be used. Do not use Teflon and WD-40 aerosol spray lubes or other petroleum chemicals as a tire lubricant. These lubricants stay on the tire beads without drying out and can cause the tire to slip on the rim and damage the valve stem on laced wheels. Some chemicals also damage the tire rubber.

3. On laced wheels, perform the following:
a. Sprinkle the tube with talcum powder and install it into the tire (**Figure 75**). The powder minimizes tube chafing and helps the tube distribute itself when inflated.

NOTE
If installing the rear tube, make sure the valve stem is correctly angled with the hole in the rim.

b. Inflate the tube to shape it against the tire. Then bleed most of the air from the tube. Too much air makes tire installation difficult and too little air increases the chance of pinching the tube.

4. Most tires are marked with a colored spot near the bead that indicates a lighter point on the tire. Align this spot as follows:
a. On the front tire of the VT1100C2 Sabre models, align the tire balance mark with the wheel mark on the brake disc side of the wheel (**Figure 65**).

11

b. On the rear tire of the VT1100C2 Sabre models, align the tire balance mark with the wheel mark on the final driven flange side of the wheel (**Figure 65**).

c. On all other models, align the tire balance mark with the valve stem (**Figure 66**).

5A. On laced wheels, perform the following:

a. Lubricate the lower bead. Then start pushing the lower bead over the rim (**Figure 76**) while inserting the air valve through the hole in the rim. Install the nut onto the valve stem to prevent the stem from sliding back into the tire.

b. Continue to push the lower bead over the rim by hand-fitting it as much as possible. The last part of the bead is the toughest to install. If necessary, grasp the spokes to steady the wheel and push the front part of the tire toward the inside of the rim with your knees. This may provide additional room at the back of the bead to help with its installation. If it is necessary to use a tire lever, use it carefully to avoid pinching the tube or tearing the tire bead.

c. When the lower bead is installed over the rim, turn the wheel over and check that the tube is not pinched between the bead and rim. If so, carefully push the tube back into the center of the tire by hand.

d. Turn the wheel back over and lift the upper bead to check the tube. Make sure the tube is laying evenly around the tire. If necessary, inflate the tube to remove any wrinkles, then bleed most of the air from the tube.

e. Turn the tire so the air valve is aligned with the rim. Also, check that the tire weight mark identified in Step 4 aligns with the valve stem hole in the rim (**Figure 66**).

f. Lubricate the upper tire bead, then start installation opposite the valve stem by hand (**Figure 77**). If necessary, relubricate the bead. Use the tire irons to pry the remaining section of bead over the rim (**Figure 78**). Remember to keep the lower bead positioned in the center of the rim when installing the upper bead.

NOTE
Do not use excessive force when using the tire irons to install the upper tire bead. Instead, use your knees to push the front part of the tire (the part closest to you) toward the inside of the rim

*and to keep the lower bead positioned in the **center** of the rim. Forcing the tire irons between the upper bead and rim because the lower bead is not properly positioned can damage the rim, cut the tire bead and pinch the tube.*

5B. On cast wheels, perform the following:

a. Place the backside of the tire into the center of the rim. The lower bead should go into the center of the rim and the upper bead outside.

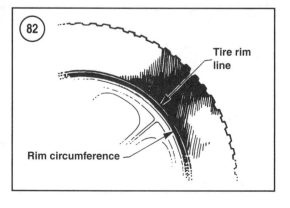

Tire rim line

Rim circumference

Use both hands to push the backside of the tire into the rim (**Figure 79**) as far as possible. Use tire irons when it becomes difficult to install the tire by hand.

b. Press the upper bead into the rim opposite the valve. Pry the bead into the rim on both sides of the initial point with a tire tool, working around the rim to the valve stem (**Figure 80**). If the tire wants to pull up on one side, use another tire iron or a knee to hold the tire in place. The last few inches are the toughest to install. If possible, continue to push the tire into the rim by hand. Relubricate the bead if necessary. If the tire bead wants to pull out from under the rim, use both knees to hold the tire in place. If necessary, use a tire iron for the last few inches (**Figure 81**).

c. Check the bead on both sides of the tire for an even fit around the rim. Align the tire weight mark with the valve stem or wheel as described in Step 4.

6. Relubricate both sides of the tire.

WARNING
Special care must be taken when inflating the tire and seating the tire beads in the next step. Never exceed 300 kPa (43.5 psi) inflation pressure because the tire could burst, causing injury. If the tire does not seat at the recommended pressure, do not continue by overinflating the tire. Doing so could cause the tire to burst, and cause injury. Deflate the tire and repeat the procedure.

NOTE
The safest way to inflate the tire is to use a clamp-on air chuck and a remote air gauge/inflator. Wear safety glasses and stand as far away from the tire as possible. Never stand directly over a tire while inflating it.

7. Lubricate both beads. Use a clamp-on air chuck and inflate the tire to seat the beads on the rim. Do not exceed 300 kPa (43.5 psi).

8. After inflating the tire, check to see that the beads are fully seated and that the rim lines are the same distance from the rim all the way around the tire (**Figure 82**). If not, deflate the tire and repeat the procedure.

9A. On laced wheels, when the beads are correctly seated, deflate the tire (but do not break the tire beads). Then inflate the tire again to help stretch the tube and seat it fully against the tire. Set the tire to the required tire pressure listed in **Table 3**. Tighten the outer valve stem nut and the valve stem cap (**Figure 83**).

9B. On cast wheels, set the tire to the required tire pressure listed in **Table 3**. Install and tighten the valve stem cap.

10. Balance the tire and wheel assembly as described in this chapter.

Table 1 TIRE AND WHEEL SPECIFICATIONS

Tire size	
Front	
VT1100C	110/90-19 62H
VT1100C2	120/90-18 65H
VT1100C3	140/80-17 69H
VT1100T	130/80R-18 66H
Rear	
VT1100C	170/80-15 77H
VT1100C2	170/80-15 77H
VT1100C3	170/80-15 77H
VT1100T	170/70R-16 75H
Tire brands	
Front	
VT1100C	Dunlop F24
VT1100C2 ACE	
1995-1996	Dunlop K177F
1997-on	Dunlop K177F, K177F WSW
VT1100C2 Sabre	Dunlop K177F
VT1100C3	
1998-2000	Dunlop D404F WSW
1998-2002	Bridgestone EXEDRA L309
VT1100T	Dunlop D206F
Rear	
VT1100C	Dunlop K555
VT1100C2 ACE	
1995-1996	Dunlop K555
1997-on	Dunlop K555, K555 WSW
VT1100C2 Sabre	Dunlop K555
VT1100C3	
1998-2000	Dunlop K555 WSW
1998-2002	Bridgestone EXEDRA G546
VT1100T	Dunlop D206A
Minimum tire tread depth	
Front	1.5 mm (0.06 in.)
Rear	2.0 mm (0.08 in.)
Wheel balance weight maximum limit	
Front	60 g (2.1 oz.)
Rear	
VT1100C2 ACE and VT1100C3	90 g (3.2 oz.)
All other models	70 g (2.5 oz.)

Table 2 WHEEL AND AXLE SERVICE SPECIFICATIONS

	Service Limit mm (in.).
Axle runout	0.20 (0.008)
Wheel runout	
Axial	2.0 (0.08)
Radial	2.0 (0.08)

Table 3 TIRE INFLATION PRESSURE[1]

	Front psi (kPa)	Rear psi (kPa)
Up to 90 kg (200 lb.) load		
VT1100C	33 (225)	33 (225)
VT1100C2		
ACE		
1995-1996	33 (225)	33 (225)
1997-on	29 (200)	33 (225)
Shadow Sabre	29 (200)	33 (225)
VT1100C3	29 (200)	29 (200)
VT1100T	33 (225)	33 (225)
From 90 kg (200 lb.) load to the maximum weight limit[2]		
VT1100C	33 (225)	41 (280)
VT1100C2		
ACE	33 (225)	41 (280)
Shadow Sabre	29 (200)	41 (280)
VT1100C3	29 (200)	41 (280)
VT1100T	33 (225)	36 (250)

1. The tire inflation pressure for original equipment tires. Refer to Table 1 in this chapter for a list   of the OEM equipped tire brands and tire sizes. Aftermarket tires may require different inflation pressures.   Refer to tire manufacturer's specifications.
2. Refer to Table 3 (Vehicle Weight Specifications) in Chapter One for the maximum weight limit for each model.

Table 4 WHEEL TORQUE SPECIFICATIONS

	N•m	in.-lb.	ft.-lb.
Brake disc bolts*	42	–	31
Damper holder plate bolts*	20	–	15
Front axle pinch bolt	22	–	16
Front axle bolt	59	–	43
Final drive unit nut	64	–	47
Rear axle pinch bolt	26	–	19
Rear axle nut	88	–	65
Rear brake arm nut			
VT1100C	22	–	16
Rear caliper stopper pin bolt*	70	–	51
Rear shock absorber lower mounting bolt	23	–	17
Spoke nipple	4.3	38	–
Valve stem nut	2.8	25	–

*Install new ALOC bolts if possible. Otherwise, clean threads on original bolts and apply a medium strength threadlock to bolt threads.

CHAPTER TWELVE

FRONT SUSPENSION AND STEERING

This chapter describes procedures for the repair and maintenance of the handlebar, front fork and steering components. Refer to Chapter Ten for front wheel and tire service.

Front suspension and steering specifications are listed in **Tables 1-3** at the end of the chapter.

> *WARNING*
> *Replace all fasteners used on the front suspension and steering components with parts of the same type. Do not use a replacement part of lesser quality or substitute design; this may affect the performance of the system or cause failure of the part that leads to loss of control of the motorcycle. Refer to the torque values specifications during installation to ensure proper retention of these parts.*

> *NOTE*
> *The ALOC fasteners identified in **Table 3** use a pre-applied threadlock. Honda specifies to replace ALOC fasteners during installation. When a replacement ALOC fastener is unavailable, remove all threadlock from the original fastener and apply a medium strength threadlock to the threads during installation.*

HANDLEBAR

Removal

1. Cover the fuel tank with a thick blanket to protect it from scratches and other damage.
2. Remove the left and right side mirrors.
3. Remove the wire harness clamps from the handlebar.
4. Disconnect the clutch switch electrical connectors at the clutch switch (**Figure 1**).
5. Disconnect the clutch cable at the lever, if necessary.
6. Remove the two clutch lever bracket mounting bolts and remove the clutch bracket holder (A, **Figure 2**) and lever bracket.
7. Remove the left handlebar switch housing screws (B, **Figure 2**) and separate the switch housing from around the handlebar.
8. Disconnect the choke cable (A, **Figure 3**) from the choke lever.

> *NOTE*
> *Loosening the choke cable locknut at the bottom of the left handlebar switch housing changes the choke cable adjustment.*

9. Disconnect the front brake light switch connectors at the switch (**Figure 4**).

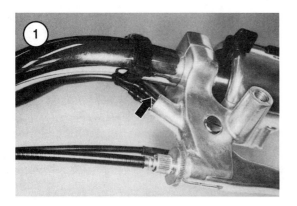

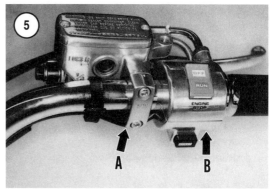

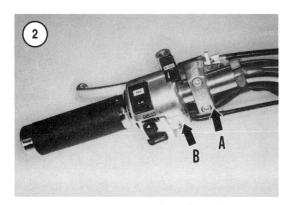

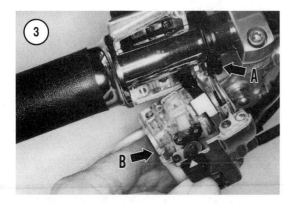

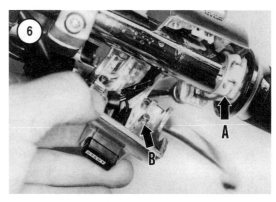

10. Remove the two master cylinder holder bolts and remove the holder and front master cylinder (A, **Figure 5**). Support the master cylinder upright so air does not enter the hydraulic system.

11. Remove the right side handlebar switch housing screws and separate the switch housing (B, **Figure 5**) from around the handlebar.

12. Disconnect the throttle cables (A, **Figure 6**) from the throttle sleeve and slide the throttle grip off the handlebar.

> *NOTE*
> *If there is not enough slack to disconnect the throttle cables at the throttle sleeve, disconnect them at the carburetor, then at the throttle sleeve. Refer to Chapter Eight.*

13. If the handlebar lower holders (**Figure 7**) are going to be removed, loosen the lower holder mounting nuts while the handlebar is still mounted in place.

14. Remove the handlebar upper holder bolt caps, bolts and holders (**Figure 8**).

15. Remove the handlebar.

12

16. To remove the handlebar lower holders (**Figure 9**) perform the following:

    a. Identify the holders so they can be installed facing in their original directions.

    b. Remove the lower holder nut, washer and lower holder.

    c. On VT1100C2 Sabre and VT1100C3 models, remove the rubber damper from top of the steering bracket.

    d. Repeat for the other holder.

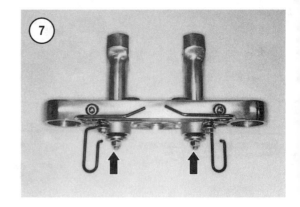

Installation

1. Clean and inspect the handlebar holders and bolts.

2. If removed, install the handlebar lower holders as follows:

    a. On VT1100C2 Sabre and VT1100C3 models, install the bushings.

    b. Install the handlebar lower holder and position it facing in its original mounting position.

    c. Install the washer and nut and tighten finger-tight.

3. Install the handlebar as follows:

    a. Place the handlebar onto the lower holders.

    b. Install the upper holders with their punch marks facing forward (**Figure 8**).

    c. Install the upper handlebar holder mounting bolts and tighten finger-tight.

    d. Align the punch mark on the handlebar with the gap between the holders as shown in **Figure 8**. The handlebar punch mark is found on either the front or rear of the handlebar.

    e. Tighten the front upper handlebar holder bolts, then the rear bolts to 30 N•m (22 ft.-lb.). Check that there is gap at the end of each holder.

    f. Install the bolt caps.

4. If the handlebar lower holders were removed, tighten the mounting nuts as follows:

    a. On VT1100C3 models, tighten to 26 N•m (19 ft.-lb.).

    b. On all other models, tighten both nuts securely.

5. Clean the inside of the throttle sleeve and the right side of the handlebar of all old grease. Then re-lubricate lightly with grease. Lubricate the cable holes in the throttle sleeve with grease.

6. Install the right side handlebar switch housing as follows:

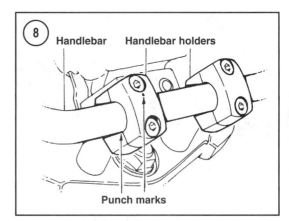

Handlebar   Handlebar holders

Punch marks

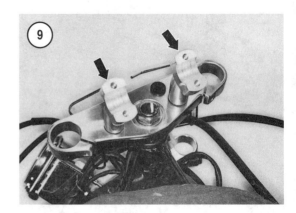

    a. Reconnect the throttle cables (A, **Figure 6**) to the throttle grip.

    b. Align the switch housing locating pin (B, **Figure 6**) with the hole in the handlebar and close the switch halves (B, **Figure 5**) around the handlebar and throttle grip.

    c. Install the front and rear switch housing screws and tighten securely.

7. Install the master cylinder as follows:

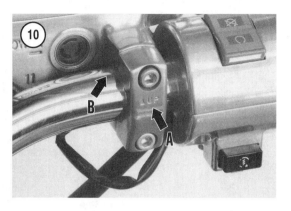

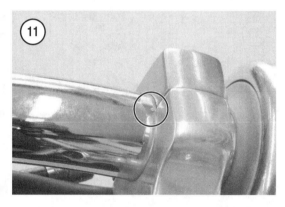

a. Clean the handlebar, master cylinder and clamp mating surfaces.

b. Mount the master cylinder onto the handlebar, then install its clamp (A, **Figure 5**) and both mounting bolts. Install the clamp with its UP mark facing up (A, **Figure 10**).

c. Align the master cylinder and clamp mating halves with the punch mark (B, **Figure 10**) on the handlebar. Tighten the upper master cylinder clamp bolt first, then the lower bolt to 12 N•m (106 in.-lb.).

8. Reconnect the front brake light switch connectors at the switch (**Figure 4**).

9. Install the left side handlebar switch housing as follows:

a. Reconnect the choke cable (A, **Figure 3**) at the choke lever.

b. Align the switch housing locating pin (B, **Figure 3**) with the hole in the handlebar and close the switch halves around the handlebar.

c. Install the front and rear switch housing screw. Tighten the front screw, then the rear screw securely.

10. Install the clutch lever bracket as follows:

a. Clean the handlebar, clutch lever bracket and holder mating surfaces.

b. Mount the clutch lever bracket onto the handlebar, then install its clamp (A, **Figure 2**) and both mounting bolts. Install the clamp with its UP mark facing up.

c. Align the end of the clutch lever bracket with the punch mark on the handlebar (**Figure 11**). Then tighten the upper holder bolt first, then the lower bolt securely.

d. Reconnect the electrical connectors at the clutch switch (**Figure 1**).

11. Install, adjust and tighten the mirrors.

12. Secure the wiring harnesses to the handlebar with the clamps.

13. If the throttle cable adjusters were loosened, adjust the throttle cables as described in Chapter Three.

14. Adjust the clutch as described in Chapter Three.

15. Check the choke cable adjustment as described in Chapter Three.

16. If air entered the front master cylinder brake line, bleed the front brake as described in Chapter Fourteen.

17. After all assemblies are installed, test each one for proper operation. Correct any problem at this time.

WARNING
An improperly installed throttle grip assembly may cause the throttle to stick open. Failure to properly assemble and adjust the throttle cables and throttle grip could cause a loss of steering control. Do not start or ride the motorcycle until the throttle grip is installed correctly and snaps back when released.

HANDLEBAR GRIPS AND WEIGHTS

End Cap Replacement

The plastic end caps (A, **Figure 12**) can be removed separately from the handlebar grips.

1. For the left end cap, use a screwdriver and pry the end cap off the handlebar grip. Install the end cap by aligning the tabs in the end cap with the grooves in the grip and push it into place.

2. For the right end cap, hold the throttle grip and turn the end cap counterclockwise to remove it. Reverse to install the cap.

Handlebar Grips Inspection

The handlebar grips (B, **Figure 12**) must be secured tightly to the left handlebar and to the throttle grip (right side). Replace cut or damaged grips because water may enter between the grip and its mounting surface and cause the grip to slip. This could cause a loss of steering control. Replace the handlebar grips as described in the following procedure.

Replacement

This section describes handlebar grip replacement and handlebar weight replacement (if used).
1A. For the left hand grip, remove the clutch holder and left handlebar switch as described under *Handlebar* in this chapter.
1B. For the right hand grip, remove the throttle grip as described under *Handlebar* in this chapter.
2. Measure the distance from the inside of the right grip to the cable flange on the throttle sleeve (**Figure 13**). This gap must be maintained to prevent the grip from contacting the switch housing.

> *NOTE*
> *If reusing the hand grips, remove them carefully to avoid damaging them.*

3. Insert a thin blade screwdriver between the grip and handlebar or throttle sleeve and spray electrical contact cleaner into the open gap (**Figure 14**). Quickly turn the grip to break the cement bond and slide it off (**Figure 15**).
4. If reusing the grips, use an electrical contact cleaner to remove all cement residue from inside the grips.
5. Replace the grips if damaged.
6. Remove all sealant residue from the handlebar or throttle sleeve.
7. To service the handlebar weight (if so equipped), perform the following:
    a. Squeeze the lock arms on the end of the handlebar weight (**Figure 16**) and pull the weight assembly from the handlebar. Refer to **Figure 17**.

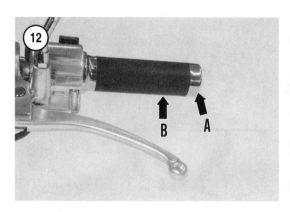

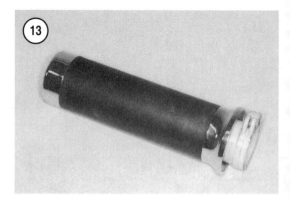

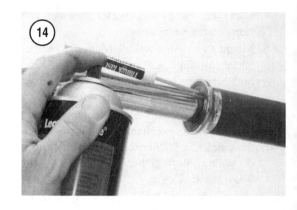

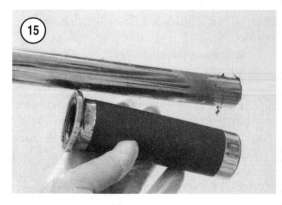

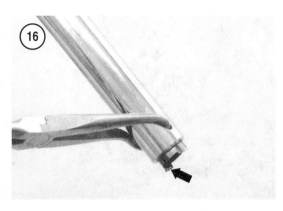

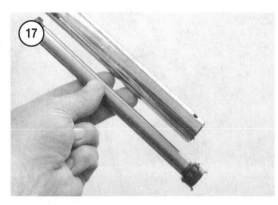

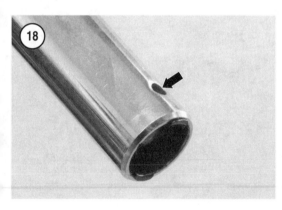

b. Inspect the handlebar weight for damage. Replace if necessary.

c. Slide the handlebar weight into the handlebar with the lock arms facing out (**Figure 17**).

d. Position the weight so the lock arms spring out and lock into the holes in the handlebar (**Figure 18**).

8. Install the left handlebar switch (**Figure 19**) before installing the grip. This prevents the grip from being installed too far onto handlebar.

NOTE
When using a grip cement in the next step, follow the manufacturer's instructions for application and drying time.

9. Apply Honda Grip Cement, ThreeBond Griplock or an equivalent grip cement onto the left side of the handlebar or onto the outside of the throttle sleeve. Install the grip as follows:

a. Install the grip with the end cap installed on the grip.

b. Install the left side grip until it almost contacts the left switch housing. When the grip is positioned correctly, remove the left switch housing and clean excess cement from the end of the grip, handlebar and left switch housing.

c. Install the right side grip onto the throttle sleeve to the dimension recorded in Step 2. Wipe off all excess cement.

WARNING
Do not ride the motorcycle until the appropriate amount of drying time specified by the manufacturer has elapsed; otherwise loose or damaged hand grips can slide off and cause loss of steering control. Make sure the hand grips are correctly installed and cemented in place before operating the motorcycle.

FRONT FORK

The following sections describe complete service and adjustment of the front forks. To prevent damaging the fork when servicing it, note the following:

1. To avoid rounding off the shoulders on the fork caps, use a 6-point socket when loosening and tightening the fork caps.

12

2. Do not overtighten the fork tube pinch bolts because this can damage the fork bridge threads and fork tubes. Always refer to the torque specifications.

3. The fork tubes and sliders are easily scratched. Handle them carefully during all service procedures.

Front Fork Removal

1. Note the routing of the throttle and clutch cables for reassembly reference.

2. On VT1100T models, remove the windshield (Chapter Fifteen).

3. Remove the front wheel (Chapter Eleven).

4. If the fork is going to be disassembled, loosen, but do not remove, the Allen bolt in the bottom of each fork tube (**Figure 20**).

5. On all models except the VT1100C3, remove the speedometer cable from its clamp or guide (A, **Figure 21**, typical).

6A. On VT1100C models, remove the brake hose from the clamp on the front fender.

6B. On all other models, remove the bolt (B, **Figure 21**) securing the front brake hose to the front fender.

NOTE
Do not remove the brake hose banjo bolt when removing the brake caliper.

7. Remove the bolts (C, **Figure 21**) and the front brake caliper. Support the caliper with a piece of stiff wire.

8. Unbolt and remove the front fender.

9. Loosen the top fork tube pinch bolt (A, **Figure 22**, typical).

10. If the fork tube is going to disassembled, loosen, but do not remove, the fork cap (B, **Figure 22**).

11. On VT1100T, VT1100C2 ACE and VT1100T models, perform the following:
    a. Remove the bolt, collar and turn signal light from the fork tube (**Figure 23**).
    b. Support the turn signal assembly with a piece of stiff wire.

12. While supporting fork tube, loosen the lower fork tube pinch bolt (**Figure 24**, typical) and remove fork tube.

NOTE
Rust and corrosion built up around the fork tube and steering stem clamp surfaces can lock the fork tube in

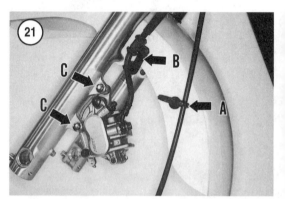

place. Support the fork tube and spray the top area of each clamp with a penetrating oil.

13. Remove the other fork tube.

Front Fork Installation

1. Clean the fork tube pinch bolts and fork bridge threads.

2. Slide the fork tube through the lower and upper fork bridges. Position the fork so the top of the fork

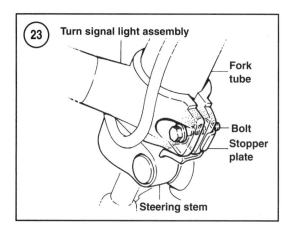

(23) Turn signal light assembly

Fork tube

Bolt

Stopper plate

Steering stem

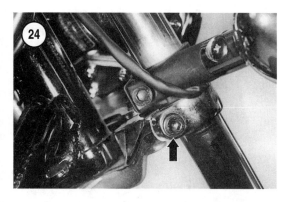

(24)

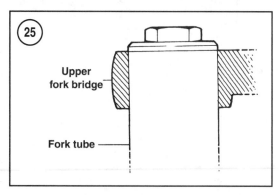

(25)

Upper fork bridge

Fork tube

a. On VT1100C2 Sabre models, tighten to 26 N•m (19 ft.-lb.).

b. On VT1100C3 models, tighten to 23 N•m (17 ft.-lb.).

c. On all other models, tighten to 11 N•m (97 in.-lb.).

NOTE
Make sure any cables or wiring harnesses are routed correctly around the fork tubes. Refer to the notes made before removing the fork tubes.

5. On VT1100T, VT1100C2 ACE and VT1100T models, install the turn signal assembly and position it with the stopper plate, collar and bolt (**Figure 23**). Tighten the front turn signal stopper plate bolt to 9 N•m (80 in.-lb.).

6. Install the front fender and the front brake hose clamp (if used). Tighten the bolts securely.

7. On all models except the VT1100C3, install the speedometer cable through its guide (A, **Figure 21** typical).

8. Install the front brake caliper using two new mounting bolts (C, **Figure 21**) and tighten as follows:

a. On VT1100C models, tighten to 45 N•m (33 ft.-lb.).

b. On all other models, tighten to 30 N•m (22 ft.-lb.).

9A. On VT1100C models, install the brake hose into its clamp on the front fender.

9B. On all other models, secure the brake hose with its clamp (B, **Figure 21**) and tighten the mounting bolt as follows:

a. On VT1100C2 ACE and VT1100T models, tighten to 12 N•m (106 in.-lb.).

b. On all other models, tighten the bolt securely.

10. Install the front wheel (Chapter Eleven).

WARNING
After installing the front wheel, operate the front brake lever to reposition the caliper pistons. If the brake lever feels spongy, bleed the brakes as described in Chapter Fourteen.

Disassembly

This section describes complete disassembly of the fork tubes. If only changing the fork oil and/or

tube is flush with the top bridge surface (**Figure 25**). Tighten the lower fork tube pinch bolt (**Figure 24**) to 49 N•m (36 ft.-lb.).

3. Tighten the fork cap (B, **Figure 22**) as follows:

a. On VT1100C2 models, tighten to 22 N•m (16 ft.-lb.).

b. On all other models, tighten to 23 N•m (17 ft.-lb.).

4. Tighten the upper fork tube pinch bolt (A, **Figure 22**, typical) as follows:

12

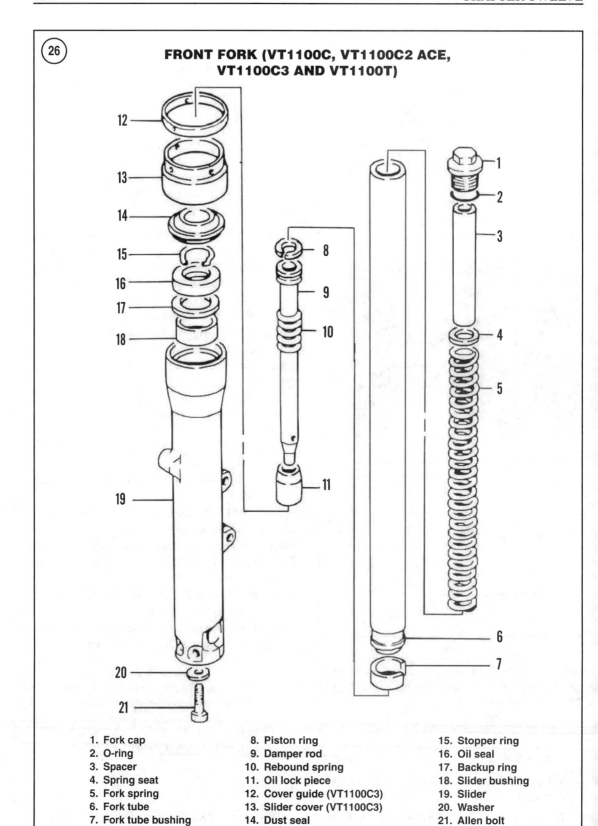

FRONT FORK (VT1100C, VT1100C2 ACE, VT1100C3 AND VT1100T)

1. Fork cap
2. O-ring
3. Spacer
4. Spring seat
5. Fork spring
6. Fork tube
7. Fork tube bushing
8. Piston ring
9. Damper rod
10. Rebound spring
11. Oil lock piece
12. Cover guide (VT1100C3)
13. Slider cover (VT1100C3)
14. Dust seal
15. Stopper ring
16. Oil seal
17. Backup ring
18. Slider bushing
19. Slider
20. Washer
21. Allen bolt

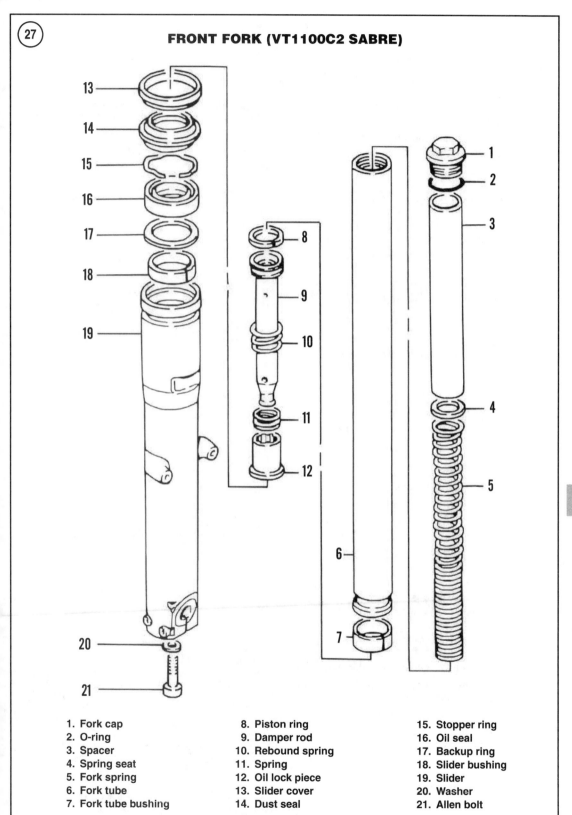

(27)

FRONT FORK (VT1100C2 SABRE)

1. Fork cap
2. O-ring
3. Spacer
4. Spring seat
5. Fork spring
6. Fork tube
7. Fork tube bushing
8. Piston ring
9. Damper rod
10. Rebound spring
11. Spring
12. Oil lock piece
13. Slider cover
14. Dust seal
15. Stopper ring
16. Oil seal
17. Backup ring
18. Slider bushing
19. Slider
20. Washer
21. Allen bolt

12

setting the oil level, begin at Step 1 and follow the required steps listed in the text.

Refer to **Figure 26** or **Figure 27**.

1. Remove the fork tube as described in this chapter.

2. Bolt a flat metal plate onto the fork tube and clamp the metal plate (**Figure 28**) in a vise to support the fork tube when loosening and tightening the fork tube Allen bolt.

> *NOTE*
> *If only changing the fork oil and/or setting the oil level, disregard the steps pertaining to loosening the fork tube Allen bolt in Step 3.*

> *NOTE*
> *Disregard Step 3 if the fork tube Allen bolt was loosened during fork removal.*

> *NOTE*
> *When loosening the Allen bolt in the bottom of the fork tube, leave the fork assembled until the Allen bolt is loosened. The internal spring pressure against the damper rod helps hold it in place as the Allen bolt is being loosened.*

3. Loosen the fork tube Allen bolt as follows:
   a. Clean the Allen bolt recess.
   b. Have an assistant compress the fork tube assembly as much as possible and hold it compressed against the damper rod. Then loosen, but do not remove, the fork tube Allen bolt (**Figure 29**).

> *WARNING*
> *The fork cap is under spring pressure. Wear safety goggles or a face shield when removing the fork cap.*

4. Slowly unscrew and remove the fork cap and its O-ring. Then remove the spacer, spring seat and fork spring (**Figure 30**). Place a plastic tie on the fork spring to identify its upper end.

5. Turn the fork tube over a drain pan and operate the fork several times to drain the oil.

> *NOTE*
> *If only changing the fork oil and/or setting the oil level, go to the **Fork Oil Adjustment** procedure at the end of*

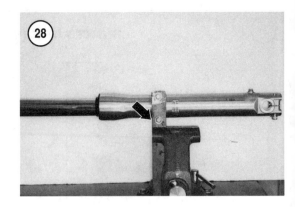
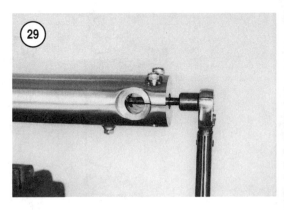
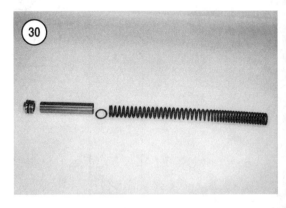
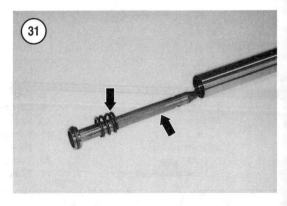

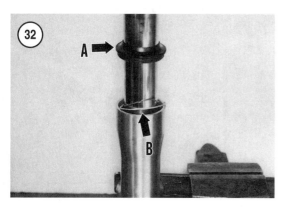

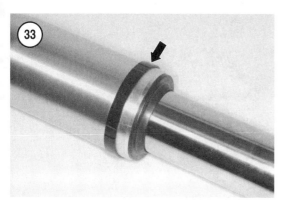

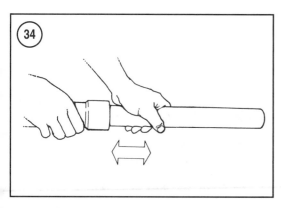

this section. If disassembling the fork, continue with Step 6.

6. On VT1100C3 models, remove the cover guide (12, **Figure 26**) and slider cover (13) from the top of the slider.

7. Remove the Allen bolt, previously loosened, and washer from the base of the slider. Discard the washer. Discard the Allen bolt if the recess in the bolt head is starting to round out.

8. Turn the fork over and slide out the damper rod and rebound spring (**Figure 31**).

CAUTION
Do not use excessive force when removing the dust seal in Step 9. Carefully pry the seal out of the slider with a suitable tool. Move the tool around the seal in small increments. It is easy to scratch and damage the slider at the top of the dust seal bore. When selecting a starting point, choose the side facing in (toward the wheel).

9. Pry the dust seal (A, **Figure 32**) out of the slider and slide it off the fork tube.

NOTE
*On the VT1100C2 Sabre, do not remove the slider cover (**Figure 33**) unless it is going to be replaced.*

10. Slip the tip of a small screwdriver behind the stopper ring and carefully pry the ring out of the slider groove (B, **Figure 32**) and remove it.

NOTE
A pressed-in bushing in the slider and a bushing on the fork tube keep the slider and fork tube from separating. To remove the fork tube from the slider, use these parts as a slide hammer as described in Step 11.

11. Hold the fork tube and pull hard on the slider, using quick in-and-out strokes (**Figure 34**). Doing so withdraws the oil seal, backup ring and slider bushing from the slider. Refer to **Figure 35**.

12. Remove the slider and pour any remaining oil in the oil pan.

13. Remove the oil lock piece from the slider if it did not come out in Step 11. A, **Figure 36** shows the plastic oil lock piece used on the VT1100C2 Sabre. All other models use an aluminum oil lock piece.

12

14. Slide off the oil seal (B, **Figure 36**), backup ring (C) and slider bushing (D) off the fork tube. Discard the dust seal and oil seal.

NOTE
Do not remove the fork tube bushing
*(E, **Figure 36**) unless it is going to be*
replaced. Inspect it as described in
this section.

Fork Inspection

When measuring the fork components, compare the actual measurements to the specifications in **Table 2**. Replace worn or damaged parts as described in this section.

1. Thoroughly clean all parts in solvent and dry them. Remove all threadlocking compound from the damper rod and Allen bolt threads.

2. Inspect the fork tube for excessive wear or scratches. Check the chrome for flaking, pitting or other damage that could damage the oil seal.

3. Check the fork tube for straightness. Place the fork tube on V-blocks and measure runout with a dial indicator. If the runout is excessive (**Table 2**), replace the fork tube.

4. Inspect the slider for dents or exterior damage. Check the stopper ring groove for cracks or damage. Inspect the oil seal mounting bore for dents or other damage.

5. Inspect the damper rod (A, **Figure 37**) for straightness, damage or roughness.

6. Inspect the piston ring (B, **Figure 37**) on the end of the damper rod for wear or damage. Replace if necessary.

7. Inspect the rebound spring (C, **Figure 37**) on the damper rod for cracks or other damage.

8. Inspect the oil lock piece (D, **Figure 37**) for wear or damage. On VT1100C2 Sabre models, check the spring installed inside the oil lock piece for cracks and other damage.

9. Measure the free length of the fork spring (**Figure 38**) with a tape measure. Replace the spring if it is too short (**Table 2**). Replace the springs as a set if they are unequal in length.

10. Inspect the fork tube (A, **Figure 39**) and slider (B) bushings for scoring, excessive wear or damage. Check for discoloration and material coating damage. If the coating is worn off so the base material is showing on approximately 3/4 of the total

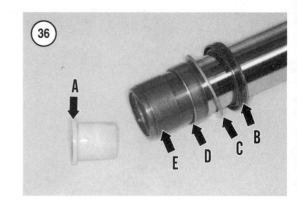

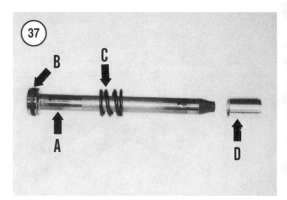

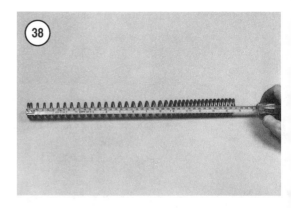

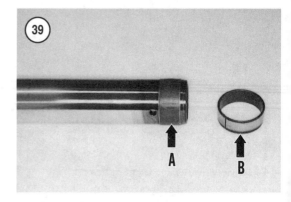

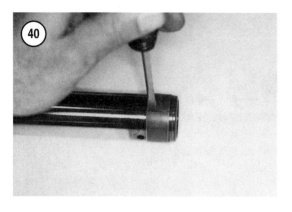

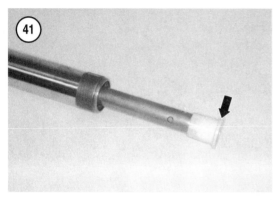

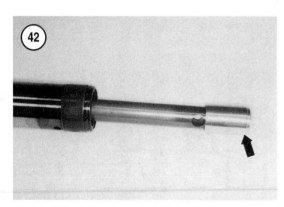

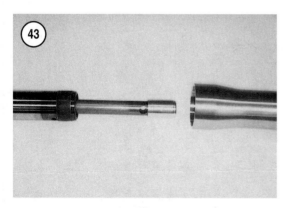

surface, the bushing is excessively worn. Replace both bushings (**Figure 39**) as a set.

11. To replace the fork tube bushing, pry its slot open with a screwdriver (**Figure 40**) and slide it off the fork tube. Clean the groove on the bottom of the fork tube, then install the new bushing until it seats fully in the groove (A, **Figure 39**).

12. Replace the fork cap O-ring if damaged or leaking.

13. On VT1100C2 Sabre models, replace the slider cover (**Figure 33**) if excessively worn or damaged.

Assembly

Refer to **Figure 26** or **Figure 27**.

1. Before assembling the parts, make sure there is no solvent left in the slider or on any part.

2. Coat the bushings with new fork oil before installation.

3. Install the rebound spring onto the damper rod and slide the damper rod assembly through the fork tube (**Figure 31**).

4. Temporarily install the fork spring, spacer and fork cap to apply tension against the damper rod.

5. Install the oil lock piece onto the end of the damper rod. Refer to **Figure 41** (VT1100C2 Sabre) or **Figure 42** (all other models).

NOTE
On VT1100C2 Sabre models, the shoulder on the oil lock piece must face toward the end of the damper rod.

6. Mount the slider in a vise by attaching a piece of metal to the fender mounting holes.

7. Carefully install the fork tube and the damper rod into the slider (**Figure 43**) until the oil lock piece bottoms against the slider.

8. Install a new washer onto the Allen bolt.

9. Install a medium strength threadlock onto the fork tube Allen bolt threads and thread the Allen bolt into the bottom of the damper rod (**Figure 44**) and tighten until the damper rod starts to turn. Have an assistant compress the fork tube as much as possible and tighten the fork tube Allen bolt (**Figure 29**) to the specification in **Table 3**.

10. Remove the fork cap, spacer and fork spring.

12

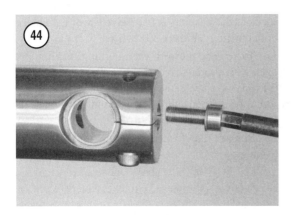

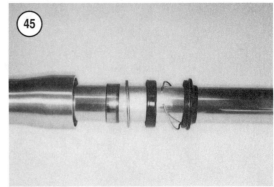

11. Using the same piece of metal to hold the fork assembly, position the slider in the vise so the fork tube faces straight up.

12. **Figure 45** shows the alignment of the bushing and seal assembly.

13. Install the fork slider bushing and backup ring as follows:

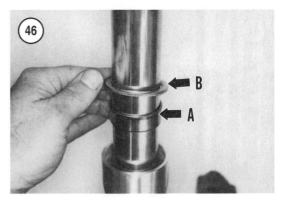

    a. Slide the bushing (A, **Figure 46**) and backup ring (B) down the fork tube. Install the backup ring with its chamfered side facing down and set it on top of the bushing.

    b. Use a fork oil seal driver (**Figure 47**) to drive the bushing into the fork slider until it bottoms out in the recess in the slider. The knocking sound made by the driver changes when the bushing bottoms out.

> *NOTE*
> *Motion Pro fork oil seal drivers, or equivalent, can be purchased from aftermarket suppliers. To select a driver, first measure the fork tube's outside diameter.*

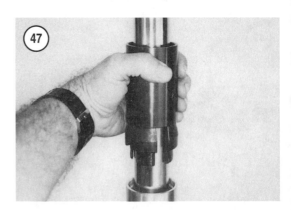

14. Install a new fork seal as follows:

    a. To avoid damaging the fork seal and dust seal when installing them over the top of the fork tube, place a plastic bag over the fork tube and lubricate it with fork oil.

    b. Lubricate the seal lips with fork oil.

    c. Install the seal (**Figure 48**) over the fork tube with its manufacturer's name and size code facing up. Slide it down the fork tube and center it into the top of the slider until its outer surface is flush with the slider's outer bore surface.

    d. Drive the oil seal into the slider with the same tool (**Figure 47**) used in Step 13.

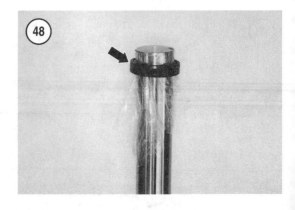

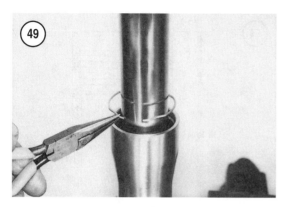

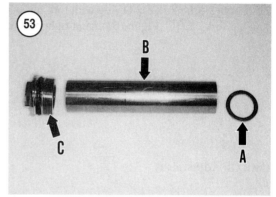

e. Continue to install the seal until the groove in the slider can be seen above the top surface of the seal.

15. Slide the stopper ring (**Figure 49**) over the fork tube and install it into the groove in the slider. Make sure the stopper ring is completely seated in the slider groove (**Figure 50**).

NOTE
If the stopper ring cannot seat completely into the slider groove, the seal is not installed far enough into the slider.

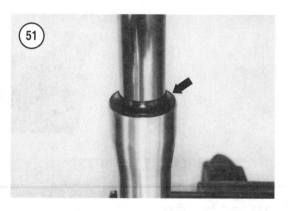

16. Slide the dust seal over the plastic bag and seat it into the slider (**Figure 51**). Remove the plastic bag.

17. On VT1100C3 models, install the slider cover (13, **Figure 26**) over the fork tube and seat it onto the slider with its punch mark facing away from the axle pinch bolts on the slider. Install the cover guide (12, **Figure 26**) and seat it into the groove in the top of the slider.

18. Fill the fork with oil and set the oil level as described under *Fork Oil Adjustment* in this section.

19. Install the spring with its closer wound spring end (**Figure 52**) facing down. If an aftermarket spring was installed, install it facing in its original position. If a plastic tie was used to identify the spring, install the spring with the plastic tie end facing up. Cut and remove the plastic tie from the fork tube.

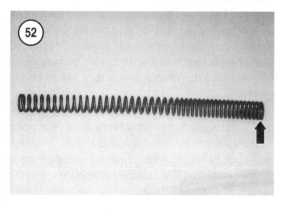

20. Install the spring seat (A, **Figure 53**) and spacer (B).

21. Install a new O-ring onto the fork cap, if needed.

22. Lubricate the fork cap O-ring with fork oil. Install the fork cap (C, **Figure 53**) hand-tight at this time.

> *NOTE*
> *The fork cap is tightened completely after the fork tube is installed onto the motorcycle.*

Fork Oil Adjustment

This section describes steps on filling the fork with oil and setting the oil level. Refer to **Table 2** for the recommended type of fork oil and the fork oil service specifications.

1. Remove the fork spring and drain the fork tube as described under *Disassembly* in this section.

2. Push the fork tube down and bottom out against the slider. Support the slider so it cannot tip over.

3. Slowly pour the recommended type of fork oil (**Table 2**) into the fork.

> *NOTE*
> *As oil replaces air during the bleeding procedure, the oil level in the fork drops. Continue to add oil to maintain a high oil level in the fork. When bleeding the fork tube, do not be concerned with maintaining or achieving the proper oil capacity. Setting the oil level determines the actual amount of oil used in each fork tube.*

4. Hold the slider with one hand and slowly extend the fork tube. Repeat until the fork tube moves smoothly with the same amount of tension through the compression and rebound travel strokes. Then stop with the fork tube bottomed out.

5. Set the fork tube aside for approximately 5 minutes to allow any suspended air bubbles in the oil to surface.

6. Set the oil level (**Figure 54**) as follows:

   a. Make sure the fork tube is bottomed against the slider and placed in a vertical position.

   b. Use an oil level gauge (**Figure 55**) and set the oil level to the specification listed in **Table 2**.

7. Complete fork assembly as described under *Assembly* in this section.

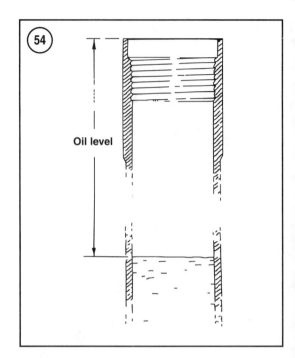

Oil level

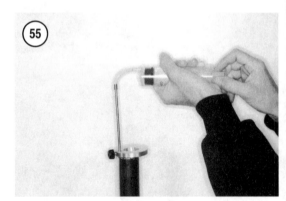

STEERING HEAD AND STEM

The steering head uses retainer-type steel bearings. Each bearing consists of an inner race, outer race and bearing. The bearings can be lifted out of their operating positions after removing the steering stem. Do not remove the lower inner race (pressed onto the steering stem) or the outer bearing races (pressed into the frame) unless they are to be replaced.

Regular maintenance consists of steering inspection, adjustment and bearing lubrication. When the steering cannot be adjusted correctly, the bearings may require replacement. However, to determine bearing condition, the steering assembly must be removed and inspected. Inspect the steering adjust-

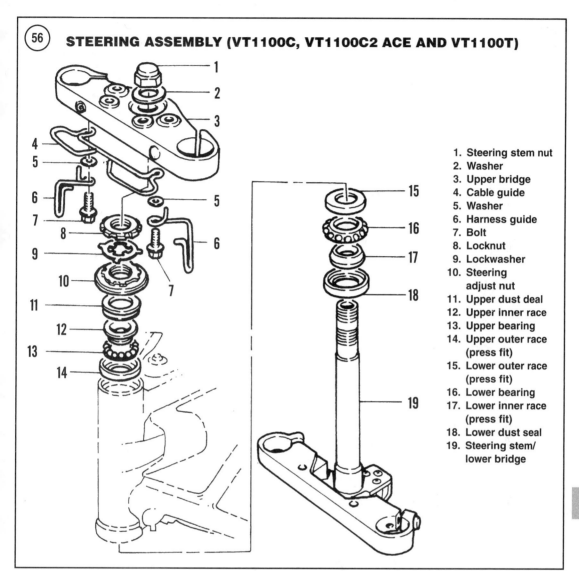

56   STEERING ASSEMBLY (VT1100C, VT1100C2 ACE AND VT1100T)

1. Steering stem nut
2. Washer
3. Upper bridge
4. Cable guide
5. Washer
6. Harness guide
7. Bolt
8. Locknut
9. Lockwasher
10. Steering
    adjust nut
11. Upper dust deal
12. Upper inner race
13. Upper bearing
14. Upper outer race
    (press fit)
15. Lower outer race
    (press fit)
16. Lower bearing
17. Lower inner race
    (press fit)
18. Lower dust seal
19. Steering stem/
    lower bridge

ment and lubricate the bearings at the intervals listed in the maintenance schedule in Chapter Three.

This section describes complete service and adjustment procedures for the steering head assembly.

Refer to **Figure 56** (VT1100C, VT1100C2 ACE and VT1100T) or **Figure 57** (VT1100C2 Sabre and VT1100C3).

Special Tools

The Honda steering stem socket (part No. 07916-3710100 or equivalent) and a spring scale are required to adjust the steering stem/bearing. These tools are shown in the appropriate procedure.

Refer to *Steering Head Bearing Race Replacement* and *Steering Stem Bearing Race Replacement* in this chapter for bearing race replacement procedures and special tools.

Troubleshooting

Before removing the steering assembly to troubleshoot a steering complaint, refer to *Front Steering and Suspension* in Chapter Two. Refer to the topic that most identifies the problem and check the items listed as possible causes.

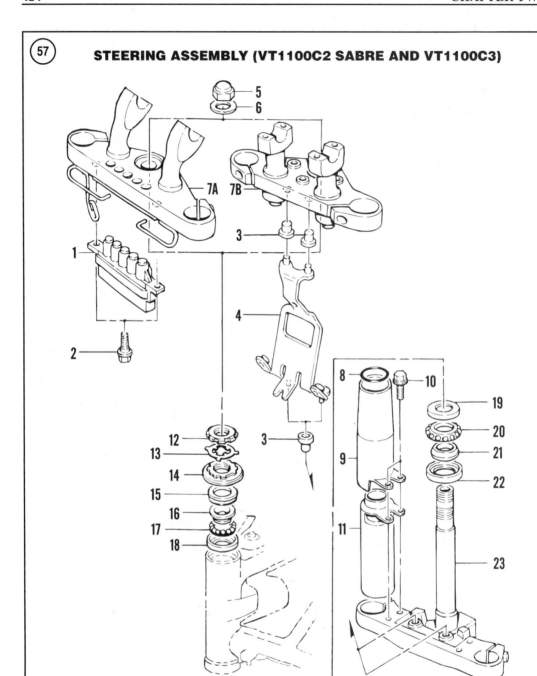

57 **STEERING ASSEMBLY (VT1100C2 SABRE AND VT1100C3)**

1. Indicator box (VT1100C3)
2. Bolts (VT1100C3)
3. Rubber grommets
   (VT1100C2 SABRE)
4. Headlight mounting bracket
   (VT1100C2 SABRE)
5. Steering stem nut
6. Washer
7A. Upper bridge (VT1100C3)
7B. Upper bridge (VT110C2 SABRE)

8. O-ring
9. Upper cover
10. Bolt
11. Lower cover
12. Locknut
13. Lockwasher
14. Steering adjust nut
15. Upper dust seal
16. Upper inner race
17. Upper bearing

18. Upper outer race
    (press fit)
19. Lower outer race
    (press fit)
20. Lower bearing
21. Lower inner race
    (press fit)
22. Lower dust seal
23. Steering stem/
    lower bridge

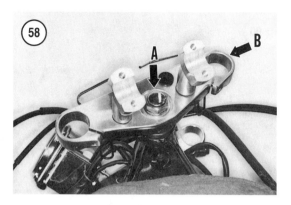

Removal

Refer to **Figure 56** or **Figure 57**.

NOTE
Note the cable and wiring harness routing from the handlebar and around the steering stem and front forks for reassembly reference.

1A. On VT1100C, VT1100C2 ACE and VT1100T models, perform the following:

   a. Remove the headlight and headlight housing (Chapter Nine).

   b. Remove the speedometer (Chapter Nine).

   c. Remove the handlebar as described in this chapter.

   d. Remove the brake hose clamp and cable guide from the steering stem (if so equipped).

1B. On VT1100C2 Sabre models, perform the following:

   a. Remove the headlight and headlight housing (Chapter Nine).

   b. Remove the handlebar as described in this chapter.

   c. Remove the turn signal assembly.

   d. Remove the bolt and the brake hose clamp from the steering stem.

   e. Disconnect the speedometer cable and the speedometer black 6-pin connector.

   f. Remove the left and right side handlebar switch wiring harnesses from the harness guide.

   g. Remove the bolts and the speedometer bracket and harness guide from the upper fork bridge.

1C. On VT1100C3 models, perform the following:

   a. Remove the headlight and headlight housing (Chapter Nine).

   b. Remove the handlebar as described in this chapter.

   c. Remove the bolt and the brake hose clamp from the steering stem.

   d. Remove the bolts and the indicator box from the upper fork bridge.

   e. Remove the throttle and clutch cables from the cables guides on the upper fork bridge.

NOTE
At this point there should be no cables, brake hose or wiring harnesses interfering with the movement of the steering stem. Check by turning the steering stem. If so, reposition the item so the steering stem can move with no interference.

2. Before loosening the steering stem nut, check the steering adjustment as described under *Steering Bearing Preload Check* in this chapter.

3. Remove the front wheel (Chapter Eleven).

4. Loosen the steering stem nut.

5. Remove the front forks as described in this chapter.

6. On VT1100C2 Sabre and VT1100C3 models, remove the mounting bolts and the upper and lower fork covers. Locate the O-rings installed inside the upper covers.

7. Remove the steering stem nut (A, **Figure 58**), washer, and the upper fork bridge (B). On VT1100C2 Sabre models, remove the headlight mounting bracket.

8. Pry the lockwasher tabs (**Figure 59**) away from the locknut grooves. Then remove the locknut (A, **Figure 60**) and lockwasher (B). Discard the lockwasher.

NOTE
Before loosening the steering adjust nut, turn the steering stem from

12

lock-to-lock to check the steering adjustment.

9. Loosen the steering adjust nut with the Honda steering stem socket (part No. 07916-3710100 or equivalent), a fabricated tool made from a piece of pipe or deep socket or a spanner wrench (**Figure 61**).

10. Support the steering stem and remove the following:

    a. Steering adjust nut and steering stem.

    b. Upper dust seal.

    c. Upper inner race and bearing assembly (**Figure 62**).

> *NOTE*
> *The upper outer race, lower outer race and lower inner race are installed with a press fit. Do not remove these parts unless they are going to be replaced.*

11. Remove the lower bearing from the lower outer race (A, **Figure 63**).

Inspection

Replace parts that show excessive wear or damage as described in this section.

> *WARNING*
> *The improper repair of damaged frame and steering components can cause the loss of steering control. If there is apparent frame, steering stem or fork bridge damage, consult with a Honda dealership or qualified frame shop for professional inspection and possible repair.*

1. Clean and dry all parts. Make certain the cleaning solution is compatible with the rubber dust seals.

2. Check the frame for cracks and fractures.

3. Inspect the steering stem nut, locknut, and steering adjust nut for excessive wear or damage.

4. Inspect the upper dust seal for tearing, deterioration or other damage.

5. Check the steering stem (**Figure 64**) for:

    a. Cracked or bent stem.

    b. Damaged lower bridge.

    c. Damaged threads.

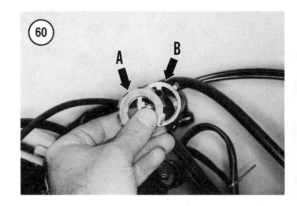

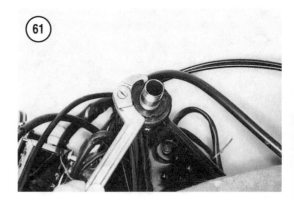

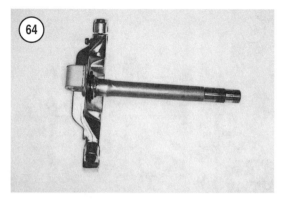

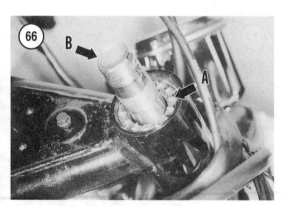

6. Check the upper bridge for cracks or other damage. Replace if necessary.

7. Inspect the bearing assemblies as follows:

  a. Inspect the bearing races for excessive wear, pitting, cracks or other damage. To replace the outer bearing races, refer to *Steering Head Bearing Race Replacement* in this chapter. To replace the lower inner bearing race, refer to *Steering Stem Bearing Race Replacement* in this chapter.

  b. Inspect the upper and lower bearings (**Figure 65**) for dents, pitting, excessive wear, corrosion, retainer damage or discoloration.

  c. Replace the upper and lower bearing assemblies at the same time.

NOTE
Each bearing assembly consists of the bearing and an inner and outer race. Always replace the bearings in upper and lower sets.

8. When reusing bearings, clean them thoroughly with a bearing degreaser and dry thoroughly. Repack each bearing with grease.

Steering Stem Assembly and Steering Adjustment

1. Make sure the upper and lower outer bearing races are properly seated in the steering head. Then lubricate each bearing race with grease.

2. Thoroughly lubricate each bearing with grease.

3. Lubricate the upper dust seal (bottom side) with grease and set aside until installation.

4. Lower bearing:

  a. Lubricate the lower outer bearing race and dust seal lip (B, **Figure 63**) with grease.

  b. Install the lower bearing (A, **Figure 63**).

5. Upper bearing and steering stem:

  a. Lubricate the upper inner bearing race and bearing with grease.

  b. Install the upper bearing (A, **Figure 66**).

  c. Install the steering stem (B, **Figure 66**) into the steering head and through the upper bearing and hold in place. Make sure the lower bearing is centered against the lower outer race.

  d. Install the upper inner race (**Figure 67**) and seat it against the bearing (**Figure 68**).

12

6. Install the upper dust seal (**Figure 69**) and seat it over the bearing assembly.

> *NOTE*
> *The steering stem, steering stem nut and steering adjust nut threads must be clean for accurate tightening of these fasteners. Any dirt, grease or other residue on the threads can affect the steering stem tightening torque and bearing preload adjustment.*

7. Lubricate the steering adjust nut threads with oil and thread it onto the steering stem (**Figure 70**). Tighten finger-tight.

8. Tighten the steering adjust nut (**Figure 70**) as follows:

   a. Use the Honda steering stem socket or equivalent to seat the bearings in the following steps. Refer to *Special Tools* in this section.

> *NOTE*
> *If the Honda tool is not available, use a spanner wrench and torque wrench (**Figure 71**) to seat the bearings. Refer to **Torque Wrench Adapters** in Chapter One for information on using these tools.*

   b. Tighten the steering adjust nut (**Figure 72**) to 21 N•m (15.5 ft.-lb.).

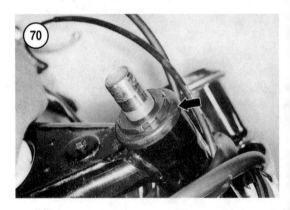

   c. Turn the steering stem from lock-to-lock five times to seat the bearings. The steering stem must pivot smoothly. Retighten the steering adjust nut to 21 N•m (15.5 ft.-lb.).

> *NOTE*
> *If the steering stem does not pivot smoothly, one or both bearing assemblies may be damaged. Remove the steering stem and inspect the bearings.*

> *NOTE*
> *Do not continue with Step 9 until the steering stem turns correctly. If there is any excessive play or roughness, recheck the steering adjustment.*

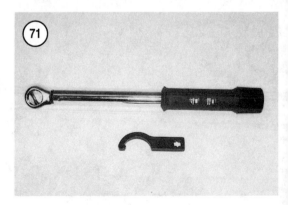

9. Align the tabs of a *new* lockwasher with the grooves in the steering adjust nut and install the lockwasher (**Figure 73**). The outer two tabs bend into the locknut grooves.

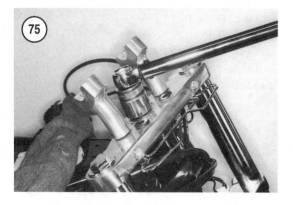

CAUTION
Never reinstall a used lockwasher be-
cause the tabs may break off, making
the lockwasher ineffective.

11. Install and tighten the locknut as follows:
   a. Install the locknut (**Figure 74**) and tighten finger-tight.
   b. Hold the steering adjust nut (to keep it from turning) and tighten the locknut approximately 1/4 turn (90°) to align its grooves with the outer lockwasher tabs.
   c. Bend the outer lockwasher tabs (**Figure 59**) up into the locknut grooves.

12A. On VT1100C2 Sabre models, install the headlight mounting bracket (**Figure 57**) onto the steering stem and install the upper bridge, washer and steering stem nut. Check that the headlight mounting bracket seats correctly into the upper and lower steering stem bridges.

12B. On all other models, install the upper bridge (B, **Figure 58**), washer and steering stem nut (A).

13. On VT1100C2 Sabre and VT1100C3 models, install new O-rings into the upper fork covers. Then install the upper and lower fork covers (**Figure 57**) and tighten the mounting bolts securely.

14. Temporarily install the fork tubes.

15. Tighten the steering stem nut (**Figure 75**) as follows:
   a. On VT1100C ACE models, tighten to 105 N•m (77 ft.-lb.).
   b. On all other models, tighten to 103 N•m (76 ft.-lb.).

16. Turn the steering stem lock-to-lock. Make sure it moves smoothly. There must be no play or binding. Note the following:
   a. If the steering stem turns correctly, continue with Step 17.
   b. If the steering stem is too loose or tight, remove the steering stem nut, washer and upper bridge. Then readjust the steering adjust nut. Repeat until the steering play feels correct. Damaged bearings and races can also cause tightness.

NOTE
If the steering adjustment is too loose,
the steering becomes unstable and
causes front wheel wobble. If the
steering adjustment is too tight, the
bearings eventually score or notch the
races. The steering then become slug-
gish because the damaged bearings

and races operate roughly against
each other. Both conditions hamper
steering performance.

NOTE
Arriving at the proper steering adjust-
ment usually comes down to the steer-
ing effort required to turn the
handlebar. The number of attempts
required to arrive at the correct steer-
ing adjustment (feel) can vary consid-
erably.

17. Install the front fork as described in this chapter.
18. Install the front wheel (Chapter Eleven).
19. Reverse Step 1 to complete installation. Refer to
the disassembly notes on the correct routing of the
cables and wiring harnesses. Tighten the front brake
hose clamp bolt (if used) to 12 N•m (106 in.-lb.).
20. Perform the *Steering Bearing Preload Check*
described in this chapter.

WARNING
Do not ride the motorcycle until all of
the lights, controls and brakes work
properly.

NOTE
The steering bearing preload check
measures the amount of weight re-
quired to move the steering stem. This
check confirms whether the steering
adjustment is correct.

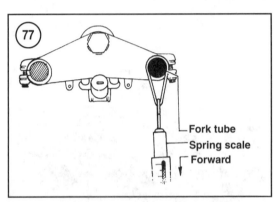

Fork tube
Spring scale
Forward

STEERING BEARING PRELOAD CHECK

Proper steering bearing preload is important because it controls bearing play and steering control.
If the preload is too loose, excessive play in the
steering allows the wheel to wobble, which is best
defined as a slight to excessive side-to-side movement or oscillation of the handlebars. A wobble may
occur at all vehicle speeds or start and stop at certain
speeds. In all respects, it is a frustrating condition
and can be difficult to troubleshoot. If the preload is
too tight, the bearings and races suffer unnecessary
wear and cause stiff and uneven steering, requiring
the rider to make a greater steering effort when turning the handlebars. Dry or damaged bearings can
cause similar conditions.

Check the steering head for looseness at the intervals specified in Chapter Three or whenever the following symptoms or conditions exist:

1. The handlebars vibrate more than normal.
2. The front fork makes a clicking or clunking
noise when the front brake is applied.
3. The steering feels tight or slow.
4. The motorcycle does not steer straight on level
road surfaces.

Inspection

When installing the steering stem assembly, the
steering bearings are preloaded (bearings placed
under pressure) by carefully tightening the steering

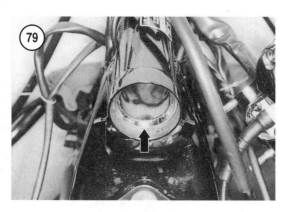

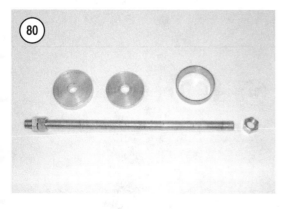

3. Attach a plastic zip tie onto one of the fork tubes (between the fork bridges). Then attach a spring scale onto the zip tie (**Figure 76**).

4. Center the wheel. Position the spring scale at a 90° angle with the steering stem (**Figure 77**). Pull the spring scale and note the reading on the scale when the steering stem begins to turn. This reading is steering stem bearing preload. Refer to **Table 1** for the correct steering preload reading.

5. If the preload reading is incorrect, adjust the steering assembly as described under *Steering Stem Assembly* and *Steering Adjustment* in this chapter. Perform the adjustment with the front fork and front wheel mounted on the motorcycle.

> *WARNING*
> *Do not ride the motorcycle until the horn, cables and brakes all work properly.*

STEERING HEAD BEARING RACE REPLACEMENT

The steering head bearing races (**Figure 78** and **Figure 79**) are pressed into the frame's steering head. The bearing races should only be removed when installing new races.

Use a threaded rod and disc tool (**Figure 80**) to install the races. When properly used, this tool exerts even pressure around the race. One disc is sized to fit the outer diameter of the races, while the other disc is slightly larger than the diameter of the steering head.

> *NOTE*
> *The following procedure describes home techniques to remove the bearing races. If removal is difficult, do not chance damage to the frame or new bearing races. Have the task performed by a Honda dealership or a qualified specialist.*

Replace both bearing races and bearings at the same time.

> *CAUTION*
> *If binding occurs when removing or installing the bearing races, stop and release tension from the bearing race. Check the tool alignment to make sure the bearing race is moving evenly in its mounting bore. Otherwise, the*

adjust nut and the steering stem nut. When the bearings are lubricated and correctly preloaded, the bearings should not move out of alignment. To check bearing preload, Honda specifies the use of a spring scale attached to one of the fork tubes. This method measures the amount of weight required to move the steering stem with the front end assembled and the front wheel off the ground. When measuring bearing preload with a spring scale, the steering stem must be free to turn without interference from cables, hoses or wiring harnesses.

A spring scale is required for this procedure.

> *NOTE*
> *This procedure must be performed with the front fork and front wheel mounted on the motorcycle.*

1. Support the motorcycle so it is sitting level with the front wheel off the ground.

2. Turn the steering stem side to side. There should be no interference or drag from a cable, wire harness or the front brake hose when the steering stem is rotated. If there still interference, reposition or remove the affecting part as required.

12

bearing race may gouge the frame mounting bore and cause permanent damage.

1. Chill the new bearing races in a freezer for a few hours to shrink the outer diameter of the race as much as possible.

2. Insert a drift into the steering head and position it on the edge of the lower race (**Figure 81**). Carefully drive out the race. To prevent binding, make several passes around the perimeter of the race. Repeat the procedure to remove the upper race.

3. Clean the race bores in the frame and check for damage.

4. To install the upper race, do the following:

   a. Place the new upper race (**Figure 82**) squarely into the mounting bore opening with its bearing side facing out.

   b. Assemble the threaded rod tool as shown in **Figure 83**.

> *CAUTION*
> *If there is any binding when installing the bearing races in the following steps, stop and release all tension from the bearing race. Check the tool alignment to make sure the bearing race is moving evenly in its mounting bore. Otherwise, the bearing race may gouge the frame mounting bore and cause permanent damage.*

   c. Hold the lower nut and tighten the upper nut to draw the race into the frame tube. Continue until the race bottoms out in its mounting bore. Remove the puller assembly and inspect the bearing race. It must seat fully and squarely in the frame tube (**Figure 78**).

> *CAUTION*
> *Do not allow the installer shaft to contact the bearing race.*

5. Reverse the tool and repeat Step 3 to install the lower race (**Figure 79**). Insert the threaded rod tool carefully through the frame to avoid scratching the upper bearing race.

6. Lubricate the upper and lower bearing races with grease.

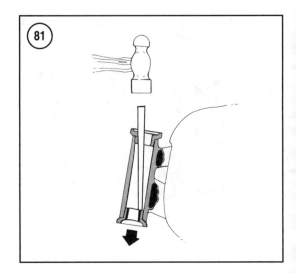

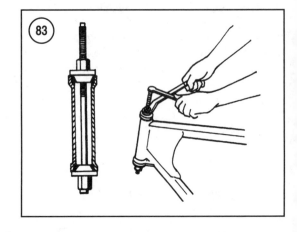

STEERING STEM BEARING RACE REPLACEMENT

The lower inner race (A, **Figure 84**) is a press fit on the steering stem. Replace the lower dust seal (B, **Figure 84**) when replacing the lower inner race.

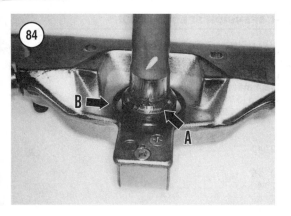

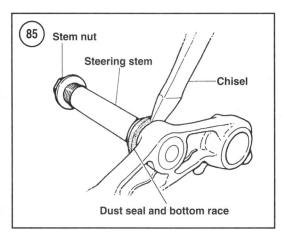

Figure 85: Stem nut, Steering stem, Chisel, Dust seal and bottom race

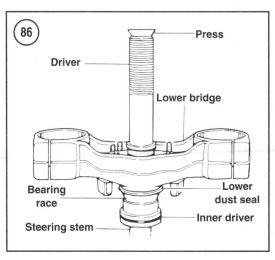

Figure 86: Press, Driver, Lower bridge, Bearing race, Steering stem, Lower dust seal, Inner driver

1. Thread the steering stem nut onto the steering stem (**Figure 85**).

NOTE
Installing the steering stem nut as described in Step 1 helps prevent damaging the steering stem threads when removing the lower inner bearing race.

WARNING
Striking a chisel with a hammer can cause flying chips. Wear safety glasses in Step 2 to prevent eye injury.

2. Remove the lower inner bearing race and dust seal with a chisel as shown in **Figure 85**. To prevent damaging the steering stem, remove the bearing race evenly. Apply pressure against the bearing race a little at a time and at different points around the bearing.

3. Discard the lower inner bearing race and dust seal.

4. Clean the steering stem with solvent and dry thoroughly.

5. Inspect the steering stem race surface for cracks or other damage. Replace the steering stem if necessary.

6. Install a new lower dust seal over the steering stem.

7. Slide the new lower inner bearing race with the bearing surface facing up onto the steering stem until it stops.

8. Install the steering stem in a press. Support the bottom of the steering stem with a bearing driver or piece of round metal. Then install a bearing driver (**Figure 86**) over the steering stem and seat it against the inner bearing race inside shoulder. Do not allow the bearing driver to contact the bearing race surface.

9. Press the lower inner race onto the steering stem until it bottoms.

10. Remove the steering stem from the press.

11. Lubricate the bearing race and dust seal (**Figure 84**) with grease.

12

Tables 1-3 are on the following pages.

Table 1 STEERING AND FRONT SUSPENSION SPECIFICATIONS

Front axle travel	
VT1100C	135 mm (5.3 in.)
VT1100C2	
ACE	124 mm (4.9 in.)
Sabre	118.4 mm (4.66 in.)
VT1100C3	95 mm (3.7 in.)
VT1100T	124 mm (4.9 in.)
Steering	
Caster angle	
VT1100C	32° 40'
VT1100C2	
ACE	32° 15'
Sabre	32° 40'
VT1100C3	32° 30'
VT1100T	32° 15'
Trail	
VT1100C	153 mm (6.0 in.)
VT1100C2	
ACE	155 mm (6.1 in.)
Sabre	161 mm (6.3 in.)
VT1100C3	144 mm (5.7 in.)
VT1100T	149 mm (5.9 in.)
Steering stem bearing preload	
VT1100C3	0.8-1.2 kg (1.8-2.6 lbs.)
All other models	0.9-1.3 kg (2.0-2.9 lbs.)

Table 2 FRONT FORK SERVICE SPECIFICATIONS

Fork oil capacity	
VT1100C	449 ml (15.2 U.S. oz.)
VT1100C2	
ACE	
1995-1998	482 ml (16.3 U.S. oz.)
1999	495 ml (16.7 U.S. oz.)
Sabre	538 ml (18.2 U.S. oz.)
VT1100C3	488 ml (16.5 U.S. oz.)
VT1100T	497 ml (16.8 U.S. oz.)
Fork oil level	
VT1100C	173 mm (6.8 in.)
VT1100C2	
ACE	
1995-1998	151 mm (5.9 in.)
1999	139 mm (5.5 in.)
Sabre	108 mm (4.3 in.)
VT1100C3	151 mm (5.9 in.)
VT1100T	140 mm (5.5 in.)
Fork oil type	Pro-Honda Suspension Fluid SS-8 or 10 wt. fork oil
Fork tube runout limit	0.20 mm (0.008 in.)
Spring free length	
VT1100C	
New	459.4 mm (18.09 in.)
Service limit	450.2 mm (17.72 in.)
VT1100C2	
ACE	
1995-1997	
New	449.4 mm (17.69 in.)
Service limit	440.4 mm (17.34 in.)
1998	
New	469.9 mm (18.50 in.)
Service limit	460.5 mm (18.13 in.)
(continued)	

Table 2 FRONT FORK SERVICE SPECIFICATIONS (continued)

VT1100C2 (continued)	
ACE	
1999	
New	447.9 mm (17.63 in.)
Service limit	438.9 mm (17.28 in.)
Sabre	
New	331.4 mm (13.05 in.)
Service limit	324.8 mm (12.79 in.)
VT1100C3	
New	429.9 mm (16.93 in.)
Service limit	421.3 mm (16.59 in.)
VT1100T	
New	475.9 mm (18.74 in.)
Service limit	466.4 mm (18.36 in.)

Table 3 FRONT SUSPENSION AND STEERING TORQUE SPECIFICATIONS

	N•m	in.-lb.	ft.-lb.
Fork cap			
VT1100C2 Sabre	22	–	16
All other models	23	–	17
Fork drain bolt	8	71	–
Fork tube Allen bolt[1]			
VT1100C	20	–	15
VT1100C2			
ACE	22	–	16
Sabre	29	–	22
VT1100C3	20	–	15
VT1100T	22	–	16
Fork tube pinch bolts			
Upper			
VT1100C2 Sabre	26	–	19
VT1100C3	23	–	17
All other models	11	97	–
Lower	49	–	36
Front brake caliper mounting bolts[2]			
VT1100C	45	–	33
All other models	30	–	22
Front brake hose clamp mounting bolt			
VT1100C2 ACE, VT1100T	12	106	–
VT1100C3[5]	–		
Front master cylinder clamp bolt	12	106	
Front turn signal stopper plate bolt	9	80	–
Handlebar upper holder bolt	30	–	22
Handlebar lower holder nut			
VT1100C3	26	–	19
All other models[5]	–		
Steering assembly[3]			
Steering adjust nut[4]	21	–	15.5
Steering stem nut			
VT1100C2 ACE	105	–	77
All other models	103	–	76

1. Apply a medium strength threadlock onto fastener threads.
2. ALOC bolts. Install new fastener during installation.
3. See text for adjustment procedure.
4. Lubricate threads with engine oil.
5. Specification not provided by manufacturer.

12

CHAPTER THIRTEEN

REAR SUSPENSION AND FINAL DRIVE

This chapter contains repair and replacement procedures for the rear wheel, hub, rear suspension, drive shaft and final drive components. Refer to Chapter Eleven for wheel and tire service procedures.

Rear suspension specifications are listed in **Table 1** and **Table 6**. **Tables 1-6** are located at the end of this chapter.

SHOCK ABSORBER

The shock absorbers are spring-loaded and hydraulically damped. Each shock has five adjustment positions for different riding and load conditions.

The shocks are sealed units. Do not replace the shock spring or disassemble the shock in anyway. Service is limited to shock adjustment and replacing the shock mount dampers installed in each end of the shock absorber.

Adjustment

Each shock absorber can be adjusted to any of 5 spring preload settings. The softest setting is No. 1 and the stiffest setting is No. 5. The standard factory setting is No. 2. Adjust the shock absorbers to best suit different load and riding conditions.

1. Remove the tool kit and assemble the spanner wrench and its extension bar.

CAUTION
Always adjust the shock absorber in single increment numbers. For example, if the shock is in position No. 2 and it is necessary to adjust the spring to position No. 5, turn the adjuster to the No., 3, No. 4 and then to position No. 5. Do not turn the adjuster directly from the No. 2 to the No. 5 position without stopping at the other adjustment numbers or the adjuster may be damaged.

2. Using the pin spanner wrench, adjust the shock absorber to the desired adjustment position (**Figure 1**).

3. Adjust the other shock to the same setting.

WARNING
Both shock absorbers must be adjusted to the same preload number or an unstable riding condition may result.

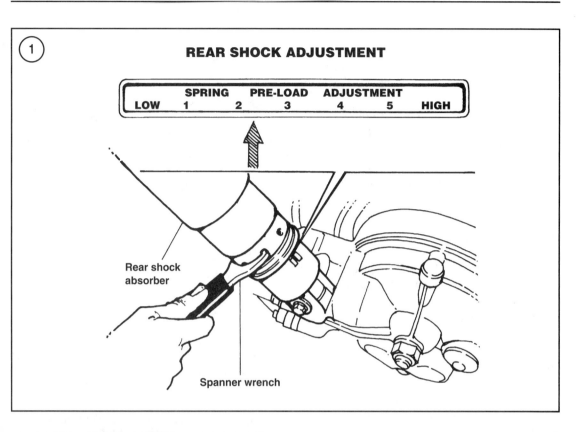

REAR SHOCK ADJUSTMENT

| LOW | SPRING 1 | 2 | PRE-LOAD 3 | ADJUSTMENT 4 | 5 | HIGH |

Rear shock absorber

Spanner wrench

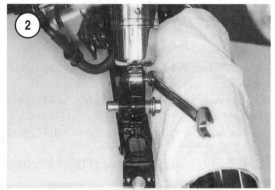

Shock Absorber Removal/Installation

1. Support the bike so that the rear wheel clears the ground.

2. On VT1100T models, remove the saddlebags (Chapter Fifteen).

3. Remove the seat if it blocks removal of the upper shock mounting bolt (Chapter Fifteen).

4. On VT1100C and VT1100C2 models, loosen the muffler fasteners to provide clearance for removing the lower shock mounting bolt (**Figure 2**).

5. On VT1100C3 models, remove the screw and the upper cover from the shock absorber.

NOTE
The left and right shock absorbers are different. Identify the shock absorbers before removing them in the following steps.

6. Remove the upper and lower shock mounting bolts (**Figure 3**) and remove the shock absorber.

7. Inspect the shock absorber as described in this section.

13

8. Installation is the reverse of removal. Note the following:

    a. Install the shock absorber with its adjustment decal facing toward the back of the motorcycle.

    b. Tighten the mounting bolts (**Figure 3**) to the torque specifications in **Table 6**.

    c. On VT1100C and VT1100C2 models, after installing the right side shock absorber, tighten the muffler fasteners as described in Chapter Fifteen.

Shock Inspection

1. Inspect the shock absorber (**Figure 4**) for oil leaks or other damage. Replace the shock absorber if it is leaking.

2. Inspect the upper and lower shock dampers for excessive wear, age deterioration or other damage. Replace the shock dampers with a press. Note the following:

    a. The shock rubber dampers are identical.

    b. The lower shock collars (**Figure 4**) are different. Identify them for reassembly.

REAR SWING ARM

Refer to **Figure 5** when servicing the swing arm in the following sections.

Special Tools

The following tools are required to remove and install the swing arm:

1. Honda pivot adjust wrench (part No. 07908-4690003 or KS-HBA-08-469). Refer to A, **Figure 6**.

2. 17 mm socket bit. Refer to B, **Figure 6**.

Removal

1. Remove the rear wheel (Chapter Eleven).

2. Remove the rear shock absorbers as described in this chapter.

3. Remove the final drive unit as described in this chapter.

4. Note how the battery breather tube (if used) and the air filter drain tube attach to the swing arm for reassembly reference.

5. On models with a rear disc brake, remove the front and rear brake hose clamps at the rear swing arm.

> *NOTE*
> *Have an assistant steady the bike when performing Step 6.*

6. Grasp the rear end of the swing arm and try to move it from side to side in a horizontal arc. There must be no noticeable side play. Then grasp the rear of the swing arm and pivot it up and down through its full travel. The swing arm must pivot smoothly. If excessive play or binding is evident and the pivot bolts are tightened correctly, inspect the swing arm bearings for severe wear or damage.

7. Remove the left and right side swing arm pivot caps.

8. Use the Honda pivot adjust wrench to loosen and remove the right pivot bolt locknut (**Figure 7**).

9. Loosen and remove the right pivot bolt (**Figure 8**).

10. Loosen and remove the left pivot bolt (**Figure 9**) and swing arm.

11. Remove the universal joint (**Figure 10**) from the swing arm.

12. On models with a rear disc brake, remove the rear brake caliper bracket stopper pin bolt from the swing arm.

> *NOTE*
> *Identify the bearings if they are going to be reused.*

13. Remove the left and right side bearings and dust seals (**Figure 11**).

Swing Arm Inspection

1. Clean and dry the parts.

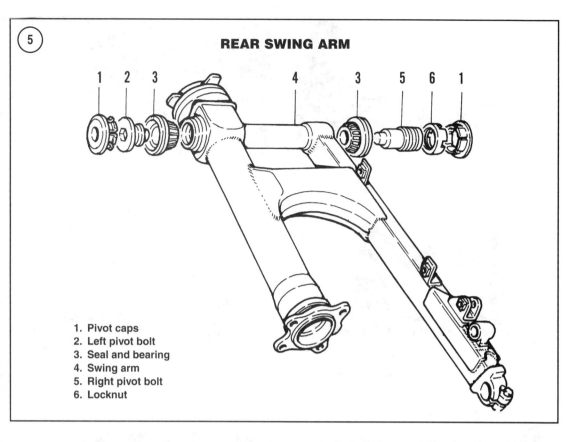

REAL SWING ARM

1. Pivot caps
2. Left pivot bolt
3. Seal and bearing
4. Swing arm
5. Right pivot bolt
6. Locknut

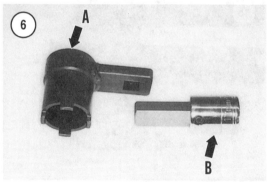

13

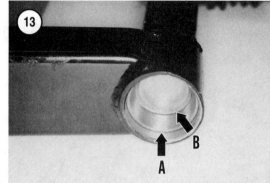

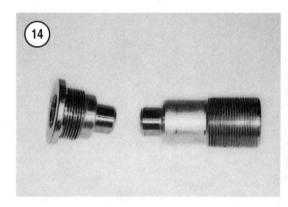

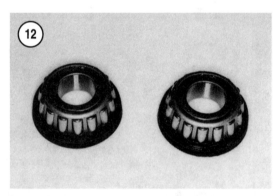

2. Inspect the swing arm for cracks and other damage.

3. Replace worn or damaged bearing dust seals.

4. Inspect each bearing (**Figure 12**) and race (A, **Figure 13**) for excessive wear, pitting or other damage. If necessary, replace the bearings and races as described under *Bearing Replacement* in this section.

5. Check that each grease retainer plate (B, **Figure 13**) fits tightly in the swing arm.

6. Inspect the pivot bolts (**Figure 14**) for excessive wear, thread damage or corrosion. Make sure the machined end on each pivot bolt is smooth. Replace if necessary.

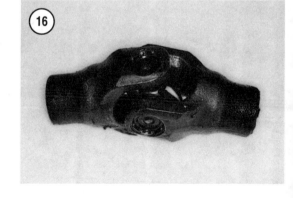

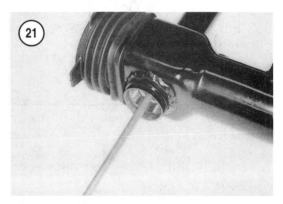

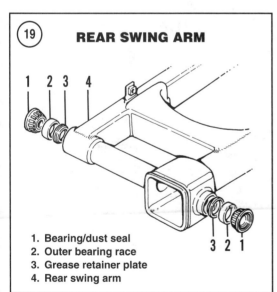

REAR SWING ARM

1. Bearing/dust seal
2. Outer bearing race
3. Grease retainer plate
4. Rear swing arm

7. Replace the boot (**Figure 15**) if damaged.

Universal Joint Inspection

1. Make sure the universal joint (**Figure 16**) pivots smoothly with no binding or roughness.

2. Inspect both universal joint spline ends for damage. If these splines are damaged, inspect the mating shaft splines for damage.

Bearing Replacement

Replace the left (**Figure 17**) and right (**Figure 18**) side bearings and races at the same time.

Refer to **Figure 19**.

1. Drill a suitable size hole through one of the grease retainer plates (**Figure 20**).

2. Insert a drift through this hole (**Figure 21**) and drive out the opposite bearing race and grease retainer plate. Refer to **Figure 22**.

3. Repeat Step 2 to remove the opposite bearing race and grease retainer plate.

4. Use a bearing driver to drive a new grease retainer and bearing race (**Figure 23**) into each side of the swing arm.

5. Lubricate each bearing race with grease.

13

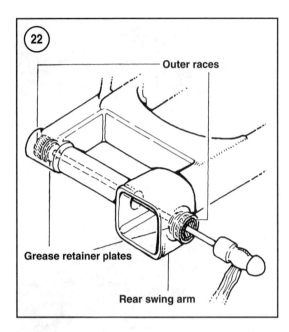

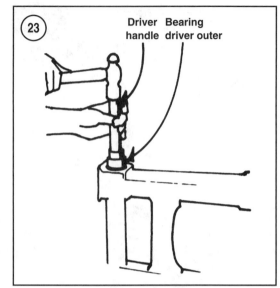

Installation

1. Remove the left crankcase rear cover as described in Chapter Fifteen.

2. Install the boot onto the swing arm with its UP mark facing up (**Figure 15**).

3. Lubricate the bearing races and bearings (**Figure 17** and **Figure 18**) with grease.

4. Install the left (**Figure 24**) and right (**Figure 25**) side bearings and dust seals into the swing arm.

5. On models with a rear disc brake, install the rear brake caliper stopper pin bolt (**Figure 26**) into the swing arm.

6. Install the universal joint partway into the swing arm (**Figure 27**).

7. Remove the drive shaft from the final drive unit as described in this chapter. Then insert the drive shaft through the swing arm (**Figure 28**) and engage it with the universal joint.

8. Lubricate the output driven gear shaft splines (**Figure 29**) with molybdenum disulfide paste.

9. Install the swing arm into the frame, while noting the following:

    a. Lubricate the machined end on both pivot bolts with grease. Do not lubricate the pivot bolt or frame threads with grease.

    b. Align the left swing arm pivot flange with the frame hole, then install the left pivot bolt (**Figure 9**).

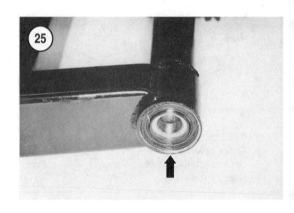

    c. Turn the drive shaft to engage the universal joint with the engine output shaft splines. Then remove the drive shaft and reinstall it onto the final drive unit as described in this chapter.

    d. Install the right swing arm pivot bolt (**Figure 8**).

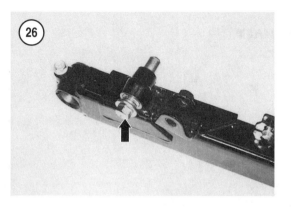

10. Install the boot over the output gearcase on the engine.

11. Tighten the left pivot bolt (**Figure 9**):

    a. On VT1100C2 ACE models, tighten to 105 N•m (77 ft.-lb.).

    b. On all other models, tighten to 103 N•m (76 ft.-lb.).

12. Tighten the right pivot bolt (**Figure 8**) to 18 N•m (159 in.-lb.).

13. Pivot the swing arm several times to help seat the pivot bearings.

14. Retighten the right pivot bolt (**Figure 8**) to 18 N•m (159 in.-lb.).

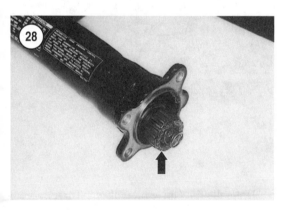

> *NOTE*
> *As shown in **Figure 30**, the Honda pivot adjust wrench effectively lengthens the torque wrench. The torque value set on the torque wrench is not the same amount of torque applied to the fastener. Recalculate the torque reading as described under **Torque Adaptors** in Chapter One.*

15. Install the right pivot bolt locknut (**Figure 31**) and hold it with a 17-mm wrench (**Figure 30**). Tighten the right pivot bolt locknut with the Honda

13

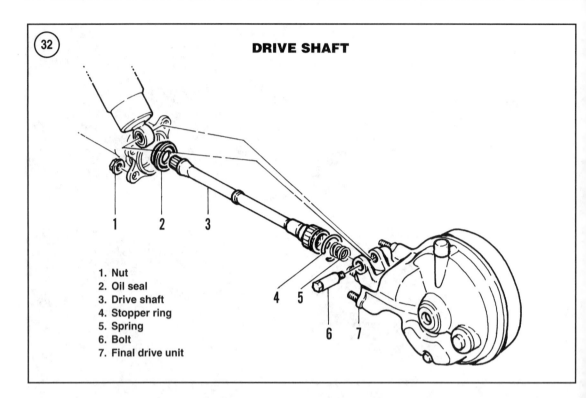

DRIVE SHAFT

1. Nut
2. Oil seal
3. Drive shaft
4. Stopper ring
5. Spring
6. Bolt
7. Final drive unit

pivot adjust wrench (A, **Figure 6**) and a torque wrench as follows:

   a. On VT1100C2 ACE models, tighten to 115 N•m (85 ft.-lb.).

   b. On all other models, tighten to 113 N•m (83 ft.-lb.).

16. Install the left and right side swing arm pivot caps.

17. On models with a rear disc brake, install the front and rear brake hose clamps onto the swing arm and secure them with new bolts. Tighten the brake hose clamp bolts 12 N•m (106 in.-lb.).

18. Install the left crankcase cover (Chapter Fifteen).

19. Reattach the battery breather tube (if used) and the air filter drain tube following notes made during removal.

20. Install the drive shaft and final drive unit as described in this chapter.

21. Install the rear shock absorbers as described in this chapter.

FINAL DRIVE UNIT AND DRIVE SHAFT

Removal

Refer to **Figure 32**.

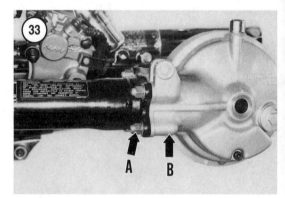

1. Drain the final drive oil (Chapter Three).

2. Remove the rear wheel (Chapter Eleven).

3. Remove the left shock absorber.

4. Remove the nuts (A, **Figure 33**) and the final drive unit (B) with the drive shaft attached.

5. Hold the final drive unit, then turn and pull the drive shaft out (**Figure 34**).

6. Remove the spring (A, **Figure 35**), stopper ring (B) and oil seal (C). Discard the stopper ring and oil seal.

7. Refer to *Final Drive Unit Overhaul* in this chapter to service the final drive unit.

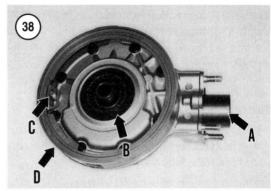

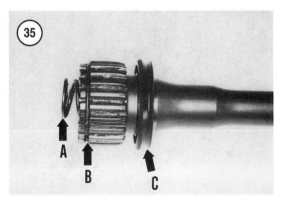

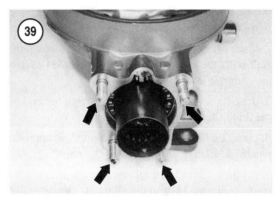

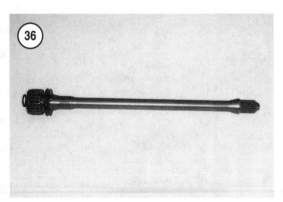

Drive Shaft Inspection

1. Clean and dry the drive shaft and spring.
2. Check the drive shaft (**Figure 36**) for damage and fatigue.

> *NOTE*
> *To inspect and service the universal joint, remove the swing arm as described in this chapter.*

3. Replace the spring (A, **Figure 35**) if damaged.

Final Drive Unit Inspection

1. Remove the distance collar (**Figure 37**) and check for damage. Reinstall the collar with the machined end going in first.
2. Turn pinion joint (A, **Figure 38**). If ring gear (B, **Figure 38**) turns roughly, perform the *Backlash Measurement* under *Final Drive Unit Overhaul* in this chapter. If necessary, disassemble unit and check for wear and damage.
3. Check for loose or damaged final drive unit studs (**Figure 39**). Remove the stud as described

under *Stud Removal/Installation* in Chapter One. Apply a medium strength threadlock onto the stud threads and install to the dimension shown in **Figure 40**.

Installation

Use molybdenum disulfide grease when grease is called for in the following steps.

1. Install a new stopper ring (B, **Figure 35**) into the drive shaft groove. The stopper ring is a loose fit as it is designed to close around the drive shaft groove when installed inside the pinion joint.

2. Pack the lips of a new oil seal with grease and install with the closed side (C, **Figure 35**) facing away from the stopper ring.

3. Install the spring (A, **Figure 35**) into the end of the drive shaft.

4. Pack 2 g (0.08 oz) of grease into the pinion joint spline (A, **Figure 38**).

5. Align the drive shaft splines with the pinion joint splines (**Figure 34**) and install the drive shaft until the stopper ring seats into the pinion joint spline groove. Lightly pull back on the drive shaft to make sure the stopper ring is properly seated in groove.

6. Tap the oil seal (**Figure 41**) into the pinion joint.

7. Pack 1 g (0.04 oz) of grease into the drive shaft splines.

8. Insert the drive shaft through the swing arm and engage with the universal joint splines. Push the final drive unit (B, **Figure 33**) studs through the holes in the swing arm and install the nuts finger-tight.

> *NOTE*
> *Do not tighten the final drive unit mounting nuts (A, **Figure 33**) until the rear wheel is installed and the rear axle nut is tightened. This sequence is described under **Rear Wheel Installation** in Chapter Eleven.*

9. Install the rear wheel and tighten the final drive unit mounting nuts as described in Chapter Eleven.

10. Install the left side shock absorber as described in this chapter.

11. Refill the final drive unit with oil (Chapter Three).

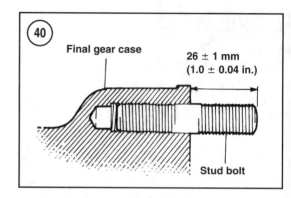

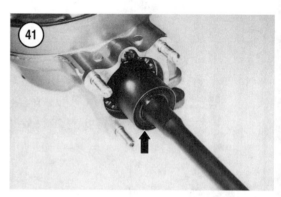

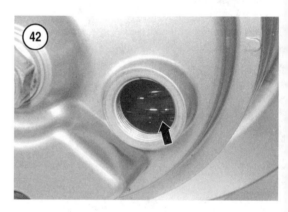

FINAL DRIVE UNIT OVERHAUL

Service Notes

Before servicing the final drive unit, note the following:

1. Refer to *Final Drive* in Chapter Two to troubleshoot the final drive unit. A new or rough sounding noise from the final drive unit is usually the first indication of a problem with the unit.

2. Ring gear removal also requires removal of the ring gear bearing. If the bearing is in good condition, it can be reused.

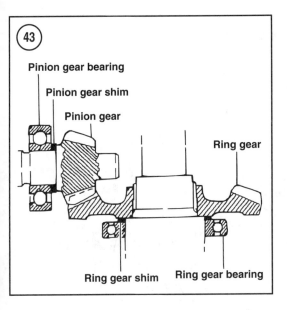

Pinion gear bearing

Pinion gear shim

Pinion gear

Ring gear

Ring gear shim   Ring gear bearing

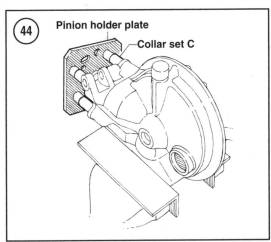

Pinion holder plate

Collar set C

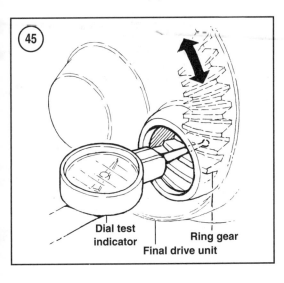

Dial test indicator

Ring gear

Final drive unit

3. The pinion gear bearing pressed onto the pinion gear can also be reused if in good condition.

4. When checking bearings, they should turn freely and without any sign of roughness, catching or excessive noise. Always replace questionable bearings.

5. Refer to the general bearing removal and installation information found under *Basic Service Methods* in Chapter One before removing or installing bearings and seals in this section.

6. Use a heat gun or shop oven when necessary to heat the parts. Do not use a torch because this heats the parts unevenly and may cause warp. When heating parts, monitor heat with heat strips available from a welding supply store or use an infrared thermometer. The text lists the temperature required to remove and install parts.

7. **Table 2** lists Honda tools required to service the final drive unit.

8. Inspect the ring gear by supporting the motorcycle with the rear wheel off the ground. Remove the oil fill cap and turn the rear wheel to inspect the gear (**Figure 42**). If wear or damage is apparent, drain the oil (Chapter Three) and inspect the oil for metal fragments and other debris.

9. Begin service by performing the *Backlash Measurement* procedure in this section.

Backlash Measurement

This procedure checks the backlash between the ring gear and pinion gear to determine gear wear and if the ring gear is running true. Measuring gear backlash is also necessary after overhaul. **Figure 43** shows ring and pinion gear engagement and the position of their adjustment shims.

Measure backlash before disassembling the final drive unit.

1. Remove the final drive unit as described in this chapter.

2. Install the Honda pinion holder plate and collar set C as shown in **Figure 44** to lock the pinion gear and remove any pinion end play.

3. Place the final drive unit in a soft-jawed vise.

4. Remove the oil fill cap.

5. Measure backlash with a dial test indicator mounted on a magnetic stand. Position the indicator so its stem is parallel to the ring gear shaft and its tip contacts the side of one gear tooth as shown in **Figure 45**.

13

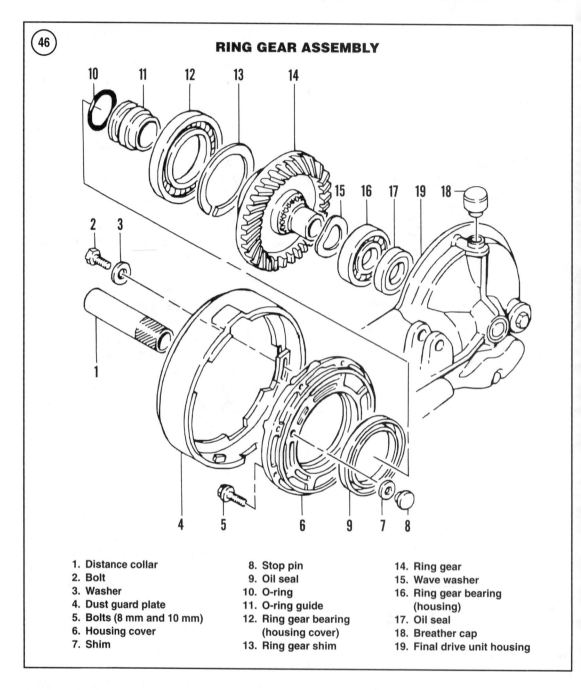

RING GEAR ASSEMBLY ㊺

1. Distance collar
2. Bolt
3. Washer
4. Dust guard plate
5. Bolts (8 mm and 10 mm)
6. Housing cover
7. Shim
8. Stop pin
9. Oil seal
10. O-ring
11. O-ring guide
12. Ring gear bearing (housing cover)
13. Ring gear shim
14. Ring gear
15. Wave washer
16. Ring gear bearing (housing)
17. Oil seal
18. Breather cap
19. Final drive unit housing

6. Move the ring gear back and forth by hand (**Figure 45**) to determine initial final drive gear backlash. Refer to **Table 3** for the specified backlash. Record the reading and perform the following:

a. Remove the dial test indicator, then rotate the ring gear and take two additional backlash readings 120° from the original measuring point. If the difference between any two readings exceeds 0.10 mm (0.004 in.), the ring

gear is running out of true. This can be caused by a damaged bearing or the bearing bore may be deformed.

b. If the backlash measurement is being performed after reassembling the final drive unit, the ring gear bearing may not have been installed correctly in its bore.

c. If the backlash reading is out of specification, but the ring gear is running true, go to Step 7.

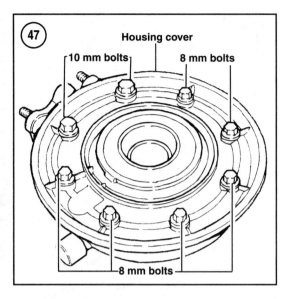

(47)

Housing cover

10 mm bolts

8 mm bolts

8 mm bolts

d. If the backlash reading indicates that the ring gear is running out of true, remove the ring gear and inspect the parts and housing for damage.

7. To correct backlash, the ring gear is removed and the proper ring gear shim installed. Note the following:

a. If gear backlash is too small, replace the ring gear shim (13, **Figure 46**) with a thinner one.

b. If gear backlash to too large, replace ring gear shim (13, **Figure 46**) with a thicker one.

c. Refer to **Table 4** for ring gear shim sizes.

d. Remove the ring gear and install the correct size shim as described in this section.

8. Reverse Steps 1-5.

Ring Gear Removal and Shim Adjustment

This procedure removes the ring gear without having to remove the pinion gear. However, if the drive unit is to be disassembled completely, remove the ring gear, then remove the pinion gear.

Refer to **Figure 46**.

1. Review *Service Notes* in this section.

2. Perform the backlash measurement described in this section.

3. Remove the distance collar (**Figure 37**).

4. Remove the bolt (C, **Figure 38**), washer and dust guard plate (D).

5. Remove the housing cover 10-mm and 8-mm bolts (**Figure 47**) in a crossing pattern and remove the housing cover (6, **Figure 46**).

6A. If the ring gear remained in the housing cover, support the housing cover in a press with the ring gear facing down. Press the ring gear out of the housing cover with a hydraulic press.

6B. If the ring gear did not remain in the housing cover, remove the ring gear and wave washer from the housing.

7. Tap the O-ring guide (11, **Figure 46**) to remove it from the ring gear. Discard the O-ring.

8. Remove the ring gear bearing (12, **Figure 46**) from the ring gear as follows:

a. Check the bearing condition before removing it.

b. Use a 2-jaw puller and remove the ring gear bearing from the ring gear.

c. Recheck the bearing to see if it was damaged during removal. If not, the bearing can be re-used.

9. Remove the ring gear shim.

10. Clean and dry the parts. Do not replace the housing cover oil seal (9, **Figure 46**) until final assembly of the final drive unit.

11. Install the correct size ring gear shim (13, **Figure 46**) as follows:

a. If the unit was disassembled to correct the backlash measurement, install the correct size shim. Refer to *Backlash Measurement* in this section.

b. If the ring gear set, ring gear bearing, pinion bearing, housing cover or housing are being replaced, install a 2.00 mm (0.079 in.) thick shim as a starting point.

12. Place the ring gear shim onto the ring gear and press the bearing onto the ring gear.

13. Lubricate a new O-ring (10, **Figure 46**) with grease and install onto the O-ring guide.

14. Drive the O-ring guide into the ring gear shaft.

15. Install the ring gear into the housing cover.

16. Check the ring gear-to-stop pin side clearance as follows:

a. Measure the clearance between the ring gear and the stop pin with a feeler gauge (**Figure 48**). Refer to **Table 3** for the recommended clearance. The shim (7, **Figure 46**) under the stop pin (8, **Figure 46**) is used to adjust the clearance.

13

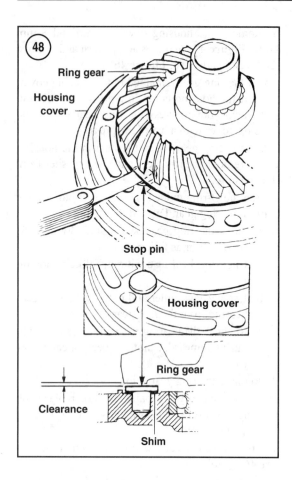

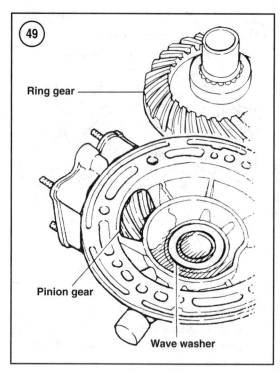

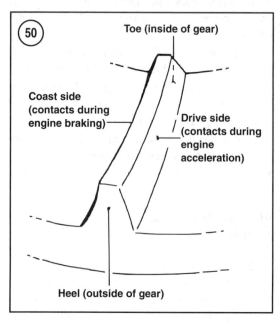

b. To adjust the clearance, remove the ring gear from the housing cover. Heat the housing cover to 80° C (176° F). Remove the stop pin (8, **Figure 46**). Install either a 0.10 mm (0.004 in.) or 0.15 mm (0.006 in.) stop pin shim to obtain the desired clearance.

c. Drive the stop pin into the cover and recheck the clearance. Repeat until the ring gear to stop pin clearance is within specifications (**Table 3**).

17. Perform the *Gear Mesh Pattern Check* in this section.

Gear Mesh Pattern Check

1. Remove the ring gear and wave washer from the housing. Refer to *Ring Gear Removal and Shim Adjustment* in this section.

2. Clean and dry the ring gear and pinion gear teeth.

3. Apply a gear marking compound to both sides of the ring gear and pinion gear teeth (**Figure 49**).

4. Install the wave washer and ring gear into the housing (**Figure 49**).

5. Lubricate the housing cover oil seal with grease and install the housing cover (**Figure 47**) onto the housing.

6. Install the housing cover bolts (**Figure 47**) and tighten in a crossing pattern and in several steps un-

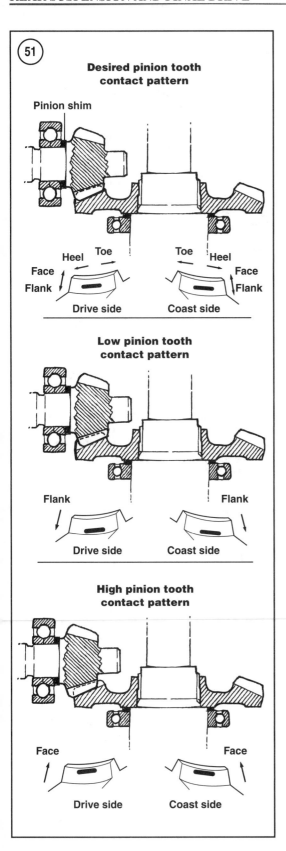

(51)

Desired pinion tooth contact pattern

Pinion shim

Heel Toe   Toe Heel
Face   Face
Flank   Flank
Drive side   Coast side

Low pinion tooth contact pattern

Flank   Flank
Drive side   Coast side

High pinion tooth contact pattern

Face   Face
Drive side   Coast side

til the housing cover contacts the housing evenly. Tighten the housing cover 8 mm bolts in a crossing pattern and in several steps to 25 N•m (19 ft.-lb.). Tighten the 10 mm bolts to 47 N•m (35 ft.-lb.).

7. Remove the oil fill cap.

8. Rotate the pinion shaft several rotations and in both directions so a pattern is evident on the ring gear teeth. View the ring gear teeth through the housing oil fill hole.

9. Examine the wear pattern on both sides of the gear teeth as follows:

    a. Refer to **Figure 50** to identify the parts of the gear teeth.

    b. The desired gear tooth wear pattern in **Figure 51** shows the pattern positioned approximately in the center of each tooth and slightly toward the flank side of the tooth.

    c. If the pinion contact pattern is low (**Figure 51**), install a thinner pinion gear shim (11, **Figure 52**).

    d. If the pinion contact pattern is high (**Figure 51**), install a thicker shim.

    e. The pinion gear and bearing must be removed to replace the shim. Refer to *Pinion Gear Removal/Installation and Shim Adjustment* in this section.

    f. Changing shim thickness 0.1 mm (0.004 in.) moves the contact pattern approximately 1.5-2.0 mm (0.06-0.08 in.). Refer to **Table 5** for pinion shim sizes.

10. Reinstall the pinion gear and bearing if they were removed, as described in this section. After obtaining a satisfactory pinion gear contact pattern, check the ring gear backlash as described under *Backlash Measurement* in this section.

11. Remove the cover and refer to *Final Drive Unit Assembly* to continue with the final assembly procedure.

Pinion Gear Removal/Installation and Pinion Shim Adjustment

Refer to **Figure 52**.

1. Review *Service Notes* in this section.

2. Remove the pinion joint nut (3, **Figure 52**) as follows:

    a. Support the housing in a soft-jawed vise.

    b. Install the Honda pinion holder plate and collar set C as shown in **Figure 53** and remove the pinion joint nut.

13

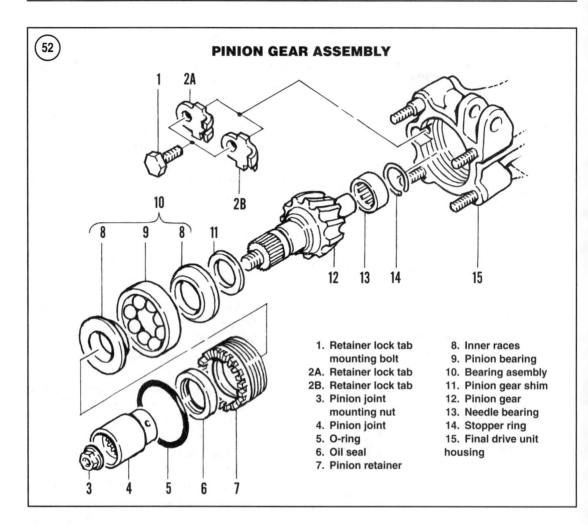

PINION GEAR ASSEMBLY

1. Retainer lock tab
   mounting bolt
2A. Retainer lock tab
2B. Retainer lock tab
3. Pinion joint
   mounting nut
4. Pinion joint
5. O-ring
6. Oil seal
7. Pinion retainer

8. Inner races
9. Pinion bearing
10. Bearing asembly
11. Pinion gear shim
12. Pinion gear
13. Needle bearing
14. Stopper ring
15. Final drive unit
housing

3. Remove the bolt and the retainer lock tab (**Figure 54**).

4. Remove the pinion retainer (**Figure 54**) with the Honda retainer wrench or an equivalent tool.

5. Assemble the following tools as shown in **Figure 55**, and remove the pinion gear assembly:

    a. Honda pinion puller base A.

    b. Honda puller shaft 22 × 1.5 × 240 mm and attachment.

6. Remove the pinion bearing (9, **Figure 52**) from the pinion gear as follows:

    a. Check the bearing condition before removing it.

    b. Remove the bearing and both races (10, **Figure 52**) with a 2-jaw puller.

    c. Recheck the bearing to see if it was damaged during removal. If not, the bearing can be re-used.

7. Remove the pinion gear shim (11, **Figure 52**).

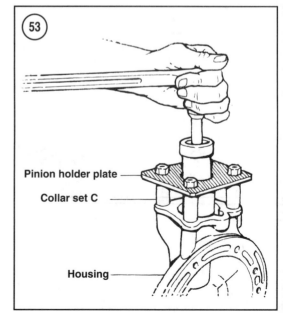

Pinion holder plate

Collar set C

Housing

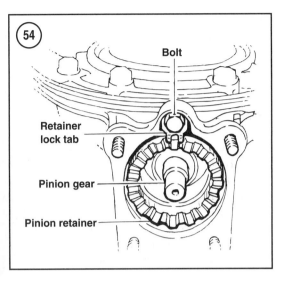

54

Bolt

Retainer
lock tab

Pinion gear

Pinion retainer

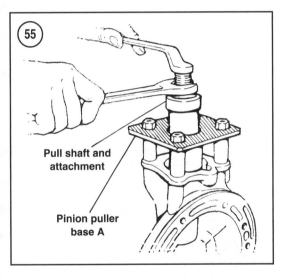

55

Pull shaft and
attachment

Pinion puller
base A

8. Inspect the pinion gear.

9. If only the bearing is being replaced, use the original shim on the pinion shaft. If the final drive housing cover or housing, ring and pinion gears or the side bearings are being replaced, install a 2.0 mm (0.79 in.) thick shim as a starting point for the gear position adjustments.

10. Clean and dry the housing and all parts.

11. Install the pinion gear shim onto the pinion gear shaft.

12. Press or drive the pinion gear bearing and both races onto the pinion gear shaft.

13. Remove and discard the O-ring (5, **Figure 52**) and seal (6, **Figure 52**) on the pinion retainer. Clean the pinion retainer and install a new seal and O-ring. Lubricate the seal lips and O-ring with grease.

14. Support the housing a soft-jawed vise.

15. Drive the pinion assembly into the housing with a bearing driver until there are enough housing threads visible above the pinion gear bearing to allow installation of the pinion retainer.

16. Thread the pinion retainer (**Figure 54**) into the housing. Use the Honda retainer wrench to tighten the pinion retainer to 108 N•m (80 ft.-lb.).

17. Engage a new retainer lock tab with the notches on the pinion retainer (**Figure 54**). Install the retainer lock tab bolt and tighten to 10 N•m (88 in.-lb.).

18. Install the pinion joint onto the pinion gear shaft.

19. Apply a medium strength threadlock onto the pinion joint nut and install it finger-tight.

20. Secure the pinion joint with the same Honda tools (**Figure 53**) used to loosen the nut. Tighten the pinion joint nut to 108 N•m (80 ft.-lb.). Remove the Honda tools.

Ring Gear Bearing and Seal Replacement

Perform the following to replace the ring gear bearing (16, **Figure 46**) and seal (17):

1. Remove the ring gear and pinion gear assemblies as described in this section.

2. Heat the housing to 80° C (176° F).

3. Tap the cover with a plastic hammer to remove the bearing. If the bearing does not fall out, remove it with a blind bearing puller.

4. Remove and discard the oil seal.

5. Clean and dry the housing.

6. Install the new seal into the housing. Coat the seal lips with grease.

7. Drive a new ring gear bearing into the housing.

8. Refer to *Final Drive Unit Assembly* to assemble the final drive housing assembly.

Final Drive Unit Assembly

1. Clean the breather passage as follows:
   a. Remove the breather cap (18, **Figure 46**) from the housing.
   b. Clean the breather passages in the housing cover and housing with compressed air.
   c. Reinstall the breather cap.

2. Replace the housing cover oil seal (9, **Figure 46**). Install the seal with its closed side facing to-

13

ward the outside of the housing cover. Lubricate the seal lip with grease.

3. Install the pinion gear assembly as described in this section.

4. Install the ring gear and wave washer into the housing cover as described in this section.

5. Clean the housing cover and housing sealing surfaces.

6. Install the two dowel pins into the housing.

7. Apply a liquid sealant, such as Yamabond No. 4, to the mating surface of the housing and housing cover. Do not apply the sealant around the two dowel pin holes.

8. Install the housing cover bolts (**Figure 47**) and tighten in a crossing pattern and in several steps until the housing cover contacts the housing evenly.

Then tighten the housing cover 8-mm bolts in a crossing pattern and in several steps to 25 N•m (19 ft.-lb.).

9. Apply a medium strength threadlock onto the 10 mm bolt threads and tighten to 47 N•m (35 ft.-lb.).

10. Make sure the gears rotate freely without binding.

11. Use a beam type torque wrench and socket and turn the pinion shaft to measure the final drive gear assembly preload. If the preload reading is not within 0.2-0.4 N•m (1.7-3.5 in.-lb.), perform the *Backlash Measurement* described in this section to determine whether the ring gear bearing is properly installed. After determining the backlash measurement, disassemble the housing and check the bearings for damage and proper installation.

Table 1 REAR SUSPENSION SPECIFICATIONS

Rear axle travel	
VT1100C3	95 mm (3.7 in.)
All other models	100 mm (3.9 in.)
Shock absorber standard preload adjuster setting	Second position

Table 2 TOOL AND PART NUMBERS FOR FINAL DRIVE UNIT OVERHAUL

Tool	Honda part number
Pinion holder plate	07924-ME40010
Collar set C	07924-ME40020
Retainer wrench	07910-ME8000
Pinion puller base A	07HMC-MM8011A
Puller shaft 22 × 1.5 × 240 mm	07931-ME4010B
	07931-HB3020A

Table 3 FINAL DRIVE UNIT SERVICE SPECIFICATIONS

	New mm (in.)	Service limit mm (in.)
Final drive gear backlash	0.05-0.15 (0.002-0.006)	0.30 (0.012)
Final drive gear backlash difference between measurements	–	0.10 (0.004)
Ring gear to stop pin clearance	0.30-0.60 (0.012-0.024)	–
Final drive gear assembly preload	0.2-0.4 N•m (1.7-3.5 in.-lb.)	–

Table 4 RING GEAR SHIM SIZES

Ring gear shim	Thickness mm (in.)
A	1.82 (0.072)
B	1.88 (0.074)
C	1.94 (0.076)
D (standard shim)	2.00 (0.079)
E	2.06 (0.082)
F	2.12 (0.083)
G	2.18 (0.086)
H	2.24 (0.088)
I	2.30 (0.091)

Table 5 PINION SHIM SIZES

Ring gear shim	Thickness mm (in.)
A	1.82 (0.073)
B	1.88 (0.074)
C	1.94 (0.076)
D (standard shim)	2.00 (0.079)
E	2.06 (0.082)
F	2.12 (0.083)
G	2.18 (0.086)

Table 6 REAR SUSPENSION AND FINAL DRIVE TORQUE SPECIFICATIONS

	N•m	in.-lb.	ft.-lb.
Damper holder plate bolt[1]	20	–	15
Final drive unit mounting nuts	64	–	47
Housing cover bolts			
8 mm	25	–	19
10 mm	47	–	35
Pinion joint nut	108	–	80
Pinion retainer	108	–	80
Pinion retainer lock tab bolt	10	88	–
Rear brake hose clamp bolt[1]	12	106	–
Rear shock absorber			
Upper mounting bolt	27	–	20
Lower mounting bolt			
Left side	23	–	17
Right side			
VT1100C3	26	–	19
All other models	35	–	26

(continued)

13

Table 6 REAR SUSPENSION AND FINAL DRIVE TORQUE SPECIFICATIONS (continued)

	N•m	in.-lb.	ft.-lb.
Swing arm[2]			
Pivot bolt			
Left side			
VT1100C2 ACE	105	–	77
All other models	103	–	76
Right side	18	159	–
Right pivot locknut			
VT1100C2 ACE	115	–	85
All other models	113	–	83
1. ALOC bolts. Install new fastener during installation.			
2. See text for tightening procedure.			

CHAPTER FOURTEEN

BRAKES

This chapter covers service, repair and replacement procedures for the front disc brake, rear disc brake, rear drum brake (VT1100C) and rear brake pedal assembly. Routine brake inspection and adjustment procedures are found in Chapter Three. The front and rear brake units are critical to riding performance and safety. Inspect the front and rear brakes frequently and repair any problem immediately.

Brake specifications are located in **Tables 1-5** at the end of this chapter.

BRAKE FLUID SELECTION

When adding brake fluid, use DOT 4 brake fluid from a sealed container. DOT 4 brake fluid is glycol-based and draws moisture, which greatly reduces its ability to perform correctly. Purchase brake fluid in small containers. Do not store a container of brake fluid with less than 1/4 of the fluid remaining.

> *CAUTION*
> *Do not intermix DOT 5 (silicone-based) brake fluid because it can cause brake system failure.*

PREVENTING BRAKE FLUID DAMAGE

Be careful not to spill any fluid because it stains or damages most surfaces. To prevent brake fluid damage, note the following:

1. Before performing any procedure in which there is the possibility of brake fluid contacting the motorcycle, cover the area with a large piece of plastic. It only takes a few drops of brake fluid to damage an expensive part.

2. When working on the brake system, fill a small container with soap and water and keep it close to the motorcycle. If brake fluid contacts the motorcycle, clean and rinse the area thoroughly.

3. To help control the flow of brake fluid when filling the reservoirs, punch a small hole into the seal of a new container next to the edge of the pour spout.

DISC BRAKE SERVICE

When working on the brake system, the work area and all tools must be clean. Any tiny particles of dirt or debris in the caliper assembly or master cylinder can damage the components and prevent the system from functioning properly.

Consider the following when servicing the disc brakes:

> *WARNING*
> *Whenever working on the brake system, do **not** inhale brake dust. Do **not** use compressed air to blow off brake parts. It may contain asbestos, which can cause lung injury and cancer. Wear a face mask that meets OHSA requirements for trapping asbestos particles, and wash hands and forearms thoroughly after completing the work. Wet down the brake dust on brake components before working on the brake system. Secure and dispose of all brake dust and cleaning materials properly.*

1. Drain and flush the brake system at the intervals specified in Chapter Three. Allowing old and contaminated brake fluid to remain in the system damages all of the systems internal surfaces.

2. DOT 4 brake fluid damages plastic, painted and plated surfaces.

3. Always keep the master cylinder reservoir and brake fluid containers closed to prevent dust or moisture from entering. This contaminates the brake fluid and can cause brake failure.

4. Handle the brake components carefully when servicing them. Use only DOT 4 brake fluid or isopropyl alcohol to wash rubber parts in the brake system. Never allow any petroleum-based cleaner to contact any of the rubber parts. These chemicals cause the rubber to swell, requiring their replacement.

5. Do not allow any grease or oil to contact the brake pads or brake shoes.

6. When cleaning the brake components, wear rubber gloves to keep brake fluid off skin.

7. Whenever loosening any brake hose banjo bolt, the brake system is opened. The system must be bled to remove air bubbles. Also, if the brake feels spongy, this usually means air bubbles are in the system. Bleed the brakes as described in this chapter.

> *WARNING*
> *Contaminated brake fluid can cause brake failure. Never reuse brake fluid and always dispose it safely in a marked container.*

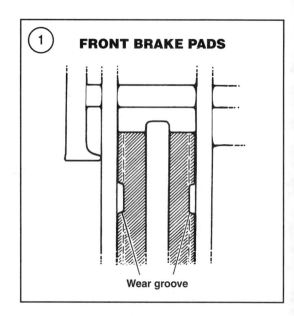

FRONT BRAKE PADS

Wear groove

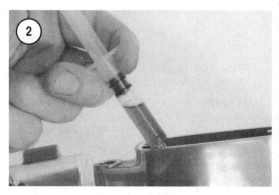

FRONT BRAKE PADS

There is no recommended mileage interval for changing the brake pads. Pad wear depends on riding habits and the condition of the brake system. As the brake pads wear, the brake fluid level drops in the reservoir and automatically adjusts for wear.

The brake pads can be replaced with the brake caliper mounted on the motorcycle.

Always replace both front brake pads at the same time. Never use one new brake pad with a used brake pad in a caliper. Doing so causes an unbalanced braking condition.

Inspection

Replace the brake pads when they are worn to the bottom of the pad wear limit groove (**Figure 1**) or when contaminated with brake fluid.

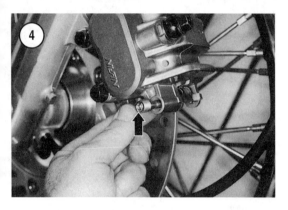

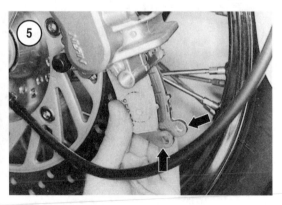

when the caliper pistons are compressed for pad re-installation. Do *not* drain the reservoir to the point where the filler and compensating ports in the bottom of the reservoir are exposed to air. When air enters the system, the system has to be bled. Reinstall the cover assembly.

3. Before removing the brake pads, note the following:

    a. Check the caliper for leaks around the brake hose banjo bolt, bleed valve and caliper pistons.

    b. Check for tar, dirt and other material stuck to the exposed part of the caliper pistons. If debris is present, remove the brake pads as described below but do not push the pistons back into the caliper (Step 4) because the debris may damage the caliper seals. After removing the brake pads, clean the exposed part of the caliper pistons with a soft brush or cloth and an aerosol vrake cleaner, then push the pistons into the caliper by hand.

CAUTION
Do not allow the master cylinder reservoir to overflow when performing Step 4. Brake fluid damages most surfaces it contacts.

4. Hold the caliper housing from the outside and push it toward its brake disc to push the pistons into the caliper to make room for the new brake pads.

NOTE
The pistons should move smoothly when repositioning them in Step 4. If not, check the caliper for a stuck piston or damaged caliper bores, pistons and seals. Repair requires overhaul of the brake caliper assembly.

Replacement

Depending on the model, the front brake caliper is mounted on either the left or right side. This procedure is applicable to all brake calipers.

1. Review the *Disc Brake Service* information in this chapter.

2. Turn the front wheel to level the master cylinder. Remove the front master cylinder cover assembly and use a syringe (**Figure 2**) to remove and discard about 50 percent of the fluid from the reservoir. This prevents the master cylinder from overflowing

5. Remove the pad pin plug (**Figure 3**), pad pin (**Figure 4**) and both brake pads (**Figure 5**).

6. Make sure the pad spring (**Figure 6**) is in good condition and installed inside the caliper. Replace the pad spring if damaged.

7. Inspect the pad pin (A, **Figure 7**) for excessive wear, corrosion or damage. Use a wire-wheel to remove corrosion and dirt from the pad pin surface. A dirty or damaged pad pin surface prevents the brake pads from sliding properly and causes brake drag and overheating of the brake disc.

8. Inspect the brake pads (B, **Figure 7**) as follows:

a. Inspect the friction material for light surface dirt, grease and oil contamination. Remove light contamination with sandpaper. If the contamination has penetrated the surface, replace the brake pads.

b. Inspect the brake pads for excessive wear or damage. Each pad should show equal amounts of wear. Replace the brake pads when the friction material is worn to the wear limit groove (**Figure 1**) on the pad.

c. Check the shim (**Figure 8**) on the backside of the inner pad for rust, corrosion and damage. Make sure the shim fits tightly on the pad.

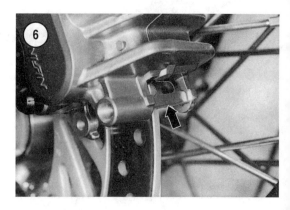

9. Inspect for leaking brake fluid around the caliper piston. If there is a leak, overhaul the brake caliper as described in this chapter.

10. Service the brake disc as follows:

a. Use brake cleaner and a fine-grade emery cloth to remove road debris and brake pad residue from the brake disc. Clean both sides of the disc.

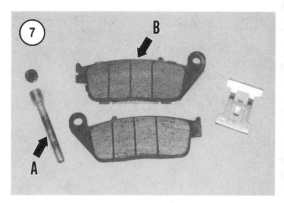

NOTE
Because different pad compounds may not be compatible, it is especially important to clean the brake disc when changing pad compounds. Old material left on the disc may contaminate the new pads.

b. Check the brake disc for wear as described in this chapter.

11. Install the brake pads into the caliper (**Figure 5**) so the friction material on both brake pads faces toward the brake disc. Install the pad with the shim on the inside of the caliper. Insert the extended arm on the end of each pad into the pad retainer in the caliper bracket (**Figure 9**).

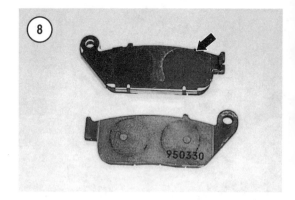

12. Push both brake pads against the pad spring and install the pad pin (**Figure 4**) through the brake caliper and brake pad holes. Tighten the pad pin finger-tight.

13. Tighten the pad pin (**Figure 4**) to 18 N•m (159 in.-lb.).

14. Install the pad pin plug (A, **Figure 2**) and tighten to the torque specification in **Table 3**.

15. Pump the front brake lever to correctly seat the pads against the disc, then check the brake fluid level in the reservoir. If necessary, add new DOT 4 brake fluid (Chapter Three).

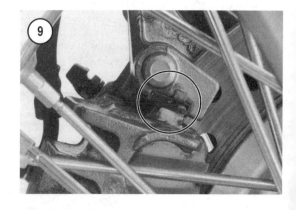

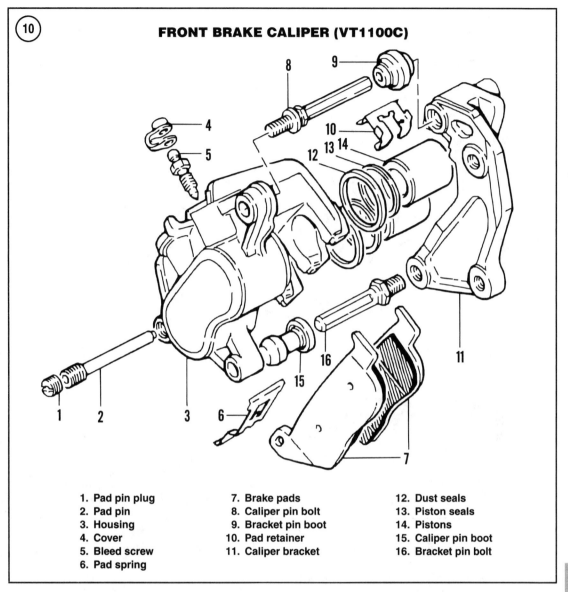

FRONT BRAKE CALIPER (VT1100C)

1. Pad pin plug
2. Pad pin
3. Housing
4. Cover
5. Bleed screw
6. Pad spring
7. Brake pads
8. Caliper pin bolt
9. Bracket pin boot
10. Pad retainer
11. Caliper bracket
12. Dust seals
13. Piston seals
14. Pistons
15. Caliper pin boot
16. Bracket pin bolt

WARNING
Do not ride the motorcycle until the brakes operate correctly.

16. Bed the pads in gradually by using only light pressure as much as possible. Immediate hard application glazes the new friction pads and greatly reduces their effectiveness.

FRONT CALIPER

On VT1100C models, the front brake caliper is mounted on the right side. On all other models, the brake caliper is mounted on the left side. All of the procedures in this section are applicable to both the left and right side mounted front brake calipers.

Refer to **Figure 10** (VT1100C) or **Figure 11** (VT1100C2, VT1100C3 or VT1100T).

Removal/Installation

1. If the caliper is going to be removed from the motorcycle, perform the following:
   a. Remove the brake pads as described in this chapter to prevent their contamination from contact with brake fluid.

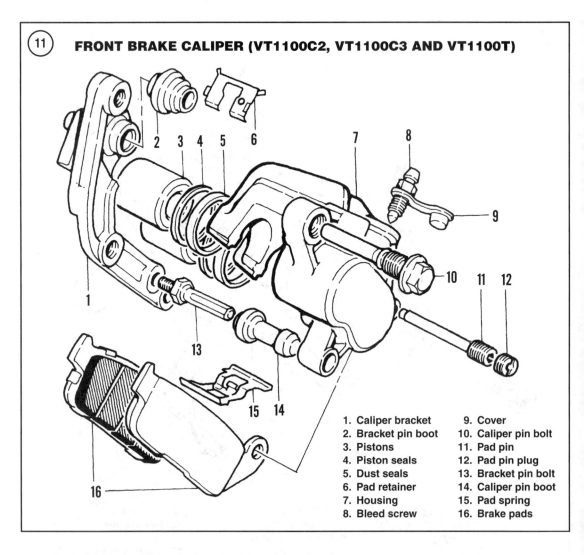

⑪ **FRONT BRAKE CALIPER (VT1100C2, VT1100C3 AND VT1100T)**

1. Caliper bracket
2. Bracket pin boot
3. Pistons
4. Piston seals
5. Dust seals
6. Pad retainer
7. Housing
8. Bleed screw
9. Cover
10. Caliper pin bolt
11. Pad pin
12. Pad pin plug
13. Bracket pin bolt
14. Caliper pin boot
15. Pad spring
16. Brake pads

b. Drain the brake fluid as described in this chapter.

2. Remove the brake hose banjo bolt and the two washers at the caliper (A, **Figure 12**). Place the loose end of the hose in a plastic bag to prevent leakage and hose contamination.

3. Remove the two brake caliper mounting bolts (B, **Figure 12**) and lift the caliper off the brake disc. Remove the speedometer cable from the guide on the caliper, if used.

4. If the brake hose was not disconnected at the caliper, insert a spacer block between the brake pads and support the caliper with a wire hook.

NOTE
The spacer block prevents the pistons from moving out of their caliper bores if the front brake is applied.

5. If necessary, service the brake caliper as described in this chapter.

6. Installation is the reverse of removal. Note the following:

a. Install the caliper assembly over the brake disc. If the pads are installed in the caliper, be careful not to damage their leading edges.

b. Install two new brake caliper mounting bolts (B, **Figure 12**) and tighten to the torque specification in **Table 3**. Position the speedometer cable into the guide on the brake caliper, if used.

c. Place a new washer on each side of the brake hose (**Figure 13**). Then thread the banjo bolt into the caliper and tighten to 34 N•m (25 ft.-lb.).

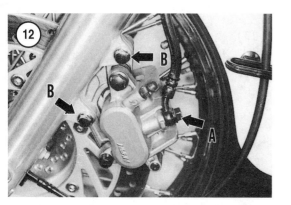

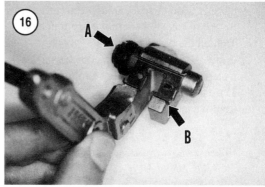

d. If removed, install the brake pads as described in this chapter.

e. If the brake hose was disconnected or it is necessary to do so, bleed the front brake as described in this chapter.

f. Pump the front brake lever to seat the pads against the brake disc.

Disassembly

Refer to **Figure 10** or **Figure 11**.

1. Remove the brake pads, pad spring and brake caliper as described in this chapter.

2. Slide the caliper bracket (**Figure 14**) from the caliper housing.

3. Remove the caliper pin boot (**Figure 15**).

4. Remove the bracket pin boot (A, **Figure 16**) and pad retainer (B).

5. Remove the pistons as follows:

> *WARNING*
> *Be careful when using compressed air. The pistons, dirt and brake fluid can fly from the caliper at great speed and cause injury. Compressed air forces the pistons out of the caliper under considerable force. Do not cushion the pistons by hand, as injury could result. Wear safety eyewear and shop gloves and apply compressed air gradually. Do not use high pressure air.*

a. Identify the pistons by marking their inner bore with a black marker so they can be reinstalled in their original cylinders.

b. Place the caliper on a workbench with the pistons facing down. Place a thick towel between the pistons and workbench. Make sure

14

there is enough space underneath the caliper for the pistons to be removed completely.

c. Tighten the bleed screw.

d. Blow the pistons out with compressed air directed into the hydraulic fluid hose (**Figure 17**).

e. Remove the pistons (**Figure 18**).

NOTE
When removing the seals in Step 6, note the piston seals are thicker than the dust seals.

6. Remove and discard the dust seals (A, **Figure 19**) and piston seals (B).

7. Remove the bleed screw and its cover from the caliper.

Inspection

When measuring the brake caliper components, compare the actual measurements to the specifications in **Table 1**. Replace worn or damaged parts as described in this section.

1. Clean and dry the caliper assembly as follows:

a. Handle the brake components carefully when servicing them.

b. Use only DOT 4 brake fluid or isopropyl alcohol to wash rubber parts in the brake system. Never allow any petroleum-based cleaner to contact the rubber parts. These chemicals cause the rubber to swell, requiring their replacement.

c. Clean the dust and piston seal grooves carefully to avoid damaging the caliper bore. Use a small pick or brush to clean the grooves. If a hard varnish residue has built up in the grooves, soak the caliper in solvent to help soften the residue. Then wash the caliper in soapy water and rinse completely.

d. If alcohol or solvent was used to clean the caliper, blow dry with compressed air.

e. Check the fluid passages to make sure they are clean and dry.

f. After cleaning the parts, place them on a clean lint-free cloth until reassembly.

CAUTION
Do not get any oil or grease onto any of the brake caliper components. These chemicals cause the rubber

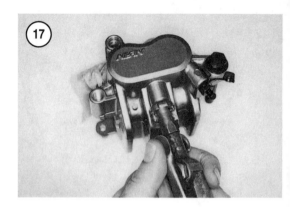

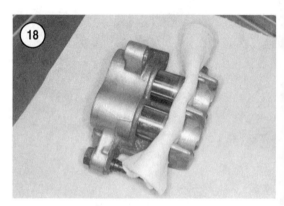

parts in the brake system to swell, permanently damaging them.

2. Check each cylinder bore for corrosion, deep scratches and other wear marks. Do not hone the cylinder bores.

3. Measure the caliper cylinder bore diameters (A, **Figure 20**).

4. Inspect the pistons for pitting, corrosion, cracks or other damage.

5. Measure each piston outside diameter (B, **Figure 20**).

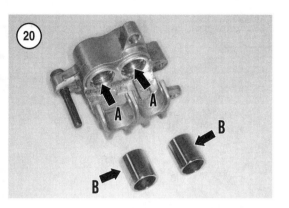

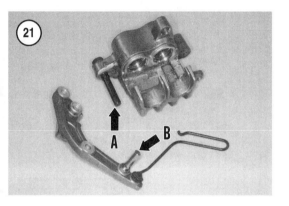

6. Clean the bleed screw with compressed air. Check the valve threads for damage. Replace the dust cap if missing or damaged.

7. Clean the banjo bolt with compressed air.

8. Inspect the caliper and caliper bracket pin bolts and pin boots as follows:

NOTE
The brake calipers are of a floating design. Pin bolts mounted on the caliper housing and caliber bracket allow the brake caliper to slide or float during piston movement. Pin boots installed over each bolt help control caliper movement by preventing excessive bolt vibration and play and to prevent dirt from damaging the bolt operating surfaces. Grooved or damaged pin bolts prevent caliper movement. This condition causes brake pads to wear unevenly, causing brake drag and overheating of the brake disc and brake fluid.

a. Inspect the pin boots for age deterioration and damage.

b. Inspect the pin bolts (A and B, **Figure 21**) for excessive wear, uneven wear (steps) and other damage. Replace damaged pin bolts as required.

NOTE
The caliper bracket pin bolt is not available for all models. Refer to a Honda dealership for availability before removing the original bolt.

9. When reinstalling or replacing damaged pin bolts, apply a medium strength threadlock onto the caliper pin bolt (A, **Figure 21**) and the bracket pin bolt (B) threads and tighten as described in **Table 3**.

Assembly

Use new DOT 4 brake fluid when lubricating the parts in the following steps.

NOTE
A front brake caliper rebuild kit for the VT1100 is available from K&L Supply and can be ordered through most Honda dealerships. The kit contains all the necessary components to rebuild the brake caliper.

1. Install and tighten the bleed screw.

2. Soak the new piston and dust seals in new brake fluid.

3. Lubricate the pistons and cylinder bores with brake fluid. Check that the surfaces are free of dust and other particles.

NOTE
The piston seals are thicker than the dust seals.

4. Install a *new* piston seal (B, **Figure 19**) into each inner bore groove.

5. Install a *new* dust seal (A, **Figure 19**) into each outer bore groove.

NOTE
Make sure each seal fits squarely in its groove.

6. Install each piston into its respective caliper bore with its open side facing out (**Figure 22**). To prevent the pistons from damaging the seals, turn them into the bore by hand.

14

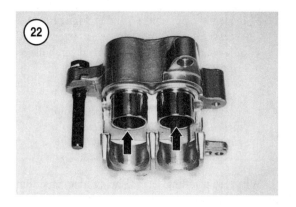

7. Apply silicone brake grease to the inside of the pin boots and along the pin bolts. Install the small boot onto the caliper bracket (A, **Figure 16**) and the large boot through the caliper housing (**Figure 15**).

8. Install the brake pad retainer (B, **Figure 16**) onto the caliper bracket. Make sure it fits tightly.

9. Align and install the caliper bracket over the caliper housing (**Figure 14**).

10. Install the pad spring, brake caliper and brake pads as described under *Front Brake Pads* in this chapter.

FRONT MASTER CYLINDER

Read the information listed under *Disc Service* in this chapter before servicing the front master cylinder.

Removal/Installation

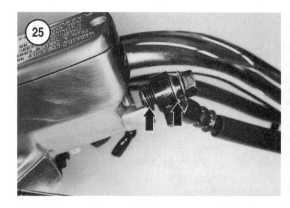

1. Remove the rear view mirror from the master cylinder.

2. Cover the fuel tank and front fender to prevent damage from brake fluid contact.

> *CAUTION*
> *Wash brake fluid off any surface immediately because it damages the finish. Use soapy water and rinse completely.*

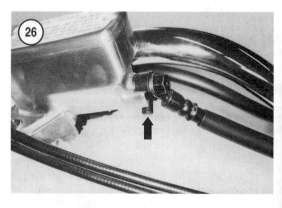

3. Clean the top of the master cylinder of all dirt and debris.

4. Turn the handlebar so the master cylinder reservoir is level. Remove the master cylinder cover assembly. Empty the brake fluid reservoir with a syringe (**Figure 1**). Reinstall the parts.

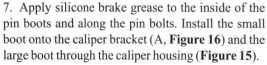

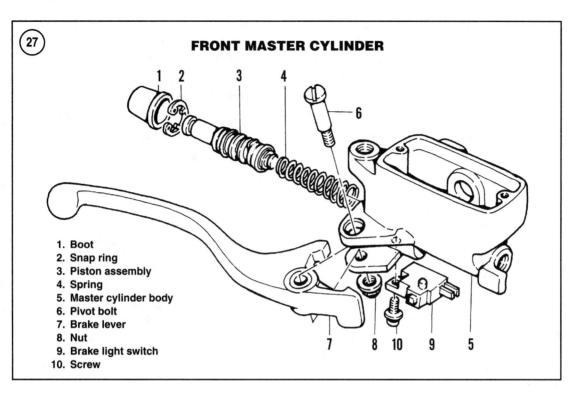

FRONT MASTER CYLINDER

1. Boot
2. Snap ring
3. Piston assembly
4. Spring
5. Master cylinder body
6. Pivot bolt
7. Brake lever
8. Nut
9. Brake light switch
10. Screw

5. Disconnect the brake light switch connectors (**Figure 23**) at the switch.

6. Remove the banjo bolt (A, **Figure 24**) and two washers securing the brake hose to the master cylinder. Cover the open end of the hose with a plastic bag to prevent leakage and hose contamination.

7. Remove the bolts and clamp (B, **Figure 24**) securing the master cylinder to the handlebar and remove the master cylinder.

8. If necessary, service the master cylinder as described in this chapter.

9. Clean the handlebar, master cylinder and clamp mating surfaces.

10. Installation is the reverse of removal. Note the following:

  a. Mount the master cylinder onto the handlebar and align the upper master cylinder and clamp mating surfaces with the punch mark (C, **Figure 24**) on the handlebar.

  b. Install the clamp (B, **Figure 24**) with its UP mark facing up and secure with the mounting bolts. Tighten the upper mounting bolt first, then the lower mounting bolt to 12 N•m (106 in.-lb.). Check that there is a gap at the bottom of the clamp.

  c. Secure the brake hose to the master cylinder with the banjo bolt (A, **Figure 24**) and two *new* washers. Install a new washer on each side of the brake hose (**Figure 25**). If the brake hose is equipped with an extended arm, position the arm against the master cylinder as shown in **Figure 26**. If there is no arm, position the curved part of the hose against the master cylinder.

  d. Tighten the banjo bolt to 34 N•m (25 ft.-lb.).

  e. Bleed the front brake as described in this chapter.

  f. Turn the ignition switch on and make sure the brake light comes on when operating the front brake lever.

Disassembly

Refer to **Figure 27**.

1. Remove the master cylinder as described in this chapter.

2. If not already removed, remove the master cylinder cover, set plate, diaphragm and float.

3. Remove the screw and the brake light switch (A, **Figure 28**).

14

4. Remove the nut, pivot bolt and front brake lever (B, **Figure 28**).

5. Remove the boot (**Figure 29**) from the groove in the end of the piston.

> *NOTE*
> *To aid in the removal and installation of the master cylinder snap ring, thread a bolt and nut into one of the clamp bolt holes and secure the bolt in a vise (**Figure 30**).*

6. Compress the piston and remove the snap ring from the groove in the master cylinder.

7. Remove the piston assembly (**Figure 31**) from the master cylinder bore. Do not remove the primary and secondary cups from the piston.

8. Remove the deflector (**Figure 32**) from the reservoir.

9. Before cleaning the master cylinder, examine the filler port (large hole) and the compensating port (small hole) in the reservoir (**Figure 33**). A plugged compensating port causes pressure to build in the brake system and results in brake drag.

Inspection

When measuring the master cylinder components, compare the actual measurements to the specifications in **Table 1**. Replace worn or damaged parts as described in this section.

1. Clean and dry the master cylinder assembly as follows:
   a. Handle the brake components carefully when servicing them.
   b. Use only DOT 4 brake fluid or isopropyl alcohol to wash rubber parts in the brake system. Never allow any petroleum-based cleaner to contact the rubber parts. These chemicals cause the rubber to swell, requiring their replacement.
   c. Clean the master cylinder snap ring groove carefully. Use a small pick or brush to clean the groove. If a hard varnish residue has built up in the groove, soak the master cylinder in solvent to help soften the residue. Then wash in soapy water and rinse completely.
   d. Blow the master cylinder dry with compressed air.
   e. Place cleaned parts on a clean lint-free cloth until reassembly.

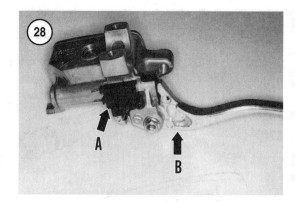

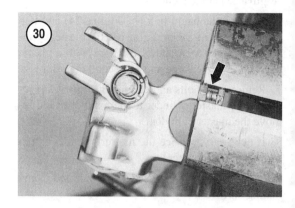

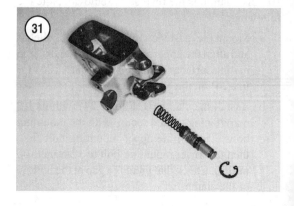

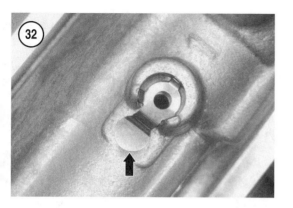

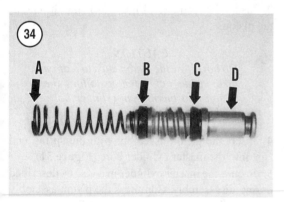

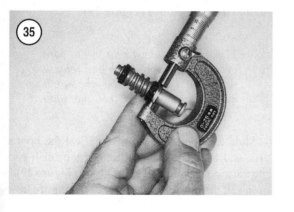

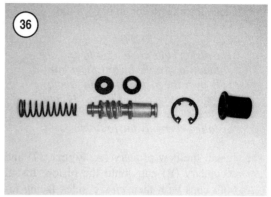

WARNING
Do not get any oil or grease onto any of the components. These chemicals cause the rubber parts in the brake system to swell, permanently damaging them.

CAUTION
Do not remove the primary and secondary cups from the piston. The cups are not available separately and must be replaced with a new piston and spring as an assembly.

2. Check the piston assembly for the following defects. Replace the piston assembly if any of these parts are worn or damaged.

    a. Broken, distorted or collapsed piston return spring (A, **Figure 34**).

    b. Worn, cracked, damaged or swollen primary (B, **Figure 34**) and secondary cups (C).

    c. Scratched or damaged piston (D, **Figure 34**).

    d. Worn or damaged boot.

3. Measure the piston outside diameter at the point indicated in **Figure 35**.

4. To assemble a new piston assembly (**Figure 36**), perform the following:

NOTE
A master cylinder rebuild kit is available from K&L Supply and can be ordered through most Honda dealerships. The kit contains all the necessary components to rebuild the master cylinder.

    a. Before installing the new piston cups, lubricate them with brake fluid. This helps to clean the cups as well as aid in their installation.

14

b. Clean the new piston in brake fluid.

NOTE
*The piston cups are a tight fit and are difficult to install. Install them carefully over the piston to avoid damaging them. Refer to **Figure 34** and **Figure 37** to make sure the cups are installed correctly the first time.*

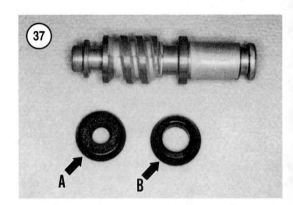

c. Install the new primary (A, **Figure 37**) and secondary (B) cups onto the piston. Install both cups with their *closed* sides facing toward the rear of the piston (opposite the spring end). If necessary, refer to the original piston assembly (**Figure 34**) for cup alignment.

5. Inspect the master cylinder bore (**Figure 38**) for corrosion, pitting and other damage. The bore surface must be smooth.

6. Inspect the threads in the master cylinder body. If damaged, chase threads with a suitable size metric tap or replace the master cylinder assembly.

7. Inspect the fluid viewing port for fluid leakage. If leakage has occurred, replace the master cylinder body.

8. Inspect the hand lever pivot hole on the master cylinder body. Check for cracks or elongation. If damaged, replace the master cylinder body.

9. Measure the master cylinder bore inside diameter (**Figure 38**).

10. Clean the filler and compensating ports (**Figure 33**) in the master cylinder with compressed air.

11. Check the brake lever assembly for the following defects:

a. Damaged brake lever. Check the pivot hole for cracks and elongation.

b. Scored or damaged pivot bolt.

12. Inspect the master cylinder reservoir diaphragm for tearing, cracks or other damage. A damaged diaphragm allows moisture to enter the reservoir and contaminate the brake fluid.

Assembly

1. If installing a new piston assembly, assemble it as described under *Inspection* in this section.

2. Lubricate the piston assembly and cylinder bore with DOT 4 brake fluid. Check that the surfaces are free of dust and other particles.

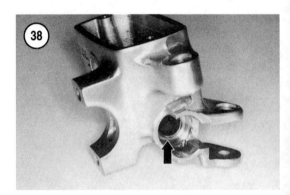

3. Install the spring (A, **Figure 34**) onto the end of the piston.

CAUTION
Do not allow the piston cups to tear or turn inside out when installing the piston into the master cylinder bore. Both cups are larger than the bore.

4. Insert the piston assembly with the spring end first into the master cylinder bore (**Figure 31**).

5. Secure the master cylinder in a vise as described during disassembly. Compress the piston assembly and install a new snap ring with the flat side facing out into the bore groove (**Figure 39**).

CAUTION
The snap ring must seat in the bore groove completely. Push and release the piston a few times to make sure it moves smoothly and that the snap ring does not pop out.

6. Slide the boot over the piston. Seat the boot's large end against the snap ring and the small end into the groove in the end of the piston (**Figure 29**).

7. Install the brake lever assembly (B, **Figure 28**):

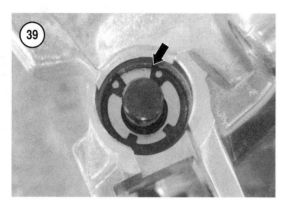

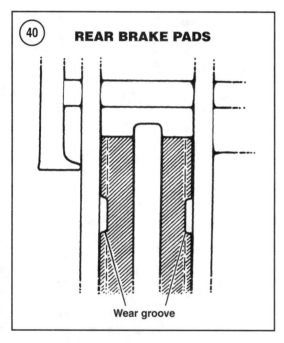

REAR BRAKE PADS

Wear groove

a. Lubricate the pivot bolt shoulder with silicone brake grease.
b. Install the brake lever.
c. Install and tighten the brake lever pivot bolt to 1 N•m (8.8 in.-lb.). Pump the brake lever to make sure it moves freely. If there is any binding or roughness, remove the pivot bolt and brake lever and inspect the parts.
d. Hold the pivot bolt, then install and tighten the brake lever pivot nut to 6 N•m (53 in.-lb.). Check that the brake lever moves freely.

NOTE
The piston assembly must move smoothly when operating the brake lever. If there is any roughness, the snap ring may have popped out of its

groove. Remove the brake lever and check the spring, piston and snap ring.

8. Install the deflector (**Figure 32**) into the reservoir.

NOTE
The deflector prevents brake fluid from spurting out the reservoir when operating the brake lever during brake bleeding.

9. Install the front brake light switch (A, **Figure 28**) and secure with the mounting screw.
10. Install the float, diaphragm, set plate and cover.
11. Install the master cylinder as described in this section.

REAR BRAKE PADS
(ALL MODELS EXCEPT VT1100C)

There is no recommended mileage interval for changing the brake pads. Pad wear depends on the riding habits and condition of the brake system. As the brake pads wear, the brake fluid level drops in the reservoir and automatically adjusts for wear.

The brake pads can be replaced with the brake caliper mounted on the motorcycle.

Always replace both rear brake pads at the same time. Never use one new brake pad with a used brake pad in a caliper. Doing so causes an unbalanced braking condition.

Inspection

Replace the brake pads when they are worn to the bottom of the pad wear limit groove (**Figure 40**) or when contaminated with brake fluid.

Replacement

1. Review the *Disc Brake Service* information in the preceding section.
2. Remove the bolt, rear master cylinder cover and spacer.
3. Remove the reservoir cover assembly. Use a syringe to remove and discard about 50 percent of the fluid from the reservoir. This prevents the master cylinder from overflowing when the caliper piston is reposition for pad reinstallation. Do *not* drain the reservoir to the point where the port in the bottom of

14

the reservoir is exposed to air. When air enters the system, the system has to be bled.

4. Before removing the brake pads, note the following:

  a. Check the caliper for leaks around the brake hose banjo bolt, bleed valve and caliper piston.

  b. Check for tar, dirt and other material stuck to the exposed part of the caliper piston. If debris is present, remove the brake pads as described below, but do not push the piston back into the caliper (Step 5). Doing so may cause the debris to damage the caliper seals. After removing the brake pads, clean the exposed part of the caliper piston with a soft brush or cloth and an aerosol brake cleaner, then reposition the piston.

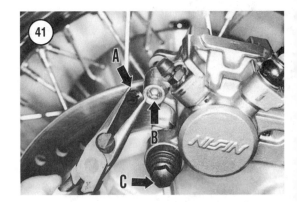

CAUTION
Do not allow the master cylinder reservoir to overflow when performing Step 5. Brake fluid damages most surfaces it contacts.

5. Hold the caliper housing from the outside and push it toward its brake disc to push the piston into the caliper to make room for the new brake pads.

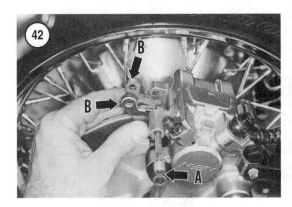

NOTE
The piston should move smoothly when repositioning it in Step 5. If not, check the caliper for a stuck piston or damaged caliper bore, piston and seals. Repair requires overhaul of the brake caliper assembly.

6. Reinstall the cover assembly removed in Step 3.
7. Remove the pad pin plug (A, **Figure 41**) and loosen the pad pin (B).
8. Remove the caliper bracket bolt (C, **Figure 41**) and pivot the caliper up.
9. Remove the pad pin (A, **Figure 42**) and both brake pads (B).

NOTE
Figure 43 is shown with the caliper removed to better show the pad spring installed position.

10. Make sure the pad spring (**Figure 43**) is in good condition and installed tightly in the caliper. Replace the pad spring if it has a loose fit or is damaged.
11. Inspect the pad pin and caliper bracket bolt (**Figure 44**) for excessive wear, corrosion or dam-

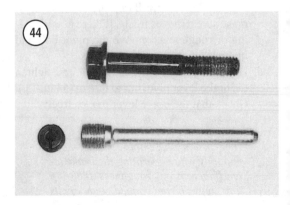

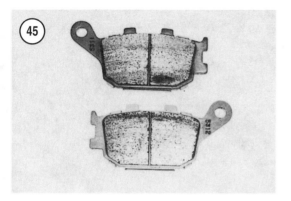

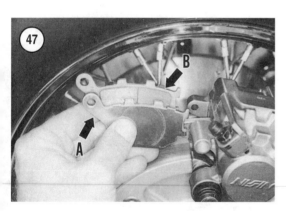

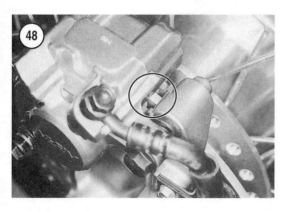

age. Use a wire-wheel to remove corrosion and dirt from the pad pin surface. A dirty or damaged pad pin surface prevents the brake pads from sliding properly and causes brake drag and overheating of the brake disc.

12. Inspect the brake pads (**Figure 45**) as follows:

   a. Inspect the friction material for light surface dirt, grease and oil contamination. Remove light contamination with sandpaper. If the contamination has penetrated the surface, replace the brake pads.

   b. Inspect the brake pads for excessive wear or damage. Each pad should show equal amounts of wear. Replace the brake pads when the friction material is worn to the wear limit groove (**Figure 40**) on the pad.

   c. Check the shim (**Figure 46**) on the backside of each pad for rust, corrosion and damage. Make sure each shim fits tightly on its pad.

WARNING
Do not use grease to hold the pad shims on the pads. Heat thins the grease and causes it to contaminate the pads and disc.

13. If brake fluid is present around the caliper piston, overhaul the brake caliper as described in this chapter.

14. Service the brake disc as follows:

   a. Use brake cleaner and a fine-grade emery cloth to remove road debris and brake pad residue from the brake disc. Clean both sides of the disc.

NOTE
Because different pad compounds may not be compatible, make sure to clean the brake disc when changing pad compounds. Old material left on the disc may contaminate the new pads.

   b. Check the brake disc for wear as described in this chapter.

15. Install the outer (A, **Figure 47**) and inner (B) brake pads into the caliper and hold them in place so the front end of each pad rests on the pad retainer (**Figure 48**) on the caliper bracket.

16. Lower the brake caliper over the brake disc and pads. Check that the front end of each pad still rests on the pad retainer (**Figure 48**).

14

17. Install the caliper bracket bolt (C, **Figure 41**) as follows:

   a. Lubricate the bolt shoulder with silicone brake grease. Do not lubricate the bolt threads.

   b. Tighten the caliper bracket bolt to 23 N•m (17 ft.-lb.).

18. Push the brake pads up against the pad spring and install the pad pin (B, **Figure 41**) through the caliper and both brake pads and thread into the caliper housing. Tighten the pad pin to 18 N•m (159 in.-lb).

19. Install and tighten the pad pin plug (A, **Figure 41**) to the torque specification in **Table 4**.

20. Pump the rear brake pedal to correctly seat the pads against the disc, then check the brake fluid level in the reservoir. If necessary, add new DOT 4 brake fluid (Chapter Three).

21. Install the master cylinder reservoir spacer, cover and mounting bolt.

WARNING
Do not ride the motorcycle until the brakes operate correctly.

22. Bed the pads in gradually by using only light pressure as much as possible. Immediate hard application glazes the new friction pads and greatly reduces their effectiveness.

REAR CALIPER
(ALL MODELS EXCEPT VT1100C)

Removal/Installation

1. Remove the brake pads as described in this chapter.

2. If the caliper is going to be removed from the motorcycle:

   a. Drain the brake fluid as described in this chapter.

   b. Remove the brake hose banjo bolt and the two washers at the caliper (**Figure 49**). Place the loose end of the hose in a plastic bag to prevent leakage and hose contamination.

3. Raise and slide the caliper (A, **Figure 50**) off the caliper mounting bracket.

4. If necessary, service the brake caliper as described in this chapter.

5. If the brake hose was not disconnected, support the caliper to prevent damaging the brake hose.

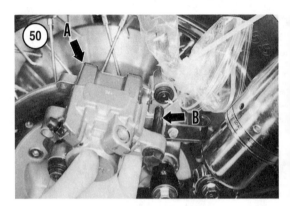
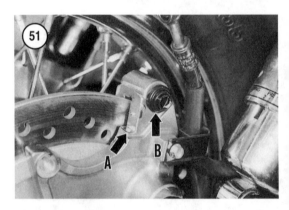

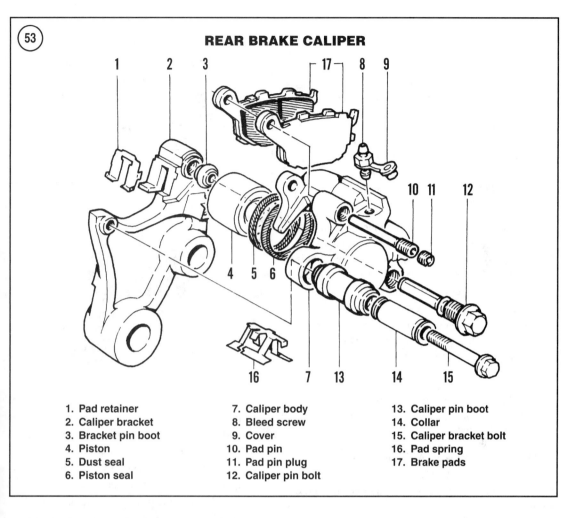

REAR BRAKE CALIPER

1. Pad retainer
2. Caliper bracket
3. Bracket pin boot
4. Piston
5. Dust seal
6. Piston seal
7. Caliper body
8. Bleed screw
9. Cover
10. Pad pin
11. Pad pin plug
12. Caliper pin bolt
13. Caliper pin boot
14. Collar
15. Caliper bracket bolt
16. Pad spring
17. Brake pads

6. Check that the pad retainer (A, **Figure 51**) is mounted tightly against the caliper bracket. Replace the pad retainer if it is loose or damaged.

7. Check that the pin boot (B, **Figure 51**) is mounted on the caliper bracket.

NOTE
If the pin boot is damaged, replace the boot and clean the caliper bracket pin bore.

8. Lubricate the caliper pin bolt (B, **Figure 50**) with silicone brake grease. If the pin boot (B, **Figure 51**) was replaced, lubricate the inside of the boot and the caliper bracket pin bore with silicone brake grease.

9. Install the caliper pin bolt through the boot and into the caliper bracket.

10. Place a new washer on each side of the brake hose (**Figure 52**). Then thread the banjo bolt into

the caliper while making sure the brake hose rests against the stop on the caliper (**Figure 49**). Tighten the banjo bolt to 34 N•m (25 ft.-lb.).

11. Install the brake pads as described in this chapter.

12A. If the brake hose was disconnected, bleed the rear brake as described in this chapter.

12B. If the brake hose was not disconnected, operate the rear brake pedal to seat the pads against the brake disc and obtain a firm pedal. If the pedal does not feel firm, bleed the rear brake as described in this chapter.

Disassembly

Refer to **Figure 53**.

1. Remove the brake caliper as described in this chapter.

2. Remove the pad spring (16, **Figure 53**), collar (14) and caliper pin boot (13).

14

3. Remove the piston as follows:

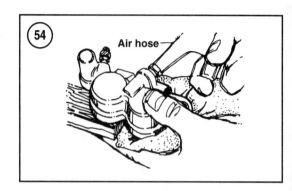

WARNING
Be careful when using compressed air. The piston, dirt and brake fluid can fly from the caliper at great speed and cause injury. Compressed air forces the piston out of the caliper under considerable force. Do not cushion the piston by hand, as injury could result. Wear safety eyewear and shop gloves and apply compressed air gradually. Do not use high pressure air.

a. Place the caliper on a workbench with the piston facing down. Place a thick towel between the piston and workbench. Make sure there is enough space underneath the caliper for the piston to be removed completely.

b. Tighten the bleed screw.

c. Blow the piston out with compressed air directed into the hydraulic fluid hose (**Figure 54**).

d. Remove the piston (A, **Figure 55**).

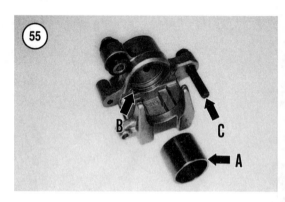

NOTE
When removing the seals in Step 4, note that the piston seal is thicker than the dust seal.

4. Remove the dust seal (A, **Figure 56**) and piston seal (B), and discard them.

5. Remove the bleed screw and its cover from the caliper.

Inspection

When measuring the brake caliper components, compare the actual measurements to the specifications in **Table 1**. Replace worn or damaged parts as described in this section.

1. Clean and dry the caliper assembly as follows:

a. Handle the brake components carefully when servicing them.

b. Use only DOT 4 brake fluid or isopropyl alcohol to wash rubber parts in the brake system. Never allow any petroleum-based cleaner to contact the rubber parts. These chemicals cause the rubber to swell, requiring their replacement.

c. Clean the dust and piston seal grooves carefully to avoid damaging the caliper bore. Use a small pick or brush to clean the grooves. If a hard varnish residue has built up in the grooves, soak the caliper in solvent to help soften the residue. Then wash the caliper in soapy water and rinse completely.

d. If alcohol or solvent was used to clean the caliper, blow dry with compressed air.

e. Check the fluid passages to make sure they are clean and dry.

f. After cleaning the parts, place them on a clean lint-free cloth until reassembly.

CAUTION
Do not get any oil or grease onto any of the brake caliper components. These chemicals cause the rubber parts in the brake system to swell, permanently damaging them.

2. Check the cylinder bore for corrosion, deep scratches and other wear marks. Do not hone the cylinder bore.

3. Measure the caliper cylinder bore diameter (B, **Figure 55**).

4. Inspect the piston for pitting, corrosion, cracks or other damage.

5. Measure the piston outside diameter (A, **Figure 55**).

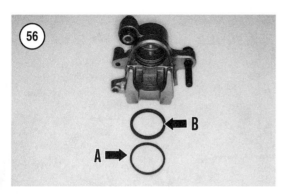

6. Clean the bleed screw with compressed air. Check the valve threads for damage. Replace the dust cap if missing or damaged.

7. Clean the banjo bolt with compressed air.

8. Clean the pin bolt hole (B, **Figure 51**) in the caliper bracket.

9. Inspect the caliper pin bolt, caliper bracket bolt and both pin boots as follows:

NOTE
The brake caliper is a floating design. A pin bolt mounted on the caliper housing and a caliper bracket bolt (and collar) that threads into the caliper bracket allow the brake caliper to slide or float during piston movement. Pin boots installed over each bolt help control caliper movement by preventing excessive bolt vibration and play and prevent dirt from damaging the bolt operating surfaces. Grooved or damaged pin bolts prevent caliper movement. This condition causes brake pads to wear unevenly, causing brake drag and overheating of the brake disc and brake fluid.

a. Inspect the pin boots (3 and 13, **Figure 53**) for age deterioration and damage.

b. Inspect the caliper pin bolt (C, **Figure 55**) for excessive wear, uneven wear (steps) and other damage. Replace the pin bolt (Step 10) if required.

NOTE
The caliper pin bolt is not available for all models. Refer to a Honda dealership for availability before removing the original bolt.

c. Inspect the collar (14, **Figure 53**) and the caliper bracket bolt (15) for corrosion or damage.

10. When reinstalling or replacing the caliper pin bolt (C, **Figure 55**), apply a medium strength threadlock onto the bolt threads and tighten to 27 N•m (20 ft.-lb.).

Assembly

Use new DOT 4 brake fluid when lubricating the parts in the following steps.

NOTE
A rear brake caliper rebuild kit is available from K&L Supply and can be ordered through most Honda dealerships. The kit contains all of the necessary components to rebuild the brake caliper.

1. Install and tighten the bleed screw.
2. Soak the new piston and dust seals in new brake fluid.
3. Lubricate the piston and cylinder bore with brake fluid. Check that the surfaces are free of dust and other particles.

NOTE
The piston seal is thicker than the dust seal.

4. Install a *new* piston seal (B, **Figure 56**) into the inner bore groove.
5. Install a *new* dust seal (A, **Figure 56**) into the outer bore groove.

NOTE
Make sure each seal fits squarely in its groove.

6. Install the piston with its open side facing out (**Figure 57**). To prevent the piston from damaging

14

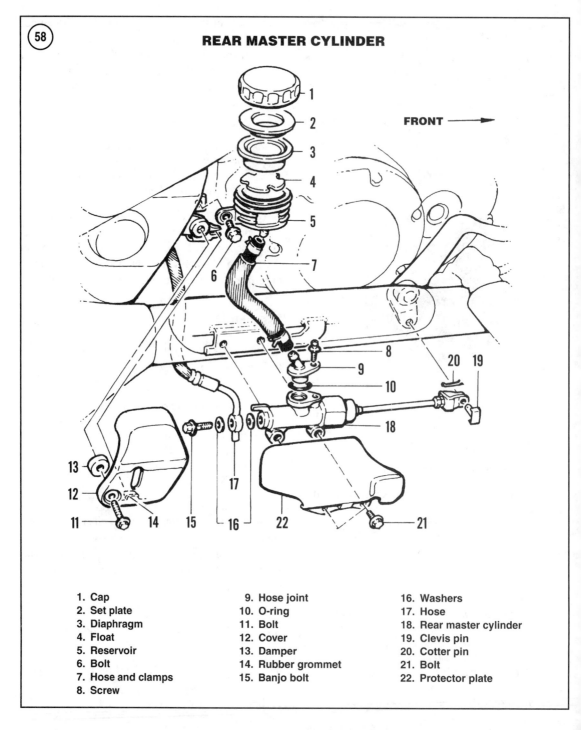

REAR MASTER CYLINDER

FRONT ——►

1. Cap	9. Hose joint	16. Washers
2. Set plate	10. O-ring	17. Hose
3. Diaphragm	11. Bolt	18. Rear master cylinder
4. Float	12. Cover	19. Clevis pin
5. Reservoir	13. Damper	20. Cotter pin
6. Bolt	14. Rubber grommet	21. Bolt
7. Hose and clamps	15. Banjo bolt	22. Protector plate
8. Screw		

the seals, turn the piston until it passes through both seals, and then push it to the bottom of the bore.

7. Apply silicone brake grease inside the pin boots and along the pin bolt and caliper bracket bolt. Install the small boot onto the caliper bracket (B, **Figure 51**) and the large boot through the caliper

housing (13, **Figure 53**). Then install the collar (14, **Figure 53**) through the caliper pin boot.

8. Install the brake pad retainer (A, **Figure 51**) onto the caliper bracket. Make sure it fits tightly.

9. Install the pad spring and brake pads as described under *Rear Brake Pads* in this chapter.

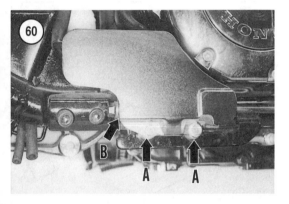

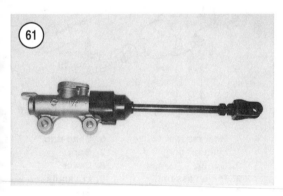

REAR MASTER CYLINDER

Read the information listed under *Brake Disc Service* in this chapter before servicing the rear master cylinder.

Removal/Installation

The rear master cylinder can be removed with the exhaust system installed on the motorcycle. The following steps show removal with the exhaust system removed for photographic clarity.

Refer to **Figure 58**.

1. If the exhaust system is installed on the motorcycle, cover it with a plastic cloth to prevent spilled brake fluid from damaging it.

> *CAUTION*
> *Wash brake fluid off any surface immediately because it damages the finish. Use soapy water and rinse completely.*

2. Drain the brake fluid from the rear brake system as described in this chapter.

3. Loosen, but do not remove, the banjo bolt (15, **Figure 58**) from the master cylinder.

4. Remove the screw and disconnect the reservoir hose joint (9, **Figure 58**) from the master cylinder. Remove the O-ring.

5. Remove the cotter pin and clevis pin (**Figure 59**) and disconnect the pushrod from the brake pedal.

6. Remove the master cylinder mounting bolts (A, **Figure 60**) and the protector plate (B).

7. Remove the banjo bolt, washers and rear master cylinder (**Figure 61**). Discard the two washers.

8. If necessary, service the master cylinder as described in this chapter.

9. Install the master cylinder and protector plate (B, **Figure 60**). Tighten the master cylinder mounting bolts (A, **Figure 60**) to 12 N•m (106 in.-lb.).

10. Connect the pushrod to the brake pedal with the clevis pin (19, **Figure 58**). Secure the clevis pin with a new cotter pin (20, **Figure 58**).

11. Reconnect the hose joint (9, **Figure 58**) as follows:

    a. Apply a medium strength threadlock onto the screw (8, **Figure 58**) and set aside until reassembly.

    b. Lubricate a new O-ring (10, **Figure 58**) with brake fluid and install it onto the hose joint (9).

    c. Connect the hose joint onto the master cylinder and tighten the screw (8, **Figure 58**) to the torque specification in **Table 4**.

12. Secure the brake hose to the master cylinder with the banjo bolt (15, **Figure 58**) and two *new* washers (16). Install a new washer on each side of the brake hose. Position the brake hose against the master cylinder as shown in **Figure 62**. Tighten the banjo bolt to 34 N•m (25 ft.-lb.).

13. Refill the master cylinder reservoir and bleed the rear brake as described in this chapter.

14. Check the rear brake pedal height as described in Chapter Three.

14

15. Turn the ignition switch on and make sure the brake light comes on when the rear brake pedal is pressed.

Disassembly

Refer to **Figure 63**.

1. Remove the master cylinder as described in this section.

2. Slide the cover (A, **Figure 64**) off the master cylinder.

3. Slide the boot (B, **Figure 64**) out of the master cylinder bore.

> *NOTE*
> *To aid in the removal and installation of the master cylinder snap ring, thread a bolt and nut into the end of the master cylinder and secure the bolt in a vise (**Figure 65**).*

4. Compress the piston and remove the snap ring (**Figure 66**) from the groove in the master cylinder.

5. Remove the pushrod and piston assembly (**Figure 66**) from the master cylinder bore. Do not remove the primary and secondary cups from the piston.

6. Before cleaning the master cylinder, examine the filler port (large hole) and the compensating port (small hole) in the master cylinder. A plugged compensating port causes pressure to build in the brake system and causes brake drag.

Inspection

When measuring the master cylinder components, compare the actual measurements to the specifications in **Table 1**. Replace worn or damaged parts as described in this section.

1. Clean and dry the master cylinder assembly as follows:

    a. Handle the brake components carefully when servicing them.

    b. Use only DOT 4 brake fluid or isopropyl alcohol to wash rubber parts in the brake system. Never allow any petroleum-based cleaner to contact the rubber parts. These chemicals cause the rubber to swell, requiring their replacement.

    c. Clean the master cylinder snap ring groove carefully. Use a small pick or brush to clean

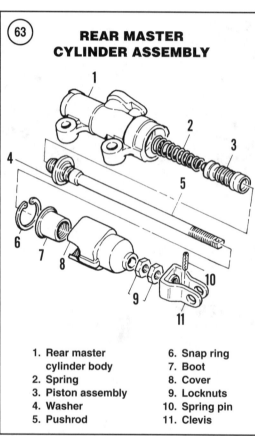

REAR MASTER CYLINDER ASSEMBLY

1. Rear master cylinder body
2. Spring
3. Piston assembly
4. Washer
5. Pushrod
6. Snap ring
7. Boot
8. Cover
9. Locknuts
10. Spring pin
11. Clevis

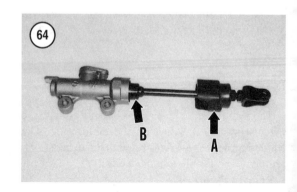

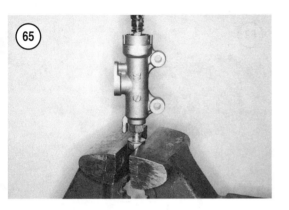

65

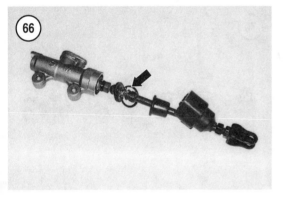

66

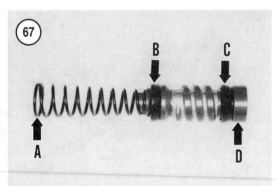

67

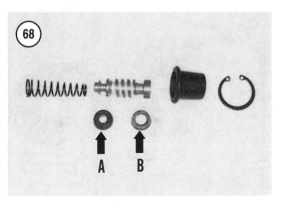

68

the groove. If a hard varnish residue has built up in the groove, soak the master cylinder in solvent to help soften the residue. Then wash in soapy water and rinse completely.
d. Blow the master cylinder dry with compressed air.
e. Place cleaned parts on a clean, lint-free cloth until reassembly.

WARNING
Do not get any oil or grease onto any of the components. These chemicals cause the rubber parts in the brake system to swell, permanently damaging them.

CAUTION
Do not remove the primary and secondary cups from the piston. The cups are not available separately and must be replaced with a new piston and spring as an assembly.

2. Check the piston assembly for the following defects. If any of these parts are worn or damaged, replace the piston assembly:
a. Broken, distorted or collapsed piston return spring (A, **Figure 67**).
b. Worn, cracked, damaged or swollen primary (B, **Figure 67**) and secondary cups (C, **Figure 34**).
c. Scratched or damaged piston (D, **Figure 67**).
d. Worn or damaged boot.
3. Measure the piston outside diameter at the point indicated in D, **Figure 67**.
4. To assemble a new piston assembly (**Figure 68**), perform the following:

14

NOTE
A master cylinder rebuild kit is available from K&L Supply and can be ordered through most Honda dealerships. The kit contains all the necessary components to rebuild the master cylinder.

a. Before installing the new piston cups, lubricate them with brake fluid. This helps to clean the cups as well as aid in their installation.
b. Clean the new piston in brake fluid.

NOTE
The piston cups are a tight fit and are difficult to install. Install them care-

*fully over the piston to avoid damaging them. Refer to **Figure 67** to make sure the cups are installed correctly the first time.*

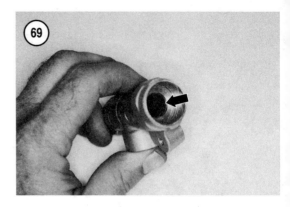

c. Install the new primary (A, **Figure 68**) and secondary (B) cups onto the piston. Install both cups with their *closed* sides facing toward the rear of the piston (opposite the spring end). If necessary, refer to the original piston assembly (**Figure 67**) for cup alignment.

5. Inspect the master cylinder bore (**Figure 69**) for corrosion, pitting and other damage. The bore surface must be smooth.

6. Inspect the threads in the master cylinder body. If damaged, chase threads with a suitable size metric tap or replace the master cylinder assembly.

7. Measure the master cylinder bore inside diameter (**Figure 69**).

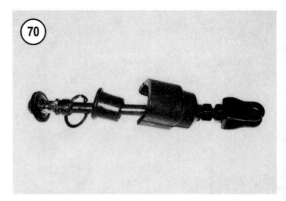

8. Clean the ports in the master cylinder with compressed air.

9. Inspect the master cylinder reservoir diaphragm for tearing, cracks or other damage. A damaged diaphragm allows moisture to enter the reservoir and contaminate the brake fluid.

10. Inspect the pushrod assembly (**Figure 70**) for:

a. Bent, corroded or damaged pushrod. The washer cannot be removed from the pushrod. If damaged, replace the pushrod assembly.

b. Damaged cover or boot. To replace the cover or boot, loosen the locknuts from the end of the pushrod and remove the clevis. Readjust the pushrod length as described under *Assembly* in this section.

c. Weak or damaged snap ring.

Assembly

1. If installing a new piston assembly, assemble it as described under *Inspection* in this section.

2. Lubricate the piston assembly and cylinder bore with DOT 4 brake fluid. Check that the surfaces are free of dust and other particles.

3. Install the spring (A, **Figure 67**) onto the end of the piston.

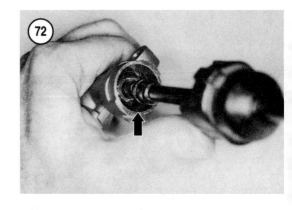

CAUTION
Do not allow the piston cups to tear or turn inside out when installing the

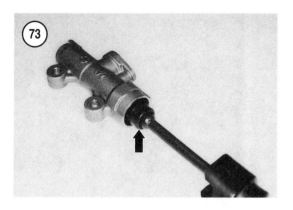

73

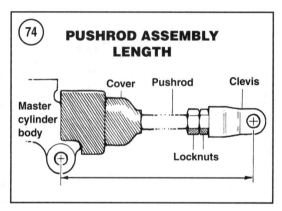

74

PUSHROD ASSEMBLY LENGTH

Master cylinder body

Cover Pushrod Clevis

Locknuts

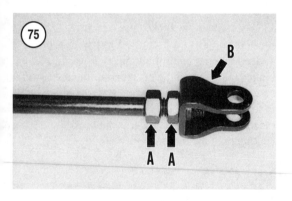

75

B

A A

the snap ring groove, then install the snap ring (**Figure 72**) into the groove.

> *CAUTION*
> *The snap ring must seat in the master cylinder groove completely. Push and release the piston a few times to make sure it moves smoothly and that the snap ring does not pop out.*

8. Apply silicone brake grease to the boot groove in the pushrod. Then slide the boot down the pushrod and seat it against the snap ring. Seat the outer end of the boot into the pushrod groove (**Figure 73**).

9. Align the cover slots with the master cylinder mounting boss, and install it onto the master cylinder (**Figure 61**).

10. Measure the pushrod length from the center of the front master cylinder mounting bolt hole to the center of the hole in the clevis (**Figure 74**). The correct length is specified in **Table 1**. To adjust, loosen the pushrod locknuts (A, **Figure 75**) and turn the clevis (B). Tighten the locknuts and recheck the pushrod length.

11. Install the master cylinder as described in this section.

REAR MASTER CYLINDER RESERVOIR

Removal/Installation

Refer to **Figure 58**.

1. Park the motorcycle on level ground.

> *CAUTION*
> *Wipe up any spilled brake fluid immediately because it stains or destroys the finish of most plastic and metal surfaces. Use soapy water and rinse thoroughly.*

2. If the exhaust system is mounted on the motorcycle, cover it with a plastic drop cloth to prevent spilt brake fluid from damaging it.

3. Drain the brake fluid from the rear master cylinder as described under *Brake Fluid Draining* in this chapter.

4. Remove the bolt and the reservoir cover.

> *NOTE*
> *Do not lose the rubber grommet installed on the reservoir cover tab.*

14

piston into the master cylinder bore. Both cups are larger than the bore.

4. Insert the piston assembly with the spring end first into the master cylinder bore (**Figure 71**).

5. Secure the master cylinder in a vise as described during disassembly.

6. Lubricate the end of the pushrod that contacts the piston with silicone brake grease.

7. Install the pushrod into the master cylinder bore and seat it against the piston. Push the pushrod to compress the piston and install the washer below

5. Remove the reservoir mounting bolt (**Figure 76**).

6. Disconnect the reservoir hose at the reservoir, then remove the reservoir.

7. Cover the exposed reservoir hose end to prevent contamination or brake fluid from leaking out.

8. Reverse these steps to install the master cylinder reservoir, while noting the following:

   a. Tighten the master cylinder reservoir mounting bolt (**Figure 76**) to 12 N•m (106 in.-lb.).

   b. If removed, install the rubber grommet onto the reservoir cover tab.

   c. Align the reservoir cover rubber grommet with the frame cutout and install the reservoir cover.

   d. Tighten the reservoir cover mounting bolt securely.

   e. Refill the brake system and bleed the rear brake as described in this chapter. Check the reservoir and reservoir hose for leaks.

> *WARNING*
> *Do not ride the motorcycle until the rear brake is working properly.*

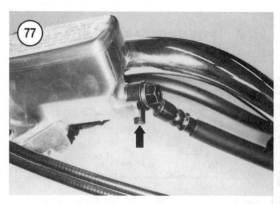

BRAKE HOSE REPLACEMENT

Check the front and rear brake hoses at the brake inspection intervals listed in Chapter Three. Replace a brake hose if it shows signs of bulging, chafing or damage. To replace a brake hose, perform the following:

1. Drape a plastic drop cloth over the areas under and around the brake hose.

> *CAUTION*
> *DOT 4 brake fluid damages the finish on plastic, painted and plated surfaces. Immediately wash spilled brake fluid off the motorcycle. Use soapy water and rinse the area completely.*

2. Drain the brake system as described in this chapter.

3. Before removing the brake hose, note the following:

   a. Record the hose routing on a piece of paper.

   b. Remove any bolts or brackets securing the brake hose to the front fender, frame or suspension component.

   c. Before removing the banjo bolts, note how the end of the brake hose is positioned against the brake unit. Refer to **Figure 77**, typical.

4. Remove the banjo bolt and two washers at the brake caliper. Hold the open end of the hose over a container and pump the brake lever or brake pedal to force fluid out of the hose. Place the loose end of the hose in a plastic bag to prevent brake fluid from leaking onto the motorcycle.

> *CAUTION*
> *Dispose of this brake fluid properly. Never reuse brake fluid.*

5. Remove the banjo bolt and two washers at the master cylinder.

6. Carefully remove the brake hose from the motorcycle.

7. Wash off brake fluid that may have leaked out the hose or brake units during removal.

8. Clean and dry the banjo bolts.

9. Reverse these steps to install the new brake hose, while noting the following:

   a. Compare the new and old hoses to make sure they are the same.

11. Refill the master cylinder and bleed the brake as described in this chapter.

> *WARNING*
> *Do not ride the motorcycle until making sure the front and rear brake are operating properly.*

BRAKE DISC

Inspection

Each brake disc can be inspected while installed on the motorcycle. Small marks on the disc are not important, but deep scratches or other marks may reduce braking effectiveness and increase brake pad wear. If these grooves are evident and the brake pads are wearing rapidly, replace the brake disc.

Table 1 lists specifications for brake disc thickness. The minimum (MIN) thickness is stamped on the outside of the disc face. If the specification stamped on the disc differs from the service limit in **Table 1**, confirm that the proper disc is installed on the motorcycle.

When servicing the brake disc, do not have the disc reconditioned (ground) to compensate for warp. The disc is thin and grinding only reduces its thickness, causing it to warp quite rapidly. If the disc is warped, replace it as described in this section.

1. Support the motorcycle with the front or rear wheel off the ground.

2. Measure the disc thickness at several locations around the disc (**Figure 79**). Replace the disc if its thickness at any point is less than the minimum allowable specification stamped on the disc or less than the service limit in **Table 1**.

3. Make sure the disc mounting bolts are tight before checking brake disc runout.

4. When checking the front brake disc, turn the wheel to one side. Position a dial indicator stem against the brake disc (**Figure 80**). Zero the dial gauge and slowly turn the wheel and measure runout. If the disc runout is excessive:

  a. Check for loose or missing fasteners.

  b. Remove the wheel and check the wheel bearings.

  c. Check the hub for damage.

5. Clean the disc of any rust or corrosion, and wipe clean with brake cleaner. Never use an oil-based solvent that may leave an oil residue on the disc.

b. Clean the *new* washers, banjo bolts and hose ends to remove any contamination.

c. Referring to the notes made during removal, route the brake hose along its original path.

d. Install a *new* washer on each side of the brake hose. Refer to **Figure 78**, typical.

e. Tighten the banjo bolts to 34 N•m (25 ft.-lb.).

10. After replacing a front brake hose, turn the handlebar from side to side to make sure the brake hose does not rub against any part or pull away from its brake unit. Check for any twisting or interference.

14

**Brake Disc
Removal/Installation**

1. Remove the wheel (Chapter Eleven).

2. Remove the bolts securing the brake disc to the wheel and remove the disc. Discard the mounting bolts. Refer to **Figure 81** (front) or **Figure 82** (rear).

3. Perform any necessary service to the hub (wheel bearing or tire replacement) before installing the brake disc.

4. Clean the brake disc threaded holes in the hub.

5. Clean the brake disc mounting surface on the hub.

6. Install the brake disc with the MIN marked side facing out.

7. Install *new* brake disc mounting bolts and tighten in a crossing pattern and in several steps to 42 N•m (31 ft.-lb.).

> *CAUTION*
> *The disc bolts are made from a harder material than similar bolts used on the motorcycle. When replacing these bolts, use Honda brake disc bolts. Never use different bolts. They do **not** properly secure the disc to the hub.*

8. Clean the disc of any rust or corrosion and spray clean with brake cleaner. Never use an oil-based solvent that may leave an oil residue on the disc.

9. Install the wheel (Chapter Eleven).

BRAKE BLEEDING

Air in the brake system increases brake lever or pedal travel while causing it to feel spongy and less responsive. Under extreme braking (heat) conditions, it can cause complete loss of the brake. Bleeding the brakes removes air from the brake system.

The brake system can be bled manually or with the use of a vacuum pump. Both methods are described in this section.

When adding brake fluid during the bleeding process, use DOT 4 brake fluid. Do not reuse brake fluid drained from the system or use DOT 5 (silicone based) brake fluid. Brake fluid damages most surfaces, so wipe up any spills immediately with soapy water and rinse completely.

General Bleeding Tips

When bleeding the brakes, note the following:
1. Cover all parts that could become contaminated by the accidental spilling of brake fluid. Wash any spilled brake fluid from any surface immediately because it damages the finish. Use soapy water and rinse completely.
2. Make sure the brake system banjo bolts and hose fittings are tight.
3. Clean the bleed screw (**Figure 83**) and the area around the valve of all dirt and debris. Make sure the passageway in the end of the screw is open and clear.
4. Use a box-end wrench to open and close the bleed screw to prevent damaging its hex-head. Replace the bleed screw if damaged.
5. Install the box-end wrench on the bleed screw before installing the catch hose (**Figure 84**).
6. Use a clear catch hose to allow visual inspection of the brake fluid as it leaves the caliper. Air bubbles visible in the catch hose indicate there still may be air trapped in the brake system.
7. Turn the handlebars to level the front master cylinder and remove the screws, reservoir cap, set plate

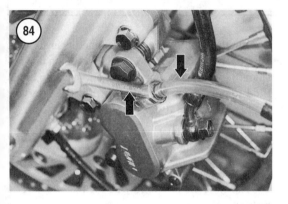

and diaphragm. Fill the reservoir to about 10 mm (3.8 in.) from the top.

8. If using a vacuum pump in the following sections, continually observe the brake fluid level in the reservoir. It drops quite rapidly. Maintain the level at 10 mm (0.39 in.) from the top of the reservoir to prevent air from drawing into the system.

9. It is possible to see air exiting through the catch hose even though no air is in the brake system. Air can enter around a loosened bleed screw or a loose-fitting catch hose. In both cases, air is being introduced into the bleed system, not from within the brake system itself. This condition can be misleading and cause excessive brake bleeding when no air is in the system.

10. Open the bleed screw just enough to allow fluid to pass through the valve and into the catch bottle. The farther the bleed screw is opened, the looser the valve becomes. This allows air to be drawn into the system from around the valve threads.

11. If air is suspected of entering from around the bleed screw, pack the area around the bleed screw threads with silicone brake grease during bleeding.

WARNING
Do not force grease into the caliper past the bleed screw threads. This can block the bleed screw passageway and contaminate the brake fluid.

12. If the system is difficult to bleed, tap the banjo bolt on the master cylinder a few times. Air bubbles can become trapped in the hose connection where the brake fluid exits the master cylinder. When a number of bubbles appear in the master cylinder reservoir after tapping the banjo bolt, air was trapped in this area. It is also helpful to tap the banjo bolt and hose connection at the brake caliper.

13. After bleeding the front brake so no air bubbles appear in the catch hose, test the feel of the brake lever. It should be firm and should offer the same resistance each time it is operated. If the brake lever feels spongy, air is trapped in the system and the bleeding procedure must be continued.

14. Tighten the bleed screw as specified in **Table 3** or **Table 4**.

15. If necessary, add DOT 4 brake fluid to correct the level in the master cylinder reservoir. It must be above the level line.

16. Test ride the motorcycle slowly at first to make sure the brakes are operating correctly.

WARNING
Do not ride the motorcycle until both brakes and the brake light are working properly.

Vacuum Bleeding
(Hand-Operated Vacuum Pump)

This procedure uses a hand-operated vacuum pump to bleed the brake system.

1A. On the front brake, turn the handlebar to level the front master cylinder. Lock the wheel in this position to prevent it from turning and causing brake fluid to spill from the reservoir. Fill the reservoir with DOT 4 brake fluid.

1B. On the rear brake, support the motorcycle on a stand to level the reservoir. Fill the reservoir with DOT 4 brake fluid.

2. Connect the discharge hose between the bleed screw and bottle. Connect the other hose between the bottle and vacuum pump. Refer to the tool manufacturer's instructions for additional information. **Figure 85** shows a typical setup.

14

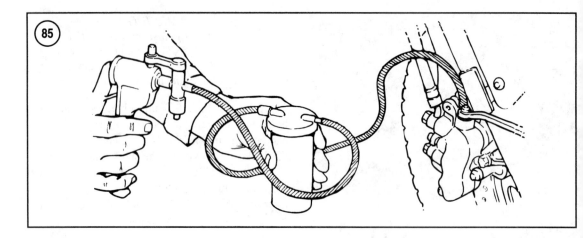

3. Secure the vacuum pump to the motorcycle with a length of stiff wire so it can be left in place when checking and refilling of the master cylinder reservoir.

4. Operate the vacuum pump to create a vacuum in the discharge hose connected to the bleed screw. Then open the bleed screw with a wrench to allow brake fluid to be drawn through the master cylinder and brake hose. If a helper is available to keep the reservoir full of brake fluid, continue operating the vacuum pump to maintain a vacuum in the hose until the system is bled. If a helper is not available, close the bleed screw before the brake fluid stops flowing from the system (no more vacuum in line) or before the master cylinder reservoir runs empty.

5. Repeat Step 5 until the brake fluid running through the discharge hose is a clear and solid stream without air bubbles.

Vacuum Bleeding
(Compressed Air Vacuum Pump)

This tool (A, **Figure 86**, typical) uses compressed air to create a powerful vacuum to drain and bleed brake systems. An air compressor (80-120 psi) is required to operate the pump. The handle (B, **Figure 86**) on top of the cover allows the user to control the amount of brake fluid removed from the system.

NOTE
This tool drains the reservoir very rapidly. Make sure to maintain the brake fluid level in the reservoir to prevent emptying the reservoir and allowing air to enter the system.

1A. On the front brake, turn the handlebar to level the front master cylinder. Lock the wheel in this position to prevent it from turning and causing brake fluid to spill from the reservoir. Fill the reservoir with DOT 4 brake fluid.

1B. On the rear brake, support the motorcycle on a stand to level the reservoir. Fill the reservoir with DOT 4 brake fluid.

2. Assemble the tool following the manufacturer's instructions.

3. Connect a box-end wrench onto the bleed screw. Connect the vacuum hose onto the bleed screw (**Figure 86**).

4. Connect a compressed air source (C, **Figure 86**) to the vacuum tool.

5. Depress the lever (B, **Figure 86**) on top of the pump, then open the bleed screw slightly. As long as the lever is depressed, a vacuum is created in the canister and brake fluid evacuates from the line. Releasing the lever stops the vacuum. This tool drains the master cylinder rapidly. If an assistant is not available to refill the master cylinder during the procedure, release the lever and tighten the bleed screw. Then refill the master cylinder and continue the procedure.

NOTE
Close the bleed screw before releasing the lever on top of the pump.

6. Continue until the brake fluid running through the vacuum hose is a clear and solid stream without air bubbles.

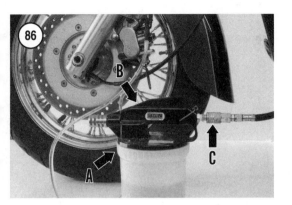

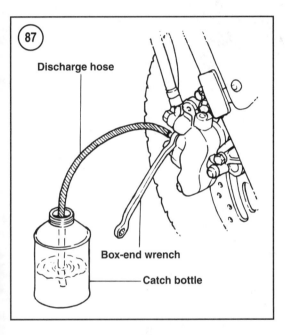

Discharge hose

Box-end wrench

Catch bottle

Manual Bleeding

This procedure requires a catch bottle, length of clear hose (discharge hose), wrench and DOT 4 brake fluid (**Figure 87**).

1A. On the front brake, turn the handlebar to level the front master cylinder. Lock the wheel in this position to prevent it from turning and causing brake fluid to spill from the reservoir. Fill the reservoir with DOT 4 brake fluid.

1B. On the rear brake, support the motorcycle on a stand to level the reservoir. Fill the reservoir with DOT 4 brake fluid.

2. Connect the discharge hose to the bleed screw on the brake caliper. Submerge the other end of the hose into the bottle partially filled with DOT 4 brake fluid (**Figure 87**). This prevents air from be-

ing drawn into the discharge hose and back into the brake caliper.

3. Apply the brake lever or pedal until it stops and hold in this position. Do not release the lever or pedal. Open the bleed screw with a wrench. When doing so, hand pressure applied against the brake lever or pedal causes it to move and force brake fluid to flow through the discharge hose. When the brake lever or pedal stops at the end of its travel, close the bleed screw, then slowly release the brake lever or pedal.

NOTE
*To prevent air from being drawn back into the caliper, close the bleed screw **before** releasing the brake lever or pedal.*

4. With the bleed screw closed, pump the brake lever or pedal a few times and release it.

5. Repeat Step 3 and Step 4 until the brake fluid running through the hose is a clear and solid stream without air bubbles.

BRAKE FLUID DRAINING

Before disconnecting a brake hose, drain the brake fluid. Doing so reduces the amount of brake fluid that can spill out when disconnecting the brake hoses and lines from the system.

1. Read the information listed under *Brake Bleeding* in this chapter for the selection, installation and operation of a brake bleeder.

2. Turn the handlebar to level the front master cylinder or support the motorcycle so the rear reservoir is level.

3. Connect a brake bleeder to the bleeder screw. Open the bleed screw and operate the bleeder until brake fluid stops flowing. Tighten the bleed screw.

4. If flushing the brake system, use DOT 4 brake fluid as a flushing fluid. Flushing consists of drawing new brake fluid into the system until new fluid appears at the caliper without the presence of any air bubbles. To flush the brake system, follow one of the bleeding procedures described under *Brake Bleeding* in this chapter.

**REAR DRUM BRAKE
(VT1100C)**

All VT1100C models use a rear drum brake (**Figure 88**). Activating the foot pedal pulls the pushrod

14

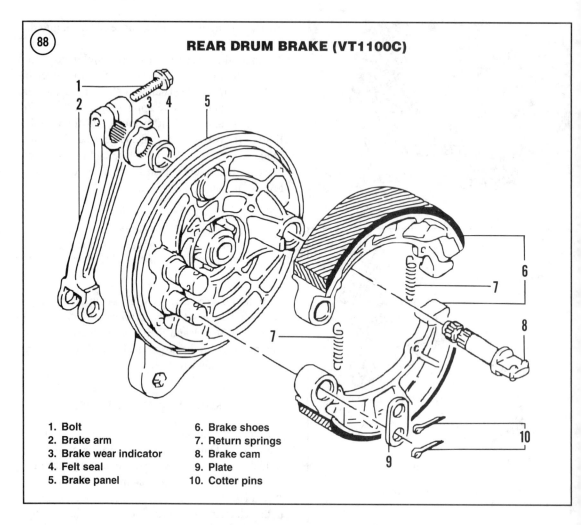

REAR DRUM BRAKE (VT1100C)

1. Bolt
2. Brake arm
3. Brake wear indicator
4. Felt seal
5. Brake panel
6. Brake shoes
7. Return springs
8. Brake cam
9. Plate
10. Cotter pins

and brake rod, which in turn rotates the brake cam in the brake drum. This forces the brake shoes out into contact with the drum.

Rear brake pedal free play must be maintained to minimize brake drag and premature brake wear and to maximize braking effectiveness. Refer to *Rear Brake Pedal Free Play* in Chapter Three for complete adjustment procedures.

WARNING
When handling the rear brake assembly, do not inhale brake dust as it may contain asbestos, which can cause lung injury and cancer. Wear a disposable face mask and wash hands and forearms thoroughly after completing the work. Wet down the brake dust on brake components before storing or working on them. Secure and dispose of all brake dust and cleaning materials

properly. Do not use compressed air to blow off brake parts.

Brake Shoe Replacement

Refer to **Figure 88** for this procedure.
1. Remove the rear wheel (Chapter Eleven).
2. Pull the rear brake panel out of the brake drum.

NOTE
When measuring the brake lining thickness, measure the lining thickness only. Do not include the brake shoe thickness.

3. Measure the brake lining thickness with a vernier caliper (**Figure 89**). Measure at several places along the brake lining. Replace the brake shoes if the lining thickness is worn to the service limit in **Table 2**.

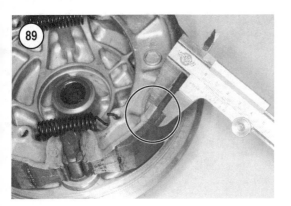

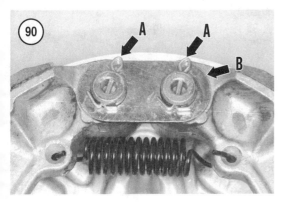

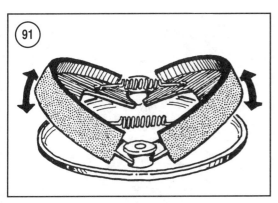

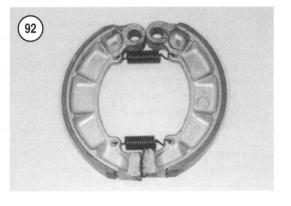

4. Mark the web portion on both shoes so the shoes can be reinstalled in their original position.

NOTE
When handling the brake shoes, place a clean rag over the linings to protect them from oil and grease.

5. Remove the two cotter pins (A, **Figure 90**) and the plate (B).
6. Spread the brake shoes (**Figure 91**) and remove them from the brake panel.
7. Disconnect the return springs (**Figure 92**) from the brake shoes.
8. Discard the brake shoes if installing new shoes.
9. Clean and dry the brake panel and springs.
10. Inspect the return springs for cracks, stretched coils or damaged spring ends. Replace both springs as a set.

NOTE
Worn or damaged return springs may not allow the brake pads to fully retract from the drum, causing brake drag.

11. Lubricate the brake cam and brake panel pivot shafts with a waterproof bearing grease.
12. Install the return springs onto the brake shoes with the open spring ends (**Figure 92**) facing away from the brake panel.
13. Spread the brake shoes (one end at a time) and install them into the brake panel (**Figure 93**). Make sure the return springs attach fully to the brake shoes.
14. Wipe excess grease from the end of the pivot shaft and brake cam.
15. Install the plate (B, **Figure 90**) and two new cotter pins. Install the cotter pins with their closed

14

sides facing out (A, **Figure 90**). Bend the cotter pin arms to lock them in place.

16. Operate the brake arm by hand, making sure it moves and returns under spring pressure.

17. Install the brake panel and rear wheel (Chapter Eleven).

Brake Arm
Removal/Installation

Refer to **Figure 88**.

1. Remove the brake shoes as described in this section.

2. Note the brake arm and brake cam alignment marks (A, **Figure 94**). Realign these marks during installation. If the marks do not align, the brake cam is incorrectly installed.

3. Remove the rear brake arm bolt (B, **Figure 94**) and brake arm (C).

4. Remove the brake wear indicator (A, **Figure 95**) and felt seal (B).

5. Remove the brake cam (**Figure 96**).

6. Clean and dry all parts (except the brake shoes and felt seal).

7. Inspect the brake arm for cracks, excessive wear or other damage.

8. Inspect the brake cam for excessive wear or damage.

9. Inspect the splines on the brake arm and brake cam for damage.

10. Inspect the brake panel bore for cracks, wear or elongation. If damaged, replace the brake panel.

11. Replace the brake wear indicator and felt seal if damaged.

12. Lubricate the brake cam with a waterproof bearing grease and install it (**Figure 96**) into the brake panel. Wipe excess grease off the brake cam and where it contacted the brake panel.

13. Install the felt seal (B, **Figure 95**) into the bore in the brake panel.

14. Install the brake wear indicator by aligning its wide tooth with the wide spline on the brake cam (**Figure 97**).

15. Install the brake arm by aligning its punch mark with the punch mark on the end of the brake cam (A, **Figure 94**).

> *WARNING*
> *When the rear brake is applied, the angle between the brake arm and brake rod must not exceed 90°. In-*

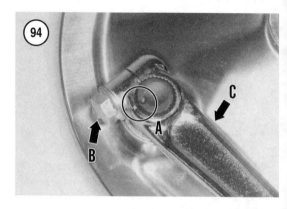

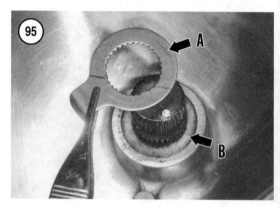

> *stalling the brake arm as described in the text maintains the correct operational relationship between the brake arm and brake cam. If the brake arm and brake rod angle exceeds 90°, the brake cam could pivot overcenter (turn horizontal) and lock the rear brake and wheel, causing the motorcycle to loose control. Do not reposition the brake arm on the brake cam to compensate for worn brake linings or a worn brake drum.*

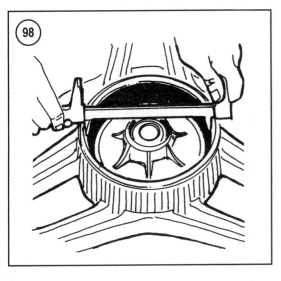

16. Install the rear brake arm bolt (B, **Figure 94**) and tighten to 29 N•m (22 ft.-lb.). Pivot the brake arm, making sure it moves without any roughness or binding. Refer to **Table 5** for torque specifications.

17. Install the brake shoes as described in this section.

Rear Brake Drum Inspection

Table 2 lists the new and service limit specifications for the brake drum outside diameter. The maximum (MAX) allowable outside diameter is embossed on the hub near the brake drum. If the specification on the hub differs from the service limit in **Table 2**, use the specification on the hub when inspecting it.

When servicing the brake drum, do not have the drum reconditioned (ground) to compensate for out-of-round or to remove wear grooves.

1. Remove the rear wheel (Chapter Eleven).
2. Clean the brake drum as follows:
   a. Turn the wheel over and pour any accumulated brake dust into a bag. Tie the bag closed and discard it.
   b. Do not clean the brake drum with compressed air. Instead spray the brake drum with a brake cleaner and allow to drain and dry.
3. Inspect the brake drum for roughness, cracks, distortion and other damage. Service the drum as follows:
   a. Remove light roughness and glaze with a fine-to-medium grade sandpaper.
   b. Replace the rear wheel if the brake drum is cracked or if the drum surface is scored heavily.
4. Measure the brake drum inside diameter with a vernier caliper (**Figure 98**). Measure at different points around the brake drum to determine any out-of-roundness. Replace the rear hub if the inner diameter exceeds the maximum allowable specification on the hub or in **Table 2**.
5. Install the rear wheel (Chapter Eleven).

REAR BRAKE PEDAL AND LINKAGE (VT1100C)

The rear brake pedal assembly consists of the rear brake pedal, middle brake arm and pivot arm. This assembly is joined together by a pushrod. The pivot arm assembly is connected to the rear brake panel by a brake rod.

Rear Brake Pedal
Removal/Installation

Refer to **Figure 99**.

1. Disconnect the rear brake light switch spring from the brake pedal.
2. Remove the rear brake light switch from the footpeg mounting bracket. Position the switch to avoid damaging its wiring harness.
3. Remove the bolts and the right footpeg.
4. Remove the rear brake pedal from the pivot shaft on the frame. Remove the cotter pin, clevis pin and separate the pushrod from the brake pedal. Discard the cotter pin.
5. Inspect and lubricate the brake pedal assembly:

14

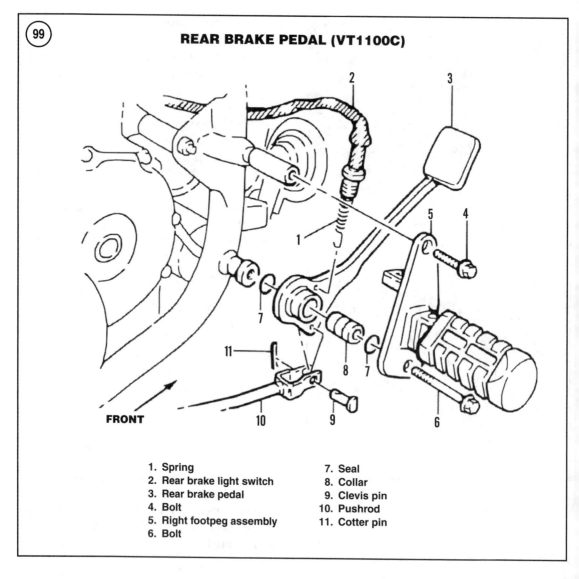

REAR BRAKE PEDAL (VT1100C)

1. Spring	7. Seal
2. Rear brake light switch	8. Collar
3. Rear brake pedal	9. Clevis pin
4. Bolt	10. Pushrod
5. Right footpeg assembly	11. Cotter pin
6. Bolt	

a. Remove the dust seals and collar from the brake pedal. Clean all parts and pivot surfaces.

b. Replace the dust seals if worn or damaged.

c. Check the brake pedal pivot bore, collar and the frame pivot shaft for excessive wear or damage.

d. Lubricate the collar and seal lips with a waterproof grease and install into the brake pedal.

6. Installation is the reverse of removal. Note the following:

a. Lubricate the frame pivot shaft with waterproof grease.

b. Tighten the footpeg mounting bolts to 39 N•m (29 ft.-lb.).

c. Secure the pushrod to the brake pedal with the clevis pin and a new cotter pin. Bend the cotter pin arms to lock it.

d. Check the rear brake adjustment. (Chapter Three).

e. Adjust the rear brake light switch (Chapter Three).

f. Apply the rear brake pedal and check that the rear brake works.

WARNING
Do not ride the motorcycle until the rear brake, brake pedal and brake light work properly.

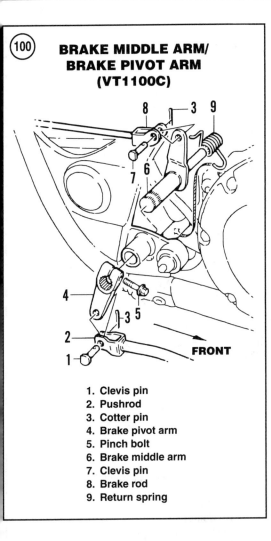

**BRAKE MIDDLE ARM/
BRAKE PIVOT ARM
(VT1100C)**

1. Clevis pin
2. Pushrod
3. Cotter pin
4. Brake pivot arm
5. Pinch bolt
6. Brake middle arm
7. Clevis pin
8. Brake rod
9. Return spring

**Brake Middle Arm and Brake Pivot Arm
Removal/Installation**

Refer to **Figure 100**.

1. Remove the exhaust system if it interferes with brake rod removal. Refer to Chapter Fifteen.

2. Remove the adjust nut (**Figure 101**) and disconnect the brake rod from the brake arm. Then remove the collar and spring.

NOTE
Before removing the brake pivot arm, find the punch marks on the brake pivot arm and brake middle arm. Both marks should align.

3. Remove the bolt and disconnect the brake pivot arm from the brake middle arm. If necessary, spread

the notch in the top of the brake pivot arm with a screwdriver.

4. Remove the brake middle arm and return spring from the frame.

5. Remove the cotter pins and joint pins securing the pushrod and brake rod to the brake middle arm. Discard the cotter pins.

6. Clean the brake middle arm and return spring. Check both parts for damage.

7. Installation is the reverse of removal. Note the following:

   a. Lubricate the brake middle arm shaft and the frame bore with waterproof grease.

   b. Install the brake middle arm through the inside of the frame. Connect the return spring to the brake middle arm and frame as shown in **Figure 100**.

   c. Use new cotter pins when connecting the pushrod and brake rod to the brake middle arm. Bend the cotter pin arms to lock them.

   d. Install the brake pivot arm by aligning its punch mark with the punch mark on the brake middle arm. Install the pinch bolt from the front side of the brake pivot arm and tighten to 26 N•m (19 ft.-lb.).

   e. Check the rear brake adjustment (Chapter Three).

   f. Apply the rear brake pedal and check that the rear brake works.

WARNING
Do not ride the motorcycle until the rear brake, brake pedal and brake light work properly.

14

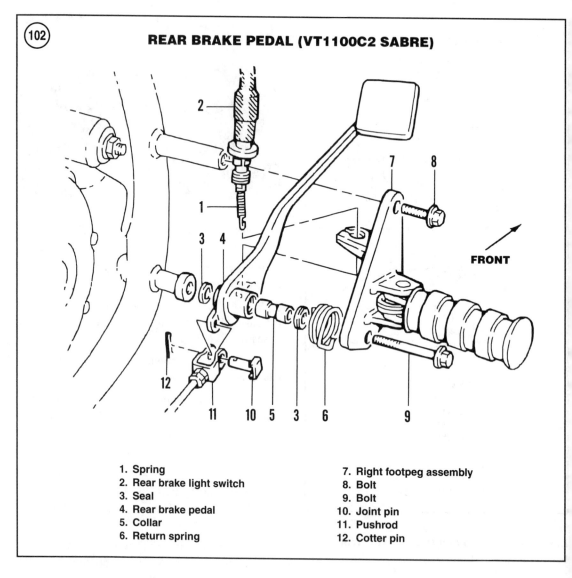

(102) **REAR BRAKE PEDAL (VT1100C2 SABRE)**

FRONT

1. Spring
2. Rear brake light switch
3. Seal
4. Rear brake pedal
5. Collar
6. Return spring
7. Right footpeg assembly
8. Bolt
9. Bolt
10. Joint pin
11. Pushrod
12. Cotter pin

REAR BRAKE PEDAL
(VT1100C2 SABRE, VT1100C2 ACE, VT1100C3 AND VT1100T)

The rear brake pedal is connected to the master cylinder pushrod mounted.

Removal/Installation

VT1100C2 Sabre

The rear brake pedal can be removed with the exhaust system installed on the engine.

Refer to **Figure 102**.

1. Disconnect the rear brake light switch spring from the brake pedal.

2. Remove the rear brake light switch from the footpeg mounting bracket. Position the switch to avoid damaging its wiring harness.

3. Remove the cotter pin, joint pin and separate the pushrod from the brake pedal. Discard the cotter pin.

4. Remove the mounting bolts, right footpeg, return spring and brake pedal.

5. Inspect and lubricate the brake pedal assembly:

    a. Remove the dust seals and collar from the brake pedal. Clean all parts and pivot surfaces.

    b. Replace the dust seals if worn or damaged.

103 **REAR BRAKE PEDAL (VT1100C2 ACE, VT1100C3 AND CT1100T)**

1. Master cylinder pushrod
2. Cotter pin
3. Clevis pin
4. Dust seals
5. Brake pedal
6. Washer
7. Snap ring
8. Brake pedal return spring
9. Brake switch return spring
10. Brake switch

c. Check the brake pedal pivot bore, collar and the frame pivot shaft for excessive wear or damage.

d. Lubricate the collar and the seal lips with a waterproof grease and install into the brake pedal.

6. Installation is the reverse of removal. Note the following:

a. Tighten the right footpeg mounting bolts securely.

b. Secure the master cylinder pushrod to the brake pedal with the clevis pin and a new cotter pin. Bend the cotter pin arms to lock it.

c. Check the rear brake adjustment (Chapter Three).

d. Adjust the rear brake light switch (Chapter Three).

e. Apply the rear brake pedal and check that the rear brake works.

WARNING
Do not ride the motorcycle until the rear brake, brake pedal and brake light work properly.

VT1100C2 ACE, VT1100C3 and VT1100T

Refer to **Figure 103**.

1. Remove the exhaust system (Chapter Fifteen).
2. Remove the bolts and the right side footpeg.

14

3. Disconnect the brake pedal return spring from either the frame or brake pedal.

4. Disconnect the rear brake light switch return spring from the brake pedal.

5. Remove the cotter pin, clevis pin and separate the pushrod from the brake pedal. Discard the cotter pin.

6. Remove the snap ring, washer and brake pedal.

7. Inspect and lubricate the brake pedal assembly:

   a. Remove the dust seals from the brake pedal. Clean all parts and pivot surfaces.

   b. Replace the dust seals if worn or damaged.

   c. Check the brake pedal pivot bore and frame pivot shaft for excessive wear or damage.

   d. Lubricate the seal lips with a waterproof grease and install them into the brake pedal bore.

8. Installation is the reverse of removal. Note the following:

   a. Lubricate the frame pivot shaft with waterproof grease.

   b. Install the snap ring into the frame pivot shaft groove with its closed side facing out. Make sure the snap ring seats in the groove completely. Replace the snap ring if it fits loosely in the shaft groove.

   c. On VT1100C2 ACE and VT1100T models, tighten the right footpeg mounting bolts to 27 N•m (20 ft.-lb.). On VT1100C3 models, tighten the right footpeg mounting bolts securely.

   d. Secure the master cylinder pushrod to the brake pedal with the clevis pin and a new cotter pin. Bend the cotter pin arms to lock it.

   e. Adjust the rear brake light switch (Chapter Three).

   f. Apply the rear brake pedal and check that the rear brake works.

WARNING
Do not ride the motorcycle until the rear brake, brake pedal and brake light work properly.

Table 1 FRONT AND REAR DISC BRAKE SERVICE SPECIFICATIONS*

	New mm (in.)	Service limit mm (in.)
Brake caliper inside diameter		
Front	27.000-27.050	27.06
	(1.0630-1.0650)	(1.065)
Rear	38.180-38.230	38.24
	(1.5031-1.5051)	(1.506)
Brake caliper piston outside diameter		
Front	26.935-26.968	26.91
	(1.0604-1.0617)	(1.059)
Rear	38.115-38.148	38.09
	(1.5006-1.5019)	(1.500)
Brake disc runout	–	0.30
	–	(0.012)
Brake disc thickness	5.8-6.2	5.0
	(0.23-0.24)	(0.20)
Master cylinder inside diameter	12.700-12.743	12.75
	(0.5000-0.5017)	(0.502)
Master cylinder piston outside diameter	12.657-12.684	12.64
	(0.4983-0.4994)	(0.498)
Rear master cylinder pushrod length		
VT1100C2 Sabre	316	–
	(12.4)	–
All other models (except VT1100C)	169	–
	(6.7)	–

*Specifications are for front and rear brake components unless otherwise specified.

Table 2 REAR DRUM BRAKE SPECIFICATIONS

	New mm (in.)	Service limit mm (in.)
Brake drum inside diameter	180.0 (7.09)	181 (7.1)
Brake lining thickness	5.0 (0.20)	2.0 (0.08)

Table 3 FRONT DISC BRAKE TORQUE SPECIFICATIONS

	N•m	in.-lb.	ft.-lb.
Banjo bolt	34	–	25
Brake disc bolts[1]	42	–	31
Brake light switch screw			
VT1100C2 ACE	1.2	10.6	–
All other models	1.0	8.8	–
Caliper bleed screw			
VT1100C2 ACE	5.5	49	–
All other models	5.9	52	–
Front brake hose clamp mounting bolt			
VT1100C2 ACE, VT1100T	12	106	–
Front brake lever			
Pivot bolt	1.0	8.8	–
Nut	6	53	–
Front caliper bracket pin bolt[2,3]	13	115	–
Front caliper mounting bolt[1]			
VT1100C	45	–	33
All other models	30	–	22
Front caliper pin bolt[2]			
VT1100C2 Sabre, VT1100C3	27	–	20
All other models	23	–	17
Master cylinder clamp bolt	12	106	–
Pad pin plug			
VT1100C2 ACE	2.5	22	–
All other models	2.9	26	–
Pad pin	18	159	–

1. ALOC bolts. Install new fastener during installation.
2. Apply a medium strength threadlock onto fastener threads.
3. This bolt is not replaceable on all models. See text for information.

14

Table 4 REAR DISC BRAKE TORQUE SPECIFICATIONS

	N•m	in.-lb.	ft.-lb.
Banjo bolt	34	–	25
Brake disc bolts[1]	42	–	31
Caliper bleed screw			
VT1100C2 ACE	5.5	49	–
All other models	5.9	52	–
Caliper bracket bolt	23	–	17
Caliper pin bolt[2,3]	27	–	20
Caliper stopper pin bolt[1]	70	–	52
Pad pin plug			
VT1100C2 ACE	2.5	22	–
All other models	2.9	26	–
(continued)			

Table 4 REAR DISC BRAKE TORQUE SPECIFICATIONS (continued)

	N•m	in.-lb.	ft.-lb.
Pad pin	18	159	–
Rear master cylinder hose joint screw[2]			
VT1100C2 ACE	1.5	13	–
All other models	2.0	18	–
Rear master cylinder mounting bolt	12	106	–
Rear master cylinder pushrod locknut	18	159	–
Rear master cylinder reservoir mounting bolt	12	106	–
Right footpeg mounting bolts			
VT1100C2 ACE, VT1100T	27	–	20
VT1100C2 Sabre, VT1100C3[4]	–		

1. ALOC bolts. Install new fastener during installation.
2. Apply a medium strength threadlock onto fastener threads.
3. This bolt is not replaceable on all models. See text for information.
4. Specification not provided by manufacturer.

Table 5 REAR DRUM BRAKE TORQUE SPECIFICATIONS

	N•m	ft.-lb.
Brake pivot arm pinch bolt	26	19
Rear brake arm bolt	29	22
Right footpeg mounting bolts	39	29

CHAPTER FIFTEEN

BODY AND EXHAUST SYSTEM

This chapter contains removal and installation procedures for the body components and exhaust system. Torque specifications are listed in **Table 1** at the end of chapter.

SEAT

Removal/Installation (VT1100C)

> *NOTE*
> *Make sure not to scratch the rear fender when removing the seats.*

1. Remove the rear seat mounting nut.
2. Raise the rear seat and pull it rearward to disconnect its hook from the bracket mounted on the front seat (**Figure 1**).
3. Remove the front seat mounting bolts and remove the front seat (**Figure 2**).
4. Installation is the reverse of removal. Note the following:

a. Check the seat mounting brackets for loose or missing fasteners. Tighten the fasteners securely.
b. Replace any missing or damaged rubber grommets mounted on the bottom of the front and rear seats.

> *CAUTION*
> *Rubber grommets missing from the bottom of the seal causes the seat to sit lower on the frame and block the air filter intake port. This affects engine performance.*

c. Insert the hook on the front seat under the frame cross member, then push the seat forward. Install and tighten the mounting bolts securely.
d. Install the rear seat between the front seat and the back rest. Push the rear seat forward to engage the hook on the seat with the bracket on the front seat. Tighten the rear mounting nut securely.

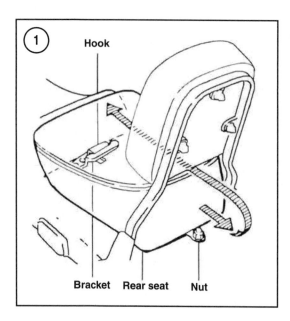

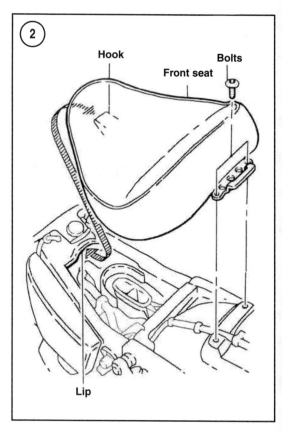

e. Pull up on the front seat to make sure it is hooked correctly under the frame cross member.

Backrest (VT1100C)

1. Remove the nuts and the backrest (**Figure 3**).
2. Installation is the reverse of removal. Apply a medium strength threadlock onto the nuts and tighten to 12 N•m (106 in.-lb.).

Removal/Installation (VT1100C2, VT1100C3 AND VT1100T)

1. Note the following before removing the seats:
   a. The VT1100C2 Sabre is equipped with a one-piece seat.
   b. VT1100C2 ACE, VT1100C3 and VT1100T models are equipped with a separate front and rear seat. Remove both seats, then separate them.

NOTE
Take care not to scratch the rear fender when removing the seat(s).

2. Remove the three mounting bolts and remove the seat (**Figure 4**, typical).
3. On VT1100C2 ACE, VT1100C3 and VT1100T models, to separate the front and rear seats, remove

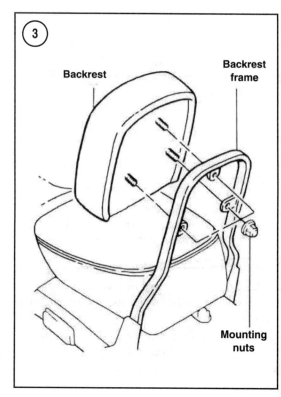

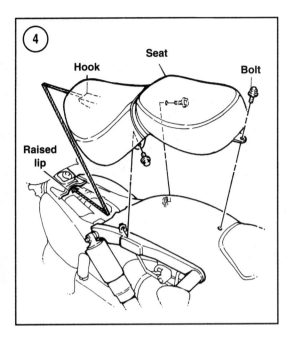

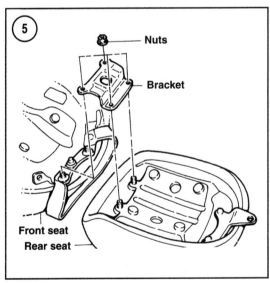

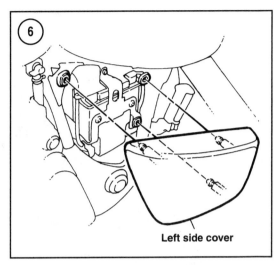

the bracket nuts, bolts (VT1100C3) and bracket (**Figure 5**, typical).

4. Installation is the reverse of removal. Note the following:

    a. If separated, secure the front and rear seats with the mounting bracket, nuts and bolts (VT1100C3). Tighten the fasteners securely.

    b. Check the seat mounting brackets for loose or missing fasteners. Tighten the fasteners securely.

    c. Replace any missing or damaged rubber grommets mounted on the bottom of the front and rear seats.

> *CAUTION*
> *Rubber grommets missing from the bottom of the seal causes the seat to sit lower on the frame and block the air filter intake port. This affects engine performance.*

    d. Insert the hook on the front seat under the frame cross member, then push the seat forward. Install and tighten the mounting bolts securely.

    e. Pull up on the front seat to make sure it is hooked correctly under the frame cross member.

SIDE COVERS

Service decals are mounted on the backside of some side covers. Install new decals when replacing the side cover.

Removal/Installation
(VT1100C2, VT1100C3 and VT1100T)

1. Left side cover:

    a. Carefully pull the side cover bosses out of the frame grommets and remove the side cover (**Figure 6**, typical).

    b. Replace any missing or damaged frame grommets.

15

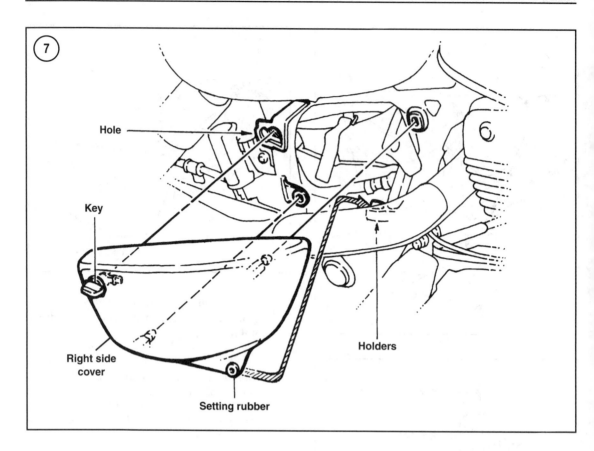

⑦

Hole

Key

Right side
cover

Holders

Setting rubber

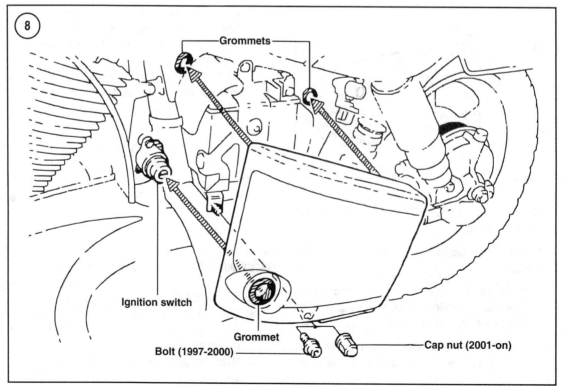

⑧

Grommets

Ignition switch

Grommet

Bolt (1997-2000)

Cap nut (2001-on)

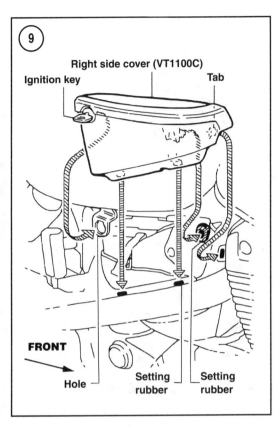

9

Right side cover (VT1100C)

Ignition key

Tab

FRONT

Hole

Setting rubber

Setting rubber

c. Installation is the reverse of removal.

2. Right side cover:

   a. Insert the ignition key into the cover lock and turn 90° clockwise (**Figure 7**).

   b. Pull the right side cover back to disconnect it from its frame damper and remove.

   c. Replace any missing or damaged frame grommets.

   d. Install the upper cover so its bosses fit into the frame grommets. Push the lock in slightly, then turn the key 90° counterclockwise to lock the cover. Remove the key from the lock.

3. Check that the side cover is mounted securely.

Removal/Installation (VT1100C)

Left side cover

1. Remove the bolt (1997-2000) or cap nut (2001-on) from the bottom of the side cover (**Figure 8**).

2. Carefully pull the side cover bosses out of the frame grommets and remove the side cover (**Figure 8**).

3. Replace any missing or damaged frame grommets.

4. Installation is the reverse of removal.

Right side upper and lower covers

The right side cover assembly consists of upper and lower covers. The upper cover must be removed first, then the lower cover.

1. Upper cover:

   a. Insert the ignition key into the cover lock and turn 90° clockwise (**Figure 9**).

   b. Pull the right side cover back to disconnect it from its frame damper and remove.

2. Lower cover:

   a. Remove the exhaust system as described in this chapter.

   b. Remove the two mounting bolts, then release the tab on the lower cover from the hook and remove the cover (**Figure 10**).

3. Installation is the reverse of removal. Note the following:

   a. Replace any missing or damaged frame grommets.

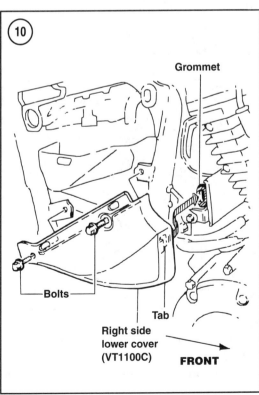

10

Grommet

Bolts

Tab

Right side lower cover (VT1100C)

FRONT

15

b. On the upper cover, inspect the lock for damage.

c. Install the upper cover so its bosses fit into the frame grommets. Push the lock in slightly, then turn the key 90° counterclockwise to lock the cover. Remove the key from the lock.

d. Tighten the fasteners securely.

STEERING COVERS

Removal/Installation

VT1100C2, VT1100C3 and VT1100T

1. Remove the fuel tank (Chapter Eight).

> *NOTE*
> *Figure 11 shows the trim clip. When installed, the screw spreads the clip arms to lock it in place.*

2. Remove the screw from each trim clip, then remove the steering cover (**Figure 12**) from the frame. Remove the trim clips. Do not pry the trim clips out without first removing the screw.

3. Installation is the reverse of removal. Note the following:

a. Replace damaged trim clips.

b. Align the holes in the steering side cover with the frame bracket holes and install the trim clips without the screws.

c. Push a screw into each trim clip to lock it.

VT1100C

1. Remove the fuel tank (Chapter Eight).

2. Remove the screw from the front of the steering cover (**Figure 13**).

3. Pry out on the rear lower end of the cover to release its grommet from the frame boss. Then release the cover from the stud on the frame and remove it (**Figure 13**).

4. Installation is the reverse of removal.

WINDSHIELD (VT1100T)

Removal/Installation

> *NOTE*
> *Make sure not to scratch the windshield when removing and installing it.*

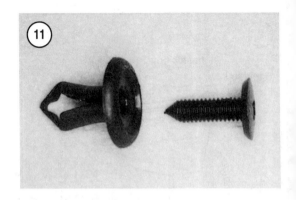

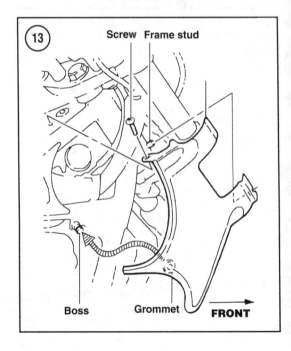

Screw   Frame stud

Boss   Grommet   **FRONT**

1. Place a towel across the front fender.

2. Remove the two nuts securing front lower part of the windshield (**Figure 14**) to the headlight mounting bracket.

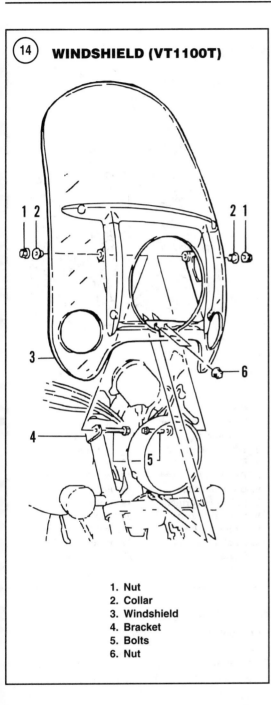

⑭ **WINDSHIELD (VT1100T)**

1 2   2 1

3

4

5

6

1. Nut
2. Collar
3. Windshield
4. Bracket
5. Bolts
6. Nut

3. Loosen the two nuts securing the windshield to the mounting brackets on the front fork tubes (**Figure 14**).

4. While holding the windshield, remove the two nuts, bolts and windshield.

5. Installation is the reverse of removal. Do not overtighten the two nuts at the bottom of the windshield.

Disassembly/Reassembly

Refer to **Figure 15** when replacing the windshield or mounting bracket assembly. Note the following:

NOTE
Make sure not to scratch the windshield when replacing it.

1. Different fasteners and grommets secure the windshield to its mounting bracket. Identify these parts for correct reassembly.
2. Check the rubber parts for wear and deterioration and replace if necessary.
3. Clean all of the fastener threads before installing them.
4. Do not overtighten the screws that secure the stay brackets and garnish strips to the windshield.

SADDLEBAGS (VT1100T)

Removal/Installation

1. Support the motorcycle on its sidestand.
2. Open the saddlebag and insert the ignition key into the cover lock and turn it counterclockwise.
3. Working inside the saddlebag, remove the four mounting bolts (**Figure 16**), then remove the saddlebag from its mounting bracket.
4. Installation is the reverse of removal.

Mounting Bracket
Removal/Installation

Refer to **Figure 17** when servicing the saddlebag mounting bracket assembly. Tighten the bolts securely.

FRONT FENDER

Removal/Installation

1. Remove the front wheel (Chapter Eleven).
2. Remove the speedometer cable (A, **Figure 18**, typical) from its guide on the front fender.
3. Remove the front brake hose clamp bolt (B, **Figure 18**, typical) at the front fender. Note the bracket installed on the inside of the front fender (**Figure 19**).
4. Remove the front fender mounting bolts and remove the front fender. On VT1100C2 Sabre mod-

15

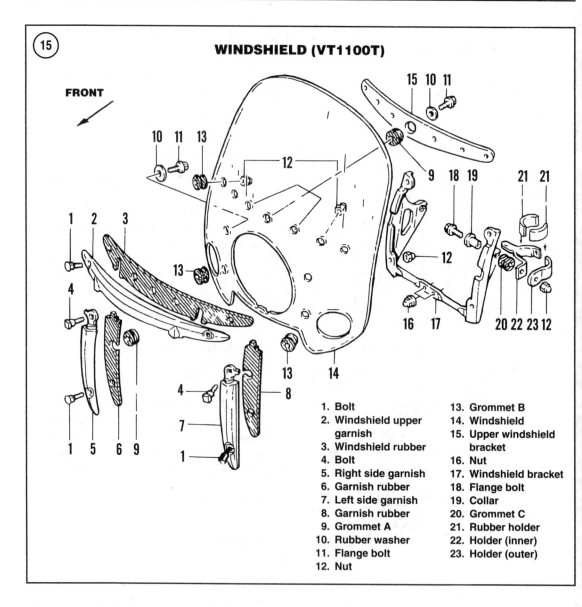

WINDSHIELD (VT1100T)

FRONT

1. Bolt
2. Windshield upper garnish
3. Windshield rubber
4. Bolt
5. Right side garnish
6. Garnish rubber
7. Left side garnish
8. Garnish rubber
9. Grommet A
10. Rubber washer
11. Flange bolt
12. Nut
13. Grommet B
14. Windshield
15. Upper windshield bracket
16. Nut
17. Windshield bracket
18. Flange bolt
19. Collar
20. Grommet C
21. Rubber holder
22. Holder (inner)
23. Holder (outer)

els, remove the brace and collars when removing the fender.

5. Installation is the reverse of removal. Note the following:

a. Clean the mounting bolt and front fork threads of all dirt and debris.

b. Tighten the fender mounting bolts securely.

c. Tighten the front brake hose clamp bolt securely.

d. Check the front brake operation before riding the motorcycle.

Fender Garnish Covers (VT1100C3)

The fender is equipped with four separate garnish covers. These covers can be replaced after removing the bolts, nuts and rubber grommets.

Fender Extension (VT1100T)

The fender extension can be replaced by first removing the three nuts. During installation, apply a medium strength threadlock onto the fender studs and tighten the nuts securely.

16 **SADDLEBAG (VT1100T)**

1. Bolt
2. Saddlebag
3. Bracket
4. Bracket
5. Heat guard

REAR FENDER

Removal/Installation

Refer to **Figure 20**, typical when removing the rear fender.

> *NOTE*
> *On VT1100T models, the rear fender can be removed with the saddlebags mounted on the motorcycle.*

1. On VT1100C models, remove the bolts, washers and backrest assembly.

2. Remove the seat(s) as described in this chapter.

3. Disconnect the taillight and brake light connectors. Position the wiring harness so it can be easily removed with the fender.

4. On VT1100C2 ACE models, disconnect the fuse box 2P-white connector from the fender stay (**Figure 21**). Push the connector tab toward the connector wires, then slide the connector off the fender tab.

> *NOTE*
> *The rear part of the fender is heavy because of the taillight assembly. When releasing the fender, do not allow the back of the fender to fall down and contact the frame and fender stays.*

> *NOTE*
> *On VT1100T models, open the saddlebags to access the fender mounting bolts.*

5. While supporting the rear fender, remove the 8 mm (A, **Figure 22**) and 10 mm (B) bolts securing the rear fender to the fender stays. Lower the rear fender onto the rear tire.

6. On VT1100C and VT1100T modles, perform Step 4 to disconnect the fuse box connector.

7. Carefully remove the rear fender (**Figure 23**) from between the fender stays.

8. Installation is the reverse of removal. Note the following:

   a. Clean and dry the mounting bolts.

   b. Check threads in the fender bolt holes for damage. Clean and dry the threads.

   c. Lubricate the 10 mm bolts threads and washer surfaces with engine oil before installing them.

   d. Install the 8 mm and 10 mm mounting bolts finger-tight before tightening them. Check the wiring harness routing.

15

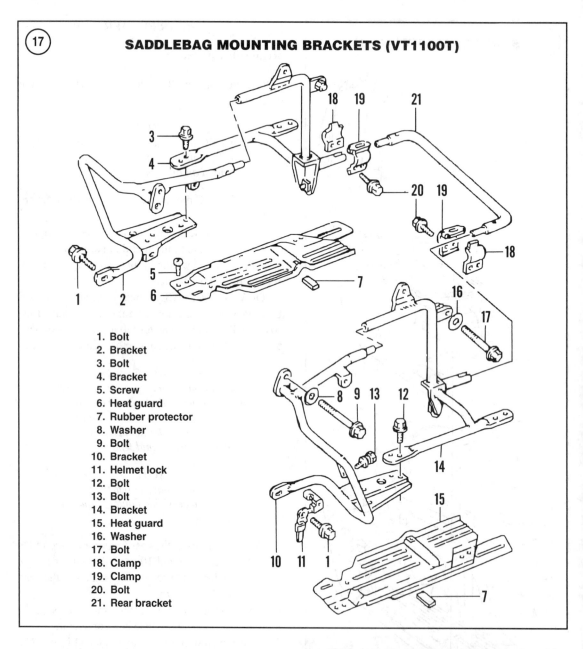

17

SADDLEBAG MOUNTING BRACKETS (VT1100T)

1. Bolt
2. Bracket
3. Bolt
4. Bracket
5. Screw
6. Heat guard
7. Rubber protector
8. Washer
9. Bolt
10. Bracket
11. Helmet lock
12. Bolt
13. Bolt
14. Bracket
15. Heat guard
16. Washer
17. Bolt
18. Clamp
19. Clamp
20. Bolt
21. Rear bracket

e. Tighten the 10 mm bolt (B, **Figure 22**) to 64 N•m (47 ft.-lb.).

f. Tighten the 8 mm bolt (A, **Figure 22**) to 26 N•m (19 ft.-lb.).

g. Check all of the rear lights for proper operation.

REAR FENDER STAY

The rear fender stays (C, **Figure 22**) are bolted to the rear frame arms and support the rear fender. On

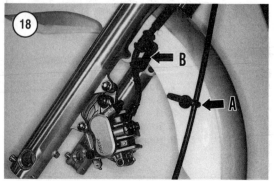

18

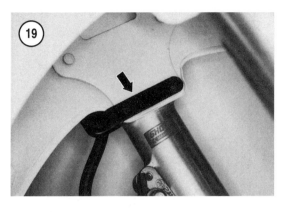

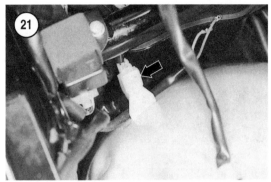

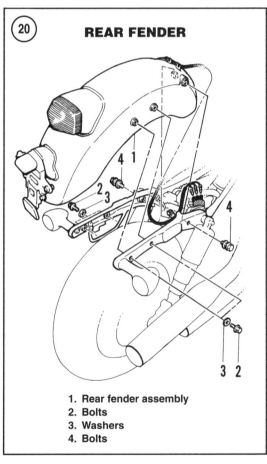

REAR FENDER

4 1

2 3

4

3 2

1. Rear fender assembly
2. Bolts
3. Washers
4. Bolts

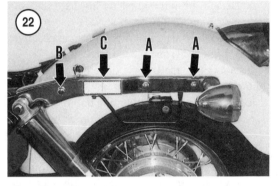

VT1100C and VT1100C2 ACE models, the rear turn signals are bolted to the stays.

Removal/Installation

> *NOTE*
> *When replacing both rear fender stays, do only one stay at a time.*

1. Remove the seat as described in this chapter.

2. Remove the rear fender as described in this chapter.

3. Support the motorcycle with a jack to control the weight on the rear of the motorcycle when removing the shock absorber(s).

4. Remove the shock absorber (A, **Figure 24**) from the side being worked on. Refer to *Rear Shock Absorber* in Chapter Thirteen.

5. On VT1100C and VT1100C2 ACE models, perform the following:

    a. Disconnect the turn signal connectors.

15

b. Detach the turn signal wiring harness from the clamp on the fender stay.

6. Remove the shock absorber 14 mm upper pivot bolt (B, **Figure 24**) and the fender stay (C).

7. Installation is the reverse of removal. Note the following:

   a. Clean and dry the mounting bolts.

   b. Check the upper shock absorber pivot bolt threads in the frame for damage. Clean and dry the threads.

   c. Lubricate the shock absorber 14 mm upper pivot bolt threads and seating surfaces with engine oil before installation.

   d. Tighten the shock absorber 14 mm upper pivot bolt to 108 N•m (80 ft.-lb.).

   e. Install the rear fender as described in this chapter.

   f. Install the shock absorber as described in Chapter Thirteen.

   g. Check the rear lights for proper operation.

FRONT FOOTREST
(VT1100C3)

This model is equipped with a floorboard type footrest assembly. The footrest assembly can be disassembled to service the pivot shaft and return spring assembly.

Removal/Installation

WARNING
Do not remove the right footrest when the exhaust system is hot.

1. For the right footrest only, loosen the exhaust system fasteners to provide clearance between the exhaust pipe and frame.

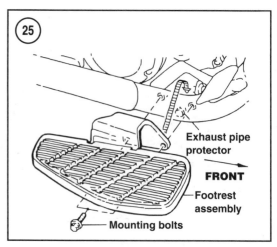

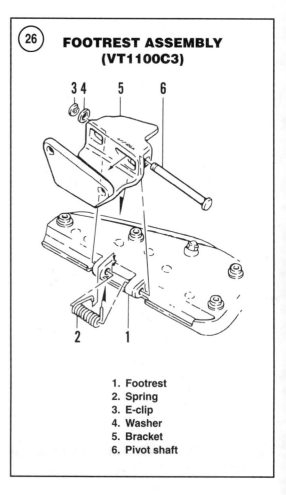

1. Footrest
2. Spring
3. E-clip
4. Washer
5. Bracket
6. Pivot shaft

NOTE
When removing the right footrest, do not damage or dislodge the rubber protector mounted on the inside of the front exhaust pipe.

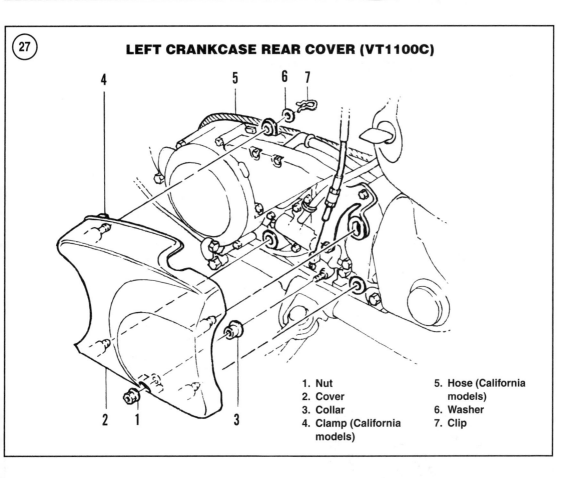

LEFT CRANKCASE REAR COVER (VT1100C)

1. Nut
2. Cover
3. Collar
4. Clamp (California models)
5. Hose (California models)
6. Washer
7. Clip

2. Remove the two footrest mounting bolts and the footrest assembly (**Figure 25**).

3. Installation is the reverse of removal. Tighten the footrest mounting bolts to 39 N•m (29 ft.-lb.).

4. Tighten the exhaust system fasteners as described under *Exhaust System* in this chapter.

Disassembly/Reassembly

Refer to **Figure 26**.

1. Remove the footrest as described in this section.

2. Remove the E-clip and washer from the pivot shaft.

3. Tap the pivot shaft out and separate the bracket and spring from the footrest.

4. Clean and dry the parts.

5. Inspect the return spring for weakness or damage. Replace if necessary.

6. Inspect the pivot shaft for wear grooves or other damage. Replace if necessary.

7. Assemble the bracket and spring onto the footrest. Insert the hooked spring end into the hole in the

footrest. Insert the straight spring end through the hole in the bracket.

8. Use a screwdriver to align the spring with the pivot holes in the bracket and footrest, then install the pivot shaft as shown in **Figure 26**.

9. Install the washer and E-clip. Make sure the E-clip correctly seats in the shaft groove.

10. Install the footrest as described in this section.

LEFT CRANKCASE REAR COVER

Removal/Installation

1. Support the bike securely on a stand.

2. Remove the left footpeg if it interferes with cover removal.

3. On California models, remove the hose from the clamp at the front of the cover.

4A. On VT1100C models, remove the clip and washer at the front upper boss (**Figure 27**).

15

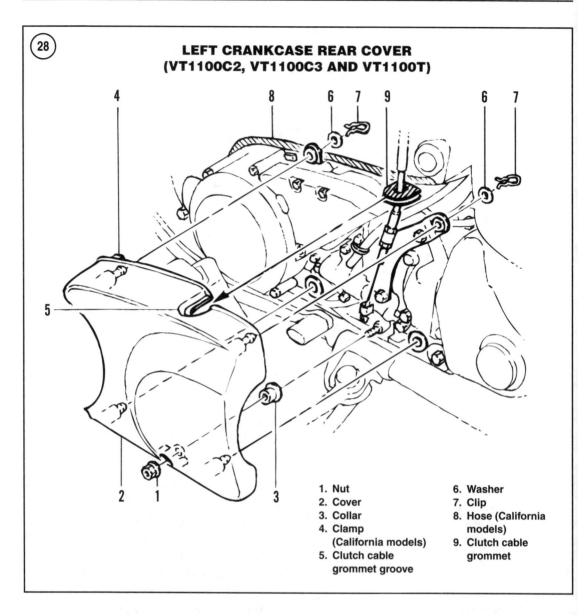

**LEFT CRANKCASE REAR COVER
(VT1100C2, VT1100C3 AND VT1100T)**

1. Nut
2. Cover
3. Collar
4. Clamp
   (California models)
5. Clutch cable
   grommet groove
6. Washer
7. Clip
8. Hose (California
   models)
9. Clutch cable
   grommet

4B. On all other models, remove the two clips and washers (**Figure 28**) securing the cover's upper front and rear bosses.

5. Remove the lower cover mounting nut (**Figure 27** or **Figure 28**) and pull the lower part of the cover out to release it from the rubber dampers. Remove the left crankcase rear cover.

6. Inspect the cover and its mounting fasteners for damage.

7. Inspect the cover mounting grommets (mounted on engine) and replace if excessively worn or damaged.

8. Reverse these steps to install the left crankcase rear cover. Note the following:

   a. On all models except the VT1100C, install the clutch cable grommet into the notch in the top of the left crankcase rear cover.

   b. Tighten the left crankcase rear cover mounting nut to 12 N•m (106 in.-lb.).

EXHAUST SYSTEM

Refer to **Figures 29-33** when servicing the exhaust system in this section.

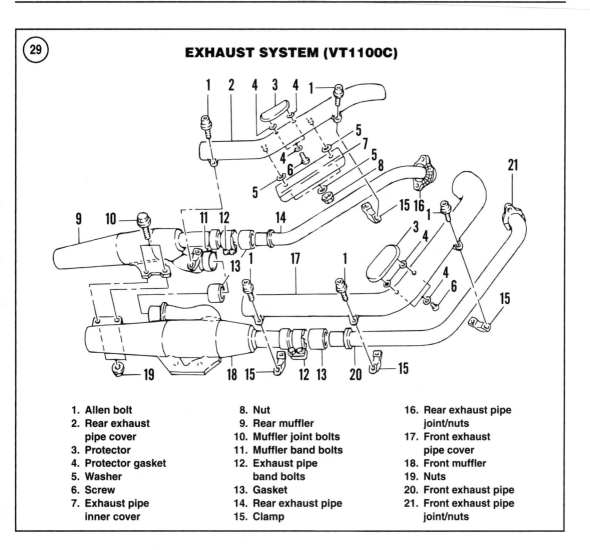

EXHAUST SYSTEM (VT1100C)

1. Allen bolt
2. Rear exhaust
   pipe cover
3. Protector
4. Protector gasket
5. Washer
6. Screw
7. Exhaust pipe
   inner cover
8. Nut
9. Rear muffler
10. Muffler joint bolts
11. Muffler band bolts
12. Exhaust pipe
    band bolts
13. Gasket
14. Rear exhaust pipe
15. Clamp
16. Rear exhaust pipe
    joint/nuts
17. Front exhaust
    pipe cover
18. Front muffler
19. Nuts
20. Front exhaust pipe
21. Front exhaust pipe
    joint/nuts

Troubleshooting

Other than normal cleaning and polishing, the exhaust system is designed to be maintenance free. However, regular inspection is required to check for loose or missing fasteners and muffler damage. Note the following:

1. A loose exhaust pipe connection at the cylinder head can cause engine backfiring or afterburn if cold air enters the exhaust system. Periodically check the tightness of these fasteners.

2. Loose or damaged muffler baffles can restrict the exhaust system and cause low power. Tap the muffler with a rubber or plastic hammer. If the muffler rattles, replace the muffler.

3. Check the exhaust pipes and mufflers for rust, holes and other damage.

Component Service

1. Because of the environment and temperature differences the exhaust system is subjected to, the fasteners may be difficult to loosen. When the exhaust system is cold, spray stubborn fastener(s) with penetrating oil. Before loosening Allen screws, clean the screw head to avoid damaging the hex recess.

2. Because exhaust components are often replaced with aftermarket parts, nonstandard fasteners may be used. While this is not a problem, fastener damage can occur if an incorrect size tool is used, especially when turning Allen head fasteners. Check the length of nonstandard fasteners to make sure they do not contact the swing arm or rear master cylinder (if so equipped).

3. Install new exhaust pipe gaskets during installation.

15

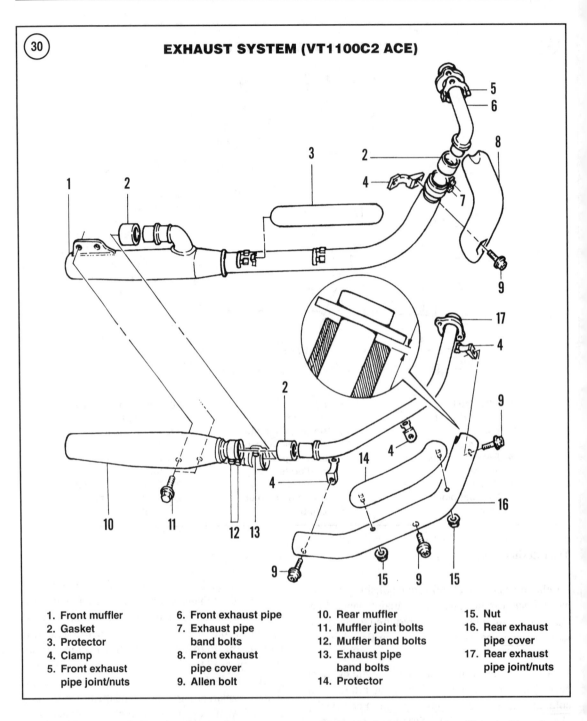

EXHAUST SYSTEM (VT1100C2 ACE)

1. Front muffler
2. Gasket
3. Protector
4. Clamp
5. Front exhaust
   pipe joint/nuts
6. Front exhaust pipe
7. Exhaust pipe
   band bolts
8. Front exhaust
   pipe cover
9. Allen bolt
10. Rear muffler
11. Muffler joint bolts
12. Muffler band bolts
13. Exhaust pipe
    band bolts
14. Protector
15. Nut
16. Rear exhaust
    pipe cover
17. Rear exhaust
    pipe joint/nuts

4. Clean fasteners of all rust and corrosion.

Exhaust Pipe/Muffler Covers and Protectors Removal/Installation

Each exhaust pipe is equipped with a cover that can be removed with the exhaust pipe assembly installed on the motorcycle. Removable clamps secure the covers to the exhaust pipes.

All exhaust pipe covers in this section are also equipped with a separate protector. The protectors sit higher than the exhaust pipes to protect them from wear or scratches. Protectors not secured with fasteners arc designed to be used one time. The lock

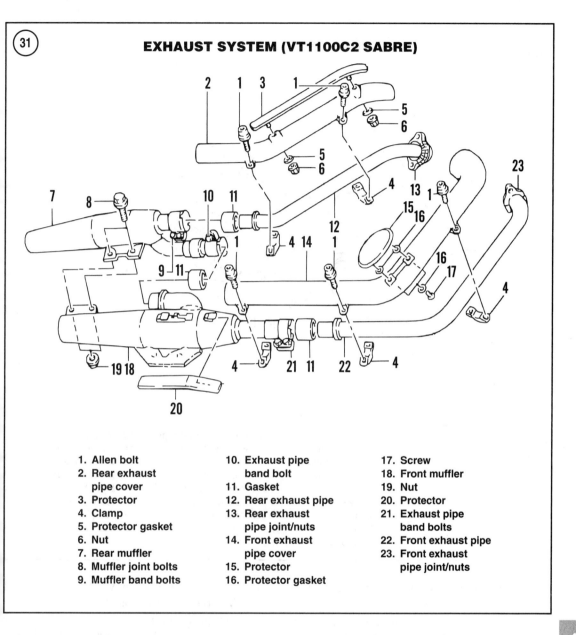

EXHAUST SYSTEM (VT1100C2 SABRE)

1. Allen bolt	10. Exhaust pipe	17. Screw
2. Rear exhaust	band bolt	18. Front muffler
pipe cover	11. Gasket	19. Nut
3. Protector	12. Rear exhaust pipe	20. Protector
4. Clamp	13. Rear exhaust	21. Exhaust pipe
5. Protector gasket	pipe joint/nuts	band bolts
6. Nut	14. Front exhaust	22. Front exhaust pipe
7. Rear muffler	pipe cover	23. Front exhaust
8. Muffler joint bolts	15. Protector	pipe joint/nuts
9. Muffler band bolts	16. Protector gasket	

tabs on these protectors are broken during removal, preventing the protectors from being reinstalled.

1. Refer to **Figures 29-33** to identify the exhaust pipe covers, protectors and individual mounting applications.

2. On VT1100C2 ACE, VT1100C3 and VT100T models, to remove the front exhaust pipe protector:

   a. Drive the protector toward the front of the engine with a plastic hammer until its lock tab breaks (**Figure 34**) and frees the protector from the exhaust pipe.

   b. Discard protector.

3. On VT1100C2 Sabre models, to remove the front muffler protector:

   a. Drive the protector toward the front of the exhaust pipe with a plastic hammer until its lock tab breaks (**Figure 34**) and frees the protector from the muffler.

   b. Discard the protector.

4. To remove the exhaust pipe covers, first remove the bolts and clamps. Then tap the cover with a plastic hammer to release it from the exhaust pipe. If the bolts are tight, lubricate them with penetrating oil.

15

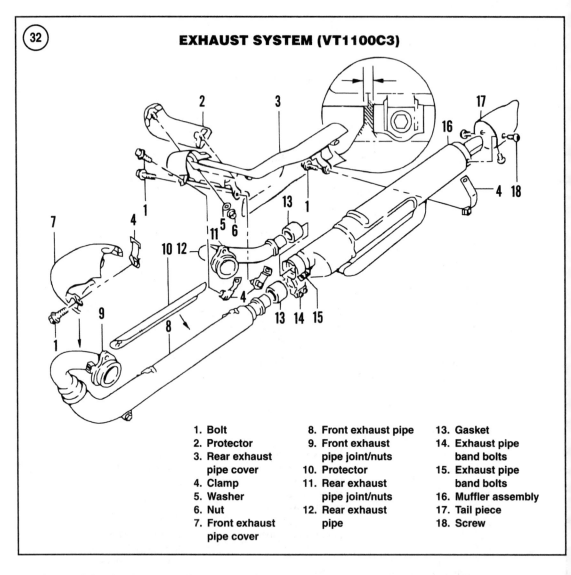

EXHAUST SYSTEM (VT1100C3)

1. Bolt
2. Protector
3. Rear exhaust pipe cover
4. Clamp
5. Washer
6. Nut
7. Front exhaust pipe cover
8. Front exhaust pipe
9. Front exhaust pipe joint/nuts
10. Protector
11. Rear exhaust pipe joint/nuts
12. Rear exhaust pipe
13. Gasket
14. Exhaust pipe band bolts
15. Exhaust pipe band bolts
16. Muffler assembly
17. Tail piece
18. Screw

5. Clean and dry the clamps and fasteners. Replace damaged or rusted parts.

6. While the covers are removed, inspect the exhaust pipes for rust and holes. Clean the exhaust pipes with steel wool.

7. If used, reinstall the gaskets or washers installed between the protectors and exhaust pipe covers. Tighten the fasteners securely.

8. Install the exhaust pipe covers as follows:

   a. If removed, install the exhaust pipes and mufflers as described in this section.

   b. Install the exhaust pipe cover over the exhaust pipe. For front cylinder exhaust pipe covers, align the holders on the inside of the cover with the exhaust pipe flange retainer tabs (**Figure 35**). On VT1100C2 ACE and VT1100T models, maintain a distance of 5 mm (0.02 in.) between the end of the cover and the exhaust pipe flange; refer to the example in **Figure 30** or **Figure 33**. For the rear cylinder exhaust pipe cover on VT1100C3 models, maintain a distance of 10 mm (0.04 in.) between the edge of the mounting stay and the cover clamp; refer to the example in **Figure 32**.

   c. Tap the cover to install it over the exhaust pipe.

   d. On the underside of the cover, attach the clamp over the hook and secure with the bolt. Repeat for each clamp.

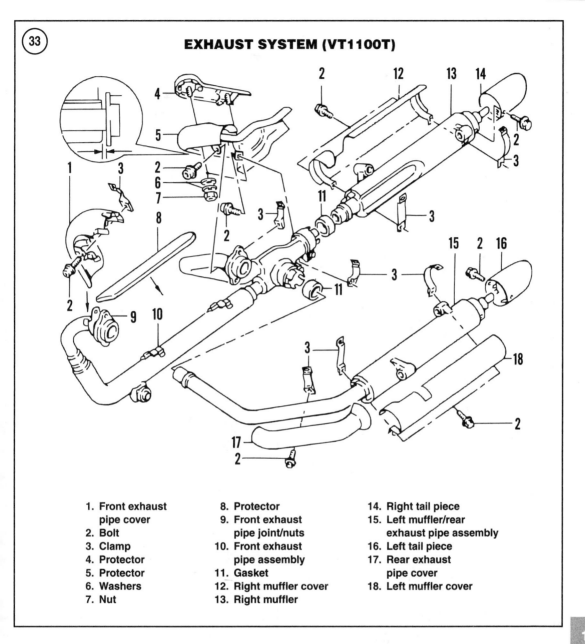

33 EXHAUST SYSTEM (VT1100T)

1. Front exhaust
   pipe cover
2. Bolt
3. Clamp
4. Protector
5. Protector
6. Washers
7. Nut
8. Protector
9. Front exhaust
   pipe joint/nuts
10. Front exhaust
    pipe assembly
11. Gasket
12. Right muffler cover
13. Right muffler
14. Right tail piece
15. Left muffler/rear
    exhaust pipe assembly
16. Left tail piece
17. Rear exhaust
    pipe cover
18. Left muffler cover

15

e. Tighten the bolts securely.

9. Reverse Step 2 or Step 3 to install the new protector. To install protectors not secured with fasteners, drive the protector in place until its lock tab snaps in place.

Exhaust System Removal

1. If necessary, remove the exhaust pipe covers and protectors as described in this section. However, the covers and protectors can be left in place.

2. On VT1100C3 models, remove the right footrest as described in this chapter.

3A. On VT1100T models, the mufflers must be removed first, then the exhaust pipes. Remove the mufflers as follows:

    a. Loosen the left muffler band bolts.

    b. Remove the right muffler band bolts.

    c. Remove the right muffler mounting bolts, washer and nut and remove the right muffler.

    d. Remove the left muffler mounting bolts and remove the muffler.

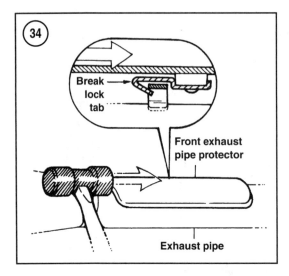

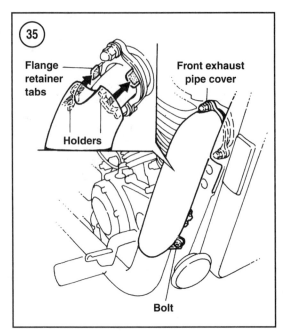

e. Remove and inspect the muffler gaskets.

3B. On all other models, if the mufflers are going to be removed later, loosen the muffler joint and band bolts.

> *NOTE*
> *On some models, the joint nuts installed at the cylinder head include a retainer and four spring washers (**Figure 36**).*

4A. On VT1100T models, remove the two exhaust pipe joint nuts at each cylinder head and remove the exhaust pipe.

4B. On all other models:

    a. Remove the exhaust pipe mounting nuts and bolts. Note the location and direction of the fasteners for reassembly.

    b. Remove the exhaust pipes and mufflers as an assembly.

5. Remove and discard the gasket (**Figure 37**) from each exhaust port.

6. Clean the exhaust port mating surfaces of all carbon and oil residue.

7. On all models except the VT1100T, if necessary, remove the mufflers from the exhaust pipes.

8. Replace the muffler gaskets if damaged or if there was an exhaust leak.

Exhaust System Installation

Refer to **Figure 29-33**.

1. Rebuildable joint nuts—If the exhaust pipe joint nuts were disassembled, assemble them in the order

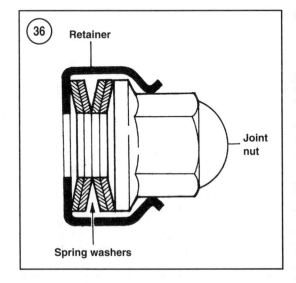

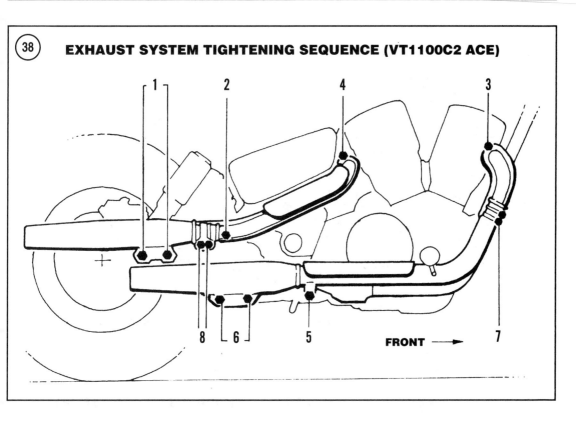

EXHAUST SYSTEM TIGHTENING SEQUENCE (VT1100C2 ACE)

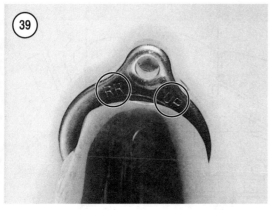

shown in **Figure 36**. Set the nuts aside until installation.

2. On all models except the VT1100T, if the mufflers were removed, perform the following:

   a. Install the muffler gaskets.

   b. Assemble the mufflers as shown in **Figure 29-32**.

   c. Temporarily tighten the muffler joint bolts and muffler band bolt.

3. On VT1100C2 ACE models, if the mufflers were removed, tighten them in the following order

before installing the exhaust assembly onto the motorcycle:

   a. Tighten the muffler joint bolts (1, **Figure 38**) to 35 N•m (26 ft.-lb.).

   b. Tighten the muffler band bolt (2, **Figure 38**) to 20 N•m (15 ft.-lb.).

4. Install a new gasket in each exhaust port (**Figure 37**). Make sure each gasket seats flush against the exhaust port mating surface.

NOTE
If the gasket does not stay in the port, apply a few dabs of grease to the side of the gasket that seats against the port. The grease burns off after running the engine for a short time.

5. Lift the exhaust assembly and install the exhaust pipes into their respective cylinder head ports. Make sure the exhaust gaskets did not fall out. Note the following:

   a. On VT1100C2, VT1100C3 and VT1100T models, each exhaust pipe flange (**Figure 39**) is marked with FR UP (front cylinder) and RR UP (rear cylinder) alignment designations. During installation, position each flange with

15

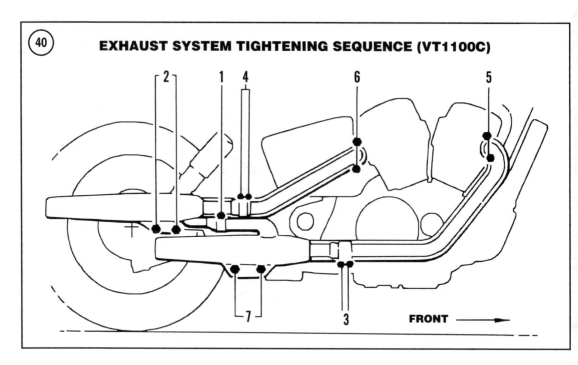

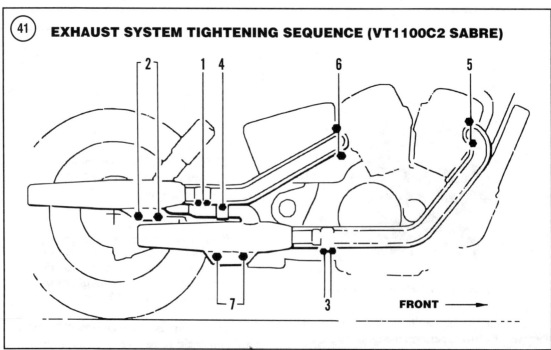

the correct mark (front or rear cylinder) facing up.

b. On VT1100C models, position each flange with its UP mark facing up.

6. Install the exhaust pipe joint nuts finger-tight.

7A. On VT1100T models, install the mufflers (**Figure 33**) as follows:

a. Install the muffler gaskets.

b. Install the left and right mufflers. Align the tabs on the right muffler with the holders on the exhaust pipe cover.

EXHAUST SYSTEM TIGHTENING SEQUENCE (VT1100C3)

FRONT ⟶

c. Install the muffler mounting bolts, washers and nuts. Temporarily tighten these fasteners finger-tight.

d. Go to Step 9E to tighten the exhaust system fasteners.

7B. On all other models, install the exhaust pipe and muffler mounting bolts and nuts finger-tight.

8. On VT1100C3 models, install the right footrest assembly as described in this chapter.

9A. On VT1100C models, tighten the exhaust system fasteners in the order shown in **Figure 40**:

  a. Muffler band bolts (1, **Figure 40**) to 20 N•m (15 ft.-lb.).

  b. Muffler joint bolt (2, **Figure 40**) to 26 N•m (19 ft.-lb.).

  c. Exhaust pipe band bolts (3 then 4, **Figure 40**) to 20 N•m (15 ft.-lb.).

  d. Exhaust pipe joint nuts (5 then 6, **Figure 40**) to 25 N•m (18 ft.-lb.). Tighten these nuts in a crossing pattern in two to three steps.

  e. Mounting bolts (7, **Figure 40**) to 26 N•m (19 ft.-lb.).

9B. On VT1100C2 ACE models, tighten the exhaust system fasteners in the order shown in **Figure 38**:

  a. The muffler band bolts (1, **Figure 38**) and muffler joint bolt (2) were tightened before

installing the exhaust system on the motorcycle. Refer to Step 3 in this procedure.

  b. Exhaust pipe joint nuts (3 then 4, **Figure 38**) to 23 N•m (17 ft.-lb.). Tighten these nuts in a crossing pattern in two to three steps.

  c. Mounting bolts (5 then 6, **Figure 38**) to 35 N•m (26 ft.-lb.).

  d. Exhaust pipe band bolts (7 then 8, **Figure 38**) to 20 N•m (15 ft.-lb.).

9C. On VT1100C2 Sabre models, tighten the exhaust system fasteners in the order shown in **Figure 41**:

  a. Muffler band bolt (1, **Figure 41**) to 20 N•m (15 ft.-lb.).

  b. Muffler joint bolts (2, **Figure 41**) to 26 N•m (19 ft.-lb.).

  c. Exhaust pipe band bolts (3 then 4, **Figure 41**) to 20 N•m (15 ft.-lb.).

  d. Exhaust pipe joint nuts (5 then 6, **Figure 41**) to 23 N•m (17 ft.-lb.). Tighten these nuts in a crossing pattern in two to three steps.

  e. Mounting bolts (7, **Figure 41**) to 23 N•m (17 ft.-lb.).

9D. On VT1100C3 models, tighten the exhaust system fasteners in the order shown in **Figure 42**:

  a. Mounting bolts and nuts (1, **Figure 42**) to 34 N•m (25 ft.-lb.).

15

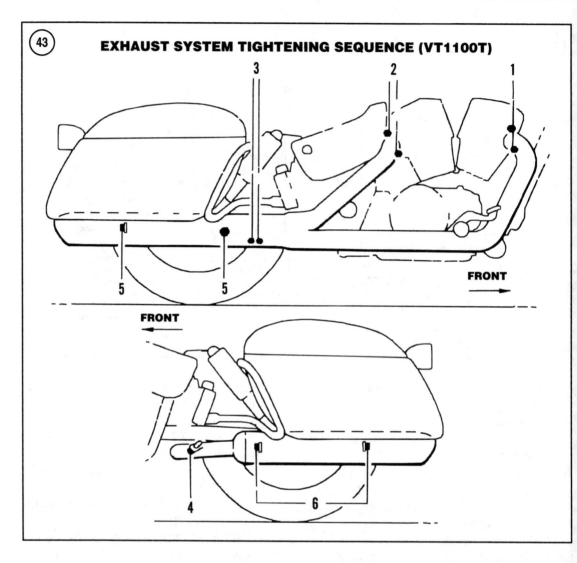

43 **EXHAUST SYSTEM TIGHTENING SEQUENCE (VT1100T)**

b. Exhaust pipe joint nuts (2 then 3, **Figure 42**) to 23 N•m (17 ft.-lb.). Tighten these nuts in a crossing pattern in two to three steps.

c. Exhaust pipe band bolts (4 then 5, **Figure 42**) to 20 N•m (15 ft.-lb.).

9E. On VT1100T models, tighten the exhaust system fasteners in the order shown in **Figure 43**:

a. Exhaust pipe joint nuts (1 then 2, **Figure 43**) to 23 N•m (17 ft.-lb.). Tighten these nuts in a crossing pattern in two to three steps.

b. Muffler band bolts (3 then 4, **Figure 43**) to 20 N•m (15 ft.-lb.).

c. Mounting bolts (5 then 6, **Figure 43**) to 26 N•m (19 ft.-lb.).

10. If removed, install the exhaust pipe covers and protectors as described in this section.

11. Start the engine and check for exhaust leaks. If grease was applied to the exhaust gaskets, allow the engine to run long enough for the grease to burn off.

Table 1 BODY AND EXHAUST SYSTEM TORQUE SPECIFICATIONS

	N•m	in.-lb.	ft.-lb.
Backrest mounting nuts			
VT1100C	12	106	–
Exhaust system			
VT1100C			
Exhaust pipe band bolts	20	–	15
Exhaust pipe joint nuts	25	–	18
Mounting bolts	26	–	19
Muffler band bolts	20	–	15
Muffler joint bolt	26	–	19
VT1100C2 ACE			
Exhaust pipe band bolts	20	–	15
Exhaust pipe joint nuts	23	–	17
Mounting bolts	35	–	26
Muffler band bolt	20	–	15
Muffler joint bolts	35	–	26
VT1100C2 Sabre			
Exhaust pipe band bolts	20	–	15
Exhaust pipe joint nuts	23	–	17
Mounting bolts	23	–	17
Muffler band bolt	20	–	15
Muffler joint bolts	26	–	19
VT1100C3			
Exhaust pipe band bolts	20	–	15
Exhaust pipe joint nuts	23	–	17
Mounting bolts and nuts	34	–	25
VT1100T			
Exhaust pipe joint nuts	23	–	17
Mounting bolts	26	–	19
Muffler band bolts	20	–	15
Front footrest mounting bolts			
VT1100C3	39	–	29
All other models[2]	–		
Left crankcase rear cover mounting nut	12	106	–
Rear fender mounting bolts			
8 mm	26	–	19
10 mm*	64	–	47
Rear shock absorber 14 mm upper pivot bolt[1]	108	–	80

1. Lubricate the bolt threads and washer surfaces with engine oil.
2. Specification not provided by manufacturer.

15

INDEX

16

16

16

16

MAINTENANCE LOG

Date	Miles	Type of Service

NOTES

NOTES

NOTES

NOTES

WIRING
DIAGRAMS

VT1100C SHADOW SPIRIT (1997-2000)

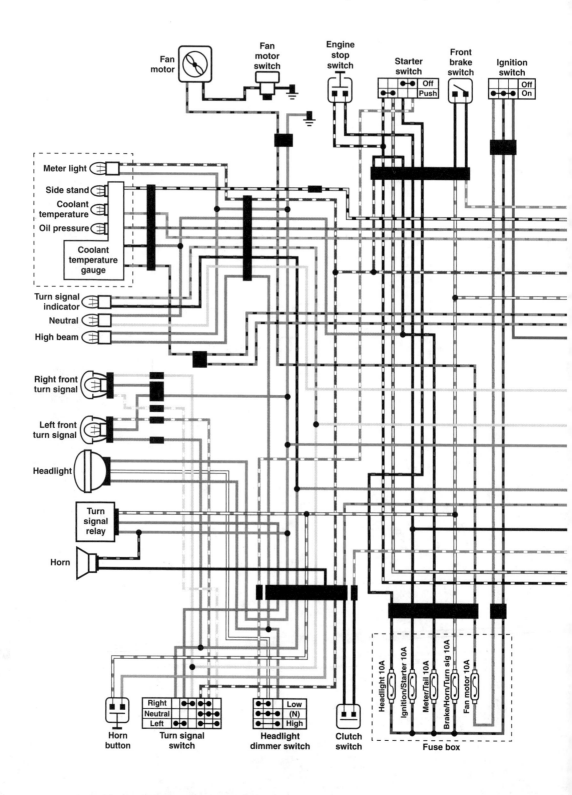

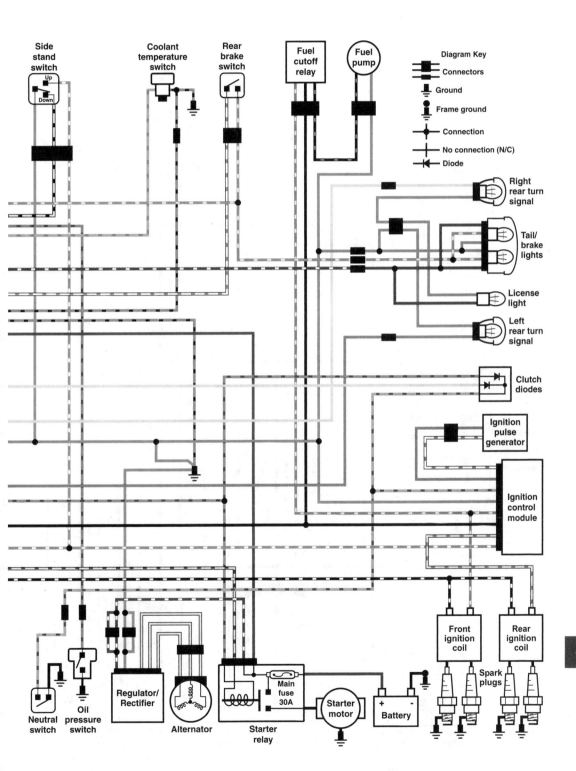

VT1100C SHADOW SPIRIT (2001-ON)

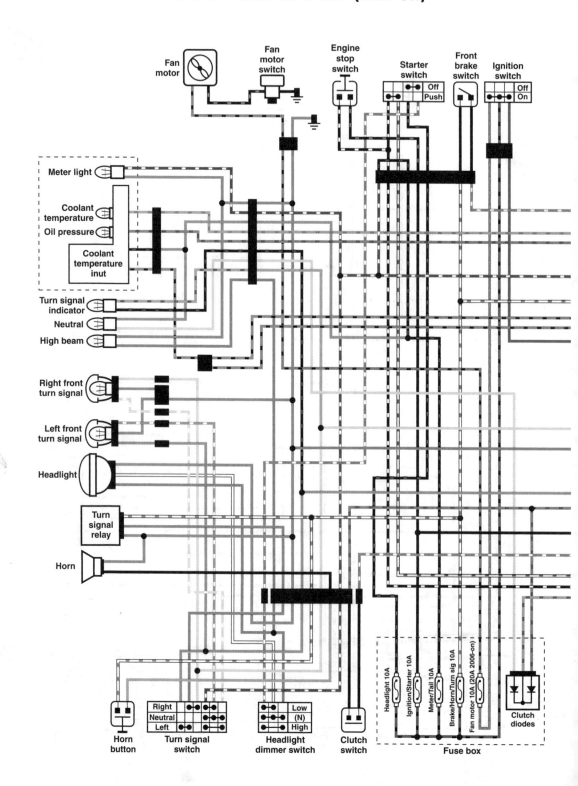

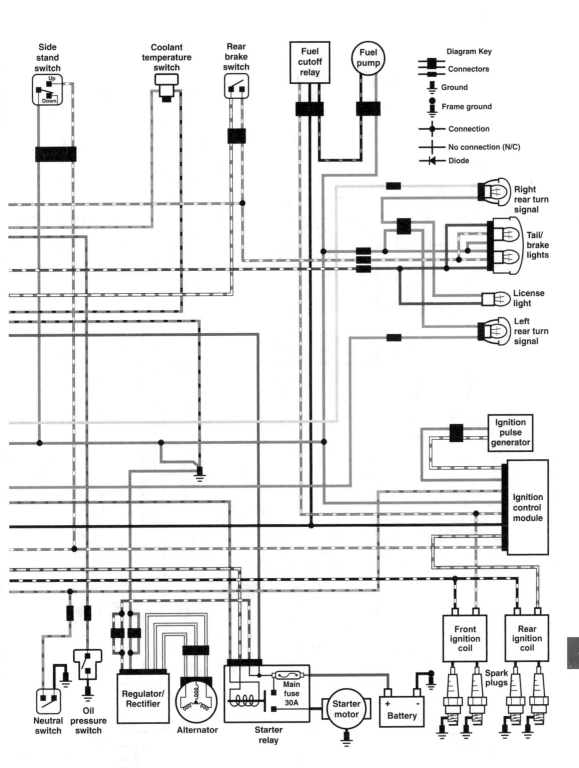

VT1100C2 SHADOW ACE (1995-1999)

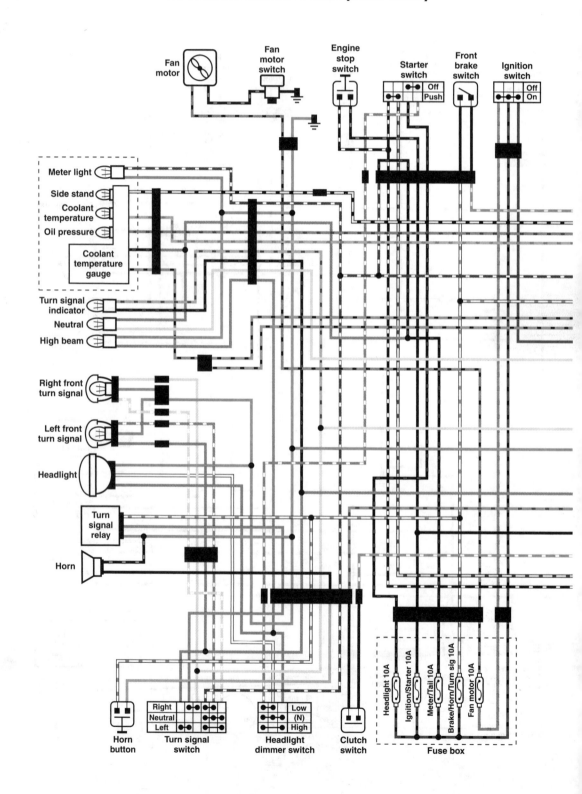

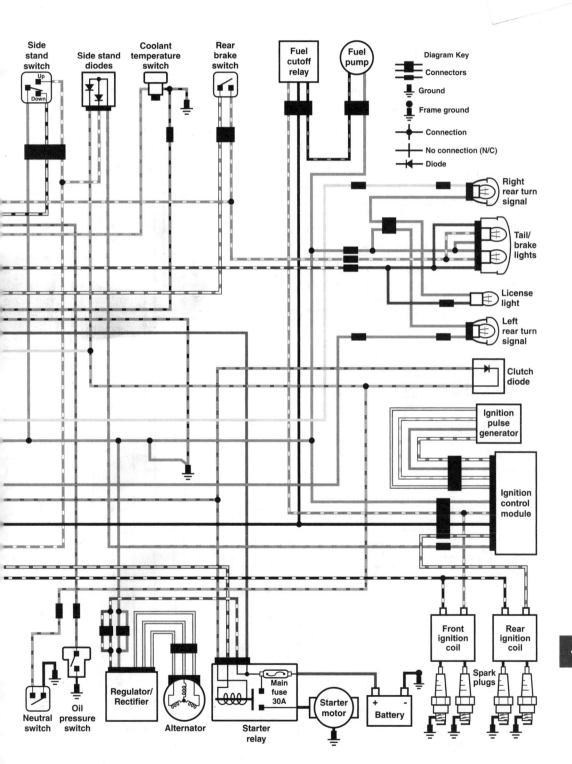

17

VT1100C2 SHADOW SABRE (2000-ON)

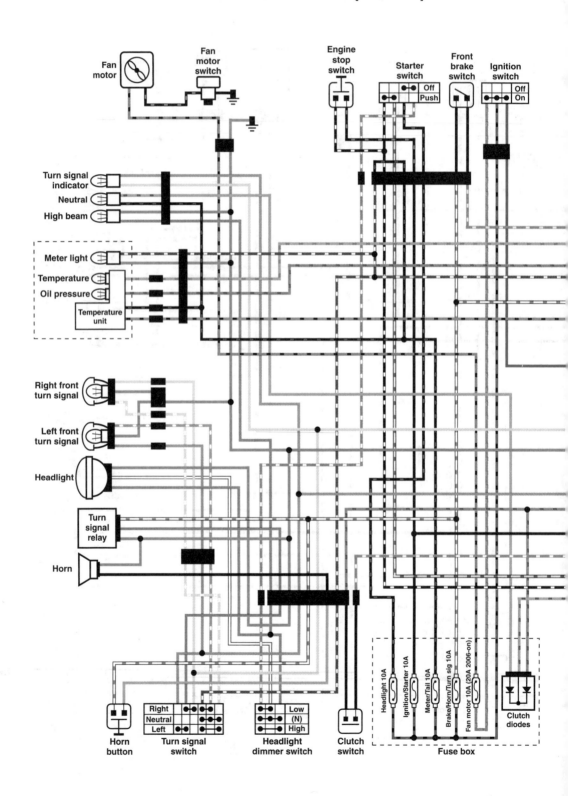

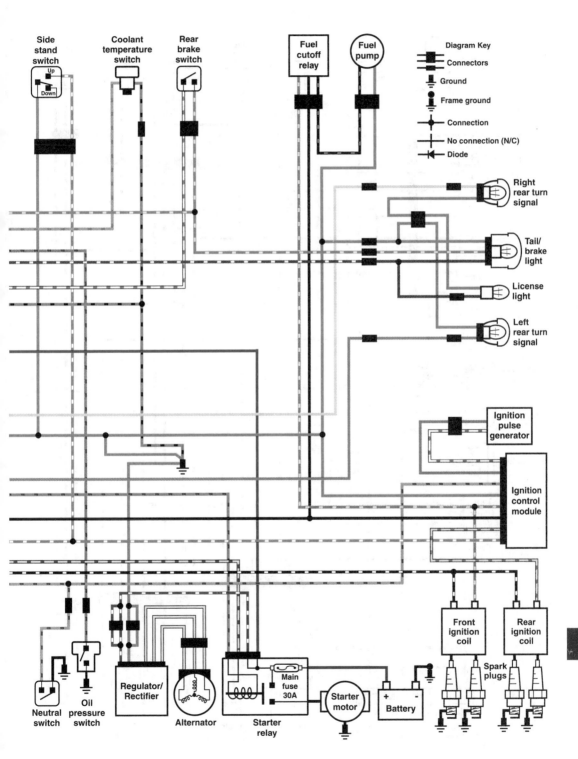

VT1100C3 SHADOW AERO (1998-2000)

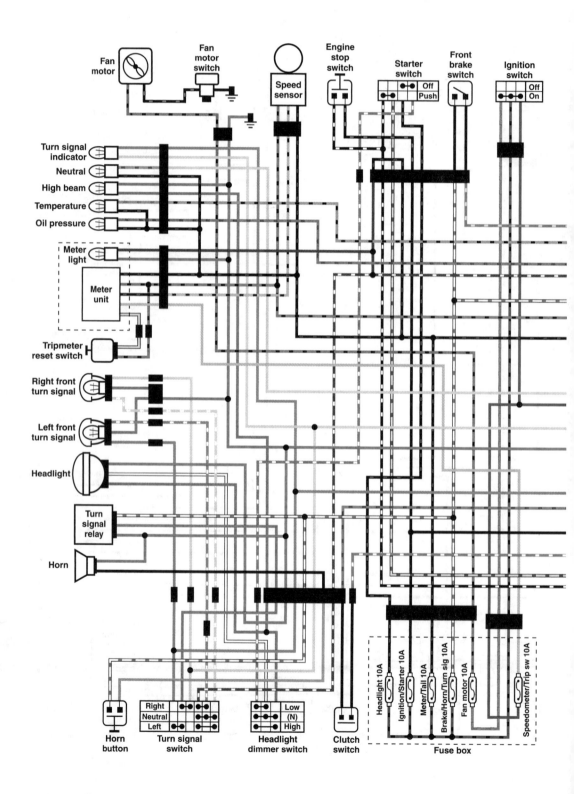

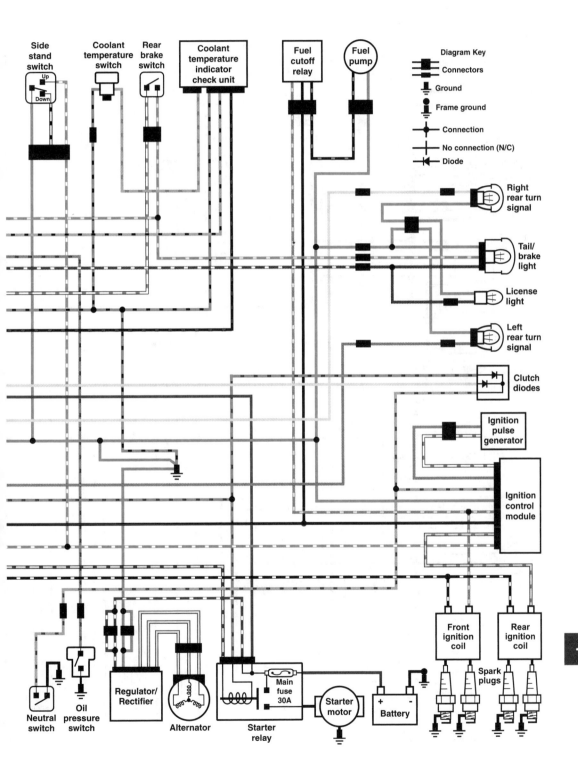

VT1100C3 SHADOW AERO (2001-2002)

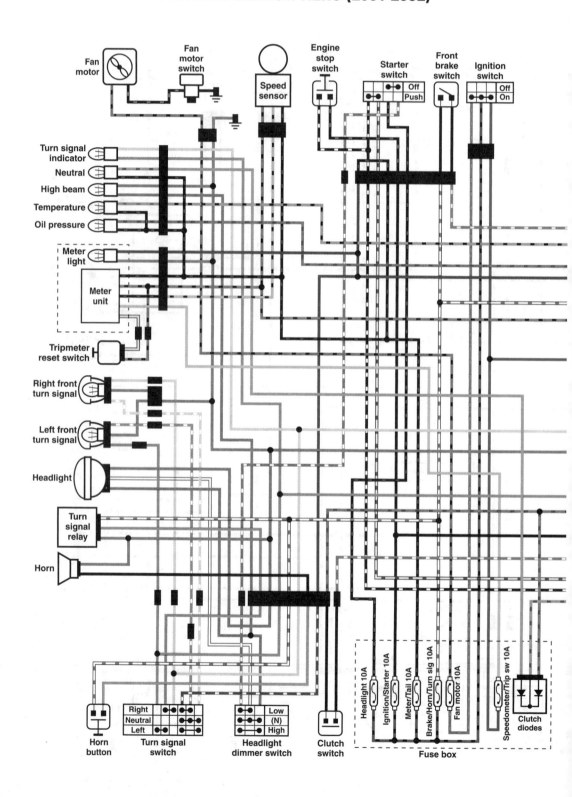

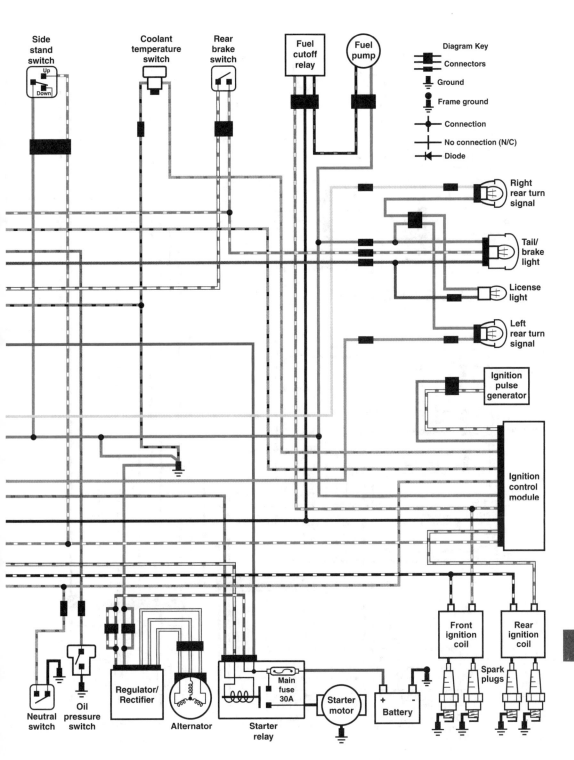

17

VT1100T SHADOW AND VT1100 ACE TOURER (1998-2000)

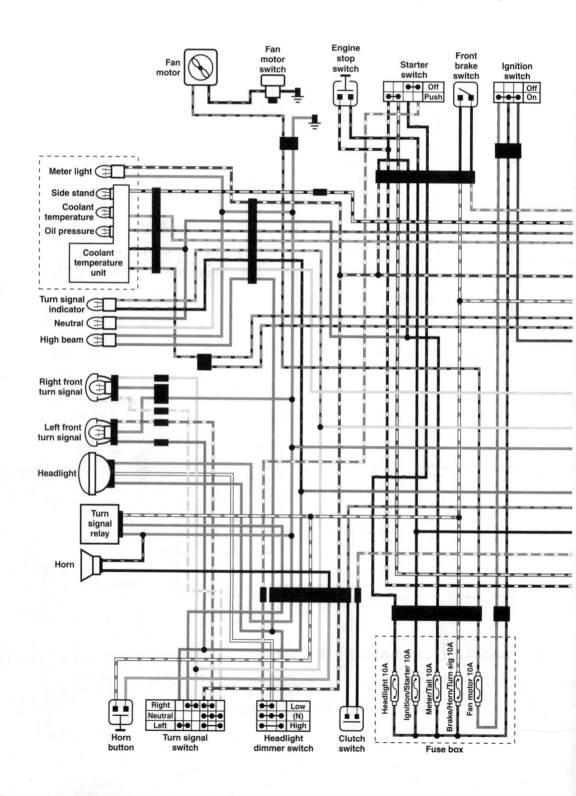

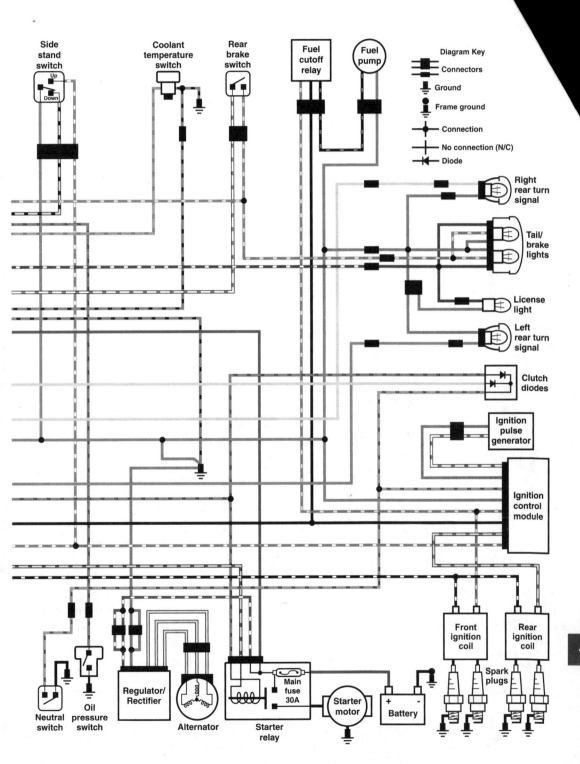

17

555

...cc Twins, 65-78
...c Twins, 64-74
... Twins, 74-77
...el 250 &
... 78-03
...ns, 78-87
...00cc Twins, 65-76
...X & GL500/650, 78-83
... VT500, 83-88

M313	VT700 & 750, 83-87
M314-3	VT750 Shadow Chain Drive, 98-06
M440	VT1100C Shadow, 85-96
M460-4	VT1100 Series, 95-07
M230	VTX1800 Series, 02-08
M231	VTX1300 Series, 03-09

Fours

M332	CB350-550, SOHC, 71-78
M345	CB550 & 650, 83-85
M336	CB650, 79-82
M341	CB750 SOHC, 69-78
M337	CB750 DOHC, 79-82
M436	CB750 Nighthawk, 91-93 & 95-99
M325	CB900, 1000 & 1100, 80-83
M439	600 Hurricane, 87-90
M441-2	CBR600F2 & F3, 91-98
M445-2	CBR600F4, 99-06
M220	CBR600RR, 03-06
M434-2	CBR900RR Fireblade, 93-99
M329	500cc V-Fours, 84-86
M349	700-1000cc Interceptor, 83-85
M458-2	VFR700F-750F, 86-97
M438	VFR800FI Interceptor, 98-00
M327	700-1100cc V-Fours, 82-88
M508	ST1100/Pan European, 90-02
M340	GL1000 & 1100, 75-83
M504	GL1200, 84-87

Sixes

M505	GL1500 Gold Wing, 88-92
M506-2	GL1500 Gold Wing, 93-00
M507-3	GL1800 Gold Wing, 01-10
M462-2	GL1500C Valkyrie, 97-03

KAWASAKI

ATVs

M465-3	Bayou KLF220 & KLF250, 88-10
M466-4	Bayou KLF300, 86-04
M467	Bayou KLF400, 93-99
M470	Lakota KEF300, 95-99
M385-2	Mojave KSF250, 87-04

Singles

M350-9	80-350cc Rotary Valve, 66-01
M444-2	KX60, 83-02; KX80 83-90
M448-2	KX80, 91-00; KX85, 01-10 & KX100, 89-09
M351	KDX200, 83-88
M447-3	KX125 & KX250, 82-91; KX500, 83-04
M472-2	KX125, 92-00
M473-2	KX250, 92-00
M474-3	KLR650, 87-07
M240-2	KLR650, 08-12

Twins

M355	KZ400, KZ/Z440, EN450 & EN500, 74-95
M241	Ninja 250R (EX250), 88-12
M360-3	EX500, GPZ500S, & Ninja 500R, 87-02
M356-5	Vulcan 700 & 750, 85-06
M354-3	Vulcan 800, 95-05
M246	Vulcan 900, 06-12
M357-2	Vulcan 1500, 87-99
M471-3	Vulcan 1500 Series, 96-08
M245	Vulcan 1600 Series, 03-08

Fours

M449	KZ500/550 & ZX550, 79-85
M450	KZ, Z & ZX750, 80-85
M358	KZ650, 77-83
M359-3	Z & KZ 900-1000cc, 73-81
M451-3	KZ, ZX & ZN 1000 &1100cc, 81-02
M452-3	ZX500 & Ninja ZX600, 85-97
M468-2	Ninja ZX-6, 90-04
M469	Ninja ZX-7, ZX7R & ZX7RR, 91-98
M453-3	Ninja ZX900, ZX1000 & ZX1100, 84-01
M409	Concours, 86-04

POLARIS

ATVs

M496	3-, 4- and 6-Wheel Models w/250-425cc Engines, 85-95
M362-2	Magnum & Big Boss, 96-99
M363	Scrambler 500 4X4, 97-00
M365-4	Sportsman/Xplorer, 96-10
M366	Sportsman 600/700/800 Twins, 02-10
M367	Predator 500, 03-07

SUZUKI

ATVs

M381	ALT/LT 125 & 185, 83-87
M475	LT230 & LT250, 85-90
M380-2	LT250R Quad Racer, 85-92
M483-2	LT-4WD, LT-F4WDX & LT-F250, 87-98
M270-2	LT-Z400, 03-08
M343-2	LT-F500F Quadrunner, 98-02

Singles

M369	125-400cc, 64-81
M371	RM50-400 Twin Shock, 75-81
M379	RM125-500 Single Shock, 81-88
M386	RM80-250, 89-95
M400	RM125, 96-00
M401	RM250, 96-02
M476	DR250-350, 90-94
M477-4	DR-Z400E, S & SM, 00-12
M272	DR650, 96-12
M384-5	LS650 Savage/S40, 86-12

Twins

M372	GS400-450 Chain Drive, 77-87
M484-3	GS500E Twins, 89-02
M361	SV650, 1999-2002
M481-6	VS700-800 Intruder/S50, 85-09
M261-2	1500 Intruder/C90, 98-09
M260-3	Volusia/Boulevard C50, 01-11
M482-3	VS1400 Intruder/S83, 87-07

Triple

M368	GT380, 550 & 750, 72-77

Fours

M373	GS550, 77-86
M364	GS650, 81-83
M370	GS750, 77-82
M376	GS850-1100 Shaft Drive, 79-84
M378	GS1100 Chain Drive, 80-81
M383-3	Katana 600, 88-96 GSX-R750-1100, 86-87
M331	GSX-R600, 97-00
M264	GSX-R600, 01-05
M478-2	GSX-R750, 88-92; GSX750F Katana, 89-96
M485	GSX-R750, 96-99
M377	GSX-R1000, 01-04
M266	GSX-R1000, 05-06
M265	GSX1300R Hayabusa, 99-07
M338	Bandit 600, 95-00
M353	GSF1200 Bandit, 96-03

YAMAHA

ATVs

M499-2	YFM80 Moto-4, Badger & Raptor, 85-08
M394	YTM200, 225 & YFM200, 83-86
M488-5	Blaster, 88-05
M489-2	Timberwolf, 89-00
M487-4	Warrior, 87-04
M486-6	Banshee, 87-06
M490-3	Moto-4 & Big Bear, 87-04
M493	Kodiak, 93-98
M287	YFZ450, 04-09
M285-2	Grizzly 660, 02-08
M280-2	Raptor 660R, 01-05
M290	Raptor 700R, 06-09
M291	Rhino 700, 2008-2012

Singles

M492-2	PW50 & 80 Y-Zinger & BW80 Big Wheel 80, 81-02
M410	80-175 Piston Port, 68-76
M415	250-400 Piston Port, 68-76
M412	DT & MX Series, 77-83
M414	IT125-490, 76-86
M393	YZ50-80 Monoshock, 78-90
M413	YZ100-490 Monoshock, 76-84
M390	YZ125-250, 85-87 YZ490, 85-90
M391	YZ125-250, 88-93 & WR250Z, 91-93
M497-2	YZ125, 94-01
M498	YZ250, 94-98; WR250Z, 94-97
M406	YZ250F & WR250F, 01-03
M491-2	YZ400F, 98-99 & 426F, 00-02; WR400F, 98-00 & 426F, 00-01
M417	XT125-250, 80-84
M480-3	XT350, 85-00; TT350, 86-87
M405	XT/TT 500, 76-81
M416	XT/TT 600, 83-89

Twins

M403	650cc Twins, 70-82
M395-10	XV535-1100 Virago, 81-03
M495-6	V-Star 650, 98-09
M284	V-Star 950, 09-12
M281-4	V-Star 1100, 99-09
M283	V-Star 1300, 07-10
M282-2	Road Star, 99-07

Triple

M404	XS750 & XS850, 77-81

Fours

M387	XJ550, XJ600 & FJ600, 81-92
M494	XJ600 Seca II/Diversion, 92-98
M388	YX600 Radian & FZ600, 86-90
M396	FZR600, 89-93
M392	FZ700-750 & Fazer, 85-87
M411	XS1100, 78-81
M461	YZF-R6, 99-04
M398	YZF-R1, 98-03
M399	FZ1, 01-05
M397	FJ1100 & 1200, 84-93
M375	V-Max, 85-03
M374-2	Royal Star, 96-10

VINTAGE MOTORCYCLES

Clymer® Collection Series

M330	Vintage British Street Bikes, BSA 500–650cc Unit Twins; Norton 750 & 850cc Commandos; Triumph 500-750cc Twins
M300	Vintage Dirt Bikes, V. 1 Bultaco, 125-370cc Singles; Montesa, 123-360cc Singles; Ossa, 125-250cc Singles
M305	Vintage Japanese Street Bikes Honda, 250 & 305cc Twins; Kawasaki, 250-750cc Triples; Kawasaki, 900 & 1000cc Fours

---

...06-84
...S Evolution, 84-99
...S/FXS Twin Cam, 00-05

M422-3	FLH/FLT/FXR Evolution, 84-98
M430-4	FLH/FLT Twin Cam, 99-05
M252	FLH/FLT, 06-09
M426	VRSC Series, 02-07
M424-2	FXD Evolution, 91-98
M425-3	FXD Twin Cam, 99-05

HONDA

ATVs

M316	Odyssey FL250, 77-84
M311	ATC, TRX & Fourtrax 70-125, 70-87
M433	Fourtrax 90, 93-00
M326	ATC185 & 200, 80-86
M347	ATC200X & Fourtrax 200SX, 86-88
M455	ATC250 & Fourtrax 200/250, 84-87
M342	ATC250R, 81-84
M348	TRX250R/Fourtrax 250R & ATC250R, 85-89
M456-4	TRX250X 87-92; TRX300EX 93-06
M446-3	TRX250 Recon & Recon ES, 97-07
M215	TRX250EX, 01-05
M346-3	TRX300/Fourtrax 300 & TRX300FW/Fourtrax 4x4, 88-00
M200-2	TRX350 Rancher, 00-06
M459-3	TRX400 Foreman 95-03
M454-4	TRX400EX 99-07
M201	TRX450R & TRX450ER, 04-09
M205	TRX450 Foreman, 98-04
M210	TRX500 Rubicon, 01-04
M206	TRX500 Foreman, 05-11

Singles

M310-13	50-110cc OHC Singles, 65-99
M315	100-350cc OHC, 69-82
M317	125-250cc Elsinore, 73-80
M442	CR60-125R Pro-Link, 81-88
M431-2	CR80R, 89-95, CR125R, 89-91
M435	CR80R &CR80RB, 96-02
M457-2	CR125R, 92-97; CR250R, 92-96
M464	CR125R, 1998-2002
M443	CR250R-500R Pro-Link, 81-87
M432-3	CR250R, 88-91 & CR500R, 88-01
M437	CR250R, 97-01
M352	CRF250R, CRF250X, CRF450R & CRF450X, 02-05
M319-3	XR50R, CRF50F, XR70R & CRF70F, 97-09
M312-14	XL/XR75-100, 75-91
M222	XR80R, CRF80F, XR100R, & CRF100F, 92-09
M318-4	XL/XR/TLR 125-200, 79-03
M328-4	XL/XR250, 78-00; XL/XR350R 83-85; XR200R, 84-85; XR250L, 91-96
M320-2	XR400R, 96-04
M221	XR600R, 91-07; XR650L, 93-07
M339-8	XL/XR 500-600, 79-90
M225	XR650R, 00-07